English population history from family reconstitution 1580–1837 is the most important single contribution to British historical demography since Wrigley and Schofield's *Population history of England*. It represents the culmination of work carried out at the Cambridge Group for the History of Population and Social Structure over the past quarter-century. Both books use Anglican parish registers to illuminate the population history of England between the sixteenth century and the mid-nineteenth century, for which period they are the prime source available. This second work demonstrates the value of the technique of family reconstitution as a means of obtaining accurate and detailed information about fertility, mortality, and nuptiality in the past. Indeed, more is now known about many aspects of English demography in the parish register period than about the post-1837 period when the Registrar-General collected and published information. Using data from 26 parishes, the authors show clearly that their results are representative not only of the demographic situation of the parishes from which the data were drawn, but also of the country as a whole. While the book largely confirms the earlier findings of the Cambridge Group, many novel and some very surprising features of the behaviour of past populations are brought to light for the first time.

English population history from family reconstitution 1580–1837 marks a further major development in the study of English population history. It will be an essential source of information for all economic and social historians.

English population history from family reconstitution
1580–1837

Cambridge Studies in Population, Economy and Society in Past Time 32

ROGER SCHOFIELD

Cambridge Group for the History of Population and Social Structure

RICHARD SMITH

Cambridge Group for the History of Population and Social Structure

JAN DE VRIES

University of California at Berkeley

PAUL JOHNSON

London School of Economics and Political Science

Recent work in social, economic and demographic history has revealed much that was previously obscure about societal stability and change in the past. It has also suggested that crossing the conventional boundaries between these branches of history can be very rewarding.

This series exemplifies the value of interdisciplinary work of this kind, and includes books on topics such as family, kinship and neighbourhood; welfare provision and social control; work and leisure; migration; urban growth; and legal structures and procedures, as well as more familiar matters. It demonstrates that, for example, anthropology and economics have become as close intellectual neighbours to history as have political philosophy or biography.

For a full list of titles in the series, please see end of book

English population history from family reconstitution 1580–1837

E.A. WRIGLEY

Professor of Economic History and Master of Corpus Christi College, Cambridge

R.S. DAVIES

Cambridge Group for the History of Population and Social Structure

J.E. OEPPEN

Cambridge Group for the History of Population and Social Structure

R.S. SCHOFIELD

Cambridge Group for the History of Population and Social Structure

CAMBRIDGE
UNIVERSITY PRESS

PUBLISHED BY THE PRESS SYNDICATE OF THE UNIVERSITY OF CAMBRIDGE
The Pitt Building, Trumpington Street, Cambridge CB2 1RP

CAMBRIDGE UNIVERSITY PRESS
The Edinburgh Building, Cambridge, CB2 2RU, United Kingdom
40 West 20th Street, New York, NY 10011-4211, USA
10 Stamford Road, Oakleigh, Melbourne 3166, Australia

First published 1997

Printed in the United Kingdom at the University Press, Cambridge

Typeset in monotype Palatino 10/12pt

A catalogue record for this book is available from the British Library

Library of Congress cataloguing in publication data

English population history from family reconstitution
1580–1837/ E. A. Wrigley . . . [et al.].
p.   cm. – (Cambridge studies in population, economy, and
society in past time; 32)
Includes bibliographical references and index.
ISBN 0 521 59015 9 (hardcover)
1. England – Population – History.   2. Mortality – England – History.
3. Fertility, Human – England – History.   4. Family reconstitution –
England – History.   I. Wrigley, E. A. (Edward Anthony), 1931–   .
II. Series.
HB3585.E54   1997
304.6'0942–dc21   96–47524 CIP
ISBN 0 521 59015 9 hardback

Contents

Figures

Tables

PART I

1

Introduction

This book is intended as a complement to the *Population history of England*. The two books are offspring of the same overall research project: to make as full use as possible of Anglican parish registers to throw light on the population history of England during the period when the registers are the prime source available. When the project was instituted more than a quarter of a century ago, it seemed likely that family reconstitution, the technique used to produce the results presented in this book, would be the chief method for the whole enterprise. Family reconstitution had then recently been perfected by Louis Henry as a technique for articulating and analysing nominal data to produce demographic information, and he had shown in his pioneering study of the parish of Crulai in Normandy that, where suitable sources existed, it could sustain a very detailed and searching examination of many aspects of the population history of a community.[1]

At that time, however, it was still not certain that English parish registers could be used for family reconstitution since the information routinely recorded in each entry was characteristically less complete than was true of the better French registers. To test the point was of

---

[1] Gautier and Henry, *Crulai*. Family reconstitution, or methods bearing a close resemblance to it, had been employed by others before Henry. As long ago as 1915 Edin had taken advantage of the excellence of Swedish population registers to publish an article about age-specific fertility in 12 parishes in Västmannland, while in 1942 Hyrenius published a study in book form based on data taken from 6 parishes in Estonia inhabited by Swedes, covering the period from 1840 to 1937, which contained much data on fertility, marriage age, and child mortality. Edin, 'Studier i Svensk fruktsamhetsstatistik'; Hyrenius, *Estlandssvenskarna*. Hyrenius also published a summary of some of his findings in 'Fertility and reproduction in a Swedish population group'. Henry was aware of the work of Hyrenius and made generous acknowledgement of it, though he was probably not aware of Edin's earlier achievements: Henry, 'La fécondité naturelle'. See also Vann and Eversley, *Friends in life and death*, pp. 22–3.

crucial importance since family reconstitution is possible only if the life histories of individuals and families can be built up accurately from the records of their birth (baptism), marriage, and death (burial); and this in turn hinges on the quality and quantity of information routinely recorded in the registers.[2] An initial experiment was made using the register of the parish of Colyton in Devon, chosen because, although registration in Colyton appeared to be almost complete and unbroken, the amount of detail given with each entry varied greatly from period to period. The experiment showed that it was possible to carry out a successful reconstitution using an Anglican register and that the demographic results appeared to be reliable, provided that certain categories of information were present to ensure accurate record linkage.[3] Many Anglican registers fall short in this regard, but there are a sufficient number meeting the necessary criteria to enable reconstitution to be carried out successfully on a substantial total of registers.

The scope of the present study

The title of this book was chosen deliberately. It indicates the scope of the work, and also hints at its limitations. Family reconstitution has proved a wonderfully fruitful technique for securing accurate and detailed information about the demography of past populations. As a result it is fair to claim that more is now known securely about some aspects of the demography of England in the period when the parish registers are the main source of information than about its demography in the post-1837 period for which the Registrar-General has collected and published information.[4]

This assertion is certain to be probed and likely to be challenged both by those harbouring doubts about the data and methods used and

[2] The general and logical issues involved in historical record linkage are discussed in Wrigley and Schofield, 'Nominal record linkage'. There is a comprehensive account of the keeping of parish registers, the legislation relating to them, and nature of their contents in Steel, *National index of parish registers*, I, esp. pp. 3–128; see also Cox, *Parish registers*; Burn, *Parish registers*.

[3] Some of these issues are discussed in Wrigley, 'Some problems of family reconstitution'. Probably the most important minimum requirement in determining whether a register is suitable for reconstitution is that entries in the burial register should record the relationship of the deceased to the head of the family. The initial results of the Colyton reconstitution were described in Wrigley, 'Family limitation', and 'Mortality in pre-industrial England'.

[4] See, for example, the discussion of entry and subsequent sterility (pp. 359–61, 381–9); of fecundability (pp. 464–501); of the seasonality of mortality (pp. 322–43); or the relationship between length of widowhood and the number of dependent children (pp. 177–82).

because it might seem folly to suppose that reliable knowledge concerning the country as a whole can be gleaned from the contents of the handful of parishes which are the sole source of the empirical information used in the study. Conscious of the need to be as explicit as possible about data and methods, and to justify the claim that the results reported may be taken as representing the characteristics of a much larger entity, we have been at pains to emulate the tradition established by Louis Henry in the first French reconstitution monograph. Gautier and Henry, in an appendix to their work, recapitulated much of the raw data which underpinned the tables and figures published in the main text.[5] Although the bulk of this book is devoted to the presentation of the nuptiality, mortality, and fertility history of England, a substantial part is given over to describing the parish registers of the 26 parishes from which data were drawn; to discussing the inherent strengths and weaknesses of the technique of reconstitution and of the methods of analysis associated with it; and to testing the claim that it is reasonable to represent the outcome as yielding a picture true of the whole country rather than a handful of parishes. Representativeness and reliability not only provide the titles of two of the chapters in the book, but are a continuing theme running throughout the whole work.

The upshot may be likened to laying the foundations and erecting the main fabric of a house, but leaving its finishing and furnishing to another day. Since demographic behaviour is so central to many aspects of the economic and social functioning of a community or of a country, this will inevitably appear to some as a job half done. Given the importance of seeking to establish the authority of the new findings to be presented, however, and the constraints of space, the choice made was to favour a strategy which has meant that discussion of wider issues of interpretation was largely eschewed. Other considerations have taken a back seat to the wish to provide as wide a range of new empirical information as possible, and to verify its accuracy. Indeed, there are many purely demographic questions, to do with the interrelationship between the behaviour of fertility, mortality, and nuptiality in early modern England which are not explored. An indication of the scope for future work is given, both scattered through the individual chapters of the book, and in the concluding chapter in a more considered fashion, but the central concern has been to establish a reliable empirical foundation for future work. To change the analogy, a vintage has been gathered in. To be appreciated in full, however, it will in due time

---

[5] Gautier and Henry, *Crulai*, annexe, pp. 241–69.

benefit from being served as a part of a spread table rather than being drunk in isolation, as in this volume.

The origins of the present study

Following the original family reconstitution study of Colyton, the embryonic Cambridge Group drew up a list of English registers that appeared to offer some promise for further reconstitution work in the sense that registration began early and that there were no significant gaps in the registers. An appeal was then made for local volunteers to help to further the work. They were asked to use standard forms on which monthly totals of baptisms, burials, and marriages were to be recorded from the start of registration until 1837, the year in which civil registration was instituted in England.[6] With an eye to reviewing other aspects of the suitability of the registers for reconstitution, they were also asked to make notes about the degree of detail found in the registers, for example whether the relationship of a deceased person to the head of his or her family was normally given in the burial register, whether the name of the mother as well as the father was recorded in the baptism register, whether occupation and place of residence were given, and so on.

The response to the appeal was far more generous than we had expected and, in the event, aggregative tabulations of many hundreds of registers were returned to the Group in the course of the next decade.[7] Not only did this make it possible to identify a few dozen registers that appeared to promise well for family reconstitution, but it rapidly became evident that the aggregative tabulations, originally conceived of simply as a means of finding good registers for reconstitution, were a most important source of information in their own right. They provided several million monthly totals of events from the mid-sixteenth to the mid-nineteenth century, and it proved irresistible to try to make the best use of such a very large body of information. Inspired by Ronald Lee's initiative in devising a method which he termed inverse projection, the technique of back projection was developed in an attempt to make the

---

[6] Strictly speaking this was the second time that civil registration was established in England. It was first instituted during the Commonwealth period and was in force from 1653 to 1660.

[7] The data used in Wrigley and Schofield, *Population history of England*, were taken from 404 parish registers, themselves selected from the total of 530 tabulations of registers available in 1974. The total has subsequently risen by about a further couple of hundred tabulations.

most of this academic windfall.[8] Much effort was expended in trying to ensure that the data used were rendered free from serious defects and representative of the country as a whole. The results were published in the *Population history of England*, based on data drawn from a total of 404 parish registers.

Back projection requires as input data only simple totals of births and deaths together with information about the size and age structure of the population in question at a point in time, and assumptions (or direct information) about certain other characteristics of the population, such as the age patterns of mortality and of net migration.[9] From these data, estimates of population size, crude birth and death rates, gross reproduction rates, expectation of life at birth (or at other ages), and net migration can be obtained for whatever time intervals are appropriate. In contrast, family reconstitution, using nominal information to create links between records relating to the same individual, produces far more detailed demographic information, for example infant and child mortality rates broken down into any convenient age divisions, or age-specific marital fertility rates.

The two principal techniques for making use of parish registers, therefore, offset each other's strengths excellently. One provides an outline sketch of a country's demographic features; the other the detail to bring out finer points of interest and to illuminate intricate issues. One depends upon counting and the relevant data can be assembled fairly rapidly; the other depends on linking and is far more labour intensive. Where both can be applied successfully a comprehensive picture of the population history of a given country or any other unit can be built up, offering the opportunity to relate demographic characteristics both to general measures of social and economic conditions countrywide and to particular issues or to the circumstances of individual families or small communities.

---

[8] Lee, 'Estimating series of vital rates'. Back projection is described in app. 15 of the *Population history of England*.

[9] Back projection in its original form was open to a number of objections. Its properties were not fully understood by either its authors or its critics. Subsequently it was developed into a form that was more satisfactory because its properties could be more closely specified and related to a large body of existing statistical theory. It was in this form that it was christened generalised inverse projection (GIP). It is a particularly valuable feature of its present form that GIP can make use of a wide range of types of empirical evidence both to help to enhance the accuracy of its results and to examine the internal consistency of such evidence. Oeppen, 'Back projection and inverse projection', and 'Generalized inverse projection'. See also Lee, 'Inverse projection and demographic fluctuations'.

In order to complete the aggregative project, reconstitution was for many years given a lower priority but yet made steady progress. This was principally due to the indefatigable efforts of a small band of volunteers working in close association with the Group who were willing to make the very large commitment of time and concentrated effort needed to carry out the family reconstitution of a parish register. Since the manual reconstitution of even a small parish means several hundred hours of tedious work, the extent of our debt to these volunteers will be obvious. Just as with the aggregative project, the entire complex structure of description and analysis that constitutes this book is erected on foundations that are a testimony to the skill and selflessness of those interested in local population history in England.

The names of those who carried out each of the 26 parish reconstitutions which provided all the data used in this book, together with the names of the parishes on which they worked, are set out in appendix 1. Our usual practice was to provide those who volunteered to undertake a reconstitution with a list of registers in their neighbourhood which appeared to promise well so far as could be judged from the preliminary aggregative exercise and from any other information that could be readily reviewed. The volunteer then chose the register of greatest interest, or the most readily accessible, carried out some further tests of suitability, and, if these proved encouraging, embarked on the reconstitution proper, using slips and forms provided by the Group (some examples are reproduced in appendix 2). Some parishes, however, were suggested by the local volunteers themselves. A standard guide to procedure was readily available,[10] and we were able to keep in close contact with our volunteers by correspondence, telephone, and personal visits, and thus to deal with the innumerable problems peculiar to each register as they arose from time to time.

The scale of both projects created problems for the Group, especially in converting the data into a machine-readable form preparatory to tabulation and analysis. Data entry for the aggregative material involved between 10 and 12 million key depressions, while that for the reconstitutions ultimately proved to require about 25 million. Since the Group was seldom in a position to allocate more than one assistant to data input, and was often unable to spare the full time of even one person to such work, giving priority to the input of the aggregative data inevitably meant relatively slow progress on reconstitution data entry. Nor was data entry the most laborious aspect of the work necessary before analysis could begin: the cleaning of the data involved a still

---

[10] Wrigley, ed., *English historical demography*, ch. 4.

greater expenditure of time.[11] But delay was not without compensations. It meant that the number of reconstitutions that could be incorporated into the data set rose slowly to about twice the level reached at the time when it was decided to give priority to the aggregative project. And this in turn led to a reassessment of the strategy for reconstitution work.

As originally envisaged, the reconstitution volume would have complemented the *Population history of England* by showing the range of demographic experience within the country, whereas the aggregative project was focused exclusively upon the characteristics of the country as whole. Thus, for example, expectation of life at birth was calculated for each quinquennium throughout the 330-year period covered by the exercise, but if such work is based exclusively on national data, it can provide no direct evidence about the extent of the *contrast* in mortality levels between, say, remote upland rural areas and densely populated market towns.[12] Within the constraints imposed by dependence upon local volunteers, the reconstitution parishes were selected with an eye to establishing the range of demographic experience in places with contrasting economic, social, and geographical characteristics. Each reconstitution was seen principally as a separate entity. This followed a well-established tradition in reconstitution work. Most published studies have related to individual parishes, and because the number of events occurring in each parish was small, it has become customary to present results for cohorts covering 50 years, 100 years, or irregular periods of similar or greater length, in order to avoid the random fluctuations in rates that would arise if results were calculated for, say, quinquennia or decennia. This is often true even of studies involving a substantial number of reconstitutions, such as Knodel's analysis of the material contained in the German *Ortsippenbücher*.[13]

Illustrating the range of demographic experience to be found in early modern England remains an important object of this book, but the increase in the number of available reconstitutions that occurred when work on the aggregative project was in full swing suggested the possibility of pooling information from the individual reconstitutions.

---

[11] The data were extensively checked for both formal and logical errors (below pp. 116–7 and app. 4). The correction of some of these, when detected, involved a considerable amount of additional work since some of the problems brought to light could only be resolved by reference to the original source.

[12] Some analysis drawing upon local data was included in the *Population history of England*, notably in a passage dealing with the structure of local crisis mortality (pp. 685–93), but the overwhelming bulk of the work used only national data.

[13] Knodel, *Demographic behavior in the past*.

This would allow the creation of a data base of sufficient size to permit rates to be calculated for much shorter periods of time, whether on a cohort or period basis. To do this would have been of limited interest if the amalgamated reconstitutions had constituted a large body of data not known to be representative of anything but the group of parishes in question. By happy coincidence, however, there is good reason to think that the characteristics of the 26 reconstitutions resemble those of the country as a whole.[14] The reconstitution data can therefore complement the aggregative findings not simply by establishing the range of local variation round a national mean, but also by throwing light on matters that could only be viewed in outline when the picture was built up from the findings of back projection, or from generalised inverse projection, the improved system which was developed to replace back projection.[15] To put the same point in another way, reconstitution data, if available in sufficient quantity and provided that they can be shown to refer to the same unit of description and analysis, can parallel as well as complement aggregative data.

An illustration may be appropriate at this point. For each total of deaths which produced a crude death rate, back projection also calculated a corresponding expectation of life at birth, and a related set of age-specific mortality rates. This could only be done, however, by assuming that, with increasing or decreasing overall mortality levels, age-specific rates changed in conformity with the pattern found in a grid of model life tables. The program moved across the grid and identified the life table that represented a level of mortality sufficient, given the age structure of the population, to 'absorb' all the deaths occurring in a given interval of time.[16] Thus it was the size of the total of deaths that determined the age-specific rates selected. There was no independent evidence about the age structure of mortality, and therefore no direct evidence to support the assumption that broadly proportionate changes occurred in the rates for all age groups. The movement across the grid of life tables imposed this result.

Reconstitution, on the other hand, produces direct evidence about changes in age-specific rates, and is particularly informative about rates in infancy and childhood, the periods of life when a very large proportion of all deaths took place.[17] It is therefore possible to determine

[14] See below ch. 3.   [15] See n 9 above.

[16] Wrigley and Schofield, *Population history of England*, pp. 730–2.

[17] For example, in the model North tables of the Princeton set with an intrinsic growth rate of 0.5 per cent per annum and a female expectation of life at birth of 35 years, circumstances that roughly fit English experience in the early modern period, the proportion of all deaths occurring to those under the age of 5 is 38 per cent. For

whether, in a period of rising mortality, the increase in death rates was spread evenly across all age groups or concentrated in, say, later childhood. The reconstitution data show, for instance, that the infant mortality rate was not at an unusual level in the late 1720s,[18] although national crude death rates were generally high in this period. In 1729, indeed, the crude death rate, at 44.7 per 1000, was the third highest annual rate in the entire period between 1541 and 1837.[19]

What holds true for the estimation of the characteristics of mortality by inverse projection methods and its more direct measurement by reconstitution also applies to fertility measurement. Although inverse projection methods yield estimates of the crude birth rate and of the gross reproduction rate, they cannot provide direct estimates of age-specific fertility rates. Indeed, in order to generate estimates of the gross reproduction rate, an assumption is made about the proportionate distribution of births among women in the childbearing age groups and, when using back projection, this distribution was invariant for any given mean age at maternity.[20] Reconstitution, however, measures age-specific marital fertility directly, and it is therefore possible to establish whether in, say, a period in which overall fertility fell, the fall was disproportionately concentrated among certain age groups or duration of marriage groups.

Reconstitution does not provide detailed and reliable information about all aspects of demographic experience in the past. The mortality of adults who married, for example, cannot normally be established with as much precision as that of infants and children, and the mortality of adults who never married cannot be studied at all. It is also impossible in most English parishes to determine the proportion of men and women who never married, a statistic of fundamental importance in the history of nuptiality. Yet it is nevertheless true that, used with precaution, family reconstitution applied to Anglican parish registers can

comparison, with an intrinsic growth rate of 0.0 per cent per annum and a female expectation of life at birth of 77.5 years, which is approximately the position in England today, the comparable proportion is only 1.4 per cent.

[18] The legitimate infant mortality rate for 1725–9 was 189 per 1000, a lower rate than for the decade of the 1720s as a whole, and lower also than the rates for the 1710s and 1730s. The rate for children aged 1–4 ($_4q_1$), on the other hand, was 135 per 1000 in 1725–9, a substantially higher rate than for the three decades from 1710 to 1739. The average rate in these three decades was 117 per 1000: tab. 6.1, p. 215.

[19] Annual crude rates are to be found in Wrigley and Schofield, *Population history of England*, tab. A3.3, pp. 531–5. Between 1727 and 1731, the crude death rate averaged 38.1 per 1000; in the five years preceding this spell of high mortality, it averaged 28.8 (1722–6); in the five succeeding years 28.0 (1732–6).   [20] Ibid., pp. 730–2.

sustain a very detailed and accurate study of a wide range of the demographic attributes of past populations.

Family reconstitution and the estimation of the demographic characteristics of a population

The technique of reconstitution is in essence the systematic assemblage and articulation of information about the life histories of families. Though it is convenient to focus on the family in identifying the building blocks used to calculate demographic rates, it is important to bear in mind that the history of the family in turn consists of the drawing together of the separate items of information that represent the lives of each individual comprising the family. The basic data are simple and stark. Life consists only of birth, marriage, and death. If the dates of birth and death (or, for those who married, of birth, marriage (or marriages), and death) of each member of a family are known, the reconstitution of that family is complete. Having once created such a skeletal history, however, much additional detail may be added, either from the parish registers themselves or from a range of other local sources. As a result, occupation; place of residence; social status; tenurial position; income and/or wealth; involvement with the poor law either as rate payer or recipient of relief; brushes with legal and ecclesiastical authority; and much else about some or all of the family members may be known: but the demographic core of the exercise is based on the three types of event that constituted the basic staging posts in the life of every man and woman.

The past histories of the lineages from which they sprang has been a matter of compelling interest to men and women of many cultures for many centuries. Both oral and written sources have been used extensively to garner such knowledge and its transmission to the next generation has often been a matter of great moment to the living. In a sense, therefore, there is nothing new about family reconstitution. The interests which are a consuming passion to many genealogists are familiar to a far wider sector of the population. A large literature has grown up intended to help those interested in their ancestry to track down all available information relevant to their pursuit, and to marshal it prudently.[21] All the difficulties arising from defective sources, haphazard survival, casual vandalism, the interference of interested

---

[21] The volumes constituting the *National index of parish registers*, published by the Society of Genealogists, are the best instance of this, but other valuable compilations made for particular purposes also exist, as for example the Mormon guide, Gardner and Smith, *Genealogical research in England and Wales.*

parties, and, not least, the wishes and prejudices of the man or woman carrying out the search, have long been familiar to experienced genealogists and local historians.

The technique of family reconstitution can thus make no claim to innovation or superiority in this regard. Henry set out the successive operations which serve to convert a scattering of entries in a parish register into a grid of information on a family reconstitution form (FRF) with great clarity,[22] but the operations described are all familiar to genealogists. Indeed Henry's first major research monograph using historical data was based on the genealogies of the bourgeois families of Geneva.[23] Yet Henry's work is rightly regarded as pathbreaking.

One difference between Henry's work and that of most genealogists lay in the unit of reference for the two types of study. As Henry's research plans took shape, he concentrated on recovering as much information as possible about the life histories of all the families living in a particular parish, whereas for genealogists the unit of reference is normally either a descent group or an ascent group. This is an important difference. It is often the case that genealogical studies, even though conducted with the greatest care and accuracy, are of limited value for demographic purposes. For example, retrospective work beginning with a survivor or survivors will tend to involve disproportionate concentration on marriages that produced offspring and hence systematically underrepresent childless couples. This will result in great difficulties in the estimation of fertility. Yet, in spite of the differences arising from the different purposes of genealogical work and reconstitution, there were few if any differences in the basic logic of the operations involved. Henry's originality lay elsewhere. He defined the circumstances in which it was legitimate to use reconstitution data as a basis for calculating demographic rates.

The problem that Henry faced and solved had long inhibited work in population history for periods before the routine taking of censuses. Most measures used in conventional demographic analysis are rates. They are calculated by drawing information from a census or its equivalent, which reveals the number at risk, and from the vital registration system, which establishes the total of events occurring to those at risk. Thus, in the simplest possible case, if the total population living in a given year is known and the total number of births taking place during the year is also known, it is easy to calculate a crude birth rate. With more detail available about the age, sex, and marital status both of the stock of population and of the flow of events, more complex

[22] Fleury and Henry, *Nouveau manuel.*   [23] Henry, *Anciennes familles genevoises.*

measures can be derived, for example age-specific marital fertility rates. If, however, information is available only about the stock of population or only about the flow of events, but not about the other quantity, the calculation of rates is less straightforward.

The former difficulty, which arises, for example, in some Third World countries which take moderately reliable censuses but do not maintain a vital registration system, attracted much attention in the decades immediately following the Second World War.[24] The latter problem is peculiar to historical studies. A system of parochial registration of baptisms (births), burials (deaths), and marriages was established in many European countries in the sixteenth and seventeenth centuries. Where registration coverage was good and consistent the parish registers provide much the same information as was later to be collected by state vital registration systems in the nineteenth and twentieth centuries. For a long time, however, it appeared to be impossible to make full use of this information for lack of periodical censuses to provide information about the population at risk.

The problem was least pressing in relation to short-term changes. If the number of births rises by 20 per cent from one year to the next, for example, though it may not be possible to establish the level of any fertility rate, there can be no doubt that a sharp rise in fertility has occurred since the stock of women of fertile age cannot have changed other than marginally from one year to the next, except under most unusual circumstances. However, even if the number of births rises dramatically by, say, 300 per cent in the course of a century, it is unsafe to draw any conclusion about the trend in fertility rates over the period, since over a period as long as a century the stock of women of fertile age may have doubled, tripled, or quadrupled, with very different implications for changes in fertility rates. For this reason, until the development of family reconstitution and, more recently, generalised inverse projection,[25] most work in historical demography had concentrated on the study of short-term variation; on such topics as the relationship between grain price fluctuations and parallel changes in the number of marriages, or in the intensity of mortality crises.

Demographers are accustomed to distinguish between *period* and *cohort* measures of population characteristics. The former are intended to capture the situation of an entire population at a point in time; the latter trace the demographic experience of a group who were all born in the same period, or married in the same period, as they pass through life

[24] For example, Mortara, *Methods of using census statistics*.
[25] Oeppen, 'Back projection and inverse projection'.

from birth to death. Period rates therefore conflate small segments of the demographic histories of many cohorts, all of which were in existence at a particular point in time. Cohort rates conflate small segments of the demographic histories of the same cohort over many time periods. The same data are common to both, though marshalled in different ways, as may be seen most readily by referring to a Lexis diagram. The differences between the two types of measure are examined in greater detail, using Lexis diagrams, in appendix 3.

Henry's contribution was to devise a satisfactory solution to the measurement of cohort rates from reconstituted families, which, given the nature of the relationship between cohort and period measures, can in principle always be converted to a period form. The life histories of the individuals comprising a family form the basic unit: a large number of such units may be combined to form a cohort. Birth and death are the events that decide the size of the numerator when calculating fertility and mortality rates, while the denominator consists of the years of exposure to the risk of an event of a particular type occurring. Between her 25th and 30th birthdays, for example, a married woman will experience five years of exposure to the risk of bearing a child. If during that period she has two children, her individual marital fertility rate will be 400 per 1000 ($2/5 \times 1000$). If, on average, all women of this age group experience the same fertility, the age-specific cohort fertility for the age group 25–9 as a whole will also be 400 per 1000.

Family reconstitution produces much information which lends itself to the calculation of cohort rates. Henry's work endowed results obtained in this way with authority because he specified the period of time that a family could be regarded as in observation in such a way as to guard against the danger that the rates calculated from FRFs might be biased.

Although the question may prove complex in detail, the fundamental point concerning Henry's rules of observation is simple. If it were true, say, that all children born in a parish continued to live there until they had reached their 15th birthday, it would be a straightforward matter to calculate age-specific mortality rates up to that age. Any child whose death was not recorded within 15 years of his or her birth could safely be assumed to have contributed a full quota of years in observation to each of the conventional age groups. For example, he or she would have contributed five years in observation to the age group 5–9. Any death occurring beneath the age of 15 would contribute years in observation appropriately to each age group on one side of the ledger and also a death to one of the age groups. For example, a child who died on his or her 7th birthday would contribute two years in observation to the age group 5–9 and one death to the same age group. From a mass of similar individual life histories, the information needed to construct a life table from birth to age 15 could be gleaned.

But children were mobile in the past, moving with their parents when their parents were alive and without their parents if their parents had died, so that it would be absurd to proceed on the assumption that all children continued to be present in a parish until their 15th birthday. In each interval of time following his or her birth a child might either survive throughout the interval while remaining in the parish, or remain in the parish but die at some time during the interval, or leave the parish. The second case is unambiguous in that an entry exists recording the death, but the first and third are hard to distinguish. At one extreme, to assume that all those who did not die remained in the parish would cause the mortality rate to be underestimated, since some of those who left the parish would have died but in circumstances which caused their burial to be registered elsewhere. At the other extreme, to assume that the last entry relating to a child represented his or her passage from observation would cause mortality to be overestimated. Both those who survived throughout their first 15 years while remaining in the parish, but later left the parish, and, equally, those who survived for a part of this period of their lives but migrated out of the parish before their 15th birthday, would normally be treated as passing out of observation at birth (baptism), since this would often be the last record of their presence in the parish, leaving only those who died in the parish, whether under 15 or at a later age, to contribute to the calculation of years in observation. The resulting mortality rates would be grossly exaggerated.

Henry's solution to this difficulty was to devise a set of rules for determining the period during which a child was in observation which avoided both hazards. The presumptive presence of a family in a parish is shown by entries in the parish register from time to time which testify to its continued existence. For example, the baptism of a child creates such a presumption, as does the burial of the earlier to die of a pair of spouses, which may be taken as defining a date up to which the family was present in the parish. As long as the event in question is unconnected with the phenomenon being measured, it is acceptable as evidence of continued presence in observation. Thus, in the case of infant and child mortality, the death of a child must not be used as evidence of continuation in observation, either for the child itself or for other children in the family, since this would cause the rate to be overestimated, as families in which infant and child deaths were frequent would contribute disproportionately to the calculation of infant and child death rates. *Mutatis mutandis* the same principles can be applied to the measurement of fertility. It was Henry's achievement to have teased out the logical problems involved in a satisfactory manner which has stood the test of time.[26]

An analogous set of problems arises in tabulating data drawn from a cohort of reconstituted families. These problems centre on truncation bias. Consider, as an example, the estimation of age at first marriage. It will be obvious that if age at marriage is calculated from links made between a baptism and the subsequent marriage of the individual concerned, no age at marriage will be known during the first 15 years of a reconstitution. Only after the first 15 years will there have been time for a man or woman to have been born and to have lived long enough to have reached a minimum marriageable age since the start of registration. Thereafter the number of known ages will gradually increase. After 25 years of registration anyone who was born and baptised in the parish and who married under the age of 25 will appear in a tabulation of known ages at first marriage. But, assuming that the maximum age at first marriage is arbitrarily taken to be 49 years, it will only be after 50 years of parochial registration that an unbiased mean age at marriage can be calculated. Any average calculated using data from the first 50 years of registration will tend to cause the mean age to be underestimated. Comparable problems affect the calculation of most demographic measures. The rules implemented to minimise the danger of truncation bias are described more fully in appendix 3.

The organisation of the book

This book is divided into three sections of unequal length, much the longest being part II, in which the chief empirical findings are described.

Part I, consisting of this chapter and the next three following, is devoted to a description of the characteristics of the reconstitution parishes and their registers, and the problems associated with the fact that the reconstitutions begin and end at widely different dates; to the discussion of the sense in which it appears to be legitimate to treat the reconstitution parishes as representative of the country as a whole; and to the testing of the accuracy of the information contained on FRFs, and hence the reliability of the results derived from family reconstitution. Jointly the next three chapters establish the validity of the findings presented in later chapters, but for those who are interested chiefly in

---

[26] The principles involved and the particular sets of rules devised by Henry are set out in Henry, *Techniques d'analyse*, esp. pt 3.

the empirical results obtained from the 26 reconstitutions, little is lost by turning directly to part II.

Part II consists of three chapters which deal successively with nuptiality, mortality, and fertility. Each chapter presents the information obtained from thousands of reconstituted families after it has been converted into the conventional measures used by historical demographers to describe the characteristics of a given population. These chapters also include additional tests of the accuracy and validity of the reconstitution material, including comparisons between the nuptiality, mortality, and fertility rates found by reconstitution in the later decades of the parish register period and the national rates published by the Registrar-General in the early decades of civil registration.

Part III contains two further chapters, the first devoted to a discussion of the implications of the new findings of family reconstitution for studies based on aggregative data using generalised inverse projection, the second to a brief review of what has been accomplished and what still remains to be done.

2

The reconstitution parishes

Parochial registration began in England in 1538; civil registration, apart from the period 1653–60, in 1837. If all registers had survived, all had been kept to a uniform, high standard throughout, and all had survived the hazards of fire, damp, rodents and insects, theft, malicious damage, and general neglect, it would be possible to select a sample of registers for a particular purpose over a particular span of years in the knowledge that all the parishes in the sample would yield information of value throughout the period in question. It would then also be possible to select a random sample from the totality of parish registers and ensure thereby that the results of the exercise would be representative of the country at large. In practice, the defects and deficiencies of Anglican registration ensure that any study which attempts to cover the bulk of the parish register period and to make use of a significant number of registers must face two difficulties: the implications of being unable to use a random sampling approach; and the need to adopt a strategy for coping with the fact that, even with care in the initial selection of registers, some will ultimately prove to be unusable for a variety of reasons over the whole or a part of the period of interest.

The first of these two questions, the problems associated with the use of information drawn from a non-random sample of registers while attempting to identify national patterns, is discussed in the next chapter. Here we concentrate on the second issue. Relatively few registers begin in 1538 and many fewer are well kept continuously from that date onwards. Problems associated with differing starting dates therefore affect any study based on a number of registers, especially if it begins as early as the late sixteenth century. Towards the end of the parish register period most parishes have registers which are unbroken in the sense that there are no significant breaks in registration, but other deficiencies

19

may obtrude, so that the closing dates of reliable registration are almost as various as the starting dates.

The set of reconstitution parishes

A total of 34 parish reconstitutions was available to the Cambridge Group when the latter stages of work on this book began. Only 26, however, were retained in a final pool.[1] The population of the 26 parishes in 1801 was 56 857, or 0.66 per cent of the national total of 8.66 million.[2] The 26 were considerably larger on average than normal. Assuming for simplicity that there were 10 000 parishes in England in 1801, the national average parish size was about 860, or only 40 per cent of 2187, which was the mean size of the 26 reconstitution parishes. There were some small parishes among the 26, but the difference in size is marked, and it is appropriate to note that the large size of most reconstitution parishes was by design.

Although by 1801 the average size of an English parish was about 860 souls, for the bulk of the parish register period a more representative figure would be about 500. In a community of 500 people in the course of a century only about 400 marriages may be expected to take place.[3] In many cases, moreover, nothing further is known of a marriage celebrated locally because the bride and groom settled elsewhere, an especially common pattern where the bride was local but the groom a 'foreigner'. To offset this, of course, many couples settled in a given parish who had been married elsewhere. But FRFs without a date of marriage yield comparatively little useful data, especially about nuptiality or fertility. Therefore, in an average sized parish useful data will be obtainable only from, say, 200–300 FRFs even over a century. And many of these will prove incomplete in some way that limits their usefulness, principally because of the high level of mobility in pre-industrial England. Thus the quantity of information that can be derived from a small parish is limited and will be subject to substantial margins of uncertainty because of the small number of cases on which particular tabulations are based. At a time when our strategy was still conceived in terms of discovering the characteristics of individual parishes rather than those of a set of reconstitutions as a whole, there

[1] See pp. 28–30 below for reasons for reducing the original 34 parishes to 26.
[2] See tab. 2.1 for details of parish populations in 1801.
[3] A crude marriage rate of 8 per 1000 would produce this total. In the seventeenth and eighteenth centuries, there was only one quinquennium, 1731–5, when the crude marriage rate exceeded 10 per 1000. The average rate over the two centuries was 8.3 per 1,000. Wrigley and Schofield, *Population history of England*, tab. A3.1, p. 528.

was every reason to concentrate principally on identifying suitable registers from relatively large parishes.

In the event chance and the particular interests of those who volunteered to take part in the project led to some small parishes being tackled. Of the 26 parishes which were ultimately retained, 2 had fewer than 500 inhabitants in 1801, and a further 4 fewer than 1000, but as many as 7 had more than 2000 inhabitants (table 2.1). In most cases, therefore, sufficient information is available for individual parishes to allow a meaningful picture of local demographic characteristics to be obtained for periods of a century or less in length.

Data entry from the 34 reconstitutions was already complete in the late 1980s and much time had been spent in identifying formal and logical errors in the data and in rectifying them.[4] Preliminary tabulations of the main fertility, mortality, and nuptiality measures had been made for each parish, so that much was already known about the characteristic levels of, say, infant mortality or marital fertility.[5] Since, however, it had become clear that much could be learnt from amalgamating the data from the set of parishes as a whole, it was necessary to find a solution to the problems presented by the wide variation in the dates at which the reconstitutions began and finished. Moreover, further testing of the quality of registration, partly in the light of the demographic tabulations already made, suggested that the start and finish dates for *reliable* results did not always coincide with the overall start and finish dates. The problem of varying start and finish dates, therefore, which would have been significant in any case, was thrown into high relief by this further work.

Table 2.1 lists the 34 parishes. The successive columns give the name of the parish (1); the hundred in which it was located (2); its county (3); the registration district to which it was allocated (4); its population in 1801 (5); its area (taken from the 1831 census) (6); the start and finish dates of the reconstitution (7); and the limits within which the data appear to be trustworthy (8). In a few cases there is no entry in the eighth column, for reasons that will appear as the discussion develops. In only 12 cases does the register appear trustworthy from start to finish, that is the dates in columns 7 and 8 coincide. It is instructive to consider the individual parishes one by one, but before doing so, an initial review of the possible solutions to the problems posed by the varying start and finish dates may be helpful.

---

[4] See app. 4.
[5] Some tabulations based on an initial set of 13 parishes were reported in Wrigley and Schofield, 'English population history from family reconstitution'.

Table 2.1 *The 34 original reconstitution parishes*

Parish (1)	Hundred (2)	County (3)	Registration district (4)	Population 1801 (5)	Area 1831 (acres) (6)	Outer limits (7)	Final limits (8)
Alcester	Barlichway	Warwicks	Alcester	1 625	1 530	1562–1841	1579–1744
Aldenham	Cashio	Herts	Watford	1 103	5 830	1559–1839	1563–1789
Ash	St Augustine Lathe, Wingham	Kent	Eastry	1 575	6 940	1654–1840	1654–1840
Austrey	Tamworth Div., Hemlingford Hundred	Warwicks	Tamworth (Staffs)	491	2 280	1559–1836	1559–1749
Banbury	Banbury	Oxon	Banbury	3 810	3 150	1564–1837	1564–1837
Birstall	Morley Wapentake	Yorks, WR	Bradford/ Dewsbury	14 657	13 180	1595–1800	1595–1800
Bottesford	Framland	Leics	Grantham (Lincs)	804	5 010	1581–1849	1581–1849
Bridford	Wonford	Devon	St Thomas	444	4 090	1538–1849	1538–1749
Colyton	Colyton	Devon	Axminster	1 641	5 430	1540–1837	1578–1789
Dawlish	Exminster	Devon	Newton Abbot	1 424	4 710	1654–1837	1654–1837
Earsdon	Castle Ward, East Div.	Northumb	Tynemouth	1 879	4 219	1594–1841	1679–1789
Eccleshall*	North Pirehill	Staffs	Stone/Newcastle-under-Lyme	3 734	20 930	1574–1783	
Gainsborough	Pts of Lindsey, Corringham W'take	Lincs	Gainsborough	5 112	7 210	1564–1812	1564–1812
Gedling	Thurgarton Wapentake, South Div.	Notts	Basford	1 530	4 490	1565–1841	1565–1841
Great Ayton*	Langbaugh Liberty, West Div.	Yorks, NR	Stokesley	1 066	5 740	1676–1837	
Great Oakley	Tendring	Essex	Tendring	769	3 090	1559–1838	1673–1789
Hartland	Hartland	Devon	Bideford	1 546	11 030	1558–1837	1597–1769
Hawkshead*	Lonsdale, North of the Sands	Lancs	Ulverstone	1 585	22 220	1568–1841	
Ipplepen	Haytor	Devon	Newton Abbot	1 033	5 090	1671–1837	1671–1789
Kenton*	Exminster	Devon	St Thomas	1 639	4 850	1694–1839	

				Acreage	Population	Dates	Outer limits
Lowestoft	Mutford and Lothingland	Suffolk	Mutford	2332	1950	1561–1730	1561–1730
March	North Witchford	Cambs	North Witchford	2514	20440	1558–1751	1558–1751
Methley	Aggbrigg Wapentake Lower Div.	Yorks, WR	Pontefract	1234	3240	1560–1812	1560–1812
Morchard Bishop	Crediton	Devon	Crediton	1698	6910	1660–1851	1660–1851
Moretonhampstead*	Teignbridge	Devon	Newton Abbot	1768	7370	1603–1837	
Odiham	Odiham	Hants	Hartley Wintney	1485	7550	1539–1849	1539–1849
Reigate	Reigate	Surrey	Reigate	2246	5900	1560–1769	1593–1729
Shepshed	West Goscote	Leics	Loughborough	2627	5280	1538–1849	1600–1849
Southill and Campton with Shefford	Wixamtree and Clifton	Beds	Biggleswade	1775	7300	1538–1841	1580–1789
Tavistock*	Tavistock	Devon	Tavistock	3420	11660	1741–1871	
Terling	Witham	Essex	Witham	708	4190	1538–1849	1564–1789
Thurleston*	Stanborough	Devon	Kingsbridge	356	2390	1650–1950	
Whickham*	Chester Ward, West Div.	Durham	Gateshead	3659	5730	1576–1779	
Willingham	Papworth	Cambs	Chesterton	795	4440	1559–1812	1587–1729

Note: the population and area data for Earsdon refer to Seaton and Hartley alone since the reconstitution relates only to this part of the parish. Acreage from the 1831 census. The column headed 'Outer limits' records the dates between which there is registration in all three series (baptisms, burials, and marriages). In many cases individual series begin before or end after the dates shown. Parishes which were not included in the final set of 26 parishes from which the empirical data used in this book were derived are indicated by an asterisk against the name of the parish.

Sources: cols. 2, 3, and 6, *1831 Census*, Enumeration abstract; col. 4, *1851 Census*, Population tables I, Numbers of inhabitants; col. 5, *1801 Census*, Enumeration.

The start and finish problem

When a similar issue arose in connection with aggregative data from the 404 parish registers whose entries formed the basis for the *Population history of England*, the solution adopted was simple in principle, if complex in detail. All of the 404 parishes were in observation during a central period from 1662 to 1811. Moving out in either direction from these two dates towards the opening and closing dates (1538 and 1837) an increasing proportion of parishes fell out of observation. To produce a consistent series of baptism, burial, and marriage totals covering the entire period, it was assumed that the proportional contribution to the total of events made by any one parish in the 10 years before it passed out of observation held good also for the sweep of years to which it made no contribution, stretching back to 1538 or forward to 1837. Thus, if parish A in which registration began in 1600 contributed 1 per cent to the total of baptisms in 1600–9, it was assumed that in each year between 1599 and 1538 it would have made the same proportional contribution if the register had been available.

The solution adopted for the aggregative study seemed inappropriate for the reconstitution study. With far fewer parishes in the sample, adopting the previous solution would have assumed a more arbitrary character, and, whereas only three weights needed to be determined for any one parish (for baptisms, burials, and marriages) in the case of aggregative tabulations, the far greater range of tabulations arising when exploiting reconstitution data would have involved a much more complex exercise.[6]

---

[6] Moreover, the nature of the assumptions needed to justify the solution adopted is different in the case of the reconstitution study from that of the aggregative study. To justify what was done in the latter case, it was only necessary to assume that the proportional contribution of the parishes exiting from observation remained the same outside the period of direct observation. In any one case this may not have been a valid assumption, but for a number of parishes the assumption is defensible. To have followed the same path with the reconstitution data set would have involved making not only this assumption but *another* in addition concerning the level of the variable in question. For example, it would be necessary in the case of infant mortality not only to establish the 'weight' of the parish in the set of parishes in the period immediately preceding passage from observation, an operation analogous to that in the aggregative exercise, but also to decide what the representative *level* of infant mortality in the parish should be relative to the larger grouping. The second is necessary since the first alone would increase the numerator and denominator equally for the calculation of infant mortality and so ensure that the new rate was, in effect, based only on the parishes remaining in observation. But to make an assumption about any rate differential multiplies uncertainty. If, for example, infant mortality was high in the last decades before passage from observation, is it plausible to assume that what may have been a relatively temporary phenomenon continued over a long period?

A different approach seemed preferable. Assuming that it was desirable to secure an unchanging set of parishes possessing the same start and finish dates, two extreme possibilities existed. The first was to confine the study to those parishes all in observation over a long common period. This would have reduced the sample to a small group, and would therefore have meant discarding a vast amount of good data. The second would have been equally wasteful: to confine the study to the brief period common to all the parishes, or even to, say, the 20 parishes with the longest common span.

The strategy actually adopted stemmed from a consideration of the dates in column 8 of table 2.1, the period of time during which the data were reliable; rather than from those in column 7 which give the whole span of the reconstitution. It represents a compromise between the two extreme possibilities. The set of parishes as a whole was divided into four groups, each with an unchanging composition over a given time span. The groups were deliberately defined to ensure that there were wide overlaps between them: they run 1580–1729, 1600–1729, 1680–1789, and 1680–1837, and consist of 15, 20, 18, and 8 parishes respectively. The composition of each group is set out diagrammatically in table 2.2, and its membership is listed. It will be clear that all the parishes in group 1 are also members of group 2, together with 5 additional parishes in which the beginning of reliable data occurred between 1580 and 1600. There are 12 parishes common to group 2 and group 3, and all 8 parishes in group 4 were also members of group 3. Only 4 parishes are members of all four groups (Banbury, Bottesford, Gedling, and Odiham); at the other extreme 6 parishes were members of only one group, 3 in group 2 (Hartland, Reigate, and Willingham) and 3 in group 3 (Earsdon, Great Oakley, and Ipplepen).

Any decision about the periodisation of the groups is inevitably somewhat arbitrary. The chief consideration affecting the choice of the starting date of group 1 was the fear that to have begun earlier would have produced major 'start-up' problems. These relate to the fact that the measurement of many demographic rates depends on the parishes having been in observation for several decades. For example, age-specific marital fertility can be calculated only if the age of the mother is known, which in turn depends on knowledge of her date of birth. A woman who was aged 25 in 1585 would have been born in 1560. To have started earlier than about 1580 would have meant a very limited and selective flow of information for several important demographic variables in the early decades of group 1. The starting date for group 2 was determined by the fact that several parishes began reliable registration between 1580 and 1600, including Birstall, which grew to become the

Table 2.2 *The four parish groups*

	1580–1729	1600–1729	1680–1789	1680–1837
Alcester				
Aldenham				
Ash				
Austrey				
Banbury				
Birstall				
Bottesford				
Bridford				
Colyton				
Dawlish				
Earsdon				
Gainsborough				
Gedling				
Great Oakley				
Hartland				
Ipplepen				
Lowestoft				
March				
Methley				
Morchard Bishop				
Odiham				
Reigate				
Shepshed				
Southill				
Terling				
Willingham				

Note: the membership of the individual groups is listed below (the four groups have 15, 20, 18, and 8 members respectively).

Group 1	Group 2	Group 3	Group 4
Alcester	Alcester		
Aldenham	Aldenham	Aldenham	
		Ash	Ash
Austrey	Austrey		
Banbury	Banbury	Banbury	Banbury
	Birstall	Birstall	
Bottesford	Bottesford	Bottesford	Bottesford
Bridford	Bridford		
Colyton	Colyton	Colyton	
		Dawlish	Dawlish
		Earsdon	
Gainsborough	Gainsborough	Gainsborough	
Gedling	Gedling	Gedling	Gedling
		Great Oakley	
	Hartland		
		Ipplepen	
Lowestoft	Lowestoft		
March	March		
Methley	Methley	Methley	
		Morchard Bishop	Morchard Bishop
Odiham	Odiham	Odiham	Odiham
	Reigate		
	Shepshed	Shepshed	Shepshed
Southill	Southill	Southill	
Terling	Terling	Terling	
	Willingham		

biggest of the parishes in the reconstitution set. Thereafter there was a lull in the arrival of new reconstitutions until the Commonwealth period. The new entrants were all in observation by 1680, however, which suggested this year as the starting date for group 3, and also for the fourth and final group which continues through to the end of the parochial registration period.

End points for the groups were chosen with similar considerations in mind. 8 parishes went out of observation between 1729 and 1789 (table 2.1), suggesting the former date as an end point for groups 1 and 2; and of the 18 parishes in group 3, 7 ceased to provide reliable data after 1789 which is therefore the end date for group 3. Only 8 survived in observation by the end of the Napoleonic war period, although all of these remained in observation thereafter until 1837, thus constituting group 4. The 7 parishes with an end date in 1789 form a relatively large group. In all these cases the original reconstitution continued to a later date but the quality of the reconstitution deteriorated in the late 1780s or soon thereafter.[7]

The long overlap in time between the successive groups was intended to make it possible to measure with confidence the degree of distortion involved in moving from one group to the next. Thus, for example, if infant mortality in group 2 were consistently 10 per cent higher than in group 3 over the period common to them both, the effect of the changing composition of the two groups is plain.

Group 4 is much smaller than the other three and therefore presents special problems. It is not small because few reconstitutions continued down to 1837: in all 19 of the 26 parishes which appear in one or more of the groups met this requirement. It is small because in so many cases (11 of the 19) the quality of the reconstitution data after 1789 became

---

[7] On the deterioration of Anglican registration, see especially Krause, 'Changes in English fertility and mortality' and 'The changing adequacy of English registration'. The final annual inflation ratios used in correcting the recorded Anglican events to produce national totals of births, deaths, and marriages in the *Population history of England* tell a similar story. In the case of baptisms the final inflation ratio in 1700 was 1.096; by 1780 this had increased to 1.177; but thereafter it jumped sharply to 1.348 in 1800. The comparable ratios for burials show the same pattern: they were 1.036, 1.094, and 1.244 respectively. But the marriage ratios displayed quite a different pattern: they were 1.010, 1.005, and 1.002 at the same dates. For a discussion of the elements comprising the final inflation ratio and for details of the ratios themselves see Wrigley and Schofield, *Population history of England*, chs. 3–5.

It should be noted that the inflation ratios used in the *Population history of England* stand in need of revision in the light of the findings of reconstitution. They do not, however, invalidate the point just made, since they alter the level of the inflation ratios but leave their general pattern largely unchanged. See below pp. 520–30.

suspect.[8] It was tempting in view of this to set 1789 as the terminal date for the whole exercise, but the subsequent half-century is of such interest that it seemed worthwhile to continue with a more restricted empirical base, even though the results might appear less authoritative.

Solving the problem of different starting and finishing dates, by defining fixed groups over particular time periods, however, still left some teasing and intractable difficulties, especially concerning the 'start-up' problem. It would be possible to ignore any event registered before the beginning of a group in, say, 1580. This would ensure that the resulting tabulations were homogeneous, but would also mean that for some types of measure the true starting date was far later than the apparent one, since, for example, with a group starting date in 1580, no age at marriage, or very few, would be known until after 1600, given that teenage marriage was almost unknown for men and rare for women. Nor could a current measure of age at marriage be calculated with confidence until much later since not until 1629 could a woman who married for the first time at age 49 appear in the data set. If 50 is taken as the maximum age at first marriage, the first year in which age at marriage could be calculated without truncation bias would be 1630.

It might seem that a difficult choice is inevitable between the frustrations of later starting dates and the hazards of allowing the shares of the parishes to change. Using age at marriage to illustrate the problem, however, exaggerates its extent. In the case of infant mortality, for example, all parishes in group 1 yield usable data from 1580, the first year of the group, because only 1 year in observation is necessary rather than the 50 years needed to secure an unbiased estimate of age at first marriage. In general, estimates of each demographic variable have been provided from the earliest feasible date even though not all parishes were initially contributing to the calculation of the measure in question. The problems of truncation bias and their solution are discussed more fully in appendix 3.

The characteristics of the individual parishes

It will be evident from a comparison of table 2.1 and table 2.2 that some of the 34 reconstitutions listed in the former do not figure in any of the groups, and that in many other cases the period of usable data (table 2.1, column 8) is shorter, and sometimes much shorter, than the period for which reconstitution data are available (table 2.1, column 7). Thus, for

---

[8] The reasons for suspecting the period after 1789 in these registers is discussed below pp. 30–8.

example, the reconstitution period for Alcester (1562–1841) is 114 years longer than the period during which the reconstitution is reliable (1579–1744), and the parish therefore figures only in groups 1 and 2 rather than in all four. By considering all 34 parishes individually, the reasons why some were rejected completely, some accepted in full, and some were accepted only in part, will become clear.

In 12 cases the dates in columns 7 and 8 in table 2.1 coincide, indicating that the reconstitution is reliable throughout its span (Ash, Banbury, Birstall, Bottesford, Dawlish, Gainsborough, Gedling, Lowestoft, March, Methley, Morchard Bishop, Odiham). In the other 22 cases there is reason to distrust the data either for the entire period covered by the reconstitution, or for part of it.

It is convenient to begin by considering the 8 cases in which no part of the reconstitution proved usable. No reconstitution was even begun unless the register appeared to be complete, or almost complete, over a long period of time; that is, there were no significant gaps in registration and no periods of obviously defective registration. It was also a precondition of reconstitution that registration should be tolerably complete in a different sense, that the information given at each entry should normally be sufficiently full to ensure that the individual concerned could be identified with confidence.[9] It follows that the difficulties which caused data to be rejected became evident only *after* the reconstitution had been carried out, and that they were in general muted and subtle. Decisions were sometimes a matter of judgement. They were always made conservatively; only those periods in a reconstitution were retained during which there appeared to be no reason for concern.

The 8 parishes rejected

These parishes fall into three groups. In 2 parishes registration began too late to qualify for any of the four groups (**Kenton** and **Tavistock**). 3 parishes suffered from persistent problems of apparent underregistration in one or more of the main series (**Eccleshall**, baptisms; **Great Ayton**, burials; **Whickham**, both baptisms and burials). In a further group of 3 parishes the level of childlessness among married women was suspiciously high (**Hawkshead**, **Moretonhampstead**, and **Thurleston**). In each of these parishes childlessness after 20 years of marriage among women marrying under the age of 25 was 11 or 12 per cent, a substantially higher figure than in other parishes. Since there were other

[9] Wrigley, 'Some problems of family reconstitution'.

reasons for doubt about each of these reconstitutions, it seemed prudent to exclude them, even though acting in this way involves a risk that genuine 'outliers' may be excluded.

The final set of 26 parishes

The location of the final set of 26 parishes is shown in figure 2.1. The map calls for little comment. The parishes are widely distributed within England. In a bald and naive sense they might be said to represent a good spread, but any initial satisfaction should be tempered by a recognition that the spread is less satisfactory for the four groups than for the set as a whole, and particularly, of course, for the fourth and smallest of the groups. And the matter is further complicated by the fact that population size is also important and this modifies the apparent significance of the locational spread. Thus there are 6 parishes in Devon, which appears too large a number for balance, but their combined population in 1801 (7786) was only half that of the single parish of Birstall (14 657). The map, in short, is useful only as a starting point for purposes of comparison and analysis.

14 of the 26 parishes were not reliable throughout the full period of reconstitution. This is true of several parishes, such as Alcester, Aldenham, and Colyton, which have been used without restriction in earlier published work based on Cambridge Group reconstitutions.[10] Discussion of the evidence for lack of reliability will be confined to baptisms and burials. This is not to suggest that marriage registration was free from defects, but failure to register marriages, or damage to marriage registers, have a less serious effect on reconstitution than similar failures in the other two registers. Missing baptisms or burials will lead to an underestimation of the level of fertility or mortality in most circumstances. Missing marriages, on the other hand, will normally reduce the quantity of usable data without affecting its accuracy. If a marriage is missing but the subsequent baptisms and burials relating to the family are registered normally, the effect is to cause the creation of an FRF which will carry all the information that would have attached to a registered marriage, except the marriage itself, though there may also be consequential loss of other detail, such as the maiden name and date of birth of the wife. As a result, there is less usable information, but the reliability of the data that can be used is unaffected.

Alcester is the first of the parishes, taken in alphabetical order, which proved to be reliable only during a part of the full period of reconstitu-

---

[10] For example in Wrigley and Schofield, 'English population history from reconstitution'.

Figure 2.1 *The location of the 26 reconstitution parishes*

tion. The reconstitution ran from 1562 to 1841, but appears unreliable until 1579 because in both the baptism and the burial registers there is evidence of defective registration. Even with the revised starting date, however, the parish qualifies for inclusion in group 1, and it is therefore unnecessary to spend time describing the reasons for distrusting the early years of registration. The change to the closing date from 1841 to

1744 (table 2.1) is much more important since it removes the parish from groups 3 and 4.

In 1730–9, 330 baptisms occurred in reconstituted Alcester families.[11] Thereafter the decadal figure fluctuated but tended to sag, falling to 268 in 1780–9, and 304 in 1790–9, an unusual feature in the later eighteenth century, when, in general, the number of baptisms was rising rapidly. The baptism rate in the 10 years 1796–1805 was only 18.3 per 1000.[12] Of itself such a low rate might not constitute ground for alarm. It might be, for example, that the parish had swung heavily to nonconformity over the preceding half century. But there was a very smart recovery in the totals of baptisms from 1805 onwards, and in the decade 1810–9 the total rose to 589, almost double that of the 1790s. Since the level of marital fertility derived from reconstitution data fell sharply between the two half-centuries 1700–49 and 1750–99, there seems good reason to doubt the validity of data drawn from the Alcester reconstitution after the mid-century. There were complete breaks in both the baptism and the burial registers in 1745–7. The end of reliable data was therefore set as 1744.

The small adjustment to the starting date for **Aldenham** need not detain us. As with Alcester, the key change is to the closing date. Here the problem lies with the burial register. The numbers of burials recorded in the Aldenham register in successive decades beginning in 1760–9 and ending in 1800–9 were 317, 302, 285, 253, and 243, though the number of baptisms was rising slightly, if irregularly. The drop in the last two decades is not pronounced and not in itself conclusive, but there was also an exceptionally sharp drop in infant mortality between 1750–99 and 1800–49 (from 141 to only 57 per 1000). The available evidence suggests that a substantial underregistration of deaths must have occurred and 1789 was chosen as the closing date for Aldenham.

Deficiencies in the registration of infant burials are, of course, to be expected in the eighteenth century in many parishes because the

[11] It should be noted that the total of baptisms on FRFs will not be the same as those recorded in the register because illegitimate baptisms are not included in the former. The comparable totals of burials will be much further apart since many individuals were buried in a parish who had not been born there, or married there, or had a child baptised there, and so their burials could not be linked to any event recorded on an FRF. See tab. 3.4, p. 55. For some parishes the full aggregative totals are known, and, where this was the case, these totals are quoted, but in others no separate aggregative count was made, and in these cases the totals quoted are those recorded on the FRFs. Where totals of the latter type are quoted, their provenance is noted.

[12] The rate was calculated by relating the number of baptisms to the population total at the census of 1801 (tab. 2.1, pp. 22–3).

lengthening customary delay in baptising children increased the risk that a child might die before baptism. In general, before about 1700 it appears to have been normal to record the burial of an unbaptised child when it died. Indeed, frequently in such cases the entry specifies that the child was unbaptised. This practice grew less common in the new century, and, since this coincided with an increasing interval between birth and baptism, the coverage of infant deaths sometimes became substantially less complete.

The degree to which registration was affected, however, seems to have varied greatly, and local customs were often deep-rooted, so that the deterioration in coverage for the country as a whole was brought about by a wide mixture of local circumstances, rather than by a uniform, progressive shift in practice. There is evidence that parents whose children were in danger of dying took steps to ensure that they were baptised early. If this were done consistently and with discretion, even a long average delay between birth and baptism need not imply extensive or serious underregistration of baptisms.[13]

The case of **Austrey** resembles Aldenham though the deterioration of burial registration appears to have occurred earlier. As with Aldenham, the number of burials fell sharply, though again not so steeply as to justify in itself the conclusion that the register had become unreliable.[14] But since the level of infant mortality also fell to an implausibly low level (from 110 per 1000 in 1700–49 to 47 per 1000 in 1750–99), it seemed prudent to disregard the post-1750 period.

Bridford, like Austrey, was a small parish with fewer than 500 inhabitants in 1801. Their registration histories were similar. The completeness of burial registration appears to have deteriorated in Bridford towards the middle of the eighteenth century, and there was at the same time an apparent fall in infant mortality, though less marked than in the case of Austrey. The decline was, however, heavily

---

[13] Wrigley and Schofield, *Population history of England*, p. 96, n. 15. On the other hand, registers occasionally contain explicit notes indicating laxity of practice. The vicar of Linton in Cambridgeshire, for example, made the following note in his register in 1780: 'N.B. It has not been usual for many years past to register sickly children who are named at home, till they are brought to church to be incorporated. Consequently all that die and are never incorporated come into the List of Burials but not of Baptisms. This circumstance should be known to the curious who may be inclined to form their ideas of population from these lists.'

[14] The totals of burials in the decades 1730–9 to 1760–9 were 62, 53, 46, and 38 while the baptism totals ran 117, 92, 102, and 121. The baptism and burial totals in this instance represent the numbers used in the reconstitution rather than the numbers recorded in the register.

concentrated in the early months of life.[15] Taken together these signs of deficiency suggest that the reconstitution post-1750 is significantly less complete than earlier.

Burial registration in **Colyton** was intermittently defective in the middle decades of the sixteenth century, notably in 1540–2, 1554–5, 1562–4, and in a scattering of years in the 1570s, especially 1574–7. The problem disappears from 1578 onwards, which explains the choice of starting date for the parish. Matters are less clear-cut in the later decades of parochial registration, but, as happened in many places, there appears to have been a weakening in burial coverage towards the end of the eighteenth century. It therefore seemed prudent to use 1789 as the stopping date. Whatever defects there may be in the Colyton register do not result in appreciable falls in either infant mortality or age-specific marital fertility, but the changes in the relative numbers of baptisms and burials recorded were so striking that it is reasonable to doubt the continued trustworthiness of the registers. In the 30-year period 1760–89 the number of baptisms averaged 346 per decade and the number of burials per decade was virtually identical at 342. The number of baptisms then rose very steeply indeed and in 1810–29 averaged 632 per decade, while the number of burials, after dipping below the previous average in 1790–1809 (294), recovered only to its former level in 1810–29 when the decadal average was 347. While so dramatic a change in the relative frequencies of baptisms and burials should not be dismissed as beyond the bounds of possibility, it suggests that it would be rash to accept them.[16]

The **Earsdon** reconstitution refers to only a part of the parish, the townships of Seaton and Hartley. The register was kept in a form which makes this feasible since place of residence was routinely recorded for each entry. Seaton and Hartley are enclosed by the rest of the parish. Treating them as a discrete unit offered the possibility of amplifying information about Seaton and Hartley families, since events occurring elsewhere in the parish could be used to supplement 'local' events, rather as if, in a conventional reconstitution, the registers of neighbouring parishes were ransacked for information. The Earsdon register

---

[15] The totals of burials and baptisms, calculated, as in the case of Austrey, from FRFs, for the decades 1730–9 to 1760–9 were 59, 61, 38, 47; and 81, 71, 85, and 88. The apparent infant death rate in the first month of life fell from 57 per 1000 in 1700–49 to 15 per 1000 in 1750–99.

[16] Especially as the number of births recorded in Colyton nonconformist registers was rising in this period though there was no comparable rise in separate nonconformist registration of burials. The disproportion between the rate of growth in the true number of births and deaths, therefore, is probably understated in the Anglican registers.

suffered sporadically from serious underregistration in the early seventeenth century, and coverage remained patchy in the burial register after the Restoration in the 1660s and 1670s, but was generally sound from 1679 onwards, which therefore represents an acceptable starting date, though there was a further lapse in burial registration in 1698–9. As happened so often elsewhere, however, there was probably a marked deterioration in registration towards the end of the eighteenth century. This is not readily visible in the aggregative totals but between the half-century 1750–99 and the succeeding period 1800–41, several demographic measures changed in a way that strongly suggests a failure in coverage. Infant mortality fell from 143 to 91 per 1000, and the death rate among children aged 1–4 ($_4q_1$) fell from 126 to 66 per 1000, while there was a simultaneous significant decline in age-specific marital fertility rates, a combination of changes that suggests that the reconstitution data should not be accepted after the end of the group 3 period.

Great Oakley suffered a collapse in registration during the Civil War and Commonwealth period, and both the baptism and burial registers were affected by further failures in the late 1660s and early 1670s, imposing a much delayed start to the period of reliable data. Burial registration weakened noticeably again after the 1780s. The number of baptisms on the FRFs showed an irregular tendency to rise in the six decades from 1770 to 1829 (239, 194, 233, 271, 301, 273), but the corresponding totals of burials linked to reconstituted families dipped very sharply in the third and fourth decades of the period before recovering after 1810 (153, 148, 111, 98, 123, 145). Although the reconstitution as a whole covered the period 1559–1838, therefore, the reliable period shrinks to 1673–1789.

The **Hartland** register began in 1558, and it may be slightly harsh to reject data from the early decades, but there are several periods in the burial register when the numbers of events recorded appear suspiciously low (for example, between September 1566 and July 1568). The last such period ran from March 1592 to February 1597. In these 60 months, constituting exactly half the decade, there were 84 burials; in the balance of the decade there were 166 burials, a substantial difference, and enough to suggest a 1597 start.[17]

Burial registration in Hartland began to deteriorate rather earlier than in most other parishes which suffered in this regard. Between 1760–9 and 1770–9 the number of burials fell by a third (from 303 to 207) while

---

[17] In the same 60 months nationally there were 498 996 deaths out of the decadal total of 1 026 597, or 48.6 per cent. Wrigley and Schofield, *Population history of England*, tab. A2.4, pp. 503–26.

the number of baptisms rose (from 359 to 394). Nor was this a temporary change that might have been due to exceptionally favourable conditions in the 1770s. The decadal average number of baptisms recorded in the parish register in the 40-year period 1730–69 was 331; the corresponding figure for burials was 281. In the next five decades, 1770–1819, the decadal averages were 423 and 238 respectively. At the same time the apparent level of infant mortality, which was a little under 100 per 1000 in 1700–49, fell to 55 per 1000 in 1750–99, and still further to 36 per 1000 in 1800–37. Hartland lay in an area that enjoyed exceptionally low infant mortality, as the returns for the early years of civil registration clearly show. In the mid-nineteenth century the rate was well under 100 per 1000.[18] There is therefore nothing implausible in the early eighteenth-century level of infant mortality revealed by reconstitution, but its subsequent apparent fall must reflect deteriorating registration. It would therefore be foolhardy to include the period after about 1770.

In **Ipplepen**, as so often elsewhere, the 1790s appear to have been a decade when burial coverage worsened. The trend in the number of baptisms was broadly flat from the 1770s to the 1820s, when the successive decadal totals of baptisms linked to reconstituted families were 161, 196, 203, 169, 198, and 213, but burials behaved differently. The comparable decadal burial totals over the same period dipped sharply in the 1790s, recovered in the 1800s, but again fell to a low level in the 1810s. The successive totals were 96, 109, 63, 96, 77, and 105. Hence the decision to treat 1789 as the closing date of reliable registration.

The **Reigate** register was intermittently defective in its early years and at times registration failed completely; for example, no burials were recorded in the years 1583–6. From 1593 onwards, however, though there were still occasional years when the register was not complete, for example in 1605 and 1618 in the baptism register, coverage appears generally satisfactory. The reconstitution of Reigate was taken only as far as 1769, which means that it cannot be included in groups 3 and 4 whose end dates are 1789 and 1837. But in any case there is some reason to doubt the quality of the reconstitution data after 1729, which is accordingly taken as the closing date. The number of baptisms recorded in the register fell from 683 in 1720–9 to no more than 488 in 1770–9 at a time when in most parishes the number of baptisms was rising strongly, and, while the burial totals showed little change over these decades, the proportion of burials that could be linked to individuals on FRFs fell sharply from almost 70 per cent in the 1720s, a typical figure for the

---

[18] In the registration district of Bideford and Holsworthy, of which Hartland formed part, the level of infant mortality in 1841, 1842, 1845, and 1846, was 71 per 1000; fig. 6.5, p. 232.

reconstitution parishes as a whole,[19] to less than 30 per cent by the 1750s. A significant percentage of burials will always fail to link to a previous baptism or marriage, of course, because of the effect of migration. In parishes where the level of immigration was high the proportion of unlinked burials may also be relatively high. But a *change* in the linkage proportion as conspicuous as that which occurred in Reigate is necessarily suspicious.

Registration in both the baptism and burial registers of **Shepshed** was often defective in the 1570s and 1580s, and the number of burials recorded in the 1590s remained modest, even though this was a decade in which mortality was commonly heavy. Prudence therefore suggests a 1600 start. Thereafter the recording of events appears to have been generally satisfactory, apart from a probable weakening of coverage in the Commonwealth period, which affected both baptisms and burials.[20]

It is convenient for the sake of brevity to refer to **Southill** as if it were a single parish, but, as will have been clear from table 2.1, this reconstitution was based on the entries in the registers of both Southill, a relatively large parish, and the small and closely linked neighbouring parish of Campton with Shefford. The parishes are treated as a single unit throughout this study. The totals of both baptisms and burials in Southill suggest that registration was frequently incomplete in the 1550s and 1560s, and, in the case of burials, the problem probably continued into the later 1570s, suggesting 1580 as a start date.[21] Southill also experienced in a particularly acute form an abrupt worsening in burial registration after the 1780s, which suggests 1789 as a closing date. The number of baptisms linked to reconstituted families was remarkably steady in number in the range 500–70 in five successive decades from the 1770s to the 1810s before rising sharply in the next two decades. The number of burials, in contrast, plummeted for three decades after the 1780s. The successive decadal figures from the 1770s to the 1820s were 262, 328, 183, 136, 187, and 262. It would plainly be unwise to trust data drawn from the period after 1790.

Baptisms in **Terling** appear to have suffered from underrecording in the late 1550s and early 1560s, suggesting that it is prudent to ignore the years before 1564. The parish also experienced the deterioration in burial registration that occurred widely late in the eighteenth century, though in Terling the nadir appears to have been reached rather later

---

[19] Tab. 3.4, p. 55.

[20] Shepshed was, however, a parish in which the proportion of the population which continued to use the Anglican rites fell substantially in the late eighteenth and early nineteenth centuries: Levine, 'The reliability of parochial registration'.

[21] The earliest surviving register for Campton with Shefford only began in 1568.

than in most other parishes. In the six decades from 1770–9 to 1820–9 the number of baptisms linked to reconstituted families showed an irregular but substantial rise (197, 181, 213, 209, 234, 283), but the number of burials over the same decades changed so implausibly as to cause distrust of any tabulations based on data after 1789 (107, 131, 96, 113, 65, 84).

Finally, there is **Willingham**. A patch of defective burial registration between 1581 and 1586 suggests delaying the start until 1587. And from the end of the 1720s a striking change in customary practice in the seasonal distribution of baptisms argues strongly against using later material. Before 1730 the distribution resembled that found elsewhere in England,[22] but thereafter there was an abrupt change. In the 1730s and 1740s well over a third of all baptisms were concentrated in September alone. In the next three decades the favoured month changed to October but the concentration became even more pronounced. In the 1760s almost a half of all baptisms (73 out of 159) took place in October. At the same time that custom began to favour baptism in a particular month there was also a sharp fall in the total number of baptisms and a sharp reduction in the apparent level of age-specific marital fertility. It therefore seemed sensible to reject all data from 1730 onwards.

There remain 12 parishes which appear to be of acceptable quality throughout the period covered by the reconstitution. It would be absurd to suppose, of course, that registration was invariably complete in these 12, or indeed in the periods that survived scrutiny in the 14 parishes just discussed. Occasional defects are usually visible in the aggregative data, as when there is a run of several months, or even of a year or two, with many fewer entries than normal or a shorter period in which there appears to have been a complete break in registration. And undoubtedly registration also fell short of complete coverage from time to time in ways that are not detectable in frequency counts of events. But any remaining defects that are recognisable in the aggregative pattern of recorded events are infrequent and small in scale, and will have only minor effects on any demographic rates based on them. Subtler forms of incompleteness that are not visible in the aggregative data will be discussed where appropriate in later chapters.

It might appear that this chapter is not placed where logic suggests it might best stand. To devote part of it to a discussion of the best strategy to adopt to overcome the problems associated with the wide range of

---

[22] That is, a marked peak in late spring and a trough in the late summer and early autumn: Wrigley and Schofield, *Population history of England*, fig. 8.1, p. 288.

dates at which reliable registration began and ended involves the assumption that the amalgamation of data from the whole set of parishes is justified. If each were to remain a separate entity for description and analysis, and no groups of parishes were to be formed, much of the preceding discussion would be otiose. Only if there is good reason to suppose that the 26 parishes, and particularly the four groups formed from them, mirror national characteristics and national demo-graphic behaviour fairly closely is it imperative to find a solution to the difficulties arising from their varying chronological coverage. However, to have dealt with the question of their representativeness first would have resulted in even more serious inconsistencies. Until the strategy of forming four groups had been decided upon, and their composition determined, tests of representativeness could not be made, either for each group or for the set of parishes as a whole. Even a matter as elementary as the exact number of usable reconstitutions could not be specified. With these issues settled, however, we can now turn to the question of the representativeness of the 26 parishes.

3

Representativeness

The slow accumulation of completed reconstitutions by the Cambridge Group was a haphazard process. Those who volunteered to undertake a reconstitution made a choice from a list of parishes which had appeared *prima facie* to possess suitable registers.[1] Alternatively, a local historian might write describing a register in which he or she was interested and suggest that a reconstitution was feasible. Such offers were normally accepted provided that further tests demonstrated that the register was indeed capable of sustaining a successful reconstitution, at least for a substantial period of time. There could therefore be no prior expectation that the set of reconstitutions would prove to reflect the behaviour of the nation as a whole. Such a coincidence was most unlikely. Nor did this seem unfortunate since the individual reconstitutions were intended to reflect extremes of local experience which would establish the extent of the variability of demographic characteristics, as they reflected local economic, geographical, and cultural peculiarities. Remote, upland pastoral economies; market towns engaged in handicraft industry and providing services; centres of early industrial growth; villages dependent chiefly on arable agriculture; such communities might be expected to differ from one another considerably.

Initial investigation, however, suggested that the improbable was happening as the total of reconstitutions reached and passed the two dozen mark. Just as with the 404 parishes which contributed data to the aggregative study,[2] so with the reconstitution parishes, an attempt was made to collect certain standard items of information to enable the distinctive features of each parish to be specified. The gradual accumulation of such information showed the closeness of the similarity

[1] See above pp. 6–8.
[2] Wrigley and Schofield, *Population history of England,* tab. 2.3., p. 39.

between the mensurable characteristics of the set of reconstitution parishes and the national whole.

In this chapter attention is focused on two indicators which offer in combination a searching test of the validity of the claim that the reconstitution parishes mirror national characteristics. The first concerns occupational structure; the second the trends and fluctuations in the totals of baptisms, burials, and marriages over the quarter millennium from 1580 to 1837. If it is true both that the workforce in the reconstitution parishes was making its living from employments whose relative importance conformed to the national pattern, and also that the trends and fluctuations in totals of events were much the same in the 26 reconstitutions as in the country as a whole, it is hard to resist the conclusion that the reconstituted parishes shared many of the characteristics that would have been displayed by a group of parishes drawn by a random sampling procedure from the 10 000 ancient parishes of England.

The occupational structure of the reconstitution parishes

The 1841 census is often regarded as the first to yield useful data on occupation. The printed tabulations are very detailed, if unstructured, for the country as a whole and at the county level, though not, unfortunately, below that level. True, since this was the first census to be based on individual household schedules, which were in turn transcribed and consolidated in enumerators' books, it is also possible, at least in principle, by using data drawn from the enumerators' books, to establish the occupational structure of any chosen areal unit smaller than the county. But this is only possible at the cost of great labour. However, the 1831 census, which has the attraction of lying just within the period covered by parish reconstitutions, though based, like the three earlier censuses, on returns made by the parish overseers rather than by individual householders, contains more occupational information about individual parishes than its predecessors. It can be used to test the representativeness of the reconstitution parishes as a group. The earlier censuses, apart from the first, attempted nothing beyond a rough classification by family into three broad categories. In 1811 the question asked was: 'What number of families in your parish, township, or place, are chiefly employed in and maintained by agriculture; how many families are chiefly employed in and maintained by trade, manufacture, or handicraft; and how many families are not comprized in either of the two preceding classes?'[3]

---

[3] *1811 Census*, Preliminary observations, p. ix.

In 1821 the same question was asked though it was expressed more concisely. In 1801 a different question had been asked: 'What number of persons, in your parish, township, or place are chiefly employed in agriculture; how many in trade, manufactures, or handicraft; and, how many are not comprized in any of the preceding classes?'[4]

In 1831 overseers were again asked the questions that had been in use from 1811 onwards but more detailed information was solicited about all males aged 20 years or more, and the results were then published in the census parish by parish rather than in county summaries. Table 3.1 provides such data for the 26 reconstitution parishes, together with the other summary information for each parish collected by the overseers, including the results of the earlier standard question about the occupation of family units. The first three columns give details of housing; columns 4–7 show the occupational picture produced by asking the 'traditional' questions; columns 8–10 give population totals; columns 11–21 deal with the occupations of the adult male population; and, finally, the last two columns 22–3 are devoted to female servants and to male servants under the age of 20. By later standards the information in columns 11–21 is sparse, and perhaps idiosyncratic, but it may nonetheless serve the present purpose well.

In considering these data in detail, it should be borne in mind that manufacturing was so defined, or so interpreted, as to include both those engaged in the new factory-based industry found in areas like Lancashire and the West Riding and those working in handicraft industry where the industry found its outlets in national or international markets (such as the framework knitters in Shepshed, for example). However, handicraft manufacture for purely local markets was *excluded* (so that trades such as those practised by blacksmiths, shoemakers, tailors, or millers would appear under handicraft rather than manufacturing). This explains the high proportion of zeros in column 15 (manufacturing).[5]

---

[4] *1801 Census*, Enumeration, unnumbered preliminary page.
[5] The formal definitions of the two categories were rather bald. Manufacture was defined as comprising those engaged in 'manufacture or in making manufacturing machinery; but not including labourers in warehouses, porters, messengers, etc.'; retail trade and handicrafts as men who were 'masters, shopmen, journeymen, apprentices, or in any capacity requiring skill in the business; but not including labourers, porters, messengers, etc.'. But Rickman's intention was made clearer by a list of the main subdivisions of retail trade and handicraft (87 in number, of which a few were further subdivided), and by the notes at the end of the county summaries which reveal how Rickman chose to make the distinction between the two groups. His intention is made especially clear, for example, in the Northamptonshire note: 'The shoemakers of Northampton, Wellingborough and Irthlingborough, in so far as they may appear to exceed the usual number

The total population of the 26 parishes in 1831 was 87 693 or 0.67 per cent of the national total of 13 091 005 (England only),[6] so that about 1 person in every 137 in the country as a whole lived in one of the 26 parishes.

Table 3.1 leaves no room for doubt that local occupational patterns were highly variable. Some parishes were still almost wholly given over to agriculture. In Ash, Bridford, Great Oakley, Hartland, and Terling, for example, the percentages of the adult male labour force engaged in agriculture were respectively 74, 84, 80, 74, and 76, while at the other extreme in Gainsborough and Lowestoft the comparable percentages were under 10. In 18 of the 26 parishes no adult males were employed in manufacture, yet in Shepshed manufacturing employed 58 per cent of adult males, and in Gedling and Birstall, the other two main manufacturing centres, the comparable percentages were 44 and 32. The third major category, rivalling agriculture in size, was retail trade and handicraft. Here the large market towns led the way. In Banbury 52 per cent of adult males were returned in this category; in Gainsborough 51 per cent; though Dawlish (46 per cent), Alcester (45 per cent), and Lowestoft (42 per cent) were not far behind. At the other extreme, Bridford, Gedling, Hartland, Shepshed, and Terling all fell in the range 13 to 16 per cent. Clearly, there could be no presumption that a chance grouping of parishes would possess a collective pattern similar to that found nationally.

Table 3.2 shows how the proportional distribution of occupations in the 26 parishes as a whole compares with the national picture and also with England without the metropolis. If the percentages in columns 6 (provincial England) and 7 (the 26 parishes) are compared, it will be seen that the overall agreement is moderately close, but that there are some discrepancies. Within agriculture, the category 'occupiers not employing labour' is somewhat overrepresented in the reconstitution parishes. Agriculture as a whole, however, is underrepresented (30.2 per cent compared with 34.7 per cent), whereas manufacturing (13.6 and 10.7 per cent) and retail trade and handicraft (30.2 and 27.9 per cent) are overrepresented. Elsewhere the differences are not pronounced except that 'others (not servants)' are again more numerous in the reconstitution parishes (7.2 per cent: 5.8 per cent).

Much of the discrepancy between the occupational structures shown in columns 6 and 7 reflects the influence of the presence of a single parish, Birstall. Birstall was by far the most populous of the reconstitu-

of shoemakers in places of similar population, and therefore produce an article consumed elsewhere, may be deemed manufacturers.' *1831 Census*, Enumeration abstract, I, pp. 446–7.   [6] It was 0.66 per cent in 1801.

Table 3.1 *The occupational structure of the reconstitution parishes in 1831*

	Houses			Families				Persons		
	(1)	(2)	(3)	(4)	(5)	(6)	(7)	(8)	(9)	(10)
Alcester	491	30	1	74	272	173	519	1121	1284	2405
Aldenham	278	28	1	161	66	66	293	771	723	1494
Ash	388	8	4	302	81	46	429	1097	1043	2140
Austrey	103	3	0	65	27	19	111	271	269	540
Banbury	1148	54	10	132	710	445	1287	2909	2997	5906
Birstall	4755	378	44	437	2685	1709	4831	12005	12098	24103
Bottesford	277	6	1	145	105	44	294	647	673	1320
Bridford	79	2	0	83	12	2	97	276	253	529
Colyton	436	20	6	144	164	139	447	1056	1126	2182
Dawlish	572	45	3	238	225	112	575	1362	1789	3151
Earsdon	450	20	0	44	117	338	499	1034	1087	2121
Gainsborough	1687	171	15	141	614	959	1714	3543	3992	7535
Gedling	473	182	7	143	310	63	516	1136	1207	2343
Gt Oakley	219	4	0	166	53	0	219	568	550	1118
Hartland	393	14	3	264	102	39	405	1101	1042	2143
Ipplepen	205	11	2	124	54	50	228	584	580	1164
Lowestoft	857	32	8	53	349	513	915	1970	2268	4238
March	1016	42	16	511	334	178	1023	2542	2575	5117
Methley	339	5	0	161	67	119	347	813	780	1593
Morchard Bishop	375	17	3	210	132	80	422	941	1062	2003
Odiham	503	13	5	246	157	104	507	1276	1371	2647
Reigate	554	14	3	211	262	171	644	1588	1809	3397
Shepshed	753	37	0	140	582	47	769	1897	1817	3714
Southill	454	5	6	289	111	111	511	1220	1275	2495
Terling	182	8	0	123	41	22	186	448	444	892
Willingham	293	1	6	169	105	54	328	707	696	1403
Total	17280	1150	144	4776	7737	5603	18116	42883	44810	87693

Notes: the column numbering indicates the following: **Houses:** (1) Inhabited; (2) Uninhabited; (3) Building **Families:** (4) Agriculture; (5) Trade, manufacture & handicraft; (6) Other; (7) Total **Persons:** (8) Males; (9) Females; (10) Total **Agriculture:** (11) Occupiers employing labour; (12) Occupiers not employing labour;

tion parishes. In 1831 it contained 27.5 per cent of the combined population of the 26 parishes: in 1801 it had contained 25.8 per cent of the combined total.[7] It lay within an area in which employment in woollen textiles was growing very rapidly in the eighteenth and early nineteenth centuries. Its size, high growth rate, and distinctive economic base meant that, of all those engaged in manufacture in the reconstitution parishes in 1831, more than 60 per cent were to be found in Birstall alone, even though the percentage of the adult male labour force in manufacturing was lower in Birstall than in either of the other two main 'manufacturing' parishes, Shepshed and Gedling. Parishes sharing the same broad characteristics as Birstall were, of course, a very important feature of economic growth in Georgian England, but Birstall

[7] Tab. 3.1, and tab. 2.1, pp. 22–3.

	Agriculture			Males aged 20 and over							Other	
(11)	(12)	(13)	(14)	(15)	(16)	(17)	(18)	(19)	(20)	(21)	(22)	(23)
8	6	57	71	89	225	39	48	8	19	499	14	110
20	2	221	243	0	80	18	1	15	23	380	5	35
41	14	344	399	0	111	6	7	6	7	536	0	89
9	9	56	74	0	35	4	3	27	5	148	6	25
25	10	123	158	125	764	106	238	66	18	1 475	6	330
142	263	383	788	1 684	1 292	118	582	809	31	5 304	14	314
26	17	110	153	0	106	10	26	24	3	322	3	57
14	8	96	118	0	20	1	0	2	0	141	0	9
50	27	130	207	0	201	16	45	34	11	514	12	88
28	43	142	213	0	272	41	32	13	16	587	6	278
16	2	42	60	47	81	13	241	13	2	457	0	34
19	23	128	170	0	916	148	420	126	18	1 798	13	385
22	43	107	172	273	99	7	51	6	7	615	0	42
13	0	202	215	0	51	1	0	0	2	269	3	33
85	31	300	416	0	93	10	0	42	4	565	0	72
39	16	102	157	0	49	17	25	10	5	263	0	38
4	9	61	74	0	417	73	382	27	19	992	5	182
78	84	369	531	0	324	22	57	42	57	1 033	52	185
26	4	137	167	0	85	10	135	16	2	415	5	37
41	15	224	280	2	88	6	22	29	0	427	0	33
23	1	273	297	3	146	27	123	27	17	640	10	90
15	5	248	268	0	283	61	129	64	22	827	26	228
27	25	138	190	553	123	14	29	37	3	949	0	33
17	4	315	336	0	152	17	74	18	18	615	9	63
20	4	154	178	0	36	3	14	4	0	235	5	18
46	50	109	205	0	103	16	1	9	0	334	0	43
854	715	4 571	6 140	2 776	6 152	804	2 685	1 474	309	20 340	194	2 851

(13) Labourers; (14) Total **Males aged 20 and over**: (15) Manufacture (16) Retail trade & handicraft; (17) Capitalists; (18) Labourers not agricultural; (19) Others (not servants); (20) Servants; (21) Total **Other**: (22) Male servants under 20; (23) Female servants. *Source*: *1831 Census*, Enumeration abstract.

clearly looms too large within the set of reconstitution parishes, threatening to suffuse with its own image any picture built up from the data from the 26 parishes.

A simple expedient was adopted to overcome this problem. Its effect is visible in columns 4 and 8 of table 3.2. If Birstall is given only half-weight in calculating the occupational structure of the 26 parishes (that is, treated as if its population in 1831 were 12053 rather than 24103 and all other totals reduced proportionately), the overall picture changes significantly. The numbers in column 4 and the percentages in column 8 are the result of giving half-weight both to Birstall and to Shepshed, a much smaller parish. Shepshed contained the second largest concentration of manufacturing employment in the 26 parishes.[8]

[8] Tab. 3.1.

Table 3.2 The occupational structure of England and of the 26 reconstitution parishes compared

		England without	26 parishes	26 parishes	Percentages from			
	England (1)	London (2)	(3)	(adjusted)[a] (4)	col. (1) (5)	col. (2) (6)	col. (3) (7)	col. (4) (8)
Houses								
Inhabited	2 326 022	2 129 356	17 280	14 525	94.4	94.8	93.0	93.2
Uninhabited	113 885	97 477	1 150	942	4.6	4.3	6.2	6.0
Building	23 462	19 376	144	122	1.0	0.9	0.8	0.8
Total	2 463 369	2 246 209	18 574	15 589	100.0	100.0	100.0	100.0
Families								
Agriculture	761 848	758 371	4 776	4 487	27.7	31.6	26.4	29.3
Trade, manufacture & handicraft	1 182 912	986 292	7 737	6 103	43.1	41.1	42.7	39.8
Other	801 076	653 317	5 603	4 724	29.2	27.2	30.9	30.8
Total	2 745 836	2 397 980	18 116	15 315	100.0	100.0	100.0	100.0
Persons								
Males	6 376 627	5 693 568	42 883	35 931	48.7	49.0	48.9	48.7
Females	6 714 378	5 925 496	44 810	37 852	51.3	51.0	51.1	51.3
Total	13 091 005	11 619 064	87 693	73 784	100.0	100.0	100.0	100.0
Agriculture								
Occupiers employing labour	141 460	141 129	854	769	14.4	14.4	13.9	13.6
Occupiers not employing labour	94 883	94 601	715	570	9.7	9.7	11.6	10.1
Labourers	744 407	741 175	4 571	4 310	75.9	75.9	74.4	76.3
Total	980 750	976 905	6 140	5 651	100.0	100.0	100.0	100.0

Males aged 20 & over	Agriculture	980 750	976 905	6 140	5 651	30.6	34.7	30.2	32.8
	Manufacture	314 106	302 272	2 776	1 657	9.8	10.7	13.6	9.6
	Retail trade & handicraft	964 177	783 422	6 152	5 444	30.1	27.9	30.2	31.6
	Capitalists	179 983	124 130	804	738	5.6	4.4	4.0	4.3
	Labourers not agricultural	500 950	410 800	2 685	2 379	15.7	14.6	13.2	13.8
	Others (not servants)	189 389	162 724	1 474	1 050	5.9	5.8	7.2	6.1
	Servants	70 629	51 729	309	291	2.2	1.8	1.5	1.7
	Total	3 199 984	2 811 982	20 340	17 213	100.0	100.0	100.0	100.0
Other	Male servants under 20	30 777	24 416	194	187				
	Female servants	518 705	429 188	2 851	2 677				

[a] The totals in col. 4 are derived from those in col. 3 by reducing the latter in each case by one half of the totals for the parishes of Birstall and Shepshed.

Source: as tab. 3.1.

The combined effect is to produce a slight overcorrection (in that the percentage in manufacturing in column 8 is *lower* than that in column 6), but the difference is slight, and this gives a generally improved agreement between the occupational structure of the reconstituted parishes and the national whole. One reason for experimenting with reweighting, of course, was that if it produced a substantially improved match with the national pattern, it would be easy to use the selected weights in any demographic calculations from the reconstitution data base, and so to endow any empirical results with a greater authority.

The percentages in column 8 of table 3.2 match those in column 6 better than do those in column 7 in every individual case except for retail trade and handicraft. Often the improvement is striking and the paired percentages are very close. The lack of agreement in retail trade and handicraft (31.6 per cent as compared with 27.9 per cent) reflects the overrepresentation of large market towns among the 26 parishes, which in turn occurred because larger than average parishes promised better for reconstitution than small ones.[9] Banbury and Gainsborough contributed 27.3 per cent to the total of employment in this category in the reconstitution parishes as a whole, although their combined population was only 15.3 per cent of the overall total (or 30.9 per cent and 18.2 per cent when Birstall and Shepshed are given half-weight). A further round of reweighting could have overcome this problem and secured a still closer match between the reconstitution parishes and provincial England, but a strongly 'interventionist' strategy seemed unnecessary.

The percentages in table 3.2 constitute a plausible case for supposing that information derived from the set of reconstitution parishes may well reflect national trends sufficiently accurately to give them a wide relevance, if judgement is based on occupational criteria. Since, however, there was only a very brief period when all 26 parishes were in observation simultaneously (table 2.2 shows that only the period 1680–1729 is common to all four groups), it is of greater operational significance to consider the occupational structure of the subsets of parishes forming the four groups rather than that of the full set of 26 parishes. They, too, should match the national pattern tolerably closely if results based on them are to command assent as a guide to national demographic trends and characteristics.

Table 3.3 sets out in summary form the same information for the four groups as was given in table 3.2, while repeating the parallel data for the country as a whole, and for the full set of 26 parishes. Groups 2 and 3 call for little comment. They include such a large number of parishes that it

---

[9] See above, pp. 20–1.

Table 3.3 The occupational structure of England and of the four parish groups compared (percentages)

	England (1)	England without London (2)	26 parishes (3)	26 parishes (adjusted)ᵃ (4)	Group 1 (5)	Group 2 (6)	Group 3 (7)	Group 4 (8)
Occupiers employing labour	14.4	14.4	13.9	13.6	12.2	13.7	13.1	12.4
Occupiers not employing labour	9.7	9.7	11.6	10.1	8.5	11.1	9.5	8.8
Labourers	75.9	75.9	74.4	76.3	79.2	75.2	77.4	78.8
Total agriculture	100.0	100.0	100.0	100.0	100.0	100.0	100.0	100.0
Agriculture	30.6	34.7	30.2	32.8	30.0	29.5	30.7	34.8
Manufacture	9.8	10.7	13.6	9.6	5.0	11.0	12.4	13.4
Retail trade & handicraft	30.1	27.9	30.2	31.6	36.7	32.7	31.1	32.4
Capitalists	5.6	4.4	4.0	4.3	5.1	4.5	4.1	4.1
Labourers not agricultural	15.7	14.6	13.2	13.8	16.5	14.0	13.9	10.1
Others (not servants)	5.9	5.8	7.2	6.1	4.5	6.7	6.5	3.7
Servants	2.2	1.8	1.5	1.7	2.2	1.8	1.3	1.4
Total	100.0	100.0	100.0	100.0	100.0	100.0	100.0	100.0
Total males aged 20 and over	3199984	2811982	20340	17213	9822	14675	12674	5076
Total population	13091005	11619069	87693	73784	41236	62088	54012	21367

ᵃ Totals for Birstall and Shepshed were halved for the calculations in col. 4 and in the groups in which they appear (for Birstall, groups 2 and 3; for Shepshed, groups 2, 3, and 4).
Note: for the composition of the four groups see tab. 2.2, p. 26.
Source: as tab. 3.1.

would be surprising if they were not broadly similar in occupational structure to the full set. Compared to the 26 parishes (column 4) they are less agricultural, but more given to manufacturing, and their overall agreement with the pattern for provincial England is as close as that for the full set. Such discrepancies as there are reflect the fact that the 'missing' parishes in the two groups were strongly agricultural, and were almost devoid of manufacturing employment. For example, the six parishes absent from group 2 (Ash, Dawlish, Earsdon, Great Oakley, Ipplepen, and Morchard Bishop) contained only 49 men engaged in manufacturing in 1831 (of whom 47 were in Earsdon), but as many as 1324 men out of an adult male labour force in the six parishes of 2539, or 52 per cent, were engaged in agriculture.

The first and last groups require more comment. In the first only 5 per cent of men were engaged in manufacture, a much lower figure than in the other groups or than in provincial England, and there was an offsetting overrepresentation of employment in retail trade and handicraft. The reason for this marked difference between the first and later groups is that neither Birstall nor Shepshed, the two parishes with the largest number of men in manufacture, is a member of group 1. The framework knitters of Shepshed and the weavers of Birstall make a big difference to the occupational balance of the set of parishes as a whole. At first glance this might suggest serious doubts about the representativeness of group 1. Alarm on this score is, however, misplaced. As a distinct category, manufacture, in the sense in which the term was used in the 1831 census, was very largely a novel feature of the later eighteenth century, the period when parishes like Birstall were growing so fast. In the Tudor and Stuart period a distinction between manufacture and retail trade and handicraft would have been much harder to draw. If the two categories are combined the difference between group 1 and the pattern in provincial England is much more muted (41.7 and 38.6 per cent, respectively).

In the final group the continued good 'fit' with provincial England may occasion some surprise since so few parishes remained in observation in this period. The total adult male labour force (5076) was less than 30 per cent of the total for the 26 parishes collectively (17 213), but, fortuitously, the occupational structure was not radically different from that of group 3. All three of the categories on which discussion has concentrated, manufacture, agriculture, and retail trade and handicraft, were more strongly represented in group 4 than in group 3, and in each case overrepresented compared with provincial England, though the difference was negligible in the case of agriculture; but the overall match

with the national template was only slightly less good than in the case of groups 2 and 3.

An acceptable similarity between each of the four groups of parishes and the country as a whole in respect of adult male occupational structure in 1831 is reassuring, but it is insufficient to underwrite large claims about their trustworthiness as a source of surrogate measures of national demographic behaviour. If the agreement had been poor, it would have cast doubt on the value of pooling the individual reconstitutions, but a fair agreement represents only a conditional endorsement of the enterprise, especially as it is impossible to conduct a similar comparison for an earlier date. The 1831 comparison relates to a single point in time and to a single, if fundamental, economic variable. It can be complemented, however, by a further comparison extending over the full time span of the reconstitutions and relating to the three basic demographic series. For each reconstitution parish annual totals of baptisms, burials, and marriages recorded on FRFs can be tabulated, similar to those produced in aggregative studies. By combining totals from the appropriate parishes, aggregative series for each reconstitution parish group can be obtained, and these can be compared with the template of national trends in baptisms, burials, and marriages that formed the empirical basis of the *Population history of England*.

This comparison forms the subject of the next section. It represents a searching test. The aggregative data were taken from 404 parishes. Of these 15 were among the 26 reconstitution parishes. That there was a limited overlap of membership between the two groups, however, does not detract from the severity of the test. It is inherently improbable that the two series should display similar trends when such a small proportion of the aggregative parishes were also part of the reconstitution set. It would be simple to demonstrate by experiment that if samples of 15 parishes were drawn at random from the aggregative parishes, and then increased in each case to a total of 26 parishes by selecting 12 further parishes from the rest of the country,[10] the resulting totals of events would often display substantially different trends from those found in the national template based on the earlier aggregative exercise. A close agreement arising by chance alone is improbable.

But a similar point can also be demonstrated directly. Suppose that

[10] The apparent illogicality of adding 12 to 15 and making 26 is explained by the fact that the 15 parishes in the aggregative set included both Campton with Shefford and Southill as two separate parishes, but, when the reconstitution of these adjacent parishes was undertaken, they were treated as a single entity, so that 12 further parishes are needed to create a total comparable to that in the reconstitution set of parishes.

the presence of 15 reconstitution parishes in the aggregative set exerted a strong influence on the behaviour of the birth, death, and marriage series of the 404 parishes and thus undermined the stringency of the test by concealing or moderating differences that would otherwise be apparent. If that were the case, removing the 15 from the set of 404 would produce a change in the patterns observable in the totals of events taken from the remaining 389 parishes. The totals of events in the latter can be inflated in such a way as to allow a direct comparison to be made with the former. The indexing process which allows such a comparison to be made is described below when the reconstitution patterns are compared with the national template.[11]

The comparison shows plainly that the two series display almost identical characteristics. Over the period 1662–1811 the average absolute difference (that is, ignoring sign) between the baptism totals in the 389 series and the 404 series was 0.129 per cent; between the burial totals 0.249 per cent; and between the marriage totals 0.267 per cent.[12] The maximum difference in any one year in the case of baptisms was 0.441 per cent; in the case of burials 0.880 per cent; and in the case of marriages 0.919 per cent.[13] That these percentage differences are so modest is not surprising, given that the 15 parishes contributed only 3.04 per cent of the total of baptisms in the 404 parishes, 3.22 per cent of the total of burials, and 2.95 per cent of the total of marriages. It is clear that the presence of a handful of the reconstitution parishes in the aggregative set makes no significant difference to the national template based on the

---

[11] See pp. 57–8.

[12] The comparison is made over the period 1662–1811, rather than over a longer period, because this was the period during which all the 404 parishes in the original aggregative set were in observation. Before 1662 and after 1811 some parishes passed out of observation. Allowance was made for this, of course, in constructing the national series in the *Population history of England,* but to extend the present comparison outside this central period would involve a series of complex adjustments to the data series without corresponding benefit. The central period is itself long and, if there had been characteristic differences between the totals and trends in the set of 389 parishes compared with the set of 404 parishes, this would be apparent during the central period. It should be noted that the construction of the national series from data taken from the 404 parishes involved a step in which the raw totals of events were weighted according to the size of the population of the parish in question in 1811. For this purpose the parishes were divided into six groups. This was done to make the distribution of parish sizes in the aggregative set mirror the national pattern. In removing the totals for the 15 reconstitution parishes from the totals for the 404 parishes, therefore, the totals in question were not those to be found in the registers of the 15 parishes, but the reweighted totals according to their populations in 1811. See Wrigley and Schofield, *Population history of England,* ch. 2, esp. pp. 45–56.

[13] In calculating these percentage differences, the 404 total was treated as 100 per cent, and the 389 total was related to this figure.

404 parishes. It follows that, if the trends in the totals of 'reconstitution' events parallel the national template, any such agreement must reinforce the strength of the claim that the demographic characteristics of the reconstitution parishes were similar to those of the country as a whole.

A comparison of national totals of events and totals from the parish groups

The national series of births, deaths, and marriages published in the *Population history of England* were derived ultimately from monthly totals of baptisms, burials, and marriages taken from 404 parish registers. The raw totals were corrected for deficient or defective registration; reweighted to offset the untypical size distribution of the parishes in the sample compared with that found in the 10 000 ancient parishes of England; inflated to overcome the problem posed by the fact that registration did not begin and end at the same dates in all parishes; multiplied by a factor designed to convert the totals for the 404 parishes into national totals; and, finally, increased to make good the growing effects of the spread of nonconformity, of the increasing delay between birth and baptism, and of other residual causes of non-registration.[14] The resulting totals were then used as input data for the back projection exercise.

For purposes of comparison with totals of events taken from FRFs, it is appropriate to use the totals obtained before the final two steps were taken (those designed to convert the totals from the 404 parishes into national totals, and those intended to offset growing nonconformity and residual causes of non-registration). The multiplication by a factor intended to produce estimated national totals is irrelevant for the present purpose, while the spread of nonconformity is to be ignored in a comparison of two Anglican data sets, and the same goes for the residual causes of non-registration. The increasing delay between birth and baptism is a different matter. The correction to the aggregative totals to counteract the effects of this change in social custom was made because the longer children lived without being baptised, the greater the danger that their early deaths would mean underregistration of births. The problem also exists in reconstitution parishes, but the danger is less acute because, if the child died before baptism but its burial was recorded (as was commonly, though not universally, the case), a 'dummy' baptism was created to parallel the burial, and when this is

---

[14] This series of operations is described in Wrigley and Schofield, *Population history of England*, chs. 2–5.

done no undercounting of births results. In view of this, it is arguable that this correction to the national series should not be excluded when making a comparison with reconstitution totals, but the issue appeared too minor to justify the extensive reworking of the aggregative data that would be needed to minimise this source of distortion when comparing the two series.

A few preliminary remarks are called for to clarify the nature of the aggregative totals obtained from the reconstitution parishes. Both baptism and burials totals will differ from those that would arise from a tabulation made directly from the registers. Although every legitimate baptism recorded in a parish register is included on an FRF in the course of reconstitution, baptisms of illegitimate children do not appear on FRFs. Baptism totals taken from FRFs, therefore, do not include illegitimate children, whereas the national totals of births relate, of course, to all children. If illegitimate births had been a constant fraction of total births this would not cause a problem since relative change over time would be the same whether illegitimate births were included or excluded, but this was not the case. During the eighteenth century, for example, the proportion of illegitimate births rose substantially.[15] If, therefore, the trend in reconstitution baptism totals were less buoyant than the national equivalent during the eighteenth century, this might simply reflect the effect of the exclusion of bastard children from the former series.

Reconstitution burials totals are affected by a different problem. Whereas all baptisms of legitimate children and all marriages must, by the rules of reconstitution, appear on an FRF, the same is not true of burials. Only those burials will appear on an FRF which can be linked to a preceding marriage or baptism. A man or woman who died and was buried in a parish but who had not been born or married there would not necessarily appear on any FRF.[16] Similarly, the burial of anyone baptised as illegitimate will not be linkable to a baptism since such a baptism will not appear on any FRF. Roughly 75 per cent of all burials can be linked to an FRF once the early decades of the reconstitution are past, and the proportion seldom varies significantly thereafter. Apart from the initial period, therefore, although the absolute total of burials on FRFs is always well short of the total to be found in the register, a

---

[15] See tab. 6.2, p. 219.
[16] Some such individuals do appear on FRFs because they had children baptised in the parish even though they were not themselves born or married there. In such circumstances an FRF is created since every legitimate baptism must be recorded on an FRF, and a father or mother who appeared on an FRF for this reason might subsequently be linked to a burial.

Table 3.4 *The proportion of all burials that were linked to an FRF*

| | Decades from start of reconstitution | | | | | | | | Start of | |
	1	2	3	4	5	6	7	8	Reconstitution	Reliable data
Alcester	0.213	0.360	0.576	0.627	0.637	0.665	0.653	0.754	1562	1579
Aldenham	0.345	0.461	0.460	0.570	0.627	0.706	0.700	0.601	1559	1563
Banbury	0.293	0.535	0.613	0.589	0.698	0.711	0.805	0.800	1564	1564
Bottesford	0.274	0.438	0.603	0.704	0.665	0.778	0.775	0.771	1581	1581
Colyton	0.420	0.504	0.652	0.764	0.803	0.836	0.839	0.866	1540	1578
Gainsborough	0.462	0.622	0.727	0.694	0.781	0.808	0.794	0.839	1564	1564
Gedling	0.130	0.594	0.534	0.711	0.733	0.719	0.790	0.860	1565	1565
Hartland	0.319	0.464	0.538	0.608	0.701	0.695	0.701	0.745	1558	1597
Odiham	0.311	0.274	0.512	0.652	0.584	0.595	0.623	0.672	1539	1539
Reigate	0.424	0.532	0.600	0.674	0.755	0.728	0.760	0.719	1560	1593
Shepshed	0.237	0.309	0.563	0.658	0.355	0.434	0.627	0.577	1538	1600
Willingham	0.522	0.733	0.714	0.763	0.786	0.706	0.777	0.802	1559	1587
Average	0.329	0.486	0.591	0.668	0.675	0.698	0.737	0.751		

Note: the proportions measured are from the start of the reconstitution, given in the penultimate column, and not from the start of reliable data, given in the final column.

Source: Cambridge Group reconstitutions.

55

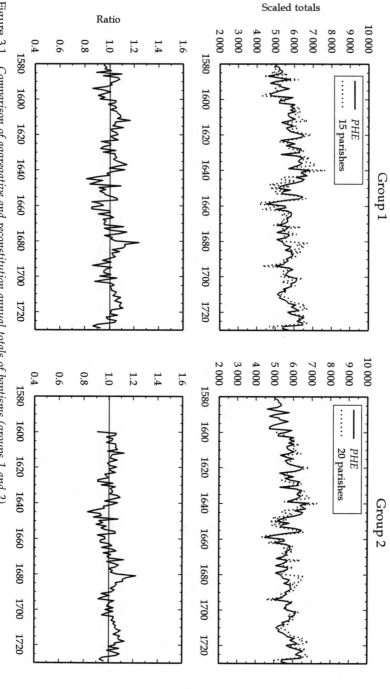

Figure 3.1 *Comparison of aggregative and reconstitution annual totals of baptisms (groups 1 and 2)*
Sources: reconstitution totals: Cambridge Group reconstitutions. National totals: Wrigley and Schofield, *Population history of England*, tab. A4.1, col. 4, pp. 537–60.

comparison of trends and fluctuations between the reconstitution totals and the national totals is meaningful. In every parish there will, however, be a 'start-up' period when the proportion of all burials that can be linked to an FRF is slowly rising, and during this period such a comparison will be uninformative. This happens because the birth or marriage of many men and women, though occurring in the parish, will have taken place before the inception of registration, so that their burials cannot be linked to any earlier record. The way in which the proportion of linkable burials slowly rises to reach a plateau after about 70 years may be seen in table 3.4.

Standard aggregative tabulations of the total of burials recorded in the registers were available for only 12 parishes, and the comparison in table 3.4 is therefore confined to these 12. The overall pattern shown in the average figures at the foot of the table is probably a reliable guide to the rise in the proportion of burials 'captured' on FRFs which normally takes place as time elapses after the start of a reconstitution.[17]

Baptisms

Comparison of the reconstitution and aggregative totals is shown graphically in the following figures. In each figure, one line represents the annual totals of events in the parishes in a given group (broken line) while the other shows the comparable national totals (solid line).[18] The reconstitution totals of Birstall and Shepshed are given half-weight for reasons set out earlier in this chapter.[19]

The left-hand panels of figure 3.1 compare the baptisms registered in the 15 parishes of group 1 over the period 1580–1729 with the totals of births over the same period in the 404 parishes of the *Population history of England*. The right-hand panels do the same for the 20 parishes of group 2. To make a comparison of the pairs of series simple, the total of events in the reconstitution parishes over the whole period covered, shown in

---

[17] It might be thought that many figures for individual decades in particular parishes would be misleading, especially in the earliest decades of registration. In the nature of the exercise it was essential to begin the comparison at the date when reconstitution started, but in several parishes some aspect of registration in the early decades of the reconstitution appeared unreliable and the start date for reliable data was therefore set later than the beginning of the reconstitution (tab. 2.1, pp. 22–3). In contrast to what might have been expected, however, the ratios are not consistently different in the two types of parish (that is those where the two dates are the same and those where they are not), and it is unlikely that the absence of this complication would have made any significant difference to the outcome of the exercise.

[18] The national totals are taken from Wrigley and Schofield, *Population history of England*, tab. A4.1, col. 4, pp. 537–60.   [19] See above pp. 43–8.

the upper panel, was inflated so that it exactly equalled the total over the same period in the aggregative series. Thus, if the overall total of baptisms in the 404 parishes between 1580 and 1729 were exactly 10 times as large as the total of baptisms in group 1 over the same period, and if the absolute total for 1610 in the latter series were 550, it would be plotted in figure 3.1 as 5500. The vertical scale is therefore keyed to the aggregative totals. Using this method of comparison implies, of course, that if, say, in the reconstitution series the totals of events were consistently below those in the aggregative series in the early years shown in a graph, there must be a compensating period later when the reverse is true. The lower panel uses the same data but shows each annual total in the aggregative series as 1.0 and plots the discrepancy between this total and the total derived from the reconstitution series as a ratio figure. This makes it easier to identify both the relative scale of discrepancies between the two series and any long-term trends in such discrepancies.

In general there is a close agreement between the trends in the two series shown in the left-hand upper panel of figure 3.1. There is no tendency for them to swing apart at either end as would happen if one were growing more rapidly than the other.

The lower left-hand panel shows that some of the individual discrepancies are substantial. In 1681 the reconstitution series was 24 per cent higher than the national series; in 1645 it was 19 per cent lower. There are also some extended periods when the reconstitution series was consistently above or below the aggregative series. Between 1607 and 1623 it was always the higher of the two, and again from 1678 to 1689, and from 1707 to 1720. Periods when there was a consistent discrepancy in the other direction were briefer, except that for almost the whole of the Civil War and Commonwealth period the reconstitution line shows values below 1.0. This is perhaps the most significant single feature of the lower panel of the graph. The pattern may be due in part to the incompleteness of baptism registration in the reconstitution parishes in this period. It is also possible that the algorithm used to detect periods of underregistration in the 404 parishes and to estimate replacement values for such periods may have produced an overcorrection. In this period many parishes had gaps in registration, or periods when registration was clearly defective, and the inflation of the raw totals of events to offset these problems shot up after 1640 from a pre-war level of 4 or 5 per cent to more than 20 per cent in every year from 1644 to 1653 with a peak value of 26.4 per cent in 1645 and 1651.[20] If the 'hole'

---

[20] Wrigley and Schofield, *Population history of England*, tab. 4.1, col. 7, pp. 537–60.

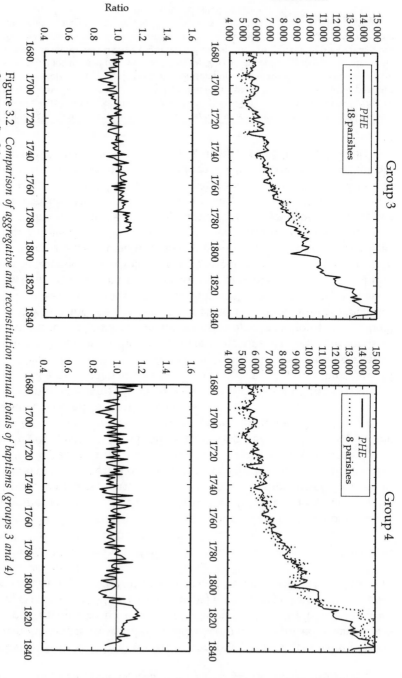

Figure 3.2   *Comparison of aggregative and reconstitution annual totals of baptisms (groups 3 and 4)*
Sources: as fig. 3.1.

between 1640 and 1660 is partly spurious, then some of the periods when the ratio is *above* unity would, of course, be reduced in length and the peaks would be less prominent. The existence of the 'hole', however, suggests that special care should be taken in interpreting fertility series derived from the reconstitutions during the period of the Civil War and Commonwealth.

The right-hand panels of figure 3.1 repeat the comparison of baptism totals for the 20 parishes of group 2 over the slightly shorter period 1600–1729. The composition of group 2 is so similar to that of group 1, differing only in the addition of a further five parishes,[21] that it is no surprise that the patterns are almost identical to those just described. In general the extreme discrepancies between the two series, as revealed in the lower panel of the figure, are less marked than with group 1, as might be expected with a larger sample of parishes and therefore some reduction in random variation, but otherwise none of the features of these panels call for further comment.[22]

Group 3, covering the years 1680–1789, consists of 18 parishes, of which 12 are common to groups 2 and 3. Figure 3.2 shows the degree of parallelism in the recorded totals for the group and the aggregative patterns. Whereas in the two previous groups the absolute totals of events varied only within narrow margins over the whole period which they covered and there was no decided secular trend, group 3 includes the decades of the middle and later eighteenth century when population growth accelerated sharply. The number of baptisms shot up, doubling over the period as a whole. The agreement between the reconstitution and national series remains reasonably satisfactory, but there is a clear long-term tendency for growth in the reconstitution series to outstrip growth in the 404 parishes. If illegitimate baptisms had been included in the reconstitution series the contrast in rapidity of growth would be still more pronounced.[23] The two lines pivot round a point about 1750 before which the reconstitution graph normally lies below the other graph, after which the reverse is the case. During the 1690s the ratio between

---

[21] Tab. 2.2, p. 26.

[22] Some light is thrown on the question of possible underregistration in the Civil War and Commonwealth period, also suggested by group 2 baptism trends, by referring to fertility data for the group. The total marital fertility rate 20–49 in the group 2 parishes for 1640–9 and 1650–9 was 7.2 and 6.5 children per woman respectively. These rates are somewhat lower than the average for group 2 as a whole (7.3). Indeed, the rate in the 1650s was marginally the lowest decennial rate in the group 2 series (1600–1729). But the discrepancy is not so large as to constitute clear evidence of registration failure. The total marital fertility rate in the 1690s, for example, was only 6.6.

[23] The scale of the rise in illegitimacy is indicated in tab. 6.2, p. 219.

the two series is on average 0.92; in the 1780s the comparable ratio is 1.08. The extremes of divergence are no more marked than in earlier comparisons but the minuses lie chiefly to the left and the pluses to the right of the pivotal date. The extent of the 'tilt' would, however, be reduced if the aggregative series had been adjusted to include a further inflation related to the increasing delay between birth and baptism.[24] The 'true' discrepancy between the series is therefore probably less marked than appears in the panels for group 3.

Table 3.5 shows that there was a great range in the growth rate of baptism totals among the individual parishes in group 3 between 1725–44 and 1770–89. At one extreme the number of baptisms in Earsdon rose by 167 per cent over this period: at the other, in Bottesford, it fell by 16 per cent. The fact that Birstall, the largest parish, grew by 92 per cent explains much of the increase in the discrepancy ratio, even though Birstall is included at half-weight. If Birstall were removed from the group, the group 3 total would grow by 35 per cent rather than 43 per cent between 1725–44 and 1770–89, and the rise in the discrepancy ratio would disappear.

The right-hand panels of figure 3.2 repeat the same exercise for the final group covering the period 1680–1837. There are only 8 parishes in the reconstitution sample in this period, and it might be expected that this would result in a poorer agreement between the two series. In fact the agreement between the two series is surprisingly good both in relation to trend and in the comparatively modest size of the discrepancies between the relative totals in the two series. There was an initial period of about 20 years during which the ratio declined fairly steadily from well above unity to well below unity, before settling down to a level close to unity for the whole of the eighteenth century. The most aberrant period begins in 1812 and continues through to the end of the series in 1837. In this period the reconstitution series initially surged abruptly ahead of the national series, reaching a peak in 1819 when there was a positive divergence of 19 per cent. The divergence stems from the marked rise in baptism totals in Banbury, Dawlish, and Bottesford. However, thereafter the reconstitution line falls back rapidly towards the aggregative series.

The comparison of the baptism totals from the reconstitution parishes with those derived from aggregative tabulations, therefore, appears to justify a degree of confidence in making use of the results obtained from group 4 in spite of its small size.

---

[24] Wrigley and Schofield, *Population history of England*, pp. 96–100, esp. tab. 4.5, p. 97.

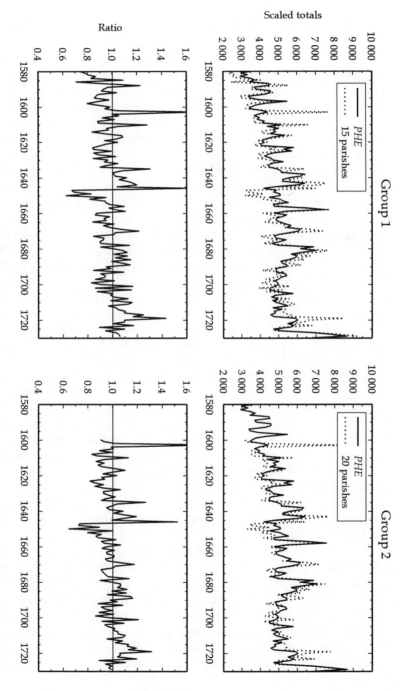

Figure 3.3 *Comparison of aggregative and reconstitution annual totals of burials (groups 1 and 2)*
Sources: as fig. 3.1.

Burials

The next series of comparisons relates to burials in the two series. The left-hand panels of figure 3.3 show that in group 1 the overall agreement is again reassuringly close. There is clearly some similarity between the behaviour of the paired baptism series and of the comparable paired burial series for this group. For example, the pattern during the Civil War and Commonwealth period, visible in the baptism series, is broadly repeated in the burial series, though in a more pronounced form since there are a few years beginning in the late 1640s when the ratio figures in the lower panel drop below 0.7 (1647, 1648, and 1650: in the last of the three it was only 0.62). It is most unlikely that the low ratio is the result of having significantly overinflated the burial totals in the aggregative series, since the crude death rate in these three years was 24.0, 23.2, and 25.2 per 1000 respectively, a relatively modest level.[25] Mortality results for this period, based on reconstitution data, must clearly be treated with considerable reserve.

The discrepancy ratio also reaches extremely high levels occasionally, notably in 1603 (1.74) and 1646 (1.66). These striking peaks arise because of exceptional epidemic mortality in one or more parishes not mirrored to the same extent in the national sample of 404 parishes (though 1603 was also a year of high mortality in the national series). In 1603, for example, there was a very severe outbreak of plague in Lowestoft. The number of burials linked to FRFs in the parish soared to a total of 269, compared with 66 in 1602 and 22 in 1604. The total of burials in group 1 in these three years was 573, 318, and 294 respectively. Of the rise of 255 burials in the 15 parishes in group 1 between 1602 and 1603, 203 is attributable to Lowestoft, and of the fall of 279 between 1603 and 1604, 247 occurred in Lowestoft.

The rather low ratios in the first two decades arise because of the 'start-up' problem already described.[26] That the effect is relatively muted is due to the fact that many of the 15 reconstitutions began well

---

[25] Ibid., tab. A3.3, p. 532. The infant and child mortality rates in these three years in the 20 parishes of group 2 were unusually low. Infant mortality, for example, averaged only 119 per 1000 in these years, compared with 174 per 1000 in the period 1640–4 and 153 per 1000 in the seven other years in the period 1645–54 (that is, in the 10-year period 1645–54, excluding 1647, 1648, and 1650). These rates relate to group 1 and to legitimate children only. For the effect of taking illegitimate infant mortality into account, see pp. 219–23 below. There was no fall in this period in the proportion of all burials recorded in the registers of the reconstitution parishes that were linked to other events on FRFs. In other words, the low level of the ratio cannot be attributed to a fall in the percentage of burials that were made use of in the process of reconstitution.

[26] See above pp. 54–7.

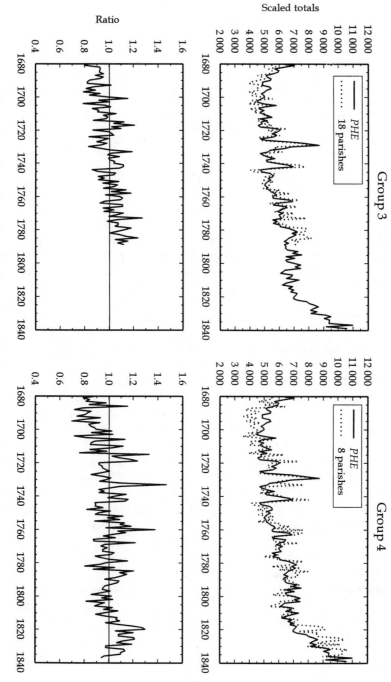

Figure 3.4 *Comparison of aggregative and reconstitution annual totals of burials (groups 3 and 4)*
Sources: as fig. 3.1.

before 1580 and had therefore reached or come close to a normal linkage percentage by the starting date of the group.[27]

As was the case with baptisms, the comparison of burial totals for group 2, consisting of 20 parishes and covering the period 1600–1729, with the 404 parish series, shown in the right-hand panels of figure 3.3, needs little additional comment, because the composition of the reconstitution sample is so little changed and the period covered is the same as for the first cohort apart from the first 20 years. Perhaps the only point worth comment is that the ratio between the two series in 1603 (1.85) is even higher than in group 1. This happens because the parish of Reigate, which is one of the five new parishes in group 2, also had a serious plague outbreak in 1603. The burials totals in Reigate in 1602, 1603, and 1604 were 27, 166, and 36. The combined burial totals in these three years for Reigate and Lowestoft were, therefore, 93, 435, and 58: the group 2 totals were 403, 786, and 375. Clearly, the surge in burial totals in Reigate and Lowestoft dominated the changes in the group as whole. Their suffering was so severe as to cause the reconstitution series to rise to a much higher peak than that found in the other series.

In group 3, covering the years 1680–1789, the 'start-up' effect is again strong, as may be seen in figure 3.4, because all six of the new parishes in the cohort began registration after 1654, and three in the 1670s. Some depression in the ratio in the early decades was therefore to be expected. Otherwise the two series agree well. The 'tilt' visible in the ratio series for baptisms is also visible in the burial series. A comparison between the two is complicated by the existence of the 'start-up' effect in the burial series (removing it would, of course, reduce the 'tilt' in the rest of the series), but clearly the phenomenon is much less pronounced in burials than in baptisms. The ratios in the lower panel are, in general, less close to unity than in the comparable baptism series, but this is to be expected in view of the generally greater volatility of burial totals from year to year.[28]

There were years of very high mortality in the late 1720s and in the early 1740s. For example, the national crude death rate was above 35 per 1000 in each year from 1727 to 1730, and stood at 34.7 and 36.7 in 1741 and 1742.[29] The two series, however, track one another closely in these years and the discrepancy ratios do not stand out as unusually high.

The narrow data base in the reconstitution series in group 4 makes for high volatility, and this is reflected in the discrepancy ratios in the right-hand panel of figure 3.4, which run at a fairly high average level.

[27] Tab. 2.1, pp. 22–3.
[28] Wrigley and Schofield, *Population history of England*, fig. 8.6, p. 316.
[29] Ibid., tab. A3.3, p. 533.

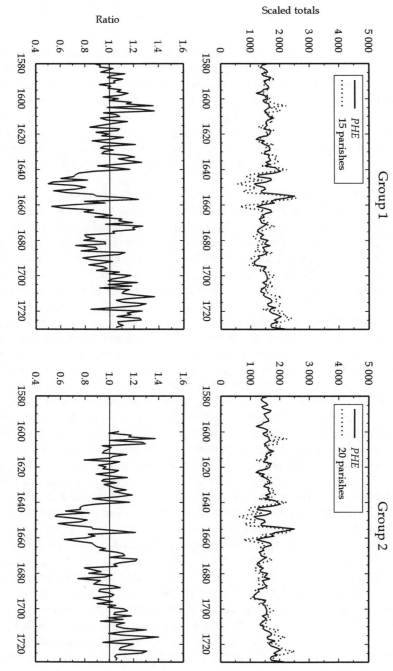

Figure 3.5 *Comparison of aggregative and reconstitution annual totals of marriages (groups 1 and 2)*
Sources: as fig. 3.1.

The 'start-up' problem is again visible, but the agreement in overall trend in the two series is encouraging. There is also a fair correspondence in the amplitude of mortality surges in the two series in bad years, such as 1729 and 1742, though there were also rogue years when the reconstitution series displays marked spikes that are not visible in the aggregative series, notably in 1818–20.

Marriages

The marriage totals from the reconstitution series should be well behaved when compared with those from the national series. There is no analogue to the problem of illegitimate children in the baptism series or to the 'start-up' problem in the burial series. On the other hand, the number of marriages was far smaller than the number of baptisms or burials, which might be expected to increase the scale of random differences between the two series.

The left-hand panels of figure 3.5 show that in group 1 this expectation is generally fulfilled. As in the other two series there is a shortfall in the reconstitution series between 1640 and 1660; this phenomenon is even more pronounced in the marriage series than in either of the other two, and for the same reason. The algorithm used in correcting the raw data in the sample of 404 parishes detected periods of defective or deficient registration in very many parishes and, to rectify such periods, subsequently inflated the recorded totals substantially; in two of the peak years, 1650 and 1651, by a factor of more than 2.0.[30] Even though marriage registration may have been somewhat less affected in the reconstitution parishes, marriage totals plummeted in them also, and in this period the discrepancy ratio is very large as a result. In 1648 it dipped as low as 0.50 and over the 12-year period 1642–53 it averaged 0.67, recovering in the Commonwealth period to 0.98 (1654–9).

A subtler problem emerged after the Restoration. For several decades after 1660 clandestine marriage was widespread in England.[31] In some cases the effects of clandestine marriage on marriage totals in the 404 parishes were interpreted as periods of underregistration by the algorithm designed to detect defective registration and replacement marriage totals were added by program to fill the 'hollows' as appropriate. The raw totals were increased by between 8 and 13 per cent in every

---

[30] Ibid., tab. A.4.1, p. 556.

[31] The nature and prevalence of clandestine marriages of various types are discussed in Gillis, 'Conjugal settlements', and *For better, for worse*, esp. ch. 3; Ingram, *Church courts, sex and marriage*, esp. pp. 212–8; Brown, 'The rise and fall of Fleet marriages'; and Boulton, 'Itching after private marryings?'.

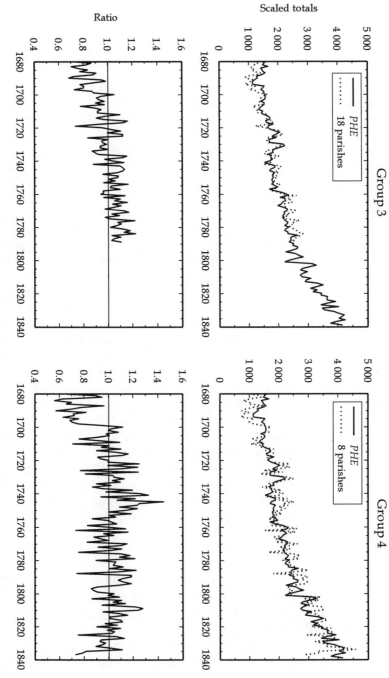

Figure 3.6 *Comparison of aggregative and reconstitution annual totals of marriages (groups 3 and 4)*
Sources: as fig. 3.1.

year from 1662 to 1695, but thereafter, initially no doubt because of the effects of the Marriage Duty Act of 1695, the annual supplement to the total of marriages added for this reason fell rapidly away to between 2 and 4 per cent.

The discrepancy ratio over the 34-year period 1662–95 suggests that clandestine marriage also affected marriage totals in the reconstitution parishes to some extent, but in this case, of course, no additions were made.[32] The shape of the trend of the ratios in the lower left-hand panel of figure 3.5 after 1660, therefore, probably reflects the influence of the changes made to the totals in the aggregative series by the replacement algorithm. The reconstitution totals, not having been amended because of clandestine marriage, tend to be relatively low down to the mid-1690s but rise thereafter.

The right-hand panels of figure 3.5 show the same exercise for group 2. The patterns are so similar to those already reviewed in discussing the first group as not to call for any further comment.

There is a tendency for the reconstitution totals in group 3 to be too low relative to the totals in the 404 parish series in the early years of the period and to be slightly too high towards its end. There is no obvious explanation for this pattern, visible in the left-hand panels of figure 3.6, though the low ratios in the early years of the cohort may be partly attributable to the effects of the treatment of clandestine marriage in the aggregative series which has already been described. Peaks and troughs agree tolerably well. The small numbers in the reconstitution series probably explain its rather more ragged and volatile behaviour. The 'tilt' in the series, visible in the case of baptisms, is somewhat less pronounced in the marriage series, where the pattern more closely resembles that in the burial series.

Finally, in group 4, shown in the right-hand panels of figure 3.6, apart from an apparent shortfall down to the 1690s, where the indirect effect of clandestine marriage may again afford a partial explanation, there is a notably good match in the long-term trends in the two series, though there were marked discrepancies between the two series in some individual years. This is hardly a surprise in view of the shrinkage in the size of group 4 compared to the other groups. Substantial annual discrepancies of this kind may be expected to occur when only 8 parishes remain in the sample.

---

[32] In some cases the effect was pronounced. In Colyton, for example, between 1665 and 1699 there were 1227 baptisms but only 128 recorded marriages, a ratio of almost 10 to 1 and a sure indication that many marriages existed that were not recorded in the Anglican register. Sharpe, 'Locating the "missing marryers"'.

What the tests of representativeness suggest

Overall, a comparison of the behaviour of totals of events drawn from the reconstitutions with the template provided by the totals of events in the set of 404 aggregative parishes is encouraging. Like the earlier analysis of occupational data from the 1831 census, it underwrites the belief that, though as a result of serendipity rather than initial design, it is reasonable to regard any findings relating to the four groups of reconstituted parishes as likely to reflect national characteristics, thus adding considerably to the interest of the exercise. Reconstitution data will not only show the range of demographic experience between parishes of different types, but also throw light on the fertility, mortality, and nuptiality characteristics of England as a whole.

This conclusion should no doubt be accepted with some reserve. It can never be possible to demonstrate conclusively that what was true of the reconstitution parishes was also true of the whole country, especially in the first two centuries of the parish register period: for the last few decades of the period the early returns of the Registrar-General offer an additional means of testing the accuracy of the rates derived from reconstitution.[33] However, it would be surprising if the underlying demographic processes that produced totals of events in the reconstitution parishes so similar in their behaviour to those found in the aggregative sample of 404 parishes were not akin to those operating nationally, especially as the occupational structure of the four groups echoes the national pattern quite closely in 1831.

The match between trends and fluctuations in the aggregative totals in the four groups and those found in the aggregative set is the more remarkable in view of the corrections made to the raw monthly totals of the 404 parishes in converting them into a series intended to represent Anglican registration nationally. The inflation of the original totals to offset the effects of defective and deficient registration and the further changes made to counteract the unrepresentative size distribution of the 404 parishes greatly enhances the plausibility of the series as reflecting national trends, but also substantially reduces the likelihood that the national pattern will be neatly paralleled in a haphazard selection of two dozen parishes. The fact that, against reasonable expectation, the match between the two series proved to be so good is not easy to explain, but it represents an opportunity too promising to be neglected.[34]

---

[33] See pp. 92–8 below.

[34] Further evidence of close similarity between the demographic characteristics of the reconstitution parishes and the country as a whole will be found on pp. 154–60, 461–4.

Table 3.5 *Baptism totals in group 3*

	Totals			Percentages		
	1680–99	1725–44	1770–89	1680–99	1725–44	1770–89
Aldenham	594	583	590	5.2	4.4	3.1
Ash	759	896	1 037	6.6	6.7	5.4
Banbury	1 323	1 399	1 867	11.6	10.5	9.8
Birstall[a]	1 174	1 867	3 588	10.3	14.0	18.8
Bottesford	575	551	462	5.0	4.1	2.4
Colyton	644	616	630	5.6	4.6	3.3
Dawlish	393	340	564	3.4	2.6	3.0
Earsdon	387	491	1 311	3.4	3.7	6.9
Gainsborough	1 694	2 165	2 808	14.8	16.3	14.7
Gedling	401	442	793	3.5	3.3	4.2
Gt Oakley	288	353	433	2.5	2.7	2.3
Ipplepen	205	223	357	1.8	1.7	1.9
Methley	415	468	594	3.6	3.5	3.1
Morchard						
Bishop	589	765	942	5.1	5.7	4.9
Odiham	576	650	1 050	5.0	4.9	5.5
Shepshed[a]	204	314	558	1.8	2.4	2.9
Southill	850	792	1 085	7.4	5.9	5.7
Terling	366	399	376	3.2	3.0	2.0
Total	11 437	13 314	19 045	100.0	100.0	100.0

[a] The absolute totals for the parishes of Birstall and Shepshed were halved.
Source: Cambridge Group reconstitutions.

Changes in the relative importance of parishes

The unchanging composition of any one group does not, of course, imply that each component parish within it makes the same proportionate contribution to events taking place in the group throughout its span. Predominantly agricultural parishes did not grow as rapidly as those in which manufacture was taking root . To illustrate the importance of this phenomenon, table 3.5 details the totals of baptisms occurring in the 18 parishes that make up group 3. Totals are given for the first 20 years of the period in question, for the last 20 years, and for a 20-year period in the middle, and the proportionate share of each parish in the total for the group in each period is shown.

The fluidity of the situation over a period as short as a century is striking. Birstall increased its proportionate share by more than 80 per cent and ended the period contributing more than one baptism in six to the group total, even at half-weight. Shepshed, though much smaller,

also advanced markedly. Earsdon, reflecting the dynamism of the coal industry, made the sharpest relative advance of all, more than doubling its share of the total. But elsewhere there were equally sharp relative declines. The absolute number of baptisms remained almost constant in both Aldenham and Colyton, and, in consequence, their percentage shares each dropped by over 40 per cent. Much the same happened in Terling, while in Bottesford the absolute number of baptisms *fell* substantially and its percentage share dropped by 52 per cent. That growth rates varied so greatly underlines the significance of the relatively close agreement between trends in the group as a whole and national trends.[35]

One further major test remains to be made before it is prudent to switch attention from preliminary issues to the substantive results obtained from the reconstitution data. It is possible to imagine a group of parishes which satisfied all feasible tests of representativeness, and which had been reconstituted with the most scrupulous care, but which could never be the source of reliable results. Suppose, for example, that the deterioration in the quality of registration in the later eighteenth century, which is clearly visible in some registers, affected all registers in some degree. If this were not detected, an apparent fall, say, in the level of marital fertility rates after 1780 might be spurious, the by-product of less conscientious registration, rather than a reflection of demographic change. Equally, and still more worrying, an apparent *absence* of change might also be spurious, concealing something which it was important to uncover. Accordingly, in the next chapter the potential causes of inaccuracy or insufficiency are reviewed, and an attempt is made to establish how far their existence may have corrupted the reconstitutions, and hence called in question the reliability of demographic tabulations based upon them.

---

[35] The absolute number of baptisms increased by 206 per cent in Birstall, and by 239 per cent in Earsdon, while there were zero growth rates in Aldenham, Colyton, and Terling, and a fall of 20 per cent in Bottesford.

4

Reliability

That family reconstitution can provide demographic information of the greatest precision and detail is not in question: nor that parish registers can provide suitable source material. Henry, indeed, perfected the method and then applied it to historical material out of frustration over the quality of contemporary sources of information suitable for the study of the fundamental characteristics of fertility and fecundity. His study of Crulai, the first application of the technique to a parish register, was a landmark in the development of historical demography.[1]

In a closed community which kept complete records of all births, deaths, and marriages, it would be possible in principle to describe and analyse any aspect of demographic behaviour exhaustively. No such community has ever existed, but the standard of ecclesiastical record keeping was sometimes very high in pre-industrial Europe, and the rules of reconstitution, by defining the periods during which an individual may properly be regarded as in observation for each type of demographic measure, largely overcome any difficulties arising from the fact that high levels of migration left most parishes very far from being closed communities.

The most unimpeachable method for concatenating information taken from baptism, burial, and marriage registers into individual life histories, however, may nonetheless fail to produce any useful results if the source to which it is applied is seriously defective. Anglican registers have a number of well-known weaknesses that may affect the accuracy or completeness of reconstitution. In general they do not compare favourably with the best continental registers, and it is therefore prudent to try to establish how far, if at all, their defects infringe the reliability of the results derived from the reconstitution of the 26 parishes.

---

[1] Gautier and Henry, *Crulai*.

High levels of migration, the presence of nonconformists, and other problems have combined to produce, so to speak, a low grade of reconstitution ore, containing much dross. Can it nonetheless produce pure metal?

The answer to this question will emerge in part in later chapters when empirical results are described and analysed, but some preliminary testing is possible. In the balance of this chapter evidence that bears on the nature and completeness of the coverage of vital events in Anglican registers is discussed. First, the baptism, burial, and marriage series for each reconstituted parish are subjected to analysis by a program designed to detect periods of underregistration in aggregative totals of events. Secondly, tests of the adequacy and accuracy of coverage of events within the Anglican section of the population are described. These involve a comparison of the last years of ecclesiastical registration with the first years of civil registration. Thirdly, the internal consistency and demographic plausibility of reconstitution data are considered. Fourthly, place of birth information in the enumerators' books of mid-nineteenth-century censuses is used as a further test of coverage. Fifthly, there follows a section devoted to the consideration of the special problems associated with the increasing delay between the occurrence of a birth and the celebration of the rite of baptism. Finally, the processing of data taken from FRFs is described and the nature of the formal and logical checks made upon the data indicated.

Indirect evidence from totals of events in the reconstitution parishes

In the *Population history of England* an algorithm for the detection of periods of defective registration in individual registers was described. The program was designed to find 'troughs' in the series of monthly totals of baptisms, burials, and marriages by moving through each series a month at a time and judging the acceptability of a test period lying ahead of the current point of reference by comparing it to a trailing period containing data that had passed the test. When a trough was found a second program generated replacement values to substitute for the originals.[2] It was therefore a simple matter to calculate for any given parish and period the length of any interval during which coverage was

---

[2] By simple geometric interpolation between the local 60-month average frequencies calculated from each end of the defective period. The replacement value for each month was further modified to impose the same proportional deviation from trend as was found in the national monthly template series during the same period of time. Wrigley and Schofield, *Population history of England*, app. 13, pp. 705–7. The method of detection of periods of defective registration is set out in ibid., app. 12.

defective in each of the three series of events and the scale of any such shortfall.

The same program can be applied to aggregative totals of events derived from the FRFs of the reconstitution parishes. In considering the results of this exercise, it should be remembered that these totals will not be the same as those which would have arisen from a simple count of events recorded in the registers of these parishes. The baptism totals taken from the FRFs exclude all illegitimate children. The burial totals fall well short of those found in the registers since only burials that can be linked to a preceding marriage or baptism appear on the FRFs. As a result about a quarter of all burials recorded in the registers are excluded from aggregative counts.[3] Only marriage totals taken from FRFs should equal marriage totals produced by a simple count of the events recorded in the parish register. To complicate matters still further, the totals of baptisms, burials, and marriages recorded on FRFs may include some events not to be found in the register of the parish in question: entries taken from the bishop's transcripts of that parish, for example, or from the registers of neighbouring parishes. The totals taken from FRFs are, however, in general little different from those recorded in the register, except in the case of burials, and any periods of defective registration are likely to be just as clear when using FRF-based counts as when using register-based counts.

For each of the reconstitution parishes, therefore, the length and scale of any troughs can be established in each of the three series. This affords an instructive check on the completeness of registration and shows whether defective registration tended to be concentrated in certain time periods. In table 4.1 the relevant data are set out in a summary form. The period 1580 to 1789 has been broken down into eight time periods (after 1789 there are no further periods of defective registration in any of the parishes whose finish date is 1790 or later).

The percentages given in table 4.1 show what proportion of the total numbers of baptisms, burials, and marriages were additions made to the recorded totals to make good shortfalls in the registers. Each percentage is the ratio of replacement totals to the final totals (that is, the events originally recorded plus replacement totals). The periodisation adopted was determined partly by the dating of the four groups. The further subdivisions were made because, as is very evident from the table, the period of the Civil War and Commonwealth was one of severe disturbance in registration, and problems continued into the 1660s and, in a more muted form, until the end of the century.

---

[3] But this need not invalidate the procedure: see pp. 63–7.

Table 4.1 *Underregistration of baptisms, burials, and marriages in 26 reconstitution parishes and in the the 404 parishes used as a source of data for the* Population history of England *(replacement totals as a percentage of recorded totals plus replacement totals)*

	1580–99	1600–39	1640–9	1650–9	1660–9	1670–99	1700–29	1730–89
26 reconstitution parishes								
Baptisms	0.93	0.21	3.01	2.61	2.42	0.43	0.14	0.02
Burials	0.81	0.11	4.68	2.81	2.68	1.41	0.76	0.03
Marriages	0.85	0.37	18.90	12.83	13.08	1.94	0.00	0.09
404 aggregative parishes								
Baptisms	4.85	4.40	15.68	16.18	6.37	2.53	1.38	0.36
Burials	5.66	4.58	22.18	22.00	7.32	4.58	1.38	0.50
Marriages	4.03	5.39	33.33	38.08	18.57	8.42	2.82	0.99

Note: see text for further details of how replacement totals were calculated. The percentages for the 26 parishes were obtained by pooling replacement totals and totals of registered events from each individual parish; those for the 404 parishes were calculated from the ratios given in Wrigley and Schofield, *Population history of England*, tab. A4.1, col. 7, pp. 537–59.
Source: Cambridge Group aggregative tabulations and reconstitutions.

The superior completeness of registration in the reconstitution parishes stands out clearly.[4] The 404 parishes were themselves a select group. Only parishes with no major breaks in registration were considered, and even so, of a total of 530 tabulations available only 404 were admitted into the final set, often because of evidence of incomplete registration.[5] Nevertheless the underregistration detection program found evidence of a significant amount of underregistration in the 404 parishes. In each of the three series the replacement percentage only dropped to less than 1 per cent after 1730. The replacement level was consistently and substantially lower in the reconstitution parishes. In the 60 years before the Civil War (1580–1639) the level was about 5 per cent in all three series in the 404 parishes but only about a tenth of that level in the 26 parishes (averaging the six readings for the three series over the two periods involved).

In the next 30 years the replacement percentages were far higher in both the reconstitution and aggregative parishes, but there were intriguing differences between the two sets of parishes. In the former 1640–69 is the only period when, in the case of baptisms and burials, the level of underregistration was other than negligible. Before 1640 and after 1670 there is little to suggest that fertility and mortality rates estimated from reconstitution data will be inaccurate because of underregistration. The replacement rate was always less than 1 per cent except for burials in 1680–99. In the aggregative parishes replacement rates were much higher in the baptism and burial series, but, as in the reconstitution parishes, pre-Civil War levels of underregistration in baptisms and burials were regained after 1670. The absolute level remained higher in the aggregative set right through to 1789, though after 1730 the absolute level in these parishes finally fell to less than 1 per cent.

Marriages were very different. Underregistration shot up to a very high level in the 1640s in both series, though to a markedly lesser extent in the 26 than in the 404 (19 and 33 per cent respectively). In the next decade the position changed substantially. In much of the decade (1653–60) civil registration replaced the Anglican ecclesiastical system.[6] In the reconstitution parishes there was a marked drop in underregistration (to 13 per cent), but in the 404 a further rise (to 38 per cent). In the 1660s the gap between the two series narrowed since the rate in the

---

[4] It would be marginally more pronounced if the 12 reconstitution parishes had been excluded from the 404 aggregative set. In principle this should have been done, but even without this added refinement the contrast is striking.

[5] Wrigley and Schofield, *Population history of England*, pp. 16–7.

[6] Burn, *Parish registers*, pp. 26–9.

reconstitution parishes was little changed from the previous decade whereas it halved in the aggregative set. Thereafter both series improved, though the change was much more marked in the reconstitution parishes. This was a period when clandestine marriage was widespread. The 'hollows' found by the algorithm used to detect underregistration sometimes reflect the unwillingness of a significant fraction of the population to contract a formal marriage by the conventional route rather than a failure of registration in the normal sense. The relatively high level of underregistration in the marriage series in the later seventeenth century may occur for this reason rather than because of a greater failure to register marriages than baptisms or burials. After 1700 underregistration was almost non-existent in the reconstitution parishes and modest in the aggregative set.

Fortunately, the high levels of marriage underregistration in the reconstitution parishes between 1640 and 1670 are, at worst, irritating rather than damaging, reducing the proportion of FRFs from which a full range of data can be extracted, without impugning the accuracy or completeness of the information that can be used. In this marriage underregistration differs from underregistration of baptisms or burials. A missing marriage has an effect similar to the migration out of the parish before their marriage of a couple who might otherwise have married there. If they had remained their presence would have added to the volume of usable data, but their absence need not affect the accuracy of the rates derived from the remaining marriages. There are simply fewer units of observation. In contrast, if a proportion of baptisms or burials are missing, this will affect the completeness of registration on a scattering of FRFs and so tend to cause fertility and mortality to be understated.

In general the inference to be drawn from table 4.1 is encouraging. The only limitations on the reliability of the reconstitution data suggested by the table are that both fertility and mortality tabulations for 1640–69 should be approached with caution. For example, an apparent slight falling away in the level of age-specific marital fertility might be spurious.[7]

Before turning to consider individual parishes, one further point may be noted. In chapter 3 totals of events in the three series taken from the

---

[7] The emperical evidence about marital fertility in this period is ambiguous. As noted above (p. 60, n.22), the total marital fertility rate 20–49 in group 2 parishes in 1640–9 was 7.2 and in 1650–9 6.5, compared with an overall rate for the whole group 2 period, 1600–1729, of 7.3. The rate in 1660–9 was 6.9. The rate in 1650–9 may reflect underregistration but the evidence is not conclusive.

reconstitutions were compared with the national series derived from the 404 parishes used the the *Population history of England*. In all three series the discrepancy ratios expressing the reconstitution totals as a proportion of the national series totals were well below 1.0 in the 1640s, 1650s, and 1660s.[8]

Table 4.2 provides some further information about underregistration in the 26 reconstitution parishes. The overall results for the pooled data have already been discussed, but it is important to consider individual parishes no less than pooled data, since it might be true that underregistration was so limited overall as to be of little moment in relation to the measurement of national trends, and yet so concentrated in a few parishes that it demanded close attention when interpreting results relating to them. The table provides details for marriages as well as for baptisms and burials, but discussion is confined to the latter two since underregistration of marriages, though far more pronounced than in the other two series, need not distort demographic measures derived from family reconstitution.

It should be noted in this connection that the periods of defective registration include both some where no events at all were recorded for months on end and others where the monthly totals fell away significantly but registration did not cease. In the former case there is rarely any doubt that events were taking place that were not entered in the parish register. In the latter, matters are sometimes less clear-cut and it is likely that replacement totals were occasionally generated and added to the originals even though no genuine lapse in registration had occurred. For example, the years 1645–7 were identified in the Colyton baptism register as defective. The totals of baptisms recorded in the register in these years (22, 27, and 35) are indeed down very sharply from the earlier part of the decade (in 1640–4 the annual average number of

---

[8] Figs. 3.1, 3.3, and 3.5, pp. 56, 62, and 66. The national series had been inflated to offset the underregistration detected in the 404 parishes, and the totals in all three series were very substantially increased as a result. Tab. 4.1 shows how great these increases were. It is therefore of interest that if the reconstitution totals are also increased in these three decades to offset the effects of underregistration by the percentages given in tab. 4.1, the discrepancy ratios are substantially changed. For example, in the group 2 baptism series the ratio of the reconstitution to the national series averaged 0.942 in 1640–9, 0.950 in 1650–9, and 0.974 in 1660–9. If the reconstitution totals are increased in the proportions suggested by tab. 4.1 (in 1640–9, for example in the ratio of 100/(100–3.01)), the discrepancy ratios rise to the following levels: 0.971, 0.975, and 0.998. The same adjustments made in burials and marriages for group 2 produce the following results for the three decades (the old ratios from chapter 3 are given in brackets in each case): burials 1.085 (1.034), 0.930 (0.904), 1.003 (0.976); marriages 0.948 (0.769), 0.980 (0.854), 1.019 (0.886)

Table 4.2 *Underregistration of baptisms, burials, and marriages in 26 reconstitution parishes (replacement totals as a percentage of recorded totals plus replacement totals)*

(1) Totals including replacement totals.
(2) Replacement totals.
(3) (2)/(1) × 100.

Baptisms

	1580–99			1600–39			1640–69			1670–9			1680–99			1700–29			1730–89		
	(1)	(2)	(3)	(1)	(2)	(3)	(1)	(2)	(3)	(1)	(2)	(3)	(1)	(2)	(3)	(1)	(2)	(3)	(1)	(2)	(3)
Alcester	657			1628			1267	18	1	414			730	4	1	926					
Aldenham	608			1302			747			210			594			804			1730		
Ash													759			1140			2969		
Austrey	187			363			313	39	13	69			185			242					
Banbury	1267			3280			2007	38	2	620	7	10	1323			2095			4760		
Birstall				3446	28	1	2552	63	3	1039			2359			3888			16554		
Bottesford	421	27	6	1060			869			238			575			815			1469		
Bridford	150			358			245			93			154			242	18	7			
Colyton	891			2482			1396	58	4	331			644			872	12	1	1863		
Dawlish													393			489			1384		
Earsdon													421	34	8	593			2567		
Gainsborough	1089			3130			2584			808			1694			3162			7223		
Gedling	290	34	12	756			592	34	6	209			401			533			1796		
Gt Oakley													288			376	9	2	1280		
Hartland				1334			935			235			546			839					
Ipplepen													205			307					
Lowestoft	908			1620			1183	239	20	494			1095			1592			948		
March	718	27	4	1399			1262	54	4	529			1065	54	5	1715					

80

Methley	347	813	772	224	413	599	1594
Morchard Bishop	751	1701	1134	285	589	1121	2562
Odiham		1780	1626	531	576	926	2588
Reigate		721	538	187	1040	1603	
Shepshed	785	1769	1036	426	398	718	2506
Southill		809	439	163	850	1265	2877
Terling	364	982	722	226	366	559	1136
Willingham					399	561	
Total	9433	30733	22219	7331	18062	27982	57806
	88	66	598	7	92	39	10
	0.93	0.21	2.69	0.10	0.51	0.14	0.02

(Individual deficiency figures shown: col 2 — 11, 13, 14 (1, 2, 1); col 3 — 48, 7 (9, 1); col 7 — 10 (0).)

Note: years in which deficiency in baptisms detected: Alcester, 1662–3, 1698; Austrey, 1664–70; Banbury, 1642; Birstall, 1616, 1639, 1643, 1644, 1653; Bottesford, 1589–90; Bridford, 1715–8; Colyton, 1645, 1646–7, 1723; Earsdon, 1697–9; Gedling, 1586–7, 1596–7, 1642–3; Great Oakley, 1670–2, 1718–9; Lowestoft, 1644, 1645, 1651–3, 1658–63; March, 1585, 1650, 1655, 1659, 1661–2, 1692, 1694–5; Reigate, 1618; Shepshed, 1613–4, 1651–4, 1779; Southill, 1645; Willingham 1630–1.

Table 4.2 (cont.)
Burials

	1580–99			1600–39			1640–9			1650–9			1660–9			1670–99			1700–29			1730–89		
	(1)	(2)	(3)	(1)	(2)	(3)	(1)	(2)	(3)	(1)	(2)	(3)	(1)	(2)	(3)	(1)	(2)	(3)	(1)	(2)	(3)	(1)	(2)	(3)
Alcester	363			916			249	35	14	351			270			868			871			1130		
Aldenham	263			768			220			204			198			584	147	25	510			1520		
Ash																492			610					
Austrey	95			230			59			55			76	31	41	196	24	12	181					
Banbury	651			1808			877	138	16	442			488			1310			1591			3717		
Birstall				1635			657			469			618			2276			2150			7956		
Bottesford	154			692			200			216			175			581			617			1063		
Bridford	69			169			59			39			56			186			199	30	15			
Colyton	588			1319			830			312			343			1090			766			1416	11	1
Dawlish																293			347			854		
Earsdon																229			359			1544		
Gainsborough	633			2366			688	27	4	800			704			2180			2697			5617		
Gedling	125			492			138			168			158			451			428			1004		
Gt Oakley																279	14	5	366	18	5	821		
Hartland				762			245			194			248			703			643					
Ipplepen																100			210			525		
Lowestoft	736			1574			233	77	33	250	73	29	255	72	28	1165			1390					
March	561	14	3	810			213			262			377	25	7	1546	86	6	1468	107	7			
Methley	228			477			170			238			183			542			420			846		
Morchard Bishop																361			397					
Odiham	441	29	7	864			226			245			246			453			726			1641		
Reigate				1297			286			263			437			551			520			1297		
Shepshed				375			179			157	72	46	124	19	15	1100			1110					
Southill	233			828			157			237			214			375			502			1292		
Terling	164			545	21	4	87			110			113			777			858			1579		
Willingham				566			140			146			199			483			392			742		
Total	5304	43	0.81	18493	21	0.11	5913	277	4.68	5158	145	2.81	5482	147	2.68	19171	271	1.41	20328	155	0.76	34564	11	0.03

Note: years in which deficiency in burials detected: Alcester, 1647–8; Aldenham, 1679–81, 1686–7, 1689–92, 1694–5, 1696–7; Austrey, 1664–9, 1685–8; Banbury, 1642, 1646, 1647–8; Bridford, 1716–21; Colyton, 1787; Gainsborough, 1640–1; Great Oakley, 1670–2, 1718–20; Lowestoft, 1643–6, 1649–50, 1651–3, 1658–63; March, 1593–4, 1661–2, 1676–7, 1692, 1694–5, 1699–1702; Odiham, 1585–6; Shepshed, 1650–5, 1661–3; Terling, 1608–10.

Table 4.2 (cont.)
Marriages

	1580–99 (1)	(2)	(3)	1600–39 (1)	(2)	(3)	1640–9 (1)	(2)	(3)	1650–9 (1)	(2)	(3)	1660–9 (1)	(2)	(3)	1670–99 (1)	(2)	(3)	1700–29 (1)	(2)	(3)	1730–89 (1)	(2)	(3)
Alcester	162			304			98	44	45	112	1	1	86	29	34	257			353					
Aldenham	212			379			63	13	21	93			72			165	32	19	186			440		
Ash																203			212			634		
Austrey	48			69			15			22	4	18	19	16	84	54	3	6	94					
Banbury	391			799			180	77	43	317	1	0	215	76	35	318	75	24	768			1788	14	1
Birstall	111			678			173	16	9	157	70	45	168			541			783			3199		
Bottesford				317			79	7	9	80	36	45	62	38	61	120			124			386		
Bridford	45	23	51	100			19			22			16			54			52					
Colyton	244			597			135	71	53	150	48	32	66	17	26	123			203			596		
Dawlish																123			128			383		
Earsdon																156			171			772		
Gainsborough	339			884			212			216			182			685			946			2247		
Gedling	112			223			55			52			77			194			204			484		
Gt Oakley																104			175			431		
Hartland				378			92			132			126			261			249					
Ipplepen																57			83			235		
Lowestoft	255			449			76	37	49	80	26	33	99	23	23	318			411					
March	165			351			125			104	21	20	125			538			616					
Methley	106			259			63	11	18	54	6	11	63			135			143			382		
Morchard Bishop																178			265					
Odiham	226			445			99			102	4	4	90	22	24	295	6	2	346			738		
Reigate				507	29	6	118			123			102			373			417			820		
Shepshed				136			35	17	49	48	20	42	31			90			162			668		
Southill	200			453			91	39	43	134	30	22	136	13	10	452			416			885		
Terling	83			210			35	10	21	38			20			77			108			337		
Willingham				244			47			45			34			116			150					
Total	2 699	23	0.85	7 782	29	0.37	1 810	342	18.90	2 081	267	12.83	1 789	234	13.08	5 987	116	1.94	7 765	0	0.00	15 425	14	0.09

Note: years in which deficiency in marriages detected: Alcester, 1643–9, 1659–62; Aldenham, 1643–5, 1659–62; Austrey, 1658–72; Banbury, 1642–3, 1646–50, 1661–4, 1679–80, 1683–5, 1691–5, 1755; Birstall, 1648–55; Bottesford, 1648–54, 1658–69; Bridford, 1580–9; Colyton, 1642–6, 1646–54, 1664–8; Lowestoft, 1640–5, 1651–3, 1658–62; March, 1651–3; Methley, 1646–50; Morchard Bishop, 1675; Odiham, 1659–62; Reigate, 1609–10; Shepshed, 1644–54; Southill, 1644–9, 1651–3, 1661–2; Willingham, 1646–9.

Source: Cambridge Group reconstitutions.

baptisms was 67), but Colyton experienced a most destructive plague in 1645–6 when approximately 20 per cent of the population died in less than a year.[9] It is possible that the direct and indirect effects of the plague account for the fall in registered baptisms.[10] The pattern of monthly totals suggests continuous registration and there were no runs of months with zero totals.

As table 4.1 made clear, baptisms were in general less affected by underregistration than either of the other two series. Table 4.2 shows that in 10 parishes (Aldenham, Ash, Dawlish, Gainsborough, Hartland, Ipplepen, Methley, Morchard Bishop, Odiham, and Terling) no detectable underregistration occurred in any period, and in 8 others (Austrey, Banbury, Bottesford, Bridford, Earsdon, Reigate, Southill, and Willingham) it was found in only one period. Great Oakley, too, belongs in this category even though two periods of underregistration are listed since the earlier of the two took place before 1680 when the parish entered group 3.[11] Only in Austrey, a very small parish, were 'missing' baptisms a high proportion of the estimated true total in the period when underregistration occurred.

In the remaining parishes there was more than one period of underregistration, but in three of them, Alcester, Birstall, and March, the underregistration total was always an insignificant percentage of total baptisms. Underregistration was somewhat more pronounced in Colyton in the 1640s,[12] in Gedling in the period 1580–99 and again in the 1640s, and there were more serious shortfalls in Lowestoft in each decade between 1640 and 1669, and in Shepshed in the 1650s. In the last four parishes fertility rates calculated for periods that include the decades to which reference has been made may fall short of their true level.

The form in which the data are presented influences the apparent pattern of percentage deficiencies, of course, since high rates of underregistration are more likely to be found in the shorter than in the

---

[9] Wrigley, 'Family limitation', p. 85; see also Schofield, 'Anatomy of an epidemic', pp. 98ff. The algorithm used in the program took into account the behaviour of registration totals in all three series. Thus a period in which the total of baptisms fell might escape being identified as a period of underregistration if burials rose at the same time; and so on. But the fall in baptisms in Colyton in the late 1640s was too great to be rescued in this way. Wrigley and Schofield, *Population history of England*, pp. 701–3.

[10] Schofield, 'Anatomy of an epidemic', p. 119.

[11] Great Oakley was not a member of either group 1 or group 2. The period 1670 99, used in the burial and marriage panels of tab. 4.2, is the only one to bridge between the time spans of two groups, and therefore can produce an anomaly of this sort, though its homogeneity in respect of underregistration makes it a sensible unit in this context.

[12] Though, for the reasons just given, it is doubtful whether there was genuine underregistration in this decade in Colyton.

longer periods. A complete cessation of registration lasting for a year would result in a replacement rate of about 10 per cent in a period lasting only a decade, assuming other years were unaffected, but a similar break occurring in a period lasting 40 years would result in a replacement rate of only 2.5 per cent, *ceteris paribus*. Since registration difficulties tended to be brief but irregular and sometimes severe, this will tend to give rise to a scattering of unusually high rates in the shorter periods, but few high rates in the longer periods. If, despite this consideration, a replacement rate of 5 per cent or more is taken as crude *prima facie* evidence of serious underregistration, then it is noteworthy that of the 16 such periods in the baptism section of the table, 5 occur in 1640–9, 3 in 1650–9, 4 in 1660–9, and only 4 at other times. Even if 1640–9, 1650–9, and 1660–9 were amalgamated into a single time block, there would still be 4 such cases out of a revised total of 8 in all. It appears clear that, when the fertility rates for individual parishes are considered, the period of the Civil War, the Commonwealth, and its immediate aftermath will need to be given special attention, especially in Austrey, Gedling, Lowestoft, and Shepshed.[13]

Although the burial totals for the reconstitution parishes taken from the FRFs, in contrast to the totals of baptisms and marriages, fall well short of those in the related registers,[14] there is good reason to think that the patterns of underregistration revealed when using them are very similar to those brought to light when using 'raw' parish register data. In 12 cases aggregative counts of burials taken direct from burial registers were available (Alcester, Aldenham, Banbury, Bottesford, Colyton, Gainsborough, Gedling, Hartland, Odiham, Reigate, Shepshed, and Willingham) and both the timing and extent of underregistration were very similar using these data to those found using the reconstitution burial totals.

[13] On marital fertility generally in the 30-year period, see p. 78 n. 7 above. The parish evidence is somewhat inconclusive. The number of woman-years at risk on which the total marital fertility rates for Austrey are based was so small, even over a quarter-century, as to prohibit their use. The most clear-cut case is that of Lowestoft. Underregistration in Lowestoft was primarily in the 1650s. In the quarter-century 1650–74 the total marital fertility rate 20–49 was only 5.7 children per woman, much lower than in any other quarter-century and well below the overall parish average (7.6). In Gedling, where underregistration was concentrated in the 1640s, the TMFR in 1625–49 was lower than the overall average for the parish (6.5 and 7.5), but the rate was as low or lower in other quarter-centuries. In Shepshed, where the deficient years were 1651–4, the TMFR in 1650–74 was very high (8.1), considerably above the overall average for the parish (7.3). Only in the case of Lowestoft, therefore, is it reasonably clear that the measurement of marital fertility is affected by putative underregistration.

[14] About three-quarters of all recorded burials can be linked to a preceding marriage or baptism and so appear on an FRF; tab. 3.4, p. 55.

Table 4.2 shows that 13 parishes have a 'clean sheet' (Ash, Birstall, Bottesford, Dawlish, Earsdon, Gedling, Hartland, Ipplepen, Methley, Morchard Bishop, Reigate, Southill, and Willingham). 6 parishes have a single period of underregistration of burials: Alcester, Bridford, Colyton, Gainsborough, Odiham, and Terling. Of these Colyton, Gainsborough, and Terling may be largely disregarded since only an insignificant shortfall occurred in each case. In the other parishes the percentage missing exceeded 5 per cent in the period in question. Alcester, in the 1640s, and Bridford, in the period 1700–29, were quite severely affected, as was Odiham in 1580–99, though less markedly. Great Oakley in 1700–29 also belongs with this group, since, although it experienced two periods of underregistration, its earlier period of underregistration does not affect any reconstitution results, as was true also of baptism underregistration in the parish.

This leaves a final group of 6 parishes where more than one period of underregistration occurred. There were five separate periods in Aldenham, though all affected the period 1670–99 when a quarter of the probable total number of burials escaped registration. In Austrey there were two such periods in the last 40 years of the seventeenth century: the first was particularly severe. Banbury's three periods all fell between 1642 and 1648 and represented a shortfall in the decade as a whole of about 16 per cent. Lowestoft suffered extensively in each of the three decades between 1640 and 1669, while March had the largest number of individual underregistration episodes, a total of six, but all were of slight import.

In summary the following parishes each suffered periods when the extent of burial underregistration exceeded 5 per cent of the presumptive 'true' total: Alcester (1640–9), Aldenham (1670–99), Austrey (1660–9, 1670–99), Banbury (1640–9), Bridford (1700–29), Great Oakley (1700–29), Lowestoft (1640–9, 1650–9, 1660–9), March (1660–9, 1670–99, 1700–29), Odiham (1580–99), and Shepshed (1650–9, 1660–9).[15] As with

---

[15] It is frequently difficult to establish unambiguously in individual parishes the effect of underregistration of burials on infant and child mortality rates both because there were substantial genuine variations in the underlying rates and because random variation was sometimes pronounced owing to the small number of deaths involved. Occasionally, however, the effect seems clear. In Aldenham, for example, there was much underregistration in the late seventeenth century, and the successive quarter-century mortality rates appear to reflect this. In 1650–74, 1675–99, and 1700–24, $_1q_0$ was 168, 83, and 140 per 1000, while $_4q_1$ for the same periods was 90, 49, and 51, and $_{10}q_5$ was 57, 28, and 28 respectively. In many other cases, however, the evidence is not clear-cut and consideration of the evidence for all the parishes with periods of underregistration yields an overall impression that rates were not affected in a consistent or significant fashion.

baptisms the periods of serious underregistration were markedly concentrated into the decades 1640–9, 1650–9, and 1660–9 which account for 9 of the 16 instances just listed, while if the three decades are amalgamated into a single period to offset the tendency of short periods to gain a disproportionate share of periods of underregistration, the mid-seventeenth century still accounts for 4 out of 11 periods of underregistration in which the shortfall exceeded 5 per cent.

Although table 4.2 contains similar information about marriage underregistration, it is not discussed here since the existence of marriage underregistration does not lead to distortion of the demographic measures derived from family reconstitution, though it will reduce the size of the available body of data that can be used, as noted above.[16]

Some issues arising from the possible underregistration of baptisms and burials and the implications of any such underregistration for the empirical results produced by reconstitution will be discussed in later chapters when the results themselves are presented. It may be appropriate to note here, however, that the damage caused by registration lapses cannot be entirely confined to the period in which the breakdown occurs. For example, if the birth of a child was recorded at a time when there was a complete break in burial registration, it is possible that the child may have died at or soon after birth, but, since this would remain unknown, he or she will be assumed to have survived and the baptism entry may later be linked to a marriage, generating a false age at marriage and, perhaps, inaccurate information about age-specific marital fertility. Many other types of mislinkage (or of failure to make a genuine link) can easily be imagined. Any such effect is most unlikely to be sufficiently serious to have an appreciable impact on the overall empirical results where underregistration was as infrequent and modest as appears to have been the case in the reconstitution parishes, but the possibility of error arising in this way should be borne in mind.

Coverage of events in Anglican registers

Effective checks upon the completeness and accuracy of parish register entries are not easy to devise, because of the nature of Anglican registration. Even if every birth were followed by a baptism and every death by a burial, an Anglican register would only mimic a state vital registration system and record every vital event in a parish where every family was Anglican. There were few such parishes in England by the

---

[16] See above p. 126–8.

early nineteenth century; nonconformists had been widely present and locally numerous ever since the Restoration, and their proportionate share of the population grew considerably over time. The presence of nonconformists led to complex and changeable registration practices. Nonconformists made selective use of Anglican rites so that the registration of baptisms, burials, and marriages was differentially affected.[17]

Coverage was least affected in the case of marriages. After Hardwicke's Act (1753) a valid marriage was possible only by Anglican rites and in prescribed circumstances, except for two numerically unimportant religious groups, the Jews and the Quakers, and members of the royal family.[18] Before Hardwicke's Act the possibility of contracting a clandestine but legally valid marriage could produce much confusion, and clandestine marriage was locally, even regionally, common in the later seventeenth and early eighteenth centuries. In such areas the number of marriages recorded in Anglican registers might fall well short of the total of unions occurring, and many of the partners to clandestine marriages were nonconformists.[19] Apart from this, however, the rise of nonconformity had little effect on marriage registration before 1753.

Nonconformity had a greater impact on registration coverage in the case of both baptisms and burials. Nonconformists began to perform baptism and to maintain their own baptism registers from the late seventeenth century onwards, and many hundreds of such registers were in use by 1800. The lack of their own burial grounds often caused nonconformists to continue to use Anglican cemeteries for decades after the founding of a local nonconformist congregation, but by the early nineteenth century both nonconformist and, in the larger towns, municipal burial grounds were increasingly widely used. Thus, because of the rise of nonconformity, the proportion of all births and deaths that were recorded as baptisms and burials in the Anglican registers was declining in the eighteenth and early nineteenth centuries, though marriage registration, at least after the passage of Hardwicke's Act, was only marginally affected.

There is a substantial element of uncertainty about the proportion of births and deaths that escaped Anglican registration because of the growing strength of nonconformity. In the context of aggregative work,

---

[17] Wrigley and Schofield, *Population history of England*, ch. 4.

[18] Quaker demographic history, however, can be studied very effectively because of the excellence of their system of record keeping: see, for example, Vann and Eversley, *Friends in life and death*.   [19] Wrigley, 'Clandestine marriage'.

where it was far more important than in the context of reconstitution,[20] estimates were made of the percentage increase in the total of Anglican events needed to reflect the growing strength of nonconformity. The full series was presented elsewhere. An impression of their scale may be gleaned from the following decadal figures: baptisms 1660–9, 0.62; 1700–9, 1.40; 1750–9, 2.04; 1800–9, 4.83; 1820–9, 6.23: burials 1660–9, 0.64; 1700–9, 1.09; 1750–9, 0.86; 1800–9, 1.69; 1820–9, 2.22.[21] These estimates were obtained by multiplying the number of surviving nonconformist registers by the average number of events recorded in a random sample of them and then making further and separate allowance for Quakers. But the full impact of nonconformity on Anglican registration was much greater than these percentages suggest, both because some nonconformist registers failed to survive or were not deposited under the mid-nineteenth-century legislation designed to secure their deposit, and also because there was probably an association between the rise of nonconformity and a more diffuse refusal to continue to conform to Anglican precepts and observances. The percentages listed therefore need to be increased substantially to capture the generalised impact of the rise of nonconformity on Anglican registration.[22]

The presence of a nonconformist alternative to Anglican registration might also involve more subtle and potentially more damaging difficulties. Suppose, for example, that a family fluctuated in its allegiance between an Anglican church and a local chapel, using, say, the parish church for the baptism of its first two children, but a local Presbyterian chapel for the baptism of the third, before reverting to the parish church for the fourth. In these circumstances measures of marital fertility would be affected, the apparent age-specific marital fertility rate would fall below its true level, and birth intervals would be overestimated. On the other hand, if a family left the Anglican church definitively and thereafter worshipped elsewhere, no longer making use of Anglican rites, the effect so far as family reconstitution is concerned is exactly the same as if the family had emigrated to a neighbouring parish, without

---

[20] Aggregative work linked to techniques such as inverse projection depends upon the availability of accurate totals of births and deaths for the population as a whole. Reconstitution depends upon accurate information about individual families. However, if some families are defective but do not enter into reconstitution tabulations because they are not in observation, data taken from families that *are* in observation may still provide accurate results, assuming that the families from which such data are drawn are representative of the population as a whole.

[21] Wrigley and Schofield, *Population history of England*, tab. 4.3, p. 94. The percentages given in the text were taken directly from tab. 4.3, except for those for 1660–9 which were obtained by interpolation from percentages for periods on either side of this decade.   [22] Ibid., pp. 90–6, 100–2, 136–43.

changing its religious affiliation. In both cases the family passes from observation. A high level of migration brings its own problems because it reduces the yield of useful information that can be obtained, and because it increases the danger that the families for which there is usable information are not representative of the whole community, but the problems associated with nonconformity need not extend further than this where there was a clean break from Anglican adherence.

In addition to the problems caused by the rise of nonconformity, there were other reasons why Anglican coverage of demographic events was likely to be incomplete. Some events escaped any form of registration because of the decline in religious observance and regular attendance at church. This phenomenon was most prominent in the towns of recent growth where large communities of recent immigrants were often ill-served with churches and chapels, especially from the later eighteenth century onwards. Changes in social custom also played a part. With each increase in the customary delay between birth and baptism, there was an increased risk that the child might die before being baptised, and a commensurate danger that its death might also pass unrecorded in the burial register. The average interval between birth and baptism rose from a few days at most in Elizabethan times to a month or more by the end of the eighteenth century.[23]

The holding of benefices in plurality, casual negligence on the part of incumbents and parish clerks, and other similar accidents that affect all recording systems to some extent, inevitably caused Anglican registration to fall still further short of complete coverage.

The existence of so many influences which reduced the completeness of Anglican coverage, and their steady increase over the post-Restoration period, however, does not necessarily imply that demographic measures based on Anglican parish registers must progressively lose validity. While it is true that Anglican registers can provide only an increasingly incomplete record of events taking place in the population as a whole, it remains possible that their coverage of events in Anglican families might remain complete, or virtually so. And if it were also true that the Anglican population did not differ significantly in its demography from the population as a whole, family reconstitution studies based on Anglican registers might still provide a sound guide to national population history.

It follows from considerations such as these that simplistic checks on the completeness of registration coverage may have little relevance. For example, the baptism rate in the parish of Gedling over the 11 years

---

[23] Berry and Schofield, 'Age at baptism'.

centring on 1801, the year of the first census, was 41.5 per 1000. The comparable rate in Banbury was 27.1 per 1000.[24] The fact that the latter rate is only two-thirds as high as the former tells us little or nothing about the adequacy of registration coverage within the *Anglican* population, however, since, quite apart from the impossibility of knowing the true birth rate in the two communities, it may be that the whole or a part of the difference relates to the proportion of the population in the two parishes that was Anglican. There was, in fact, a long-established Presbyterian chapel in Banbury, and a Wesleyan chapel was founded in 1804, followed by an Independent chapel in 1810.[25] Only if the coverage of events occurring in the *Anglican* community was poor will the usefulness of results derived from family reconstitution be seriously infringed.

The completeness of Anglican registration in the reconstituted parishes

It is to be expected that coverage was significantly better in the reconstitution parishes than in the general run of Anglican registers because the reconstitution parishes were chosen with some care. Work on them began only after they had survived simple tests for good coverage and fullness of information. And after reconstitution had been carried out, further tests were made in the light of the demographic characteristics revealed by tabulations based on the FRFs. In several cases this led to the removal of the parish from the reconstitution set, or to the identification of periods when the data appeared to be unreliable, and so to a reduction in the time span from which data were drawn.[26] Of the 34 reconstitutions initially available, only 26 were retained, and out of a combined total of 6556 years initially in observation in these 26 parishes, 1227, or 19 per cent, were excluded because there seemed reason to doubt their reliability.[27]

There is therefore good reason *prima facie* to expect that the standard of registration in the reconstitution parishes is unusually high compared with the Anglican norm, but this still leaves open the possibility that registration remained too incomplete to produce trustworthy results. In most periods the lack of a reliable alternative data source makes it impossible either to test effectively the completeness of

[24] These rates were obtained by adding to the total of baptisms included in the reconstitution in these years the total of illegitimate baptisms entered in the parish register over the same period to obtain an overall baptism total.

[25] *Lists of non-parochial registers.*   [26] See above pp. 30–9.

[27] The full list of 34 parishes is given in tab. 2.1, pp. 22–3, while the 26 parishes which survived testing are listed in tab. 2.2, p. 26.

Anglican registration by direct comparison with independent evidence, or to establish whether the demography of the Anglican community was similar to that of the population as a whole.[28] For the bulk of the parish register period, therefore, the testing of registration must depend on the plausibility and internal consistency of the results obtained. Before making tests of this sort, however, we may first consider the evidence for congruity between the evidence drawn from family reconstitution about mortality and fertility in the early nineteenth century and that provided by the early returns of the Registrar-General. Both tests depend upon the consideration that, although the *totals* of baptisms and burials taken from Anglican registers will normally fall short of the totals of births and deaths occurring in a parish, the *rates* derived from Anglican reconstitution should be closely similar to those for the community as whole. If they are not, it must be doubtful whether Anglican registers provide good coverage.

Reconstitution data and the Registrar-General's early returns

For the 8 reconstitutions that form group 4 and whose coverage extends down to 1837, a check on the quality of burial registration in each parish is feasible since civil registration began in that year and mortality rates are available from this source shortly thereafter. This permits a comparison of infant and child mortality rates obtained for each parish by family reconstitution with the rates for the civil registration districts in which they were located. An indirect check on baptism coverage, and thus on fertility estimates, is also possible by comparing the totals of legitimate births actually registered in the early years of civil registration with the totals that would have occurred if the age-specific marital fertility rates revealed by reconstitution had obtained in the English population in 1851. Similarly, the accuracy and representativeness of reconstitution data for age at marriage can be compared with information gathered by the Registrar-General in the 1840s. These tests, and other comparable tests, are considered in turn.

---

[28] Though, of course, the fact that the great majority of the population were Anglicans must go far to ensuring a strong similarity, even if nonconformist demography had possessed unusual features; Urdank, *Religion and society*, esp. ch. 5, examines evidence suggesting that the demography of nonconformist communities was distinctive. The form of Quaker record keeping makes it possible to specify the demographic charactistics of Quaker communities in Britain and in Ireland more confidently than those of any other nonconformist group, and to do so from the mid-seventeenth century onwards: Vann and Eversley, *Friends in life and death.*

Table 4.3 *Infant and child mortality (1000q$_x$) in 8 reconstitution parishes and in the registration districts in which they were situated*

	Months					Years			
	0	1	2	3–5	6–11	0	1–4	5–9	10–4
Parishes									
Ash	41	8	8	25	29	106	78	32	39
Banbury	54	18	9	27	50	148	107	44	38
Bottesford	45	22	10	36	27	134	57	34	23
Dawlish	18	5	7	23	34	84	85	13	18
Gedling	46	20	16	22	43	140	82	18	15
Morchard Bishop	23	9	5	11	36	82	48	26	14
Odiham	18	7	5	12	35	74	65	19	26
Shepshed	74	28	11	26	51	179	85	43	34
Average	40	15	9	23	38	118	76	29	26
Corresponding registration districts									
Eastry	37	14	12	28	38	122	81	32	24
Banbury	55	20	14	27	45	152	103	36	29
Grantham	51	18	11	32	34	138	90	32	24
Newton Abbot	28	12	8	22	31	97	103	38	20
Basford	68	21	14	25	43	161	112	41	25
Crediton	34	10	6	17	25	89	86	31	16
Hartley Wintney	41	12	6	23	28	106	74	29	25
Loughborough	75	28	17	30	54	189	119	43	26
Average	49	17	11	25	37	132	96	35	24

Note: for the reconstitution parishes the data all refer to the period from 1825–37. For the registration districts the rates for months within the first year of life and for the first year of life itself are averages of those for the individual years 1841, 1842, 1845, and 1846; for the age groups 1–4, 5–9, and 10–4 the rates are averages of the seven years 1838–44. The former were derived from totals of births and of deaths within the first year of life from Registrar-General, *Fifth annual report*, Abstract of births, Abstract of ages at death; *Sixth annual report*, Births in 324 statistical districts, Ages at death; *Eighth and ninth annual reports*, Abstracts of births and deaths at different ages. The latter were calculated by combining information about the age structure in 1841 and death totals in 1838–44 published in the *Ninth annual report*, app., Tables of rates of increase and of the population, deaths, and rates of mortality, at different ages.
Sources: Cambridge Group reconstitutions and the *Annual reports* of the Registrar-General listed above.

Infant and child mortality

Perhaps the most sensitive test of death registration is the infant mortality rate, and especially the rate within the early months of life. The burial of a child who died very young, and particularly of a child who did not survive long enough to be baptised, was more likely to go unremarked in the register than a death at an older age when the individual concerned had become a widely known member of the local community.

Table 4.3 contains details of infant and child mortality in each of the 8 reconstitutions in question. The table also contains comparative data for the registration districts created by the Registrar-General within which the 8 parishes were located. It is clearly desirable that the two sets of data should relate to time periods as closely similar as possible. For the reconstitution parishes the period in each case begins in 1825 and ends with the beginning of civil registration in 1837. For the registration districts the choice of period is circumscribed by the available data. No detailed tabulations of infant mortality are available for any unit smaller than the registration district, and, during the nineteenth century, the Registrar-General rarely published detailed breakdowns of infant mortality within the first year of life, even for units as large as the registration district. Fortunately, he did so for a scattering of years very early in the civil registration period, 1841, 1842, 1845, and 1846, though not again for some time.[29] The coverage of childhood mortality was less restrictive. Rates between age 1 and age 15 are therefore based on deaths occurring in the seven-year period 1838–44.

The population totals given in table 4.4 show that the parishes comprised only a small proportion of the populations of the registration districts of which they formed part. Overall the 8 represent 10.4 per cent of the combined population of the registration districts, the individual percentages ranging between 4.6 (Gedling in Basford) and 26.9 (Odiham in Hartley Wintney). It would therefore be no surprise if there were significant, genuine differences in infant mortality between individual parishes and the registration districts in which they lay, though it might also be expected that on average the rates in the two groups would be similar, unless reconstitution parishes were known to be systematically different from their immediate regions, for example by being more rural, or having a different occupational structure. Judgement is further complicated by the fact that the registration district data refer to only four years, and by the difficulty of knowing, especially for local areas,

---

[29] The Registrar-General did, however, also make summary returns with the same age breakdown within the first year of life by consolidating data for the years 1839–44 for each registration district. These data were published in Registrar-General, *Eighth annual report*, Abstract of deaths in the six years 1839–44, at different ages under one year. Since registration of burials is generally supposed to have been worst at the start of civil registration, however, the data for the years quoted in the middle 1840s were preferred for the present purpose.

Table 4.4 *Populations of 8 reconstitution parishes in 1831 and of the registration districts in which they were situated*

Parish	Registration district	Population Parish	Registration district	Parish as percentage of registration district
Ash	Eastry	2 140	23 922	8.9
Banbury	Banbury	5 906	26 801	22.0
Bottesford	Grantham	1 320	22 890	5.8
Dawlish	Newton Abbot	3 151	40 926	7.7
Gedling	Basford	2 343	51 474	4.6
Morchard Bishop	Crediton	2 003	21 765	9.2
Odiham	Hartley Wintney	2 647	9 830	26.9
Shepshed	Loughborough	3 714	24 696	15.0

Note: registration districts were not, of course, designated until after the beginning of civil registration in 1837, but their populations at earlier dates were calculated retrospectively and published in the census of 1851.
Sources: *1831 Census*, Enumeration abstract; *1851 Census*, Population tables I, Numbers of inhabitants in the years 1801, 1811, 1821, 1831, 1841, 1851.

whether there was any significant trend in the level of infant mortality during the early decades of the nineteenth century.[30]

Examination of table 4.3 shows that there is a marked resemblance between the infant mortality rates in the reconstitution parishes and those in the larger units within which they lay, both when individual pairs are taken, and when overall averages are considered. The infant mortality rates shown in the table were on average somewhat lower in the reconstitution parishes than in the corresponding registration districts (118 and 132 per 1000 respectively), but the agreement between the rates from the two sources is much closer than appears from this comparison because the reconstitution rates refer exclusively to legitimate children, whereas the Registrar-General's data refer to all children. The ratio of illegitimate to all births can be calculated for each registration district from data published by the Registrar-General for 1847, 1848, and 1849, and it is probable that the illegitimate infant mortality rate was about twice that for legitimate children.[31] It is therefore simple to calculate a revised infant mortality rate for each registration district. If this is done, the average legitimate infant

[30] In general, infant and child mortality appears to have reached a low point early in the nineteenth century and was on a rising trend from then until the middle decades of the century. See below tabs. 6.3 and 6.10, pp. 224, 250–1.   [31] See below pp. 221–2.

mortality rate in the registration districts falls to 123 per 1000, a level only slightly higher than that in the reconstitution parishes.[32] The mean absolute discrepancy in the paired infant mortality rates (using the revised registration district rates) was only 8 per 1000. The pattern of mortality in the first month of life, the most sensitive to the effects of underregistration, was also notably similar in the two series. In table 4.3 the reconstitution and registration district averages for first month mortality are 40 and 49 per 1000, respectively, but if a comparable adjustment were made to the average first month rate for the registration districts, these rates also would be very close to each other.

Table 4.3 also gives details of child mortality. It was generally higher in the registration districts than in the reconstitution parishes, but once again individual pairs tend to resemble each other quite closely.[33] The average level in the reconstitution parishes was 79 per cent of that in the registration districts for the age group 1–4, 83 per cent for the age group 5–9, and 108 per cent for the age group 10–4. The average rate for the whole period from the 1st to the 15th birthday ($_{14}q_1$) in the reconstitution parishes was 85 per cent of that in the corresponding registration districts. Mortality rates in infancy and childhood appear to have been rising in England in the second quarter of the nineteenth century after reaching a low point early in the century, so that the agreement between the reconstitution rates and those drawn from the Registrar-General's returns may be even closer than appears from a direct comparison. There is particularly good reason to think that early childhood mortality rates rose sharply in the middle decades of the nineteenth century.[34]

Since the early nineteenth century was the period when parochial registration might have been expected to be at its weakest, the implica-

[32] The individual revised rates per 1000 were as follows: Eastry 115; Banbury 139; Grantham 129; Newton Abbot 93; Basford 147; Crediton 84; Hartley Wintney 101; Loughborough 172.

[33] It is further reassuring that the relationship between infant and child mortality in the reconstitution parishes conforms fairly closely to that found in level 13 in the North set of the Princeton model life tables (the same is true of the registration districts, though in this case the pattern resembles level 12 rather than level 13). Since it is likely that if there was any underregistration of deaths the problem would be heavily concentrated in the early months of life, the fact that the level of infant mortality relative to mortality a little later in life broadly conforms to expectation enhances the probability that registration was substantially complete. Indeed, in terms of the North model life tables, infant mortality, both in the reconstitution data and in the registration districts, was distinctly too high relative to mortality at ages 1–4 and 5–9 rather than the reverse.

[34] See below tabs. 6.3 and 6.10, pp. 224 and 250–1. See also Huck, 'Infant mortality'; and Laxton and Williams, 'Urbanization and infant mortality'. The probability that death rates in the age group 1–4 were rising rapidly just as the parish register era was drawing to a close is discussed on pp. 258–60.

tion of table 4.3 is encouraging for the reliability of information derived by family reconstitution for earlier periods when parish registration was subject to fewer influences tending to impair its completeness. To make this claim is not, of course, to suggest that parochial registration was in general full and accurate. The available evidence suggests that acceptable results *may* be secured from reconstitutions based on Anglican registers if care is taken in selecting and testing them, and not that Anglican registration was generally reliable. Patently it was not.

Fertility

A test of the credibility of fertility rates derived from reconstitution data at the end of the parish register era is also possible. The Registrar-General took much less interest in fertility than in mortality in the early decades of civil registration. The high level of mortality, and its wide variation between different social groups and geographical areas, were matters of wide concern. The death rate was a focus of attention; the birth rate was not. Accordingly, detailed measures of fertility were not published. No age-specific marital fertility rates were published, nor is it possible to calculate them from the material published in the Registrar-General's *Annual reports*. Nevertheless, the plausibility of the age-specific rates derived from reconstitution data can be tested, if only indirectly.

Such a test can be undertaken because the decennial censuses contained breakdowns of the population by sex, age, and civil status. It is therefore possible to calculate the number of legitimate live-born children who would have been born if the English population in 1851 had experienced the same age-specific fertility rates as those calculated for an earlier period by using data from the Anglican parish registers. The birth total derived in this fashion can then be compared with the total of legitimate births which were recorded by the civil registration system. The reconstitution-based fertility rates are drawn from a much larger number of parishes than the infant and child mortality rates which have just been considered. This was possible because experiment showed that in the case of fertility it was unnecessary to use the four groups employed in the study of mortality and nuptiality because there were no 'group' differences in fertility rates.[35] In consequence only 9 of the 26 reconstitution parishes made no contribution to the fertility rates used in making the comparison. This exercise is reported in detail in the

[35] See below p. 357.

chapter of this book devoted to fertility,[36] but it may be of interest to summarise the findings in this context.

If the age-specific rates found in the later decades of the parish register period (1780–1829) are applied to the population of married women recorded in the 1851 census, they imply a birth total 9.9 per cent larger than the total actually registered over the five-year period 1849–53, expressed as an annual average.[37] The scale of the difference may be due in part to the fact that marital fertility was higher in the late eighteenth and early nineteenth centuries than earlier in the parish register period, and may have been higher than in the mid-nineteenth century. But even if the age-specific rates to the period 1700–49 had been used, a period of somewhat lower fertility, they would still have produced a birth total 6.2 per cent higher than that recorded by the Registrar-General.[38]

There are a number of possible reasons for these discrepancies,[39] but the comparison does nothing to injure the conclusion that parish registers, if selected and used with discretion, can yield reliable information about fertility no less than about mortality.

Nuptiality

A similar claim can be made for the accuracy of reconstitution estimates of age at marriage. There is an encouragingly good fit between the average age at marriage of men and women derived from reconstitution data in the early decades of the nineteenth century and such marriage age information as was collected and published by the Registrar-General in the early years of civil registration. The closeness of agreement between the two data sources can be tested for each of the four marriage rank combinations, bachelor/spinster; widower/spinster; bachelor/widow; and widower/widow. The relevant comparisons are made in the chapter devoted to nuptiality.[40]

Internal consistency and demographic plausibility

The suitability of Anglican parish registers as a source of information about the demography of populations in the past has been questioned from time to time. For example, Razzell has recently attempted to discredit the quality of parochial registration, especially for the study of mortality.[41] The method he employed was derived from one of the

---

[36] See below pp. 462–4.   [37] Tab. 7.38, p. 463.   [38] Ibid.   [39] See pp. 463–4 below.
[40] See esp. tabs. 5.9 and 5.10, pp. 156 and 159, and accompanying text.

techniques devised by Henry to measure the scale of register deficiencies. It depends upon the supposition that parents did not give the same name to two children in their family unless the first to receive the name was dead. If, therefore, a name is given for a second time to a child on an FRF without the burial of the first child having been recorded, it is to be presumed that a failure in registration has occurred. A more searching method of testing the issue that concerned Razzell exists. This is a convenient juncture, therefore, at which to consider the adequacy of burial registration during the parish register period as a whole, rather than at its end, and at the same time to assess the legitimacy of Razzell's claims.

Consider, first, Henry's 'repeated first name' test. Pursuing a suggestion made by Houdaille, Henry noted that birth intervals could be divided into three types, according to the fate of the next youngest child of the same sex: where the earlier child of the pair was known to have died, where the earlier child was known still to be living, and where no information existed to determine whether or not the earlier child had survived until the birth of the later child.[42] The next step was to establish for each of these three categories the proportion of cases in which the younger child was given the same name as the older one. It is then a simple matter to estimate in what proportion of 'unknown' cases the older child of the pair had died before the birth of the younger child, even though there was no burial record of the death. The formula suggested by Henry for this purpose reflects the self-evident point that evidence of a repeated first name without an intervening death in the case of 'fate unknown' children is evidence of registration failure only to the degree that the proportional frequency of such cases *exceeds the proportional frequency of similar cases where the earlier child is known to have survived.*[43] If there are no instances of a repeated first name where the earlier child is known to have survived, all repeated first names are evidence of underregistration of deaths in the 'fate unknown' category, but when first names are sometimes repeated even though the earlier child is still living, this may substantially reduce the implied level of underregistration, or even eliminate it completely.

Razzell made no reference to Henry in his article and it is therefore

[41] Razzell, 'The growth of population'.
[42] Henry, *Manuel de démographie historique*, pp. 22–3.
[43] Henry's formula is the following: $u = (1 - a)l + ad$, where l is the proportion of cases where the same name is used for a younger sibling when the older sibling is still living; d is the corresponding proportion where the older child is dead; u the corresponding proportion where the fate of the older child is unknown; and a is the proportion of older children who have died among those whose fate is unknown.

uncertain whether he was aware of the logic of Henry's approach, but it seems probable that he was not, since his analysis of data concerning repeated first names begins with a piece of evidence that is damaging to his subsequent discussion, though quoted as if it reinforced his claim. He notes that, of 2221 children named in sixteenth-century Essex wills, only 0.5 per cent of living siblings shared the same name.[44] This information is quoted as reinforcing the belief that all cases of repeated first names among 'fate unknown' children can be treated as cases of burial underregistration, but a moment's reflection in the light of Henry's formula shows that this is an unwarranted assumption. If 0.5 per cent of living siblings shared the same first name at the time when their father made his will, the use of model life tables shows that, at the point in time when the younger of two siblings was baptised, the comparable percentage would be about 1.2 per cent.[45] If we further note that in the period 1538–1837 there were 12 192 baptisms in Colyton, and that in this period Razzell found 188 cases of same name siblings where there was no recorded burial for the older child of the pair (or 376 individuals, representing 3.1 per cent of all baptisms),[46] the potential significance of the Essex will information is plain, if the reasoning used by Henry is understood and the validity of his formula therefore accepted.[47]

Evidence from Essex is of limited relevance to Devon, nor is it necessarily apt to use data drawn from wills in relation to same name repetition in parish registers, and therefore the degree to which Razzell's estimates are misleading is uncertain, but it is clear that evidence of repeated first names which fails to take account of the significance of the deliberate use of the same name at baptism, even though an older sibling of the same name was still living, is a broken reed. It is, indeed, more than likely that the improvement in the

[44] Razzell, 'The growth of population', pp. 752–3.
[45] This is the result of a rough-and-ready calculation in which the mean age at paternity was assumed to be 37.5 years, mortality levels were assumed to be those of the Princeton model North level 7 life table, and the older same sex sibling was assumed to be 5 years old at the time of the birth of his younger brother or sister. The result is not greatly sensitive to the particular assumptions made.
[46] Razzell, 'The growth of population', tab. 4, p. 755.
[47] Finlay showed an acute awareness of this issue when he used Henry's method to investigate the scale of underregistration in London in the seventeenth century. Following his calculation of the apparent level of underregistration in several London parishes in the seventeenth century, he comments on the fragility of his estimates, chiefly because of the difficulty of knowing in how many cases a younger child may have been given the same name as an older sibling even though the older child was still living. Finlay, *Population and metropolis*, pp. 45–9.

registration of burials, which Razzell believed that he detected, reflects the decreasing frequency with which parents used the same name twice for living children rather than a decline in underregistration. But it is unprofitable to pursue the issue further using this method since a better alternative exists, a method whose nature was also sketched by Henry.[48]

This alternative method also depends upon dividing birth intervals into three categories similar to those described above: where the earlier child is known to have died within the first year of life; where the earlier child is known to survived its first year; and where the fate of the earlier child is unknown. The average birth interval in the first case will be much shorter than in the second because the abrupt cessation of breastfeeding enforced by the infant death led to a new conception much sooner than where the child survived its first year. There remains the third case. In a world in which registration was perfect, an infant whose date of death was unknown but whose family had been resident in the parish until after its first birthday, could be assumed to have passed its first birthday and to have migrated elsewhere later in life, dying 'abroad'. But if registration were not good an unknown date of death might connote either migration or a death which escaped registration.

This suggests a method of identifying the scale of any underregistration of infant deaths. The third category (fate of child unknown) should display the same birth interval characteristics as the second category (known to have survived the first year of life) if all the children in the third category did indeed survive their first year, as would happen in the 'perfect registration' case. But if the third category includes a proportion of cases in which the child died in infancy but without the event being recorded, then the birth intervals in this category will display a mixture of the characteristics of the first and second categories, and it is a relatively straightforward matter to estimate the implied proportion of deaths which were missed. Approaching the question in this fashion, for example, Henry concluded that in the case of Crulai it was necessary to increase the recorded total of infant deaths by 11.5 per cent to offset the underregistration revealed by a comparison of the birth interval distributions in the three

---

[48] Henry, *Manuel de démographie historique*, pp. 22–5. The use of the repeated first name method is also problematic for other reasons. For example, defining what should constitute a repeated first name raises difficulties. Some common names existed in variant forms with varying degrees of stability of usage: for example, Margaret, Meg, Peggy, and so on. It is impossible to be sure what the 'right' solution to this problem is, yet varying solutions will result in differing estimates of the frequency of repeated first names.

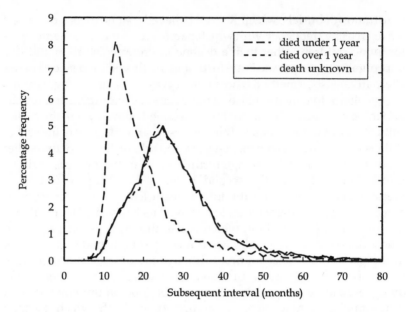

Figure 4.1 *The distribution of birth intervals where the previous child died when aged under 1, when the previous child survived, and when the fate of the previous child is unknown*

Note: last birth intervals and birth intervals from dummy marriages excluded. No data were taken from Birstall in order to preserve parity with similar exercises in ch. 7, dealing with fertility.

Source: Cambridge Group reconstitutions.

categories.[49] This approach has the great attraction, compared with the repeated first name method, that the test is based on all birth intervals falling within very broad categories and numbered in tens of thousands, rather than on a relatively small and selected set of intervals.

If there were gross differences between the birth intervals in the second and third categories, the means would differ. The question of any possible difference between the means in these two categories is important in the context of birth interval analysis, and is discussed below when analysing fertility. It is demonstrable that the means are closely similar, when appropriate allowance is made for the effect of last birth intervals and if the comparison is made parity by parity between births in the two categories.[50] For the purposes of chapter 7 this test was sufficient. In the present context it is of interest to press the matter a little

---

[49] Ibid., p. 25.   [50] See below pp. 439–43.

further and to consider the frequency distribution of the birth intervals in question as well as their means.

The birth intervals shown in figure 4.1 are drawn from the entire reconstitution data sets of all the parishes during their respective periods of sound data, except for Birstall.[51] Last birth intervals and birth intervals from dummy marriages are, however, excluded. The reasons for their exclusion are discussed elsewhere.[52] In addition, parity 1 birth intervals were excluded (that is, birth intervals between first and second births) because they were significantly shorter than birth intervals of higher parity, but they formed differing proportions in categories 2 and 3, which would have distorted comparison of the two categories. All three categories of birth interval are shown in figure 4.1. There were 5492 birth intervals in category 1, 12360 in category 2, and 21449 in category 3, a total of 39301 birth intervals. The effect of the interruption of breastfeeding on the time to next conception is very clear from the difference between the category 1 line and either of the other two. The category 1 line reaches a much earlier and much more pronounced peak than does either of the other lines.

Of prime interest in relation to the question of the possible under-registration of infant deaths, however, is the comparison of the category 2 and category 3 lines. They appear closely similar, peaking at almost the same point, maintaining similar overall shapes, and having very similar means. The mean of category 2 birth intervals is 30.01 months; that of category 3 birth intervals, 29.88 months, a difference of only 0.13 months, or 4 days. The category 2 birth interval is the equivalent of 913 days, so that the mean length of a category 3 birth interval is only 0.43 per cent shorter than that of a category 2 birth interval. However, a more formal test of their similarity, using the Kolmogorov–Smirnov test, barely fails to reject the null hypothesis that the two samples were drawn from identical populations at the 5 per cent level of significance (prob > KSa = 0.0641). Category 3 is very like category 2, but the KS result raises the possibility that, instead of all children in category 3 surviving to beyond their first birthday, a proportion may have died as infants, but without their deaths having been recorded.

A more detailed examination of the data, however, suggests a different conclusion, since a breakdown of the data by period shows

[51] The periods of sound data are those within the final limits shown in tab. 2.1, pp. 22–3. The reason for excluding Birstall from the analysis of fertility is described on p. 356 below. For the sake of consistency with the fertility calculations involving birth intervals, Birstall was also excluded from the data used in fig. 4.1, although its inclusion in this context would have been perfectly proper.   [52] See below, p. 442.

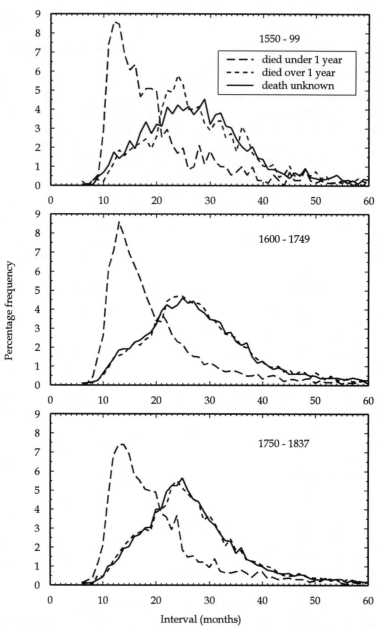

Figure 4.2 *The distribution of birth intervals where the previous child died when aged under 1, when the previous child survived, and when the fate of the previous child is unknown, by time period*

Note: last birth intervals and birth intervals from dummy marriages excluded. No data were taken from Birstall in order to preserve parity with similar exercises in ch. 7, dealing with fertility.

Source: Cambridge Group reconstitutions.

that the result for the period as a whole is misleading. The reason is simple. From the mid-seventeenth century until the end of the eighteenth century birth intervals in England gradually became shorter.[53] Towards the end of the parish register period the proportion of all birth intervals in the third 'unknown' category rose substantially, so that the proportion of birth intervals in the later decades of the period as a whole is greater in category 3 than in its comparator, category 2. This exaggerates the difference between the two categories if the overall data set is used. The problem can be overcome by using appropriate subperiods within which the problem does not arise, or is much reduced. Experiment suggests that the characteristics of the frequency distribution of birth intervals are best explored by using three subperiods; 1550–99, 1600–1749, and 1750–1837.

The distribution of birth intervals in each of the three categories for each of the three subperiods is shown in figure 4.2. The number of birth intervals is, of course, smaller in the panels of figure 4.2 than in the whole period, shown in figure 4.1, and the lines present a less smooth outline, especially in the pre-1600 period when the birth interval totals were much smaller than in either of the two later periods. The percentage distributions of category 2 and category 3 birth intervals appear very similar in the later periods, but coincide less well in the first period. What the eye suggests is confirmed by the Kolmogorov–Smirnov test. In the two later periods there is no reason to suppose that the populations from which the samples were drawn differed from one another ($KS = 0.4046$ in 1600–1749, and $KS = 0.4603$ in 1750–1837). A comparison of their means is similarly reassuring. In 1600–1749 the category 2 mean was 30.46 months; the category 3 mean 30.45 months, while in the period 1750–1837 the comparable figures were 29.14 and 29.23 months. In the latter period, therefore, the category 3 mean was actually the *higher* of the two. In these periods, therefore, there is no evidence of failure to register infant deaths. If category 3 birth intervals consisted of a mixture of intervals following an infant death and intervals in which the earlier child did not die, the birth interval distributions and the means of category 2 and category 3 would differ, and the line representing the latter would lie to the left of the line representing the former since it would include some intervals of a category 1 type.

In the earliest period the issue is more open. Kolmogorov–Smirnov does not reject the null hypothesis ($KS = 0.0509$), but there is a suggestion in the shape of the line representing the 'unknown' birth intervals

---

[53] Tab. 7.36, p. 447.

that some infant deaths were not registered. It is therefore instructive to consider how large any such underregistration might be. One way of estimating this is to establish what blend of birth intervals following an infant death and birth intervals in which the earlier child is known to have survived would best mimic the 'unknown' line.

An estimate of the extent of the 'contamination' of children who survived beyond their first birthday by children who died in infancy may be obtained by regression.[54] It suggests that the proportion of all births in category 3 which were followed by an infant death was 8.50 per cent. This in turn permits an estimate to be made of the extent to which infant mortality as a whole may have been underestimated in the period before 1600. The total of birth intervals in all three categories is 2932. Of these 456 consist of known infant deaths (category 1). None of the births in category 2 resulted in an infant death since all are known to have survived their first year. There are 1572 birth intervals in category 3. If 8.50 per cent of these intervals followed an unregistered infant death, the number of such deaths would have been 134. This suggests, therefore, that 29.4 per cent should be added to the total of infant deaths to make good those deaths missed because of defective recording ($134/456 = 0.2939$), a very substantial adjustment. It should be noted, however, that the mean birth intervals in category 2 and category 3 in this period were notably similar (30.41 and 30.51), and that the latter was actually the higher of the two rather than the lower, as would be expected if many intervals in the category had followed an infant death. Given the conflicting nature of the conclusions suggested by the two tests, and the relatively modest number of birth intervals in this earliest period, it is prudent to reserve judgement about the possible scale of underregistration before 1600. After that date, however, there seems no good reason to question the adequacy of the registration of infant deaths.

The comparison of infant mortality in reconstitution parishes early in the nineteenth century with the early returns of the Registrar-General, and the estimate of the underregistration of infant deaths based on birth interval analysis, therefore, are in broad agreement. Both suggest that any underregistration of infant deaths in the 26 reconstitution parishes

---

[54] Using the model $Y = ax_1 + bx_2$, subject to the constraint that $a + b = 1$: where Y is the category of birth intervals in which the fate of the child is unknown; a is the proportion of children dying under 1; b is the proportion of children surviving their first year; x_1 is the percentage frequency distribution of birth intervals following an infant death (category 1); and x_2 is the percentage frequency distribution of birth intervals following the birth of a child known to have survived its first birthday (category 2).

must have been relatively modest in scale, except possibly in the sixteenth century.

The conclusion that suitably chosen parish registers can yield data of high quality is strengthened by other aspects of the internal consistency of the demographic data yielded by family reconstitution, and this makes it possible to rebut some of the criticisms that are occasionally aired about such data. Take, for example, an argument made by Razzell about trends in marriage age over time. He expressed dissatisfaction with the reconstitution data on age at first marriage. His thesis was that marriage age in the seventeenth and eighteenth centuries was rising rather than falling as suggested by reconstitution evidence. He supposed marriage age to have risen by about 1.5 years between the late seventeenth century and the inception of civil registration, whereas reconstitution data suggests a fall in marriage age of 2.5–3.0 years.[55]

Razzell considered the linkage process which associates a particular baptism with a subsequent marriage to be flawed in ways which cause the apparent trend in marriage age to be misleading.[56] Yet there is a simple test based on the internal consistency of reconstitution data which shows that mislinkage can only have been a rare phenomenon. If, when the major fall in mean age at marriage occurred during the eighteenth century, the apparent trend was spurious, this would be reflected in the pattern of age-specific fertility rates. For example, suppose that, at a time when the calculated mean age at marriage was 26, the true age was only 23. This would mean that, on average, women who were apparently, say, 47 years of age would be only 44. Towards the end of the childbearing years age-specific rates fell very rapidly, and therefore, if births to women who were in reality 44 were being tabulated as relating to women aged 47, the calculated age-specific rates in the 45–9 age group would be greatly overstated. *Ceteris paribus*, if the true mean age at marriage were constant at 23 years, but mislinkage in reconstitution showed an apparent fall from 26 to 23 years during the eighteenth century, it is to be expected that the age-specific marital fertility rate for women aged 45–9 would fall sharply, since at the beginning of the period it would have been distorted by counting women as substantially older than their true age but towards the end of the period this anomaly would disappear. In practice, although age at marriage changed considerably in England during the parish register period, the age-specific rate for the 45–9 age group was remarkably

[55] Razzell, 'The growth of population', pp. 750–2. Reconstitution marriage age data are set out in tab. 5.3, p. 134.   [56] Ibid., pp. 749–50.

stable, fluctuating close to 20 per 1000 throughout. The rate in the next lower age group, 40–4, was about six times higher than that for 45–9, so that even minor inaccuracies in calculated ages would be sure to result in implausible rates.[57]

One further example of a finding of reconstitution whose nature increases confidence in the general accuracy and completeness of the information generated may be noted, drawn from the analysis of fertility and related issues undertaken in chapter 7. The analysis of fecundability carried out there contains, as a novel feature, an attempt to measure fecundability throughout the course of marriage, as well as at its beginning, the conventional point at which to analyse fecundability. This can be done by studying the frequency distribution of birth intervals following an infant death.

Models of fecundability which yield frequency distributions of birth intervals following marriage suggest, on reasonable assumptions about the relevant fertility parameters, that about 2 per cent of first birth intervals will exceed 60 months in length.[58] The situation following an infant death was not unlike that between marriage and first birth in that the death of the infant caused breastfeeding to cease and induced an early return of fecundable cycles. The fact that the proportion of birth intervals longer than 60 months following an infant death was less than 1.4 per cent suggests that few births failed to appear as baptisms on their FRFs.[59] Poor registration, by omitting some births from a sequence, would have caused an excess of long birth intervals, but such intervals were no more common than would be expected in circumstances where registration was punctilious.

---

[57] Tab. 7.37, p. 450. More direct checks upon the accuracy of links made in the course of reconstitution between baptisms and marriages are also possible if a suitable source of information exists. There was a period when this was possible in Colyton because of the nature of the information given in the register. This showed that in the 62 cases in which the accuracy of the link could be checked, in only 3 cases was it incorrect. Wrigley, 'Some problems of family reconstitution', p. 211.

[58] Wilson both discusses such models and refers to evidence that in Germany in the later eighteenth and nineteenth centuries a figure of about 2 per cent was normal. Wilson, 'Marital fertility in pre-industrial England', p. 112 and app. 4.

[59] Tab. 7.41, p. 498. It will be remarked that in this table the proportion of first birth intervals (that is, measured from marriage to first birth) of more than 60 months was somewhat higher. The frequency distribution of this interval has been commonly used in the study of fecundability. The fact that there was a higher proportion of 'long' birth intervals in this category is probably due to the existence of a prenuptial birth in a proportion of cases, which would cause what was in reality a second or later birth interval to be counted as a first birth interval, which in turn would raise the percentage of intervals longer than 60 months. See pp. 467–72.

The evidence of the mid-nineteenth-century enumerators' books

One further general test of completeness of registration coverage in reconstitution parishes may be briefly considered. From 1841 onwards the basic data from which census tabulations were built up were obtained by circulating to each household an individual schedule to be filled in by the household head, rather than by requiring the overseers of the poor to make a general return. The information set down on the schedules was then copied by the census enumerators into standard ledgers, termed enumerators' books, to consolidate the data into a form which lent itself to further analysis, and also in order to check and regularise the information. Among the standard questions to be answered for everyone counted in the census was one relating to age and another to place of birth. It is therefore possible to draw up a list of natives of a parish and, by subtraction, to estimate their years of birth. Armed with such a list, the proportion of those born in the parish whose baptism is recorded in the parish register appears easy to determine either decade by decade, or divided into other convenient time periods, for example, before and after Rose's Act, or before and after the inception of civil registration in 1837.

As might be expected, the apparent simplicity of the test dissolves rapidly on further examination. It is demonstrable, for example, that the longer an immigrant from elsewhere continued to live in a parish, the more likely he or she was to claim to have been born there. Or again, statement of age was not always accurate, or consistent from one census to the next.[60] This latter characteristic causes problems in defining the 'search area' within which it is proper to seek a baptism to match someone present at a census. Further, though most people continued to use the same first name throughout their lives, though often in a variant form from the baptism entry, there were some who changed the name by which they were commonly known. Other complications exist, and any such exercise is liable to remain inconclusive, because most parishes contained a nonconformist minority who were recorded in the census, but who were less likely than the Anglican community to appear in the Anglican baptism register. Sometimes a surviving nonconformist register can be helpful, but where none survives and especially where the nonconformists were themselves divided between several different chapels, it may be difficult to draw confident conclusions about the completeness of Anglican coverage.

Nevertheless, three studies of reconstitution parishes in the set of 26

---

[60] The accuracy of statements both about place of birth and about age are discussed in Wrigley, 'Baptism coverage in early nineteenth century England'.

have been made using the enumerators' books as a check upon the completeness of baptism registration. These were for Shepshed and Bottesford in Leicestershire; for Colyton in Devon; and for Methley in the West Riding of Yorkshire.[61] They are broadly reassuring. In the cases of Bottesford, Colyton, and Methley, Anglican coverage was generally high. For example, in the parish register period before 1837 more than 90 per cent of those who claimed to have been born locally in Colyton in the 1851 census could be traced to a baptism register, and it is likely that the true percentage of missing events was lower, perhaps much lower, than might appear, because of the fallibility of the linkage procedure for the reasons just given. The situation in Bottesford and Methley was very similar. Moreover, the completeness of reconstitution was greater than the overall linkage percentage might suggest because 'missing' baptisms were commoner in migratory families and these families contributed little data to reconstitution tabulations. The proportion of missing baptisms was far higher in Shepshed, a parish in which nonconformity was rife, but Levine concluded that 'the deficiencies in Shepshed's registration system were not as serious as they first appeared because a great deal of the leakage was occurring among families which, for the purpose of reconstitution, can be regarded as non-essential'.[62]

Because the enumerators' books do not specify the religion of the individuals listed in them, only the proportion of *all* those claiming local birth found in the parish register can be established. In relation to family reconstitution, however, the point at issue is not what proportion of *all* those living at a given census and claiming birth in the parish can be traced in the parish register, but what proportion of *Anglicans* can be so traced.[63] Bearing this point in mind, evidence provided by enumerators' books to test registration coverage is again encouraging, though the uncertainties associated with it should certainly be recognised.

Delayed baptism and dummy births

It will be convenient at intervals later in this work to consider particular questions of deficiency and bias in reconstitution data in connection with particular measures of demographic behaviour, but it is appropri-

---

[61] Ibid.; Levine, 'The reliability of parochical registration'; and Yasumoto, *Industrialisation, urbanisation and demographic change*, pp. 3–5

[62] Levine, 'The reliability of parochial registration', p. 118.

[63] This point appears not have been fully appreciated by Razzell when making a comparison of burials in the Anglican register of Colyton in the period 1837–51 with the civil registers for the same period: Razzell, 'The growth of population', pp. 755–6.

ate to deal with one such topic at this juncture, since it is perhaps the weightiest single reason for anxiety about Anglican registration coverage.

In the sixteenth century baptism commonly followed close upon birth, but the interval betweeen the two events widened with the passage of time. Since it was rare to record the dates of both birth and baptism in the baptism register, information on the average delay to baptism is scattered and intermittent but it seems clear that by the later eighteenth century the two were separated by fully a month on average, and in many individual cases the interval was far longer.[64] Moreover, local custom varied greatly. At one extreme, in some parishes births were commonly 'saved up' for baptism at a fixed point in the year, which gave rise to a very marked bunching in the seasonal distribution of baptisms and long delays for individual children,[65] while elsewhere the interval remained brief and relatively uniform. In principle, even a long average delay before baptism need not lead to any loss of coverage, provided that parents were astute in recognising when their infant was in danger of death and prompt in securing his or her baptism. There is evidence that this strategy was pursued to good effect in many individual cases;[66] but it is unrealistic to expect that all infant deaths could be anticipated in this fashion. As a consequence some children will have died unbaptised. In addition there are instances in every register of another type of child burial not preceded by a baptism. This happened when a family which had recently moved into the parish lost a child who had been born and baptised elsewhere, or when a local family was absent from the parish for a while, baptised a child in another parish and had returned to their home parish by the time the child died.

When an unbaptised child died it seems to have been customary in many parishes, at least until late in the seventeenth century, to record his or her burial; often the register entry refers explicitly to the fact that the child had died unbaptised. In such circumstances, if the name of the father of the child was given in the register (or, better still, the names of

---

[64] Berry and Schofield, 'Age at baptism'; Wrigley and Schofield, *Population history of England*, pp. 96–100.

[65] As, for example, in the Feast Week in July in Melbourn, Cambridgeshire, where over a third of all baptisms for the year took place when the custom was at its most influential in the 1780s; Mills, 'The christening custom at Melbourn', tabs. 2 and 8, pp. 13 and 19. The phenomenon was even more marked in Willingham in the 1760s when almost a half of all baptisms took place in October: see p. 38 above.

[66] See Wrigley and Schofield, *Population history of England*, pp. 96–7 n. 15.

both parents), the family of the dead child is usually identifiable. Where this was the case a dummy birth entry was created and given the same date as the burial, thus raising both the number of births on the FRF and the number of those dying in the first day of life. Indeed, whether or not a child burial entry was specifically said to relate to an unbaptised child, if it could be linked to its appropriate family, but not to a particular baptism in that family, a dummy birth was created and given the same date as the burial, provided that there was an appropriate space in the existing sequence of children in the family to accommodate the newly added birth. Such action often referred to a case where an unbaptised child was buried but was not described as unbaptised in the register, but it might also refer to a child who had been baptised elsewhere but had died at some time after the family had moved or returned to the parish. In the former case the action taken will produce broadly the 'right' solution; the total of deaths in the first day of life will be exaggerated, but the total in the first month will be approximately correct; in the latter case the inaccuracy will be greater.

The proviso that there should be an appropriate space in the existing sequence of baptisms, however, is important and reduces the likelihood of mistakenly assuming that the burial entry is evidence of death very early in life. Where a child clearly belonged to a particular family but the timing of the burial entry prohibited the creation of a dummy birth of the same date, a suitable space earlier in the sequence of baptisms was sought and a dummy birth was created, but in this case, of course, the baptism and burial dates would differ. The first type of dummy birth can conveniently be termed 'standard' and the second type 'transposed': the two types were given different 'weights' so that they could be included in or excluded from demographic tabulations as appropriate (*70 and *71 respectively).

The relative frequency of dummy births of these two types at different periods is set out in table 4.5. The time periods given in the table were chosen to ensure that the set of parishes contributing to the totals was unchanging within each period. They therefore correspond to the parish groups described above in chapter 2.[67] The trend of change is not greatly dissimilar however measured, but the apparent prevalence of dummy births differs according to the method of measurement employed (last six columns of table 4.5). It is probable that the pattern visible in columns 9 and 10, where the median is used, is the best guide to the secular trend in the number of standard and transposed dummy births.

---

[67] Except for the period 1680–1729, a period when all 26 parishes were simultaneously in observation.

Table 4.5 *Proportion of all births (baptisms) on FRFs that were dummy births*

	(1) No. of parishes in observation	(2) Total no. of births (baptisms)	(3) Dummy births *70	(4) Dummy births *71	(5) (3)/(2) ×100	(6) (4)/(2) ×100	(7) Unweighted mean of individual parish percentages	(8)	(9) Median of individual parish percentages	(10)
							*70	*71	*70	*71
1580–99	15	9885	312	156	3.2	1.6	2.9	1.7	2.7	1.5
1600–29	20	22417	838	308	3.8	1.4	3.5	1.3	2.8	0.9
1630–79	20	37072	1843	618	5.0	1.7	4.4	1.6	3.3	1.1
1680–1729	26	44845	1691	627	3.8	1.4	3.1	1.2	2.5	0.9
1730–89	18	50593	1206	517	2.4	1.0	2.1	0.8	1.8	0.7
1790–1812	8	10272	371	100	4.0	1.0	2.9	0.8	1.6	0.4
1813–37	8	16019	84	39	0.6	0.2	0.4	0.2	0.4	0.2

Source: Cambridge Group reconstitutions.

113

The tendency for the percentage of dummy births to rise over the first century is what might have been expected on general grounds. *Ceteris paribus*, a steady, if modest, lengthening in the mean interval between birth and baptism would tend to increase the percentage of standard dummy births (the proportion of transposed dummy births was always low and changed little before the later eighteenth century). But the rise in the percentage of standard dummy births did not continue into the eighteenth century: the average percentage measured overall (column 5) falls, slowly in the two periods 1680–1729 and 1730–89, but then, after a marked recovery in 1790–1812, very sharply in the final period, 1813–37.

The interpretation of these data calls for circumspection. The rise in the average figure in column 5 in the penultimate period may be disregarded. It comes about because only 8 parishes remained in observation after 1790, and the biggest of these, Banbury, which contributed almost a quarter to the total of births in this period, had a very high percentage of dummy births (8.3 per cent). Significantly, the median (column 9) shows a continued fall, rather than a marked rise, in this period. At first sight the explanation of the fall in the eighteenth century might seem to lie in the increasing unwillingness of incumbents to record the burial of unbaptised children. There is evidence for this both in the sense that it becomes rarer to find references to the burial of unbaptised children during the eighteeenth century, and from the comments which incumbents occasionally made in their registers.[68] But there is an important offsetting consideration that suggests caution in supposing that increasingly neglectful registration explains the fall in the percentage of dummy births created to match an infant burial. The overall level of infant mortality peaked early in the eighteenth century and thereafter tended to fall, though only modestly, but the level of mortality within the first month of life fell strikingly. The reconstitution data suggest a fall from 106.3 to 48.7 per 1000 between 1700–24 and 1825–37.[69] There is good reason to believe that even so marked a fall is genuine.[70] Clearly, if the level of infant mortality early in the first year of life fell sharply, the impact of delayed baptism on the apparent rate of infant mortality would also be reduced. This change implies that some, even much, of the fall in the percentage of dummy births in the eighteenth and early nineteenth centuries may be genuine rather than a reflection of changed social custom and registration practice.

The very low percentage for the final period 1813–37 in table 4.5,

---

[68] See p. 33, n. 13 above.   [69] Tab. 6.4, p. 226 below.   [70] See below pp. 223–42.

however, does reflect a change in registration practice. Under Rose's Act, from 1813 onwards parishes were required to keep register books consisting of printed *pro forma* sheets. The prescribed form of entry for burials included a section for the age of the deceased, an item of information that had rarely been recorded previously, but there was no field for the names of the father and mother of the deceased, though it had been common practice in the past to record the names of one or both parents when a child died.

The absence of information about parentage necessarily makes the treatment of the burial of an infant problematic where there is no suitable baptism entry to which the burial entry can be linked. Linkage to the family rather than to the individual is more difficult. It might therefore be expected that the percentage of dummy births would fall sharply, and it is reasonable to fear a fall in the completeness of coverage of births as a result. But it must be recalled that table 4.3 gives little ground for supposing that the true level of infant mortality was higher than the rates calculated from family reconstitution, which in turn implies that few births were missed by relying on the baptism register. If they had been missed, thus increasing the number of unlinked infant deaths, the calculated infant mortality rate would have fallen short of the levels revealed by the new civil registration system. It should also be emphasised once more, however, that the parish registers used for family reconstitution were an elite set selected with care and extensively tested. The problems associated with delay in baptising children were, therefore, probably much less prominent and serious in these parishes than in the Anglican registration generally.

Overall, it seems appropriate to conclude that the loss of coverage and therefore the degree to which fertility measures were affected by delayed baptism, though hard to quantify, is probably slight in the reconstitution parishes. Any such effect would necessarily tend to be proportionately greater in the measurement of infant mortality than in measuring fertility. For example, in the simplest case, if a register which had previously recorded the burial of all unbaptised children suddenly ceased to do so, and if there had been 20 such entries for every 980 recorded baptisms at a time when infant mortality was at 160 per 1000 births, the abrupt cessation of the practice (entailing the disappearance of dummy births and the associated early deaths from the reconstitution) would reduce the total of births by 2 per cent, but the level of infant mortality by 12.5 per cent. Even in the case of infant mortality, however, the evidence of table 4.3 suggests little cause for alarm, and the fertility comparison exercise described above, and detailed in table 7.38, contains no hint that fertility rates based on Anglican registration were below their true level.[71]

The processing of data taken from FRFs

There must always be a risk that error is introduced into any exercise based on very large data sets by the successive stages of data copying, data articulation, and data processing. Thus, even if Anglican registration were as complete and detailed as would be required to sustain the most demanding demographic measures, the tabulations based upon them might still be defective if significant inaccuracies were introduced while processing the data. It would be idle to suppose that a procedure as complicated as family reconstitution can escape difficulty on this score. There are numerous opportunities for error at all stages in the exercise.

The basic operations constituting reconstitution by hand make heavy demands on the concentration of the person concerned, both in following the rules governing the construction of the links out of which the history of a family is built up, and in preserving accuracy in the course of the innumerable clerical operations involved. But errors affecting the accuracy of data are likely to occur at all stages of the process of reconstitution. Information may be mistranscribed from the register to the extraction slip, from the extraction slip to the FRF, and from the FRF to a machine-readable form of the data. Errors arising at the first two stages occur pen in hand, at the third at a keyboard, but they are all similar in nature. Some of these errors will never be detected but will survive to reduce the accuracy of the data used in the calculation of demographic measures. Others, however, can be brought to light by

---

[71] One other possible reason for doubt about the accuracy of rates derived from reconstitution should be mentioned. It affects only the measurement of infant and child mortality. The rules of manual reconstitution prescribe that where, say, a given baptism can be linked to more than one child burial, no link should be made. This is a necessary rule because cases of far greater complexity than the illustration just given are common and it is virtually impossible to act consistently when reconstituting by hand. When the record linkage is done by computer, however, there is no such limitation. Algorithms have been written to ensure consistency which can deal with all possible combinations of possible links. More probable links can be preferred to less probable ones, resorting in a limiting case to a random choice if competing possibilities are equally strong (see, for example, Schofield, 'Automated family reconstitution', for a brief description of linkage strategy). It is to be expected, therefore, that computerised record linkage must yield higher infant and child mortality rates than manual reconstitution, when applied to data from the same register. Such tests as have been carried out so far, however, reveal very little difference in the rates produced by the two methods.

appropriate logical and formal checks made by program after the reconstitution data have been rendered into a machine-readable form. Once identified the source of the error can normally be established and a correction made.

The detection of formal errors is a routine matter. For example, it is important to ensure that in fields that should contain only alphabetic information, such as names, there are no numerical data; and in date fields, only numerical data with appropriate values, as, for example, 1–31 for days, 1–12 for months; and so on. Some forms of logical error can also be detected, and, their detection can significantly improve the empirical findings embodied in reconstitution tabulations. For example, no date of death is admitted which is greater than the date of birth plus 105 years; no woman can marry at less than 15 years of age; no child may remain linked to a family if its presence would imply that the mother was 50 years of age or more when the birth took place; and so on. It would be wearisome to describe all these tests in the main text of this chapter, but they are specified in full in appendix 4.

It should be noted that information may be known with varying degrees of accuracy. A date, for example, may be known only to the month rather than the day. Again, additional information which is not routinely recorded, and for which there is therefore no reserved information field on the FRF, may nonetheless be sporadically available, and useful where known. Such information was recorded by a system of flagged information fields, or flags, and may be of great value in subsequent tabulation and analysis. The systems of date weights and flags are described and illustrated in appendix 2.

Conclusion

A definitive estimate of the scale of inaccuracies in the reconstitution data is not feasible, though many other tests might be made which could further limit any remaining uncertainties. Some further tests will be presented seriatim as the findings are presented. Thus, for example, models of fecundability can be used to test the closeness with which birth interval data conform to expectation.[72] Others could have been made directly upon the reconstituted families themselves rather than upon the tabulated results. For example, many married men left wills at their death in which their children were named as beneficiaries under the will. Where a family was apparently in observation throughout the duration of the marriage, any child named in a will should also appear

---

[72] See below pp. 464–501.

on the FRF, and should not have been buried before the date of the father's death. Similarly, if a detailed listing of inhabitants survives for a parish, a comparable check is possible. Where a reconstitution was taken down to the end of the parish register period or beyond, the enumerators' books of the 1841 census, or of a later census, can be made to serve the same purpose. The results of such a test for 4 of the 26 reconstitution parishes have been reported,[73] but many others could be carried out.

All such tests can be valuable: but all prove to be less straightforward and conclusive than might appear at first blush. It would have been possible to have carried out more tests than are reported in this chapter and elsewhere later in the book, and it is likely that some would have proved valuable in supplementing and extending knowledge of the strengths and weaknesses of the reconstitution data. There is, however, a danger of declining marginal returns to extra effort. We take the view that, just as the tests described in the last chapter justify a provisional conclusion that the four groups should yield results that are broadly representative of the country as a whole, so the tests of reliability described in this chapter suggest that the empirical findings based on the 26 reconstitution parishes are unlikely to be seriously defective, and this view is strongly buttressed by the further evidence of the accuracy and internal consistency of the nuptiality, mortality, and fertility findings to be presented in the next three chapters.

[73] See above pp. 109–10.

PART II

5

Nuptiality

All beings that enter life must later leave it. Between birth and death some, but not all, will play a part in ensuring that, though they may die, their species will continue. In some animal species only a tiny fraction of each new generation plays a part in engendering its successor because so few survive the early perils of life and become sexually mature. Even in the unhealthiest environment, however, the erosion of each new generation by death is relatively mild in the case of man. Even where expectation of life at birth is as low as 20 years, for example, about a third of new-born children will survive to the age of 25 years.[1] To survive to maturity, however, is not always enough to ensure an opportunity to reproduce even when the man or woman in question is well able to do so physiologically. It may also be necessary to marry. Reproduction outside marriage occurred in all societies, but in many it was rare and might involve punishment for one or both parents and serious disabilities for the child. If marriage was not a *sine qua non* for reproduction, therefore, it was often almost so.

In most societies, restricting reproduction very largely to those who were married did not exclude many young men and women from the opportunity to reproduce since almost all who reached maturity without marked physical or mental handicaps were assured of marrying, but parts of western Europe formed an exception to this rule since there a substantial proportion of each rising generation never married, often more than 10 per cent, sometimes as much as 25 per cent. Hajnal drew attention to this fact in a famous article in which he used census data to show that outside western Europe in the middle decades of the

[1] For example, the figure for female children with $e_0 = 20$ years in model North of the Princeton life tables is almost exactly one third. Coale and Demeny, *Regional model life tables*, p. 220.

121

twentieth century very few men and women remained single in adult life. Only 1 per cent of Egyptian women were unmarried in the age group 45–9 and only 2 per cent of men in the same age group in 1947.[2]

In general, custom decreed that women should marry by the time they were sexually mature or soon thereafter. In western Europe, however, there was often a long interval between menarche and marriage. The average age at marriage was normally within the range between 23 and 27 years, whereas in eastern Europe it was much lower. Hajnal noted that in Serbia over the period 1886–1905 it was just less than 20 years and in India far lower still.[3] For example, in the state of Berar the proportion of women never married in the age group 15–9 was less than 4 per cent in every census between 1881 and 1931, with the exception of 1901 when it was slightly higher.[4]

West European men also married late in life. They were usually a little older than their wives, but the wife was not infrequently the older of the two. The age gap between spouses was commonly much greater in other societies and women were less frequently older than their husbands. This pattern was characteristic of Mediterranean Europe, for example. The nature of the institution of marriage in western Europe was such, therefore, that many men and women, though adult and healthy, had little chance of contributing to the next generation by procreation. Even those who succeeded in marrying might have relatively small families because most married so long after reaching sexual maturity. A woman marrying at, say, 26, for example, will already have exhausted more than 40 per cent of the fertility potential available to her as a young girl of 17, yet 17 was a relatively high average female age at marriage in India or in many other countries in the past.[5]

The pattern that Hajnal identified was of long standing in England. It prevailed throughout the early modern period and may have been present also in the later medieval period.[6] Such nuptiality patterns were not universal in English society. Hollingsworth has shown that in late Tudor and Stuart times the daughters of noble families married young,

---

[2] Hajnal, 'European marriage patterns', tab. 4, p. 104.   [3] Ibid., p. 109.
[4] Dyson, 'The historical demography of Berar', tab. 1, p. 153.
[5] The figure of 40 per cent was arrived at by using a representative schedule of age-specific marital fertility rates for early modern England (see tab. 7.37, p. 450 below). To make a simple calculation of this sort is unrealistic in that at a given age the marital fertility rates of women who had married early tended to be lower than those marrying later in life at a given age. Thus the rate at age 35–9 for women who had married in their teens might be appreciably less than for women who had married in their late 20s. The figure of 40 per cent may therefore be somewhat higher than the 'true' figure, but the contrast is nonetheless striking.
[6] Smith, 'Some reflections', and 'Fertility, economy and household formation'.

with a preponderance of teenage brides, though by the mid-eighteenth century elite practice had ceased to diverge so markedly from the national norm.[7] For those who commanded great resources, the timing of marriage might be a matter of choice, and either family interest or custom might dictate early marriage. For most couples intent upon marriage, however, the possibility of achieving their aim depended upon the assembling of the resources and the acquisition of the skills needed to embark upon the enterprise. It is perhaps significant that the Prayer Book of 1549 uses this terminology in describing the frame of mind proper to those contemplating matrimony.[8] Marriage was an assertion of independence both economically and from parental ties. It involved establishing a new household, with a new household head, whereas in many other societies a couple on marriage joined an existing household and the husband might wait many years before becoming its head.[9]

To establish a new household involved substantial initial expense and a relatively high level of continuing cost. In most cases it meant the purchase, or acquisition in other ways, of such things as pots, pans, fire irons, mugs, platters, cutlery, chairs, tables, chests, beds, and bedlinen as well as the ability to meet rent payments or their equivalent. In many cases there were parallel equipment costs because the household was also a workshop – a loom, a knitting frame, a set of carpenter's or shoemaker's tools. The more expensive items might be rented rather than bought but, whatever the particular situation, there were both setting up costs and subsequent running costs to be met. A farming household needed farm equipment and in addition there was stock to be bought as well as a continuing commitment to be met in the form of rents, rates, tithes, payments in kind, etc.

Just as important as the saving necessary to pay for the cost of setting up a household was the acquisition of the skills required to be confident of running it independently. Service in husbandry or an apprenticeship

---

[7] Hollingsworth, *Demography of the British peerage*, tabs. 2 and 5, pp. 11 and 15. Later elite practice again diverged from the patterns of the population at large. In the nineteenth century marriage occurred later in life among noble families than in the mass of the population. See also Stone, *Family, sex and marriage*, esp. pt 4.

[8] 'whiche holy estate . . . is not to bee enterprised, nor taken in hande unaduisedlye, lightelye,or wantonly, to satisfie mens carnal lustes and appetites, like brute beasts that have no understanding: but reuerentely, discretely, aduisedly, soberly, and in the feare of God'. *The first and second prayer books of Edward VI*, p. 252.

[9] The nature of the rules governing the north-west European simple household system and of the contrast between it and joint household systems is elegantly set out in Hajnal, 'Two kinds of pre-industrial household formation'. See also Laslett, 'Introduction: the history of the family'.

were periods of training during which a young man became sufficiently a master of a related set of production skills to be able to operate on his own with a fair chance of success. His bride must know how to bake bread, prepare and cook food, mend clothes, and perhaps also how to spin thread or make lace, or how to run a dairy parlour or a poultry yard. Apprentices and servants were debarred from marriage, but having served out their terms, and in part because they now possessed the production skills required for independence, they might venture upon it.[10] The combination of having jointly saved enough to embark on a marriage, and sharing the skills necessary to run a household, made a couple eligible to marry. Arthur Young made clear the implied time scale of the process for those who could expect little or nothing from their parents. He estimated that a pastoral farm of 12 acres would cost £65-5-0 in a first year, including stock, implements, and rent; an arable farm of 16 acres £91. Kussmaul suggests that such sums were within the joint saving capacity of a young man and a young woman in service over a period of 10 years or so.[11]

Acquiring the resources and skills necessary for marriage was apt to be a protracted process for both potential partners, but the length of time involved varied, not only from couple to couple for myriad reasons, many inconsequential, but also systematically over time and between different groups. Husbandmen, carpenters, miners, and fishermen, for example, might differ in the speed with which they habitually acquired the skills and assembled the resources needed for marriage. Or again, in periods of lowered real wages and with uncertain prospects for employment or for the sale of produce, plans to marry might miscarry and the event itself be postponed or cancelled.

In most societies marriage was an archway through which all or almost all passed in their journey through life if they survived beyond childhood. In western Europe the archway was set further down the road and did not fully span it: many did not pass through, some from unfettered choice, others because the pressure of circumstance forced them aside. To oversimplify in the interests of clarity, it might be said, in short, that in most of the major cultures of the past, marriage, at least for

[10] Kussmaul, *Servants in husbandry*, pp. 83–5. On the scale of the institution of service in husbandry in England and some comparative data for other countries, see Laslett, 'Characteristics of the western family'. The circumstances which led to a servant girl with several years of service behind her being more 'marriageable' than a less experienced servant girl are vividly described by Sundt, drawing upon his fieldwork experience, in *On marriage in Norway*, pp. 157–62. He was describing nineteenth-century Norway, rather than early modern England, and many of the courtship rituals were different in the two settings, but the considerations which caused many young men to prefer older to younger brides were not dissimilar.

[11] Kussmaul, *Servants in husbandry*, pp. 81–2.

women, was triggered by the approach to or the attainment of menarche. Physiological change provoked individual and family action backed by social sanctions. To avoid shame the family had to arrange a match. In contrast, in England, and in some other parts of western Europe, marriage was triggered by economic circumstances and was accordingly a movable feast, since both the particular circumstances of individual couples and the general circumstances of the economy changed and fluctuated over time.[12]

To describe the distinctive nature of west European marriage in these terms is, of course, to oversimplify. The decision to marry always reflects a vast range of pressures and incentives of which only a limited number are economic. Social custom, established conventions, personal preferences and sexual drives, family exhortation, and prejudice all play a part. Because many of these are imponderable, it does not follow that they are unimportant. Introspection immediately suggests otherwise. Yet there were close links between economic circumstances and marriage decisions in western Europe in the past.[13] Because of the nature of the institution of marriage, the decision to marry was peculiarly susceptible to economic pressures.

Marriage held the centre of the demographic stage in early modern England because fluctuations in nuptiality produced closely similar movements in fertility. Marital fertility changed only modestly between the middle of the Tudor period when it can first be measured with confidence and the onset of the definitive fall in marital fertility about 1870 when more and more couples began to practise family limitation within marriage.[14] A sharp rise in marriage age or in the proportion never marrying therefore implied a matching fall in fertility as the

---

[12] Although it serves a useful purpose to express this contrast so starkly, it is, of course, too forcefully put. Moreover, what is regarded as 'economic' is often a matter of taste. For example, in an agricultural setting where farm holdings represented 'niches', the death of a member of the older generation might be the reason for a marriage opportunity opening up to a member of the younger generation. Here marriage is jointly conditioned by economic and demographic circumstances. These issues figure largely in Macfarlane, *Marriage and love in England*.

[13] An early examination of this link may be found in Thomas, *Swedish population movements*, and it was a main theme of much French writing in the early postwar decades, well exemplified in Goubert, *Beauvais et le Beauvaisis*. There is a vast literature on the topic. Galloway has recently brought together much comparative data about price fluctuations and movements of demographic indices, including marriages, within an econometric framework in 'Basic patterns', especially fig. 1, p. 286 and app. tab. 1. For a recent overview of the subject, see Schofield, 'Family structure', esp. pp. 282–5.

[14] Wilson and Woods, 'Fertility in England', tab. 1, p. 403. This characterisation appears a little too simple in the light of new knowledge about changes in marital fertility. See pp. 449–54 below for evidence that age-specific marital fertility rates were less invariable than once seemed likely.

proportion of the fertile period that the average woman spent in marriage fell. Conversely, a fall in marriage age or in celibacy meant a rise in fertility. The secular fluctuations in nuptiality and thus in fertility could be very substantial. An illustrative calculation in an earlier examination of this issue suggested, for example, that the rise in nuptiality in the eighteenth century was sufficient to increase fertility by about 50 per cent from its low point in the middle decades of the seventeenth century.[15]

In principle, of course, even such wide swings in fertility might have been exceeded by still more dramatic mortality changes but in practice for much of the early modern period the former were more influential than the latter in affecting trends in the intrinsic growth rate. Using the results of back projection applied to aggregative data, for example, it appeared that between 1680 and 1810, a period during which the intrinsic growth rate rose from zero to 1.5 per cent per annum, about two-thirds of the increase was attributable to fertility change, and thus chiefly, if indirectly, to the rise in nuptiality which took place during the eighteenth century.[16]

Marriage was, of course, also of central importance in a wider social context. It was not just the means by which genes passed from one generation to the next but also an important vehicle for the transmission of property, and the prime means by which the socialisation and education of children took place. Each new marriage resulted in the formation of a new building block in the social, economic, political, and demographic fabric of the community.

The special characteristics of the reconstitution marriage data

In establishing the demographic characteristics of a population from reconstitution data, the study of nuptiality enjoys an advantage over the study of fertility or mortality that simplifies the discussion of long-term nuptiality trends in England. It will be recalled from the discussion in chapter 2 that in many parishes reliable registration begins only some time after the earliest years of the reconstitution and that, similarly, it may cease before the reconstitution ends.[17] This was one reason for the

[15] Wrigley and Schofield, *Population history of England*, tab. 7.15, p. 230. The gross reproduction rate rose from an average of 1.91 in the quarter-century 1649–73 to 2.94 in the quarter-century 1804–28, though a small part of the rise was due to the rapid increase in illegitimate fertility over the period rather than to fertility increase within marriage.
[16] This question is discussed with illustrative calculations in ibid., pp. 265–9.
[17] Tab. 2.1, pp. 22–3.

adoption of the device of using parish groups to marshal the data so that over the time period covered by a particular group its composition did not change. For example, the abrupt shrinkage in the number of parishes in observation in moving from group 3 (1680–1789) to group 4 (1680–1837) does not occur because many reconstitutions stopped in 1789, or soon thereafter, but because there is reason to doubt the reliability or completeness of the information in the registers from 1790 or thereabouts. If, say, the burial of young children is no longer fully recorded after a particular date, it would be foolish to continue to attempt to measure child mortality after that date. Similarly, marital fertility cannot be estimated with confidence if baptisms are no longer reliably set down. In such periods of defective registration, however, it does not follow that estimation of marriage age will also be seriously affected. It is true, of course, that if a child is born but not baptised, survives childhood and marries, no link can be made between a baptism and a marriage record relating to that man or woman, and so he or she will not enter into the calculation of marriage age for the period. But, provided that the failure to record baptism is not selective, the effect will be to reduce the number of known ages at marriage rather than to distort the estimation of marriage age.

Not all dangers are avoided. It is conceivable, for example, that a defective burial register may mean that, say, a girl died and was buried in childhood but that this escaped registration and that in consequence her baptism is incorrectly linked to a subsequent marriage. But there is no systematic tendency for marriage age to be distorted by continuing to make use of marriage ages even in periods when registration was unsatisfactory for other purposes. The whole reconstitution period in each parish can therefore be used to provide information about age at marriage. And this in turn means that, for example, group 3, instead of ending in 1789 can be allowed to continue through to 1837. Some problems remain. One or two reconstitutions within the set of parishes comprising group 3 ended before 1837 and care must therefore be taken to avoid the danger that compositional change is mistaken for 'real' change, but the broader empirical base afforded by the 18 parishes of group 3, rather than the 8 parishes of group 4, represents an important advantage.

In considering the empirical data contained in the tables in this chapter and in the next two chapters, dealing with mortality and fertility, it should be remembered that all data from Birstall and Shepshed are given only half-weight. Apparent discrepancies between, for example, row or column totals and the sum of individual cells are to be attributed to the rounding of the subtotals in the cells which may occasionally result in small anomalies of this type.[18] The measures taken to avoid truncation bias in measuring nuptiality, mortality, and fertility are described in appendices 3 and 10.

Nuptiality trends and characteristics

It is convenient to begin with an overview of the long-term pattern of nuptiality change in England, and to do so by considering decadal data relating to marriages between spinsters and bachelors. Table 5.1 sets out the relevant information for groups 1, 2 and 3: 1580–9 is omitted from group 1 because there were so few known ages in that decade. In considering the data it should be borne in mind that it is normally easier to be certain about the marriage rank of women than of men when using Anglican parish register material. If a link can be made between a female baptism and a marriage entry it is almost always safe to assume that the marriage is a first marriage since a woman on marriage assumed the surname of her husband. Only, therefore, if a woman had previously married a man of the same surname and so had the same surname both as a spinster and as a widow is there a danger of mistaking a second for a first marriage, even if the marital status of the bride was not specified in the marriage entry. In the case of men, in contrast, it is less easy to be sure of marriage rank. Since a man's surname did not change on marriage, it is not possible to be certain of his marital status unless the marriage entry defines it by referring to the groom as bachelor or widower. This information became more common after the coming into effect of Hardwicke's Act in 1754 but was very rare before that date. Where the register does not specify marital status on marriage, therefore, there is a danger, in the case of a groom, of making a link from his baptism to a marriage other than his first and assuming that he was a bachelor because no earlier marriage is known, even though he had in fact been married previously in a different parish and was remarrying in the parish of his birth. No doubt some mistakes were made in identifying bachelors for this reason but it is probable that such mistakes were few in number, since the difference in age between spinsters and bachelors calculated from reconstitution data is remarkably similar to that found in the early years of the Registrar-General's returns.[19]

---

[18] For a discussion of the reasons for giving half-weight to Birstall and Shepshed, see pp. 43–8 above.

[19] See below tab. 5.10, p. 159. The difference in marriage age between bachelors and spinsters was 1.1 years both in the reconstitution data and in the Registrar-General's returns for 1846–8. It was 1.0 year in his data for 1839–41. Close agreement is to be

It is clear at a glance from table 5.1 that the level and trend in ages at marriage is closely similar in the three groups in the periods of overlap between them but that in order to produce a single series of figures for the whole period some 'splicing' of the data taken from the different groups is necessary. First, however, there is a preliminary difficulty to be overcome. It relates to the composition of the sets of parishes making up each group at the beginning and the end of the period that it spans. One reason for constituting the groups was, of course, to avoid compositional problems by keeping the same set of parishes in observation continuously throughout a particular period.[20] Such problems cannot, however, be entirely avoided in some kinds of tabulation. For example, although all the parishes in group 2 were producing reliable data from a date before 1600,[21] not all could contribute to the calculation of marriage age from that date. The reason is that only after 50 years have elapsed from the start of a reconstitution can age at marriage be calculated without danger of downwardly biasing the resulting estimate (assuming that the estimate is a period measure relating to the date of the marriage rather than a cohort measure relating to the date of birth).[22]

This problem would be present in any case even if marriage age had been calculated for all four groups and if the 'final limits' shown in table 2.1 had been used, but it is more acute given the strategy adopted in this chapter of using data from within the wider span of the 'outer limits' from each parish and because of opting to use a 'long' group 3 rather than group 4 to obtain information after 1790. With these relaxations compositional problems are more obtrusive.

In order to appreciate the nature of the solution adopted, consider table 5.2. It shows the proportional decadal contribution to the total of female marriage ages made by each parish in group 2. Only from the 1640s onwards are all the 20 parishes represented in the table. Before that date some parishes are missing; the earlier the decade the greater the incompleteness. Birstall is missing in the 1630s, then both Birstall and Bottesford in the 1620s, until in the first decade of the century only half the parishes are in observation. Apart from illustrating the problem

expected by this late date since marital status was often given for both brides and grooms in parish registers by the early nineteenth century, but there was no suspicious change in marriage age difference in the wake of Hardwicke's Act, as might have been expected if widowers had previously sometimes been misidentified as bachelors (tab.5.1, p. 130).

[20] See above pp. 24–8 for a fuller discussion of the reasons for constituting the parishes into four groups as a basic strategy for the analysis of the reconstitution data.

[21] See the 'final limits' in tab. 2.1, pp. 22–3.

[22] This truncation problem is discussed in app. 3.

Table 5.1 Mean age at marriage in bachelor/spinster marriages (years)

	Group 1				Group 2				Group 3			
	Bachelors		Spinsters		Bachelors		Spinsters		Bachelors		Spinsters	
	Age	No.	Age	No.	Age	No.	Age	No.	Age	No.	Age	No.
1590–9	29.3	73	25.6	97								
1600–9	28.3	91	25.7	147	28.3	104	25.8	165				
1610–9	27.4	257	25.7	306	27.4	347	25.8	389				
1620–9	27.4	263	25.1	338	27.4	346	25.3	416				
1630–9	27.2	365	25.1	490	27.4	448	25.3	566				
1640–9	27.3	229	25.8	299	27.5	333	25.8	417				
1650–9	27.4	332	25.2	344	27.5	462	25.6	486				
1660–9	27.1	224	25.9	275	27.4	381	25.9	430				
1670–9	27.5	244	26.2	324	28.0	400	26.2	468				
1680–9	27.1	231	25.4	272	27.7	375	25.8	436	27.2	241	25.3	278
1690–9	26.1	223	25.6	260	27.1	370	25.9	431	27.0	226	25.5	267
1700–9	27.3	279	25.8	383	27.4	431	26.0	575	27.7	300	25.8	393
1710–9	27.0	321	26.4	409	27.3	524	26.3	639	27.5	413	25.9	497
1720–9	27.2	359	26.2	425	27.0	533	25.9	635	27.1	464	25.9	571
1730–9									27.0	477	25.4	637
1740–9									26.6	498	24.7	632
1750–9									26.2	543	24.9	722
1760–9									26.0	727	24.4	877
1770–9									26.2	745	24.2	953
1780–9									26.0	789	23.9	1058
1790–9									25.4	938	23.9	1145
1800–9									25.7	698	24.2	929
1810–9									25.6	621	23.6	832
1820–9									25.6	685	23.9	857
1830–7									25.3	572	23.2	770

Table 5.2 *Percentage share of each parish in totals of female marriage ages in group 2 (bachelor/spinster marriages)*

	1600–9	1610–9	1620–9	1630–9	1640–9	1650–9	1660–9	1670–9	1680–9	1690–9	1700–9	1710–9	1720–9
Alcester	2.4	3.9	3.9	5.3	5.5	6.4	5.4	7.1	4.8	4.2	6.3	6.9	4.1
Aldenham		11.3	6.3	4.8	3.4	4.5	2.1	4.1	3.0	3.7	2.1	2.8	3.3
Austrey		1.8	1.4	0.5	2.2	1.0	0.2	0.2	1.6	1.2	1.2	1.6	1.6
Banbury		4.6	11.8	14.7	7.4	9.7	5.8	6.2	4.6	3.5	7.3	8.5	8.2
Birstall					5.8	4.9	12.5	10.6	11.1	16.0	16.4	16.4	18.1
Bottesford				4.6	4.6	2.3	1.9	6.2	3.4	2.8	3.8	2.0	3.5
Bridford	4.9	4.4	1.7	2.8	1.4	1.9	0.7	1.9	1.1	0.7	1.9	0.6	1.3
Colyton	37.7	13.4	10.3	10.4	3.6	8.0	3.3	2.4	3.0	2.8	2.6	1.3	2.8
Gainsborough		7.7	15.4	13.8	17.5	13.4	13.3	11.8	14.7	11.4	12.2	11.9	12.3
Gedling		2.8	3.1	3.0	2.4	3.1	5.4	3.4	6.0	2.6	2.8	4.5	3.5
Hartland	6.1	7.7	7.9	6.5	9.4	11.1	12.8	7.9	11.7	9.8	6.6	8.1	5.7
Lowestoft		5.4	5.1	4.2	3.1	2.7	5.8	6.6	3.4	8.8	8.9	7.0	8.0
March	1.8	3.9	4.1	3.0	5.5	2.5	5.8	4.1	3.0	4.9	4.0	3.3	3.1
Methley		5.4	3.9	4.9	2.4	3.3	5.6	4.9	3.4	2.3	2.8	2.7	3.8
Odiham	17.0	6.7	5.1	7.1	8.6	6.6	4.0	4.7	4.6	4.4	4.5	4.9	3.9
Reigate		8.0	5.8	3.5	9.4	9.5	8.4	10.1	11.9	10.0	6.8	7.7	5.8
Shepshed	2.7	0.8	2.0	1.4	0.8	1.0	0.9	1.3	0.9	2.0	2.0	1.4	2.4
Southill	14.0	4.9	5.5	5.7	2.9	3.1	3.3	4.9	3.7	4.6	5.4	4.2	5.8
Terling	11.6	2.6	3.9	1.8	1.2	2.5	1.6	0.9	2.1	2.6	0.9	1.9	1.7
Willingham	1.8	4.9	2.9	1.9	2.9	2.7	1.4	0.9	1.8	1.9	1.6	2.3	1.1
	100.0	100.0	100.0	100.0	100.0	100.0	100.0	100.0	100.0	100.0	100.0	100.0	100.0
N	165	389	416	566	417	486	430	468	436	431	575	639	635

Source: Cambridge Group reconstitutions.

131

of the composition of the group in the early decades, the table also provides points of interest substantively, such as the rising share of Birstall with the early development of domestic manufacture, or the very severe relative decline of Colyton following the huge loss of life in the plague epidemic of 1645–6 when a fifth or more of the population died within a period of 12 months.[23] But in this context the compositional question has priority.

It is feasible to make an approximate correction for a 'missing' parish by establishing its proportional contribution to the total of events in the group as a whole in a particular base period close to the point in time at which it passes out of observation, and for the same period to measure the difference between marriage age in the parish in question and marriage age in the group as a whole minus that parish. On the assumption that the parish would have made the same proportional contribution to the group total during the period when it was not in observation and that the same difference between its mean age at marriage and that of the rest of the group obtained, a corrected value for the group can be estimated. The procedure is described in appendix 5.

Although the problem of missing parish data can be overcome by calculating the probable effect of the absence of particular parishes, it would be unwise to make use of this device unless the number of missing parishes is relatively small. In group 2 in 1600–9 as many as half of the parishes were making no contribution to the group totals. This is too high a proportion to suggest that a reliable estimate can be made for this decade, and, accordingly, no estimate of marriage age was attempted for this decade. The same problem affects the composition of group 1 parishes almost as severely, since group 2 consists of the parishes in group 1 with five additions. The decade 1610–9 thus becomes the first decade in the consolidated series intended to capture national trends, and all the decadal data are therefore drawn from groups 2 and 3.

Just as there was a problem in generating dependable estimates of

---

[23] Wrigley, 'Family limitation', p. 85. This estimate is confirmed in Schofield's much more exhaustive analysis of the available data; Schofield, 'Anatomy of an epidemic', esp. pp. 98, 119. The example of Colyton also illustrates the difficulty of drawing straightforward conclusions from apparently simple patterns in the data, however. There is no doubt that the population of the parish was substantially lower in the second half of the seventeenth century than before the plague, but the fall is much exaggerated in the table because clandestine marriage was widespread in Colyton in this period. Significantly the baptism/marriage ratio rose to 9.6 in the period 1665–99 from 4.4 in the period 1600–39. This was not because families were unusually large in late seventeenth-century Colyton. On the contrary age at first marriage for women rose to a very high level in the parish at this period (tab. 5.18, pp. 184–5). It was because many marriages went unrecorded in the Colyton register.

marriage age in the early decades of group 2, there was also a problem in the final decades of group 3. All the parishes constituting group 3 had been in observation for 50 years or more by the decade 1730–9, the first after the end of the group 2 period, and all remained in observation until the end of the eighteenth century, but thereafter a few parishes began to drop out of observation because of an early end to the reconstitution. The three affected were Birstall, where the reconstitution ended in 1800, and Gainsborough and Methley, in both of which the reconstitution finished in 1812. Revised overall estimates of marriage age were therefore required from 1800 to take account of Birstall, and from 1810 in the other two cases. The nature of the exercise needed to achieve this end was, however, the same as for the missing parishes in the early period for group 2 and needs no further comment.

There remains the question of 'splicing' data taken from group 3 to those taken from group 2. It seemed sensible to use group 2 as the 'base' series, since group 2 is the largest group and conforms quite well to the national pattern in such matters as occupational structure and aggregative demographic trends.[24] Down to 1730, therefore, group 2 data are used in the final estimates of marriage age, and the question of splicing reduces to finding an appropriate adjustment for group 3 data after 1730. Table 5.1 shows that mean ages in group 2 and group 3 were not greatly different during the overlap period between the two series, but that whereas male ages in group 3 tended to be slightly the higher of the two, the opposite was true of female ages. A more complete picture of the relative level of ages in the two series can be obtained by moving outwards from 1730 in both directions to discover how greatly and how consistently the means in the two series differed. This is feasible because the same method used to adjust for compositional changes in the parishes constituting group 2 in its early decades, and group 3 in its later decades, can also be used to generate marriage age data for group 2 after 1730 and for group 3 before 1730.[25] This compensates for the absence of 'real' data from some parishes in any given quinquennium. The parishes for which a substitute figure must be calculated for group 2 in, say, 1740–4 can readily be identified from the 'outer limits' dates for the individual parishes given in table 2.1.

This exercise revealed a notably stable relationship between the means in the two series. Over the 30-year period centred on 1730 (1715–44) the group 3 mean for grooms was 0.15 years higher than that of group 2. If the period was extended to 40, 50, 60, 70, and 80 years, in each case centred on 1730, the differences were 0.12, 0.10, 0.11, 0.12, and

---

[24] Tab. 3.3 and figs. 3.1, 3.3, 3.5, pp. 49 and 56, 62, 66.   [25] See app. 5.

Table 5.3 *Mean age at marriage in bachelor/spinster marriages: original data and final estimates (years)*

(1) Uncorrected mean ages from group 2 (1610–9 to 1720–9) and group 3 (1730–9 to 1830–7) (tab. 5.1, p. 130).
(2) Changes made to offset compositional change among the parishes in group 2 and group 3 (see pp. 129–32).
(3) Effect of 'splicing' group 3 to group 2 (see pp. 133–4).
(4) Final figures.

	Males				Females			
	(1)	(2)	(3)	(4)	(1)	(2)	(3)	(4)
1610–9	27.4	27.5		**27.5**	25.8	25.6		**25.6**
1620–9	27.4	27.6		**27.6**	25.3	25.2		**25.2**
1630–9	27.4	27.3		**27.3**	25.3	25.2		**25.2**
1640–9	27.5	27.4		**27.4**	25.8	25.7		**25.7**
1650–9	27.5			**27.5**	25.6			**25.6**
1660–9	27.4			**27.4**	25.9			**25.9**
1670–9	28.0			**28.0**	26.2			**26.2**
1680–9	27.7			**27.7**	25.8			**25.8**
1690–9	27.1			**27.1**	25.9			**25.9**
1700–9	27.4			**27.4**	26.0			**26.0**
1710–9	27.3			**27.3**	26.3			**26.3**
1720–9	27.0			**27.0**	25.9			**25.9**
1730–9	27.0		26.9	**26.9**	25.4		25.5	**25.5**
1740–9	26.6		26.5	**26.5**	24.7		24.8	**24.8**
1750–9	26.2		26.1	**26.1**	24.9		25.0	**25.0**
1760–9	26.0		25.9	**25.9**	24.4		24.5	**24.5**
1770–9	26.2		26.1	**26.1**	24.2		24.3	**24.3**
1780–9	26.0		25.9	**25.9**	23.9		24.0	**24.0**
1790–9	25.4		25.3	**25.3**	23.9		24.0	**24.0**
1800–9	25.7	25.4	25.3	**25.3**	24.2	23.9	24.0	**24.0**
1810–9	25.6	25.2	25.1	**25.1**	23.6	23.5	23.6	**23.6**
1820–9	25.6	25.3	25.2	**25.2**	23.9	23.7	23.8	**23.8**
1830–7	25.3	25.0	24.9	**24.9**	23.2	23.0	23.1	**23.1**

Source: Cambridge Group reconstitutions.

0.04 years respectively. The six comparable figures for brides were 0.12, 0.12, 0.13, 0.10, 0.12, and 0.11 years but in this case the group 3 mean was always *lower* than that for group 2. In view of these findings it seemed reasonable to *decrease* all male means in group 3 by 0.1 years and to *increase* female means by the same amount.

The elements now exist to enable final estimates of marriage ages to be derived by successive modifications of the figures presented in table

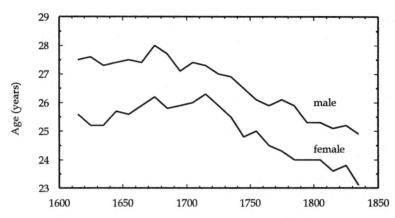

Figure 5.1 *Mean age at first marriage: bachelor/spinster marriages (decennial data)*

Note: each reading refers to the decade beginning in the year indicated: thus the 1620 reading refers to 1620–9, and so on.
Source: tab. 5.3.

5.1. The successive steps are set out in table 5.3 and the final figures are also shown graphically in figure 5.1.

The final figures do not greatly differ from those given in table 5.1, in part because the changes made to offset compositional changes affect data from only a small number of parishes, and in part because marriage ages in groups 2 and 3 were closely similar. The overall pattern of long-term change is very simple. For the century from the 1610s to the 1730s there was very little change in the average age at which spinsters and bachelors married. For men the average always lay between 27.0 and 28.0 years; for women between 25.2 and 26.3 years. Thereafter a major change occurred. Male age at marriage fell from about 27 to about 25 over the final hundred years from the 1730s to the 1830s. The fall was almost over by the 1790s. Female marriage age fell even more markedly from a peak of more than 26 years early in the eighteenth century to about 23.5 years in the last three decades, and again the fall was chiefly concentrated in the half-century after 1730.

The early plateau was not quite flat. In the 30-year period from 1660 to 1689, when the series peaked, the male age at marriage averaged 27.7. In the last three decades covered in the table, from 1810 to 1837, it averaged 25.1, suggesting a peak to trough fall of 2.6 years. Similarly, female marriage age reached a peak in the 30 years from 1690 to 1719, when it was 26.1 years, and then fell to an average of 23.5 in the period 1810–37, again a fall of 2.6 years. It is, however, probably more justifiable to view the first 120 years of the period as without significant trend in the case of male marriage age. In the case of women there is a stronger suggestion of upward movement during the seventeenth century (the average in 1610–29, for example, was 25.3 years compared with a figure of 26.1 years in 1690–1719). It is possible that during the middle and later decades of the seventeenth century the high level of emigration to North America and, at times, to Ireland, and the fact that it was predominantly a movement of young men, caused the sex ratio in the marriageable age groups to fall. Other things being equal, this would tend to reduce marriage opportunities for young women and to cause the age at marriage of spinsters to rise.

At first blush, the fall in marriage age in the course of the eighteenth century, which is the dominant feature of figure 5.1, though unambiguous, might not be regarded as large enough to be considered a change of the first importance. To draw such an inference, however, would be mistaken. If the fall in female age at first marriage is taken as 2.6 years (from 26.1 to 23.5 years between 1690–1719 and 1810–37), the implications for changes in the general level of fertility are highly significant. *Ceteris paribus* such a fall will increase the gross reproduction rate significantly. Suppose, for example, that the age-specific marital fertility rates for the five-year age groups 20–4 to 45–9 were 410, 370, 310, 250, 130, and 20 per 1000 respectively. These rates for the successive five-year age groups are those obtaining in early modern England in a stylised form.[26] A woman marrying at the average age prevailing late in the seventeenth century (26.0 years) and surviving throughout the rest of her childbearing period in marriage would bear 5.03 children: her great-great-granddaughter, making a comparable marriage early in the nineteenth century at the then average age of 23.5 years, and enjoying equal good fortune in the length of her marriage, would bear 6.02 children, an increase of 20 per cent. This calculation implies an impressive change but still understates the 'real world' change because in some cases marriages were broken by death before the end of the period of childbearing. The fertility of those marrying late was more severely affected proportionately than that of those marrying early. A fall in marriage age therefore increased the number of years of childbearing that the average bride could expect to experience by a greater percentage than that obtained by assuming that every bride survived in marriage to age 50. In addition, of course, other things being equal, a higher proportion of each cohort would marry and embark on a reproductive career when brides married early rather than late. If these

[26] See tab. 7.1, p. 355.

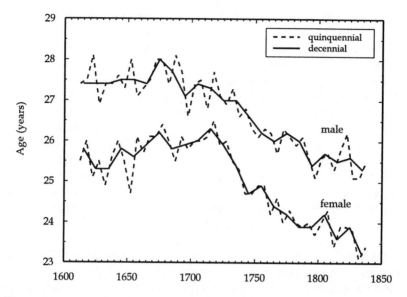

Figure 5.2   *Mean age at first marriage: bachelor/spinster marriages (quinquennial and decennial data)*

Note: each reading refers to the decade or quinquennium beginning in the year indicated: thus the 1620 reading refers to 1620–5 or 1620–9 as appropriate.
Source: Cambridge Group reconstitutions.

factors are taken into account the differential widens to about 23 per cent.[27]

In figure 5.2 quinquennial and decennial marriage age data are compared. These data are uncorrected. They are drawn from group 2 down to 1729 and from group 3 beyond that date. Figure 5.2 was included in order to make it easy to judge whether aggregating the data into ten-year blocks tends to obscure important shorter-term changes in marriage age: it is therefore the comparison of the two lines that is important and corrections designed to eliminate the 'overlap' problem are unimportant.

In general there is little difference between the two quinquennial figures that make up a decade and the related decennial figure. In the male series there were two decades in the seventeenth century, the 1620s and the 1650s, when a decennial figure almost identical to those for the decennia on either side was made up of a high average age at

[27] The calculation was made using the Princeton North female model life tables with an expectation of life at birth of 35 years.

marriage in the early years of the decade balanced by a much lower figure in the later years. Similarly, in the 1690s the rather low decennial figure occurred only because of the plunge in marriage age in the second half of the decade. In the 1710s there was a parallel but opposite pattern with the latter half of the decade showing a much higher figure than the first half. These were the only cases, apart from the 1820s, where the two quinquennial figures differed by a year or more, thus making the decennial figure potentially misleading. Occasionally, the adjacent quinquennial figures belonging to different decades were similar to each other but not to those of the decades of which they formed part. For example, there was a modest local 'peak' between 1815 and 1824, when the average age reached 26 years, which is not visible in the decennial data. But none of these slight digressions from the pattern visible in the decennial data was pronounced, and all may be in part due to random effects rather than the economic or other pressures of the time.

The female marriage age figures are very 'well-behaved'. There are even fewer marked contrasts between the pattern suggested by decennial data and that visible in the quinquennial data in the female series than in the male. There was one decade, the 1650s, when the two quinquennial figures were more than a year apart, but apart from this perhaps the only other feature worthy of notice is the evidence of a modest rise in the average age of female marriage in the seventeenth century, which is more clearly visible in the quinquennial data.[28] Over the period 1620 to 1654 the average age of spinster brides marrying bachelor grooms was 25.3 years: over the following quarter-century it was 26.1 years, a wider difference than that suggested by the decennial series.

There are circumstances in which it is to be expected that some aspects of nuptiality are best analysed using cohort rather than period data. For example, if the number of men in a given cohort is severely depleted by war deaths, but the number of women in the same cohort is little changed, a cohort approach may yield insights less readily secured when using period measures. With this point in mind, quinquennial and decennial data for cohorts were compared with period data. If the latter are offset by 25 years to reflect in a rough and ready way the modal interval between birth and marriage for the two sexes, it is straightforward to establish whether the cohort series differed significantly from the period series. The tables and graphs used to make the comparison are not reproduced here, since, with rare exceptions, the mean ages in

---

[28] It may well be that marriage opportunities for women were more seriously affected than those for men during the seventeenth century because of the trends in both external and internal migration: Smith, 'Influences exogènes et endogènes', pp. 182–9.

the two series were closely similar for both the quinquennial and the decennial data. The only discrepancy worthy of note, however, is intriguing. The mean age at marriage of the male cohort born in 1670–4 was more than 2 years higher than the period mean for 1695–9, the most appropriate comparator using a 25-year offset (28.7 years compared to 26.6 years). No other difference approached this magnitude: most were very small. The period mean was exceptionally low. No earlier quinquennium yielded a lower figure, nor any later one until the 1720s.

The Marriage Duty Act was passed in 1695, levying taxes on births, marriages, and deaths, and imposing a poll tax on bachelors. It therefore created an incentive for unmarried men to marry and it is possible that this is reflected in the low male mean age at marriage for the quinquennium immediately following its coming into force. There is a hint of the same phenomenon in the comparable female quinquennium but the effect is much less pronounced, as might, indeed, be expected. It would be premature, however, to claim that the observed cohort/period contrast is attributable to the Marriage Duty Act. A larger body of data is needed before such a claim could be adequately tested. This would enable the means for individual years to be calculated and any shift in the distribution of marriage ages to be identified with confidence. The present data, however, suggest a possibility that might repay further investigation.[29]

The frequency distribution of age at marriage in bachelor/spinster marriages

The same information that makes possible the calculation of an average age at marriage can, of course, also be displayed as a cumulative frequency distribution and be used to calculate quartiles, deciles, medians, and so on. For example, the seemingly small changes in mean age at marriage during the eighteenth century shown in table 5.3 can also be analysed in terms of the distribution of marriage ages for the two sexes before, and after, the main changes had taken place. In table 5.4 these distributions are shown for the period 1600–1724, during which average ages at marriage changed little and were relatively high, and for the period 1775–1837, when again there was little change in marriage age but the average age had fallen substantially. All data refer to

[29] The individual male means for 1690–9 are as follows. The numbers on which they are based are given in brackets. It will be clear that the number of cases is too small to inspire much confidence in the resulting means. 1690: 27.7 (45); 1691: 28.3 (32); 1692: 28.3 (38); 1693: 25.8 (23); 1694: 28.0 (24); 1695: 26.0 (42); 1696: 26.2 (45); 1697: 27.1 (37); 1698: 26.5 (48); 1699: 27.3 (32).

bachelor/spinster marriages. The earlier figures are taken from group 2 and the later figures from group 3; both are given uncorrected, that is without modifying the original data as was done in preparing the final estimates of marriage age in table 5.3. The corrected and uncorrected figures, however, differ only marginally and any such difference would be swamped by the great fall in marriage age during the eighteenth century. The picture given by table 5.4 may therefore be taken as a broadly reliable guide to the changes which took place. Within each panel the average age at marriage scarcely altered, as is clear from the figures in the final column, nor did the distribution of marriage age change significantly. The final row in each panel, where the totals for the periods comprising each panel are reexpressed in an indexed form, may be taken as showing the extent of the change brought about by the abrupt fall in marriage age in the middle decades of the eighteeenth century.

For both sexes the changes were striking. The proportion of men marrying in their teens doubled between the two periods, and the proportion marrying between the ages of 20 and 24, always the most important group, rose substantially, from just over a third to almost a half. Above the age of 25 proportions fell. The total of male marriages above that age declined from 603 in every 1000 in the earlier period to only 431 in the later. Female trends were similar to male. Teenage brides were always more common than teenage grooms, but in the later period marriage before age 20 became so common that the 15–9 age group became the third largest, and only fell short of the 25–9 age group by a whisker. The 20–4 age group became increasingly dominant and, as with bachelor grooms, came to comprise almost half of all marriages in the later period. Meanwhile marriages contracted at age 25 and above fell from 493 per 1000 to only 318 per 1000.

The characteristics of bachelor/spinster marriages may be further explored by considering the pattern of marriage for the two sexes taken jointly. Table 5.5 gives the relative frequencies of age at marriage combinations between bachelors and spinsters, and figure 5.3 displays the same information in the form of a data surface. Since, as was clear from table 5.4, there was very little variation in the pattern during the period down to the end of the first quarter of the eighteenth century, the first panel of table 5.5 shows the pattern for group 2 as a whole and therefore refers to the period 1600–1729. The second panel shows the same data for 1775–1837 when marriage patterns were again relatively unchanging; these data are taken from group 3. As may be seen from a comparison of the row and column totals in table 5.5 with the last rows of the four panels in table 5.4, the overall patterns are closely similar in

Table 5.4 *The distribution of marriage age among brides and grooms in bachelor/spinster marriages*

	Under 20	20–4	25–9	30–4	35–9	40–4	45 and over	Total	Average age at marriage (years)
					Males				
Group 2 1600–1724									
1600–24	22	201	212	111	34	14	12	605	27.7
1625–49	34	372	324	142	71	19	12	972	27.3
1650–74	39	361	381	151	75	23	19	1047	27.6
1675–99	41	333	310	161	56	25	15	941	27.5
1700–24	54	453	412	185	76	32	23	1233	27.3
1600–1724	190	1720	1639	750	312	113	81	4798	27.5
Per 1000	39	358	341	156	65	23	17	1000	
Group 3 1775–1837									
1775–99	151	1057	555	193	103	37	25	2121	25.7
1800–24	154	761	439	181	64	33	15	1644	25.7
1825–37	99	450	243	84	32	17	8	931	25.2
1775–1837	404	2268	1237	458	199	87	48	4696	25.6
Per 1000	86	483	263	97	42	18	10	1000	
					Females				
Group 2 1600–1724									
1600–24	108	264	222	106	24	12	4	739	25.6
1625–49	163	473	358	149	48	16	8	1213	25.5
1650–74	154	449	331	155	60	22	7	1177	25.8
1675–99	132	421	303	131	60	18	8	1072	26.0
1700–24	147	589	470	198	76	29	8	1515	26.1
1600–1724	704	2196	1684	739	268	97	35	5716	25.8
Per 1000	123	384	294	129	47	17	6	1000	
Group 3 1775–1837									
1775–99	528	1281	595	189	70	25	13	2701	24.0
1800–24	436	1011	483	161	45	20	7	2162	23.9
1825–37	288	607	214	76	24	11	5	1225	23.4
1775–1837	1252	2899	1292	426	139	56	25	6088	23.9
Per 1000	206	476	212	70	23	9	4	1000	

Source: Cambridge Group reconstitutions.

the two bodies of data, though the former is based on less than half as many cases as the latter since the ages of both bride and groom must be known for a marriage to appear in table 5.5.

The great bulk of the marriages always occurred in the north-west

Table 5.5 *Age at marriage combinations for bachelor/spinster marriages: proportional distribution*

		Husband					
	Under 20	20–4	25–9	30–4	35–9	40 and over	All
1600–1724 (N = 2054)							
Under 20	9	55	44	15	6	5	133
20–4	17	163	132	47	17	8	383
Wife 25–9	7	104	115	51	19	9	305
30–4	3	35	40	21	13	10	121
35–9	—	11	11	10	5	3	39
40 and over	0	4	5	4	2	3	19
All	37	371	346	147	62	37	1 000
1775–1837 (N = 2309)							
Under 20	32	127	35	10	3	2	207
20–4	38	278	126	36	10	10	497
Wife 25–9	8	77	69	30	12	5	200
30–4	3	17	27	12	7	3	69
35–9	0	3	4	6	3	3	17
40 and over	0	1	2	2	2	3	11
All	81	502	263	95	36	23	1 000

Note: the numbers in each cell indicate the proportion of marriages having a given combination of spouses' ages at marriage in every 1000 marriages taking place. A dash in a cell indicates that no marriages took place; a nought in a cell indicates that there were some marriages in the cell but fewer than 1 per 1000 after rounding. The effect of rounding means that row and column cells do not always sum to the marginal totals. The boxes enclose the smallest number of cells whose combined total exceeds 500, or one half, of the total of marriages.
Source: Cambridge Group reconstitutions.

corner of each table, that is among brides and grooms who were under the age of 30, but the degree of concentration in this corner changed over time. In the seventeenth and early eighteenth centuries 354 out of every 1000 marriages took place outside the block of 9 cells (3 x 3) in the north-west corner of the upper panel. In the lower panel the comparable figure was only 210. First marriages between bachelors and spinsters became increasingly youthful. The 4 cells representing marriages in which both partners were under 25 accounted for 244 in every 1000 marriages in the earlier period, but for 475 in the later. Yet another way of bringing home the same point is to identify the group of cells which jointly account for half or more of all marriages. These are indicated in

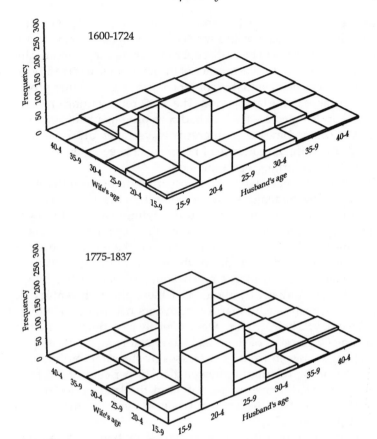

Figure 5.3   *Marriage age combinations: bachelor/spinster marriages*
Source: tab. 5.5.

table 5.5 by being boxed. The closer concentration of marriage in a short span within the lifetimes of brides and grooms is indicated by the fact that only three cells are needed to include more than half the marriages in the second period compared to four cells in the first period (the totals in the boxed cells are 514 in the upper panel and 531 in the lower). And, whereas in the first period the four cells were those representing marriages between brides and grooms who were over 20 and under 30, in the second period two of these cells disappear (those relating to marriages between brides aged 25–9 and grooms aged either 20–4 or 25–9), to be replaced by the cell representing marriages between grooms aged 20–4 and brides who were under 20.

The same data are pictured as a surface in figure 5.3, where the upper figure represents the earlier and the lower figure the later period. Inevitably, only a part of the surface can be made visible if a three-dimensional effect is to be realised, but the increasing concentration of marriages in the south-west corner of the lower figure is readily visible. The four blocks nearest to this corner comprise a far higher proportion of all marriages in the later period. The block representing grooms aged 20–4 and brides aged 20–4, which had been prominent but not dominant in 1600–1724 becomes a comparative skyscraper in 1775–1837. The marked rise in the importance of marriage between men in their early 20s and teenage brides also stands out.

The change in marriage patterns occurred quite abruptly. Although it is not possible to demonstrate the point from the data set out in table 5.5, similar tables for quarter-centuries within each of the two long periods represented in the table show little change (as is clear also from table 5.4). But between the two periods there was a very marked change. In the middle decades of the eighteenth century young men and women began to marry much younger than in the five or six preceding generations. By the end of the eighteenth century 70 per cent of all spinsters who married bachelors had done so before their 25th birthday. Their grooms were scarcely less quick to marry: approaching 60 per cent of them had stood before an Anglican minister to exchange vows in front of witnesses by the same birthday. At the other end of the distribution fewer than 10 per cent of the brides of table 5.5 married above the age of 30 in the later period, compared with 18 per cent in the earlier, while for grooms the comparable percentages were 15 and 25.

Information drawn from frequency distributions is displayed in a more complete form in table 5.6 where, once again, the data are in their 'raw' state without any of the corrections embodied in table 5.3. Any 'join' problems have been ignored. The virtual absence of change in marriage behaviour in bachelor/spinster marriages during the seventeenth and early eighteenth centuries is further underlined by presenting the data in this form. From the second quarter of the eighteenth century, however, the age structure of marriage became steadily more youthful. For example, whereas in 1700–24 only 15 per cent of grooms had married for the first time by the end of their 21st year, the comparable figure in 1800–24 was 27 per cent. Similarly, the pace of marriage quickened so notably for brides that whereas at the end of their 19th, 20th, and 21st years in 1700–24 only 9, 16, and 23 per cent of those marrying for the first time had reached the church porch, by 1800–24 the proportions had risen to 19, 29, and 40 per cent. The middle decades of the eighteenth century again appear as the period of most rapid change. Brides and grooms married at ever younger ages until the end of the parish register period, but the momentum of change was much reduced after the third quarter of the eighteenth century, especially in the case of men.

The composition of groups 2 and 3 was not, of course, the same.[30] Their characteristics may best be compared in the overlap period 1700–24. The differences were not marked but do again reveal the curiosity that while men in group 3 were slightly older at marriage in this period than those in group 2, the reverse was true of women.[31] Fortunately, it is reasonable to ignore any 'join' problems since the major changes in marriage occurred wholly within the group 3 period.

Throughout the whole parish register period it was rare to a degree for a man to marry when less than 18. Normally, less than 1 per cent of grooms were beneath this age, and the great fall in marriage age during the eighteenth century made no difference to this figure. Marriage began earlier for women, but under 2 per cent married before reaching their seventeenth birthday, a figure that again changed little over time, and only at the very end of the period were significantly more than 10 per cent married when less than 19 years of age.

The distribution of marriage age as a whole is most readily appreciated by considering summary measures such as the deciles and quartiles. This forcefully underlines the stability of marriage patterns in the group 2 period. The first and ninth deciles for both spinsters and bachelors scarcely altered over five quarter-centuries. The first decile for bachelors varied only between 21.1 and 21.8 years without evidence of trend; the ninth decile only between 34.9 and 35.3 years. For spinsters the comparative figures were 19.4 and 20.1, and 28.5 and 29.0 years. The medians, quartiles, means, and modes were, of course, similarly without significant change. In the group 3 period, in contrast, there were striking changes. Marriage was increasingly compressed into a briefer and briefer time span. The ninth decile for bachelors fell from 35.4 years in 1700–24 to 32.1 years in 1825–37, while the first decile fell from 21.3 to 19.9 years. The span of time separating the first from the ninth decile fell from 14.1 to 12.2 years. Only a comparatively small change in the first decile was possible since hardly any men married before their eighteenth birthday (1.4 years), but the ninth decile fell by 3.3 years. The quartiles and the median changed as might be expected in view of the relative changes in the first and ninth deciles. The third quartile, the median, and the first quartile fell by 2.9, 2.4, and 1.8 years respectively

---

[30] 12 parishes were common to groups 2 and 3. Group 2 had 20 members; group 3 18 members (tab. 2.2, p. 26).   [31] The same feature is visible in tab. 5.1, p. 130.

Table 5.6 *Cumulative frequency distribution of bachelor/spinster marriages (per 1000); medians, quartiles, deciles, means, and modes*

| | N | Per 1000 marriages Age | | | | | | | Years | | | | | | |
		15	16	17	18	19	20	21	1st decile	1st quart.	Median	3rd quart.	9th decile	Mean	Mode
Males: group 2															
1600–24	605	2	3	10	20	36	63	113	21.8	23.7	26.7	30.6	34.9	27.7	24.6
1625–49	972	1	2	7	20	35	67	127	21.5	23.2	26.2	30.0	35.1	27.3	23.9
1650–74	1047	2	4	7	13	37	73	137	21.5	23.6	26.2	30.1	35.3	27.6	23.5
1675–99	941	2	6	8	16	44	87	140	21.2	23.4	26.2	30.5	35.2	27.5	23.6
1700–24	1233	2	6	12	21	43	91	153	21.1	23.2	25.9	30.1	35.2	27.3	23.2
Females: group 2															
1600–24	739	7	22	43	70	146	206	272	19.5	21.7	25.0	28.7	32.9	25.6	23.7
1625–49	1213	4	17	42	80	134	211	294	19.4	21.5	24.7	28.5	32.6	25.5	23.1
1650–74	1177	6	22	48	79	131	190	261	19.4	21.8	24.8	28.7	33.7	25.8	22.8
1675–99	1072	6	17	38	69	123	183	258	19.5	21.9	24.8	28.8	34.1	26.0	22.6
1700–24	1515	5	12	29	57	97	164	235	20.1	22.2	25.2	29.0	33.8	26.1	23.3
Males: group 3															
1680–99	467	0	4	9	25	53	101	160	21.0	23.1	25.6	29.5	34.1	27.1	22.6
1700–24	959	1	2	8	18	39	86	142	21.3	23.4	26.3	30.2	35.4	27.5	23.8
1725–49	1192	2	3	7	18	47	97	167	21.1	22.9	25.5	29.2	34.1	26.8	23.0
1750–74	1621	0	2	9	22	49	114	212	20.8	22.4	24.7	28.1	33.3	26.1	21.9
1775–99	2121	2	4	9	27	71	143	261	20.5	21.9	24.3	27.9	33.0	25.7	21.4
1800–24	1644	1	2	9	36	93	163	276	20.1	21.8	24.4	28.3	32.9	25.7	21.6
1825–37	931	0	4	13	41	106	184	287	19.9	21.6	23.9	27.3	32.1	25.2	21.3

Females: group 3

1680–99	544	9	18	47	86	157	213	300	19.1	21.4	24.2	28.2	33.7	25.4	21.9
1700–24	1 178	4	12	35	67	112	181	251	19.8	22.0	25.0	28.8	33.6	25.9	23.1
1725–49	1 551	6	16	37	77	142	221	305	19.5	21.4	24.1	28.1	32.6	25.2	21.9
1750–74	2 053	5	19	45	96	170	262	368	19.1	20.9	23.3	27.1	31.5	24.5	21.0
1775–99	2 701	6	22	53	111	196	307	422	18.8	20.5	22.8	26.4	30.5	24.0	20.5
1800–24	2 162	4	19	57	112	202	305	411	18.8	20.5	22.9	26.2	30.4	23.9	20.9
1825–37	1 225	7	17	56	140	235	345	463	18.6	20.1	22.4	25.4	29.9	23.4	20.3

Note: the means are uncorrected for compositional effects and 'splicing', unlike those in tab. 5.7. The mode was taken as mode = mean − 3 (mean − median).

Source: Cambridge Group reconstitutions.

147

over the same period. For spinsters the changes mirrored those for bachelors, but were slightly more pronounced. The ninth decile fell by 3.7 years, the first decile by 1.2 years, while the third quartile, the median, and the first quartile fell by 3.4, 2.6, and 1.9 years between 1700–24 and 1825–37. The interval between the first and ninth deciles fell from 13.8 to 11.3 years, or by almost 20 per cent.

Other marriage rank combinations

The measurement of age at marriage is least problematic in the case of bachelor/spinster marriages both because they were always far more numerous than other categories and because a higher proportion of these marriages yield marriage ages in the course of reconstitution than those in other categories. Since Anglican marriage registers did not record age at marriage regularly or systematically during most of the parish register period,[32] establishing the age of the bride or groom depends on making a link from the marriage entry to a preceding baptism. For both sexes the registers pose problems in establishing age at marriage in cases where the individual had been married previously. It was far more common for women to be explicitly identified as a widow in a register than for men to be described as a widower, and in that respect female remarriage poses fewer problems than male. But, since a woman's surname changed each time she married, a widow's baptism can only be traced if the history of any previous marriage or marriages is known, and, as remarriage often meant moving from one parish to another, missing links are common. For men the difficulty lies in the fact that, since widowers were seldom designated in the register as such until after Hardwicke's Act, a groom can only be identified as a widower if the existence of an earlier marriage is known and it is clear that the wife in that marriage had died. As a result, it is harder to establish age at marriage for widows and widowers than for spinsters and bachelors, and such marriages are therefore underrepresented compared with bachelor/spinster marriages. The proportion of all marriages in which one or both spouses were widowed appears to have been substantially higher in the sixteenth and seventeenth centuries than later on, and it is frustrating that the age of widowed brides and grooms is known less frequently than that of spinsters and bachelors.[33] Nevertheless, reconstitution reveals much about other marriage rank combinations. Table 5.7 and figure 5.4 set out their salient features.

[32] They did so more frequently, however, after the provisions of Hardwicke's Marriage Act came into force in 1754 than previously.

[33] Wrigley and Schofield, *Population history of England*, pp. 258–9.

Table 5.7 *Mean ages at marriage for four marriage rank combinations (years)*

Bachelor/spinster: 1/1. Bachelor/widow: 1/2+. Widower/spinster: 2+/1.
Widower/widow: 2+/2+.

	1/1		1/2+		2+/1		2+/2+	
	M	F	M	F	M	F	M	F
Mean ages								
1610–24	27.6	25.5	28.5	37.8	39.1	28.2	43.5	38.1
1625–49	27.3	25.5	29.0	37.8	39.8	29.1	43.4	40.5
1650–74	27.6	25.8	28.3	37.4	39.4	29.4	46.3	42.6
1675–99	27.5	26.0	30.1	39.9	39.5	29.6	45.2	40.2
1700–24	27.3	26.1	29.0	35.4	39.9	29.7	45.4	42.5
1725–49	26.7	25.3	28.1	36.1	39.7	28.6	46.4	42.8
1750–74	26.0	24.6	29.4	34.2	39.3	28.1	47.0	41.7
1775–99	25.6	24.1	31.3	34.5	39.5	28.8	46.3	40.3
1800–24	25.3	23.8	28.4	34.2	40.0	29.8	46.4	43.2
1825–37	24.8	23.3	30.4	35.7	38.1	27.8	51.7	39.5
Totals on which the means were based								
1610–24	501	574	38	23	59	46	10	12
1625–49	972	1 213	63	44	181	115	41	20
1650–74	1 047	1 177	50	57	186	128	39	20
1675–99	941	1 072	22	33	171	123	43	18
1700–24	1 233	1 515	46	42	179	139	27	21
1725–49	1 192	1 551	57	46	178	128	30	20
1750–74	1 621	2 053	72	77	160	173	68	62
1775–99	2 121	2 701	75	64	225	240	75	46
1800–24	1 644	2 162	56	48	163	156	54	51
1825–37	931	1 225	26	22	65	77	24	14

Note: the data are taken from group 2 parishes to 1700–24 and from group 3 parishes thereafter. In the case of bachelor/spinster marriages corrections for compositional change and 'splicing' were made in the same way as those made in tab. 5.3.
Source: Cambridge Group reconstitutions.

The data in table 5.7 are given in quarter-century blocks since the number of cases is too small to justify finer time divisions. The patterns revealed in the table were remarkably stable over time. In marriages between widowers and widows, the average age of the groom was always in the mid-40s, ranging between 43 and 47 (except for the final, shorter period when the numbers are small), while that of the bride was somewhat lower, predominantly between 40 and 43. Such stability is, perhaps, somewhat surprising both because the very marked improvement in adult mortality in the eighteenth century might have been

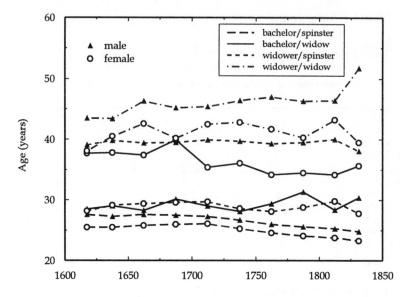

Figure 5.4　*Mean age at marriage for four marriage rank combinations*
Source: tab. 5.7.

expected to result in a tendency for age at remarriage to rise,[34] and also because the conventional interval between the loss of a spouse and contracting a new marriage lengthened substantially between Elizabethan times and Regency England.[35] Offsetting these influences to some degree, was the fall in age at first marriage in the eighteenth century which, other things being equal, would have tended to lower the age of widowhood and thus of remarriage.

As might be expected, in 'mixed' marriages where one partner had been married previously but the other was marrying for the first time, the widowed partner was somewhat younger than in widower/widow marriages (2+/2+), while the single partner was somewhat older than in bachelor/spinster marriages (1/1). In the case of widower/spinster marriages (2+/1), the average age of the groom, with a quite remarkable constancy, was 39 years in almost every subperiod, about 5 years less than when widowers married widows. Their brides averaged about 29 years of age, or 4 years older than when spinsters married bachelors. In the reverse situation a broadly similar pattern existed. Bachelors who married widows (1/2+ marriages) were 28–30 years old. Initially they

[34] For details of the fall in adult mortality rates, see tab. 6.26, p. 303, and accompanying text.
[35] See below pp. 172–82.

were only slightly older than bachelors who married spinsters (only 1.1 years older on average in the first three subperiods), but later the gap increased considerably (to 4.8 years in the last three subperiods). Their brides were approximately 36 years old, again roughly 5 years less than the age of widows who married widowers. In this last case, marriage age may have fallen in the eighteenth century, but the numbers involved are small and the apparent fall may be spurious. They suggest, however, a marked fall in the mean gap in age between brides and grooms in the 1/2+ marriage category between the early seventeenth and the early nineteenth century. The greater stability of ages in the 2+/1 marriage category very probably reflects the much larger number of cases involved. If numbers were equally large for 1/2+ and 2+/2+ marriages, these categories might well also show a comparable stability.

In general, as may be seen in figure 5.4, stability was the order of the day. No other marriage rank combination appears to have followed the numerically dominant 1/1 category in experiencing a clear fall in mean age at marriage.

The age gap between spouses

Conventions about an acceptable difference in age between bride and groom vary greatly in different societies. Since it was normal in many societies for women to marry soon after reaching sexual maturity but common for men to marry much later, in such societies grooms were often much older than their brides and it was therefore unusual for the bride to be the older of the two. The west European readiness to countenance much later marriage for women both tended to result in small age gaps between spouses and caused marriages in which the wife was older than her husband to occur much more frequently than was commonly the case elsewhere.

Table 5.8 sets out the pattern of age difference between spouses in early modern England in summary form. It shows the distribution of age differences in five-year blocks. To simplify comparison the data in each column have been expressed in such a way that they sum to 1000. The mean and median intervals for each combination of marriage ranks are also given together with the total number of cases on which each distribution is based. The distributions in the two panels are derived from data drawn from group 2 (1600–1729) and group 3 (1750–1837). In the earlier period there was little change in marriage age, while in the middle decades of the eighteenth century there was a rapid fall in marriage age, so that the two panels should reflect the 'before' and 'after' situation effectively. Although the parish composition of the two groups differed, there was, as we have seen, a close similarity between them in nuptiality characteristics during the period of overlap between them.[36]

There are substantial numbers of cases only for 1/1 and 2+/1 marriages, and for all marriages combined. In other categories the numbers are small and any evidence of change may therefore be unreliable. The simplest summary measure is the mean difference in age of bride and groom. There is a consistent tendency in each marriage rank combination for this mean to fall between the earlier and later periods. The mean difference in the case of 1/1 marriages, for example, fell from 5.3 to 4.3 years. Equally consistent across categories was the rise in the proportion of all marriages in which the groom was older than his bride. In the case of 1/2+ marriages the change was very marked, from 23.5 to 37.8 per cent. But less pronounced change was taking place in the other marriage rank combinations as follows: 1/1 61.0 to 64.8 per cent; 2+/1 80.7 to 84.6 per cent; 2+/2+ 54.0 to 72.2 per cent; and for all marriages combined 62.1 to 65.6 per cent. Median differences were broadly stable over time except for 1/2+ marriages. As might be expected the median figures closely resemble the differences between the mean ages at marriage for the several marriage rank combinations shown in table 5.7, except that the striking fall in the median in 1/2+ marriages is not fully matched in the behaviour of the means (in table 5.7 the average difference in the means for bachelors and widows in 1/2+ marriages fell from −8.6 years in the period 1610–1725 to −4.8 years in the period 1750–1837). It is likely that the fall is overstated in the median figures which are based on a much smaller number of cases.

Table 5.8 shows that the shape of the distribution of age differences was changing. For example, in the 1/1 category, in the later period, 69.8 per cent of all differences fell within the range +4 years to −4 years whereas in the earlier period the comparable figure was only 58.5 per cent. Towards the centre of the distribution the change was even more marked. In both periods more age differences were concentrated into the same set of six contiguous single year categories stretching from +3 to −1 (+3, +2, +1, +0, −0, −1), than into any other set covering the same number of years, but in the earlier period this span included only 40.1 per cent of the total compared with 51.3 per cent in the later period. To include over 50 per cent of cases in a consecutive run of years in the earlier period, it would be necessary to take 8 rather than 6 years (from +4 to −2). In the earlier period there was a substantially higher proportion of large age gaps, both plus and minus, in all categories.

[36] See pp. 129–35 above.

Table 5.8 *Age difference between spouses by marriage rank combinations (male age minus female age)*
Bachelor/spinster: 1/1. Widower/spinster: 2+/1. Bachelor/widow: 1/2+
Widower/widow: 2+/2+.

Years	1/1	2+/1	1/2+	2+/2+	All/all
1600–1729					
+15 and over	35	263	0	159	61
+10–4	64	156	0	127	73
+5–9	181	212	84	190	182
+0–4	330	176	151	63	305
−0–4	255	101	176	238	236
−5–9	91	69	235	159	93
−10–4	34	15	168	32	35
−15 and over	10	8	185	32	14
All	1 000	1 000	1 000	1 000	1 000
N	2054	267	60	32	2 411
Cum. total husband older (per 1000)	610	807	235	540	621
Mean abs. difference (yrs)	5.3	11.2	9.0	9.8	6.1
Median difference (yrs)	1.6	7.9	−7.5	6.0	1.9
1750–1837					
+15 and over	26	232	14	130	41
+10–4	43	156	35	139	52
+5–9	154	221	119	222	158
+0–4	425	237	210	231	405
−0–4	273	98	315	111	260
−5–9	58	36	224	111	61
−10–4	17	16	70	37	18
−15 and over	4	4	14	19	4
All	1 000	1 000	1 000	1 000	1 000
N	3 110	224	72	54	3 460
Cum. total husband older (per 1000)	648	846	378	722	656
Mean abs. difference (yrs)	4.3	10.6	5.7	9.2	4.8
Median difference (yrs)	1.5	7.5	−1.4	5.7	1.7

Note: the 1600–1729 panel uses group 2 data; the 1750–1837 panel group 3 data.
Source: Cambridge Group reconstitutions.

Marriage ages from reconstitution compared with the Registrar-General's returns

Independent evidence with which to test the accuracy of the nuptiality levels and trends shown in table 5.3, and further amplified in the subsequent tables, is lacking for most of the parish register period, but at its end the ages at marriage of men and women found in the reconstitutions can be compared with those recorded in the early reports of the Registrar-General. Or, to put the point in a different way, just as there is an issue relating to the 'splicing' of data from group 3 on to those from group 2, so there is also a question about the 'join' between the reconstitution estimates and the information about age at marriage collected by the Registrar-General in the early years of the new civil registration system after 1837. If it were true, for example, that *trends* in marriage age were correctly identified using reconstitution material but that the *level* was either overstated or understated, and that the national level in the late 1830s and 1840s was known from the Registrar-General's returns, then, after adjusting the reconstitution series to match the information drawn from the early years of state registration, a reliable series might still be constructed stretching back over the two preceding centuries.

Unfortunately, in his early *Annual reports* the Registrar-General displayed little interest in attempting to establish marriage age patterns, though marriage totals were recorded in considerable detail. Even if he had evinced an interest in marriage age, however, it would have been difficult to provide reliable information because there was no requirement to state age at marriage initially, and the proportion choosing to do so was at first quite low.[37] In a few years in the 1840s, however, tables were published giving details of the patterns to be found in the four basic marriage rank combinations: bachelor/spinster (1/1), bachelor/widow (1/2+), widower/spinster (2+/1), and widower/widow (2+/2+). In each case the table took the form of a cross-tabulation in which each cell showed the total number of marriages taking place between brides and grooms in five-year age blocks. Thus, for example,

---

[37] Because few data were published, the only series of marriage age coverage that can be constructed on a uniform basis is that which relates the number of marriages in which husband and wife both stated their exact age to the total of all marriages. In the first year for which there is a marriage tabulation, 1846, only 16.7 per cent of all couples both stated their exact age. Thereafter the proportion at first rose rapidly, but coverage remained significantly defective throughout the balance of the nineteenth century, and was still not complete even on the eve of the Great War. In 1848 the percentage had risen to 24.2 and in 1851 to 36.5. Subsequent percentages were as follows: 1860, 62.5; 1870, 69.9; 1880, 81.8; 1890, 96.7; 1900, 98.6; 1910, 99.1.

the total of marriages between brides who were aged 25–9 and grooms who were 35–9 would occupy one cell in the table. The row and column totals, therefore, show the total number of brides and grooms in each five-year age group. Average ages were not given, but can be calculated readily by assuming that within each five-year block the average age was at the midpoint of the period. Those aged 20–4, for example, were assumed to have married on average at age 22.5, and so on. In the case of the first age group, consisting of those whose age was less than 20 years, it was assumed that the average age was 18.5 years. The results of the exercise are shown in table 5.9.

The second panel of the table shows that although the average ages given are based on substantial numbers of cases, they represent only a small fraction of the national totals of marriages in each category, though the position had improved markedly in 1848 compared with the two previous years. For a marriage to figure in the Registrar-General's table, of course, the ages of both spouses had to be known, so that the coverage is even poorer than would have been the case if average ages had been calculated from individual cases where the bride or groom gave her or his age when the marriage was registered. The value of these data therefore rests on the assumption that those who chose to give their age were a random sample of the whole population. It is clearly reasonable to be doubtful whether this was the case since occupation, education, religion, area of residence, and several other influences may have affected response rates and, if such factors were associated with differing ages at marriage, the published figures would not match the behaviour of the population as a whole, though it is mildly reassuring that the substantial improvement in coverage in 1848 was not accompanied by any significant change in average ages.

Taken at face value, however, the average ages in the table strongly support the reconstitution estimates (third panel of table 5.9). Over the period 1800–37 the average age at marriage of spinsters and bachelors in the reconstitution parishes was 23.7 and 25.1 years respectively in marriages between spinsters and bachelors. The comparable figures taken from the Registrar-General's returns were 24.0 and 25.4 (using the adjusted figures from which first marriages taking place above the age of 50 have been eliminated, since such marriages were very rare on FRFs[38]). In each case the reconstitution figures are the lower of the two,

---

[38] In principle there should be no first marriage on an FRF in which the bride or groom was aged 50 or more. This is a guiding rule in the construction of the links between baptisms and subsequent marriages from which all information on age at marriage is derived; Wrigley, 'Some problems of family reconstitution', pp. 133–4. A tiny number of first marriages contracted at a greater age are nevertheless to be found on the FRFs.

Table 5.9 *Mean age at marriage for four marriage rank combinations from reconstitution data and from the Registrar-General's returns (years)*

Bachelor/spinster: 1/1. Bachelor/widow: 1/2+. Widower/spinster: 2+/1.
Widower/widow: 2+/2+.

Mean age at marriage (Registrar-General's returns)

	1/1		1/2+		2+/1		2+/2+	
	M	F	M	F	M	F	M	F
1846	25.4	24.0	31.6	33.9	38.0	31.3	46.3	42.8
1847	25.4	24.0	31.7	34.3	38.2	31.3	46.7	43.0
1848	25.5	24.0	31.6	33.9	37.9	30.9	46.7	42.3
Average 1846–8	25.5	24.0	31.6	34.0	38.1	31.2	46.5	42.7

(1) Totals on which means were based   (2) All marriages   (3) (1)/(2) × 100

	1/1			1/2+			2+/1			2+/2+		
	(1)	(2)	(3)	(1)	(2)	(3)	(1)	(2)	(3)	(1)	(2)	(3)
1846	20 519	121 324	16.9	871	5 997	14.5	1 970	12 212	16.1	996	6 131	16.2
1847	20 450	112 576	18.2	874	5 705	15.3	1 947	11 667	16.7	949	5 897	16.1
1848	27 483	113 284	24.3	1 316	5 920	22.2	2 969	12 702	23.4	1 620	6 324	25.6

Registrar-General's data compared to reconstitution data

	1/1		1/2+		2+/1		2+/2+	
	M	F	M	F	M	F	M	F
Reconstitution 1800–37	25.1	23.7	29.0	34.7	39.5	29.2	48.0	42.4
R-G's returns 1846–8	25.5	24.0	31.6	34.0	38.1	31.2	46.5	42.7
R-G's returns adjusted	25.4	24.0	30.8			30.5		

Proportionate share of different marriage rank combinations

	1/1	1/2+	2+/1	2+/2+	All
R-G's returns 1846–8	82.7	4.2	8.7	4.4	100.0
Reconstitution 1800–37 M	86.9	2.8	7.7	2.6	100.0
F	90.2	1.9	6.2	1.7	100.0

Note: in the top panel of the table the averages for 1846–8 are unweighted averages of the three years. Since the number of events was much larger in 1848 than in the two previous years, this seemed the appropriate procedure. In the third panel the adjusted figures are those that result from removing all first marriages in which the bride or groom was 50 years of age or older. In the reconstitution data there are in principle no first marriages above the age of 50 (see p. 155 n. 38 above), so that the adjusted figures are more

and in each case the difference was about 0.3 years. The differences are modest, though it would be imprudent to lay great stress on their close agreement, if only because it is impossible as yet to adduce independent evidence of the extent of changes, if any, in marriage age between 1800–37 and the later 1840s. Nevertheless, it seems fair to conclude that the Registrar-General's tabulations tend to increase confidence in the reconstitution estimates as a guide to national patterns for earlier periods.

The Registrar-General's data for other marriage rank combinations also agree fairly well with reconstitution estimates. For 1/2+, 2+/1, and 2+/2+ marriages, average ages at marriage in 1846–8 for men and women were as follows (the figures in brackets represent the comparable figures obtained by reconstitution for 1800–37): 31.6, 34.0 (29.0, 34.7); 38.1, 31.2 (39.5, 29.2); 46.5, 42.7 (48.0, 42.4). The agreement between the equivalent average ages is close in the four cases where widows or widowers are involved, with the reconstitution figure usually the higher of the two.[39] The mean absolute difference in these four cases is 0.98 years, or taking sign into account, +0.83 years, but the agreement is much closer for widows (mean absolute difference 0.50 years, or, taking sign into account +0.20 years), than for widowers (1.45 and +1.45 years respectively).

Where bachelors or spinsters were marrying widows or widowers the agreement is less close with the reconstitution figure the lower of the two. In these cases, however, as may be seen on the bottom row of the panel, the difference is appreciably reduced by adjusting the civil

[39] The ages for all reconstitution marriage rank combinations in England are closely similar to those in Germany in the eighteenth and nineteenth centuries, described in Knodel and Lynch, 'The decline of remarriage', tab. 4, p. 41.

Notes to table 5.9 *(cont.)*

closely comparable to the reconstitution data than the unadjusted figures. In practice there are a very small number of brides and grooms aged 50 or more at first marriage due to errors that escaped uncorrected or that were introduced in amending original errors. For example, in group 2 there were 2 brides aged 50 or more in bachelor/spinster marriages and 4 such brides in widower/spinster marriages. There were 27 grooms aged 50 or more in bachelor/spinster marriages and 1 such case in bachelor/widow marriages. These totals should be compared with the overall totals of marriages in the four categories of 6049, 588, 5051, and 234 respectively. The reconstitution figures are weighted averages of the ages at marriage for 1800–24 and 1825–37 given in tab. 5.7. In the bottom panel the R-G's data for 1846–8 refers to all marriages taking place in the three-year period.
Sources: Cambridge Group reconstitutions; Registrar-General, *Ninth, tenth, and eleventh annual reports,* Ages of men and women married in England . . . distinguishing bachelors, spinsters, widowers, and widows.

registration figure to eliminate grooms and brides marrying above the age of 50. The differences then become 1.8 years for bachelors and 1.3 years for spinsters (compared with 2.6 and 2.0 years before adjustment).

The bottom panel of the table confirms what might be expected because of the nature of the reconstitution process. 1/1 marriages are overrepresented, and other marriage categories underrepresented in reconstitution material because it is easier to make a link from a baptism to a subsequent marriage than to continue the chain of connection on through one or more remarriages. It is also clear that the 'chaining' process involves greater difficulty for women than for men because of the successive changes of surname involved. Thus the age of a larger percentage of widowers than of widows is known and 1/2+ marriage percentages for women are relatively much further below the expected figure set by the civil registration data than are the percentages for men in 2+/1 marriages. For the reason already given, of course, it is debatable how safely the Registrar-General's data can be used as 'target' figures.

The early returns of the Registrar-General offer a further opportunity to estimate marriage age in the period immediately after the institution of a system of civil registration. In the the *Fourth annual report* he remarked, 'As the age at which marriages take place, in connexion with the increase in population, is supposed to have a great influence upon the misery or happiness of the people, I wish I could have stated the ages of the persons who were married in every county; but the exact ages were only specified in a small number of districts.'[40] He then appended three tables relating to these districts. The heading of the first of the three records the 'ages of males and females in marriages which occurred in districts varying greatly in situation and character throughout the whole Kingdom, and including every marriage in such districts'.[41] This table provides marriage age tabulations for 10 019 marriages in 1839–40 and for 5560 marriages in 1840–1. The districts in which the marriages were recorded are not named, though it is evident from the sharp drop in the number of events between the two years that complete returns were available for a much smaller number of districts in the second than in the first year. It is not clear whether the returns for 1840–1 were from a subset of the districts for which returns were available from the previous year, though it is perhaps natural to assume that this is likely to have been the case. In 1839–40 the total of marriages in the districts represented in the table were 8.06 per cent of the total of 124 329 marriages in England and Wales in that year. This source therefore provides information about all marriages in some registration districts,

---

[40] Registrar-General, *Fourth annual report*, p. 8.   [41] Ibid., tab. (f), p. 10.

Table 5.10 *Mean age at marriage for bachelors, widowers, spinsters, and widows from reconstitution data and from the Registrar-General's returns (years)*

	Bachelors	Widowers	Spinsters	Widows
R-G's data 1839–40	25.6	39.5	24.4	39.2
R-G's data 1840–1	25.4	40.6	24.5	38.7
Average of 1839–40 and 1840–1	25.5	40.1	24.5	38.9
R-G's data 1846–8	25.8	40.9	24.7	38.5
Reconstitution 1800–37	25.3	42.3	24.2	38.7

Note: The Registrar-General's data for 1846–8 were calculated from the second row of the third panel of tab. 5.9 (that is, uncorrected for first marriage above the age of 50). This ensures that the two sets of data drawn from the Registrar-General's returns are directly comparable, but, as may be seen by comparison with tab. 5.9 (third row, third panel), slightly overstates the differences between these data and those drawn from reconstitution in the case of bachelors and spinsters. The relative frequency of the different types of marriages in 1846–8 is set out on the first row of the bottom panel of tab. 5.9.
Sources: Registrar-General, *Fourth annual report*, tab.(f), p. 10; tab. 5.9; and Cambridge Group reconstitutions.

whereas the data used in table 5.9 gave information about some marriages in all registration districts.

In the *Fourth annual report* the Registrar-General gave the totals of marriages contracted by bachelors, widowers, spinsters, and widows in five-year age groups from 15 to 85 and average ages can therefore be calculated by the same method used in constructing table 5.9. The information is less complete, however, in that no breakdown is provided between ages for bachelors who married spinsters and those who married widows, and so on. Nevertheless a comparison is possible between these data and those given in table 5.9. On the assumption that the relative frequency of 1/1, 1/2+, 2+/1, and 2+/2+ marriages was the same in 1839–41 as in 1846–8 (bottom panel of table 5.9), the average age at marriage of bachelors, widowers, spinsters, and widows for 1846–8 can be recalculated, as can also average ages for the reconstitution data for 1800–37 (third panel, table 5.9). The results are shown in table 5.10.

There is a very close agreement between the Registrar-General's data for the two periods at either end of the 1840s. While it is possible that neither data set was representative of the country as whole but that both diverged in the same way from the true picture, it seems more likely that both were effectively random samples drawn from the national pool of marriages (and also that there was little change in marriage age over this short period). The reconstitution data are also remarkably close to the pattern found in the Registrar-General's returns, except in the case of widowers. The evidence of table 5.10, therefore, both strengthens the probability that age at marriage in the 1840s can be established with fair confidence for the country as a whole, and also does nothing to undermine the belief that at the end of the time span covered by reconstitution, the age structure of marriage for each combination of marriage ranks estimated from the FRFs closely mirrored the national pattern.

Sources of bias in the estimation of age at marriage

The close accord between reconstitution marriage ages for the early nineteenth century and the marriage data in the early returns of the Registrar-General is encouraging since doubts have sometimes been expressed about the trustworthiness of reconstitution-derived demographic estimates, given that they may reflect the experience of an unrepresentative minority of the whole population. Those who remain in their parish of birth figure much more prominently than migrants in many measures. Indeed, in the case of marriage age calculations almost all the data relate to men and women born in a given parish who subsequently married there.

Recently, Ruggles has given a new precision to unease on this score, using English reconstitution data to exemplify the problems involved. He investigated the effect of migration in causing average ages at first marriage when taken from reconstitution material to result in underestimation of the true level of marriage age. To enable the phenomenon to be measured accurately, he conducted a microsimulation exercise in which a population of about 50 000 married couples was endowed with demographic characteristics similar to those found in England in the early eighteenth century.[42] He incorporated into the microsimulation migration propensities believed to represent behaviour in seventeenth-century England, and showed that the potential difference between what can be measured and what one might wish to measure is very substantial. On the 'medium migration' variant of his model the difference in mean age at first marriage measured from the whole simulated population, including both those who migrate and those who do not, and the mean age based only on those marrying in their parish of birth was 2.9 years in the case of women and 2.3 years in the case of men.[43]

---

[42] Ruggles, 'Migration, marriage, and mortality'.   [43] Ibid., tab. 4, p. 512.

There is no reason to doubt the accuracy of Ruggles's microsimulation. If it captured the reality of the historical past it would suggest great caution in making use of reconstitution data as a guide to marriage age. Ruggles has unquestionably rendered a great service to reconstitution work by pursuing this topic with rigour. However, although Ruggles's logic appears sound, the English past is not mirrored in his microsimulation. Since the reasons for the mismatch between logic and fact are instructive, a brief account of them is included here. A fuller discussion has already been published elsewhere.[44]

Ruggles pointed out that the extent by which the 'true' age at marriage[45] was underestimated in reconstitution studies could be estimated not only indirectly by microsimulation but also more directly by calculating two mean ages at marriage. The first mean was based on all first marriages occurring in a particular parish (measure A), the second on the subset of these marriages in which the wife (if female marriage age is at issue) survived to age 50 or more (measure B). The difference between the two means will provide a measure of the extent to which migration and mortality distort the measurement of marriage age: 'By eliminating those who migrated or died during the marriage years, we eliminate the possibility of censoring.'[46]

Mortality, like migration, may cause the true age at marriage to be underestimated since those who die unmarried in the age groups during which marriage occurs will include some who would have married if they had not died. In this context, however, the effect of mortality in distorting mean age at first marriage can be ignored. Indeed, it would be inconvenient if it were not present since, for example, the effect is also present in the marriage ages tabulated by the Registrar-General and comparison with his data is facilitated by the fact that the two measurements are made on the same basis. But any migration effect needs to be carefully quantified.

Ruggles's own estimate of its extent led him to conclude that the difference between measure A and measure B in the 26 reconstitution parishes was 1.34 years. This figure included both the mortality and the migration effect, however, and since the former may be estimated at 0.7 years, the migration effect is reduced to 0.64 years.[47] This figure is far lower than any suggested by Ruggles's microsimulation, much lower

---

[44] Wrigley, 'The effect of migration'.

[45] Ruggles made the reasonable assumption that it would be of interest to know the mean age at marriage of an entire cohort born in a given parish, whether or not the marriages took place in the parish. It is this value that I have in mind in referring to a 'true' age at marriage.   [46] Ruggles, 'Migration, marriage, and mortality', p. 511.

[47] Ibid., tab. 5, p. 513.

even than his 'low migration' alternative. In noting this, Ruggles suggested as a plausible reason for the discrepancy that migration and marriage were not independent of each other, as he had assumed in his microsimulation. If there were a close link between the two, the discrepancy could clearly be much lower or even eliminated.

Further analysis of the reconstitution data and examination of the methods and assumptions used by Ruggles shows, however, that the difference between the measure A and measure B averages, both for women and for men, is considerably smaller even than he supposed, no larger indeed than would be expected from the mortality effect alone.[48] Measure A and measure B, when correctly calculated, differ by only 0.8 years in the case of women and 0.7 years in the case of men, a discrepancy no greater than can conservatively be attributed to the effect of mortality. The further reduction occurs chiefly because of an error in identifying individuals who had been married and had survived to reach the age of 50. Their original specification led to an association between late marriage and the likelihood of inclusion in the group of survivors to age 50 and thus caused Ruggles to overestimate their mean age at marriage.[49] The means derived from reconstitution are, therefore, when accurately measured, almost exactly those that would arise if the marriage ages both of those born and married in the parish, and of those born in the parish but married elsewhere, were known and had been jointly tabulated. Moreover, this phenomenon is not a peculiarity solely of English reconstitutions. Desjardins has shown that the same is true of the French Canadian population in the period 1680–1740. The demonstration of the absence of a 'Ruggles' effect is even more telling in this than in the English case, since the French Canadian data enable the subsequent histories of men and women who left their place of birth and later married elsewhere to be traced. In the case of men the difference between the two groups was 0.3 years; in the case of women the marriage ages of migrants and non-migrants were identical.[50] Desjardins remarked that 'migration censoring did not lead to significant bias that needs to be corrected in the present case'.[51]

Furthermore, in the English case there is additional evidence to substantiate the conclusions to be drawn from the calculation of measure A and measure B means. The census enumerators' books of the

---

[48] Wrigley, 'The effect of migration'.   [49] Ibid., pp. 85–6

[50] Desjardins, 'Bias in age at marriage', tab. 3, p. 168.

[51] Ibid., p. 168. The study covered a substantial population. The mean ages at marriage were calculated from 13 218 male ages at marriage (5593 migrants; 7625 non-migrants), and 14 102 female ages at marriage (5417 migrants; 8685 non-migrants). Ibid., tab. 3, p. 168.

1851 census contain information which makes it feasible to calculate the singulate mean age at marriage of the local born still resident in each small area and for migrants to the area. This can be done for both sexes. The singulate mean ages at marriage are almost identical for the local born and migrants both in the case of men and of women.[52] This exercise, however, brought to light a striking difference between 'stayers' and 'leavers' in a different aspect of nuptiality. Although female mean age at first marriage in the two groups was alike, the proportion never married was not. About 16 per cent of the local born women in 1851 were never married compared to only 9 per cent of migrants (the comparable male figures were 11 and 10 per cent). The detailed age-specific figures which can be constructed from the census data suggest that migration did indeed influence female marriage patterns substantially, though not in the manner suggested by Ruggles's microsimulation.[53]

The absence of the sort of migration effect that Ruggles expected to be present is probably due to three main factors. First, inasmuch as migration takes place *before* the age range within which marriage occurs, it will not affect a calculation of mean age based only on those marrying in their home parish.[54] Only migration occurring part way through the marriageable age groups will introduce distortion. Service in husbandry was very common for both sexes in the past and often involved a definitive move from the home parish at an early age.[55] Second, as Ruggles himself suggested, there was probably a strong link between migration and marriage, and therefore the assumption in his microsimulation of their independence was misplaced. Third, return migration of natives to their home parish while still unmarried, followed by their subsequent marriage at the local church, would raise mean age at marriage calculated from reconstitution data. Return migration has the reverse effect to the migration effect upon which Ruggles concentrated. There is indirect evidence in the data drawn from the 1851 census enumerators' books that this third factor may have been significant.[56]

The close coincidence between the naively observed mean age at marriage taken from reconstitution data and the true mean is the result of a particular combination of historical circumstances; in short, of chance. In some historical settings it is possible that a wide divergence between measure A and measure B might be visible in the fashion modelled by Ruggles. In the case of early modern England, however, it

---

[52] Wrigley, 'The effect of migration', tab. 6, p. 93.   [53] Ibid.
[54] On the neutral assumption that the marriage regime outside the parish is the same as that within it.   [55] Wrigley, 'The effect of migration', pp. 89–90.
[56] Ibid., pp. 92–4.

appears that the very close agreement between reconstitution-derived marriage age estimates and the early returns of the Registrar-General, described in the previous section, which suggested confidence in reconstitution results, is not misleading. Though the logic of Ruggles's argument casting doubt on the value of reconstitution marriage data is impeccable, the assumptions which he used, though reasonable enough in the abstract, did not parallel English experience.

The changing relative frequency of different marriage rank combinations

A comparison of the evidence drawn from reconstitution with the early returns of the Registrar-General suggests that the age of brides and grooms in all marriage rank combinations except those between bachelors and spinsters changed little, if at all, between the early seventeenth and nineteenth centuries. On the other hand, the relative frequency of the different marriage rank combinations did change, as may be seen in table 5.11. Unfortunately, however, it is clear from the bottom panel of table 5.9 that frequencies derived from family reconstitution are a poor guide to the true situation. Bachelor/spinster marriages are overrepresented in the total. Other marriage rank combinations are underrepresented but in differing degrees. Both tables show, moreover, that the frequencies measured from male and female data differ substantially when they should be identical. They differ because these totals depend on the number of links made in the reconstitution process and the marriage rank is normally only unambiguously clear as a result of making a link from a baptism to a marriage. Thus the number of cases depends on the number of links made, and both the absolute number that can be made and the relative number in different marriage categories differ between men and women.

With such recalcitrant data it must be doubtful whether anything of value can be learned from the changing relative frequency of marriage rank combinations. As an illustration of the possible implications of the patterns visible in table 5.11, however, the following observations may be made.

The fourth panel of table 5.9 suggests that the true proportion of bachelor/spinster marriages is approximately 95 per cent of the proportion found in the reconstitution data.[57] In that case table 5.11 suggests that the proportion of all marriages that were between bachelors and spinsters in the early seventeenth century was about 75 per cent of the

---

[57] Because the Registrar-General's bachelor/spinster percentage was 82.7 when the reconstitution percentage was 86.9, and $827/869 = 0.95$.

Table 5.11 *Relative frequency of different marriage rank combinations (per 1000 marriages)*

Bachelor/spinster: 1/1. Bachelor/widow: 1/2+. Widower/spinster: 2+/1. Widower/widow: 2+/2+.

	1/1		1/2+		2+/1		2+/2+	
	M	F	M	F	M	F	M	F
1610–49	790	873	54	33	129	79	27	16
1650–99	796	856	29	34	143	96	33	14
1700–49	824	886	35	25	121	77	19	12
1750–99	847	878	33	26	87	76	32	20
1800–37	869	902	28	19	77	62	26	17

Note: the proportions should be read as follows: out of every 1000 male ages at marriage known in 1610–49, 790 fell into the 1/1 category, 54 into the 1/2+ category, 129 into the 2+/1 category, and 27 into the 2+/2+ category.
Source: tab. 5.7.

total (790 × 0.95 = 750). Bachelor/spinster marriages became an increasingly prominent feature of the nuptiality scene between 1600 and 1800. Table 5.11 also suggests a parallel decline in the relative importance of both bachelor/widow and widower/spinster marriages over the two centuries covered by the table. The proportionate share of both categories roughly halved, but widower/widow marriages were an unchanging fraction of the total.[58]

These comments are based, however, on the figures relating to males in each category. Using female proportions the changes all appear much less dramatic, though the trends are in the same direction. It is possible that the male figures are the better guide to secular change, just as they are a better guide to the position in the early nineteenth century (table 5.9, bottom panel). The very different impression conveyed by the male and female series, however, suggests that to describe the estimates as conjectural at best is perhaps to overstate their claim to attention. Yet it is beguiling to try to estimate the extent of the changes. In the 1840s, for example, widower/spinster marriages were still fairly common at just

---

[58] These percentages and trends over time are similar to those found in eighteenth- and nineteenth-century Germany, though at the beginning of the eighteenth century in Germany the proportion of bachelor/spinster marriages was remarkably low, only 67 per cent of the total; Knodel and Lynch, 'The decline of remarriage', tab. 4, p. 41. In seventeenth-century France, especially in the wake of epidemics, remarriages sometimes comprised an even higher proportion of all marriages. At times of crisis on occasion fewer than half of all marriages were bachelor/spinster marriages, and even in less troubled periods such marriages were often only 60 to 65 per cent of the total; Cabourdin, 'Remariage', pp. 311–4. See also Bideau, 'Widowhood and remarriage'.

under 9 per cent of the total (table 5.9). In the early seventeenth century they may have constituted about 15 per cent of the total, allowing for the understatement of the frequencies of marriage rank combinations that involved widows or widowers when using reconstitution material. Or again, if one assumes that widower/widow marriages remained a constant proportion of the total throughout, and accepting the estimate of bachelor/spinster marriages in the early seventeenth century as only 75 per cent of the total, it follows that whereas in the 1840s only about 10.9 per cent of all those marrying (male and female combined) were widowed, two hundred years earlier the comparable figure was 14.7 per cent.[59] In Elizabethan times the 'widowed' figure was probably still higher.[60]

Other things being equal, the sharp improvement in adult mortality in the 'long' eighteenth century might account for many of the changes that occurred, but changes in social attitudes and personal preferences may also have played a part.[61] It is frustrating to be unable to delineate them more precisely at present, but useful perhaps to indicate their possible scale.

Marriage age and birth parity

Since marriage and the transmission of resources between the generations are closely connected, it is often supposed that the opportunity to marry and the timing of marriage is affected by birth parity, that, for example, oldest sons will marry at an earlier age than their younger brothers because they possess the wherewithal to do so from parental provision, where younger brothers are partly or wholly dependent on their own efforts. Or, alternatively, it may be thought that oldest sons

[59] In the 1840s 82.7 per cent of all marriages were bachelor/spinster, 4.4 per cent widower/widow. Since all other marriages involved one partner who had previously been married, the overall percentage of brides and grooms combined who were widowed will have been $4.4 + (100 - (82.7 + 4.4))/2 = 10.85$. A similar calculation for the earlier period yields a total of 14.7.

[60] In the *Population history of England* it was necessary to attempt an estimate of this percentage in the mid-sixteenth century. Such fragmentary evidence as was available led to the adoption of a figure of 30 per cent for the proportion of all those marrying who were widows or widowers. The estimate of 14.7 per cent relating to a period about three-quarters of a century later suggests that the estimate of 30 per cent may have been too high, though later French and German evidence shows that remarriages could be a very high proportion of all marriages (p. 165, n. 58). Both English estimates are supported by such flimsy and uncertain evidence that the only safe inference is that more work on the subject is needed.

[61] See below pp. 280–93 for a description of the scale of the changes in adult mortality in the course of the eighteenth century.

are inhibited by their position in the family because they must wait for the older generation to die or to retire before being in a position to marry whereas younger brothers are freer to choose. Social convention may also play a part. Younger sisters may be debarred from entering the marriage market while older sisters remain unmarried; and so on. Demography, no less than economic circumstances and social convention, has also often been invoked as a contribution to the explanation of the timing of marriage. The death of a father, by releasing resources, may make feasible a marriage that would otherwise have had to be postponed, or, alternatively, may make marriage more difficult by depleting family resources, or by obliging a daughter to assist her widowed mother.

English family reconstitution data do not permit an effective investigation of this issue in relation to the question of whether or not sons or daughters *ever marry*, but their *age at marriage* in relation to birth rank and family circumstances can be studied. The following tables are intended to enable two topics to be examined: the effect of birth rank, or more exactly rank in the family among children not known to have died, on the timing of marriage, and the effect of the death of the father on the age at which his children married.

Table 5.12 is based on the assumption that it is convenient to study marriage age by relating it to the size of the sibling group to which an individual belonged at the time he or she reached his or her eighteenth birthday. This birthday was chosen as a starting point since it represents the age at which marriage became a serious possibility. Very few women and almost no men married when under 18. In other words, it reflects the assumption that a boy born as the third son in a family whose two older brothers were both dead by the time he reached the age of 18 should be regarded as a first son at that time. The top panel of the table refers to sons: the lower panel to daughters. Thus the third line of the top panel relates to families in which there were three surviving sons at the time that the son in question became 18, and shows that the average age at first marriage of the young man who was the first son in such families was 26.5 years; of the young man who was the second son 26.9 years; and of the young man who was the third son 26.7 years. In defining the size of the set of male siblings, only those alive when the son in question became 18 are counted, except that an older brother who had married but subsequently died is included on the grounds that he would have claimed a share of the patrimony which would not usually return to the family's pool of resources on his death. The determination of ego's rank in the family is made exclusively at the time of his 18th birthday. Thus it is possible for two successive sons both to be counted, say, as the second

Table 5.12 *Mean age at marriage by parity among surviving siblings of the same sex and by size of same sex sibling set* (years)

Size of same sex sibling set when ego aged 18	Ego's parity among same sex siblings at age 18										All	
	1		2		3		4		5 and over			
	Mean	N	Mean	N	Mean	N	Mean	N	Mean	N	Mean	N
Men												
1	26.8	1676									26.8	1676
2	26.9	1238	26.4	994							26.7	2232
3	26.5	801	26.9	645	26.7	559					26.6	2005
4	26.3	445	26.6	358	26.6	306	25.8	261			26.3	1369
5 and over	25.1	255	25.6	256	26.5	232	25.9	223	26.2	251	25.8	1212
All	26.6	4413	26.5	2252	26.6	1096	25.9	482	26.2	251	26.5	8492
Women												
1	25.1	2165									25.1	2165
2	25.0	1602	25.1	1352							25.1	2954
3	24.8	960	25.1	865	25.3	791					25.1	2616
4	24.5	500	24.8	463	24.8	386	24.8	335			24.7	1684
5 and over	24.6	293	24.8	306	24.8	261	25.2	267	24.6	317	24.8	1442
All	24.9	5519	25.0	2984	25.1	1437	24.9	602	24.6	317	25.0	10861

Note: discrepancies between cumulated individual cell totals and row and column totals sometimes appear quite marked in this table (e.g. the cumulative total of the cells on the '5 and over' male row is 1217, compared with the row total of 1212). These are due, as in several other tables, to the half-weights attaching to Birstall and Shepshed, since totals are rounded up to the nearest whole number when not printed to the first decimal place. The problem is more marked on the '5 and over' row than elsewhere because the totals appearing in the cells in the table are themselves the result of aggregating totals in the original table for parities 5, 6, 7, and 8 and over.
Source: Cambridge Group reconstitutions.

168

son if an older brother died unmarried between the dates when the two became 18.

The last row and penultimate column in each panel show respectively the average ages at first marriage of sons and daughters of successive parities and the average age of particular sibling set sizes. The data were drawn from all parishes and all periods. They were not divided by parish group and the absolute values of the average ages shown are subject to the biases introduced by such factors as the differing length of the periods of reconstitution in different parishes. But the *relative* ages are unaffected by combining the data in this way, which has the advantage of maximising the number of observations.

Neither the row nor column averages suggest either for sons or daughters any clear association between age at first marriage and family characteristics. In pre-industrial England neither the number of siblings of the same sex within a family, nor the rank of individuals within the sibling set appears to have had a significant influence upon the timing of marriage. Nor does the examination of the average age figures along each successive row suggest that within sibling sets of a given size there was any tendency for those born early or late within the family to differ from others in marriage age. Certainly any patterns are very muted and it would require a far larger data set to confirm them. In the panel relating to daughters there is a slight hint of declining age at marriage with increasing sibling group size, but examination of parallel tabulations for individual half-centuries suggests that this is due to the greater frequency of large families in the later eighteenth and early nineteenth centuries when age of marriage was generally lower. The separate tabulations for successive half-centuries show the same general absence of pattern. Finally, if sons and daughters are consolidated together into combined sex sibling sets and the exercise is repeated, there is still no evidence that rank within the family makes any significant difference to marriage age.[62]

A second issue related to the demography of the family can also be examined. Table 5.13 shows the average ages at marriage of bachelors and spinsters according to their age at the death of their fathers. The successive columns show average ages at marriage when the father had died before the individual in question reached the age of 18, when he died between the individual's 18th and 23rd birthdays, between his 23rd and 28th birthdays, when the individual was 28 or older, and, finally, when the date of death of the father was unknown. In other words, the tabulation is prospective. If age at marriage were measured

---

[62] These tabulations are not reproduced in tab. 5.12.

Table 5.13 *Mean age at marriage by age at father's death (years)*

	Age at father's death (years)									
	Under 18	N	18–22	N	23–7	N	28 and over	N	Not known	N	All	N
Sons	27.3	889	27.0	369	27.3	336	27.6	1578	27.6	724	27.5	3896
Daughters	26.0	1106	26.1	385	25.8	469	26.1	1942	26.3	944	26.1	4845

Source: Cambridge Group reconstitutions.

according to whether the individual's father was alive or dead when he or she married, it is probable that the average age would be higher in the latter than in the former case since the older an individual at marriage, the more likely that his or her father had died. Any marriage taking place less than 75 years before the end of a reconstitution was excluded from the tabulation to ensure that a family in which the father attained an advanced age before dying was as likely to be included as one in which he died young.

Once again, there is a notable absence of any evidence that age at marriage was affected by the variable under examination. This is true of both sons and daughters. Those whose parents were already dead at the time when they reached an age to marry were neither precipitated into making an early marriage nor prevented from doing so, and the same holds true of each of the other categories relating to the death of the father. Although the data for half-century periods are not shown, they, too, fail to reveal differences in average age at marriage for either sex according to when the father died. As with the previous tabulation, it may be that if it were possible to examine particular economic or social groupings within the population differences in marriage characteristics might appear, but the gross picture suggests either that such differences were absent, or that if practice in one group favoured, say, early marriage following the death of the father, there must have been countervailing tendencies elsewhere.

In general, therefore, it seems that neither the place of the child within the sibling group nor the timing of the father's death had any effect on age at marriage sufficiently strong and consistent to show through in aggregate reconstitution data, and this finding holds true equally for young men and young women.

Remarriage

Some aspects of remarriage are difficult to study effectively using reconstitution data. Just as it is impossible to establish the proportions of single men and women ever marrying, so it is *a fortiori* beyond reach to discover what proportion of those who were widowed later remarried. On the other hand, it is readily possible to measure the interval of time that elapsed between becoming a widow or widower and making a further marriage, and how the interval varied over time or according to the circumstances of the widowed person. The average *absolute* interval may understate the true figure. Only those remarriages which took place within the parish can be used in the estimation of average

Table 5.14 *Remarriage intervals (months)*

	Male		Female	
	Mean	N	Mean	N
1580–99	19.4	19	17.1	11
1600–49	21.2	218	32.2	98
1650–99	25.0	247	40.8	98
1700–49	26.3	351	47.6	128
1750–99	33.6	465	45.5	207
1800–37	37.3	192	55.3	73
All	29.0	1 492	43.7	615

	All		Under 30		30–9		40–9		50 and over	
	Mean	N	Mean	N	Mean	N	Mean	N	Mean	N
Male										
1580–1649	21.1	237	26.1	52	17.8	99	16.9	56	31.1	30
1650–1749	25.8	598	24.4	144	24.3	234	31.8	128	23.3	92
1750–1837	34.7	657	37.3	155	34.9	252	34.2	149	30.9	101
All	29.0	1 492	30.4	351	27.8	585	30.4	333	27.8	223
Female										
1580–1649	30.7	109	31.4	32	29.7	48	39.6	20	13.9	9
1650–1749	44.6	226	51.5	63	45.2	105	39.3	43	27.1	15
1750–1837	48.0	280	54.0	97	49.0	119	39.7	55	22.4	9
All	43.7	615	49.4	192	44.1	272	39.5	118	22.2	33

Note: the data are cohorted by date of becoming a widow or widower. All marriages ending less than 10 years before the end of a reconstitution are excluded (to avoid truncation effects on the measurement of the remarriage interval towards the end of the data). All parishes were included for the full term of their reconstitution (see tab. 2.1, pp. 22–3).
Source: Cambridge Group reconstitutions.

remarriage intervals, and, because the chance of migrating from the parish was presumably greater the longer the interval to remarriage, the true figure will be higher than the measured figure, unless marriage and migration were as closely linked for widows as for spinsters. No evidence at present exists to resolve this question but, in any case, *relative* intervals are unlikely to be affected by this consideration, so that, for example, the estimation of the effect of the number of surviving children on the remarriage interval should be free from difficulty on this score.

Table 5.14 shows the patterns of change in remarriage intervals during the parish register period. In very general terms, and concentrating initially on all remarriages in each period, the patterns are simple. The top panel of the table shows that the mean interval to remarriage lengthened considerably for both sexes between the early seventeenth and the early nineteenth century, almost doubling in each case (no reliance should be placed on the means for the earliest period, 1580–99, which are based on very few cases). The interval was always longer for widows than for widowers, being usually about half as long again for the former as for the latter. In detail, however, it is clear that the simplicity of the overall picture needs to be qualified. For example, after 1750 there appears to be only a modest further rise in the remarriage interval for women, but a more pronounced change for men in the two periods that followed, but a later and more pronounced change for women.[63]

Reference to the second panel of the table shows that this difference between widows and widowers is not an artefact of changing proportions of widows and widowers in the several age groups: indeed, controlling for age, the contrast is heightened.[64] In each age group the interval to remarriage lengthened in the case of men but in the case of women the interval stabilised between 1650–1749 and 1750–1837. The apparent change for women after 1800, visible in the upper panel of the table, may be an artefact of small numbers.

Differences between the sexes were not confined to change over time. There was also a systematic difference between widows and widowers in remarriage interval by age at widowhood. The interval for widowers was much the same whatever the age at which they lost their spouse, indeed the overall figures in each age group are so closely similar as to suggest virtual identity. In the three century-long periods viewed separately there is more variation, with a hint that the interval was longest among elderly widowers in the earliest period. Later they became the quickest to remarry, but this apparent pattern may be an aberration resulting from the small number of cases. In the case of

---

[63] The pattern of remarriage intervals found in pre-industrial England may well not have been characteristic of pre-industrial Europe generally. In Anhausen in Bavaria, for example, in the eighteenth century the mean interval to remarriage for widowers was only 4.5 months and for widows just under 16 months. Both the length of the intervals and the proportionate difference between widowers and widows form a marked contrast with England in the same period; Knodel, 'A Bavarian village', tab. 5C, p. 364. There is much disparate information about remarriage in the past in Dupâquier *et al.*, eds., *Marriage and remarriage*.

[64] The periods in the second panel are a century rather than a half-century in length because the number of cases in some half-centuries is modest even when no division by age at widowhood is made, as may be seen in the top panel: when divided by age, the numbers are too small to yield dependable results.

Table 5.15 *Distribution of remarriage intervals (per 1000)*

Male

	Months since widowhood										N	Mean (mths)
	0–	2–	4–	6–	12–	18–	24–	36–	48–	60 and over		
Age at widowhood under 30												
1580–1649	58	154	231	442	615	673	750	827	904	1000	52	26.1
1650–1749	56	132	257	479	604	653	785	889	924	1000	144	24.4
1750–1837	0	26	103	271	355	497	665	755	819	1000	155	37.3
All	31	88	185	382	496	587	727	821	875	1000	351	30.4
Age at widowhood 30–9												
1580–1649	20	253	384	556	737	798	879	899	929	1000	99	17.8
1650–1749	26	111	197	427	577	675	765	897	927	1000	234	24.3
1750–1837	8	83	147	294	425	540	667	762	829	1000	252	34.9
All	17	123	207	392	539	638	742	839	886	1000	585	27.8
Age at widowhood 40–9												
1580–1649	107	286	393	607	732	750	821	929	946	1000	56	16.9
1650–1749	31	94	148	367	531	586	750	820	844	1000	128	31.8
1750–1837	13	47	114	262	409	524	685	765	866	1000	149	34.2
All	36	105	174	360	511	586	733	814	871	1000	333	30.4
Age at widowhood over 50												
1580–1649	67	67	233	400	533	567	667	800	833	1000	30	31.1
1650–1749	65	130	315	522	674	717	804	870	880	1000	92	23.3
1750–1837	20	109	158	317	515	584	693	782	871	1000	101	30.9
All	45	126	233	413	583	637	735	821	870	1000	223	27.8
All												
1580–1649	55	228	333	523	684	730	810	878	916	1000	237	21.1
1650–1749	40	115	219	442	589	657	773	875	901	1000	598	25.8
1750–1837	9	65	131	285	419	533	674	764	842	1000	657	34.7
All	29	111	198	385	529	614	735	826	877	1000	1492	29.0

Female

	0-	2-	4-	6-	12-	18-	24-	36-	48-	60 and over	N	Mean (mths)
					Months since widowhood							
Age at widowhood under 30												
1580–1649	31	63	188	344	469	531	719	781	844	1000	32	31.4
1650–1749	0	0	64	254	318	349	508	587	635	1000	63	51.5
1750–1837	10	21	31	93	196	289	454	608	660	1000	97	54.0
All	10	21	68	188	281	349	516	630	682	1000	192	49.4
Age at widowhood 30–9												
1580–1649	0	42	125	396	521	688	750	771	833	1000	48	29.7
1650–1749	0	29	95	219	371	438	571	638	705	1000	105	45.2
1750–1837	17	34	59	177	286	361	538	639	714	1000	119	49.0
All	7	33	85	232	360	449	588	662	732	1000	272	44.1
Age at widowhood 40–9												
1580–1649	0	50	100	150	300	400	600	700	800	1000	20	39.6
1650–1749	0	0	70	209	419	512	651	698	744	1000	43	39.3
1750–1837	18	55	91	255	309	418	600	709	800	1000	55	39.7
All	9	34	85	220	348	449	619	703	780	1000	118	39.5
Age at widowhood over 50												
1580–1649	0	111	222	667	667	778	889	1000	1000	1000	9	13.9
1650–1749	0	133	333	468	468	533	733	867	895	1000	15	27.1
1750–1837	0	111	111	111	444	778	889	889	889	1000	9	22.4
All	0	121	242	424	515	667	818	909	939	1000	33	22.2
All												
1580–1649	9	55	147	358	477	596	725	780	844	1000	109	30.7
1650–1749	0	22	97	243	372	434	530	650	708	1000	226	44.6
1750–1837	4	36	57	161	264	361	532	650	718	1000	280	48.0
All	8	34	88	226	342	429	584	673	737	1000	615	43.7

Note and sources: see tab. 5.14.

widows, however, the overall figures suggest a marked tendency for the remarriage interval to decline with age. Young widows waited longer to remarry than those who lost their husbands later in life, though this pattern is less clear in the earliest period, when in any case the number of cases is too small to support confident assertion. The contrast between widows and widowers in this regard was so marked that, in spite of the substantially higher overall average remarriage intervals among the former, widows above the age of 50 had a shorter remarriage interval than widowers. The difference in remarriage interval between widows and widowers narrowed steadily with age. If the male and female means in the four age groups (under 30, 30–9, 40–9, and 50 and over) are expressed as a ratio to one another with the male figure as 100, the successive ratios in the four age groups are 163, 159, 130, and 80.

Changes in the mean interval to remarriage reflect a changing distribution in the length of the individual intervals contributing to the mean. In table 5.15 the distribution of intervals is shown for each of the main age at widowhood categories and for all age groups combined.

As was to be expected in view of the similarity in the level and trend of mean intervals for widowers of various ages visible in table 5.14, the patterns in the individual age at widowerhood categories are similar and it is, therefore, possible to focus chiefly on the overall pattern. In the period 1580–1649 half of the widower remarriages had taken place within a year of widowhood, whereas in 1750–1837 a comparable proportion was not reached until two years had elapsed. In the earlier period only about 8 per cent of remarriages took place more than five years after the end of the previous marriage, whereas in the later period the equivalent figure was 16 per cent. Very rapid remarriage was never common: in late Elizabethan and early Stuart England about 6 per cent of male remarriages took place within two months of the death of the wife, but by the end of the eighteenth century the figure was down to about 1 per cent.[65]

The comparable figures for widows are apt to be more volatile because remarriage intervals are known for only 40 per cent as many widows as widowers. The overall pattern reveals a median interval in the earliest period of about 19 months which had lengthened to about 34 months in 1750–1837. Much higher proportions of widows than

---

[65] It is difficult to make an exact comparison with Knodel's German villages because of differences in the presentation of data, but it seems safe to say both that the distribution of intervals to remarriage and trends over time were similar for the two countries, if they are offset by a century or so (that is, seventeenth- and eighteenth-century England resembled eighteenth- and nineteenth-century Germany); Knodel and Lynch, 'The decline of remarriage', tab. 5, p. 44.

widowers married after more than five years of widowhood: in the earlier period 16 per cent, in the later period 28 per cent. Rapid remarriage was rarer for widows than for widowers. In 1580–1649 33 per cent of widowers remarried within six months of losing a wife, compared with 15 per cent of widows within the same interval of losing a husband; by 1750–1849 the comparable percentages were 13 and 6.[66]

Table 5.15 confirms that there was a sharp decline in the remarriage interval with increasing age at widowhood. The figures for all time periods combined, for example, show that only 52 per cent of all those who were widowed under 30 and later remarried had done so by the end of the third year of widowhood, whereas the comparable percentages for those widowed 30–9, 40–9, and 50 and over were 59, 62, and 82. Broadly comparable discrepancies may be found in the three time periods taken separately but the patterns are irregular because the number of events in some cells is very small.

The family circumstances of widowed men and women varied greatly, of course, and there has been much discussion of the degree to which the presence of dependent children might either hasten or delay remarriage. Were widowers encumbered with young children especially anxious to effect a rapid remarriage? Were widows in similar circumstances less readily able to remarry? Table 5.16 provides some answers to questions such as these. In it widows and widowers are divided into those who had 0, 1, 2, and 3 or more children surviving under the age of 10 at the time that they were widowed. The number of cases is too small to make it sensible to subdivide the data by time period.

The picture appears simple. The number of dependent children that a widower had when losing his wife made very little difference to the speed with which he remarried; nor did his age affect matters. Making some allowance for random effects where numbers are small, there is a notable absence of change in the remarriage intervals listed in the second column of the table. All the individual figures are close to the grand mean of 29 months. For widows it was very different. The smaller the number of dependent children, the shorter the interval to remar-

---

[66] Although the number of remarriages is too small to support a study of interparochial differences, it is clear that remarriage characteristics were broadly similar in all the reconstitution parishes. This represents a striking contrast with France. Flandrin quotes figures for the proportion of all remarrying widowers who did so within six months of the death of their spouse. All the six studies upon which he drew related to the seventeenth and eighteenth centuries but the percentage of those remarrying within six months varied greatly, from 6 per cent at Bilhères d'Ossau to 80 per cent in the parish of St Georges in Lyon; Flandrin, *Families in former times*, p. 115.

Table 5.16 *The burden of dependency (number of surviving children under 10) and remarriage interval by age at widowhood (months)*

	Widowers		Widows	
	N	Mean	N	Mean
Under 30				
0 ch.	159	31.3	40	33.0
1 ch.	101	27.5	78	48.3
2 ch.	54	33.0	38	59.8
3 or more ch.	37	30.2	36	59.0
All	351	30.4	192	49.4
30–9				
0 ch.	161	23.9	55	32.5
1 ch.	133	26.9	61	37.9
2 ch.	130	28.9	64	43.8
3 or more ch.	161	31.5	92	55.5
All	585	27.8	272	44.1
40 and over				
0 ch.	323	27.9	84	25.7
1 ch.	90	29.8	29	36.0
2 ch.	56	31.3	22	47.4
3 or more ch.	87	33.2	16	72.0
All	556	29.3	151	35.7
All				
0 ch.	643	27.8	179	29.4
1 ch.	324	27.9	168	42.4
2 ch.	240	30.3	124	49.3
3 or more ch.	285	31.8	144	58.2
All	1 492	29.0	615	43.7

Source: Cambridge Group reconstitutions.

riage. The combined figures for all age at widowhood groups show that a widow with three or more dependent children took twice as long to remarry as one who was without any young children. The patterns in the different age at widowhood groups all reflect this characteristic, though they also reveal a further feature: with the same burden of dependent children, the older a widow the more likely she was to remarry relatively quickly. Perhaps it was generally the case that the older a widow, the greater her wealth and hence her 'attractiveness'. Conceivably, the knowledge that older widows would have few if any further children may also have entered into the calculations of suitors. The pattern is perfectly regular in the case of widows with no dependent child or with only one child, though less clear where the dependency burden was larger.

Since there are several factors which may have been responsible for the changing length of the remarriage interval for men and for women, it is helpful to make use of a method of estimating the relative importance of each factor net of the effect of the others. The set of remarriage intervals was classified by sex, by age at widowhood, by the time period in which widowhood occurred, and by the number of dependent children. The factors were interrelated in ways which make it difficult to disentangle their separate effects, and may result in false conclusions being drawn. Some clear patterns were visible in the tabular data, but it is evident that some apparently strong relationships may have been due to an interrelation between the explanatory variables. For example, older widows and widowers are likely to have more surviving children. Age and number of dependents are interrelated. It is, therefore, appropriate in estimating the relative importance of each factor, to control for interconnections between the factors.

The effect of each factor, or 'class', on the remarriage interval was measured using the method of least squares to fit general linear models.[67] Separate estimators were run for widows and for widowers, and for each sex the factors, or classes, that were regarded as influencing the length of the remarriage interval were reduced to four: the time period in which the remarriage occurred, the age of the widowed person, the number of dependent children, and the economic type of the parish in which the marriage took place. The factors were broken down as follows: the parish register period as a whole was divided into three subperiods (before 1650, 1650–1749, and 1750 onwards), age at widowhood into four age groups (20–9, 30–9, 40–9, and 50 and over), the number of dependent children into five categories (0, 1, 2, 3, and 4 or greater), and the economic type of the parish into four groups (agricultural, manufacturing, retail and handicraft, and other). Since the general linear model was fitted over the whole range of remarriage intervals, the number of observations was quite large: 1492 for men and 615 for women.

The analysis was performed by estimating the main effect of each of the four classes on the remarriage interval net of the effect of other classes. The results are shown in table 5.17, where for each level of every class its least-squares mean is shown. The procedure takes full account of the unbalanced nature of the design, and calculates the least-squares

---

[67] The procedure was GLM in SAS, as there were unequal numbers of observations for the different combinations of class variables.

Table 5.17 *The effect of period, age, number of dependent children, and parish occupational type on mean interval to remarriage*[a]

	Widowers		Widows	
	Months	Pr > F	Months	Pr > F
Period				
Before 1650	22.9	0.00	37.0	0.02
1650–1749	27.9		49.1	
1750 onwards	35.8		49.5	
Age				
20–9	30.4	0.49	52.6	0.13
30–9	27.3		44.5	
40–9	30.0		45.3	
50 and over	27.8		38.5	
Dependent children				
0	26.9	0.68	29.1	0.00
1	27.2		38.6	
2	29.5		46.7	
3	29.6		48.5	
4 and over	31.1		63.1	
Occupational type[b]				
Agricultural	33.8	0.05	51.9	0.14
Manufacturing	28.4		42.9	
Retail trade and				
handicraft	26.6		40.8	
Other	26.6		45.2	
Mean interval	29.0		43.7	

[a] The method of estimation used in calculating the means shown in this table was the SAS general linear models procedure: least-squares means.
[b] Agricultural parishes were those where 60 per cent or more of the adult male labour force in 1831 were engaged in agriculture; manufacturing where more than 30 per cent were engaged in manufacture; retail trade and handicraft where more than 40 per cent were engaged in retail and handicraft employment. In no case did any parish qualify under more than one head.
Source: Cambridge Group reconstitutions.

mean that would have been observed if the design had been balanced. This means, for example, that it captures the characteristics of a remarriage occurring after 1750, no matter what the distribution of remarriages happened to be by age of the widow or widower, the number of dependent children, or the economic type of the parish. In this manner, the procedure attempts to overcome the distortion which is apt to appear in a simple tabulation as an unfortunate consequence of an unbalanced design.

The overall average remarriage interval was considerably shorter for widowers (29.0 months) than for widows (43.7 months). The significance of any apparent difference associated with the four classes may be judged from the columns headed 'Pr > F'. A low value in these columns indicates a clear net effect on the length of the remarriage interval; a high value that no firm conclusions should be drawn. Using the conventional 5 per cent significance level, values of 0.05 or lower are needed to justify the view that the finding is statistically significant. Using this criterion, it is clear that the remarriage interval for widowers lengthened significantly over time, from 22.9 months in the period before 1650 to 35.8 months in the period after 1750. More doubtful is the effect of the economic type of the parish. Although the remarriage interval for men in 'agricultural' parishes was considerably longer than in 'retail and handicraft' or 'other' parishes (33.8 months compared to 26.6 months), the probability that there was a net effect on the remarriage interval is only just significant at the 5 per cent level. Neither the age at which widowers remarried, nor the burden of dependent children they were shouldering, had a clear net effect on the length of the interval to remarriage.

For widows the position was substantially different. As with men, the interval to remarriage for widows was affected by the period in which they lived, but the timing of the change differed. Between the first and second subperiods there was a 12-month increase in the interval, compared with a 5-month rise for widowers. But between the second and third subperiods widowers experienced an increase of a further 8 months, while the interval to remarriage for widows remained essentially the same.

Age as well as period may have had an influence on female remarriage: the older the widow the shorter the period before remarriage. This result, however, is not statistically significant (0.13), and may have been produced by controlling for crossed effects between the factors.[68] The two sexes display similar patterns so far as the economic type of the parish is concerned. There was a considerably longer interval to remarriage in 'agricultural' than in any other type of parish, but this difference, though more pronounced in the case of widows, was not sufficient to produce a statistically significant result (0.14). Here, too, the result may be an artefact of controlling for interactions.

---

[68] If the period after 1750 is considered in isolation, the tendency of the interval to remarriage to fall within each category of dependency burden is clear-cut.

There was, however, one striking difference betweeen widows and widowers. The number of dependent children both had the strongest effect of any single factor on the length of the remarriage interval for widows, and clearly distinguished female from male remarriage patterns. Widows with no dependent children at all behaved in this respect just like widowers. Their average interval to remarriage was 29.1 months (the overall average for men was 29.0 months). Thereafter, as the number of dependent children increased, a widow's chance of making a swift remarriage declined *pari passu*, until, where she was burdened by four or more children, the average interval to remarriage was as much as 63.1 months. Moreover, it is probable, though not demonstrable from reconstitution data, that a long interval to remarriage was also associated with a decreased chance of ever remarrying. For widows the effect of the number of dependent children was both regular and strong: the probability that it was due to chance was insignificant.

In summary, therefore, the length of the interval to remarriage was affected both by period and by the number of dependent children in the case of widows. For widowers it was affected by period but not by the number of dependent children:[69] it may also have been influenced by the economic type of the parish or residence, but this is less certain. Childless widows and widowers of all types showed very similar characteristics.

Parochial trends and characteristics

Information about marriage age in bachelor/spinster marriages in the 26 reconstitution parishes is set out in table 5.18. Because of the relatively small number of marriages in the smaller parishes the data are given for half-century periods. Even so there were some periods in particular parishes when fewer than 25 marriages occurred, and in such cases no mean age is given in the table. For this reason and because of the wide differences in the dates at which reconstitution began and ended, it is only in the period 1700–49 that the full set of 26 parishes figures in the table.

---

[69] These patterns appear to differ from those in eighteenth- and nineteenth-century Germany where the number of surviving children at widowhood was inversely related to the chance of remarriage for both widows and widowers. The English data allow only the measurement of interval to remarriage and number of surviving children and not the chance of remarrying, but since the interval to remarriage and chance of remarrying are related, it seems very likely that English and German widowers behaved differently; Knodel and Lynch, 'The decline of remarriage', tab. 10, p. 53; Knodel, *Demographic behavior in the past*, p. 182.

In spite of the changing composition of the list of parishes in different periods, however, some patterns are clear. The evidence of falling marriage age after 1700 is widespread. If Birstall, Lowestoft, March, and Reigate are ignored because they are not represented in all three periods after 1700, the age of brides fell between 1700–49 and 1750–99 in 21 of the 22 parishes and was unchanged in the 22nd (Willingham); in the case of grooms the comparable figures were 17 cases of decline and 5 cases of increase. Between 1750–99 and 1800–37 there were 16 falls and 6 rises in average age at marriage for brides; 19 falls and 3 rises for grooms. In these 22 parishes the unweighted average of the individual parish means for men and women in 1700–49, 1750–99, and 1800–37 were 27.5, 26.5, 25.7; and 26.0, 24.6, and 23.7 years respectively. The comparable figures intended to represent the national picture were 27.0, 25.9, and 25.1 years; and 25.7, 24.4, and 23.6 years.[70] Both the level and the trends were similar in the two series, suggesting a marked homogeneity in marriage behaviour throughout the country.

Although it is pressing the data hard to do so, it is of interest to examine the uniformity of trend over shorter time periods, quarter-centuries rather than half-centuries. Since the number of marriages over a quarter-century is small in some cases, there is clearly a risk of random effects obscuring any underlying uniformities, but the pattern visible in table 5.19 is once more clear-cut. It suggests strongly that the tendency for marriage age to decline was maintained from the beginning of the eighteenth century right through until the end of the parish register period in 1837. The number of parishes in this tabulation is 3 fewer than in considering the half-centuries from 1750 onwards (19 rather than 22) because the reconstitutions of Gainsborough, Methley, and Willingham all cease before the final period 1825–37.

Though the downward trend in marriage age after 1700 appears to have been notably uniform across all 26 reconstitution parishes, it might, of course, have been more pronounced in some kinds of parish than in others. To test this possibility, it is convenient to divide the parishes into four groups: agricultural (those where 60 per cent or more of the adult male labour force in the 1831 census were engaged in agriculture); retail trade and handicrafts (those with 40 per cent or more in this category at the same census); manufacturing (30 per cent or more); and the rest.[71] As in the analysis of data from table 5.18, and for the same reason, data from only 22 of the 26 parishes could be used. Of the 22, 8 were agricultural on this definition (Aldenham, Ash, Bridford, Great Oakley, Hartland, Morchard Bishop, Terling, and Willingham), 4

---

[70] Tab. 5.3, p. 134, averaging the individual decennial figures for the periods in question.
[71] The criteria for the first three groups are such that no parish qualified under more than one head.

Table 5.18 Mean age at marriage in bachelor/spinster marriages in the 26 parishes (years)

	Male					Female				
	1600–49	1650–99	1700–49	1750–99	1800–37	1600–49	1650–99	1700–49	1750–99	1800–37
Alcester	29.9	27.7	27.1	27.4	24.8	25.5	27.0	28.1	24.7	23.9
Aldenham	28.5	29.1	28.1	27.2	25.8	25.0	25.6	25.8	24.1	22.9
Ash			27.6	26.8	25.4			25.6	24.3	23.6
Austrey			31.8	29.1	28.2	25.7	28.4^a	28.2	24.9	25.7
Banbury	26.3		26.4	26.2	25.1	25.3	25.3	25.8	24.8	23.5
Birstall		28.3	26.8	25.1			25.8	24.7	23.2	
Bottesford	30.3*	27.7	28.4	28.9	26.9	25.9*	25.5	27.2	26.3	24.1
Bridford	28.1	26.8	27.7	27.0	26.0	25.7	26.0	25.5	24.7	24.9
Colyton	26.8	28.0	26.9	27.7	26.8	26.7	28.3	28.1	26.6	24.2
Dawlish			27.4	26.0	25.7			27.0	24.9	24.4
Earsdon		25.9	26.8	25.9	27.2		22.2	24.9	23.7	24.1
Gainsborough	26.9	26.9	27.4	26.0	25.9*	24.5	25.1	25.2	24.8	24.3*
Gedling	28.2	29.6	28.6	25.8	24.6	27.4	26.8	26.1	24.5	23.1
Great Oakley			26.2	24.7	24.8			22.9	22.7	22.6
Hartland	28.9	30.5	29.5	27.4	27.6	27.3	28.4	27.7	26.4	24.8

Ipplepen	24.5		28.2	27.4	27.3			26.1	24.1	24.6
Lowestoft	25.9	25.7	25.3					25.2		
March	29.8	25.4	24.4			24.6	24.7	24.3		
Methley		27.8	29.9	26.8	24.1*	26.3	24.6	26.0	24.3	21.6*
Morchard Bishop			26.3	25.7	25.4	25.0	27.1	26.0	25.0	25.1
Odiham	27.6	26.6	26.4	26.6*	26.3	25.1	25.2	25.6	24.4	22.9
Reigate	26.4	26.4	25.9	25.4		24.8	24.8	25.9	23.8*	
Shepshed			28.2		24.2	28.6	26.5	27.1	24.6	23.7
Southill	27.3	26.8	26.6	24.7	23.5	25.3	24.4	24.4	23.3	22.4
Terling	25.0	24.9	24.4	25.3	25.0	24.7	23.1	24.1	22.8	23.2
Willingham	26.5	25.9	25.8	24.9	24.4*	24.3	24.9	24.3	24.3*	22.4

[a] In this instance the mean was based on fewer than 25 marriages (19) but, since the means on either side were based on 25 or more cases, this figure has been retained.

Note: no means have been entered in the table unless they were based on at least 25 marriages (but see note [a]). An asterisked figure, which only occurs in the first or last period for which there are data for the parish, indicates that the data on which the figure was based were drawn from a quarter-century or less within the half-century period (for example, an asterisk against a mean for 1600–49 indicates that all the data came from within the period 1625–49, while an asterisk against a mean for 1800–37 indicates that all the data came from within the period 1800–24).

Source: Cambridge Group reconstitutions.

Table 5.19 *Age at marriage trends in bachelor/spinster marriages*

	1700–24/ 1725–49	1725–49/ 1750–74	1750–74/ 1775–99	1775–99/ 1800–24	1800–24/ 1825–37
Male					
Age rising	8	4	8	4	6
Age falling	11	12	11	15	13
No change	0	3	0	0	0
Female					
Age rising	6	3	4	8	7
Age falling	13	16	13	11	11
No change	0	0	2	0	1

Note: the data are drawn from the 19 parishes in which the reconstitution covered the whole period from 1700 to 1837. The numbers in the table indicate the totals of parishes in which mean age at marriage was rising, falling, or stationary between successive quarter-centuries. The 19 parishes are Alcester, Aldenham, Ash, Austrey, Banbury, Bottesford, Bridford, Colyton, Dawlish, Earsdon, Gedling, Great Oakley, Hartland, Ipplepen, Morchard Bishop, Odiham, Shepshed, Southill, and Terling.
Source: Cambridge Group reconstitutions.

fell into the category of retail trade and handicraft (Alcester, Banbury, Dawlish, and Gainsborough), 2 were manufacturing (Gedling and Shepshed), and 8 were 'other' (Austrey, Bottesford, Colyton, Earsdon, Ipplepen, Methley, Odiham, and Southill). In table 5.20 the average ages at marriage for each of the four groups in the three half-century periods after 1700 are set out.

There are suggestive hints in the table but the small number of parishes involved precludes all strong statements. In all four groups average marriage age fell steadily throughout the period both for men and for women. The fall was most pronounced in the manufacturing group (which, however, contained only 2 parishes), followed by the 'other' group. But marriage age in both these groups was high initially, especially for men, so that mean age at marriage by the end of the period was not strikingly lower than in the other two groups. Indeed, in the case of the 'other' group, male age at marriage was higher than anywhere else in 1800–37 and female age was the equal second highest at that time. The fall in marriage age was least pronounced in the agricultural group, though the difference between this group and that consisting of those in retail trade and handicraft was slight. In general these two groups were closely similar to each other. Female marriage age was somewhat lower in the agricultural group than in the other three in the early eighteenth century, and, though the subsequent fall

Table 5.20 *Mean age at marriage in parish groups according to occupational structure (bachelor/spinster marriages; age in years)*

	Male			Female		
	1700–49	1750–99	1800–37	1700–49	1750–99	1800–37
Marriage age						
Agricultural	27.0	26.1	25.6	25.2	24.3	23.7
Retail trade &						
handicraft	27.1	26.4	25.4	26.5	24.8	24.0
Manufacturing	28.4	25.6	24.4	26.6	24.6	23.4
Other	28.1	27.2	26.3	26.3	24.7	23.7

	1700–49/	1750–99/	1700–49/	1750–99/
	1750–99	1800–37	1750–99	1800–37
Change over time				
Agricultural	−0.9	−0.5	−0.9	−0.6
Retail trade &				
handicraft	−0.7	−1.0	−1.7	−0.8
Manufacturing	−2.8	−1.2	−2.0	−1.2
Other	−0.9	−0.9	−1.6	−1.0

Note: the ages quoted are unweighted averages of the mean ages of the parishes comprising each group.
Source: Cambridge Group reconstitutions.

was not marked, it was sufficient to keep bridal age lower in this group than in any other except for manufacturing in the final period. Overall, though, the uniformity rather than the diversity of experience among the 26 parishes, whatever their occupational type, is the strongest impression given by the table.

If small numbers of events make for difficulties in attempting to establish trends over time in marriage age in individual parishes when using data from bachelor/spinster marriages, they prohibit the study of time trends in other marriage rank combinations. It may be of interest, nonetheless, to extend further the study of the uniformity of parish-level experience by tabulating the data relating to other marriage rank combinations for each reconstitution as a whole, and this is done in table 5.21.

In many cases the number of marriages on which the averages shown in table 5.21 were based is so small as to render the result virtually meaningless. This is especially true of the bachelor/widow and widower/widow marriage rank combinations where the total number of cases was frequently fewer than 10. Widower/spinster marriages were commoner, however, and the averages in the columns relating to

Table 5.21 *Mean age at marriage in bachelor/spinster (1/1), bachelor/widow (1/2+), widower/spinster (2+/1), and widower/widow (2+/2+) marriages by individual parishes (years: all periods combined)*

| | Mean age at marriage (years) | | | | | | | | Totals | | | | | | | |
| | Male | | | | Female | | | | Male | | | | Female | | | |
	1/1	1/2+	2+/1	2+/2+	1/1	1/2+	2+/1	2+/2+	1/1	1/2+	2+/1	2+/2+	1/1	1/2+	2+/1	2+/2+
Alcester	27.3	28.3	38.1	46.9	26.0	38.4	28.4	43.2	443	20	65	13	601	24	58	10
Aldenham	27.8	32.6	39.9	54.5	24.7	39.6	28.7	42.6	325	18	57	23	433	14	38	12
Ash	26.4	28.9	38.8	42.4	24.3	39.1	29.1	43.8	466	17	40	15	642	22	46	10
Austrey	29.2	35.0	40.7	50.2	26.2	31.2	33.2	47.4	133	8	19	3	233	3	12	3
Banbury	26.0	27.8	39.3	44.5	24.7	38.0	29.1	41.0	1089	64	190	60	1473	44	161	39
Birstall	26.0	29.3	39.7	45.1	23.9	32.2	28.9	37.2	1868	27	164	36	2140	25	146	26
Bottesford	28.2	31.2	40.4	40.5	25.7	35.3	27.2	48.3	408	9	78	8	521	7	41	1
Bridford	27.6	31.7	45.4	43.6	25.3	36.8	30.0	50.4	181	7	16	2	241	4	16	2
Colyton	27.2	26.2	42.9	43.4	26.5	33.7	31.8	35.4	668	25	84	24	800	15	74	10
Dawlish	26.2	31.6	38.9	44.1	25.2	35.7	30.1	42.3	319	9	23	7	451	18	21	6
Earsdon	26.6	28.6	38.0	44.8	24.0	32.8	26.9	45.3	719	23	40	2	835	31	35	5
Gainsborough	26.6	29.2	39.5	46.7	24.8	35.3	27.6	41.1	1204	121	247	88	1728	112	248	73
Gedling	26.3	34.3	39.2	47.0	24.5	35.7	29.5	43.7	583	27	82	22	712	27	58	9
Great Oakley	24.9	28.0	39.0	41.6	22.7	30.1	26.2	37.4	180	11	21	11	267	7	25	7
Hartland	28.8	32.8	42.4	49.2	26.9	39.0	30.4	44.9	963	16	88	10	1053	26	61	10

Ipplepen	27.5	41.5	36.4	—	24.6	34.7	30.3	47.0	169	3	12	—	253	7	18	3
Lowestoft	25.3	26.7	34.9	42.8	24.9	34.0	29.5	41.1	317	14	37	31	353	21	47	22
March	25.2	27.6	32.1	35.0	24.8	40.5	27.3	38.4	234	9	38	6	284	8	33	3
Methley	27.9	27.5	39.8	38.5	25.2	—	27.6	—	310	7	39	3	426	—	22	—
Morchard Bishop	25.7	32.4	42.9	49.9	25.1	35.8	32.3	43.6	767	14	85	19	907	16	71	23
Odiham	26.6	29.5	38.3	50.4	24.4	36.9	29.2	42.3	719	33	65	18	899	31	57	17
Reigate	26.3	26.2	38.8	41.9	25.0	37.8	28.1	35.7	560	36	72	23	608	16	57	7
Shepshed	25.6	30.6	39.9	48.5	24.7	35.8	28.9	45.5	423	12	41	9	521	6	29	6
Southill	25.3	30.6	39.3	50.9	23.7	36.2	27.9	44.8	585	20	86	16	803	17	76	11
Terling	25.0	26.4	37.0	40.7	23.3	26.3	26.8	44.1	285	12	33	6	365	3	27	6
Willingham	25.5	28.4	35.3	46.2	24.1	36.1	25.3	37.8	230	12	21	6	267	8	14	2

Source: Cambridge Group reconstitutions.

this type of marriage are fairly stable. In the case of male marriages in this category, for example, in only 6 of the 20 parishes in which the average age of widower grooms was based on 25 or more marriages was the mean either more than 5 per cent above or more than 5 per cent below the long-term average for such marriages revealed in table 5.7. The comparable figure for female marriage ages was 7 parishes (out of 19).[72]

The patterns visible in the national data reviewed earlier in this chapter are also normally mirrored at the parish level. Thus bachelors marrying widows were almost invariably older than those who married spinsters, and widowers marrying spinsters were equally regularly younger than those who married widows. The same held true for brides. Spinsters marrying widowers were always older than those marrying bachelors, and widows marrying bachelors were younger than those marrying widows with only two exceptions.[73]

Finally, it may be of interest to provide a visual impression of the degree of uniformity in the trend in marriage age in the 26 parishes. Figure 5.5 presents data in the form of 50-year moving averages of the mean age of brides and grooms in bachelor/spinster marriages in each of the parishes. The parishes have been grouped as in table 5.20 with the four parishes which were excluded from that tabulation added to their appropriate groups (Birstall to manufacturing; Lowestoft to retail trade and handicraft; March and Reigate to 'other'). Displaying the information in this way brings to light several features which were not visible when the occupational groupings were characterised by their parish means as in table 5.20, though it should always be remembered that in some small parishes the number of ages at marriage, even over a period as long as 50 years, may be very small and the danger of random fluctuation correspondingly great. For example, the total number of male ages at marriage in bachelor/spinster marriages in Austrey in 1700–49 was only 26 and of female ages 49, whereas in the same period in Birstall the male and female totals were 482 and 625.

In the agricultural group perhaps the most striking feature is the convergence towards a low age at marriage at the end of the parish register period, a feature especially prominent among males. In the early nineteenth century every parish except Hartland lay within the range 25–7 years for male age at marriage. This stands in vivid contrast

---

[72] The long-term averages were taken as the average of the 10 quarter-century figures listed for widower/spinster marriages in tab. 5.7, p. 149.

[73] The two exceptions were March and Reigate, and in both cases very small numbers were involved (8 bachelor/widow marriages and 3 widower/widow marriages in March; 16 bachelor/widow and 7 widower/widow marriages in Reigate).

with the situation in 1700 when there was a wide spread of mean ages. If the number of available parishes were greater it would be of interest to pursue two possibilities suggested by the male agricultural panel: that trends in East Anglia (Terling, Willingham, and Great Oakley, where male age at marriage was broadly unchanging) were different from areas further west; and that parishes in which mortality was high tended to be characterised by early marriage even in the seventeenth century (Great Oakley and Willingham in the agricultural set and elsewhere March and Lowestoft). The number of parishes, however, is too small to be more than suggestive in either case. The tendency to convergence is less pronounced in female marriage age in the agricultural parishes, nor is the division into high and low marriage age groups in the late seventeenth century so clear-cut.

The manufacturing parishes are few in number and the pattern of change is simple. Before the advent of large-scale employment of a proto-industrial type all three parishes were late marrying. Marriage age plunged in the course of the eighteenth century, though by the early nineteenth century, when the fall was bottoming out, age at marriage was only slightly lower than in the other groups. The three display great uniformity but the small number of parishes precludes confident generalisation.

The retail trade and handicraft group includes one particularly striking feature, the remarkable period in Alcester in the late seventeenth century and early eighteenth century when male age at marriage had fallen into a prolonged trough while female marriage age in contrast was rising to a marked peak. In the period 1660 to 1719, the mean age of marriage of grooms in bachelor/spinster marriages was 26.9 years (N = 137), but their brides were on average 1.2 years older at 28.1 years (N = 201). Such a reverse age gap was not unique. There was a similar episode in much the same period in Colyton but in Alcester the phenomenon is especially interesting, since throughout the seventeenth century male marriage age was falling continuously, while female age rose equally steadily. Apart from seventeenth-century Alcester, however, retail trade and handicraft formed a relatively homogeneous group. Marriage age fell significantly during the eighteenth century. As in the case of the agricultural parishes there was a marked convergence of lines on the graph towards the end of the period, leaving little difference between the parishes by 1800.

The 'other' group was, as might have been expected, a somewhat miscellaneous set of parishes with a fairly wide spread of average ages at marriage, though there is once again evidence of falling marriage age and of convergence during the eighteenth century, more marked in the

Male

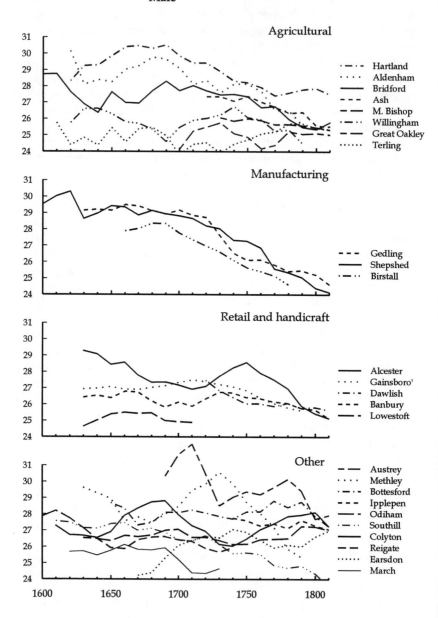

Figure 5.5 *Mean age at first marriage in the 26 reconstitution parishes:*
bachelor/spinster marriages (years)
Note: the data used in the figure are 50-year moving averages, plotted every 10 years.

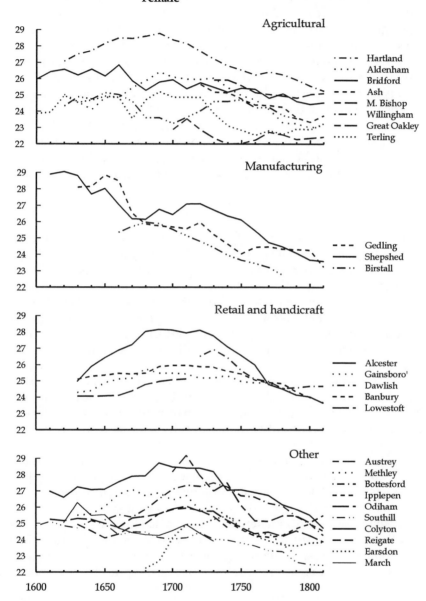

Female

Agricultural

- Hartland
- Aldenham
- Bridford
- Ash
- M. Bishop
- Willingham
- Great Oakley
- Terling

Manufacturing

- Gedling
- Shepshed
- Birstall

Retail and handicraft

- Alcester
- Gainsboro'
- Dawlish
- Banbury
- Lowestoft

Other

- Austrey
- Methley
- Bottesford
- Ipplepen
- Odiham
- Southill
- Colyton
- Reigate
- Earsdon
- March

Note to figure 5.5 (*cont.*)
Thus a reading plotted at the year 1650 represents the average of the 5 decennial figures for the decades 1630–9 to 1670–9.
Source: Cambridge Group reconstitutions.

case of women than of men. The relatively large number of parishes in the group, however, would tend to result in a wider dispersion of average ages, *ceteris paribus*. Some features, that are not readily visible because the graph is rather crowded, are worthy of note. Age at marriage of both spinsters and bachelors in Southill, for example, showed an almost perfectly regular decline from start to finish, a very unusual characteristic. Young men and young women in the mining parish of Earsdon did not marry earlier than those in other parishes.[74] The male curve in Colyton traces out a curious roller coaster path which may reflect the local employment opportunities for men in the parish.[75] These, and other similar features that might be picked out, serve to underline the impression of variety as a defining feature of this group.

Conclusion

The scope of this chapter has been largely restricted to the attempt to provide reliable estimates of the trends in marriage age and related matters over the period of almost a quarter of a millennium during which the parish registers are the chief source of demographic information. The main findings will occasion little surprise. It has been known for some time that average ages at marriage were fairly high in the seventeenth and early eighteenth centuries and that there was a sharp fall in marriage age during the middle decades of the eighteenth century.[76]

The evidence presented in this chapter confirms both the dating of the change and the extent of the fall, about three years from peak to trough. Since there is an excellent accord between the marriage age series derived from reconstitution and the early returns of the Registrar-General at the point in time when the two series meet, it is likely that the level as well the trend of estimated marriage ages are well captured by reconstitution data; nor do fears that mean marriage age based on 'stayers' must be too low appear well founded. The fall occurred in the age range when fecundity is high in women, and therefore resulted in a marked increase in overall fertility. The marriage age change alone was sufficient, *ceteris paribus*, to raise fertility by more than a fifth.[77] The reproductive careers of many women, of course, began before marriage. By the end of the eighteenth century, indeed, it is probable that about a

---

[74] The low female figures in the first decades are based on a very small number of cases.
[75] There is suggestive information about both male and female employment opportunities in Colyton in Sharpe, 'Literally spinsters'.
[76] For example, Wrigley and Schofield, 'English population history from family reconstitution', tab. 2, p. 162.   [77] See above p. 136.

quarter of all first births were illegitimate and a further quarter were prenuptially conceived.[78] The steep rise in illegitimate fertility, which was closely linked to the fall in marriage age, boosted the rise in legitimate fertility considerably, adding perhaps a further 5 per cent to overall fertility.[79] Thus, in explaining the rapid acceleration in population growth in England in the course of the eighteenth century, the change in marriage age and other changes closely associated with it must be accorded a central role, though the surge in general fertility produced by these changes was further boosted by a rise in marital fertility; births to the average couple succeeded one another at a brisker tempo than earlier and the fecundity of long-married women declined less steeply with age in the later eighteenth century than had been the case in earlier periods.[80]

In view of the evident importance of nuptiality change in influencing population trends, it is particularly disappointing that English reconstitution material yields no information about changes in the proportion of men and women who never married. The available evidence suggests that during the seventeenth century changes in proportions never marrying were much more significant than changes in the mean age at marriage in altering overall fertility levels.[81] In the eighteenth century, in contrast, the fall in marriage age dominated nuptiality change and thus fertility. The proportion of women never marrying appears to have risen greatly during late Tudor and early Stuart times, reaching a peak of over 20 per cent among those reaching adult years in the middle decades of the seventeenth century, but to have fallen to less than 10 per cent by the end of the century. Thereafter there was little further change before the middle of the nineteenth century.[82]

The marked fall in age at marriage that occurred in eighteenth-century England appears to have been remarkably uniform both geographically and in socio-economic terms. The 26 reconstitution parishes comprise a wide spread of social and economic characteristics and were well scattered throughout England, yet their nuptiality

[78] Wrigley, 'Marriage, fertility and population growth', pp. 155–63.
[79] Wrigley and Schofield, *Population history of England*, tab. 7.29, p. 267.
[80] For the change in birth intervals over time, tab. 7.36, p. 447; for overall fecundity by age at marriage, tab. 7.14, pp. 390–1.
[81] Weir, 'Rather never than late'; Schofield, 'English marriage patterns revisited'.
[82] Schofield, 'English marriage patterns revisited', tab. 2 and pp. 8–14, and 'Family structure', fig. 8.8 and pp. 296–304. The estimates of proportions never marrying given in this paper would change somewhat with more recent estimates of age at marriage and of the gross reproduction rate. See, for example, the revised gross reproduction rates in app. 9, which reflect the application of generalised inverse projection to revised aggregative data.

history is relatively homogeneous. The timing and extent of the fall in marriage age was not greatly different between, say, agricultural parishes and small market towns, nor between different regions. There is a hint that the fall was greater in parishes with a growing rural handicraft industry than elsewhere and perhaps that by the end of the parish register period women were marrying earlier in these parishes than in others, but uniformity rather than variety of experience is the predominant impression. When sufficient evidence has been accumulated from the reconstitution of other parishes, some of the modest differences visible in the 26 may appear to understate the true extent of variation by occupational type or region, but it is also possible that what now appear as modest differences may later be attributed to random factors.

It is unclear whether this finding, if confirmed, is damaging to the view that marriage behaviour was heavily influenced by economic opportunity.[83] On the one hand, it may be argued that, since the demand for labour and its remuneration was very different in different parts of the country and between different types of employment, it is surprising that this was not reflected in greater differences in the level and trend of marriage age across the country. On the other hand, the argument might be reversed. Since marriage behaviour was sensitive to economic influences, the absence of large interparochial differences in nuptiality may reflect a relatively uniform and efficient labour market in a country where the scale of migration was sufficient to equalise opportunity. On this view, the very different rates of growth of population in the different parishes might prove to be the mechanism which indirectly secured homogeneity in marriage characteristics.

[83] It is opportune in this context to mention that a number of tabulations of marriage data were made that have not been reported in this chapter because they revealed little of interest, and pressure on space suggested that no reference should be made to them. Occasionally, however, a negative finding can be illuminating. One such arose from a tabulation intended to bring to light any seasonality in age at first marriage. The seasonality of marriage totals was striking and has long been remarked. It was examined at length in Wrigley and Schofield, *The population history of England* (esp. pp. 298–305). Since the marked seasonal peak of marriages in the late autumn was closely related to the annual round of hiring fairs for servants in husbandry, and consisted largely of the marriages of those who had decided to strike out independently as married couples, it seemed possible that the mean age of brides and grooms marrying in this season of the year might differ from those marrying at other times. But there is nothing in the reconstitution data to suggest that mean ages at first marriage for either sex were any different in October and November from other months, nor indeed that any other months were consistently different from the overall pattern. (The closeness of the link between leaving service and marrying is described in Kussmaul, *Servants in husbandry*, pp. 83–5.)

Reinforcing this uncertainty is the difficulty of securing information about proportions never marrying of equal accuracy to that about age at marriage. The work of Weir and Schofield has shown good reason to suppose that age at marriage changed little during the seventeenth century, but that there were major changes in the proportions never marrying, and that in the eighteenth century the reverse was true. But estimates of the proportions never marrying are, in a sense, a residual derived from information about estimates of the gross reproduction rate, the mean age at maternity, and the mean age at marriage, and are therefore inherently less dependable than a variable that can be observed directly.[84] Levels of nuptiality in a population are the joint function of age at marriage and proportions marrying, and any discussion that takes into account only one of these two variables is inevitably incomplete. This is particularly true of a situation in which the relationship between the two itself changes radically, as appears to have happened in early modern England. Indeed, identifying the reason for this change may well be the key to a satisfactory understanding of the links between economic pressures and marriage decisions.[85]

Much remains to be done if the history of English nuptiality in the early modern period is to be fully elucidated. Enough is known, however, to make it certain that during the 'long' eighteenth century (between the last quarter of the seventeenth century and the first quarter of the nineteenth century) the scale of the fall in age at first marriage for women was sufficient to account for a large fraction of the acceleration in the population growth rate that occurred during this period, a period during which the intrinsic growth rate rose from zero to the highest level ever experienced in England, about 1.75 per cent per annum.[86] A history of English population in this period in which nuptiality did not figure prominently would resemble the proverbial production of *Hamlet* without the prince of Denmark.

[84] Weir, 'Rather never than late'; Schofield, 'English marriage patterns revisited'.
[85] In this connection, see Goldstone, 'The demographic revolution in England', and Schofield, 'British population change, 1700–1871'.
[86] Wrigley and Schofield, *Population history of England*, fig. 7.11, p. 242.

6

Mortality

It has long been conventional to subdivide the description and analysis of demographic behaviour under three main heads: fertility, mortality, and nuptiality (a fourth head, migration, is also frequently employed, but has a more uncertain status). Of these, in historical studies, it was mortality which for long attracted the lion's share of attention. There was no analogue in the comparatively even tenor of annual totals of births and marriages for the dramatic, unpredictable surges of mortality which might sweep away a tenth, a quarter, a third of the entire population of a community in a matter of weeks. Pestilence, famine, and the ravages associated with war could bring with them suffering and loss on a scale that challenges even the most vivid imagination and eloquent pen to describe in terms that can do justice to the magnitude of the human disaster involved. Such episodes were not only poignant and eye-catching but were often taken to have dominated population trends.

Until comparatively recently, moreover, both general theorising about population behaviour in pre-industrial societies and also the nature of the techniques available for analysing historical data tended to cause attention to be focused on mortality.[1] It was once commonplace to assume without question, for example, that it was a fall in mortality that initiated the series of related changes often labelled the demographic transition.[2] Population growth rates were envisaged as rising in the later

---

[1] Two of the most influential writers who have emphasised mortality as the key to understanding many aspects of population change and also wider historical change are McNeill, *Plagues and peoples*, and, more trenchantly if less convincingly, McKeown, who summarised his views in *The modern rise of population*.

[2] This view took root in the wake of the writings of Thompson and especially Notestein. There is an excellent description and critique of their views in Woods, *Theoretical population geography*, pp. 159–73. See also, for example, Notestein, 'Population: the long view'.

eighteenth century because of declining death rates, followed only after a considerable time-lag by a fall in birth rates, thereby provoking the huge rise in numbers experienced almost throughout Europe during the nineteenth century. Flinn provided an ingenious and appealing variant to this general thesis by suggesting that in its early stages the mortality fall occurred because of the attenuation of the severity of crisis mortality. The periodic surges in mortality became less frequent and less violent, thus reducing the overall level of death rates, even though the base level may initially have remained unchanged.[3]

Technical constraints also tended to foster work on mortality since before the development of methods such as family reconstitution and inverse projection short-term changes in demographic rates were far easier to estimate than long-term changes. Since the size of the population at risk could not vary much in the course of a year, it was safe to assume that a tripling in the number of deaths must indicate a comparable rise in mortality rates, whereas a tripling in the number of deaths over a period of a century was perfectly consistent with an unchanging level of mortality, or even with a decrease. In the absence of means of estimating the population at risk as well as the total of events, long-term change in demographic rates was hard to measure. The parish registers were a ubiquitous and tolerably reliable source of information about totals of events but there were few census-like sources to provide information about population totals. It was almost inevitable that what was accessible should be assumed to be important. Mortality crises were visible and mensurable. Other aspects of demographic behaviour were not. It was tempting, therefore, to assume that mortality, and especially crisis mortality, was the prime regulator of population behaviour as a whole.

Such an approach to the understanding of population change and the functioning of the demographic system was also supported by the popularity of a broadly 'Malthusian' paradigm. Inasmuch as Malthus has frequently been understood to have believed that population must always tend to outstrip available resources, thus creating a tension between production and reproduction that could only be resolved by a periodic pruning back of numbers through mortality surges, it was attractive to think in terms of populations perpetually teetering on the edge of a Malthusian precipice over which the most vulnerable were doomed to plunge from time to time when the advent of a severe epidemic or the occurrence of a run of poor harvests provoked an abrupt rise in the number of deaths. If, as Malthus had suggested, populations, when unhindered by resource constraints, tend to rise

[3] Flinn, 'The stabilisation of mortality'.

exponentially whereas output could at best rise by arithmetic progression, it was natural to believe that periodic mortality crises were the
means by which the two were kept in balance.[4]

The fruits of the deployment of new techniques of using parish
register data and of more searching statistical investigations of the
relationship between price changes and mortality fluctuations have
been such as to force a reconsideration of many old verities.[5] Among
west European populations the positive check, as Malthus himself came
to realise, was often less influential than the preventive check in
effecting an accommodation between population and resources.[6]
Though a fall in mortality was often dominant, the acceleration in
population growth which began in the later eighteenth century and
continued throughout the nineteenth century was not always due to a
combination of reduced mortality and an unchanging fertility level.[7]
When severe mortalities occurred they were often unconnected with the
harvest failure or the pressure of population on resources.[8] Adam Smith
had taken it for granted that changes in the supply of labour, or, in other
words, population trends, were determined by the necessary tendency
for mortality to fall and for fertility to rise when real wages improved

[4] 'Population, when unchecked, increases in a geometrical ratio. Subsistence increases
only in an arithmetical ratio. A slight acquaintance with numbers will show the
immensity of the first power in comparison of the second . . . This implies a strong and
constantly operating check on population from the difficulty of subsistence. This
difficulty must fall somewhere; and must necessarily be severely felt by a large portion
of mankind.' Malthus, *Essay on population* (1798), p. 9.

[5] English data suggest, for example, that harvest fluctuations and the associated price
changes explain only about a sixth of the annual variance in mortality, a smaller figure
than the comparable statistic for fertility. Wrigley and Schofield, *Population history of
England*, p. 371 (the chapter in which these data are presented was written by Prof. R.
Lee).

[6] In the sixth edition of the *Essay on population*, the last to be published during his lifetime,
Malthus conducted in book II an extensive review of the checks to population in the
various states of Europe, having previously conducted a similar review of other parts of
the world in book I. He concluded, 'In comparing the state of society which has been
considered in this second book with that which formed the subject of the first, I think it
appears that in modern Europe the positive checks to population prevail less, and the
preventive checks more than in past times, and in the more uncivilized parts of the
world.' He went on to identify delay in marriage as 'the most powerful of the checks,
which in modern Europe keep down the population to the level of the means of
subsistence'. Malthus, *Essay on population* (1826), p. 315.

[7] See, for example, Wrigley and Schofield, *Population history of England*, fig. 7.13, p. 246.

[8] The debate about the role of crises of subsistence in influencing population trends has
been most intense and extended in France, a debate often regarded as having sprung
from a seminal article by Meuvret (Meuvret, 'Les crises de subsistance'). For a summary
of the present state of the debate, see Cabourdin, 'Qu'est-ce qu'une crise?'. See also
Galloway, 'Basic patterns'; Walter and Schofield, 'Famine, disease and crisis mortality'.

with the opposite occurring when they fell.[9] A growing body of empirical studies of mortality began to call in question any simple and predictable relationship between economic and demographic trends, and to do so even more clearly for mortality than for fertility.

It has become necessary to view mortality in a different light. Its links with economic conditions were complex and sometimes took an opposite form from that once thought universal, and it was clearly heavily affected by other aspects of social structure and personal behaviour which had little connection with economic conditions. Moreover, many important mortality changes were the result of factors apparently exogenous to any aspect of the structure and functioning of human society and economy, such as the advent of new or the disappearance of old pathogens, or climatic change. With the development of a range of models purporting to capture the nature of the relationships between demographic, economic, and social variables in the past, it has become common to attempt to distinguish between endogenous and exogenous influences, and to make the distinction central to the working of the system as a whole. Exogenous influences can be made to 'drive' a system whose functioning may remain difficult to explain in their absence.[10] But it can prove teasingly difficult to establish a convincing distinction between endogenous and exogenous variables.[11]

A full discussion of these issues is beyond the scope of this chapter, but a brief survey of some of them may provide an appropriate background to the description of mortality levels and trends.

Mortality and economic circumstances

As a first approximation to the truth it might seem axiomatic to suppose that the higher the output of goods and services per head achieved by a society, the lower would be the level of mortality. A well-nourished, well-clad, well-housed population that can also afford wood for heating and cooking must surely experience a lower level of mortality than one that lacks adequate food, clothing, shelter, and fuel. Since health was so greatly affected by the abundance or scarcity of these four necessities of life the assertion seems to brook no argument. Nor indeed is it reasonable to demur if the claim is made in isolation. But a rising level of

---

[9] He remarked in the course of a pithy discussion of this issue that 'the demand for men, like that for any other commodity, necessarily regulates the production of men'. It was Smith's view that this ensured a broadly constant level of real wages corresponding to the conventional subsistence level in that community. Smith, *Wealth of nations*, I, p. 89.

[10] Lee, 'Population homeostasis'.   [11] Smith, 'Influences exogènes et endogènes'.

prosperity was often so strongly associated with other changes with very different implications for mortality that the relationship between economic advance and mortality trends in the past is best regarded as uncertain and ambiguous.

A number of closely interlinked features of pre-industrial economies in which real incomes were rising served to counteract the benefits which flowed from an increased ability to purchase goods and services. Rising real incomes meant a change in the structure of demand away from necessities and above all food in favour of manufactured goods and services. This in turn reduced the share of agriculture in total employment and increased the share of secondary and tertiary industry. Employment in the two latter forms of activity, however, normally implied a shift of population from country to town, and the urban environment was usually far less healthy than a rural setting. This was a topic that attracted the interest of William Farr in the mid-nineteenth century and led him to propose an empirical law linking the level of mortality to population density. In deriving this relationship he was, of course, using data collected by the Registrar-General in the middle decades of the nineteenth century.[12] On the assumption that Farr's relationship was broadly true in earlier periods, it suggests that if a move from a rural setting to an urban setting implied a 50-fold increase in the prevailing density of population it would mean moving to an environment in which the prevailing level of mortality was 60 per cent higher; a 250-fold increase in density would imply a rise of over 90 per cent; while for a 1000-fold increase the corresponding rise would be about 130 per cent. Moves from country to town often did imply increases in the ambient density of population of these orders of magnitude or greater, and the contrast between rural and urban death rates suggests that Farr's law may have 'saved the phenomena' quite effectively for earlier centuries than the nineteenth.[13]

---

[12] Farr had initially favoured an empirical law linking the level of mortality to the 6th root of the density of population, but later, with the benefit of data drawn from 593 registration districts covering the whole country excluding London, he suggested the 12th root as capturing the link best. However, though he termed his formula the 12th root, in fact it was approximately the 8th root, $x^{0.12}$. This formula captured the relationship in mid-nineteenth-century England quite satisfactorily when the registration districts were divided into seven groups by density of population (ranging between 166 and 65823 persons per square mile), and it was this formula which was used in the illustrative calculation in the text above. Farr, *Vital statistics*, pp. 165, 174–5.

[13] The overall density of population in early modern England was about 100 persons per square mile, or about 0.15 persons per acre. The density of population in London within the Walls at the end of the seventeenth century was about 185–190 persons per acre, or rather more than 1000 times greater. The acreage of London within the Walls is given as

The reasons for the positive association beween population density and mortality are not far to seek. A contaminated water supply is the vehicle by which many pathogens find a means of entry into the body. Water-borne diseases included some that were major killers in their own right, and many more that weakened their victims and left them a relatively easy prey to diseases that made their entry in other ways. At urban levels of population density it is both difficult and relatively expensive to ensure a supply of pure water, even when the danger of impure supplies is known. Where the link was not understood and where the disposal of sewage and other waste matter was haphazard, water-borne diseases were likely to be prevalent.

Even if the water supply had been pure, however, urban living conditions were likely to produce higher mortality than country life. Infectious and contagious diseases spread readily in large and tightly packed populations. The most destructive epidemic diseases recurred more frequently in towns than in the country, and might be endemic in urban settings though only occasional visitors to rural areas. The universal ailments of childhood, measles, whooping cough, scarlet fever, and the like, attacked children at younger ages in an urban setting than in rural areas and were more likely to prove fatal as a result. Since most serious diseases were either endemic or returned frequently in towns but recurred only at longer intervals elsewhere, the same prosperity that boosted town growth simultaneously tended to increase mortality rates, especially among children and recent immigrants from the countryside.

Associated with the changes which altered the balance between rural and urban population totals, there was another change brought about by any increase in prosperity with unfavourable implications for the death rate. Higher purchasing power meant more trade, and more trade meant a wider and more vigorous circulation of people. More contact meant greater risk of infection and contagion. So far from health and wealth moving hand in hand, they could easily march in opposite directions. The importance of this apparently perverse effect of an increasingly sophisticated economy was demonstrated several decades ago by Utterström in an article in which he showed that western Sweden, though remote, poor, and exposed to periodic famine by its isolation and primitive agriculture, was nevertheless characterised by lower death rates than those to be found in the east of the country where there were prosperous towns, incomes were higher, communications

370 acres in the *1831 Census*, Enumeration abstract, I, p. 372. The population of London within the Walls in 1695 was estimated as almost 70 000 by Glass in *London inhabitants within the Walls 1695*, p. xx.

were relatively good, and food shortages could be far more easily mitigated by import and exchange.[14]

Subsequent studies have often provided further illustrations of the phenomenon to which Utterström drew attention. For example, the remarkable healthiness of many frontier settlements in colonial North America in spite of their comparatively primitive material circumstances was as much a function of the infrequency of contact with the outside world as of plentiful food supply.[15] The history of the parish of Hartland in a remote part of north Devon provides a small illustration of the same point. The death rate in Hartland was low throughout the parish register period and the parish enjoyed a remarkable freedom from epidemic outbreaks.[16] In the pre-industrial world there was a price to be paid for economic progress. Standards of living might rise but life itself be abbreviated in the process.[17]

The severity of the 'urban' penalty should not be underestimated. Rough-and-ready calculations suggest that in the later seventeenth century London was absorbing up to half of the natural increase of population occurring elsewhere in England.[18] Several thousand young people were needed each year simply to offset the surplus of deaths over births occasioned by the unhealthiness of the metropolis, and several thousand more to enable the city to grow. The city was not merely a demographic sump, but a growing sump. Even in the absence of urban growth, however, the impact of its urban sector on the demography of a country could be striking. De Vries has shown that the burden imposed on the rest of the country by the mortality surpluses occurring in the cities had much to do with the failure of the Dutch population to grow in the eighteenth century, following the huge rise in urban population in the late sixteenth and seventeenth centuries.[19] That

---

[14] Utterström, 'Some population problems in pre-industrial Sweden'.

[15] Much evidence is summarised in Dobson, 'Mortality gradients'.

[16] Wrigley, *Population and history*, pp. 70–4: see also tab. 6.16, pp. 270–1.

[17] If the 'standard of living' is taken to reflect not earnings in a unit interval of time (such as wages paid per week or per year) but earnings over a lifespan, it is plain that it may rise on one measure while falling on the other. A rise in mortality may more than cancel out a rise in the real wage conventionally measured. This and cognate issues are explored in Jackson, 'Inequality of incomes'.   [18] Wrigley, 'London's importance', pp. 46–8.

[19] De Vries, *The Dutch rural economy in the golden age*, pp. 113–8. Where there is large-scale international migration, of course, any such calculation becomes much more complicated.

The issue of the characteristics of urban demography in the early modern period, and particularly the question of the interpretation of mortality data, has proved controversial, however. Sharlin gave a stimulating new turn to the debate 20 years ago: Sharlin, 'Natural decrease in early modern cities'. See also van der Woude, 'Population developments in the northern Netherlands'.

large clusters of population usually suffered from high mortality rates is clear. Whether there was a relatively smooth gradient in mortality rates with, say, market towns unhealthier than villages, and villages in turn less healthy than the hamlets or scattered farmsteads, or whether, alternatively, there were threshold levels of population density at which mortality suddenly worsened is less clear, but a steady gradient linked to density seems probable.[20] Supporting evidence for this view may be found in an exercise reported in the *Population history of England*. In the 404 parishes from which data were drawn, 44 per cent of the variation in crisis mortality was attributable to the population size of the parishes. While this finding may contain a spurious element arising from the way in which mortality crises were identified, it is likely that the greater density of settlement and the greater exposure to infection associated with life in the larger parishes caused population size to be a prime factor in determining the incidence of crisis mortality.[21]

The list of factors associated with economic development which may have a bearing on mortality might be extended almost indefinitely. They are too numerous to be treated exhaustively. One further preliminary point should be made, however. A distinction between endogenous and exogenous influences on mortality is often made for analytical purposes and acting in this way has an attractive simplicity. But it may prove difficult to maintain the distinction unambiguously. Changes in the disease environment, for example, such as the advent of new and dangerous infections like syphilis or cholera, are in one sense exogenous changes in relation to the economy. Their appearance and any effect that they may have on mortality are not an aspect of the functioning of the economy in the same sense as fluctuations in the level of real wages. But the appearance of a new disease may be the indirect effect of economic growth because the development of trade will lead as surely to the exchange of pathogens as to the exchange of goods. It would be difficult to argue, for example, that the advent of syphilis to Europe from the Americas was an exogenous influence on mortality while at the same time treating the increase in agricultural output due to the introduction of the potato as endogenous to the economic system.

None of the foregoing is intended as a denial that economic conditions affected mortality levels powerfully in the past. An undernour-

[20] The definition of what should be understood by 'density' is, however, problematic. The number of people per inhabited room, the number per house or other residential unit, and the number per acre may all in various ways influence disease transmission and so morbidity and mortality rates. It is quite possible for there to be severe overcrowding in the first sense of the term even in a sparsely populated rural area, and vice versa.
[21] Wrigley and Schofield, *Population history of England*, pp. 692–3.

ished population fell victim to disease more readily than one with access to an abundance of food. Damp, cramped housing led to ill health and early death. Where fuel was beyond the pockets of the poor and in consequence food was not well cooked and houses went unheated in winter, suffering and disease were widespread. A man or woman clad in verminous rags and forced to go barefoot was exposed to the risk of disease and hypothermia to a far greater degree than another who went well shod and warmly clothed.[22] For the individual it was better to be wealthy than to be poor if one wished to live long and to be untroubled by infection. But for society as a whole the balance of advantage was harder to strike. Increasing wealth bore an ambiguous relationship to improved mortality.

Mortality, social conventions, and life styles

No less complex than the web of linkages connecting economic circumstances and mortality in the past were the comparable effects of social conventions and the habits and attitudes with which they were associated. Life styles were then at least as influential as they now are in determining exposure to injury, illness, impairment, and death. Aristocratic families in England possessed the means to secure all manner of material benefits and personal services but expectation of life at birth among the aristocracy appears to have lagged behind that of the population as a whole until well into the eighteenth century.[23] Although the changes which then caused an increasing difference in life expectancy to develop are obscure, it is far more likely that they had to do with life style than that they were the result of a further increase in the relative income gap between the elite and the rest of the population.

The importance of social conventions in relation to mortality levels is

---

[22] For discussions of the types of disease whose virulence was increased by malnutrition and of those where this was not the case, see Rotberg and Rabb, eds., *Hunger and history*. This book was the upshot of a conference held in Bellagio. There is a convenient table summarising the views of the participants about the degree to which nutrition influences susceptibility to different diseases on p. 307. The contributed pieces by McKeown and Scrimshaw are of particular interest. See also Livi-Bacci, *Population and nutrition*, and Walter and Schofield, 'Famine, disease and crisis mortality', pp. 17–21.

[23] According to Hollingsworth's analysis, any increase in expectation of life at birth among the British peerage was modest and uncertain until the cohort born in 1725–49 and was only clear-cut in the following cohort, born in 1750–74: Hollingsworth, *The demography of the British peerage*, tabs. 42 and 43, pp. 56–7. Expectation of life in the English population as a whole was higher than among the peerage in the seventeenth and early eighteenth centuries, and only began to fall behind the peerage towards the end of the eighteenth century: tab. 6.27, p. 308.

especially clear in the case of infant mortality. Infant mortality rates in pre-industrial European communities varied very widely, roughly between 100 and 400 per 1000. In consequence, infant deaths were a substantial, sometimes a very large proportion of all deaths, and the level of infant mortality exercised a powerful influence on expectation of life as a whole.[24] Infant mortality today is frequently employed as a key measure of the degree of backwardness of different groups or societies. Whatever the merits of this assumption in the contemporary world, it is doubtful whether it can be justified for earlier periods because the level of infant mortality was so heavily affected by breastfeeding customs. Where breastfeeding was universal and pro-longed, infant mortality was normally quite low: where it was brief, and especially where children were weaned at birth, it was much higher.[25] The alternatives to breast milk were much inferior nutritionally. Infants weaned early in life were very likely to ingest pathogens along with their food, and at the same time lacked the protection provided by the transfer of antibodies in breast milk available to those who were still suckled.

It is scarcely surprising that there were large differences in the level of infant mortality between areas where breastfeeding was normally continued for 18 months or more, which appears to have been the case in early modern England,[26] and those where it was confined to the first few weeks of life or was not practised at all. But whether or not mothers fed their children at the breast and for how long breastfeeding continued were matters of habit and convention. Breastfeeding might be more universal and more prolonged in poor, remote, and 'backward' popula-

---

[24] Where infant mortality rates were as high as 350–400 per 1000, and assuming that the population was not actually decreasing, it is obvious that infant deaths must represent a minimum of 35 to 40 per cent of all deaths. Where such levels obtained in periods of population increase still higher percentages must have prevailed. Knodel's work on Bavaria in the nineteenth century suggests that such high percentages were not simply a theoretical possibility: Knodel, 'Infant mortality', tab. 1, p. 299. Even where the infant mortality rate was at a modest level, say 150 per 1000, and assuming that births outnumbered deaths in the ratio of 4 to 3, infant deaths would have been 20 per cent of all deaths.

[25] Knodel, *Demographic behavior in the past*, pp. 395–405. Knodel concludes, p. 405, 'In brief, the evidence relating to infant mortality and birth intervals points clearly to a substantial physiological impact related to breastfeeding and the associated period of postpartum non-susceptibility. . . Factors other than the physiological impact through breastfeeding may also operate, but these are more difficult to determine and are unlikely to be of major importance.' For a review of this issue and the literature relating to it, Huffman and Lamphere, 'Breastfeeding performance and child survival'.

[26] See pp. 489–92 for indirect evidence that the average length of breastfeeding in the reconstitution parishes was about 19 months.

tions than elsewhere, and in consequence levels of infant mortality might either bear no consistent relationship with the degree of economic or social 'advance' in a population, or the relationship might be the reverse of that suggested by conventional arguments. Within the same community, indeed, if women in elite groups were more reluctant to suckle than their social inferiors, their children might well experience a poorer chance of surviving to their first birthday as a result.[27]

Other customary practices also exercised a powerful influence on mortality. Childbed rituals provide a good example. For both mother and child the dangers of infection were deeply affected by such customs, ranging from the mode of severance of the umbilical cord, with its associated risk of tetanus, to much less specific hazards or benefits associated with the feeding of the mother, the length and severity of her confinement, the number and nature of those present during delivery, early suckling practices, and so on.[28] Many other social customs, however, influenced mortality, perhaps more importantly than vivid, but occasional events like confinement. The manner in which food was prepared and eaten, for example, influenced the risk of infection by certain types of pathogens and might play a major role in deciding whether a diet was well balanced or not. Many such customs, though perceived as stemming from, say, religious precepts, may reflect the unconscious effects of trial and error with what was beneficial or deleterious to health, continued over many generations, but whatever their origins, their existence influenced the physical well being of the population.

Other examples of personal or community customs which influenced mortality could be multiplied almost indefinitely. Alcohol consumption is a convenient illustration of the point. Heavy alcohol consumption can exact a severe toll in morbidity and mortality. Muslim society was free from this problem since alcohol was forbidden to believers. At the other extreme, there can be little doubt that a combination of the availability of

[27] For example, in Nedertorneå in northern Sweden the infant mortality of farmers was higher than that of proletarians throughout the first two-thirds of the nineteenth century. At the other extreme of the country the same was also true of Fleninge, though here the overall level of infant mortality was far lower, barely a third of the rate in Nedertorneå during the first half of the century; Brändström and Sundin, 'Infant mortality in a changing society', tab. 1, p. 77. It is of interest to note that Knodel concluded that in the German parishes which he studied in the eighteenth and nineteenth centuries, 'all social strata within a village appeared to have shared a more or less common risk of child loss', because local breastfeeding customs were common to all groups; Knodel, *Demographic behavior in the past*, p. 447. For a general survey of infant feeding and weaning, see Fildes, *Breasts, bottles and babies*.

[28] Wilson, 'Childbirth', and 'Participant or patient?'.

very cheap gin of dubious quality and the absence of any effective social sanction on heavy drinking was a contributory factor to the strikingly high level of death rates in London in the second quarter of the eighteenth century.[29] The *surmortalité* of men in the middle years of life attracted much comment in nineteenth-century France. This appears to have been due to their drinking habits. Alcoholism has remained a major cause of sex differential mortality in France.[30] Men also pay a heavy penalty for smoking more than women.

It is a matter of opinion whether the behaviour of an early modern community under a perceived threat from disease is most conveniently treated as an element in its range of social conventions, an aspect of its political organisation, or as a separate category of social activity to be labelled medicine and public health. The imposition of any modern categorisation of behaviour on to the past is debatable. If contemporaries regarded an epidemic visitation as a manifestation of divine displeasure at their falling away from the light, for example, it is artificial to analyse the episode without regard to their conception of its origin. In whatever manner such behaviour is categorised, however, its significance in influencing mortality is clear.

Nor can there be any doubt that the increasing willingness of governments to attempt to deal with some kinds of epidemic disease by administrative action played a part in reducing the toll of some of the major killing diseases. Methods of enforcing quarantine regulations and of establishing *cordons sanitaires* became increasingly effective. This was notably true in the case of plague.[31] At a later date when inoculation became known as an effective method of combating smallpox, many parishes considered it sensible to pay for a general inoculation from the poor rates as a protective measure for the community as a whole.[32] A change in perception of the propriety of attempting to control disease was no less important than the power to do so. Inoculation against smallpox affords an unusually straightforward illustration of this point, but such a change operating more diffusely probably influenced many aspects of morbidity and mortality towards the end of the parish register period.

---

[29] Landers' work suggests that the crude death rate in London in the 20-year period 1730–49 was 47.3 per 1000; Landers, *Death and the metropolis*, tab. 5.6, p. 175.

[30] See, for example, the data relating to death rates caused by alcoholism and cirrhosis of the liver for men and women in France between 1925 and 1978 in Vallin and Meslé, *Les causes de décès*, figs. 37 and 38, pp. 190–1.

[31] Slack, *The impact of plague*, pt 3, and esp. pp. 313–26.

[32] Razzell, *The conquest of smallpox*, esp. ch. 5.

The reconstitution data and techniques of analysis

Reconstitution data possess both strengths and weaknesses for the study of mortality. Their strengths will become clear as the tabulated results are presented. Three of their limitations merit a brief preliminary review.

First, there is a significant difference in the techniques used to estimate infant and child mortality on the one hand, and adult mortality on the other. Almost all children whose birth is recorded on FRFs remain in observation during the first year of life and, though the proportion in observation thereafter steadily declines as families move elsewhere, coverage remains substantial throughout childhood. Very few children left the parental household before the age of 10, so that if there is evidence that a family continued to reside in the parish it is highly probable that its children were present until that age. Movement away from the parental household into service caused a few children to leave home between the ages of 10 and 15, but there seems good reason to treat the mortality rates for the age group 10–4, measured from FRFs, as dependable in spite of this.[33] Infant and child mortality can therefore be captured by following the classic rules expounded by Henry, though in the knowledge that with the elapse of time each family was increasingly likely to have left the parish and in so doing to have reduced the proportion of a given birth cohort which remains in observation.

The measurement of adult mortality requires the use of a different technique and remains somewhat more problematic. Those who remained unmarried escape the net altogether. Their deaths were, of course, recorded in parish registers just like those of any other members of the Anglican communion, but since there is no way of establishing how long an unmarried person had been resident in the parish before death, still less of measuring the period of residence of

---

[33] If this were not so, the agreement beween reconstitution rates and those drawn from model life tables would be unlikely to be so good. See below pp. 261–3. Very few deaths occurred in the age group 10–4, which was normally the age group with the lowest death rate. There is only a limited amount of information about the percentage of children still living with their parents by age of child for English communities in the past. Wall quotes data from five communities between the late seventeenth and mid-nineteenth centuries. On average 89 per cent of boys and 93 per cent of girls aged 10–4 were living with their parents. Some of those not with their parents were no doubt with grandparents and therefore often still in the same community. However, he warns that the nature of the lists may have caused the percentages to be overstated. Wall, 'Age at leaving home', tab. 2, p. 190. If there were youngsters of this age who died while out in service, however, it may well have been normal to take them to their home parish for burial.

someone who lived for a time in the parish but then left it to die elsewhere (whose period of residence should therefore be included in any total of years lived in observation), no rates relating to the unmarried can be calculated. The position is more promising for those who were baptised in the parish and subsequently married there, and whose ages at marriage are therefore known. If, for example, such individuals always thereafter remained in the parish until their deaths, it would be a straightforward matter to treat them as entering into observation on marriage and tabulate years lived and deaths occurring in each successive age group. Accurate mortality rates could then be derived at least for those who were born and subsequently married in a parish.

Migration complicates the picture, however. Those who left their parish of birth to settle elsewhere are lost to view. The larger the proportion of cases where migration has led to a missing date of death, the greater the importance of finding a way of dealing with the problem which does not lead either to a biased estimate of adult mortality on the one hand, or to an estimate with unacceptably wide margins of error on the other. It is always possible to identify a date up to which the person in question was resident in the parish even if this is no later than the date of the marriage, but when thereafter death took place is unknown in the case of migrants from the parish.

Several methods of making the best of the available data relating to married adults have been suggested. Henry proposed a solution that depended upon making maximum and minimum estimates of the level of mortality. For each individual whose date of death was unknown he established the latest date at which he or she was still alive, and, where known, the earliest date before which he or she had died. The former gave the most pessimistic solution to the question of when the individual had died (that is that he had died immediately after the last known recorded event relating to him). The latter gave the most optimistic possibility: that the individual had died immediately before this date. If no such terminal date were known, the individual was assumed to have lived to 80 years. Since the latter, in particular, is clearly a limiting possibility rather than a realistic assumption, Henry also suggested a way of reducing the gap between the maximum and minimum estimates to more plausible limits.

Henry restricted the population included in his analysis to those who were born and had married in the parish, and, in the case of women, restricted the sample further to those who married a man who had been born in the parish. In parishes where migration was comparatively rare the resulting maximum and minimum estimates might differ only slightly.[34] The higher the prevailing level of migration, however, the greater the margin of uncertainty.

The most important advance in estimating adult mortality since Henry's original discussion was made by Blum.[35] Like Henry his analysis is confined to natives of a parish who also marry in it. Blum approached the problem by confining his attention to mortality taking place within the parish. His innovation lay in focusing attention upon the estimation of the total period spent at risk in the parish *both* by those who died there *and* by those who died elsewhere. In other words, he drew attention to the fact that it is essential to quantify the time spent in the parish before their departure by those who subsequently leave, since this represents a part of the collective period of risk experienced both by 'stayers' and by 'leavers' to which the deaths of 'stayers' should be related in order to calculate a parish mortality rate. Migrants from the parish are at risk to die as long as they stay in the parish, and mortality will be overestimated if such exposure is ignored. It is straightforward to calculate the period from marriage to the date of the event that last testifies to the presence of an individual in the parish, but account must also be taken of the further period of residence which will occur before departure takes place. The nature of Blum's method and the methods used to generate the adult mortality estimates reported in this chapter are described in detail in appendix 6.

In brief, Blum's solution to the estimation of maximum exposure was to assume that the subsequent family history of migrants was like that of those who remained in the parish until their death. If a migrant had not moved, further events relating to his or her family would have been recorded according to the pattern that holds for those who did not migrate. The date at which the next such event would have occurred can be established by drawing upon information from the families of stayers and this date sets an upper limit to the period of exposure of the migrant. If he or she had not migrated, in other words, it is reasonable to suppose that a further event would have appeared on the relevant FRF just as it did on the FRFs of those who remained behind.[36]

Blum's method has recently been the subject of critical analysis by

---

[34] Henry, *Manuel de démographie historique*, pp. 113–6.
[35] Blum, 'Estimation de la mortalité locale'. (An English language version of this article was subsequently published; Blum, 'An estimate of local adult mortality based on family cards'.)
[36] The nature of the problem posed by migrants to the estimation of adult mortality is succinctly described in Ruggles, 'Migration, marriage, and mortality', esp. pp. 514–21, where a range of possible solutions is also evaluated.

Ruggles. Ruggles attempted to show by simulation that in places where emigration levels were low Blum's method of estimating maximum exposure to produce an estimate of minimum mortality could actually result in estimates of male mortality that were slightly *higher* than the true level.[37] The nature of Ruggles's critique is also summarised in appendix 6.

The second problem associated with the use of family reconstitution data relates to the relatively small number of parishes in the data set. If, for example, one wished to test the empirical law relating population density to mortality suggested by William Farr, it would be desirable to have a much larger sample of parishes representing the whole spectrum of settlement sizes and densities. The very small number of parishes in the size categories that are represented precludes confident generalisation. *Mutatis mutandis* this problem arises in many contexts.

Thirdly, a cognate difficulty arises from the small number of deaths upon which mortality rates in some age groups are based, especially where rates relating to quinquennia or, still more, to even shorter periods are concerned. The behaviour of the annual totals of deaths in the reconstitution data set bears a close resemblance to national patterns, as we have already noted.[38] In the reconstitution parishes the annual totals of deaths recorded on FRFs was substantial (normally ranging between 350 and 600 a year in groups 2 and 3, for example), but the totals of deaths where the *age* of the deceased is known was substantially smaller, and the numbers in particular age groups much smaller still. For example, it is clear from aggregative data that the year 1729 was a year of high mortality.[39] Reconstitution data show that 1729 was a year in which infant mortality was somewhat higher than normal (the infant rate for legitimate children was 225 per 1000 compared with an average for the 1720s of 193 per 1000). They also suggest, intriguingly, that mortality in the age group 10–4 was unusually low (20.3 per 1000 compared with 23.1 per 1000 in the decade of the 1720s). But it would be unwise to suppose that equal confidence can be placed in the two rates, since the latter estimate is based on a total of only 4 deaths whereas the infant mortality estimate is based on 108 deaths. This makes the discussion of short-term changes in age-specific mortality problematic, though for longer periods, with larger totals of deaths, the difficulty largely disappears.

---

[37] Ibid., pp. 515–7.   [38] See above pp. 63–7.

[39] National aggregative data suggest that the crude death rate was 44.7 per 1000 in 1729 compared with a decadal average for the 1720s of 32.8 per 1000; Wrigley and Schofield, *Population history of England*, tab. A3.3, p. 533.

Infant and child mortality

Overall patterns of infant and child mortality

It has long been conventional to describe infant and child mortality by dividing the early years of life into four main age groups, 0–1, 1–4, 5–9, and 10–4 years. The first two of these categories are sometimes then further subdivided: infant mortality in order, say, to distinguish neonatal mortality from mortality later in the first year of life; and early childhood mortality between the ages of 1 and 5 because rates in the early part of this age period are much higher than those towards its end. Since the rates for the individual years of life in the two later age groups are normally very similar it is less common to subdivide them.

Such conventional partitioning of infant and child mortality makes a convenient beginning, but it is important to bear in mind its arbitrary nature. There might be more in common between mortality trends in months 6–11 and 12–7, for example, than between months 0–5 and 6–11, if, say, weaning took place between 9 and 15 months. Or again, the effects of the emergence or disappearance of a destructive disease which has a strongly age-specific incidence may be muffled by the normal age divisions but appear more clearly if different divisions are constructed *ad hoc*. We shall therefore begin by following the conventional path, but later consider less common age divisions.

Table 6.1 shows infant and child mortality rates by decade and by quarter-century for the period 1580–1837. The data for 1580–99 were taken from group 1 parishes, those for 1600–1729 from group 2, those for 1730–89 from group 3, and for the remaining period from group 4. There was therefore a 'join' problem arising from the fact that the composition of the four groups differed.[40] Group 4 in particular contains a much smaller number of parishes than the other groups, and, although it is a subset of the parishes in group 3, it has only a limited overlap in membership with groups 1 and 2.[41] To construct a single decennial series from data from all four groups, adjustments to the raw rates were made by calculating the ratio between rates in any two adjacent groups during a 50-year overlap period and inflating or deflating rates accordingly. Group 2, which contains the largest number of parishes of any of the four groups, was used as a base and data drawn from other groups were adjusted to conform with group 2 in order to provide a

---

[40] See above pp. 24–8 for a full discussion of the composition of the groups and the rationale of constructing long-run series using data from all four groups.

[41] Banbury, Bottesford, Gedling, and Odiham were members of both group 1 and group 4. There was the same common membership of groups 2 and 4 with the addition of Shepshed.

Table 6.1 *Infant and child mortality ($1000q_x$): rates and years of exposure on which rates were based*

	Rates				Exposure			
	$_1q_0$	$_4q_1$	$_5q_5$	$_5q_{10}$	$_1q_0$	$_4q_1$	$_5q_5$	$_5q_{10}$
1580–9	168.4	87.5	38.4	15.4	3344	10516	8757	5281
1590–9	173.0	81.4	54.4	22.3	3793	10414	8447	5450
1600–9	165.4	90.7	46.2	30.3	4997	15171	11740	7587
1610–9	166.7	77.2	32.5	16.2	5175	16783	14191	8679
1620–9	153.4	81.0	33.3	19.8	5271	16925	14992	10186
1630–9	160.3	97.8	51.4	26.8	5695	18344	15029	10037
1640–9	150.2	108.1	48.9	32.5	5183	16492	13955	9481
1650–9	164.3	108.3	47.4	25.8	4840	15994	13939	9674
1660–9	169.3	112.7	52.8	27.5	4865	14910	12637	8708
1670–9	168.2	106.8	51.9	28.4	5114	16035	13137	8403
1680–9	201.9	130.0	58.7	31.4	5341	16213	13384	9136
1690–9	174.9	87.3	31.4	20.9	4880	15631	13637	8940
1700–9	174.1	98.0	42.3	27.1	5163	16372	13833	9409
1710–9	203.3	118.7	47.7	30.8	5256	16052	14085	10074
1720–9	193.3	121.3	44.2	23.1	5262	16744	13679	9224
1730–9	195.1	111.6	55.0	32.3	5217	15906	13394	9316
1740–9	186.6	122.9	52.3	25.0	5248	16539	15043	10732
1750–9	159.6	96.1	33.7	26.3	5772	18686	16755	11665
1760–9	165.6	112.8	41.2	23.6	6151	19182	16919	12438
1770–9	158.8	114.4	50.2	29.4	7005	21703	18531	12769
1780–9	163.4	108.2	32.7	24.7	7557	23382	19725	13509
1790–9	151.3	97.1	30.7	17.1	3167	10334	9442	6957
1800–9	136.6	95.0	21.0	16.6	3259	10549	9622	7220
1810–9	133.1	103.1	27.4	26.4	4162	12731	10505	7218
1820–9	144.7	103.0	32.8	25.4	4550	14489	12259	7530
1830–7	140.4	88.8	34.1	34.1	3233	10487	8648	5632
1580–99	170.7	84.5	46.3	18.9				
1600–24	165.2	81.6	36.1	22.7				
1625–49	153.3	100.0	48.0	27.0				
1650–74	166.7	111.1	50.9	26.1				
1675–99	185.4	107.6	45.9	27.4				
1700–24	190.7	107.9	46.4	27.0				
1725–49	190.8	121.0	50.1	28.4				
1750–74	162.8	107.3	41.1	25.7				
1775–99	156.7	107.7	34.7	22.7				
1800–24	136.0	98.0	25.7	20.0				
1825–37	144.1	98.3	34.7	34.7				

Note: legitimate births only.
Source: Cambridge Group reconstitutions.

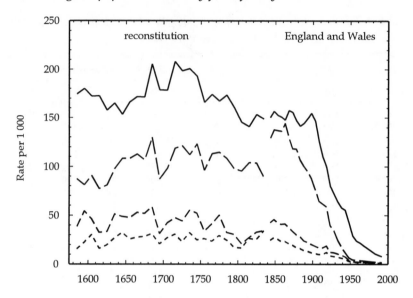

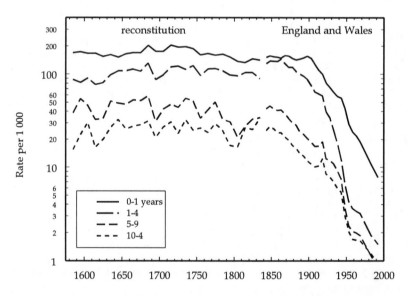

Figure 6.1   *Infant and child mortality (1000q_x): (upper panel, natural scale; lower*
panel, log scale)

Sources: reconstitution data: infant mortality, tab. 6.3; child mortality, tab. 6.1. England and
Wales data: *The Chester Beatty life tables* and its *Supplement*.

consistent series. A fuller description of the method used and some worked examples may be found in appendix 7. The number of years of exposure, on which the rates given in the left-hand top panel of table 6.1 were based, is shown in the right-hand top panel. The sharp increase in the totals of exposure between 1590–9 and 1600–9 and the even sharper fall between 1780–9 and 1790–9 occur because of a change from one group to another. Thus, the second change took place because there were far fewer parishes in group 4 than in group 3.[42] The absence of any sharp change between 1720–9 and 1730–9 shows that group 2 and group 3 were of very similar size.

Figure 6.1 shows the reconstitution decennial rates both on a natural scale (upper panel) and on a logarithmic scale (lower panel): the latter enables the relative scale of changes in the rates to be more readily addressed. To make the comparison of reconstitution and national infant mortality rates more meaningful, the reconstitution rates include a correction for illegitimate births, which is described in the next section. They are taken from table 6.3 rather than table 6.1. National data derived from the Registrar-General's annual returns are also shown from 1841 onwards. It is clear at a glance that the 'fit' between the reconstitution-based estimates and the Registrar-General's early returns is very close in the case of infant mortality, but much less good for early childhood mortality. This issue is less straightforward than might appear, however, especially in relation to $_4q_1$, and is considered in greater detail below.[43]

Infant mortality

From table 6.1, it is clear at a glance that infant mortality in England was never high by the standards of many pre-industrial communities, or indeed by comparison with those widely prevalent in Europe in the nineteenth century. This average situation did not arise because infant mortality was uniformly low in England in the past. Some individual parishes among the 26 had consistently high rates. In Gainsborough, for example, the rate averaged 261 per 1000 over the century and a half from 1600 to 1749. In other parishes the rate was high throughout the whole period of the reconstitution. In Lowestoft (1561–1730) it was 215 per 1000. Gainsborough and Lowestoft were both substantial urban places, but, although the rate was usually lower in rural parishes, this was not always the case. In March (1558–1751), for example, a large parish with a predominantly agricultural labour force in 1831, though including a

---

[42] See tab. 2.2, p. 26 above.   [43] See pp. 258–61.

market town, infant mortality was notably severe at 269 per 1000;[44] in the smaller and more deeply rural parishes of Great Oakley and Willingham (1673–1789 and 1587–1729), which were also low-lying like March, the rate was 243 and 193 per 1000 respectively.[45]

Infant mortality in London, which can be estimated from the bills of mortality, was at times at fearful levels. For the city as a whole in the early eighteenth century the rate was between 350 and 400 per 1000, and presumably higher still in the poorest and least salubrious parts of the city.[46] Marshland areas could be almost equally fatal: there the mortality table, like the water table, was apt to be very high.[47] Even in areas where infant mortality was in general very low, the rate was much higher in special circumstances. For example, the death rate of twins, who were exposed to far greater risk than singleton births, was well over 400 per 1000 nationally over most of the parish register period, and was seldom less than 300 per 1000 even in parishes in which the overall infant rate was only in the range between 100 and 150 per 1000.[48]

Though the prevailing level of infant mortality was never high in England, it changed significantly over time. The period as a whole may be divided into four broad subperiods. The first, covering the century from 1580 to 1679, was a period of relatively low rates. The average decennial rate over the ten decades was 163.9 per 1000, and there was a 30-year spell from 1620 to 1649 when the average rate was only 154.6. Thereafter rates rose sharply. In the next 70 years, 1680–1749, the average rate was 189.9 per 1000, and during this period the rate in every decade was higher than the highest decennial rate in the preceding century. The highest decennial rates (1680–9 and 1710–9) were above

[44] See tab. 3.1, pp. 44–5, above. March appears as a market town in Adams, *Index villaris*, p. 232.

[45] The variability of mortality by parish and the reasons why it was so marked are discussed, for south-east England, in Dobson, 'The last hiccup of the old demographic regime'.

[46] Landers concludes that infant mortality in the 1730s and 1740s was 'somewhere above 300 per thousand'; Landers, *Death and the metropolis*, p. 192. Laxton and Williams estimate infant mortality as about 400 per 1000 in these decades, which appear to have represented the peak in infant mortality in London in the early modern period; Laxton and Williams, 'Urbanization and infant mortality', fig.7, p. 126 (see also p. 257 n. 89 below).

[47] For example, even as late as in the years about 1800 Dobson found that infant mortality rates (taken as burials under 1 year per 1000 baptisms in parishes in which age at death was routinely recorded) averaged 292 per 1000 in nine coastal and marshland parishes in south-east England (the individual rates ranged between 200 and 377 per 1000; the parishes in question were South Benfleet; Little Clacton; Minster-in-Sheppey; Canewdon; St Clement's, Sandwich; Burnham; Strood; Tollesbury; and Southchurch). Dobson, 'Population, disease and mortality', tab. 6.27, p. 167.

[48] See tab. 6.8 and fig. 6.13, pp. 244 and 280.

Table 6.2 *Illegitimacy ratios, legitimate, and overall infant mortality rates*
($1000q_x$) by quarter-century

	Illegitimacy ratio (per cent)[a]	Legitimate infant mortality rate[b]	Overall infant mortality rate[c]
1580–99	3.76	170.7	177.1
1600–24	3.57	165.2	171.1
1625–49	2.63	153.3	157.3
1650–74	1.35	166.7	169.0
1675–99	1.84	185.4	188.8
1700–24	2.31	190.7	195.1
1725–49	2.91	190.8	196.4
1750–74	4.64	162.8	170.4
1775–99	5.93	156.7	166.0
1800–24	6.18	136.0	144.4
1825–37	5.27	144.1	151.7

Note and sources:
[a] The rates for 1580–1749 are taken from Adair, 'Regional variations in illegitimacy', tab. 2.1, p. 63. Adair provides decennial figures referring to 1581–90, 1591–1600, etc. The 25-year rates were calculated by averaging the rates over the three relevant decades, giving half-weight to the half-decade. The ratios for 1750–1834 are taken from Laslett, 'Comparing illegitimacy over time', tab. 1.1(a), pp. 14–5. The five relevant quinquennial ratios were averaged for each 25-year period and then multiplied by 1.20 (see text for explanation). The last figure in this column refers to the period 1825–34.
[b] Tab. 6.1, p. 215.
[c] The overall rate was calculated by applying the legitimate infant mortality rate to the percentage of total births that were legitimate, and double the legitimate rate to the percentage of births that were illegitimate. The two elements were then summed to produce an overall rate. For evidence of the relative level of legitimate and illegitimate infant mortality, see text.

200 per 1000. After 1750, however, the rate fell abruptly. For the next 40 years, 1750–89, it fell to a new plateau, averaging 162.9 per 1000, a return to the level found in the first period. In the final half-century, 1790–1837, infant mortality was again sharply lower averaging 141.2 per 1000. The lowest point occurred in the first two decades of the new century and was followed by a slight rise.

The size of the swings in infant mortality over the 250-year span covered in table 6.1 was therefore substantial. In the period 1790–1837 the rate was less than 75 per cent of the level reached in 1680–1749. Expressed in terms of the model West variant in the Princeton model life tables, this corresponds to a difference of about seven years in expectation of life at birth.

In considering these secular swings in infant mortality, it should be borne in mind that the data refer to legitimate children only. Illegitimate children do not appear on FRFs. If the illegitimacy ratio had been constant over time this fact would have no bearing on *relative* changes in the overall infant mortality rate, even though illegitimate children suffered a much higher risk of dying than others early in life. But, since the ratio varied substantially over time, it cannot be ignored in this context. Taking it into account raises the level of the infant mortality rate but slightly reduces the amplitude of the fluctuations of the overall rate. The scale of the effect may be seen in table 6.2, which shows quarter-century illegitimacy ratios and legitimate infant mortality rates, and revisions of the latter taking account of the former to produce overall rates.

Laslett pioneered work on the secular trends in national illegitimacy ratios, and his work has recently been considerably extended and in some respects revised by Adair. In table 6.2 the ratios for the early quarter-centuries are taken from Adair's work, which, however, covers the period only to the middle of the eighteenth century. After 1750 the ratios are taken from Laslett's final reworking of his data but in each case Laslett's figure has been multiplied by 1.2, to correct for the many illegitimate children that Adair has shown were missed in the earlier work. During the period of overlap between the two series (1580–1749) Adair's ratios exceed Laslett's on average by 20 per cent, which suggests using a multiplier of 1.2 to produce a single consistent series. Adair's ratios are always higher than Laslett's in the overlap period between the two series but the ratio between paired figures varies substantially, perhaps because of the relatively small numbers involved, especially in Laslett's data.[49]

The figures in the first column of table 6.2 may underestimate the true level of illegitimacy. For example, when returns based on their parish registers were requested from incumbents throughout the country under the provisions of the 1841 census, they showed that in 1840, 5.77 per cent of children baptised were illegitimate, whereas the civil registration figure for 1842 was 6.7 per cent (a very stable figure which varied little during the balance of the 1840s). It is quite possible, however, that the ecclesiastical returns were made with less care and precision than Adair achieved and it is unclear that any further correction to figures based on his work would be justified.[50]

---

[49] For example, in each quinquennium between 1640 and 1714 there were always fewer than 200 illegimates in the numerator of the ratio and in two of the quinquennia fewer than 100: Laslett, 'Comparing illegitimacy over time', tab. 1.1(a), p. 14.

[50] Glass, *Numbering the people*, pp. 185–6 and pp. 198–200 nn. 25–7. In this passage Glass provides an admirable discussion of the complexities of registration deficiencies in this and other contexts, and notably issues related to the underregistration of illegitimate

The overall infant mortality rates were obtained by assuming that the rate prevailing among illegitimate children was double the rate for legitimate children. Because of problems of registration coverage and because the mothers of illegitimate children were more likely to move soon after lying-in than others, it is not feasible to measure the level of illegitimate infant mortality accurately from parish register material. Nor was this a matter which attracted the attention of the Registrar-General in the early decades of civil registration. However, the question was taken up in some detail in the *Thirty-eighth annual report*. Unfortunately, this analysis contained no data for the country as a whole, but was devoted exclusively to 24 registration districts in 1875, 12 with very high overall infant mortality rates, averaging 203 per 1000 live births, and 12 with unusually low rates, averaging 107 per 1000. In the first group the legitimate infant mortality rate averaged 192 per 1000, while the illegitimate rate averaged 388 per 1000; in the second the comparable rates were 97 and 239 per 1000 respectively.[51] In 1906–10, by which time

children in the parish registers. An earlier ecclesiastical enquiry carried out as part of the 1831 census suggested an illegitimacy ratio of 5.02 per cent in 1830 (ibid., p. 186). This occurred at a period when a direct comparison with Laslett's series is possible. His figure for 1830 was 4.83 per cent, suggesting that his series was broadly representative of the Anglican parish registers as a whole, but this is an aberrantly high figure within his series and, in view of the small numbers involved and the likelihood that the true ratio changed very little from year to year, it is probably more informative to compare the 1831 census figure with the average for adjacent years in his series. Over the period 1825–34 the ratio averaged only 4.39 in his series; Laslett, 'Comparing illegitimacy over time', tab. 1.1(b), p. 16. Given the indeterminacy of the evidence it seemed unwise to carry out any further inflation to the ratios in col. 1 of tab. 6.2, though it is also probable that these ratios are below rather than above the true figures.

[51] The registration districts differed greatly in population size. In some cases, therefore, the rate was based on relatively few deaths. The highest rate in the high mortality districts was in Driffield at 596 per 1000 but this was based on only 57 illegitimate births, of which 34 died before reaching their first birthday. The illegitimate death rate in the 12 low mortality districts was sometimes based on a far smaller number of deaths (for example, in Reeth on 2 deaths and in Ledbury and Wetherby on 4 deaths). If rates are calculated for the high and low mortality districts as a whole, however, to ensure that substantial numbers are involved, much the same picture emerges. The illegitimate and legitimate rates in the less healthy districts were 390.4 and 198.0 per 1000; in the more healthy districts 261.4 and 98.5 per 1000 respectively. This again suggests that a ratio of 2:1 between the two rates is plausible. Registrar-General, *Thirty-eighth annual report*, tab. K, p. xlv and tab. L, p. xlvi.

It may be noted that the ratio between the legitimate and illegitimate rates in England appears to have been higher than in some other areas of Europe in the nineteenth century. In Prussia in 1877–81, for example, the two rates were 183.8 and 329.1 per 1000. The illegimate rate was therefore 79 per cent higher than the legitimate: Pearl, *Human biology*, tab. 32, pp. 134–5 (the Prussian combined sex rates were calculated from the male and and female rates on the assumption of a sex ratio at birth of 105:100). In

the Registrar-General was collecting these data on a national basis, the illegitimate infant mortality rate was still almost exactly twice that for legitimate children, so that it seems safe to assume that the appropriate multiplier for the parish register period was at least as high as this, though it is certainly a question which would benefit from further research.[52]

The overall infant mortality rate was only marginally different from the legitimate rate in the late seventeenth and early eighteenth centuries, when the legitimate rate was at a peak, because illegitimacy was uncommon at that time (table 6.2). The rate for 1675–99 is increased by less than 2 per cent as a result of taking illegitimacy into account; the rate for the two following quarter-centuries by 2.3 and 2.9 per cent. Thereafter there was a sharp rise, reaching a maximum in 1800–24 at 6.2 per cent. The peak to trough fall measured on the legitimate rate alone was 28.7 per cent (from 190.8 per 1000 in 1725–49 to 136.0 in 1800–24), but using the estimated rates for overall infant mortality the fall is reduced, though only slightly, to 26.5 per cent (from 196.4 per 1000 in 1725–49 to 144.4 per 1000 in 1800–24). Similarly, a revision of the calculation made above relating to the periods 1680–1749 and 1790–1837 suggests that overall infant mortality fell between the two periods from 194.4 to 149.8 per 1000, a fall of 22.9 per cent compared with 25.6 per cent in the earlier calculation. The extent of the 'leverage' exerted by the prevalence of illegitimacy is readily visible in figure 6.2.

Revision of the infant mortality rate to take account of illegitimacy emphasises the similarity between the level of the rate derived from reconstitution and that found in the early years of civil registration. The published rates in the *Annual reports* reveal an infant mortality rate of 148 per 1000 in 1841–5 and 158 per 1000 in 1846–50, but these rates are affected by underregistration both of births and of infant deaths and Glass's revised figures, which attempt to correct for these deficiencies and are probably substantially closer to the truth, are 147 and 148 per 1000 respectively for the two quinquennia.[53] These figures may be compared with the reconstitution-based estimate of 152 per 1000 for the period 1825–37 (table 6.2).[54] The excellence of the 'fit' between the level

Amsterdam in 1895–9 the illegitimate rate was 83 per cent higher than the legitimate (258.0 and 141.3 per 1000): Vandenbroeke, van Poppel, and van der Woude, 'De zuigelingen- en kindersterfte', tab. 5, p. 479.

[52] The illegitimate and legitimate rates in 1906–10 were 224 and 113 per 1000 respectively. Glass, *Numbering the people*, pp. 197–8 n. 15.   [53] Ibid., tab. 1, p. 182.

[54] The calculation can, of course, be reversed. On the assumption that the illegitimacy ratio in the 1840s was 6.8 per cent and the overall infant mortality rate 148 per 1000, the national infant mortality rate for legitimate children was 138.6 per 1000, compared with a figure of 140.4 per 1000 from reconstitution data for 1830–7 (tab. 6.3). The average

and trend of infant mortality in the later decades of the parish register period and the early decades of national data is very clear in figure 6.1.

Because of the relatively small numbers of illegitimate baptisms on which Laslett and Adair based their estimates of the illegitimacy ratio, it seemed prudent to discuss the impact of illegitimacy on the overall infant mortality rate over quarter-century periods, as in table 6.2. It may be of interest, however, to include a table showing revised estimates of the decennial infant mortality rates given in table 6.1, taking illegitimacy into account, even though the illegitimacy ratios for the individual decades are based on small numbers of events.[55] The results are shown in table 6.3 and figure 6.2.

It should be emphasised that many of the infant mortality rates quoted hereafter refer to *legitimate* children only. For some purposes, therefore, it may be advisable to make a mental adjustment to the rates shown in a table to take account of this. For example, the overall infant mortality rates in individual parishes, shown in table 6.16, were all somewhat higher than those listed, which refer only to legitimate children.

The changes in the overall infant mortality rate, though substantial, comprise, and in a sense conceal, much more striking changes in the rates for periods within the first year of life, as may be seen in table 6.4.

The table shows that rates in the second half of the first year of life, which were at a very modest level before 1675, rose substantially thereafter so that in the quarter-century 1725–49 they were roughly twice as high as in 1600–24; and that thereafter rates remained high by the standards of late Tudor and early Stuart England, rising to a record level in the last period 1825–37. Rates in the second and third months of life and in the second trimester (90–179 days) did not show such marked long-run changes. In the second and third months the rates peaked in the early eighteenth century. In the second trimester the rate reached a plateau after 1675, changing little thereafter. In this it resembled rates in the second half of the first year of life, but it had earlier risen less steeply.

In the first month of life, however, matters were very different. There was little variation round an average rate of just over 100 per 1000 from 1580 until 1750, but thereafter an uninterrupted fall so that in the latest period, 1825–37, the neonatal rate was less than half its prevailing level before 1750. Table 6.4 also shows the level of endogenous infant mortality in each period. All infant mortality can be divided into two

illegitimacy ratio in the years 1845–9 was 6.76 per cent; Registrar-General, *Annual reports* (8th to 12th).

[55] As noted above, p. 220 n.49, the total number of illegitimate baptisms from which decennial ratios were calculated was sometimes less than 200.

Table 6.3 *Illegitimacy ratios, legitimate, and overall infant mortality rates*
(1000q_x) by decade

	Illegitimacy ratio (per cent)[a]	Legitimate infant mortality rate[b]	Overall infant mortality rate[c]
1580–9	3.46	168.4	174.2
1590–9	4.05	173.0	180.0
1600–9	4.02	165.4	172.0
1610–9	3.46	166.7	172.5
1620–9	2.89	153.4	157.8
1630–9	2.87	160.3	164.9
1640–9	2.27	150.2	153.6
1650–9	1.17	164.3	166.2
1660–9	1.37	169.3	171.6
1670–9	1.68	168.2	171.0
1680–9	1.70	201.9	205.3
1690–9	2.06	174.9	178.5
1700–9	2.31	174.1	178.2
1710–9	2.23	203.3	207.9
1720–9	2.49	193.3	198.1
1730–9	2.78	195.1	200.5
1740–9	3.25	186.6	192.6
1750–9	4.02	159.6	166.0
1760–9	4.98	165.6	173.8
1770–9	5.34	158.8	167.3
1780–9	6.00	163.4	173.2
1790–9	6.12	151.3	160.6
1800–9	6.36	136.6	145.3
1810–9	5.82	133.1	140.8
1820–9	6.06	144.7	153.5
1830–7	6.00	140.4	148.8

Note and sources:
[a] For sources, see note and sources to tab. 6.2.
[b] See tab. 6.1, p. 215.
[c] For the calculation of the overall rate, see note and sources to tab. 6.2.

elements, endogenous and exogenous. The latter refers to deaths caused by the invasion of the body by external agents, for example infections such as smallpox or tuberculosis; the former to prematurity, the birth trauma itself, or inherited genetic defects which were fatal to the new-born child. The distinction may be arbitrary but has proved illuminating at times.

The endogenous mortality estimates were obtained by using a method devised by Bourgeois-Pichat. He plotted the rising total of deaths within the first year of life on a graph in which the horizontal

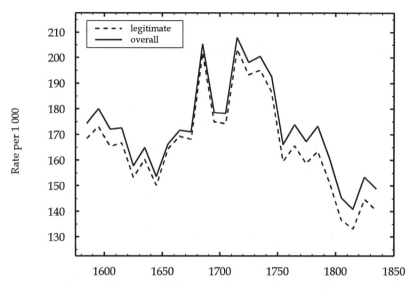

Figure 6.2   *Legitimate and overall infant mortality (1000q_x)*
Sources: tabs. 6.1. and 6.3.

axis, representing days within the first year of life, had been subjected to a logarithmic transform.[56] Bourgeois-Pichat's object was to enable the endogenous component in infant mortality to be identified, even in the absence of cause of death information. The points representing cumulative mortality between the first and twelfth month of life normally (though not invariably) lie close to a straight line, when applied to historical data. On the assumption that virtually all deaths after the end of the first month of life are from exogenous causes, it is plausible to argue that by extending the line back to the vertical axis, the exogenous component of infant mortality will continue to be captured. The height of the intercept will then represent the level of endogenous mortality, while the balance of first month mortality is taken as exogenous. The salient features in the secular development of endogenous and exogenous infant mortality are shown in figure 6.3 in which each line represents a least-squares quadratic best fit with the data points for a particular period based on the cumulative totals of deaths at 30, 60, 90, 180, 274, and 365 days.[57] A quadratic best fit line was preferred to a

[56] Bourgeois-Pichat, 'La mesure de la mortalité infantile'. The transform is $P(n) = \log^3$ (n + 1) where n is the age in days.

[57] The data plotted in fig. 6.3 are based on life table d_x's rather than upon deaths because the disappearance from observation of some families in the course of the first year of life of the child makes it desirable to avoid dependence on raw totals of events.

Table 6.4 *Mortality within the first year of life (1000q_x)*

	Days within the first year of life									$_1q_0$	Endogenous	Exogenous
	0–1	1–6	7–29	0–29	30–59	60–89	90–179	180–273	274–365			
1580–99	34.8	30.0	40.7	101.9	17.5	12.2	25.0	11.9	12.3	170.7	77.6	93.1
1600–24	44.9	31.6	35.8	108.2	15.9	10.1	18.6	11.5	9.5	165.2	88.5	76.7
1625–49	45.1	24.5	28.0	94.5	13.5	8.4	18.7	12.3	13.8	153.3	80.0	73.3
1650–74	52.5	25.2	30.2	104.2	16.2	9.3	19.1	14.1	13.0	166.7	87.3	79.4
1675–99	50.9	28.9	34.1	109.7	17.8	13.1	24.6	16.0	16.6	185.4	88.3	97.1
1700–24	31.6	33.9	44.7	106.3	19.3	14.1	26.1	21.2	17.5	190.7	84.0	106.7
1725–49	29.6	34.1	41.5	101.6	20.0	13.8	26.8	22.5	20.4	190.8	80.5	110.3
1750–74	22.6	28.3	29.8	78.5	16.0	11.6	25.7	22.6	19.1	162.8	61.3	101.5
1775–99	31.9	15.8	25.2	71.3	17.2	11.0	26.6	23.0	17.7	156.7	52.6	104.1
1800–24	22.4	11.5	24.4	57.3	14.1	10.9	23.6	21.0	16.8	136.0	41.0	95.0
1825–37	6.2	16.6	26.6	48.7	17.1	10.7	27.1	27.2	22.3	144.1	33.3	110.8

Note: legitimate births only. The rates have been adjusted in the same way as those in tab. 6.1 to overcome the problem of 'joins' between the four groups.
Source: Cambridge Group reconstitutions.

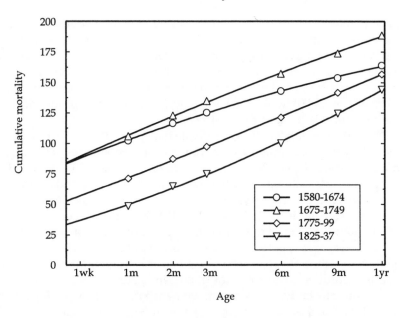

Figure 6.3   *Biometric analysis of infant mortality* $(1000d_x)$
Source: Cambridge Group reconstitutions.

linear form because some of the nineteenth-century data shown in subsequent figures were markedly curvilinear in shape. In figure 6.3 the points representing each period fall very close to a straight line so that the estimated level of endogenous mortality is much the same whichever method is used, though the line for the first period, 1580–1674, is slightly convex to its upper surface and that for the last period, 1825–37 is marginally concave.

Figure 6.3 reveals a striking pattern of change over time. Between the early decades of the seventeenth century and the period of peak infant mortality a century later the line representing cumulative infant mortality rotates upwards round its intercept on the vertical axis. Thereafter, from the peak period to the last decades covered, the intercept moves rapidly down the vertical axis but the lines showing cumulative mortality remain roughly in parallel with each other. The rise in infant mortality during the seventeenth century was confined to an increase in the exogenous component of the overall rate. As table 6.4 shows, endogenous mortality was high from the beginning. It varied only slightly in the individual quarter-century periods falling within the late sixteenth, seventeenth, and early eighteenth centuries, and was closely similar in the two long periods 1580–1674 and 1675–1749, but the overall rate rose from 164 to 189 per 1000. Endogenous mortality therefore constituted 51 per cent of the total rate before 1650, but only 44 per cent in the succeeding period. Between 1625–49, when the overall infant mortality rate was low (153 per 1000), and its peak a century later in 1725–49 (191 per 1000), exogenous mortality rose by 51 per cent (from 73 to 110 per 1000), while the endogenous rate was almost identical in the two periods (80 and 81 per 1000).[58]

When the major fall in the overall rate took place after 1750, however, the fall was concentrated exclusively in the endogenous rate which tumbled from 81 per 1000 in 1725–49 to only 33 per 1000 in 1825–37. Exogenous rates altered little after their major rise in the middle decades of the seventeenth century. The exogenous rate in the four quarter-centuries starting in 1750–74 was 102, 104, 95, and 111 per 1000.

The nature of the changes that took place over the quarter-millennium, however, are perhaps better captured in figure 6.4. In this figure endogenous mortality has been plotted against exogenous mortality by quarter-centuries: vertical movement indicates a rise or fall in exogenous mortality, horizontal movement a rise or fall in endogenous mortality. The scale on both axes is the same. After an initial period when the points are closely bunched exogenous mortality increased without significant alteration in the level of endogenous mortality, but after 1725–49 there is a dramatic change. Exogenous mortality stabilises, apart from a rise in the final, short period, but the level of endogenous mortality falls steadily and substantially.

Before considering this picture in greater detail and discussing the possible reasons for so striking a change, it is convenient first to consider whether these findings can be regarded as trustworthy, both by reviewing evidence relating to birth interval characteristics and by making use of the early returns of the Registrar-General. Only when the reliability of the endogenous infant mortality rates has been established, is it sensible to consider causation.

Plausible reasons for reservations about the data spring readily to mind. Any child who had survived long enough to have acquired a name and become an individual personality, a constituent member of the community, was unlikely at death not to be accorded recognition by a formal burial. But a child who died very early in life before a baptism ceremony had been performed was more ambiguously placed.

---

[58] It is of interest to note that, in the seventeenth century, infant mortality among the ruling families of Europe reached its highest level for the whole period since 1500, and that the whole of the substantial rise (from 193 per 1000 in 1500–99 to 246 per 1000 in 1600–99) occurred after the end of the first month of life; Peller, 'Studies on mortality', tab. 4, p. 452.

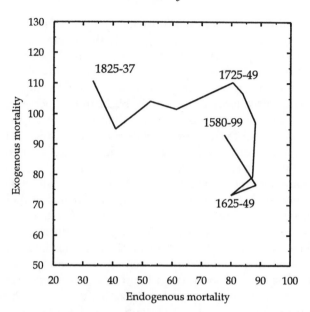

Figure 6.4   The relative movements of endogenous and exogenous infant mortality (1000d$_x$)
Source: Cambridge Group reconstitutions.

In the early decades of parochial registration it was customary to baptise children soon after birth, and it was also quite common for the parish minister to bury a child even though he or she had not been baptised, and to enter the burial in his register as 'an unbaptised son/daughter of . . .'. The average gap between birth and baptism grew slowly longer, however, and by the later eighteenth century was perhaps a month long on average and much longer in many individual cases.[59] Moreover, parish ministers often ceased to record the burials of unbaptised children.[60]

If it were true that more children were dying before baptism and that such deaths were likely to go unrecorded in the burial register, not only would this cause infant mortality as a whole to be underestimated but the fall would all be concentrated in the endogenous component of the total when using the Bourgeois-Pichat method of identifying it. Deaths

---

[59] Berry and Schofield, 'Age at baptism', tab. 2, p. 458.
[60] Failure to record the burial of unbaptised children was widespread but reconstitution parishes were much less affected than most others, since the registers in the reconstitution parishes were unusually well kept. See above pp. 74–87.

which should have figured within the totals for the first month of life would be missed, thus depressing both the overall rate and the endogenous rate by the same margin. The pattern of change during the eighteenth century revealed in figure 6.3 is suspiciously like that which would have arisen from a progressive weakening in the coverage of deaths taking place early in life before baptism had occurred.

A further complication must be noted. Before the coming into force of Rose's Act in 1813 it was rare for age at death to be recorded in the burial register. The age attributed to a dead child is therefore taken as the interval in time between two events recorded in the register. Usually the two dates are for baptism and burial, though occasionally dates of birth or death may be recorded and where these were available, they were, of course, used in preference to baptism or burial dates. In the great majority of cases, however, before 1813 age at death was obtained by subtracting the baptism from the burial date. The latter invariably occurred soon after death and therefore represents only a minor problem.[61] The former, on the other hand, was governed by custom. In the sixteenth century baptisms followed soon after birth but by the later eighteenth century there was frequently a delay of weeks or even months before baptism occurred. In particular cases the effect of delayed baptism in causing the age of the child to be underestimated could clearly be dramatic. A child of, say, two months might appear to be only a few days old. But an earlier investigation of the probable scale of the overall effect suggested that any distortion is relatively modest because of the nature of the transpositions that would occur and the characteristics of parochial registration.[62]

Finally, and less seriously, the likelihood that in some parishes registration coverage deteriorated during the Civil War and Commonwealth period has already been remarked. It is possible that the infant

---

[61] Only a few of the reconstitution parishes recorded both dates of death and dates of burial, and then chiefly in the later eighteenth century or the early nineteenth century. The only 4 parishes to record significant numbers of cases were Birstall, Colyton, Earsdon, and Odiham. There were 3086 cases in all and the mean interval between the two events was 3.4 days. Of the total 1191 cases were in the second half of the eighteenth century, when the mean interval was 3.3 days, and 1701 in the first half of the nineteenth century, with a mean interval of 3.6 days. The information was recorded too spasmodically to permit any confident inferences, other than that burial was almost never delayed for longer than a week.

[62] A full examination of this issue would unbalance the present discussion, but an estimate of its scale may be found in Wrigley, 'Births and baptisms', esp. pp. 295–310. One of the complicating factors is the existence of evidence that parents who knew that their child was in danger of dying made haste to have it baptised which would, of course, reduce any misestimation of age at death if he or she did subsequently die.

and child mortality rates for the 1640s and 1650s fall short of their 'true' level by about 3 per cent as a result.[63]

Despite these considerations, however, there is weighty evidence that the changes shown in table 6.4 bear a close resemblance to the true course of events. A first point to note is that there is strong, if indirect evidence from the analysis of birth interval data that few infant deaths failed to be registered. Birth intervals may be divided into three categories: those where the infant died in the first year of life, those where it is known to have survived the first year because its date of death is known; and those where the fate of the infant is unknown but it is presumed to have survived infancy and subsequently migrated from the parish to die elsewhere. The mean subsequent birth interval was short in the first category because the non-susceptible period was not extended by lactation. In the other two categories the mean interval should be the same since in both cases the earlier child survived. If some of those whose fate is unknown had died in infancy but their deaths had gone unrecorded in the burial register, the mean interval in the second category would be shorter than that for those known to have survived their first year. The scale of any difference of means will provide a clue to the extent of underregistration. Equally, the absence of any significant difference would be evidence that all those children whose date of death is unknown survived infancy, and that few if any infant deaths went unrecorded. It is therefore reassuring that the means were similar.[64]

The most persuasive support for the view that reconstitution data are reliable, however, is afforded by the Registrar-General's early annual returns. Although he displayed a far greater interest in mortality than in either fertility or nuptiality, and often went to great lengths to assemble information on particular causes of death or aspects of its incidence, the Registrar-General did not normally seek to subdivide mortality within the first year of life. Only for a few scattered years in the 1840s were such breakdowns provided but they are of the highest value in this connection. Their existence makes it possible both to establish the apparent level of endogenous infant mortality in England as a whole and to test whether registration coverage was adequate in the individual reconstitution parishes.

The latter exercise has already been described in an earlier chapter as

---

[63] See tab. 4.1, p. 76, and pp. 85–7.

[64] This summary is oversimplified. The crude means were not identical. The birth interval where the earlier child is *known* to have survived was about 0.4 months longer than where the date of the earlier child's death is unknown. But the apparent difference is misleading and the 'true' difference is negligibly small and may well not exist at all. The evidence for this assertion is set out in detail above pp. 98–107.

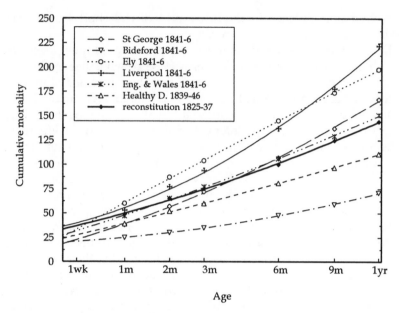

Figure 6.5   *A comparison of endogenous and exogenous infant mortality in the last years of reconstitution data with data taken from the Registrar-General's returns for the 1840s (1000d_x)*

Notes: the lines labelled 1841–6 represent rates obtained by consolidating data for the four years 1841, 1842, 1845, and 1846. The line for the Healthy Districts is based on data for all 8 years, 1839–46.

Sources: Cambridge Group reconstitutions. Data for 1841, 1842, 1845, 1846: Registrar-General, *Fifth annual report*, Abstract of births, Abstract of ages at death; *Sixth annual report*, Abstract of births, Abstract of ages at death; *Eighth annual report*, Abstract of births and deaths at different ages; *Ninth annual report*, Abstract of births and deaths at different ages. Data for 1839–46: Registrar-General, *Thirty-eighth annual report*, p. l, tab. N.

part of a generalised testing of the reliability and completeness of registration in the reconstitution parishes.[65] It suggested that very few infant deaths escaped registration in the reconstitution parishes since both the overall rates and the rates for each subdivision of the first year of life were closely similar in the parishes and the civil registration districts of which they formed part.[66] Figure 6.5, displaying the information in the same way as in figure 6.3, shows the national pattern for England and Wales in the 1840s, and for a small number of

[65] See above pp. 92–7.
[66] Detailed mortality data were not published for smaller areas by the Registrar-General.

registration districts within the country with widely different infant mortality rates, in addition to the reconstitution-based rate for 1825–37, the reconstitution period closest in time to the early returns of the Registrar-General. The rate for the Healthy Districts in 1839–46 is also shown. The national level of endogenous mortality, based on data for the years 1841, 1842, 1845, and 1846 is closely similar to the reconstitution-based estimate for 1825–37 (27 and 33 per 1000 respectively).

The lines representing the registration districts are also based on data for 1841, 1842, 1845, and 1846 and are interesting both as illustrating the broadly similar levels of endogenous mortality in places with widely differing overall infant mortality, and for comparison with some of the individual parishes. Of all the reconstitution parishes, for example, Hartland in Devon had the lowest infant mortality. In the period 1675–1749 the rate was 94 per 1000 (table 6.16). Hartland was situated in what later became the registration district of Bideford and Holsworthy where infant mortality in the 1840s was only 71 per 1000. The parish of March was at the other extreme with an infant mortality of 311 per 1000 in 1675–1749. It lay in the registration district of Ely, North Witchford, and Wisbech where the infant mortality rate was still as high as 198 per 1000 in the 1840s, not far short of Liverpool (222 per 1000), the unhealthiest large city in England for infant life. St George in the East was a poor area in east London and had one of the highest infant rates of any London registration district, though still well below the level of Liverpool or the Fens. The Healthy District data confirm the relative constancy of endogenous mortality, even though overall infant mortality varied very widely. In general places with high overall infant mortality also had above average endogenous mortality but the variation in the latter was modest, from 36 per 1000 in Liverpool to 20 per 1000 in Bideford and Holsworthy, though overall infant mortality in Liverpool was the higher of the two by 150 per 1000.

Figure 6.5 illustrates a point that could be further confirmed by using data from a larger number of registration districts, that a low endogenous mortality of about 20–35 per 1000 prevailed generally in England by the mid-nineteenth century, whatever the overall level of infant mortality. Sometimes the points representing the cumulative totals of deaths for a particular registration district are not 'well behaved' by Bourgeois-Pichat's criterion. There is a pronounced curvature in the line representing Liverpool, for example, though not in Ely where infant mortality was almost as high. Different methods of estimating endogenous mortality where the points representing mortality within the first year do not conform to a straight line will produce somewhat different results. All solutions to problems of estimation of this sort are arbitrary but the impression of a widely prevalent low endogenous rate and of a close similarity between estimates of endogenous infant mortality derived from civil registration data and those taken from reconstitution would survive whatever method were employed.

If the Registrar-General's returns are trustworthy it is difficult not to conclude that the reconstitution-derived endogenous rates are also reliable and therefore that the massive fall in endogenous rates suggested in figure 6.3 is genuine.

The proviso about the trustworthiness of the Registrar-General's returns deserves to be heeded. Glass concluded that deaths were underregistered in the early years of civil registration and that any such loss was probably largely confined to deaths at very young ages.[67] This might lead to a substantial underestimation of the true level of endogenous mortality. After 1846 for many years the Registrar-General did not publish breakdowns of deaths within the first year of life, so that the issue of the effect of any improvement in registration coverage on the apparent endogenous rate cannot be pursued as might be wished. It is therefore of interest to note that when the Registrar-General's returns next allow a comparable estimate to be made, in 1875, both the overall level of infant mortality and the level of endogenous mortality were virtually identical to those prevailing in the 1840s, as may also be seen in figure 6.6. Moreover, there was the same marked convergence to a similar level of endogenous mortality between Liverpool at one extreme and the Healthy Districts at the other as had been evident 30 years earlier. Neither Liverpool nor the Healthy Districts had changed much in the interim, as a comparison of figure 6.6 with figure 6.5 will show. In 1875 it is unlikely that any significant deficiency in registration still subsisted since the 1874 Act was by then in operation, an act that is generally reputed to have reduced underregistration to negligible levels.[68] The very close similarity of the endogenous rates for the 1870s

---

[67] He concluded, partly relying on the view of the Registrar-General's office at the time, that deaths were underregistered by 2 per cent and that all or almost all were infant deaths, but he was influenced also by the consideration that making this correction resulted in an infant mortality rate for 1841–5 which was closely similar to those for the next three quinquennia, an assumption that would be more difficult to sustain now in the light of the reconstitution evidence for rising infant mortality in the second quarter of the nineteenth century. Glass, 'Under-registration of births', pp. 84–5.

[68] The main difficulty had lain with the registration of births. Before the 1874 Act responsibility for ensuring full registration had rested with the registrars of births. The 1874 Act placed this responsibility upon parents, the occupier of the house in which the birth took place, or those attending the birth or having charge of the child. Glass, 'Under-registration of births', p. 70, and *Numbering the people*, p. 181.

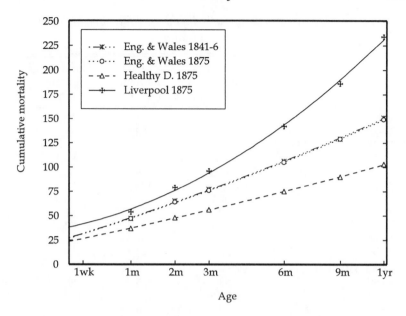

Figure 6.6   *Endogenous and exogenous infant mortality: the stability of nineteenth-century patterns (1000d_x)*
Sources: 1841–6 data: as fig. 6.5; 1875 Healthy Districts data: Registrar-General, *Thirty-eighth annual report*, p. xlix, tab. M.

to those of the 1840s tends to enhance the claim of the latter to reliability, and therefore indirectly to underwrite the reconstitution mortality estimates.

There is also evidence of a different kind to support the view that there was a large fall in endogenous infant mortality in the eighteenth century. Endogenous deaths included many that were related to the birth trauma itself and its surrounding circumstances. It is therefore likely that they were linked, at least in part, to the factors which determined the level of maternal mortality. Maternal mortality is considered in some detail later in this chapter, but it is worthy of note that over much the same period as endogenous mortality was falling, maternal mortality was also falling and in much the same proportion. Table 6.5 shows the maternal mortality rate for successive quarter-centuries beginning in 1580, together with the endogenous infant mortality rate and the rate for the first month and the first week of life. The closeness of fit between changes in the maternal rate and changes in the other two rates can be judged more conveniently by indexing them (lower panel of table 6.5). The index is based on the average rate for the

Table 6.5 *Maternal mortality, early infant mortality, and endogenous infant mortality*

	Maternal mortality[a]	Infant mortality 0–6 days[b]	Infant mortality 0–29 days[b]	Endogenous infant mortality[b]
1580–99	12.3	63.8	101.9	77.6
1600–24	12.8	75.1	108.2	88.5
1625–49	14.0	68.5	94.5	80.0
1650–74	17.0	76.3	104.2	87.3
1675–99	15.6	78.3	109.7	88.3
1700–24	13.4	64.5	106.3	84.0
1725–49	12.3	62.7	101.6	80.5
1750–74	9.5	50.2	78.5	61.3
1775–99	9.0	47.2	71.3	52.6
1800–24	6.3	33.6	57.3	41.0
1825–37	4.7	22.6	48.7	33.3
Indexed data: 100 = (1650–74 + 1675–99)/2				
1580–99	75	83	95	88
1600–24	79	97	101	101
1625–49	86	89	88	91
1650–74	104	99	97	99
1675–99	96	101	103	101
1700–24	82	83	99	96
1725–49	75	81	95	92
1750–74	58	65	73	70
1775–99	55	61	67	60
1800–24	39	44	54	47
1825–37	29	29	46	38

[a] Per 1000 birth events.
[b] Per 1000 births.
Note: the rates refer to legitimate births only.
Sources: Cambridge Group reconstitutions and tabs. 6.4 and 6.29.

two quarter-centuries 1650–74 and 1675–99. There is a strikingly good fit between the maternal rate and the infant rate in the first week of life. First month mortality conforms less well, neither rising before the peak period nor falling after it as sharply as the first week rate. The indexed endogenous rate usually lies between the other two, with perhaps a somewhat closer resemblance to the first month than to the first week index. The maternal mortality rate and the endogenous, exogenous, and overall infant mortality rates are also shown graphically in figure 6.7. It is plain that maternal mortality and endogenous mortality moved in close sympathy but that exogenous mortality moved quite independently.

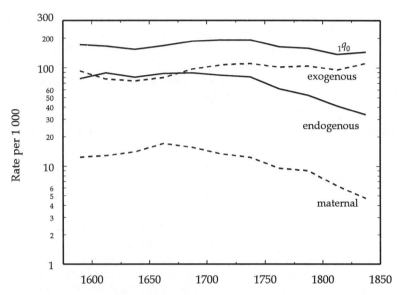

Figure 6.7   *Maternal mortality, endogenous, exogenous, and total infant mortality*

Sources: tabs. 6.1 and 6.5.

The close similarity between trends in maternal mortality and endogenous infant mortality suggests the possibility of a common influence on both, and appears to rule out certain factors as capable of accounting for both. If, for example, it were argued that the fall in maternal mortality was due to a large fall in deaths from puerperal fever, it could not be held that this also explained more than a small part of the fall in infant mortality. Since the absolute chance of death in childbirth was far lower than the chance of death early in infancy (figure 6.7), even a large proportionate saving in maternal life would affect the life chances of only a small percentage of babies.[69]

The chief components of endogenous mortality are often taken to be prematurity/low birth weight, inherited genetic defect, and the birth trauma (interpreted broadly to include, for example, deaths from umbilical tetanus). There is no apparent reason to think that there was any great change in the first two of these three factors in the course of the eighteenth century. Nor, if there were change in these two, would any

---

[69] It does not follow, of course, that, say, a fall in puerperal fever was *not* the cause of the improvement in maternal mortality, but if this *were* the case the similarity in the extent of the fall in early infant and maternal mortality would be the result of coincidence rather than common causation.

such change necessarily produce commensurate changes in maternal mortality. The third factor appears at first sight a more promising possibility. For example, more, and more competent, midwives might effect improvements in childbed practice of benefit both to mother and child.[70] The history of maternal mortality is discussed at length later in this chapter, where it appears from an odds ratio analysis that the fall in maternal mortality in the eighteenth century has much in common with general patterns of adult mortality decline. This in turn suggests either that the level of endogenous infant mortality may be heavily influenced by the health of the mother during pregnancy, or, if this proves not to be a sustainable hypothesis, that the causes of the falls in the two types of mortality were different, even though the two mortality trends were so similar.

Before leaving the question of the estimation of early infant mortality, one further point should be noted since it also has an important bearing on the completeness of parochial registration. As may be seen in table 6.6, mortality within the first month of life, which had moved within a narrow range in every decade from the 1580s to the 1740s (between a maximum of 118.4 per 1000 in 1680–9 and almost identical minima of 93.2 in 1640–9 and 92.8 in 1740–9), dropped sharply to 77.1 in the 1750s, and thereafter continued on an irregular downward trend until in the 1820s and 1830s it averaged 46.6 per 1000. The rate for the first day of life, however, followed a different pattern. It rose from an initially relatively modest level between 1580 and 1609, to reach a higher but uneven plateau during the decades between 1610 and 1700, before plunging rapidly to only about half its previous height between the 1730s and 1770s. Then followed three decades in which it rose somewhat, only to plummet to unprecedented lows in the final quarter-century.

That first day mortality should have fallen during the eighteenth century is not surprising, especially if the possible link beween early infant death and maternal mortality is borne in mind,[71] but that it should suddenly fall to a far lower level early in the nineteenth century does not conform with other mortality trends and seems inherently implausible. The explanation lies in the vagaries of Anglican registra-

---

[70] New techniques for delivering obstructed births gradually became more widely known in the early eighteenth century, involving such manoeuvres as podalic version, Deventer's manoeuvre, or midwifery forceps. Or again, a decline in customary childbed rituals may have made for more hygienic deliveries, and perhaps better nutrition for mother and child. Several of these issues are discussed in Wilson, 'Participant or patient?', and *Man-midwifery*.

[71] The fall was abruptly, if briefly, reversed in the 1790s and 1800s. It is not clear whether this was an aberration or a phenomenon which would repay further investigation.

Table 6.6 *Mortality within the first month of life (1000q$_x$)*

	Days within the first year of life				
	0–1	1–6	0–6	0–29	$_1q_0$
1580–9	35.7	25.1	59.9	97.9	168.4
1590–9	33.9	35.1	67.9	106.1	173.0
1600–9	41.3	34.7	74.5	106.7	165.4
1610–9	48.1	30.9	77.6	110.9	166.7
1620–9	40.2	25.9	65.1	95.9	153.4
1630–9	45.3	25.6	69.7	99.9	160.3
1640–9	50.1	23.1	72.1	93.2	150.2
1650–9	56.9	22.6	78.2	103.1	164.3
1660–9	50.9	27.8	77.3	106.8	169.3
1670–9	49.0	25.5	73.2	99.8	168.2
1680–9	55.5	29.3	83.2	118.4	201.9
1690–9	45.7	30.0	74.3	106.0	174.9
1700–9	31.3	33.4	63.6	100.0	174.1
1710–9	34.6	32.7	66.1	112.6	203.3
1720–9	32.2	36.9	67.9	107.2	193.3
1730–9	28.6	36.7	64.2	105.9	195.1
1740–9	26.1	30.7	56.0	92.8	186.6
1750–9	20.4	29.0	48.8	77.1	159.6
1760–9	22.7	30.7	52.6	81.0	165.6
1770–9	27.0	21.2	47.6	73.8	158.8
1780–9	29.9	16.8	46.3	75.8	163.4
1790–9	35.8	12.9	48.3	66.6	151.3
1800–9	41.8	8.7	50.1	70.4	136.6
1810–9	17.6	13.1	32.5	55.8	133.1
1820–9	5.8	15.0	20.7	45.8	144.7
1830–7	4.8	15.7	20.5	47.4	140.4

Note: legitimate births only. The rates have been adjusted in the same way as those in tab. 6.1 to overcome the problem of 'joins' between the four groups.
Source: Cambridge Group reconstitutions.

tion practice. As has been explained above,[72] burials which could be linked to a particular family, but for which there was no matching baptism, were, where appropriate, treated as evidence of a death occurring very soon after birth and before baptism could be performed. A dummy birth was then created and given the same date as the burial. All such cases, therefore, contribute an infant death on the first day of life to the infant mortality total, though in many cases the death must have occurred later than the first day. To be able to take this action,

[72] See pp. 110–2.

however, depends upon the burial record containing the name of one or both parents. It is this information that enables a link to be made to a particular FRF.

Under the provisions of Rose's Act (1812) information about parentage was no longer routinely recorded when a child was buried, but age at death was given. This ends the tendency to overestimate first day mortality. After January 1813 such deaths are distributed over the first few days and weeks of life rather than being concentrated in the first day alone. From 1813, therefore, there was a fall in the number of deaths in the first day of life, balanced, however, to some extent by an offsetting rise in the rest of the first month. Thus, in 1800–9 the first day rate was 41.8 per 1000, but was no more than 4.8 per 1000 in 1830–7, a fall of 37.0 per 1000. The first month rate fell more modestly, however, from 70.4 to 47.4 per 1000, a fall of only 23.0 per 1000.

That the distribution of deaths within the first month of life is plausible after 1813, the date of the coming into force of Rose's Act, may be seen from a comparison of the distribution of infant deaths from the reconstitution parishes with that found later in the century in Prussia as may be seen in table 6.7. It is clear at a glance that the two distributions are notably similar. The percentages of deaths occurring in the first day (4.5 in Prussia; 4.1 in the reconstitution parishes) are almost identical and the same is true for the first month (31.6 and 33.3 respectively). The circumstances of life in Prussia in 1877–81 may have been very different from those in England (for example, the legitimate infant mortality rate in those years in Prussia was considerably higher, at 184 per 1000,[73] than in England about 1840 when it was *c.* 145 per 1000). It would be helpful, of course, to have civil registration data for England in the 1840s to afford a more meaningful comparison, but the Registrar-General provided no such detailed breakdowns of English infant mortality. Even so, the comparison of reconstitution data with Prussian material tends to support the view that the registration of burials in English parish registers that survive tests for underregistration and unreliability was tolerably complete.[74]

The significance of the substantial fall in infant mortality in England

---

[73] See p. 221 n. 51 above.

[74] Further support is afforded by nineteenth-century Swedish data. In 1860–6 when the overall infant mortality rate was 133 per 1000, the proportion of all infant deaths occurring in the first week of life was 15.8 per cent, and in the first month 35.3 per cent. The comparable English figures in tab. 6.7 are 14.6 and 33.3 per cent. The Swedish data come from the work of Berg and were reproduced in Brändström and Sundin, 'Infant mortality in a changing society', tab. 2a–e, pp. 80–1.

Table 6.7 *Proportionate distribution of deaths within the first year of life in Prussia and in the English reconstitution parishes (percentages)*

Age in days	Prussia[a]	England[b]
0	4.5	4.1
1–6	8.9	10.5
7–29	18.2	18.7
30–59	11.5	11.5
60–89	9.4	8.1
90–179	20.6	17.4
180–365	26.9	29.6
Total	100.0	100.0

[a] Legitimate live-born children. In calculating a rate for the sexes combined from data relating to male and female births a sex ratio of 105:100 was assumed. The data refer to the years 1877–81.
[b] The data refer to the years 1813–37 after the coming into force of Rose's Act.
Sources: Pearl, *Human biology*, tab. 32, pp. 134–5; Cambridge Group reconstitutions.

in the course of the eighteenth century deserves emphasis. *Ceteris paribus* a fall of about 50 per 1000 in the infant mortality rate will have a considerable impact on population growth rates. For example, a fall in infant mortality from *c.* 200 to *c.* 150 per 1000 in a population with a zero growth rate, which was approximately true of England in the later seventeenth century,[75] is closely equivalent to increasing the number of births by more than 6 per cent, and at the levels of fertility and mortality prevailing in late seventeenth-century England, when the crude birth and death rates were both about 30 per 1000,[76] would cause a stationary population to rise by more than 20 per cent in the course of a century.

The striking improvement in mortality in the early weeks of life is unlikely to have been indirectly due to a sustained rise in living standards, or to have been a reflection of a significantly healthier, taller,

[75] The average intrinsic growth rate in the ten quinquennia 1651–6 to 1696–1700 was almost exactly zero. Wrigley and Schofield, *Population history of England*, tab. A3.1, p. 528.
[76] Ibid., tab. A3.1, pp. 528–9.

and better nourished population.[77] The fall in first month mortality did not begin until the mid-century, though mortality within the first week began to fall half a century earlier, whereas real wages had probably been rising since the mid-seventeenth century at the latest.[78] Moreover, the fall in first month mortality continued during the second half of the eighteenth century when living standards were probably no longer improving and may have been falling. If the circumstances that resulted in such a remarkable fall in maternal mortality at much the same time were better understood, it would be clearer whether the same causes might partly explain the fall in early infant mortality.[79]

The mortality of multiple births

Birth was always a perilous time for both mother and child in the past but far more so if she were carrying more than one child. Twins and triplets were far less likely to survive than other children and their mothers also suffered a greatly increased risk of death. Reconstitution is well suited to the study of this phenomenon but the number of multiple births in most individual reconstitutions is too small to allow any but the simplest general measures of mortality. When several reconstitutions are combined, however, the number of cases rises to a level that allows a more detailed analysis.

[77] During the first half of the eighteenth century real wages rose but thereafter their movement at the national level becomes uncertain. In the agricultural south there was probably regression, in parts of the industrial north advance. The real wage series constructed by Phelps Brown and Hopkins was based on southern craftsmen's wages in the eighteenth century; it suggests a substantial fall in real wages between the middle decades of the eighteenth century and the early 1800s. But in parts of the north real wages were moving in the opposite direction. Phelps Brown and Hopkins, *A perspective of wages and prices*, fig. 3, p. 19; Botham and Hunt, 'Wages in Britain'. Overall, during the century as a whole, it would be difficult to present a convincing case for marked improvement on present evidence. Data relating to achieved final height are available only for the last decades of the century. They suggest that English people were slightly better nourished than their neighbours on the continent, though they grew less tall than the Scots and Irish. Achieved final height was probably rising rather than falling at least until the generation reaching maturity in the 1820s, though thereafter there may have been regression; Floud, Wachter, and Gregory, *Height, health and history*, fig. 7.1, p. 289. However, there is very clear evidence that men who came from the cities were significantly shorter than their rural contemporaries, and inasmuch as the proportion of the population living in towns rose substantially during the eighteenth century the overall national trend will have been flat at best during the period when infant mortality fell so considerably; ibid., pp. 200–6; Wrigley, 'Urban growth and agricultural change', tab. 2, p. 688.

[78] Wrigley and Schofield, *Population history of England*, fig. 1, p. xxii.

[79] Possible explanations of the fall in maternal mortality are discussed below pp. 316–8.

In the reconstitution data set as a whole there were a total of 172 517 birth events of which 2338 were twins and 24 were triplets. There was in addition one set of quadruplets. Twin births were therefore 1.36 per cent of all birth events or 1 in 74, a ratio within the range observed in other populations. Similarly the ratio of triplets to all multiple births, at 1 in 98 is close to normal.[80]

In table 6.8 all the available data for twins from each parish are consolidated together, abandoning the familiar device of eliminating compositional distortions by grouping the data. This maximises the quantity of information available but should be used only with discretion to study change over time because the parish composition of the set changes.

In the first two columns of the table the overall mortality rate for twins is set out. Over the whole parish register period the rate exceeded 400 per 1000 with relatively little change over time apart from the final period, though with a suggestion that twin mortality peaked at the same time as infant mortality in the later seventeenth and early eighteenth centuries. In the second to fifth panels of the table the rates of four types of twins are given. Throughout the table the numbers at risk refer to

---

[80] It should be noted that parish registers are not always explicit in describing twin births as such, so that in many instances two children were treated as twins solely because they were baptised on the same day, but this does not appear to have given rise to significant misallocation.

Comparison with data for other populations involves some rather arbitrary decisions. For example, in England and Wales in the period 1950–4 there were 3 406 384 live births, 43 668 twin maternities, and a total of 44 085 multiple birth maternities. But in a substantial number of cases the multiple maternities resulted in stillbirths. Among the twin maternities, for example, there were 829 cases in which both children were stillborn. In such cases a parish register would be unlikely to contain any record since neither child would have been baptised. In a further 3154 cases one of the twins was stillborn and the other live-born. In a parish register the surviving twin might have been baptised without any indication that it was a twin birth. On the assumption that the least misleading comparison should be based on cases where both children in a twin pair were live-born, and making a suitable allowance to convert the total of live births into maternities giving rise to live births (that is, reducing the total of live births to reflect the number of multiple maternities giving rise to live births), twin maternities were 1.18 per cent of the total in England and Wales in 1950–4, or 1 in 85 (on the alternative assumption that stillborn twins would be missed in parish registration but that cases where one twin was stillborn but the other live-born would be recorded in such a way as to make it clear that a twin birth was involved, the comparable figures are 1.27 per cent and 1 in 79). The calculation of a ratio of triplets to all multiple births in a way that allows a meaningful comparison with the parish register data is also fraught with difficulties, but the ratio was probably about 1 in 107. The data were taken from Registrar-General, *Statistical review of England and Wales*, Tables Part II Civil, tab. DD (for the years 1950 to 1954).

Table 6.8 *The infant mortality of twins ($1000q_x$)*

	All		FF		FM		MF		MM	
	N	Rate	N	Rate	N	Rate	N	Rate	N	Rate
Before 1600	435	398	122	404	86	354	86	416	138	392
1600–49	782	388	214	329	148	256	147	376	221	416
1650–99	1023	447	314	451	196	409	195	384	267	429
1700–49	1081	452	322	458	208	457	207	456	335	432
1750–99	845	414	248	351	170	423	169	381	258	492
1800–37	510	279	153	319	102	212	101	225	155	315
All	4676	410	1373	398	909	372	904	384	1374	423

Note: legitimate births only. The numbers are totals of births rather than birth events. The FM rate refers to female individuals in mixed sex twin births; the MF rate to males in the same context. The 'All' totals exceed the sum of the other four categories because in some cases the sex of one or both twins is not known. For further comments see text.
Source: Cambridge Group reconstitutions.

individuals rather than to birth events. Thus, there were a total of 909 FM cases, that is 909 female children born in sets of twins where the other child was male. The apparent illogicality that there are odd numbers at risk in some instances, or that there were 909 FM cases but only 904 MF cases, arises because in a small number of cases the weight attached to a particular date may cause a particular child to be excluded. A similar consideration explains why the cumulative total number of individuals in the four panels detailing the four possible individual states in sex combinations of twins (4560) is less than the total in the first panel, which refers to all twins (4676). In a significant number of cases, especially before 1700, the sex of neither twin may be known. Almost all such cases soon resulted in an infant death. The infant mortality rate of the 116 children who appear only in the left-hand panel was about 930 per 1000.

The death rate in single sex twins was higher than in mixed sex pairs, no doubt because the former included many monozygotic pairs while the latter were all dizygotic. On the assumption that the death rate of dizygotic twins in single sex twins was the same as in mixed sex twins, and further that there were as many dizygotic children in single sex as in mixed sex twin pairs, it is a straightforward matter to estimate the level of monozygotic mortality even though it cannot be directly observed.[81] For female infants the dizygotic rate was 372 per 1000, and the monozygotic rate 449 per 1000, while for male infants the comparable rates were 384 and 498 per 1000. To attempt to pursue the matter further by studying change over time is hazardous because of the relatively small numbers involved when the sexes are studies separately. If this is nonetheless attempted, the monozygotic rate is normally, though not invariably, the higher of the two (for example, if the period is divided into three century blocks, 1550–1649, 1650–1749, and 1750–1837, resulting in six estimates in all, three male and three female, the monozygotic rate is the higher in five or the six cases). If the two monozygotic rates (male and female) are averaged in each period and compared to the averages of the two dizygotic rates, the hint of an intriguing pattern appears. Over the same three century blocks the monozygotic joint rate is remarkably stable at 470, 472, and 474 per 1000 respectively while the dizygotic rate is rather more variable at 342, 432,

---

[81] Cavalli-Sforza and Bodmer, *The genetics of human populations*, p. 567, describes the reasons for supposing that the number of monozygotic twins can be established approximately in this fashion. The implied rate of monozygotic twin maternities is 0.27 per cent of all maternities, a rate slightly lower than that observed in modern populations, where in Caucasoid populations it appears generally to fall in the range 0.35 to 0.40. Ibid., tab. 9.13, p. 568.

and 334 per 1000, a pattern broadly reminiscent of infant mortality generally. Moreover, if the same calculation is made for the second half of the last period, 1800–37, the former rate remains very high, at 533 per 1000, but the latter falls to a much lower level, 219 per 1000. It is possible, therefore, that the monozygotic rate was more resistant to decline than the dizygotic rate, but a study on a far larger scale would be needed to confirm this.

Table 6.8 shows that the overall twin mortality rate dropped abruptly at the end of the period. In 1750–99 it was 414 per 1000; in 1800–37 only 279 per 1000. The extent of the fall is probably exaggerated in the table since there was compositional change in the parishes from which the data were drawn. Once again small numbers preclude a firm assessment, but it may be significant that if twin mortality rates are calculated for groups 1, 2, 3, and 4 there is little difference between groups 1, 2, and 3 in periods of overlap between adjacent groups, but during the eighteenth century the rate in group 4 was about 60 per 1000 lower than in group 3. It is quite possible, therefore, that without this complication the fall would appear much more modest with the early nineteenth-century rate perhaps 80 per 1000 lower rather than 140 per 1000 lower.

Table 6.9 makes it clear how heavily the deaths of twins were concentrated into the first days and weeks of life. For comparison the rates that applied to all births in the same body of data are given, and also the ratio between the twin rate and the overall rates at each age. It is therefore readily visible that first day mortality in the two groups did not differ very markedly (though it should be recalled that the overall first day mortality includes the deaths of many 'dummy' births and that many of these probably died in the first week of life rather than on the first day).[82] Thereafter, however, the pattern is fairly simple: the ratio between the two rates was initially very high but steadily declined with the increasing age of the child. Mortality in the first month, excluding the first day, was almost five times as high among twins as among all births. In the second month the ratio of the two rates fell to less than three, and had fallen further to about two in the third trimester of life. It declined again in the fourth trimester to the point where the twin rate was only about 80 per cent higher than the overall rate, and there was a further small fall in the ratio in the second year of life.

The age of the mother is known in less than a quarter of all recorded cases of twins, so that no elaborate examination of the effect of age upon twin mortality is possible. However it seems unlikely that this was a

---

[82] See pp. 110–2 for a discussion of the circumstances that led to the creation of 'dummy' births.

Table 6.9 *The mortality of twins and of all children compared* $(1000q_x)$

						Days						
	0	1–6	7–29	30–59	60–89	90–179	180–273	274–365	366–457	458–548	549–730
Twins											
(a) Simple	59	116	147	41	29	50	34	27	28	18	31
Cumulative	59	168	290	319	339	372	393	410	426	437	454
All											
(b) Simple	34	25	31	16	11	22	17	15	14	11	19
Cumulative	34	58	87	101	111	130	145	158	169	179	194
Ratio of (a) to (b)	1.74	4.72	4.70	2.63	2.66	2.28	2.05	1.83	2.01	1.58	1.67

Note: legitimate births only. The total number of twin births was 4560: the total of all births 172 517.
Source: Cambridge Group reconstitutions.

247

major factor in determining mortality levels. The overall twin mortality rate was 398 per 1000.[83] The rate for twins whose mother's age was unknown was identical. The rates per 1000 for the successive five-year age groups by age of mother, from 15–9 to 45–9, were as follows (totals of cases in brackets after the rate): 379 (16), 435 (117), 409 (241), 401 (294), 378 (237), 361 (32), 417 (14).

The age of the mother was, however, important in other contexts. The reconstitution data show, for example, that young mothers were more likely to have all male twins than all female, but that with increasing age the pattern was reversed. If the numbers of FF, MF, and MM twins are expressed as percentages, in the age groups 15–29 the relative frequency of the three types was 28.7, 38.6, and 32.7; in the age groups 35–49 the percentages change to 32.9, 39.7, and 27.5.[84]

Maternal mortality is discussed below, but it is of interest to note here that the maternal death rate associated with twin births was much higher than in the case of singleton births; the former rate was three times the latter.[85] It is a striking illustration of the hazards faced by twins that in every case in which the mother of twins died in childbirth both twins also died (81 cases in all).

Mortality in childhood

In order to gain an impression of the history of child mortality as a whole it is convenient to consider next the changing pattern of rates for the age groups 1–4 (and its subdivisions), 5–9, and 10–4, confining the review to general patterns and reserving until later the treatment of more particular issues. With the benefit of an overview, other matters may be seen in perspective.

Table 6.10 shows the pattern of change in child mortality over the parish register period by decade, and also, to capture change in a summary form, by quarter-century. The problem of the 'join' between groups 1, 2, 3, and 4 was resolved in the same way as for infant mortality.[86] Summary measures covering both the last 10 years of childhood from 5 to 14 and the whole of the first 15 years of life are also included.

The probability of dying falls steadily with increasing age during childhood. In most populations the risk of dying in a given interval of

---

[83] This rate is calculated solely from cases where the sex of both twins was known and is therefore slightly lower than the rate quoted in tab. 6.8.

[84] The total number of twin pairs on which these percentages are based was 188 for 15–29 and 177 for 35–49. Given these small numbers, finer subdivisions did not seem appropriate.　　[85] Tab. 6.30, p. 320.　　[86] The details may be found in app. 7.

time reaches its nadir in the age group 10–4. In this age group it is low even when mortality in general is severe. In the quarter-millennium covered in table 6.10 only about 1 child in 40 died in the course of moving from age 10 to age 15, a marked contrast with the comparable risk in moving from age 1 to age 5 when the risk was 1 in 10, and a still greater contrast with the risk in moving from birth to age 1, which was about 1 in 5 or 1 in 6. Allowing for the different width of the age intervals in question, the risk of dying per unit interval of time was about 35 or 40 times as great in the first year of life as in a year of life in the early teens.

It is convenient to concentrate initially on the broad sweep of change shown in the lower panel of table 6.10, giving data by 25-year periods. In the age group 1–4 the mortality rate rose by almost 50 per cent between the early seventeenth century and the second quarter of the eighteenth century. Thereafter it declined somewhat, though only modestly, falling from about 120 per 1000 to about 100 per 1000 over the following century. The pattern of change was far from uniform, however, in the individual years of life within the age group. In the second year of life the rate changed dramatically between 1580–99 and 1725–49, rising by over 60 per cent. The second quarter of the eighteenth century was a period of high mortality in all the individual years in this age group. In all of them the rate was either the highest of any quarter-century, or very close to the peak rate. But in general this peak was followed by a fall to lower levels by the early nineteenth century. In the second year of life, however, the fall after 1750 was very slight, about 10 per cent. Indeed the behaviour of the rate for this age group suggests that it reached a plateau late in the seventeenth century and did not decline thereafter. This pattern of change is reminiscent of the pattern in the second half of the first year of life, shown in table 6.4. There, too, the rate, which was initially low, had almost doubled by 1725–49, and thereafter remained high. To bring out the distinctiveness of this pattern a fuller breakdown of the data is given in table 6.11.

Table 6.11 subdivides both the second half of the first year of life and the second year of life to make it easier to consider the distinctive mortality history of this age range, which occupies columns 3–7. Columns 1–2 and 8–9 provide information for earlier and later age periods The ratio figures in the second panel of the table are intended to bring this out. In all age groups the early eighteenth century was a high water mark but the 'before' and 'after' figures differed markedly. The most distinctive age group was perhaps that in the third column representing mortality in the third quarter of the first year of life. In this age group mortality rose by almost 90 per cent between the first century (that is, the average of the first four rows) and the

Table 6.10 Child mortality ($1000q_x$)

	$_1q_1$	$_1q_2$	$_1q_3$	$_1q_4$	$_4q_1$	$_5q_5$	$_5q_{10}$	$_{10}q_5$	$_{15}q_0$
1580–9	35.8	27.6	14.5	12.5	87.5	38.4	15.4	53.2	281.6
1590–9	32.9	22.9	12.8	15.3	81.4	54.4	22.3	75.5	297.7
1600–9	36.6	28.0	16.5	12.7	90.7	46.2	30.3	75.1	298.1
1610–9	35.2	18.4	13.1	12.7	77.2	32.5	16.2	48.2	268.1
1620–9	34.7	22.5	13.8	12.5	81.0	33.3	19.8	52.4	262.8
1630–9	41.4	27.6	19.6	12.8	97.8	51.4	26.8	76.9	300.6
1640–9	42.4	27.7	21.2	21.4	108.1	48.9	32.5	79.8	302.6
1650–9	44.4	32.0	22.0	14.4	108.3	47.4	25.8	71.9	308.4
1660–9	43.9	35.8	21.8	16.1	112.7	52.8	27.5	78.8	321.1
1670–9	43.7	32.3	21.3	13.8	106.8	51.9	28.4	78.7	315.6
1680–9	57.6	36.7	20.5	21.6	130.0	58.7	31.4	88.2	366.9
1690–9	37.0	22.4	18.5	12.2	87.3	31.4	20.9	51.6	285.8
1700–9	42.5	25.1	19.3	14.7	98.0	42.3	27.1	68.3	305.9
1710–9	52.2	24.5	29.4	17.9	118.7	47.7	30.8	77.0	352.0
1720–9	54.5	31.1	22.3	18.9	121.3	44.2	23.1	66.2	338.1
1730–9	53.0	27.4	19.2	16.6	111.6	55.0	32.3	85.5	346.1
1740–9	56.1	33.2	22.6	16.7	122.9	52.3	25.0	76.1	340.8
1750–9	43.6	25.5	17.3	13.2	96.1	33.7	26.3	59.1	285.3
1760–9	51.4	30.2	21.2	14.7	112.8	41.2	23.6	63.8	307.0
1770–9	50.6	30.0	25.0	13.6	114.4	50.2	29.4	78.1	313.2
1780–9	49.5	30.5	18.9	13.5	108.7	32.7	24.7	56.6	296.1
1790–9	48.3	26.8	14.0	11.3	97.1	30.7	17.1	47.3	270.0
1800–9	46.8	25.8	13.9	11.6	95.0	21.0	16.6	37.3	247.8
1810–9	45.8	26.4	16.6	18.3	103.1	27.4	26.4	53.0	263.6
1820–9	52.2	24.9	14.9	14.8	103.0	32.8	25.4	57.4	276.8
1830–7	46.5	19.3	13.8	11.9	88.8	34.1	34.1	67.0	269.2

250

1580–99	34.3	25.3	13.7	13.8	84.5	46.3	18.9	64.3	289.5
1600–24	35.7	22.0	13.7	12.7	81.6	36.1	22.7	58.0	277.8
1625–49	40.5	27.5	19.9	15.9	100.0	48.0	27.0	73.8	294.2
1650–74	43.7	34.3	22.5	15.4	111.1	50.9	26.1	75.6	315.3
1675–99	47.2	29.5	19.2	16.0	107.6	45.9	27.4	72.0	325.4
1700–24	47.6	24.8	23.7	16.3	107.9	46.4	27.0	72.2	330.2
1725–49	55.7	31.5	21.6	17.7	121.0	50.1	28.4	77.1	343.6
1750–74	48.4	27.9	21.4	13.9	107.3	41.1	25.7	65.7	301.8
1775–99	50.7	30.2	18.0	13.0	107.7	34.7	22.7	56.6	290.1
1800–24	47.7	25.5	14.6	13.6	98.0	25.7	20.0	45.2	255.9
1825–37	48.7	22.0	15.3	15.7	98.3	34.7	34.7	68.2	280.8

Note: legitimate births only. They were adjusted in the same way as those in tab. 6.1 to overcome the problem of 'joins' between the four groups.

Source: Cambridge Group reconstitutions.

Table 6.11 *Infant and early childhood mortality (1000q_x)*

	Days							Years	
	(1) 60–89	(2) 90–179	(3) 180–273	(4) 274–365	(5) 366–457	(6) 458–548	(7) 549–730	(8) $4q_1$	(9) $5q_5$
1580–99	12.2	25.0	11.9	12.3	10.0	11.3	15.2	84.5	46.3
1600–24	10.1	18.6	11.5	9.5	10.2	9.9	16.3	81.6	36.1
1625–49	8.4	18.7	12.3	13.8	13.0	10.5	17.8	100.0	48.0
1650–74	9.3	19.1	14.1	13.0	13.4	10.8	20.4	111.1	50.9
1675–99	13.1	24.6	16.0	16.6	15.2	13.0	20.0	107.6	45.9
1700–24	14.1	26.1	21.2	17.5	16.6	12.1	19.9	107.9	46.4
1725–49	13.8	26.9	22.5	20.4	22.1	14.1	24.8	121.0	50.1
1750–74	11.6	25.7	22.6	19.1	17.6	13.5	22.6	107.3	41.1
1775–99	11.0	26.6	23.0	17.7	16.1	13.5	23.2	107.7	34.7
1800–24	10.9	23.6	21.0	16.8	15.7	13.1	19.7	98.0	25.7
1825–37	10.7	27.1	27.2	22.3	14.6	15.0	19.7	98.3	34.7
Indexed data 100 = (1700–24 + 1725–49)/2									
First 4 rows 1580–1674	71.6	76.9	56.9	64.2	60.1	80.9	78.2	82.4	93.9
Last 4 rows 1750–1837	79.3	97.1	107.2	100.1	82.6	105.0	95.5	89.8	70.6
Ratio of last 4 rows to first 4 rows	1.108	1.264	1.886	1.560	1.375	1.299	1.221	1.090	0.752

Note: legitimate births only. The rates have been adjusted in the same way as those in tab. 6.1 to overcome the problem of 'joins' between the four groups.
Sources: Cambridge Group reconstitutions and tab. 6.10.

early eighteenth century and thereafter rose a little further (last four rows).

Moving out in both directions from this age group the pattern of relative change after the period of peak rates between 1700 and 1750 is similar. The fall from the high mortality levels of the early eighteenth century becomes more pronounced away from the third column so that in the second month of life (column 1) the fall was about 20 per cent from its peak level, and in the age group 5–9 (column 9) the fall was about 30 per cent. In columns closer to column 3 the fall was less marked. The five age groups from column 3 to column 7 formed a central 'ridge' in this respect. In all these age groups the fall after 1750 was slight (though the individual figures are variable): in them the ratio figure for the last century of the period was 98.1 on average. In general, then, beween the sixth and twenty-fourth month mortality showed no improvement after 1750, whereas at younger and older ages the improvement was quite marked.

An increase between the early seventeenth century and the high point a hundred years later was common to all nine columns but was much more strongly marked beween 6 and 15 months than at younger or older ages. In the three age groups comprising this age band mortality increased on average by almost two-thirds between the first century (1580–1674) and the peak period (1700–49). Away from this central age range of dramatic mortality deterioration in Elizabethan and Stuart times, the rise in death rates was much less marked. In the two youngest age groups mortality rose by about one third. Between 18 months and 5 years the rise was consistently about one fifth, while between the ages of 5 and 10 years it was well short of one tenth.

The third panel of table 6.11 tells the same story in a different way. The rates for the first four periods and the last four periods were averaged and the relationship between them expressed as a ratio. In the youngest age group the rate in the last century was only 11 per cent higher than in the first. At the other end of the age spectrum, in the age group $_5q_5$, the later rate was substantially the *lower* of the two. But, especially in the second half of the first year of life, the rise was pronounced: 89 per cent in the third quarter, 56 per cent in the fourth.

Change in the third, fourth, and fifth years of life may be traced by reverting to table 6.10. It shows a somewhat different character from that in slightly younger children. Quarter-century rates rose during the seventeenth century though less markedly than $_1q_1$ but thereafter tended to fall so that rates in 1800–24 were not much higher than in the early seventeenth century, though at the very end of the reconstitution period rates may have been rising once more (this feature is visible in $_1q_3$

and $_1q_4$ and very marked indeed in later childhood, $_5q_5$ and $_5q_{10}$). As evidence of a difference between $_1q_1$ and the later rates in the age group 1–4 it is noteworthy that, using the device employed in the bottom panel of table 6.11, the ratio of the last century rate to that in the first century was 1.27 in the case of $_1q_1$, whereas for the next three age groups, $_1q_2$, $_1q_3$, and $_1q_4$, the comparable ratio figures were 0.97, 0.99, and 0.97.

The rate for the age group 5–9 was in general more stable than any other childhood rate. Apart from a sharp dip in 1600–24, the rate varied little before 1750, though falling sharply thereafter to reach a very low level in the early decades of the nineteenth century, before rising again at the end of the parish register period.

Young teenagers ($_5q_{10}$) appear to have enjoyed very low mortality rates in late Elizabethan England but thereafter there was a fairly steady deterioration in mortality experience for a century, followed by some recovery in the later eighteenth century, though the rate rose to its highest level of the whole series in 1825–37, when it was almost at the same level as $_5q_5$, an inherently implausible finding. The absolute number of deaths even over a full quarter-century was quite low in this age group because the mortality rate was so modest (and still lower in a truncated period such as 1825–37, when the total number of deaths in the age group 10–4 in the eight parishes forming group 4, on which the rate was based, was only 68), and fluctuations in the rate are correspondingly hard to interpret with confidence. The small number of events probably accounts for the absence of a fall in the mortality rate between the two age groups, but, in view of the fact that both $_5q_5$ and $_5q_{10}$ were rising, it seems legitimate to conclude that rates in later childhood were rising, perhaps quite sharply, in the second quarter of the nineteenth century.

If the course of change is approached through the behaviour of decennial rather than quarter-century rates, the chief conclusion must be that using a larger scale map to survey the terrain does not change the picture greatly. In general trends were regular and uniform even when measured in these shorter units of time. The tendency towards rising mortality during the seventeenth century is plain in decennial data, for example, though perhaps a little less readily visible, and the balancing fall in the later eighteenth century is also clear.

But the decennial figures do bring to light a feature concealed by 25-year rates. During the period when child mortality rates were at their height between 1680 and 1750 there were substantial fluctuations in the rates, hidden by quarter-century divisions. In the age group 1–4, for example, rates were high in the 1680s, 1710s, 1720s, and 1740s. In all these decades $_4q_1$ was close to 120 per 1000 or above it. $_1q_1$ was higher in these decades than at any other time (except that it was also very high in the 1730s and 1820s) and the other early childhood rates, especially $_1q_2$, displayed a similar pattern. The 1690s and 1700s, on the other hand, were a benign period: $_4q_1$ in these decades was only about three-quarters as high as in the high-mortality decades on either side and proportionately mortality rates later in childhood were even lower, especially in the 1690s. The quarter-century rates contain little hint of this, however. They were almost identical during the three quarter-centuries between 1650 and 1725 before rising to a substantially higher level in 1725–49. The stability of this rate thereafter, which is a feature of the quarter-century rates, however, is fully confirmed in the decennial data.

In general terms the decennial behaviour of $_5q_5$ and $_5q_{10}$ shows much the same pattern as that described for $_4q_1$ and its components. Because the number of deaths involved is much smaller in the two higher age groups it is to be expected that their variability when compared with the same rates calculated for longer periods of time would be greater, but since much of this is attributable to randomness, little should be read into it. Two of the later decades are worthy of note, however. Both in the 1750s and in the 1790s and 1800s rates throughout childhood were very low: these decades rivalled the 1690s in this respect. Lower rates are not otherwise found without going back to the early seventeenth century. The mortality rate $_{14}q_1$ in 1750–9 was 149.5 per 1000, in 1790–9 139.8, and in 1800–9 128.8 per 1000, whereas the comparable rate for the three decades 1760–89 was 170.8 and that for the closing quarter-century of the parish register period, 1810–37, was 151.6.[87] It is also notable that the decennial data firmly underwrite the impression given by the quarter-century material that child mortality above the age of 5 years was rising sharply as the parish register period neared its end.

The overall patterns of mortality in later childhood are perhaps most easily appreciated by reviewing changes in $_{10}q_5$ and $_{15}q_0$. They reveal an early rise to a plateau that changed little between the second quarter of the seventeenth century and the middle of the eighteenth century, followed by a marked fall during the next half-century but with a return to levels approaching those of the earlier plateau at the very end of the period. This late rise parallels the changes in infant mortality but is more pronounced: the rise in $_4q_1$ was too slight to be significant.

The reality of a nadir in infant and child mortality early in the nineteenth century seems clear and the subsequent reversal was substantial. The overall mortality level of infancy and childhood, $_{15}q_0$,

[87] These rates were calculated as the averages of the decades in question. In the later of the two periods 1830–7 was treated as forming 80 per cent of a decade and a suitable divisor employed.

Table 6.12 *Overall childhood mortality*
(1000q_x)

	$_{10}q_5$	$_{15}q_0$
1580–99	64.3	295.0
1600–24	58.0	282.9
1625–49	73.8	297.6
1650–74	75.6	317.1
1675–99	72.0	328.2
1700–24	72.2	333.8
1725–49	77.1	348.1
1750–74	65.7	308.1
1775–99	56.6	297.9
1800–24	45.2	263.1
1825–37	68.2	287.2

Note: the infant mortality rate which
forms part of $_{15}q_0$ is an overall rate
including illegitimate children. The rates
were adjusted in the same way as those
in tab. 6.1 to overcome the problem of
'joins' between the four groups.
Sources: tabs. 6.2 and 6.10.

was at its height in the second quarter of the eighteenth century, when it
stood at 344 per 1000 (348 per 1000 if illegitimate infant mortality is
taken into account).[88] By 1800–24 it had fallen to 256 (263), but then rose
to 281 (287) in 1825–37, still well short of the height reached a century
earlier but a significant rise nonetheless. The comparable figure from the
third English life table is 315 per 1000 (this life table was based on births
and deaths occurring in England and Wales in the 17-year period
1838–54).

These data suggest the possibility of a substantial worsening of
mortality in infancy and childhood in the first half of the nineteenth
century. The analysis by Laxton and Williams of the London bills of
mortality shows a very similar pattern. From a high point during the
first 15 years of the period for which age-specific data are available in
these returns, when infant mortality averaged about 400 per 1000
(1728–42), the London rate fell to only about 130 per 1000 in 1815–24,
only to rebound to about 140 per 1000 in the 1830s and to over 160 per
1000 in the 1840s. This finding is the more persuasive in that the infant
mortality rate calculated from the bills of mortality in the 1840s matches

[88] See above tab 6.2, p. 219, and associated text.

the Registrar-General's data for London in that decade very closely.[89] Recent work by Huck shows similar trends in a number of English industrial parishes.[90] Nor was the trend peculiar to England in this period. The rise in the second quarter of the century appears also to have occurred in Scotland.[91]

The mortality estimates for the period after 1790, which reveal a nadir in infant and child mortality rates in the early nineteenth century, are based, of course, on data taken from only 8 parishes (those forming group 4) and there might therefore seem reason to regard them with reserve. One or two parishes, if they were relatively large in population, might dominate the picture produced from a consolidated data set drawn from the 8 parishes. But the pattern across the parishes is clear-cut and conforms to the pattern for group 4 as a whole.

Consider the three successive periods 1775–99, 1800–24, and 1825–37. The expected pattern is a fall in rates from the first to the second period, followed by a rise betweeen the second and the third. There are four rates in question, $_1q_0$, $_4q_1$, $_5q_5$, and $_5q_{10}$, and therefore a total of 32 rate change patterns to be observed in the 8 parishes (8 × 4). The possible combinations in the movement of rates between the first and second periods and between the second and third periods are down/up, up/up, up/down, and down/down. The expected pattern is, of course, the first. This occurred in 20.5 cases, up/up in 6.5 cases, up/down in 3 cases, and down/down in 2 cases (the halves arise when a rate does not change between successive periods). In almost two-thirds of the cases therefore the pattern was as expected. A simpler measure can also be used. Of the 32 rate movements from the first to the second period, 22.5 were down and 9.5 were up; and from the second to the third 27 were up and 5 were down. There is thus strong evidence that the changes observable in the

[89] Laxton and Williams, 'Urbanization and infant mortality', fig. 7, p. 126. The London bills state the number of deaths of children in the first two years of life, and any estimate of infant mortality based on them must therefore make an assumption about the proportion of the total of deaths under two which referred to infants under one. Laxton and Williams made maximum and minimum assumptions about this proportion and thus maximum and minimum estimates of the infant rate. The rates quoted above were calculated by eye from the graph which they published and are therefore approximate. It was assumed that a rate half-way between their maxima and minima is the most plausible.

[90] Huck, 'Infant mortality'. Huck's findings echo those of Armstrong, using the exceptionally detailed and reliable data available for Carlisle, though Armstrong covered a longer period. He showed that between the 1780s and the early 1840s the mortality rate of children under 5 rose by more than one fifth. Armstrong, 'Mortality in Carlisle', tab. 3, p. 104.

[91] Flinn *et al.*, *Scottish population history*, pp. 368–79, and notably tabs. 5.5.1, 5.5.2, and 5.5.3, pp. 377–8, containing data relating to mortality in Glasgow.

Table 6.13 *Comparison of reconstitution mortality estimates with the third English life table* $(1000q_x)$

	Third English life table	Reconstitution estimates 1825–37
$_1q_0$	149.5	151.7
$_4q_1$	133.7	98.3
$_5q_5$	46.6	34.7
$_5q_{10}$	25.6	34.7
$_{10}q_5$	71.0	68.2
$_{15}q_0$	315.4	287.2

Note: the reconstitution mortality rate $_1q_0$ is an overall rate including illegitimate children.
Sources: tabs. 6.2 (infant mortality) and 6.10 (child mortality). The q_xs of the third English life table were calculated from the l_xs in Registrar-General, *Supplement to sixty-fifth annual report*, pt 1, tabs. H and I, pp. xlviii–li.

consolidated data were also normally paralleled in the individual constituent parishes.

In spite of the frailty of the empirical base represented by data drawn from the 8 parishes of group 4, a comparison of the estimates of infant and child mortality derived from reconstitution for the period 1825–37 with the rates in the third English life table, which relate to the 17 years 1838–54, is moderately reassuring as to the validity of estimates derived from group 4 material.

Table 6.13 contains details of the rates for the conventional age divisions. The infant rates are closely similar in the two columns of the table, and, if the rates for the later years of childhood, $_5q_5$ and $_5q_{10}$, are combined as $_{10}q_5$, the similarity is again marked. For reasons already discussed the amalgamation of these two age groups into a single entity makes good sense in view of the comparatively small number of deaths involved in the calculation of reconstitution-based rates.[92] But there is a much larger divergence between the two columns in the case of $_4q_1$. Here the reconstitution-based rate is much lower than that of the third English life table, and it is this difference which accounts for the lower level of $_{15}q_0$ in the reconstitution column. Nor was this a temporary situation found only in 1825–37. In no decade in the entire quarter-millennium of parish register coverage was $_4q_1$ in the reconstitution-based estimates as high as in the third English life table (figure 6.1).

[92] See above pp. 254–5. Over a longer period of time, of course, with larger numbers of events, the relative levels of $_5q_5$ and $_5q_{10}$ were 'normal'. For example, over the period 1775–1837 (including, therefore, the period 1825–37), the rates were 31.2 and 24.3 per 1000.

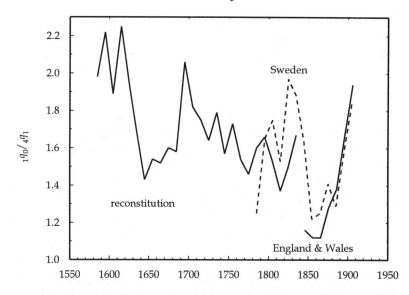

Figure 6.8 *The changing ratio of infant to early childhood mortality in England and Sweden* ($_1q_0/_4q_1$)

Notes: the English reconstitution data refer to decades running 1580–9 to 1820–9, and then 1830–7. The English national data from the civil registration period refer to decades running 1841–50 to 1901–10. The Swedish data refer to 5-year periods centring on the year '5', 1783–7 to 1903–7.

Sources: English reconstitution data: tabs. 6.1 and 6.3. English national data: *The Chester Beatty life tables*. Swedish data: Keyfitz and Flieger, *World population*, pp. 462–93.

In this respect the reconstitution parishes appear to be markedly different from the country a whole, a difference made all the more likely because the 26 reconstitution parishes do not include any from a big city or major new industrial area, and it was in such areas that early childhood mortality was so high relative to infant mortality.[93] But this appearance is deceptive. Woods has recently devoted much attention to the analysis of the relationship between mortality rates in different age groups, making extensive use of the $_1q_0/_4q_1$ ratio in this connection.[94] Figure 6.8 summarises the history of this ratio in England and Sweden.

The scale of the changes in the ratio between the mid-eighteenth and early twentieth centuries and the remarkably close similarity in the trend of the ratio in the two countries are evident. The latter may in time

[93] Woods, 'On the historical relationship between infant and adult mortality', pp. 204–7.
[94] Ibid. Prof. Woods was most generous in making available his working papers on this issue. It was he who appreciated the significance of a comparison of English and Swedish data as reflected in fig. 6.8. Fig. 6.8 is his work, though the data are very slightly modified from his original analysis. It is a pleasure to acknowledge his generosity.

provide important clues to the simultaneity of changes in the type and virulence of prevalent fatal diseases in different countries. In this context, however, the prime interest of the figure lies in the evidence it affords of a very striking change in the ratio just at the time when the parish register era was ending and the age of civil vital registration was beginning.

In the English series the last 'reconstitution' reading, which refers to the years 1830–7, is 1.67 while the next 'national' readings, for 1840–9, 1850–9, and 1860–9, are 1.16, 1.12, and 1.12. The infant mortality rates in the four periods were almost identical (149, 154, 152, and 153 per 1000 respectively), so that the change in the ratio is due solely to the rise in early childhood mortality. The English data taken in isolation would simply suggest that the reconstitution parishes were unrepresentative of the country as a whole because $_4q_1$ was understated in the parochial data. Taken in conjunction with the Swedish series, however, this inference appears less justified. The Swedish ratios for the same four decades, referring in each case to the five-year period centring on the midpoint of the decade (1833–7, 1843–7, etc.), were 1.88, 1.63, 1.22, and 1.25 respectively. For the whole of the period from 1790 to the First World War the ratio series for the two countries run closely in parallel, and it is therefore reasonable to view the marked change in the English ratio in the transition from reconstitution to civil registration not as the result of the unrepresentative nature of the parish register data, but as evidence of a major rise in early childhood mortality, which happened to coincide with the change from one data source to another. The sharp fall in the Swedish ratio occurred a little later than in England but the prior and subsequent trends in the two series were notably similar. It should be noted, however, that the change in the Swedish ratio was not simply due to a rise in $_4q_1$, as in England, but to a combination of falling infant mortality and rising early childhood mortality.

A judgement about the success with which the reconstitution early childhood mortality rates mirror national experience is therefore nicely balanced. The reconstitution parishes in question were broadly representative of the registration districts in which they were located, and these were districts in which early childhood mortality was lower than the national average.[95] This creates a strong presumption that the

[95] For a comparison of infant and child mortality in the parishes and registration districts, see tab. 4.3, p. 93. In the registration districts containing the 26 reconstitution parishes there were only two cases where $_4q_1$ in 1838–44 was higher than the rate in the third English life table (North Witchford and Bradford/Dewsbury, the registration districts containing the parishes of March and Birstall). The average level of $_4q_1$ in the 26 registration districts was only 98.3 per 1000, compared with 133.7 per 1000 in the third

reconstitution series does not reflect national experience, at any rate towards the end of the parish register period when a rising proportion of the population lived in large urban or industrial agglomerations. On the other hand, the evidence of figure 6.8 shows that the difference in early childhood mortality rates in the two columns of table 6.13 may reflect a genuine, abrupt rise in death rates in this age group occurring in the middle decades of the nineteenth century.

Age patterns of mortality and model life tables

The process of bringing the microscope closer and closer to the object of study can, of course, be extended further by studying quinquennial data, though inevitably the rates are more affected by random influences as the unit of time becomes shorter. Before considering such data, however, it is convenient to compare the pattern of infant and child mortality rates in the reconstitution sample with those to be found in model life tables. Model life tables attempt to distil the essence of large quantities of empirical data concerning the age and sex patterns of mortality by using a variety of statistical techniques to capture the regularities which may be supposed to underlie the observed rates. It has been remarked previously that at the time when Farr constructed the third English life table the age pattern of mortality in England bore a strong resemblance to that of model North in the Princeton life tables.[96] How are the changes in the age pattern of rates in infancy and childhood best characterised relative to those in the Princeton series? Table 6.14 is intended to address this issue.

In model West terms the major anomaly lies in the relatively severe mortality experienced above the age of 5 compared with that earlier in life. The age group 5–9 in particular suggests a far more severe regime than 0–1 or 1–4. The relative levels of infant and early childhood mortality fluctuate but without ever moving very far apart, but there is a pronounced change in the next higher age group, while mortality in the early teens in model West terms usually lies somewhere between the levels found in the first and second five years of life.

English life table (tab. 6.13). For the sources used to calculate the mortality rates for 1838–44 see source notes to tab. 4.3.

[96] The correspondence is not perfect. In the middle years of life (from 25 to 54) the male rates in the third English life table are slightly more severe than would be expected from rates at other ages, and this feature is very much more pronounced in the case of female rates, which from age 20 to 55 are substantially more severe than would be expected from rates at other ages and the use of the North table: see Wrigley and Schofield, *Population history of England*, tab. A14.1, p. 709.

Table 6.14 *Comparison of the age pattern of English infant and child mortality (1000q_x) with Princeton model life tables*

					Level in model									
					West					North				
	$_1q_0$	$_4q_1$	$_5q_5$	$_5q_{10}$	$_{15}q_0$	$_1q_0$	$_4q_1$	$_5q_5$	$_5q_{10}$	$_{15}q_0$	$_1q_0$	$_4q_1$	$_5q_5$	$_5q_{10}$	$_{15}q_0$
1580–99	177.1	84.5	46.3	18.9	295.0	9.9	11.9	5.5	11.6	10.2	8.6	13.2	11.3	13.7	10.9
1600–24	171.1	81.6	36.1	22.7	282.9	10.3	12.1	8.1	9.9	10.6	8.9	13.5	13.3	12.1	11.4
1625–49	157.4	100.0	48.0	27.0	297.6	11.1	10.5	5.1	8.2	10.1	9.8	12.1	11.0	10.5	10.8
1650–74	168.9	111.1	50.9	26.1	317.1	10.4	9.6	4.5	8.5	9.4	9.1	11.2	10.5	10.8	10.1
1675–99	188.8	107.6	45.9	27.4	328.2	9.2	9.8	5.6	8.0	9.0	7.9	11.4	11.4	10.3	9.7
1700–24	195.1	107.9	46.4	27.0	333.8	8.9	9.8	5.5	8.2	8.8	7.5	11.4	11.3	10.5	9.6
1725–49	196.3	121.0	50.1	28.4	348.1	8.8	8.8	4.7	7.6	8.3	7.4	10.4	10.6	10.0	9.1
1750–74	170.4	107.3	41.1	25.7	308.1	10.3	9.9	6.8	8.7	9.7	9.0	11.5	12.3	11.0	10.5
1775–99	166.0	107.7	34.7	22.7	297.9	10.6	9.8	8.5	9.9	10.1	9.3	11.5	13.6	12.1	10.8
1800–24	144.4	98.0	25.7	20.0	263.1	12.0	10.7	11.3	11.0	11.4	10.7	12.2	15.5	13.2	12.1
1825–37	151.7	98.3	34.7	34.7	287.2	11.5	10.6	8.5	5.5	10.5	10.2	12.2	13.6	7.9	11.2

Note: the reconstitution mortality rates $_1q_0$ are overall rates including illegitimate children. The rates for the sexes combined for model West and model North were taken as the average of the male and female rates in the model life table except that for $_1q_0$ and $_{15}q_0$ the ratio of males to females was taken as 105:100. The rates were adjusted in the same way as those in tab. 6.1 to overcome the problem of 'joins' between the four groups.
Sources: tabs. 6.2 and 6.10; Coale and Demeny, *Regional model life tables*.

Viewed in model North terms, the pattern appears quite differently: now all three childhood rates are in moderately close agreement with each other throughout the 250-year period (the $_5q_{10}$ rate in 1825–37 is the sole major exception). But infant mortality is substantially more severe than the childhood rates would have suggested in all periods but especially in the first half-century and again in the later seventeenth and early eighteenth centuries. By the early nineteenth century, however, $_1q_0$ grows less anomalous when compared to $_4q_1$. Plainly, English infant and child mortality in the early modern period did not conform either to model West or to model North, though edging closer to the model North pattern in the late eighteenth and early nineteenth centuries. Indeed, mortality in infancy and childhood in the English historical past does not appear to have resembled the patterns found in any of the families of tables which were extrapolated from more recent data in the Princeton tables. In model East terms, for example, the English rates in later childhood were notably severe, but infant rates were very modest.[97]

Infant and child mortality rates can also be summarised as $_{15}q_0$. Expressed in either West or North terms the swings over time are significant without ever appearing very dramatic. In both cases the extreme values are three levels apart (11.4 and 8.3 in West; 12.1 and 9.1 in North), equivalent to a difference in expectation of life at birth of approximately 7.5 years.

Short-term changes in infant and child mortality

The variability of mortality in the short term was normally greater than that of either nuptiality or fertility. The mean annual percentage deviations of the crude death rate from its own centred 25-year moving average reached a high level at times during the parish register period. Using data from the 404 parishes which formed the empirical basis of the *Population history of England*, for example, the annual deviation was more than 30 per cent in the decade of the 1550s, and over the quarter-century 1550–74 averaged almost 18 per cent before falling to about 12 per cent in each of the next four quarter-century periods. It then fell sharply to 9 and 6 per cent respectively in 1675–99 and 1700–24, but rebounded to 12 per cent in 1725–49, before declining gently thereafter to about 4 per cent by the middle of the nineteenth century.[98] Because of the much smaller number of events in the reconstitution data set annual

---

[97] The question of the characteristic change in the 'shape' of mortality by age in early modern England is discussed further below pp. 282–5.
[98] Wrigley and Schofield, *Population history of England*, tab. 8.7, p. 317.

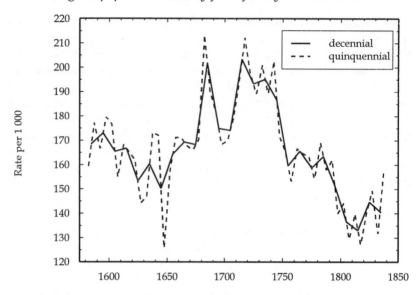

Figure 6.9   *Infant mortality (1000q$_x$): decennial and quinquennial rates
compared*
Note: legitimate births only.
Source: Cambridge Group reconstitutions.

variation cannot be studied, but some issues can be taken further using quinquennial rates to supplement the earlier discussion based on 10-year and 25-year rates.

In general quinquennial infant mortality rates do not differ greatly from the rates for the decade of which they form part. The decennial and quinquennial rates are shown in graphical form in figure 6.9. Discussion here is largely confined to those cases where the two quinquennial rates which together make up a decade differ markedly from each other.

The earliest period that attracts attention is 1620–39. Legitimate infant mortality was low in these decades with rates in 1620–9 and 1630–9 at 153.4 and 160.3 per 1000 respectively, but the decennial rates conceal the depth of the trough in infant rates since the successive quinquennial rates during the period from 1620–4 to 1635–9 were 162.0, 144.2, 146.8, and 173.1 per 1000 respectively. In the 10-year period from 1625–34, therefore, the rate was only 145.5 per 1000. It was again at an exceptionally low level in the quinquennium 1645–9 at 125.8 per 1000, even though the rate for the 1640s as a whole was 150.2. No other quinquennium experienced a rate as low as these three quinquennia until very late in the eighteenth century and between them they largely account for the generally low level of the decennial rates between 1620 and 1650. The low rates in these three quinquennia were the result of falls in both the endogenous and exogenous components of infant mortality in roughly equal proportions.

After 1680 for a period of 70 years infant mortality rose to significantly higher levels than previously except in the 1690s and 1700s when the decennial rate, though still higher than in the pre-1680 period, was appreciably lower than in the other four decades of this middle period. Within the 70 years a few quinquennia are worthy of note. In the periods 1680–4 and 1715–9 the rate rose above 210 per 1000. The 'full' infant rate, including illegitimate infant mortality was, of course, still higher, about 215–20 per 1000. These were the peak quinquennia of the whole quarter-millennium. At the other extreme, the low decennial rates in the 1690s and 1700s occurred only because rates were back to pre-1680 level in the two quinquennia from 1695 to 1704 (168.4 and 169.8 per 1000 respectively). And when the quinquennial data are consulted, the end of the period of high rates can be seen to have taken place earlier than indicated by decennial rates. The rate in 1740–4 was still as high as 202.6 per 1000 but in the second half of the decade it had fallen to 171.7 and thereafter remained close to this level, if a little below it, for the next 35 years.

Childhood rates may be reviewed in the same fashion. They are shown in figure 6.10. The period of low mortality in the early seventeenth century is visible earlier in $_4q_1$ than in $_1q_0$. The decennial rate was low in the 1610s and 1620s (table 6.10). Quinquennial rates enable the period of consistently low early childhood mortality to be identified as 1605–34 when $_4q_1$ averaged only 80.0 per 1000. As with infant mortality, $_4q_1$ was again low in 1645–9 (79.1 per 1000), but in between these two periods of low rates there was a spell when early childhood mortality shot up to a far more severe level (112.3 per 1000 in 1635–9 and to the highest level of the whole quinquennial series, 135.4, in 1640–4). After a brief remission in 1645–54, quinquennial rates moved to a substantially higher level throughout the period 1655–89 (averaging 116.9 per 1000), preceding the rise in infant mortality by a quarter of a century. The rate dipped for a 15-year period 1690–1704 (89.4 per 1000) but was then continuously above 100 per 1000 from 1705–9 to 1750–4 with an exceptionally high peak, the second highest of the series, in 1725–9 (135.2). Thereafter the rate fell back slightly, but, as we have seen previously, unlike infant rates or those of later childhood, $_4q_1$ remained close to its high level of the later seventeenth and early eighteenth centuries during the balance of the parish register period. Between 1760–4 and 1830–4 the quinquennial rate averaged 104.5 per 1000

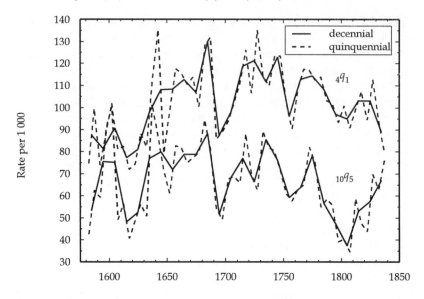

Figure 6.10   *Child mortality (1000q_x): decennial and quinquennial rates compared*
Source: Cambridge Group reconstitutions.

compared to 116.9 for the period 1655–89 and 115.4 for the period 1705–54.

The quinquennial rates for $_{10}q_5$ are based on rather small numbers of deaths (characteristically totals in the range 60–130 down to 1780 and only about 30–70 thereafter, the period when the rates are derived from the group 4 parishes). This limits the confidence that can be placed in a comparison of decennial and quinquennial rates. With this *caveat*, however, the following points may be noted. The quinquennial rate was very high indeed from 1595 to 1604, exceeding 100 in 1600–4, a feature cloaked by the decennial rates, but from 1605 to 1634 the rate was consistently low, averaging only just over 50 per 1000 and including in 1615–9 the fourth lowest rate of the entire quinquennial series. In 1635–9 the rate increased very sharply to over 100 again and remained generally at a high level until 1685–9. Both 1600–4 and 1635–9 were quinquennia in which plague was locally prevalent.[99] The average over the period 1635–89 was 81.3 (with a lowest rate of 61.1 in 1650–4). There then ensued a period of 40 years, 1690–1729, when rates were much lower, averaging 62.6 per 1000, if a brief surge back to a high level in 1715–9 is excluded. Thereafter the decennial and quinquennial rates tell

[99] For the period 1600–4, see p. 268.

Table 6.15 *Extended periods when infant and child mortality was consistently high* $(1000q_x)$

	$1q_0$	$4q_1$	$5q_5$	$5q_{10}$	$15q_0$
1679–86	211.2	125.4	58.5	35.2	373.3
1716–21	220.1	121.2	53.1	38.4	376.0
1727–33	212.2	132.1	49.6	32.7	371.3

Note: legitimate births only. The rates shown are averages of the years in question. The data are all drawn from group 2 except for the period 1730–3 for which group 3 provided the data. The group 3 material was adjusted to overcome the 'join' problem in the same way as for the material in tab. 6.1. *Source*: Cambridge Group reconstitutions.

a similar story, except that the quinquennial rates reveal that the period of very low rates began in 1795 and lasted until 1824, though 1810–4 was a local 'spike'. Excluding 1810–4, the average level of the quinquennial rate for 1795–1824 was only 41.1 per 1000. Both decennial and quinquennial rates strongly support the impression that rates in later childhood were rising strongly from the start of the nineteenth century until the end of the parish register period

Quinquennial rates in general, therefore, though somewhat more volatile than decennial rates, do not substantially modify the patterns visible in the decennial figures other than to identify the 'edges' of the plateaus already described and to demonstrate the existence of minor hillocks and depressions in the landscape.

There were three extended periods of high mortality lasting for more than 5 but fewer than 10 years, 1679–86, 1716–21, and 1727–33. Details are given in table 6.15. The age pattern of mortality was remarkably similar in all three periods. The overall level of infant and child mortality, $15q_0$, was almost identical in all three, and in all three mortality rates were consistently high in every year.[100]

[100] The three periods in question were not all periods when mortality in general was high. The average level of the crude death rate (CDR) in 1679–86 was 34.4 per 1000, a very high level for early modern England generally, as is shown by the fact that the 10 years on either side of the high mortality period experienced a far lower level of CDR: in 1674–8 and 1687–91 the CDR averaged 28.1 per 1000. In the next period of high infant and child rates from 1716 to 1721, however, the CDR averaged only 28.8 per 1000 and was slightly below the level in the 10 years surrounding this period, when the CDR was 29.4 per 1000. The last period, 1727–33, was like the first in this respect. The CDR was very high indeed, averaging 35.6 per 1000, whereas in the 10 years surrounding 1727–33, it stood at 28.3 per 1000 on average. Wrigley and Schofield, *Population history of England*, tab. A3.3, pp. 532–3. See also, ibid., tab. A10.4, pp. 660–1 for a convenient tabulation of the prevalence of local mortality crises by quinquennia.

There were also cases where a brief spurt of high mortality occurred, whose severity is not evident in the quinquennial rates. In the late sixteenth century, for example, ${}_{15}q_0$ was as high as 403.3 per 1000 in 1588, and was also high in 1596–7, averaging 375.6. Shortly afterwards, in 1603, chiefly because of plague in Lowestoft and Reigate, mortality rose higher than in any other year with ${}_{15}q_0$ at the crippling level of 510.0 per 1000 (infant mortality was high in this year, at 223.1 per 1000, but this level was exceeded in a scattering of other years between 1580 and 1730: it was the quite exceptional level of ${}_{4}q_1$, ${}_{5}q_5$, and ${}_{5}q_{10}$, each of which was higher in 1603 than in any other year, which caused the overall rate to be so high).[101] Other, similar examples can be found in 1642–3, 1658–9, 1695, and 1741–2.[102] In these years ${}_{15}q_0$ lay in the range from 350 to 420 per 1000. There were no later years in which the toll of young life approached this level.

Viewed overall, perhaps the single most striking feature of the general movements in infant and child mortality from the period when they were at their highest level early in the eighteenth century to the end of the parish register period is the degree to which change was dominated by the fall in the neonatal rate. In the first half of the eighteenth century this rate stood at 104.0 per 1000 and the rate for infancy and childhood as a whole (${}_{15}q_0$) stood at 336.9 per 1000. At the end of the period in 1825–37, the two rates were 48.7 and 280.8 respectively.[103] But for the fall in neonatal mortality, therefore, there would have been almost no change in mortality under the age of 15 between the beginning and the end of the last 150 years of the parish register period, though there was a short period of significantly lower mortality early in the nineteenth century.

Infant and child mortality in individual parishes

The device of summarising infant and childhood mortality in a single rate can also be employed to illustrate the extent of the contrast in mortality experience between the 26 parishes. In table 6.16 ${}_{15}q_0$ is given for each of the 26 parishes for the period 1675–1749, together with the rates for the conventional age divisions. In this period all the parishes

[101] The three rates were, respectively, 179.8, 150.0, and 95.3 per 1000. The total of burials recorded on Lowestoft FRFs averaged 35.4 in the five years 1598–1602 but jumped to 269 in 1603; in Reigate the comparable figures were 25.2 and 166. For the prevalence of plague generally in this period, see Creighton, *Epidemics in Britain*, I, ch. 10.
[102] Wrigley and Schofield, *Population history of England*, tab. A3.3, pp. 532–3.
[103] All these rates refer to legitimate children only (tabs. 6.4 and 6.10).

were in observation either throughout or for all but a few years (detailed in the table notes). The relative level of mortality in the parishes is therefore more accurately captured than would be the case if the rates referred to the whole reconstitution period in each parish, since this varied considerably from parish to parish.[104] The parishes are set out in descending order of overall mortality and against each is given comparable rates for the registration district within which the parish was situated for certain years soon after the beginning of civil registration.

The scale of the discrepancy between $_{15}q_0$ in March at the top of the table and Hartland at the bottom is striking; the figure for the latter is less than 40 per cent of that for the former. Parishes like March and Gainsborough suffered from very high infant and child death rates. Only about 40 per cent of female babies in these parishes would have reached the mean age at maternity (using Princeton model North life tables and taking the mean age at maternity as 32 years). Assuming that 10 per cent of each generation never married, and ignoring illegitimacy, this implies that a total marital fertility rate of a little over 5.6 would be needed to ensure replacement. At the level of marital fertility rates prevailing in early modern England, and assuming a mean age at marriage of 26, it is readily apparent that the populations of parishes such as these would have experienced difficulty in avoiding population decline unless net migration were positive.[105] Equally, similar calculations make it clear that there must have been substantial out-migration from parishes like Hartland in the absence of any rapid local build-up of numbers.

Comparison of the registration district rates from the mid-nineteenth century with those of the reconstitution parishes in 1675–1749 is instructive, though it is perhaps safer to avoid comparisons of individual parishes with the associated registration district, since, although a process of averaging is likely to make comparison of a number of parishes with their registration districts meaningful (that is, on average

[104] See tab. 2.1, pp. 22–3.

[105] At the rates prevailing in early modern England a woman marrying at age 26 might expect to bear 5.04 children if she survived in marriage throughout the childbearing period. The marital fertility rates for the age groups 25–9 to 45–9 used in this calculation were 365, 315, 250, 130, and 20 per 1000 respectively. These are rounded numbers close to those found to prevail in English parishes in the parish register period. See tab. 7.1 p. 355. Though infant and child mortality rates were high in March and Gainsborough, they were still higher in some other towns and cities, and above all in London, where in the early eighteenth century infant mortality was probably in excess of 400 per 1000. Laxton and Williams, 'Urbanization and infant mortality', fig. 1, p. 111.

Table 6.16 *Infant and child mortality in the 26 reconstitution parishes in 1675–1749 and in the registration districts in which they were located in the 1840s ($1000q_x$)*

	Reconstitution parishes 1675–1749					Registration districts 1838–44				
	$_1q_0$	$_4q_1$	$_5q_5$	$_5q_{10}$	$_{15}q_0$	$_1q_0$	$_4q_1$	$_5q_5$	$_5q_{10}$	$_{15}q_0$
March	311	161	83	52	497	195	142	56	33	370
Gainsborough	270	185	74	33	468	141	90	40	22	266
Great Oakley	269	150	48	39	431	123	90	36	27	251
Lowestoft	246	141	45	34	403	132	64	26	16	221
Alcester	236	119	53	44	390	133	79	33	28	249
Willingham	222	109	66	33	374	138	93	43	22	268
Banbury	209	127	35	29	352	139	103	36	29	277
Bottesford	167	99	49	49	321	144	90	32	24	264
Earsdon	163	111	41	20	301	146	126	40	28	303
Terling	176	83	42	21	292	139	91	41	30	272
Reigate	147	89	57	33	291	103	68	33	17	205
Southill	172	79	39	25	285	154	99	32	26	281
Colyton	125	106	48	39	285	105	101	35	22	241
Ipplepen	125	95	45	42	275	98	103	38	20	237
Morchard Bishop	131	104	43	20	269	87	86	31	16	204

Methley	134	99	28	22	258	164	116	43	23	309
Birstall[a]	128	93	41	20	256	170	141	38	28	333
Shepshed	139	86	34	11	247	178	119	43	26	325
Dawlish	108	81	31	33	231	98	103	38	29	244
Ash	121	71	37	17	228	107	81	32	24	224
Austrey	118	64	41	24	227	131	89	34	22	252
Gedling	112	71	48	14	225	159	112	41	25	302
Aldenham	130	61	37	11	222	154	90	30	23	270
Bridford	92	68	49	16	208	112	107	37	22	253
Odiham	96	64	29	22	197	101	74	29	25	212
Hartland	94	77	23	16	196	80	84	38	22	207

[a] Birstall straddled two registration districts, Bradford and Dewsbury. The rates given in the right-hand panel for Birstall are an average of the rates in the two registration districts.

Note: legitimate births only. The registration districts in which the parishes were located are listed in tab. 2.1. In the following cases the period of observation for the parish ended before 1749: Alcester (1744); Lowestoft (1730); Reigate (1729); Willingham (1729).

Sources: Cambridge Group reconstitutions. The mortality data for registration districts relate to the years 1838–44. These were combined with age data from the 1841 census to obtain the rates shown. The sources used are detailed in the source notes to tab. 4.3, p. 93.

the parishes will constitute a random sample drawn from the associated registration districts), this will not be true of individual cases.[106]

If, notwithstanding the hazards involved, a comparison of groups of parishes with 'their' registration districts is made, some suggestive trends become evident, as may be seen in table 6.17. Consider four groups of parishes; those in which the proportion of the adult male labour force engaged in agriculture exceeded 60 per cent in the 1831 census; those where the proportion in manufacturing exceeded 30 per cent; those where the proportion in retail trade and handicraft was over 40 per cent; and all remaining parishes.[107]

In the table the groupings have been simplified to exclude the low-lying parishes, where mortality was very high (Great Oakley, Willingham, and March: the first two from the agricultural group, the last from the 'other' group), and Dawlish, which was most untypical of the retail trade and handicraft group. It would be unwise to read too much into the patterns visible in these four groups since they have been arbitrarily 'purified' and the number of parishes is too small for there to be any certainty that they were typical of the categories into which they fall, yet the apparent patterns are intriguing.

The second and third groups make a striking contrast. The second group (manufacturing) consists of only 3 parishes (Birstall, Gedling, and Shepshed). The average level of $_{15}q_0$ in these parishes in the later seventeenth and early eighteenth centuries was only 76 per cent of the level reached in their registration districts in the mid-nineteenth century (the average rates were 243 and 320 respectively). In the earlier period, proto-industrial development, if present at all, was very limited. The arrival of domestic manufacture on a large scale appears to have been associated with a marked worsening in infant and child mortality.[108] In contrast, in the third group (retail trade and handicraft), consisting of 4 parishes in table 6.17 (Alcester, Banbury, Gainsborough, and Lowestoft), $_{15}q_0$ in the earlier period was 59 per cent higher than in the later period (47 per cent if Dawlish is included the group). The respective rates were 403 and 253 (or, including Dawlish, 369 and 251). In market towns, therefore, there may have been a marked improvement in mortality early in life, though it is also possible that the registration districts in which the parishes were located were much less urban than these market towns and that the fall in mortality is therefore exaggerated.

---

[106] Additional details of the registration districts and parishes may be found in tab. 2.1, pp. 22–3.

[107] Details of parochial occupational structure in 1831 may be found in tab. 3.1, pp. 44–5.

[108] This was Levine's conclusion in his study of Shepshed: Levine, *Family formation*, tabs. 5.7 and 5.17, pp. 68 and 86.

Change over time was much less spectacular in the other parish groupings. In the agricultural group over 60 per cent of the adult male population was engaged in agriculture in 1831 in each of the parishes. It is safe to assume that they were also predominantly agricultural in nature 150 years earlier (Aldenham, Ash, Bridford, Hartland, Morchard Bishop, and Terling). In these parishes there was virtual stasis (the average rates were 236 per 1000 in the reconstitution parishes and 238 per 1000 in the registration districts about 150 years later). If Great Oakley and Willingham are included in the group (both low-lying parishes in which mortality improved very markedly during the eighteenth and early nineteenth centuries) the difference increases, with a fall in $_{15}q_0$ of 14 per cent (278 and 244 per 1000). The 9 remaining 'other' parishes (Austrey, Bottesford, Colyton, Earsdon, Ipplepen, Methley, Odiham, Reigate, and Southall) are a miscellaneous group, consisting of parishes with a less clear-cut employment structure in 1831. Their rates were slightly higher than in the agricultural group but their history was otherwise similar in that $_{15}q_0$ was only slightly higher (by 6 per cent) in the earlier than in the later period (271 and 256 per 1000), but this difference is roughly doubled if March is included in the set (this results in rates of 294 and 267 per 1000). March was a third low-lying parish in which mortality appears to have fallen very substantially in the eighteenth century.

Table 6.17 suggests that the parishes that were later to be the site of rapid proto-industrial growth were indistinguishable from agricultural parishes in the late seventeenth century; that market towns were far more unhealthy than rural areas in this period; and that 'other' parishes, as might be expected, lay between the two extremes. By the mid-nineteenth century little had changed in agricultural parishes; there may have been striking progress in reducing mortality in market towns, but advance in this category was offset by a marked deterioration in manufacturing parishes; while 'other' parishes displayed intermediate characteristics and, like agricultural parishes, showed little change from the earlier period. There is evident danger in comparing parishes in one period with registration districts at another, but to ignore the apparent patterns entirely would be to carry caution to excess.

None of the apparent trends, if confirmed, is surprising. Manufacturing, especially of the domestic type, was often associated with overcrowding and sometimes involved great pressure on living standards as competition from factory-made goods became more acute. On the other hand, mortality improved markedly in many towns both large and small during the eighteenth century. Infancy and childhood in London, for example, were far less hazardous in the early nineteenth century

Table 6.17 *Infant and child mortality in four types of local economy: the period 1675–1749 and the mid-nineteenth century compared* $(1000q_x)$

	Reconstitution parishes 1675–1749					Registration districts 1838–44				
	$1q_0$	$4q_1$	$5q_5$	$5q_{10}$	$15q_0$	$1q_0$	$4q_1$	$5q_5$	$5q_{10}$	$15q_0$
Agricultural	124	77	38	17	236	113	90	35	23	238
Manufacturing	126	83	41	15	243	169	124	41	26	320
Retail trade & handicraft	240	143	52	35	403	136	84	34	24	253
Other	139	90	42	31	271	127	96	35	23	256

Note: legitimate births only. The rates given are unweighted averages of the rates of the individual parishes or registration districts in question. Great Oakley and Willingham have been omitted from the agricultural group. If they had been included the five reconstitution rates for this group would have been 154, 90, 43, 22, and 278, respectively. Similarly, March was omitted from the 'other' group: if it had been included the rates would have been 156, 97, 46, 33, and 294; and Dawlish from the trade and handicraft group which would otherwise have had the following rates: 214, 131, 48, 35, and 369. See text for details of the composition of each group, the criteria which divided the parishes, and the reasons for excluding parishes from some of the groups. The registration districts in which the excluded parishes lay were excluded from the tabulations in the right-hand panel of the table, though this made little difference to the resulting rates.
Sources: See tab. 6.16.

274

than they had been a hundred years earlier.[109] The causes of the improvement in urban mortality are currently obscure but its scale marks this out as a topic of great importance. Perhaps the benefits of substituting brick for wood in house construction may supply a part of the answer.[110] The absence of much change in rural areas is again, *prima facie*, unsurprising. The real wages of labourers and craftsmen, at least in the south of England, were probably lower in the early nineteenth century than they had been in the early eighteenth.[111] In the absence of major changes in other aspects of the social and physical environment in which they lived, and of significant advances in hygiene or medical care (except, perhaps, in relation to smallpox inoculation and vaccination), marked improvement in mortality early in life is improbable, at least for 'endogenous' reasons.

Endogenous and exogenous infant mortality rates can, of course, be calculated for each parish for the same period as the rates given in table 6.17. They are plotted against one another in figure 6.11. In the main the data are well ordered. Low levels of endogenous mortality were associated with low exogenous mortality and, equally, where one was high, so was the other (adj.r^2 = 0.51). Only Great Oakley lies any distance from the regression line. The economic type of each parish is indicated, using the same categories as previously, though marshland parishes are additionally identified since their environmental circumstances appear to have marked them out so distinctively.

The contrasts and similarities in overall infant mortality in these groups of parishes have already been discussed. Figure 6.11 does not suggest that the relationship between endogenous and exogenous mortality was distinctively different in any of them. The figure does show, however, that in a period when national endogenous rates were high and invariant the endogenous rates for individual parishes varied very widely. Agricultural and 'other' parishes, clustering in the south-west corner of the figure, experience endogenous rates lying chiefly beween 25 and 75 per 1000. On average these rates were substantially higher than the national level in the mid-nineteenth century, but far closer to that level than might have been expected in view of the level of

[109] Laxton and Williams, 'Urbanization and infant mortality', pp. 124–7.
[110] On the scale of the substitution which took place, see especially Falkus and Jones, 'Urban improvement'; Power, 'East London housing'; or, more generally, Chalklin, *Provincial towns*, and Porter, 'Cleaning up the Great Wen'.
[111] The Phelps Brown and Hopkins index of real wages, which refers chiefly to building craftsmen in the south of England, averaged 66 in 1740–59 compared with 58 in 1810–29; Phelps Brown and Hopkins, *A perspective of wages and prices*, app. B, tab. 3, pp. 30–1.

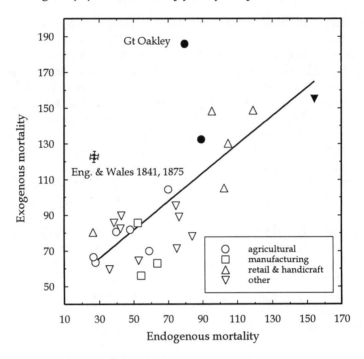

Figure 6.11   *The relative levels of endogenous and exogenous mortality by parish*
(1000d$_x$)
Note: lowlying parishes are indicated by solid symbols.
Source: Cambridge Group reconstitutions.

the national rate (over 80 per 1000) in the late seventeenth and early eighteenth centuries.[112] At the other extreme, market towns, with much handicraft and retail trade employment, suffered very high levels of endogenous infant mortality in this period, though more probably because of their size than because of the nature of employment within them. In three of the five cases the rate exceeded 100 per 1000. The 'manufacturing' parishes had yet to develop distinctive occupational patterns and, appropriately, displayed patterns similar to those to be found in agricultural parishes, while life in marshy areas was plainly hazardous for infants in the late seventeenth and early eighteenth centuries.

There remains the question of how closely the information contained in table 6.16 complements the estimates of overall 'national' mortality

[112] Tab. 6.5, p. 236.

Table 6.18 *Proportionate changes in infant and child mortality compared*
($1000q_x$)

	$_1q_0$	$_4q_1$	$_{10}q_5$	$_{15}q_0$
Reconstitution parishes (1675–1749) and their registration districts (1840s)				
(1) 1675–1749	167	100	72	304
(2) 1840s	132	98	60	264
Ratio (2)/(1)	0.79	0.98	0.83	0.87
'National' estimates				
(1) 1675–1749	193	112	74	337
(2) 1825–37	152	99	68	287
Ratio (2)/(1)	0.79	0.88	0.92	0.85

Note: the infant rates refer to all children both legitimate and illegitimate. In the case of the rate in the top row of the top panel the overall rate was calculated from the legitimate rate by assuming that over the period 1675–1749 the percentage of all births that were illegitimate was 2.35 and correcting accordingly (see tab. 6.2, p. 219, and associated text).
Sources: for upper panel tab. 6.16: for lower panel tabs. 6.1 and 6.2.

trends contained in tables 6.3 and 6.10. If it is reasonable to suppose that *on average* the registration districts mirrored conditions in the reconstitution parishes, then the trends in infant and child mortality between the late seventeenth and mid-nineteenth centuries that can be calculated from the data in table 6.16 should parallel those described earlier in this chapter, which were derived from splicing data taken from the four groups of reconstitution parishes. This supposition is tested in table 6.18.

The upper panel of table 6.18 shows average levels of $_1q_0$, $_4q_1$, $_{10}q_5$, and $_{15}q_0$ from the 26 parishes listed in table 6.16 for the period 1675–1749 and the average levels of the same rates in the registration districts in the 1840s. The ratios between the comparable rates in the two periods are also listed. Thus, infant mortality in the reconstitution parishes was 167 per 1000 in the late seventeenth and early eighteenth centuries compared with a figure of 132 per 1000 in the corresponding registration districts in the mid-nineteenth century, which produces a ratio of 0.81 between the two ($132/167 = 0.79$). In the lower panel of the table the comparable rates drawn from tables 6.1 and 6.2 are shown. In this case the first set of rates refers to the same period as in the upper panel, 1675–1749, while the second set refers to the last period for which there is reconstitution data, 1825–37, and the ratios between the two sets of rates are also given. We have already seen that mortality rates in 1825–37 in the 8 parishes forming group 4 were very similar to the comparable rates in the registration districts to which they belonged in the 1840s,[113] so that any comparison of the ratios in the two panels should not be vitiated by the fact that the later period is not identical in the two cases.

That the comparable absolute rates in the two panels differ is not surprising. In the calculation of an average rate from the data in table 6.16, parishes with small populations and low infant mortality rates in the late seventeenth century, like Bridford, Gedling, Methley, Aldenham, and Shepshed, have equal weight with much larger parishes where infant mortality was more severe, whereas the 'national' rates derived from the four reconstitution groups were based on pooled data and therefore represent a weighted rather than an unweighted average. But the scale of the relative shifts in the mortality rates is broadly reassuring. The major fall in neonatal infant mortality affected the rates in both panels of the table. In both the fall in infant mortality was much sharper than mortality reductions at later ages, and the proportionate shift was similar in the two series. In both panels $_4q_1$ fell only modestly, though the fall was substantially greater in the lower than in the upper panel. The reverse held true in the case of $_{10}q_5$. Here the fall was greater in the upper than in the lower panel. Over the whole age range from the first to the fifteenth birthday the relative movements largely offset one another, so that the fall in $_{14}q_1$ was similar in the two cases (7 per cent in the 'reconstitution' case, 11 per cent in the other). The overall fall in mortality, captured by $_{15}q_0$ was also much the same in the two panels; 13 per cent in the upper panel, 15 per cent in the lower panel.

Other features of early modern mortality can also be examined conveniently using parochial data rather than national estimates. For example, the close relationship between maternal mortality and endogenous infant mortality appeared from the study of time trends in the two series.[114] It can also be examined spatially, so to speak. Figure 6.12 plots maternal mortality against endogenous infant mortality with each dot representing a parish. Just as table 6.5 showed that as maternal mortality fell sharply in the course of the eighteenth century there was a very similar fall in endogenous infant mortality, so figure 6.12 shows that parishes in which maternal mortality was severe were places in which endogenous infant mortality was high, while equally parishes in which one of these two rates was low were usually also fortunate in respect of the other rate. Both rates refer to the whole period of sound reconstitution data in each parish in order to maximise the number of cases of maternal death in small parishes. The consistency of the relationship given the limited number of deaths in the smaller parishes

---

[113] Tab. 4.3, p. 93.   [114] Tab. 6.5, p. 236.

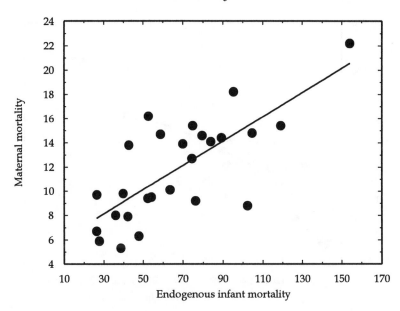

Figure 6.12   *The relative levels of maternal mortality and endogenous infant mortality by parish (rates per 1000)*
Source: Cambridge Group reconstitutions.

is notable (adj.r^2 = 0.54), especially in view of the relatively small number of maternal deaths on which some of the rates were based (for example, the rates in Ipplepen, Bridford, and Dawlish were based on 4, 9, and 23 maternal deaths respectively, whereas those for Banbury, March, and Gainsborough were based on 178, 198, and 357 maternal deaths).

In similar vein figure 6.13 shows that parishes which suffered the highest *overall* infant mortality rates had exceptionally high *twin* mortality in infancy, and where one rate was low, so was the other. The circumstances and social practices which caused one rate to be relatively high or low affected the other similarly (adj.R^2 = 0.59). Twins were always at much greater risk than singletons, but the absolute level of the twin rate was subject to variation apparently in response to much the same influences as determined the overall infant rate.[115]

[115] Once again both rates were calculated for the whole period of the reconstitution in each parish, so that the periods covered may differ considerably from parish to parish (see tab. 2.1, pp. 22–3). The regression line in fig. 6.13 is a quadratic best fit. Its form suggests the possibility that twin mortality had asymptotic tendency where very high values were involved, an intrinsically probable finding (linear and quadratic best fit lines were almost indistinguishable in figs. 6.11 and 6.12 and in each case a linear regression line was shown in the figure and the adjusted r^2 refers to a linear regression).

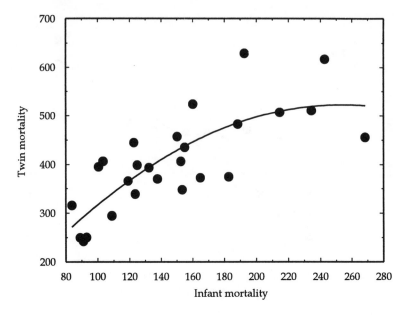

Figure 6.13   *The relative levels of overall infant mortality and the infant mortality of twins by parish (1000qₓ)*

Source: Cambridge Group reconstitutions.

Adult mortality

With adult, no less than with infant and child, mortality, it is essential to establish whether there was a significant difference in mortality level between the four groups in overlap periods between them. In this way consistent rates can be obtained for the whole of the parish register period by calculating inflation ratios to bring rates for other groups into alignment with those for group 2. The measurement of differences in level between successive groups proved a relatively straightforward matter when dealing with infant and child mortality. In this case a 50-year overlap period common to each successive pair of groups was identified and made the basis for a comparison. For example, the inflation ratio for the overlap period for group 2/group 3 was based on the period rates to be found in the period 1680–1729. The nature of the exercise is described in appendix 7. A comparable exercise for adult mortality is inherently more difficult and complex. This, too, is described in appendix 7. It consisted in identifying a Lexis parallelogram of data which is common to a pair of successive groups. The parallelogram has a base 50 years wide, and the comparison, which is made

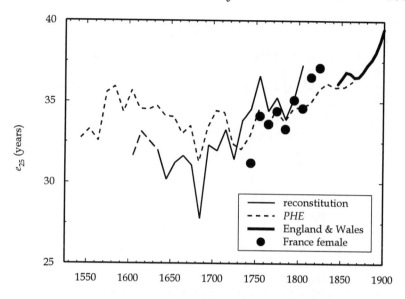

Figure 6.14 *Expectation of life at age 25 (e₂₅)*

Sources: the back projection estimates are taken from the detailed tables of output which lay behind the summary statistics published in Wrigley and Schofield, *Population history of England*, tab. A3.1, pp. 528–9. The data for England and Wales for the later nineteenth century: *The Chester Beatty life tables*. The French data: Blayo, 'La mortalité en France', tab. 12, p. 139. Cambridge Group reconstitutions.

using cohort rates, therefore reflected the experience of two cohorts, one drawn from each group, over an 80-year period.

The problems involved in estimating adult mortality rates extend well beyond those associated with the changing composition of the parishes in observation. In appendix 6 these problems, and the solutions adopted for present purposes, are described in detail. That a comparatively confident solution is possible is due principally to the advances made by Blum in defining the nature of the fundamental issue and in suggesting a method of overcoming a difficulty which had limited previous use of adult mortality data drawn from family reconstitution studies.[116]

Figure 6.14 provides a summary view of trends in adult mortality from the early seventeenth to the early nineteenth century, expressed as estimates of the expectation of life at age 25. For reasons made clear in appendix 6, the technicalities of deriving accurate estimates of adult

[116] The problem and the nature of Blum's solution to it were described in outline earlier in this chapter: see above pp. 212–3.

mortality preclude the estimation of rates based entirely on empirical data for any decades earlier than 1640–9 or later than 1800–9: the pre-1640 reconstitution estimates shown as a broken line in the figure involved, for some age groups, extrapolation from empirical data from other age groups.[117] In addition to the reconstitution estimates figure 6.14 also shows the estimates of e_{25} from aggregative data using the technique of back projection and taken from the *Population history of England*, some early national data derived from the Registrar-General's returns for the middle and later decades of the nineteenth century, and eighteenth-century French data published by Blayo. In considering the back projection estimates it should be borne in mind that these are not, of course, based on age-specific data.[118]

The overall pattern of change visible in figure 6.14 was of deteriorating mortality during the seventeenth century with a pronounced low point during the 1680s, followed by a marked rise during the first half of the eighteenth century, which had, however, largely levelled off in the second half of the century. From its lowest point in the 1680s to the high point in 1750–9, the rise in e_{25} was almost 9 years, from 27.8 to 36.6 years, though if the comparison is made between the mid-seventeenth century and the 1750s, the rise is much more modest, since e_{25} in 1640–59 was 31.4 years, a level only 3 or 4 years short of some decadal figures recorded in the later eighteenth century. The worsening of mortality in the course of the seventeenth century was quite severe.

In the period from 1640 to 1689, when e_{25} averaged just over 30 years, it was at roughly the equivalent of level 5 in the model North Princeton tables. When adult mortality was at its peak in the 1680s, and e_{25} was less then 28 years, it was at about level 2 in the North tables. By the later eighteenth century, on the other hand, with e_{25} at roughly 35 years, the situation was equivalent to that found in level 9 of the North tables. Since each level in the Princeton tables is equivalent to a difference of about 2.5 years in expectation of life at birth, if adult mortality data were the sole guide to mortality change in England in the later seventeenth and early eighteenth centuries, the rise in e_0 would appear to have been very sharp and pronounced, at least 10 years, and possibly more than 15 years, depending on whether the estimate was based on lengthy

---

[117] The method employed was the Brass standard logit system, fitting the model by minimising the *relative* squared errors rather than the squared errors, that is $\left(\dfrac{o-e}{e}\right)^2$ rather than $(o - e)^2$. This method of fitting appealed because it gives as much weight to the mortality rates in age groups where the absolute rate was low, such as $_5q_5$, as to those in age groups where the rate was high, such as $_5q_{75}$. The system is described in Brass, 'On the scale of mortality'.   [118] See p. 518.

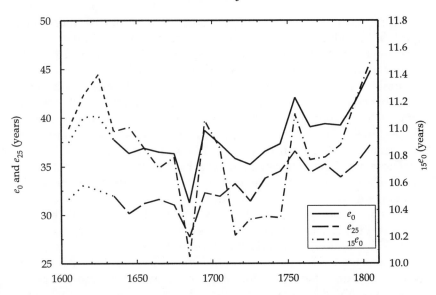

Figure 6.15 *A comparison of childhood and adult mortality*
$(e_0, {}_{15}e_0, \text{ and } e_{25})$
Source: Cambridge Group reconstitutions.

periods, or from the trough to the later eighteenth-century plateau. It is not surprising that Razzell, dependent only on evidence relating to adult death rates, was led to suggest that there were great changes in mortality overall in the early eighteenth century and to wonder 'whether this fall in mortality was sufficient to account for the whole of the population growth in question'.[119]

The period from about 1680 to 1750 was, however, a most unusual episode in English population history, as is plain in figure 6.15. In general, and in conformity with expectation, trends in mortality early in life paralleled the comparable movements in adult mortality. Thus, $_{15}e_0$ and e_{25} were in harmony during most of the seventeenth century, and the two were again moving broadly in parallel in the later eighteeenth

---

[119] Razzell, 'The growth of population', p. 765. The evidence for e_{25} cited by Razzell related to adult males who were drawn from particular groups, such as Members of Parliament, members of tontines, the aristocracy, and Scottish advocates. In all these groups there was a marked improvement in mortality in the early eighteenth century, but, where the evidence permits a judgement, little further improvement after 1750. His evidence from marriage licences in east Kent also suggested a big improvement largely confined to the first half of the eighteenth century. Ibid., tab. 10, p. 765 and tab. 6, p. 761.

century, but there was no comparable parallelism in the intervening period. In both series the 1680s were a nadir, and in both there was a marked bounce-back in the succeeding decade, but the period 1710–49 was the most sustained period of unfavourable infant and child mortality in the early modern period. As a result, of course, the striking improvement in adult mortality was not reflected in a parallel gain in overall life expectancy, as the line representing e_0 demonstrates.[120] Expectation of life at age 25 improved in a most striking fashion, but expectation of life at birth failed to follow suit.

These developments can be viewed in quite a different light, however. The early eighteenth century might be regarded as the period in which, for the first time, a 'modern' mortality regime emerged in England. If the Princeton tables are regarded as encapsulating the mortality experience of many countries over the past century or so, then, judged by modern standards, the seventeenth century was a very odd period. In the 1680s, for example, adult mortality was at about level 2 of the model North tables, but infant and child mortality, summarised as $_{15}q_0$, was at about level 8 whereas by the 1750s adult was at about level 9, and infant and child mortality was at about level 11, a very much smaller discrepancy. Thereafter, adult and child rates were, by the standards reflected in the Princeton tables, in tolerable conformity with each other. In the seventeenth century this was not so. Viewed in this way, the early eighteenth century was not an aberration, but rather a period of transition from the old to a more modern demographic regime.

The mortality history of England in the early modern period has far-reaching implications for the interpretation of partial data from other periods. For example, although there is little or no source material which can throw light on infant and child mortality in medieval times, there is a comparative abundance of sources which can be used to determine levels of mortality among adult males, though drawn from particular groups within the population rather than from the population as a whole.[121] Such studies have often concluded that mortality was high or very high, and have tended to assume that what was true of adult males was true of the population at large. It is now clear that great

---

[120] In calculating e_0, the rates for the age groups 15–9 and 20–4, for which the direct evidence is scanty when using reconstitution data, were obtained by using the method described on p. 282 n. 117 above.

[121] See, for example, Peller, 'Studies on mortality'; Russell, *British medieval population*; Hatcher, 'Mortality in the fifteenth century'; Harvey, *Living and dying in England*, pp. 112–29; and the survey of the problems involved in making inferences about mortality in the medieval period in Smith, 'Demographic developments'.

caution must be exercised in extrapolating from evidence about adults to children, and vice versa. In periods when adult male mortality was high, the same may have been true of the population as a whole, but this was not necessarily so. A low level of e_{25} is not incompatible with a relatively high level of e_0.

The factors which may have determined long-run trends in English mortality rates as a whole are as yet far from clear. The prolonged deterioration during the bulk of the seventeenth century cannot be associated with any parallel economic change. Real wages appear to have been rising from before the middle of the century, and possibly almost throughout the century.[122] Autonomous change in the virulence of some diseases, such as smallpox and dysenteric illnesses, has been suggested as a possible cause. Occasionally, climatic change surfaces as a further possibility. Equally, the substantial improvement, which, by the end of the eighteenth century, had produced a milder mortality regime than at any time in the preceding two centuries, has been the subject of much speculative discussion, but a decisive breakthrough in its understanding still remains to be made. That the improvement was so marked is the more surprising since it took place against the tide, so to speak, in that some of the changes taking place during the century, and particularly the marked increase in urbanisation, might have been expected to have caused mortality to rise rather than to fall, *ceteris paribus*.

Whatever puzzles surround secular mortality trends in other periods of English history, however, pale in comparison with the first half of the eighteenth century, since, if it is difficult to explain trends in mortality in all age groups when they were consistent with one another, it is likely to prove far more difficult to do so when trends in childhood rates were moving in the opposite direction to those later in life. Unravelling these complexities may prove an especially fruitful field for future research, since the fact of divergence in trend may make it easier to distinguish between convincing and unconvincing explanations. Where trends in all age groups are similar, blanket explanations are attractive; where they are not, a more subtle and complex approach is likely to prove necessary.

Other features of figure 6.14 call for comment. It is, for example, striking that the level and trend in female e_{25} in France in the eighteenth century should have been so similar to that in England (French male e_{25} can be traced with confidence only over a much shorter period because

---

[122] The evidence is presented and discussed in Wrigley and Schofield, *Population history of England*, pp. 312–3, 431–5, 638–41.

of the very heavy military losses during the revolutionary and Napoleonic wars). It is hard not to suppose that common influences were at work. The substantially worse French expectation of life at birth in the eighteenth century contrasts with the position for adult mortality. It is apparent, of course, that it was largely the result of more severe infant and child mortality. If this phenomenon were better understood, it might also help to provide a clue to the conundrum of the divergence in the trends of childhood and adult mortality rates in England in the first half of the century.

The aggregative estimates of e_{25} taken from the *Population history of England* were included in figure 6.14 to provide some basis for locating the new work in relation to the old, but any comparison of the two is complicated by the method of construction of the latter. An extended discussion of findings based on aggregative and reconstitution data will be found in chapter 8. A full comparison is a complex affair. In order to make a preliminary assessment of the two series, it should be recalled that the back projection estimates were not based upon totals of deaths in particular age groups, but upon totals of all deaths in each period of time. Given a knowledge of population size and age structure produced by the process of back projection, the program which embodied the technique then selected that mortality level from within a family of life tables which was needed in order to absorb the known totals of deaths for the period, which in turn yielded a set of mortality rates and associated statistics, such as e_{25}.[123] The aggregative-based rates are therefore not based on direct observation in the same sense as the reconstitution-based rates. If, for example, there were a significant change in the relative level of infant and child mortality on the one hand, and adult mortality on the other, this would not be detected by back projection, but would be immediately apparent in reconstitution rates. It is therefore possible for there to be a 'crossover' between estimates derived by the two methods, such as is visible on figure 6.14, due to difference of method rather than 'real' differences. Thus, the far more pronounced rise in e_{25} in the reconstitution series in the early eighteenth century is to be explained by this point. Since infant and child mortality did not improve in this period, and expectation of life at birth changed little, the method of construction of the back projection estimates necessarily meant that an aggregative-based e_{25} would also show little change.

Another point of comparison is less problematic. The shorter-term trends in the two series of estimates are broadly similar. In both, for

[123] Ibid., app. 15.

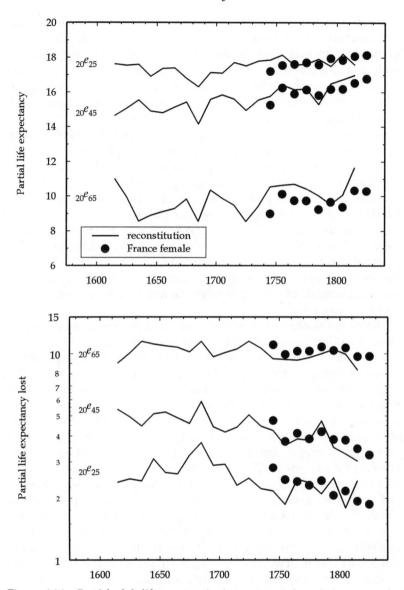

Figure 6.16   *Partial adult life expectancies ($_{20}e_{25}$, $_{20}e_{45}$, and $_{20}e_{65}$): (upper panel, years lived; lower panel, years lost)*

Sources: Blayo, 'La mortalité en France', tab. 12, p. 139. Cambridge Group reconstitutions.

example, the decade of the 1680s was a period of very high mortality, and other rises and falls tend to be coincident, though the relative scale of the changes may vary. Given the close similarity in the trends and patterns in the raw totals of events in the 26 reconstitution parishes and the 404 aggregative parishes, which has already been explored,[124] the existence of a comparable similarity in the fluctuations in the estimates of e_{25} should, however, occasion little surprise.

Before considering age-specific adult mortality rates, it is convenient to present another set of summary statistics in graphic form. Figure 6.16 shows the trends in partial life expectancies revealed by reconstitution. The data are given for three age groups, 25–44, 45–64, and 65–84. A partial life expectancy provides information about the number of years lived by the average person between two points in the life cycle. Thus, if there were no deaths at all in a population between the ages of 25 and 45, the partial life expectancy for that age group would be 20 years. Equally, a partial life expectancy of 10 years would mean that death reduced the numbers within the age group so substantially that only one half of the potential number of years that might be lived within the age group in question was actually lived.

The figure contains two panels, one showing the number of years lived, the other the number lost. The reason for using both forms is to provide alternative ways of considering the extent of any improvement or deterioration in mortality. The upper panel, showing years lived within the age group, can be misleading. For example, a major improvement in mortality might raise $_{20}e_{65}$ from 10 to 15 years, a gain of 5 years. If at the start of the same period $_{20}e_{45}$ stood at 15 years, it is obvious that it could not also increase by 5 years, and the improvement in mortality might therefore appear to be less in this age group. However, if $_{20}e_{45}$ rose to 17.5 years, this might be taken as an equivalent improvement, since this, too, would halve the gap between the current state of affairs and the complete elimination of mortality in the age group. The lower panel, therefore, presents the data in a form which makes it easier to appreciate the relative degree of success in reducing mortality in the three age groups. The data plotted are the number of years lost to death in each age group, and the vertical axis is logarithmic, so that relative movements of equal magnitude will cover the same vertical distance. Judged in this fashion progress was least in the most elderly group and more pronounced in the two younger age groups, a feature not readily appreciated in the upper panel plots. Some other features of the figure may be significant. For example, the severity of the

---

[124] See figs. 3.1–3.6, pp. 56, 59, 62, 64, 66, 68, above.

deterioration in mortality in the 1680s is clearly visible in the two younger partial life expectancies, but was more muted amongst the elderly. It would be unwise to read too much into this or other similar features of the plotted data, however, given the relatively small totals of deaths and years at risk which lie behind them.

It is again encouraging that the English reconstitution data and the estimates of French female partial life expectancies agree so closely.

Table 6.19 contains the raw material from which the summary statistics plotted in the three preceding figures were obtained. The rates in particular age groups are apt to vary considerably from one decade to the next because they are based on comparatively small totals of deaths and are therefore subject to random variation. In most decades the total of person-years of exposure in each age group lies between 1000 and 2000 from the age group 25–9 to the age group 60–4, declining rapidly thereafter to about 100 person-years in the age group 80–4. The totals are somewhat smaller in the earliest and latest decades. The totals of death are normally in the range between 30 and 80 for the several age groups, though sometimes the total in the highest age group 80–4 is a little smaller. It should be emphasised that the rates shown in the table are those obtained directly from the deaths and years of exposure of husbands and wives observed on FRFs, and not the rates which result from combining two separate male and female sets of life tables. Male lives are slightly overrepresented as a result, probably because it was more common for a wife to move on marriage to her husband's parish, if they were not from the same parish, than vice versa. The male overrepresentation is relatively slight, however, so that to have used the alternative strategy would have produced only minor changes to the rates shown in the table.

Since decennial rates are subject to random movement, it is more meaningful to consider longer periods of time when the rates are based on substantially larger totals of years of exposure and of events. In table 6.20 attention is focused on two long spans of time, 1640–89 and 1750–1809. Reference to figure 6.14 and table 6.19 will show that within these periods e_{25} fluctuated but without decided trend, and that they were the periods of lowest and highest e_{25} respectively. The rates shown are averages of the decadal rates in the periods in question.

In the earlier of the two periods e_{25} was 30.4 years; in the later period 35.4 years, a difference of exactly 5 years. The individual rates for each 5-year age group were invariably lower in the later than in the earlier period. In the age groups below 65 the rates in 1750–1809 were usually 25–35 per cent lower than in 1640–89, averaging 30 per cent lower, though in the highest age groups the differences narrowed sharply.

Table 6.19 *Adult mortality, sexes combined* $(1000q_x)$

	1640–9	1650–9	1660–9	1670–9	1680–9	1690–9	1700–9	1710–9	1720–9	1730–9	1740–9	1750–9	1760–9	1770–9	1780–9	1790–9	1800–9
25–9	79.1	65.1	54.0	87.3	94.1	82.3	46.8	53.9	59.5	45.6	47.9	39.0	56.8	58.9	53.6	72.8	40.1
30–4	72.5	54.4	84.2	89.8	109.2	65.2	101.1	54.7	57.4	69.7	56.8	48.2	68.6	62.0	43.3	59.8	42.5
35–9	109.1	99.4	81.7	87.4	109.7	84.7	111.2	73.2	96.7	59.3	70.8	54.7	68.0	70.7	61.5	62.2	56.6
40–4	107.0	86.8	91.5	85.8	92.9	95.0	91.6	100.4	79.4	75.0	72.9	78.1	89.7	57.5	84.1	42.6	56.7
45–9	105.7	120.7	108.8	101.6	138.1	100.2	100.9	94.1	110.3	107.5	97.0	75.1	89.3	88.8	121.4	81.0	78.3
50–4	155.3	143.0	140.5	109.3	164.5	127.2	90.2	135.7	140.8	97.1	99.0	106.5	107.8	104.6	115.5	96.6	75.8
55–9	222.4	192.4	188.2	191.2	230.1	152.2	169.7	140.4	221.3	168.0	175.2	119.6	134.0	126.6	161.2	95.8	107.1
60–4	146.6	242.9	236.5	218.7	285.7	203.7	185.0	207.6	239.8	200.5	216.0	171.6	179.4	143.5	215.3	163.7	159.3
65–9	334.4	280.0	293.2	272.5	297.3	242.1	275.5	326.8	311.1	298.4	235.7	224.2	227.0	236.1	235.0	266.8	237.2
70–4	389.7	464.5	414.8	399.8	488.1	335.6	317.4	346.2	513.5	359.0	336.8	341.1	327.8	365.1	377.1	426.1	417.3
75–9	554.7	546.0	455.1	426.7	590.2	457.8	544.4	432.9	542.1	474.6	463.5	436.3	398.3	434.3	532.9	496.8	335.5
80–4	500.0	622.0	646.5	639.7	728.7	605.6	595.4	508.5	704.8	625.1	469.7	544.4	642.9	548.1	604.3	596.3	709.1
e_{25}	30.2	31.2	31.6	31.1	27.8	32.3	32.0	33.3	31.4	33.8	34.5	36.6	34.4	35.3	33.9	35.2	37.3
$_{20}e_{25}$	16.9	17.4	17.4	16.8	16.3	17.1	17.1	17.7	17.5	17.8	17.8	18.1	17.5	17.6	17.9	17.5	18.2
$_{20}e_{45}$	14.9	14.8	15.1	15.4	14.2	15.6	15.8	15.6	15.0	15.6	15.8	16.4	16.1	16.2	15.3	16.5	16.7
$_{20}e_{65}$	8.9	9.1	9.3	9.8	8.5	10.4	9.9	9.5	8.5	9.4	10.5	10.6	10.7	10.4	10.0	9.5	10.1

Source: Cambridge Group reconstitutions.

Table 6.20 *Adult mortality, sexes combined: England and France (1000q$_x$)*

	England					France
	(1)	(2)	(3) (2)/(1) ×100	(4) 3rd ELT modified	(5) (2)/(4) ×100	(6)
	1640–1689	1750–1809				1740–89
25–9	75.9	53.6	71	47.8	112	56.1
30–4	82.0	54.1	66	52.6	103	62.7
35–9	97.4	62.3	64	58.4	107	71.9
40–4	92.8	68.1	73	66.2	103	86.2
45–9	115.0	89.0	77	76.8	116	101.1
50–4	142.5	101.1	71	94.3	107	119.1
55–9	204.9	124.1	61	123.3	101	148.6
60–4	226.1	172.1	76	170.7	101	203.4
65–9	295.5	237.7	80	242.8	98	285.5
70–4	431.4	375.8	87	350.7	107	381.0
75–9	514.5	439.0	85	480.9	91	511.5
80–4	627.4	607.5	97	618.9	98	646.5
e_{25}	30.4	35.4		36.3		33.4
$_{20}e_{25}$	17.0	17.8		18.0		17.6
$_{20}e_{45}$	14.9	16.2		16.5		15.7
$_{20}e_{65}$	9.1	10.2		10.2		9.6

Note: the third English life table in col. 4 (1838–54) was modified in that the rates for all age groups above the age of 50 were taken from the life table of 1891–1900 to produce a more accurate picture.
Sources: England: cols. 1 and 2, Cambridge Group reconstitutions; col. 4, Wrigley and Schofield, *Population history of England*, tab. A14.3, p. 711. France: Blayo, 'La mortalité en France', tab. 12, p. 139. Blayo only provides data for both males and females for the period 1740–89, though female rates are given for a longer period. Male rates for later decades are disturbed by the effects of the revolutionary and Napoleonic wars. A rate for the sexes combined was calculated as an average of the rates for males and females. This represents an approximation only.

A comparison of the rates in column 2 with those in column 4 is particularly interesting, since it shows that adult mortality rates in the 60-year period 1750–1809 bore a remarkably stable relationship to those in the third English life table.[125] Mortality was a little higher in the earlier period, though the differences were very slight above the age of 55. Since there had also been little change between columns 1 and 2 in

[125] The rates shown in col. 4 are taken from the 3rd English life table up to the age of 50: above that age they are taken from model North of the Princeton tables since there is reason to believe that this captures the situation in mid-nineteenth-century England better than the rates published in the 3rd ELT. Wrigley and Schofield, *Population history of England*, pp. 709–12, esp. tab. A14.3, p. 711.

the higher age groups, this might suggest that death rates among the elderly were more 'sticky' than those of younger men and women. However, the conclusion that death rates in the higher age groups were 'sticky' is affected by the method of comparison used. If a comparison of the two series is made, not by using percentages, but by calculating the odds ratios between the two series, a somewhat different picture emerges. For example, the odds for the age group 45–9 in 1640–89 is 0.1299 (115/(1000 − 115)) while that for 1750–1809 is 0.0977 (89/(1000 − 89)). Therefore, using odds ratios, the figure equivalent to the figure of 77 in column 3 is 75 ((0.0977/0.1299) × 100). These two figures are closely similar, but, whereas the percentage figure for 75–9 is 85, the odds ratio-based figure is 74. The series based on odds ratios is much 'flatter' than the percentage series, apart from the final figure for the age group 80–4. From an odds ratio perspective, therefore, the decline in adult mortality between 1640–89 and 1750–1809 is relatively uniform across all age groups. The average figure based on odds ratios for the six age groups 25–9 to 50–4 in column 3 is 68; that for the next five age groups 55–9 to 75–9 is 71, a very modest change, whereas the comparable average percentages, given in column 3 of table 6.20, are 70 and 78, suggesting that mortality in the higher age groups was falling substantially less than amongst younger adults. Since the odds for a given age group express the likelihood of dying in relation to the likelihood of surviving, the odds ratio for that age group in two different periods of time captures the nature of the change taking place in a different fashion from the percentage change method. Viewed in this light, the experience of all the adult age groups was similar.

The similarity in the pattern of the rates in the two series in relation to one another serves to increase confidence in the reliability of the reconstitution estimates, and suggests that adult mortality changed relatively little in the early nineteenth century, in very marked contrast with the rapid change which had taken place a hundred years earlier.[126]

The rates for the sexes combined for France in the later eighteenth century, shown in column 6 of table 6.20, invariably lie between those for England in 1640–89 and 1750–1809, with the trivial exception of the highest age group. This suggests that the structure of the rates was very similar in the two countries, and that mortality in France was somewhat

---

[126] It should be noted that the rates shown in tabs. 6.19 and 6.20 were taken directly from the combined data for men and women. They are therefore marginally affected by the fact that the relative contribution of the two sexes was not uniform throughout the whole age range. Experiment showed, however, that if the rates for the two sexes were first calculated separately and then combined as a joint life table the resulting rates were almost unchanged.

more severe than in England in the later eighteenth century, given that the second English period and the French period are very similar and that rates in England changed little over the period.[127]

The anomalous nature of mortality changes in the first half of the eighteenth century has already been noted. Adult mortality improved rapidly; mortality earlier in life moved in the opposite direction. The effect of these different trends may be highlighted by considering infant and childhood mortality in the periods before and after the early eighteenth century, in the same manner as has just been done for adult mortality. This helps to establish the extent of the contrast. Adult rates in the period 1750–1809 were about 30 per cent lower than they had been in the period 1640–89 between the ages of 25 and 65, though above 65 the fall was appreciably smaller. If the same comparison is made for rates earlier in life the fall is less uniform and often much more modest. In 1640–89 the average level of the four infant and childhood rates, $_1q_0$, $_4q_1$, $_5q_5$, and $_5q_{10}$, was 173.5, 113.2, 51.9, and 29.1 per 1000 respectively, while in 1750–1809 the average rates were 164.4, 103.9, 34.9, and 23.0 per 1000. The percentage falls in each case, therefore, were 5.2, 8.2, 31.8, and 20.9 per cent respectively. Adult rates fell far more dramatically than rates under the age of 5, though in later childhood the scale of the fall was similar to that in later life. The fall in $_1q_0$ and $_4q_1$ was very slight by comparison. The modest scale of mortality decline in children under 5 exerts great leverage on an overall measure like expectation of life at birth. Given that death rates were high early in life, the proportion of each cohort surviving to adult years will not increase significantly in these circumstances, and even dramatic improvements in death rates in later life must have only a limited impact. Those who are already dead, so to speak, are incapable of benefiting from improved mortality in the higher age groups.

Overall mortality

Since earlier sections have yielded information about mortality up to the age of 15 and from the age of 25 onwards, it is a comparatively trivial matter to generate estimates of e_0 and so complete the review of mortality for the parish register period. The gap was filled by estimates for $_5q_{15}$ and $_5q_{20}$ obtained by using Brass life table parameters to generate estimates based on the observed rates in all the other age groups.[128]

---

[127] If English rates are calculated for exactly the same period as the French, they are, in general, closer to the French rates than those for the period 1750–1819, though still below them.   [128] For fuller details see p. 282 n. 117.

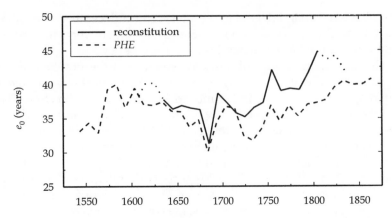

Figure 6.17   *Expectation of life at birth (e_0): reconstitution and back projection estimates*

Sources: Wrigley and Schofield, *Population history of England*, tab. A3.1, pp. 528–9. Cambridge Group reconstitutions.

Direct evidence for these two age groups is slight because relatively few men and women were married in their teens and early twenties. There were few brides and even fewer grooms under the age of 20. For the next age group 20–4 the total of years of exposure of married men and women rises considerably, but the evidence for men is still limited in volume, while for women, it should be remembered that only a minority of the age group were married, and that those who were married had often been pregnant at marriage and therefore often had a first child with its attendant risks within the age group. The death rates of married women in this age group were therefore especially likely to be unrepresentative. In this case also, therefore, inference from a knowledge of age-specific rates on either side of the gap seemed preferable to the use of empirical evidence. Any uncertainties are limited by the fact that age-specific rates in these age groups were amongst the lowest in the entire age span. The results may be seen in figure 6.17 and table 6.21.

In figure 6.17 the solid line represents the decennial reconstitution data. Before 1640–9 the solid line is continued backwards for a further half-century but the estimates are inherently less reliable because, although infant and child mortality can be measured directly throughout this period, some adult rates have to be estimated, given the nature of the process by which they are generated.[129] The estimates for the period after 1800–9 are also shown as a broken line, in this case because

[129] See above pp. 281–2 and app. 6.

Table 6.21 *Expectation of life at birth (e_0):*
sexes combined (years)

1600–9	37.5	1710–9	35.8
1610–9	40.1	1720–9	35.2
1620–9	40.2	1730–9	36.6
1630–9	37.8	1740–9	37.3
1640–9	36.4	1750–9	42.1
1650–9	36.9	1760–9	39.0
1660–9	36.5	1770–9	39.4
1670–9	36.3	1780–9	39.2
1680–9	31.3	1790–9	41.7
1690–9	38.7	1800–9	44.8
1700–9	37.3		

Source: Cambridge Group reconstitutions.

the estimates of e_0 are extrapolations from the infant and child mortality rates. The reconstitution estimates are plotted against the comparable back projection results using the aggregative data described in the *Population history of England*. The latter are included only to orientate the reconstitution results, since in chapter 8 new estimates based on revised aggregative data and produced by generalised inverse projection rather than back projection will be described. The new estimates represent a better template against which to judge the consonance of reconstitution and aggregative estimates than the old back projection results. Nevertheless the old estimates make a useful background against which to set the new estimates. There is little to report in this connection which has not been remarked previously when discussing the mortality of children or adults. When combined into a single series, the age-specific rates derived from the reconstitution parishes imply changes in expectation of life at birth broadly similar to those which were produced by back projection until the later eighteenth century. The reconstitution estimates are slightly the higher of the two throughout the first century and a half, but in the last half-century the gap widens. A main reason for the discrepancy lies in the nature of the new knowledge gained from reconstitution about mortality trends in the early nineteenth century, but the exposition of this point and its implications belongs to chapter 8.

Figure 6.17 shows that the seventeenth century was an era of steadily worsening mortality until the 1680s, while from the second quarter of the eighteenth century there was considerable, if somewhat erratic, improvement. In between there were some violent swings in e_0. There had been a very marked improvement in the 1690s following the

Table 6.22 Age- and sex-specific infant and child mortality $(1000q_x)$

	$_1q_0$		$_4q_1$		$_5q_5$		$_5q_{10}$		$_{10}q_5$	
	M	F	M	F	M	F	M	F	M	F
1580–99	174.9	163.0	87.0	81.2	49.3	43.2	18.1	19.7	66.6	62.1
1600–24	162.6	141.7	76.9	86.1	39.2	32.9	20.3	25.3	58.7	57.3
1625–49	148.8	132.0	103.3	95.8	47.5	48.4	28.6	25.4	74.8	72.6
1650–74	160.9	141.9	114.4	106.9	46.0	55.7	26.7	25.6	71.4	79.9
1675–99	195.0	160.6	107.8	107.0	46.0	45.7	26.9	28.0	71.7	72.3
1700–24	195.0	182.7	110.3	105.2	47.7	45.1	24.2	30.0	70.7	73.8
1725–49	207.4	172.3	121.3	121.0	53.9	46.4	29.4	27.0	81.7	72.2
1750–74	172.9	151.8	100.5	114.5	41.9	40.3	26.4	25.0	67.3	64.3
1775–99	165.9	146.0	106.0	108.2	33.7	37.1	20.2	26.5	53.2	62.6
1800–24	146.4	124.5	97.0	100.3	23.6	27.8	19.6	20.6	42.7	47.8
1825–37	151.3	136.3	98.4	98.9	37.7	30.8	23.2	46.5	60.1	75.9
Male/female ratios										
1580–99	1.073		1.071		1.142		0.919		1.072	
1600–24	1.148		0.894		1.192		0.802		1.023	
1625–49	1.127		1.079		0.981		1.127		1.030	
1650–74	1.134		1.071		0.824		1.041		0.893	
1675–99	1.215		1.007		1.008		0.962		0.991	
1700–24	1.067		1.049		1.058		0.805		0.959	
1725–49	1.204		1.002		1.162		1.087		1.132	
1750–74	1.139		0.877		1.041		1.058		1.047	
1775–99	1.136		0.980		0.908		0.760		0.849	
1800–24	1.176		0.967		0.846		0.952		0.892	
1825–37	1.110		0.995		1.223		0.499		0.791	

Note: legitimate births only. The rates have been adjusted in the same way as in tab. 6.1 to overcome the problem of 'joins'

296

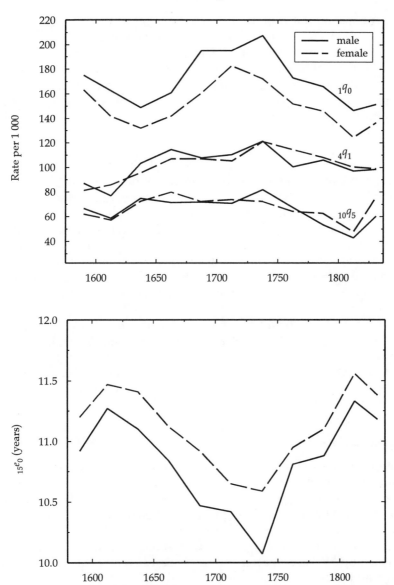

Figure 6.18   *Male and female infant and child mortality ($1000q_x$) (upper panel), and partial life expectancies ($_{15}e_0$) (lower panel)*

Note: the infant mortality rates refer to legitimate children only.
Source: Cambridge Group reconstitutions.

exceptional mortality of the 1680s, but the improvement did not hold, and by the 1720s e_0 was at the second lowest point of the whole series. The scope for improved life expectancy which was opened up in the first half of the eighteenth century by the striking improvement in adult mortality was largely offset until the 1750s by the prolonged period of high infant and child rates which characterised the early decades of the century.

Male and female mortality

In all populations more male than female children are born. The ratio is usually about 105 : 100. In most populations the male surplus at birth is eroded by higher male mortality until eventually the numerical advantage shifts to favour females over males. In societies where mortality rates are generally high the crossover age may be very low. For example, in the Princeton model West life tables, at level 6 (female e_0 32.5 years), and assuming a sex ratio at birth of 105, the male surplus disappears in the course of the first year of life. Where absolute age-specific rates are very low, as in wealthy countries today, the male surplus persists until far later in life (in the model West tables with a female e_0 of 77.5 years until about age 60). In some populations, however, discrimination in feeding, attention, medical care, or other matters may distort the 'natural' pattern and cause female age-specific rates to exceed male rates at ages where they might be expected to be lower than male rates or on a par with them.

Infancy and childhood

Reconstitution can, of course, throw light on the relative level of male and female mortality in the past. In table 6.22 the conventional infant and child rates are shown for quarter-century periods for each sex, together with ratios expressing their relative level. They are shown in graphical form in the upper panel of figure 6.18, with the two highest age groups collapsed as $_{10}q_5$ in the interest of clarity, while in the lower panel the partial life expectancy over the first 15 years of life is shown for boys and girls.

The most conspicuous feature of the table is the gradual deformation in the relative level of male and female mortality by age over time. Within the first year of life male rates were always substantially higher than female and the pattern did not change between the sixteenth and nineteenth centuries. At higher ages, however, the male/female ratio did change, especially after 1750, in ways that disfavoured girls, and the

Table 6.23 *Male/female mortality ratios from English family reconstitutions and in Princeton model life tables*

	$_1q_0$	$_4q_1$	$_{10}q_5$
1580–1749	1.138	1.025	1.014
1750–1837	1.140	0.955	0.895
Level 8 North	1.168	1.045	1.003
Level 8 West	1.163	1.001	0.916

Note: the ratios in the top panel of the table are the averages of the quarter-century ratios given in tab. 6.22.
Sources: tab. 6.22; Coale and Demeny, *Regional model life tables*, pp. 9, 227.

higher the age group the greater the female disadvantage, both relatively and absolutely. Over the whole span of childhood, however, as the lower panel of the figure shows clearly, girls always enjoyed a distinct advantage over boys.

To make the patterns readily visible they are set out in summary form in the top panel of table 6.23, with $_5q_5$ and $_5q_{10}$ collapsed as $_{10}q_5$ in the interest of capturing both the scale of the change and its more marked character in the higher age groups.

The male/female ratio in infant mortality showed no significant trend over time and was close to the levels found in model North and model West at a broadly appropriate expectation of life at birth (37.5 years for women). In both the higher age groups, however, the ratio changed quite markedly after 1750 with a sharp rise in the relative level of female mortality, reminiscent of a shift from a North to a West pattern in terms of the Princeton tables, but more pronounced. Before 1750, as may be seen in figure 6.18, male rates were usually slightly higher than female rates though the differences were neither marked nor consistent. After 1750 female rates rose above male, and above the age of 5 the margin of female disadvantage increased. The ultimate cause of the change is unclear. A possible proximate cause is suggested by the information in table 6.24.

Table 6.24 shows that respiratory tuberculosis claimed a steadily rising proportion of all deaths in each successive age group from birth to adolescence in England and Wales in 1861 (though the *absolute* rate was actually higher in the first year of life than in any subsequent age group until the late teens). It also shows that the rate for girls was generally higher than that for boys and that in the age group 10–4 it was almost twice as high. In the later teens, indeed, more than half of all the girls who died were victims of respiratory tuberculosis. In 1861 death rates

Table 6.24 *Respiratory tuberculosis in England 1861 (m_x)*

	Male			Female		
Age	All causes (a)	Respiratory tuberculosis (b)	(b)/(a) × 100	All causes (a)	Respiratory tuberculosis (b)	(b)/(a) × 100
0	0.19911	0.00158	0.83	0.15714	0.00158	1.01
1–4	0.03568	0.00096	2.69	0.03507	0.00104	2.97
5–9	0.00674	0.00050	7.42	0.00678	0.00057	8.41
10–4	0.00433	0.00070	16.17	0.00436	0.00130	29.82
15–9	0.00644	0.00249	38.66	0.00702	0.00359	51.14

Source: Preston, Keyfitz, and Schoen, *Causes of death*, pp. 224–7.

from respiratory tuberculosis were probably already in sharp decline: at all events they were much lower in 1871 than they had been 10 years earlier.[130] Assuming that rates had reached a peak earlier in the century, and that during the later eighteenth century they were climbing towards that peak, there was likely to have been a shift in the ratio of male to female deaths in later childhood of the sort which is visible in table 6.23.

The infant mortality rates set out in table 6.22 show that the male rate was always higher than the female rate and that the differential was broadly constant over time. Figure 6.19 and table 6.25 show how male and female endogenous and exogenous rates varied over time. The male/female ratio shown in the third panel of the table was more stable for exogenous than for endogenous mortality. The exogenous ratio showed no trend over time, whereas the endogenous ratio rose markedly from the late sixteenth century, when it was close to unity, to reach a peak in the first half of the eighteenth century, before falling back in the early nineteenth century to its starting level. The average level of the two ratios, however, was almost identical. Plainly, exogenous mortality affected boys more severely than girls. The significance, if any, of the changing ratio in endogenous mortality is unclear. Figure 6.19 plots the same information, using the same method employed in figure 6.4. The lines that represent the two sexes parallel each other closely. In the seventeenth and early eighteenth centuries change was largely confined to exogenous rates: thereafter to endogenous rates. There are, however, some dissimilarities which might repay more detailed analysis with a larger data set. For example, male endogenous mortality

---

[130] Preston, Keyfitz, and Schoen, *Causes of death*, pp. 224–31.

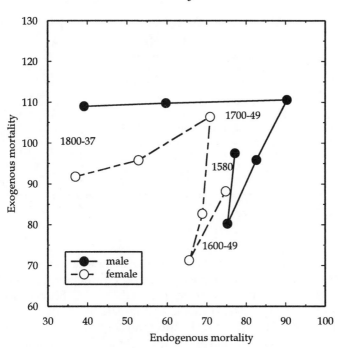

Figure 6.19   *The relative levels of male and female endogenous and exogenous*
infant mortality (1000d$_x$)
Source: Cambridge Group reconstitutions.

improved substantially more than female in the last century of the parish register period, but the reverse was true of exogenous mortality. Male rates showed no improvement, where female rates improved significantly.

Adulthood

Unlike the data relating to infant and child mortality, adult mortality data produced by reconstitution relate only to those who married. Among this population, however, there were substantial contrasts between the mortality experience of the two sexes. In table 6.26 three sets of male and female rates are set out, for the whole period 1640–1809, and for the two subperiods which were used in the earlier section on adult mortality, 1640–89 and 1750–1809. The latter were the two periods in which mortality was at its height and at its lowest respectively, and

Table 6.25 *Male and female endogenous and exogenous infant mortality* (1000d_x)

	Endogenous		Exogenous		Ratio M/F	
	M	F	M	F	Endogenous	Exogenous
1580–99	77.2	74.9	97.5	88.2	1.03	1.11
1600–49	75.3	65.6	80.3	71.2	1.15	1.13
1650–99	82.7	68.9	95.8	82.7	1.20	1.16
1700–49	90.4	70.9	110.5	106.4	1.28	1.04
1750–99	59.8	52.9	109.7	95.7	1.13	1.15
1800–37	39.2	37.0	109.0	91.8	1.06	1.19

Note: legitimate births only.
Source: Cambridge Group reconstitutions.

they are long enough to remove much of the random variability from the decennial data. Since they also represent the beginning and the end of the data, they may be expected to reveal any significant change over time in the relative levels of male and female mortality.

The earlier section devoted to adult mortality showed that mortality rates fell very markedly between the earlier and later periods shown in table 6.26, and the same was true of the male and female rates which jointly comprise the overall rates and which moved in sympathy with the overall rates. There is, however, no evidence of any significant change in the *relative* levels of male and female rates. In both periods, as overall, female rates were far above male rates in the main childbearing age groups, but, in general, well below male rates thereafter. Female rates above the age of 45 were not invariably lower than male rates. The female rate was the higher of the two in the age groups 65–9 and 75–9 in the parish register period as a whole, but it is probable that both this and the remarkably high male/female ratio for the age group 55–60 are the result of random influences on relatively small bodies of data. A better guide to the broad plausibility of the male/female ratios of mortality rates is the average ratio for each age group from 45 upwards. The ratios are given in columns 9 and 10 of table 6.26 and show the position for the reconstitution data as a whole and for a modified version of the third English life table. Because the 3rd ELT was derived from a massively larger body of data, the ratios in column 10 are much less variable than those in column 9. However, the average of the ratios from 45–9 to 80–4 is 108 for the reconstitution data and 107 for the 3rd ELT. The averages are sufficiently similar to encourage the belief that the underlying pattern of comparative death rates of the two sexes above the age of childbearing changed very little if at all over time.

Table 6.26 *Adult mortality, male and female (1000q_x)*

	1640–1809		1640–89		1750–1809		3rd ELT extended			
	(1) M	(2) F	(3) M	(4) F	(5) M	(6) F	(7) M	(8) F	(9) (1)/(2)	(10) (7)/(8)
25–9	39.1	74.8	50.9	99.1	25.8	73.4	46.7	49.0		
30–4	55.3	79.0	60.3	92.6	37.2	70.5	51.5	53.6		
35–9	71.6	89.0	85.5	111.3	57.8	67.1	58.1	58.7		
40–4	84.1	83.8	90.9	95.6	68.5	68.0	67.5	64.9		
45–9	106.1	95.7	114.8	114.8	99.0	77.5	80.8	72.8	111	111
50–4	127.5	110.6	154.4	126.6	116.3	83.3	101.0	87.1	115	116
55–9	182.6	139.7	216.3	189.0	133.1	113.0	130.1	116.6	131	112
60–4	203.3	189.3	221.8	232.6	182.8	160.0	176.9	165.7	107	107
65–9	259.0	267.7	286.3	310.3	222.1	254.5	246.8	240.9	97	102
70–4	387.1	374.4	454.9	406.5	372.7	380.0	355.7	348.7	103	102
75–9	469.3	476.0	492.7	555.3	423.9	451.8	489.3	477.3	99	103
80–4	609.7	596.4	537.2	766.0	643.5	556.2	626.2	615.9	102	102

Sources: Cambridge Group reconstitutions (cols. 1–6). Cols. 7 and 8: from 25–9 to 45–9, taken from the third English life table, Wrigley and Schofield, *Population history of England*, tab. A14.1, p. 709; from 50–4 to 80–4 extended from Princeton model North tables in the manner described in ibid., pp. 711–3.

In the main childbearing age groups, on the other hand, the patterns in the reconstitution data appear different from those in the 3rd ELT. In the mid-nineteenth century female mortality rates were higher for women than for men, but the differences were modest. The comparable ratios in the reconstitution data were far higher. In the first age group, 25–9, indeed, the female rate in the parish register period as a whole was almost double the male rate. In some degree this may be due to random factors, but the differences are too large and too consistent for them to play a major part in explaining such a marked disparity. Another factor has greater weight. The reconstitution rates refer, of course, to married women only. Since childbearing was largely confined to married women, the additional risks attendant upon childbearing were born almost exclusively by them. In the youngest age group, 25–9, a large proportion of the age group was unmarried. As a result in the 3rd ELT the childbearing penalty is diluted since over 40 per cent of the women in the age group were single.[131] With increasing age married women

---

[131] In 1851 in England and Wales 39.8 per cent of the 25–9 age group were single and 1.9 per cent widowed: Mitchell, *British historical statistics*, ch. 1, tab. 5, p. 21.

became steadily more representative of their age groups as a whole, and, in parallel, the difference in the ratio of male to female mortality between the reconstitution data and the 3rd ELT became steadily less pronounced.

The risk directly associated with childbearing can, of course, be quantified. For example, if one assumes for simplicity of calculation that the risk averaged 12 per 1000 live births over the parish register period as a whole,[132] then over a five-year period in which on average two births would have taken place, there would be 24 deaths among every 1000 married women entering the age group. While this factor would not eliminate the difference between male and female mortality rates in the prime years of childbearing, it would go much of the way to doing so. However, the risk in the younger age groups is understated by such a calculation, because the first child was frequently prenuptially conceived and born early in the marriage. The mean interval to first birth in bachelor/spinster marriages in which the wife was aged 25–9 at marriage was 16.6 months, and shorter still where the bride was younger.[133] Since the measure of exposure to the risk of dying begins with the date of the marriage, the risk associated with childbirth in the younger age groups, in which most marriages took place, was more heavily concentrated per unit of time than would appear from the initial calculation of two births in a five-year period. Finally, the risk associated with a first birth was about 50 per cent higher than the average for births of all parities.[134] If these considerations are taken into account the scale of the difference between male and female mortality rates in the twenties and early thirties is less surprising.[135] Excluding such risks the difference might well be similar to the relatively slight female *surmortalité* found in teenagers during much of the early modern period, but especially in the early nineteenth century.[136]

Figure 6.20 provides, in the upper panel, a summary of the comparative male and female partial expectations of life, paralleling figure 6.16 above; and in the lower panel, life expectancy at age 25 for the two sexes. Between 25 and 45 there was a marked male advantage. In the next 20

---

[132] Tab. 6.29, p. 313.   [133] Tab. 7.35, pp. 440–1.   [134] Tab. 6.31, p. 321.

[135] It should be noted that the high female mortality rates in the age groups in which most marriages were taking place are not a function of the decision to assume that women whose partners were born in another parish, and for whom their marriage was the last recorded event, left the parish immediately after their marriage. Even if they had not been made the subject of this special rule in calculating imputed exposure, the resulting change in mortality rates would have been slight. For a discussion of the rules relating to the determination of the length of the period of exposure to death on the part of men and women who married in the parish but subsequently migrated to die elsewhere, see app. 6.   [136] Tabs. 6.22 and 6.23, pp. 296 and 299.

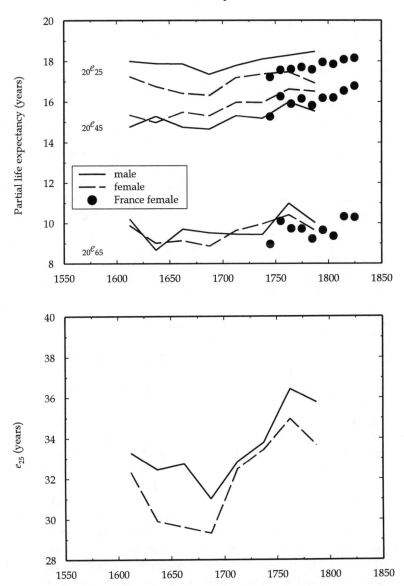

Figure 6.20   *Male and female partial life expectancies ($_{20}e_{25}$, $_{20}e_{45}$, and $_{20}e_{65}$)*
(upper panel), and expectation of life at age 25 (e_{25}) (lower panel)
Sources: Blayo, 'La mortalité en France', tab. 12, p. 139. Cambridge Group reconstitutions.

years of life the tables were turned: women could expect to survive more successfully throughout middle age. Between 65 and 85 the position was less clear-cut. The very marked advantage enjoyed by women in these age groups in the twentieth century does not appear. It is significant in this regard that the relative advantage of women over men declined steadily from the age group 50–4 onwards in the 3rd ELT and was modest in old age (table 6.26, column 10). Measured by e_{25}, there was a male advantage in adult life expectancy at all periods, though the difference became very slight in the first half of the eighteenth century.

It is likely that further work on adult partial life expectancies will yield much of interest. Young adults, like children, experienced worsening mortality during the seventeenth century. This trend was more pronounced for women than for men, as was the subsequent improvement. The difference between male and female trends may well be explained by a deterioration in maternal mortality in the seventeenth century, followed by a very marked reduction in its toll in the next century.[137] Between the ages of 45 and 65, in contrast, the seventeenth century saw no increase in mortality, and thereafter a steady and substantial improvement, common to both sexes. In the oldest of the three age groups it is difficult to detect any unambiguous change in the case of men. Mortality rates for women declined slightly in the eighteenth century, but were little if any better in 1800 than they had been in the early seventeenth century.

Male and female mortality rates for each age group can, of course, be combined into a single expression in the form of an expectation of life at birth. Rates for the age groups 15–9 and 20–4 can be estimated in the manner already described above for overall rates.[138] The outcome, shown in figure 6.21 and in table 6.27, shows that the advantage built up in infancy and childhood was sometimes sufficient to cause female life expectancy to exceed male, in spite of the heavier female mortality in middle life, but more often the reverse was the case. It is probable, however, that if rates could be calculated for the whole female population in the early adult years, and not just for married women, a small female advantage would show through, especially as the level of the observed rates for women in the childbearing age groups influences the calculation of the imputed rates for women in the age groups 15–9 and 20–4 for which empirical data were not available. The fact that female rates in the childbearing years are based exclusively on married women, who were differentially exposed to the hazards of pregnancy and delivery, must tend to exaggerate the level of female mortality at

---

[137] Tab. 6.29, p. 313.   [138] See p. 293.

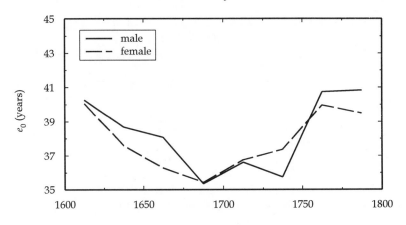

Figure 6.21   *Male and female expectation of life at birth (e_0)*
Source: Cambridge Group reconstitutions.

this time of life. When presented in this form, with estimates covering 25-year blocks of time, the starkness of the contrast between the periods before and after 1750 comes out very clearly. In the form in which the data were presented earlier for the sexes combined (figure 6.17), the point is less easily appreciated. Despite the very marked gains in adult life expectancy in the first half of the century, an overall advance was frustrated by the worsening of mortality early in life, but when these rates improved, the general improvement was dramatic, a rise of five years for men, though substantially less for women.

Maternal mortality

Today the chance of dying in childbed is very low. In England and Wales in 1988 it was only 0.06 per 1000 births, yet 70 years earlier, in 1920–9, it was roughly 70 times greater, at 4.1 per 1000. In this respect women in the 1920s were little better off than those in the mid-nineteenth century: in England and Wales in 1850–9 the maternal mortality rate had been 4.9 per 1000 live births, having varied only modestly in the intervening period.[139] Even this rate was low compared

[139] For recent maternal mortality rates, UN, *Demographic Yearbook 1989*, pp. 364–7; the rates for the 1850s and 1920s are taken from Loudon, *Death in childbirth*, app. 6, tab. 1, pp. 542–4. While it is true that decadal average rates did not change greatly in the later nineteenth and early twentieth centuries, individual annual rates still varied widely. The rate in 1874, for example, was as high as 6.9 per 1000 births, yet in 1878 it was only 3.7 per 1000; ibid.

Table 6.27 *Expectation of life at birth*
(e_0): *male and female (years)*

	M	F
1625–49	38.7	37.6
1650–74	38.1	36.3
1675–99	35.4	35.4
1700–24	36.6	36.8
1725–49	35.8	37.4
1750–74	40.7	40.0
1775–99	40.8	39.5

Source: Cambridge Group reconstitutions.

with that prevailing in earlier centuries, and since most women in early modern England married in their early or mid-twenties and, if they survived the childbearing years, were exposed to the risks of childbirth on half a dozen occasions or more, maternal mortality was a substantial danger to married women.[140]

Before a national vital registration system was created in 1837 only one source consistently recorded causes of death: the London bills of mortality. Though the interpretation of the terms used to describe the causes of death in the bills presents serious difficulty in most cases, 'childbed' was a fairly unambiguous descriptor, and so the number of burials recorded under this head are likely to be reasonably close to the mark. The number of burials due to 'childbed' per 1000 baptisms has been calculated for the four 'half-centuries' from 1657 to 1830 as follows: 21.0, 14.5, 11.4, 9.2.[141] The rate for the final period 1800–30 is somewhat higher than the rates for London recorded in the early years of vital registration (the rate for the period 1840–7, for example, was 6.1 per 1000), but encourages a belief that rates calculated from the bills of mortality were broadly accurate.[142] The London rate, however, was higher than elsewhere in the country and cannot be regarded as a good guide to the level or even perhaps to the trend of the national rate.

[140] On the perception of the danger of childbirth among women exposed to this risk in the early modern period, see Wilson, 'The perils of early modern procreation', and, more generally, the essays in Fildes, ed., *Women as mothers in pre-industrial England*.

[141] The periods in question are 1657–99, 1700–49, 1750–99, and 1800–30. Marshall, *Mortality in the metropolis*, pp. 70–1, 73 (baptisms); unpaginated tables after p. 82 (deaths in childbed). The numbers of baptisms were 540 474; 822 361; 844 262; and 703 696.

[142] The rate was obtained by relating deaths in childbirth to the totals of births for the London Division: all data were taken from Registrar-General, *Annual reports* (8th to 10th).

Since specific identification of maternal mortality is absent in other sources, it is necessary to estimate the national rate indirectly by counting the deaths of women in the period immediately following a birth as maternal mortality. This is to follow a well-worn path. For example, the International Federation of Gynaecology and Obstetrics (IFGO) defines maternal mortality as comprising 'the death of a woman while pregnant or within 42 days of termination of pregnancy irrespective of duration and site of pregnancy'.[143] This alternative approach, therefore, includes both deaths directly caused by childbirth and all others within a stated span of time following childbirth, presumptively on the ground that pregnancy and childbirth may increase the chance of dying from other causes, such as infectious disease.

A maternal mortality rate of this sort can be calculated from reconstitution data by treating any death of a married woman within a specified period after the birth of a child as a maternal death. There are, however, a number of awkward problems associated both with the calculation of the rate and with its interpretation. First, there is no agreement about the length of the specified period. The IFGO standard of 42 days was followed by Knodel and Imhof, while most French scholars have adopted a period of 60 days, and Perrenoud based his Genevan estimates on a period of 30 days.[144] We have chosen to use the longest of the alternatives, 60 days, but, given the relatively high level of adult mortality in the past, this suggests making an allowance for mortality from other causes which would have occurred in any case in the 60-day period, and subtracting it from the observed rate.

Second, the date which opened the 60-day interval during which a maternal death might occur was the date of baptism, not birth. If an infant died very young and escaped being recorded in either the baptism or the burial register, a maternity would be missed, and any associated mortality misallocated. Moreover, the lengthening delay between birth and baptism could cause the observational period to be displaced with a consequent loss of accuracy. In practice, however, neither problem is serious in England until the later eighteenth century. Before that date an infant dying before baptism was frequently entered in the burial register, and in the process of family reconstitution this would lead to the creation of a 'dummy' birth.[145] Nor was baptism delay

---

[143] This definition is also adopted by the World Health Organisation. It is qualified by the clause, 'from any cause related to, or aggravated by, the pregnancy or its management, but not from accidental or incidental causes'. WHO, *Manual of causes of death*, p. 772.

[144] Imhof, 'La surmortalité des femmes mariées'; Perrenoud, 'Surmortalité féminine'. French scholars include Bideau, 'Accouchement naturel'; Bardet *et al.*, 'La mortalité maternelle autrefois'; Gutierrez and Houdaille, 'La mortalité maternelle en France'.

[145] For further information about 'dummy' births, see pp. 110–2 above.

a major problem in the early parish register period. In the late sixteenth century children were baptised soon after birth, though the interval had lengthened to 8 days in the late seventeenth century, and to 26 days in the late eighteenth century.[146]

Third, and much more serious, is the fact that English parish registers did not usually record stillbirths, but the risk of a maternal death was much higher with stillbirths than in the case of live births.[147] English baptismal registers omit precisely those maternities in which the mother's life was most at risk. Consequently, maternal rates based solely on register entries would undoubtedly be too low. To correct for this, the proportion of all maternal deaths associated with stillbirths and with undelivered pregnancies must be established.

Fortunately, Swedish data provide what is needed. Swedish registers are of excellent quality and the Swedish and English mortality regimes in the eighteenth and nineteenth centuries appear to have been similar. Moreover, there was a rough parity in national maternal mortality rates in the two countries in the mid-nineteenth century.[148] The results of a study of all maternal deaths in nine parishes in contrasting social and economic contexts in southern Sweden between the mid-eighteenth and mid-nineteenth centuries are summarised in table 6.28. Almost a quarter of maternal deaths following a live birth occurred on the day of birth and a further 20 per cent in the next three days. Approaching a half of all maternal deaths, therefore, occurred within 4 days and 75 per cent within 2 weeks. Very few maternal deaths (only 2 per cent) occurred more than 60 days after childbirth. In the case of stillbirths, a much higher proportion of maternal deaths, 53 per cent, occurred on the day of delivery, probably because obstetrical problems both killed the foetus and caused the immediate death of the mother as well.

The Swedish data suggest that the maternal mortality rate associated with stillbirths was about eight times higher than with live births, and that stillbirths resulted in about 18 per cent of all maternal deaths.

---

[146] The figures cited are for the median birth–baptism interval in the median parish for 1650–99 and 1771–89; Berry and Schofield, 'Age at baptism', p. 458.

[147] For example, Eccles found maternal mortality rates for stillbirths in three northern parishes of 57, 64, and 137 per 1000 for the period 1629–1750, as compared with the range 10–15 per 1000 generally found in reconstitution studies in the same period; Eccles, 'Obstetrics in the seventeenth and eighteenth centuries', pp. 8, 10.

[148] For the excellence of the Swedish parish registers, see Schofield, 'Did the mothers really die?', p. 236. For the similarity of English and Swedish mortality regimes, see Wrigley and Schofield, *Population history of England*, fig. 7.13, p. 246. For the similarity of maternal mortality rates, see Registrar-General, *Seventeenth annual report*, p. 72, and *Thirty-ninth annual report*, p. 279, for England, and Schofield, 'Did the mothers really die?', tab. 9.1, p. 238.

Table 6.28 *Maternal deaths in nine Swedish parishes in the later eighteenth and early nineteenth centuries: interval from delivery to death by age, and those dying undelivered by age (all figures in the top panel of the table are percentages)*

| Interval from delivery to death (days) | Live births and stillbirths by age of decedent | | | | | | Live births | Stillbirths | Illegitimate | Multiple |
	Under 25	25–9	30–4	35–9	40–9	All				
0	24	26	27	30	34	29[a]	23	53	39	33
1–3	18	28	20	14	11	19	20	14	22	8
4–6	15	2	12	14	14	11	11	14	11	8
7–14	21	16	22	19	23	20	21	12	17	8
15–30	9	19	12	13	14	14	16	2	6	25
Over 30	12	9	7	10	5	8	9	6	6	17
0–30	88	91	93	90	95	92	91	94	94	83
0–42	94	98	96	93	98	96	95	100	94	83
0–60	100	100	99	96	98	98	98	100	100	92
N	33	57	74	70	44	279[a]	228	51	18	12
Percentage dying undelivered (of total deaths following live births, stillbirths, and undelivered)										
	13	17	28	19	41	27			14	0
All deaths (following live births, stillbirths, and undelivered)										
N	38	69	103	87	75	381[b]			21	12

[a] Includes one case with age not stated.
[b] Includes nine cases with age not stated.
Source: Swedish parish archives cited in Schofield, 'Did the mothers really die?', tab. 9.4, p. 243.

Consequently, maternal mortality rates based on registers that record live births alone would need to be inflated by about 22 per cent to take account of the maternal deaths that took place after stillbirths.[149] However, there was a further hidden dimension to maternal mortality: no less than 27 per cent of Swedish mothers dying from maternal causes died undelivered. The marginal notes in the register often attest to this fact. And this danger increased with age: no less than 41 per cent of maternal deaths of women in their 40s were of this type. In registers less informative than the Swedish such deaths will appear to be unrelated to childbearing and so will fail to be included in estimates of maternal mortality. The potential combined shortfall is serious: a register which included only live births, as in normal Anglican practice, would miss 40 per cent of the total of maternal deaths.[150]

Further analysis showed that the proportional division of maternal deaths beween live births, stillbirths, and undelivered pregnancies was not constant, but varied according to the overall level of maternal mortality. The Swedish data suggest that over a range of maternal mortality rates between extremes of 4.0 and 14.3 per 1000, the total rate could be predicted fairly accurately from the live-born maternal rate by increasing the latter by 7 per cent and adding a further constant of 2.73 per 1000.[151]

The Swedish data provide a basis for correcting English maternal mortality rates derived from live births alone. Table 6.29 shows the successive steps needed to estimate a corrected rate, and the resulting rates for each quarter-century. The mortality rate for women dying within 60 days of childbirth is given in the first column. In the second column this rate is reduced to reflect the 'background' mortality that would have occurred in the 60-day period in any case. This column, in other words, shows maternal rather than overall mortality. The difference between the rates in the first two columns is the rate at which the *husbands* of the women in question died in the same 60-day period. Admittedly this is only an approximate method as it assumes that the mortality of husbands was the same as that of their wives, and also ignores the fact that husbands were older than their wives by roughly two years, but it is sufficiently accurate for the present purpose. The third column shows the final estimated maternal mortality rate after increasing the rates in the second column by the amounts suggested by

[149] $100 \times 18/82 = 22$.   [150] That is, using the data in tab. 6.28, $40 = (381 - 228)/381 \times 100$.
[151] Total maternal mortality rates (TMMR) were regressed against live-birth-based rates (LBR) using ordinary least squares and the following relation was obtained: $TMMR = 1.07 \times LBR + 2.73$ (adj. $r^2 = 0.95$): Schofield, 'Did the mothers really die?', pp. 245–6.

Table 6.29 *English maternal mortality rates (per 1000 birth events)*

	Woman dies within 60 days of live birth (1)	Rate corrected for background mortality (2)	Rate corrected for stillbirth and no birth (3)[a]	Number of live birth events on which rates based
Before 1600	11.1	9.0	12.3	14 839
1600–24	11.6	9.4	12.8	17 892
1625–49	13.4	10.6	14.0	18 717
1650–74	15.9	13.4	17.0	18 544
1675–99	14.6	12.0	15.6	21 122
1700–24	12.8	10.0	13.4	21 842
1725–49	11.2	9.0	12.3	21 432
1750–74	7.7	6.3	9.5	21 130
1775–99	7.1	5.8	9.0	24 806
1800–24	4.6	3.4	6.3	16 470
1825–37[b]	3.2	1.8	4.7	11 178
Total	8.5	10.5	11.8	207 969

[a] 1.07 × rate in col. 2 plus 2.73. For further details see text.
[b] It should be noted that the rate for 1825–37 includes data for a few additional years after 1837 in the case of some parishes. Where the reconstitution extended down to, say, 1840 the additional information was used to maximise the number of observations available.
Note: legitimate births only.
Source: Cambridge Group reconstitutions.

Swedish experience. The final column shows the number of live births upon which the rates were calculated. The data are drawn from all the reconstitution parishes rather than taking data from the four groups for different periods. This maximises the quantity of data available and does not appear to introduce bias into the resulting series, even though the composition of the data changes as parishes enter or leave observation.[152]

The maternal mortality rate is also shown in figure 6.22. The rate rose steadily from the first quarter of the seventeenth century to a peak of 17.0 per 1000 in the last quarter of the century. Thereafter it fell, almost

[152] It is difficult to establish the absence of bias definitively since the number of maternal deaths in overlap periods is relatively small compared with similar exercises relating, say, to infant mortality. There is a possibility, of course, that the relationship that captures Swedish experience so neatly is inappropriate for English data, but it is plain that correcting English data in this way is preferable to quoting them without making any allowance for stillbirths and undelivered pregnancies.

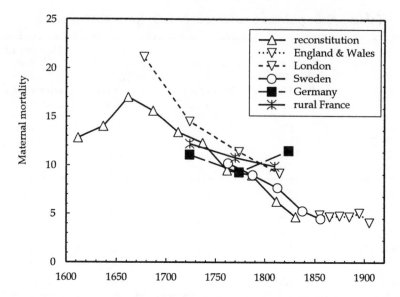

Figure 6.22   *Maternal mortality: English data and international comparisons (per 1000 live birth events)*

Notes: the data in the figure are shown as points connected by lines but in each case they refer to time periods as follows: English reconstitution: 1600–24 by quarter-century to 1800–24, then 1825–37; English national: 1850–9 to 1900–9 by decade; London: 1657–99, 1700–49, 1750–99, 1800–30; Sweden: 1751–75 to 1826–50 by quarter-century, then 1851–60; Germany: 1700–49 to 1800–49 by half-century; rural France: 1700–49, 1750–89, 1790–1829.

The English reconstitution data, the English national data, the London data, and the Swedish data were taken from the sources quoted without further correction. In each of these cases either corrections to the raw data had already been made (English reconstitution), or there is reason to think that the original data do not stand in need of correction. In the case of the German data (taken from the six parishes of Kappel, Rust, Braunsen, Massenhausen, Middels, and Öschelbronn) and the French data (taken from a number of family reconstitutions), correction like that applied to the English reconstitution data is needed since the rates quoted in the sources were based on deaths of mothers within a given period after childbirth. The formula quoted above (p. 312 n. 151) was therefore used to allow for maternal deaths which did not follow a live birth (which meant using the observed rather than the 'corrected' data in the case of France (see Gutierrez and Houdaille in the source note below). A further correction is, however, needed because some of those who died within the 60-day period after the birth of the child would have died in any case. Blayo provides mortality data on which an appropriate correction can be based. Death rates (m_x) from the Princeton North tables were selected to reflect the changing level of e_{30} in France as follows: 1700–49, level 4; 1750–89, level 6; 1790–1829, level 8. In the absence of direct evidence about an appropriate mortality correction for the German parishes, it was assumed that adult mortality rates were similar to those in France and the following levels were therefore used: 1700–49, level 4; 1750–99, level 6; 1800–49, level 8.

halving over the next century, and halving again between 1750–74 and 1825–37, when it was only 4.7 per 1000.[153] Thus the long period of stability in the maternal mortality rate from the 1850s until the 1930s was preceded by a quarter-millennium in which the rate first rose and then fell steeply.

Since the quoted rates are the product of a series of corrections, it is important to test their plausibility, both against contemporary data for other populations, and by examining such features as the rate according to the age of the mother and the multiplicity and parity of the child. Figure 6.22 compares the reconstitution estimates with rates of other populations, namely London (from the 1650s); a number of French family reconstitutions (from 1700); a set of six German parishes (from 1700); national data for Sweden (from 1751); and national data for England and Wales (from 1850).

The national data for England and Sweden tend to confirm the plausibility of the estimates derived from the 26 reconstitutions. First, the reconstitution-based rate of 4.7 per 1000 for the period 1825–37 is only a trifle lower than the English national rate of 4.9 per 1000 for 1850–9. Second, from 1750 onwards the reconstitution-based rate lies uncannily close to the Swedish national rate; the Swedish rate falls at much the same speed, and is never more than 1.4 per 1000 away from the English rate. It is particularly reassuring to find the same steep decline in the Swedish data, which comprise by far the best set of observations of the incidence of maternal mortality in a large population during this period.

Comparison with rates based on smaller population units is also illuminating. Although the French reconstitution-based rates began at a similar level to the English parishes in the early eighteenth century, they experienced a much slower decline, so that by the early nineteenth century the rural French rate was just under 10 per 1000 while the

---

[153] It should be noted that the rate for 1825–37 includes data for a few additional years after 1837 in the case of some of the parishes. Where the reconstitution extended down to, say, 1840 the additional information was used in order to maximise the number of observations available.

Notes to figure 6.22 (*cont.*)

Sources: English reconstitution: tab. 6.24; English national: Loudon, *Death in childbirth*, app. 6, tab. 1, pp. 542–3; London: Marshall, *Mortality in the metropolis*, pp. 70–1, 73 (baptisms), unpaginated tables after p. 82 (deaths in childbed); Sweden: Schofield, 'Did mothers really die?', tab. 9.1, p. 238; Germany: Knodel, *Demographic behavior in the past*, tab. 5.1, p. 105; rural France: Gutierrez and Houdaille, 'La mortalité maternelle en France', tab. 1, p. 978, and Blayo, 'La mortalité en France', tab. 16, p. 141.

English rate was 6.3 per 1000. It thus appears that in France the maternal death rate was also improving, though less rapidly than in England or in Sweden. In the six German parishes, however, there was not even a modest improvement between the early eighteenth and the early nineteenth centuries. The maternal mortality rate in the period 1800–49 was 11.5 per 1000 compared to the slightly lower rate of 11.1 per 1000 for 1700–49, though in the intervening half-century the rate was distinctly lower, at 9.3 per 1000.[154] Finally, the reconstitution-based English rates are consistently lower than those calculated from the deaths attributed to childbed in the London bills of mortality. It is probable that the London rate understates the true level of maternal deaths in that deaths arising from complications during pregnancy may well not have been classified as maternal deaths. Any correction here, however, would be hazardous, especially as there was also underrecording of births. The comparison is reassuring nonetheless, since the London rate was certainly higher than the national average. The excess of the London rate averaged about 30 per cent over the four comparison periods, a level similar to the metropolitan excess over the national rates in the Registrar-General's returns in the mid-nineteenth century.[155]

At first sight the most puzzling feature of the secular changes in the

---

[154] There was a similar absence of improvement but at a considerably higher absolute level in the ruling families of Europe which were the subject of Peller's attention. The maternal death rate (taken as all deaths of mother within two months of the birth of a child) in the periods 1500–1699, 1700–99, and 1800–99 was 20.6, 20.4, and 16.2 per 1000 in these families; Peller, 'Studies on mortality', p. 442.

[155] As an example of the extent of the difference between the maternal mortality rate in London and that in the country as a whole after the inception of civil registration, there were 507 deaths in 'childbirth' in London in 1847 and 68 331 births, while in England and Wales in the same year the comparable figures were 2432 and 539 965, yielding rates of 7.45 and 4.50 maternal deaths per 1000 live births respectively.
It may be of interest to note that the estimated English rates also seem quite reasonable even in the context of a generally low level of obstetrical knowledge and skill. For example, a report based on 1897 home deliveries among the London poor in the years 1774–81 noted that 94.5 per cent had 'natural labours, not attended with any particular danger', 3.3 per cent had 'preternatural or laborious births, or suffered in consequence of labour' but 'recovered with little more than the common assistance', and only 2.2 per cent had deliveries which were 'attended with particular difficulty or danger'; Bland, 'Some calculations', pp. 358–60. Thanks are due for this reference to Irvine Loudon of the Wellcome Unit for the History of Medicine, Oxford. This assessment is close to a modern estimate of the percentage of women who face danger in childbed, and suggests that only 22 per 1000 would have been seriously at risk of dying from maternal complications. Wilson notes that 96 per cent of modern births are normal and spontaneous while the remaining 4 per cent involve serious obstruction; 'William Hunter and the varieties of man-midwifery', pp. 344–5.

maternal mortality rate in England was its rise during the seventeenth century, since there seems no good reason to suppose, for example, that obstetrical practice deteriorated at this time. However, during this period the general level of mortality also rose (tables 6.3 and 6.10). Recent research has shown that women in their third trimester of pregnancy, or newly delivered, are several times more likely than others of the same age to become infected by, and to die of, diseases that were common in England in the past, such as tuberculosis, smallpox, and influenza. This is because pregnancy suppresses cell-mediated immunity in a way which permits foetal retention, but interferes with resistance to specific pathogens.[156] The existence of a 'pregnancy-associated immune deficiency syndrome' (PAIDS) might help to account not only for the rise in maternal mortality rates during the seventeenth century, assuming that exposure to infectious disease increased, but also for the consistently higher maternal mortality rates found in London and in other pre-industrial cities where exposure to infection was higher than in the countryside. Puerperal fever induced by streptococcal infection may well have been the most important single cause of maternal deaths. Maternal mortality rates were not simply an index of the level and diffusion of obstetrical knowledge and skills: indeed, they were probably little affected by them. Other factors in the social, economic, and political domains were more important because they influenced the incidence of, and exposure to, infectious disease.[157]

Just as an increase in exposure to infectious disease may serve in part to explain the rise in maternal mortality in the seventeenth century, so it may also explain much, indeed perhaps all, of its subsequent decline. Adult mortality fell very substantially during the first half of the eighteenth century. Female $_{20}e_{25}$, for example, rose from 16.3 years in 1675–99 to 17.5 years in 1750–74. This may appear unimpressive, but can equally well be viewed as moving from a position in which 3.7 years out of a possible maximum of 20 were lost to death to a position in which only 2.5 years were so lost. The latter figure is only two-thirds as large as the former. In the most important childbearing age groups from 25 to 40 the five-year age-specific mortality rates fell by 32 per cent on average.[158] The fall in maternal mortality was even steeper than this, however, so that it might appear that part of the decline in the former to

---

[156] Weinberg, 'Pregnancy and resistance to infectious disease'.

[157] The ways in which patterns of mortality are structured by different dimensions of the social order are discussed in Schofield, 'Family structure', and by Walter and Schofield, 'Famine, disease and crisis mortality'.

[158] Tab. 6.26, p. 303, gives additional details of the extent of the fall in adult female mortality rates, though for somewhat different time periods.

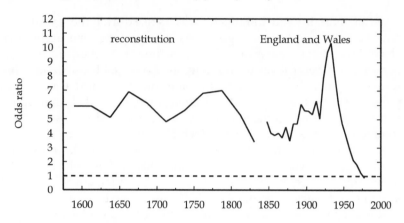

Figure 6.23　*The maternal to male mortality odds ratio*
Note: the calculation of the male mortality rate in the parish register period, which is a paternal mortality rate covering the same period in the lives of fathers as that used to calculate the maternal mortality rate for mothers, is explained in the text relating to tab. 6.29 on pp. 312–3 above. The male mortality rate for the civil registration period is the rate for men aged 30–4 ($_5m_{30}$).
Sources: maternal mortality rates: Loudon, *Death in childbirth*, app. 6, tab. 1, pp. 542–5. Male mortality rates for the parish register era: Cambridge Group reconstitutions; for the civil registration era: *The Chester Beatty life tables*.

unprecedentedly low levels by the early nineteenth century must be attributed to improvements in the management of childbirth, chiefly, perhaps, because of 'a significant rise in the number, status, skill, and efficiency of English midwives'.[159] However, the view taken of this issue depends in part on the method of analysis employed. The value of the odds ratio in offering an alternative perspective to that of percentage change was clear in discussing the age pattern of mortality decline.[160] It is equally useful in this context, as may be seen in figure 6.23.

The male mortality rate is the difference between the rates shown in the first two columns of table 6.29, as explained in the accompanying text, while the maternal rate is that given in column 3 of the same table. The ratio plotted in the figure is the odds ratio between the maternal rate and the male rate. The fact that the ratio is so stable throughout the parish register period suggests that the same influences may have been at work in reducing both. If the PAIDS factor were the major influence in determining the level of maternal mortality, a largely unchanging odds ratio is to be expected. On the other hand, if the maternal mortality rate were strongly influenced by the direct and immediate hazards of childbirth, through protracted or difficult labour, an unchanging odds

---

[159] Loudon, *Death in childbirth*, p. 161.　　[160] See above p. 292.

ratio is more surprising, since there is no apparent reason to expect changes in such hazards to mirror changes in the prevalence and virulence of infectious disease.

Figure 6.23 also shows that the odds ratio did not change significantly until well into the twentieth century. The subsequent very steep rise may possibly reflect the hazards associated with the procuring of abortions during the interwar period, when they were illegal but widely practised where contraception had failed.

The risk of death in childbed varied substantially according to the circumstances of the birth. The most striking instance of this is to be found in the case of multiple births. Since single births form the great majority of all births the maternal mortality rate for single births was very close to the overall rate: they were 11.5 and 11.8 per 1000 respectively over the whole period covered by reconstitution. The rate for multiple births, however, was much higher at 33.5 per 1000 deliveries. Table 6.30 shows that the rate for multiple births was always higher than that for singleton births. But the differential decreased over time. In the period before 1650 the former was 48.6 per 1000 and was about four times as high as the singleton rate. In the following century it fell substantially to 35.5 per 1000, and in the final period the fall accelerated. The rate almost halved to 18.8 per 1000. By this time the multiple birth rate was less than two-and-a-half times the singleton rate. The maternal mortality rate for multiple births probably peaked earlier than the overall rate.[161] Any PAIDS effect may have been swamped by other factors. The fact that the ratio of the rate for multiple births to that for singleton births declined suggests a greater relative improvement in the handling of multiple births.

Age of mother and parity, no less than multiplicity, normally influenced the risk of childbirth in the past. Of all births, the first is usually the most dangerous. As may be seen in table 6.31, over the whole reconstitution period the risk to the mother at a first birth was 45 per cent greater than the average, a larger differential than in the French parishes where the comparable figure was 38 per cent for the period 1700–1829.[162] After the first birth the rate dropped to about 86 per cent of the overall average level, remaining near this level for all subsequent

---

[161] The rates for half-century periods suggest that it was at its peak in the first half of the seventeenth century, when it stood at 53.3 per 1000, but rates calculated for relatively short periods may be untrustworthy since the number of cases was small.

[162] Gutierrez and Houdaille, 'La mortalité maternelle en France', tab. 13, p. 987, using the 'observed' rather than the 'corrected' rates. In the six German parishes (1700–1899) the penalty attaching to a first birth was substantially lower, at 22.7 per cent; Knodel, *Demographic behavior in the past*, tab. 5.1, p. 105. The overall rate was estimated for 60 days from the first 'confinement order' in fig. 5.1, p. 111, multiplied up from the 42-day rate to equal the 60-day rate.

Table 6.30 *Maternal mortality rates by birth multiplicity (per 1000 birth events)*

| | Single births | | Multiple births | |
	Rate	No. of birth events	Rate	No. of birth events
Before 1650	12.6	50 702	48.6	746
1650–1749	14.2	81 635	35.5	1 307
1750–1837[a]	7.7	72 648	18.8	936
All	11.5	204 985	33.5	2 989

[a] It should be noted that the rate for 1825–37 includes data for a few additional years after 1837 in the case of some parishes. Where the reconstitution extended down to, say, 1840 the additional information was used to maximise the number of observations available.
Note: legitimate births only. Rate corrected for stillbirths and no births.
Source: Cambridge Group reconstitutions.

parities apart from the sixth parity but the dip at this parity may well be adventitious. In French and German parishes it was normal for the rate to rise rather than fall at higher parities.[163] A possible reason for this puzzling contrast is that the English rates were based on live birth events, corrected by the standard formula, whereas the comparable data for other countries came from sources in which at least some stillbirths were recorded. As noted above, it was evident from the Swedish data that the proportion of maternal deaths not associated with live births was especially high for women in their 40s. Since higher parities would be drawn differentially from this age group, there is a strong possibility that the lack of any parity effect in the English data may be due to the increasing proportion of women dying after a stillbirth or undelivered in the later age groups.

In an attempt to overcome this problem, the English live-birth maternal mortality rates were tabulated by age. When they are corrected by applying age-specific omission rates calculated from the Swedish data, the resulting age profile of maternal mortality has a more plausible shape, as may be seen in table 6.32. The index numbers imply no significant effect of age on the rate up to age 35. In almost all historical studies the rate rises for mothers from age 35 onwards. In France in the

---

[163] France: Gutierrez and Houdaille, 'La mortalité maternelle en France', p. 987. Germany: Knodel, *Demographic behavior in the past*, fig. 5.1, p. 111.

Table 6.31 *Maternal mortality rates by parity of birth (per 1000 birth events)*

| | Parity | | | | | | | |
	1	2	3	4	5	6	7 and over	All
Rate	17.0	9.7	10.2	10.4	9.9	8.6	10.1	11.7
Index	145	83	87	89	85	74	86	100
Birth events	29 106	22 621	17 799	13 772	10 336	7 427	12 523	113 584

Notes: legitimate births only. Rates corrected for stillbirths and no births.
Source: Cambridge Group reconstitutions.

321

period 1700–1829 women in their 40s had a maternal mortality rate 43 per cent above the overall average, while in the six German parishes the rate was 56, and in the nine Swedish parishes 70 per cent above average.[164] In England, there was a high rate for women aged 45–9, but, because the rate for women aged 40–4 was only modestly higher than the overall rate and many more children were born to women in their early 40s than in their late 40s, the overall rate for women in their 40s was only 28 per cent above the overall average. The English pattern was not, however, unique. Rates in Rouen in the period 1650–1792 were even more uniform. The maternal mortality rates were virtually the same for all age groups (nor was there any increase in rates by parity).[165]

Seasonal mortality

General patterns

The overall pattern of seasonality of deaths was simple and stable in early modern England. The data presented in the *Population history of England*, which were drawn from a sample of 404 parishes, show that over each of six successive half-centuries beginning in 1540 and ending in 1834, the mortality minimum was reached in midsummer, and that the maximum occurred in the late spring.[166] July was the least mortal month in each period except 1750–99, when the minimum was in August, while the peak values occurred either in March (1540–99, 1800–34), or in April (1600–49), or the two months were equal first (1650–99, 1700–49, 1750–99). Indexed on the average number of deaths in each month, and after correction for the varying length of the month, the peak value in each period lay in the range 114 to 121, with a mean of 117, while the minimum value lay in the range 81 to 87, with a mean of 83. There was thus an average peak to trough ratio of 1.41. Of all the 404 parishes in the sample, 31.2 per cent reached a peak of mortality in April during the period as a whole (1540–1834), and 71.5 per cent in February, March, or April. The comparable low point in mortality occurred in 39.6 per cent of all parishes in July, and in 70.1 per cent of all parishes in July, August, or September.[167] The pattern of seasonality found in the aggregative data is shown in figure 6.24.

---

[164] Gutierrez and Houdaille, 'La mortalité maternelle en France', pp. 982–3; Knodel, *Demographic behavior in the past*, data from fig. 5.1, p. 111 expressed as a percentage of the overall rate calculated from tab. 5.1, p. 105. For an indirect estimate for the nine parishes in southern Sweden, see sources listed under fig. 6.22, p. 314.
[165] Bardet *et al.*, 'La mortalité maternelle autrefois', p. 44.
[166] Wrigley and Schofield, *Population history of England*, tab. 8.3 and fig. 8.2, pp. 293–4.
[167] Ibid.

Table 6.32 *Maternal mortality rates by age of mother (per 1000 birth events)*

				Age				
	15–9	20–4	25–9	30–4	35–9	40–4	45–9	All
Rate per 1000 live births	8.1	7.4	7.6	7.0	8.0	6.8	12.7	7.5
Inflation factor	1.3	1.4	1.5	1.6	1.6	2.0	2.0	1.6
Total rate	10.5	10.4	11.4	11.2	12.8	13.6	25.4	12.0
Index	88	87	95	93	107	113	212	100
Birth events	1672	11427	18010	16938	12784	6097	1067	67995

Note: legitimate births only. For description of inflation factor see text.
Source: Cambridge Group reconstitutions.

323

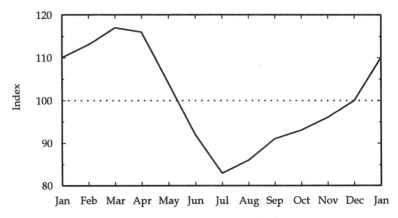

Figure 6.24   *The seasonality of all deaths at all ages in early modern England,*
1540–1834 (monthly average = 100)
Note: the index numbers are averages of half-century indices covering the periods
1540–99, 1600–49 . . . 1750–99, 1800–34. They are corrected for the varying length of the
month. The original data were drawn from 404 English parishes.
Source: Wrigley and Schofield, *Population history of England*, tab. 8.3, p. 294.

The absence of significant change in seasonality over time found in
the aggregative data is mirrored also in the reconstitution material.
Figure 6.25 shows that there was no major change in either the timing or
the scale of seasonal peaks and troughs in overall mortality after 1650.
The period before 1650 appears at first blush to be different. There was a
much less pronounced winter peak, balanced by a more clear-cut
autumn peak in September than was found later. The slightly higher
September peak may well reflect the fact that plague was still present in
England in this first period, since a late summer peak in mortality was a
common feature of plague.[168] The absence of the normal mortality peak
in March, on the other hand, is spurious, the product of a truncation
effect. In the early years of any reconstitution, although the deaths of the
elderly no less than the young will be recorded in the parish register,
their age will be unknown since they will have been born before the start
of registration, whereas the age of a young child can be established,
because he or she will have been born after the start of registration. It is
therefore inevitable that young children will be heavily overrepresented
among deaths of known age in the early decades of reconstitution.
Comparison with figure 6.26 will show that this must tend to result in a

[168] It may, however, also reflect the seasonal incidence of other epidemic diseases,
especially diarrhoeal infections: Wrigley and Schofield, *Population history of England*,
pp. 657–9.

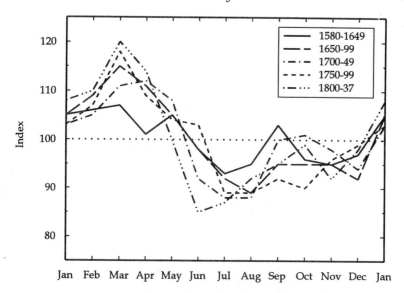

Figure 6.25   *The seasonality of deaths by half-century periods (monthly average = 100)*
Note: corrected for the varying length of the month.
Source: Cambridge Group reconstitutions.

seasonal mortality pattern like that for the period before 1650 in figure 6.25. The apparent contrast between the pre-1650 period and later periods should therefore be discounted. Even after 1650, a few parishes had still not been in observation long enough to avoid the truncation effect, but they constituted too small a proportion of the total to exercise a significant influence on the seasonal pattern. If the remaining four periods are compared with the seasonal pattern for the whole post-1650 period, none of the four differs from the period as a whole to a statistically significant degree.[169]

When seasonality of death is cross-classified by age at death using reconstitution data, it becomes apparent that the pattern visible in deaths at all ages combined is not mirrored in each separate age group. In figure 6.26 the seasonality of death in broad age groups is shown, together with the overall aggregative pattern from figure 6.24, while in table 6.33 the reconstitution data are shown in tabular form.

Some of the age groups in the figure and the table cover a wide age span. These divisions were adopted, however, only after experiment

[169] Tests conducted on the infant rates and on adult mortality confirm this point.

Table 6.33 *Seasonality of deaths by age*

	Jan.	Feb.	March	April	May	June	July	Aug.	Sept.	Oct.	Nov.	Dec.	N	Prob.	Stan. dev.
0–4	103	108	114	109	103	93	89	90	99	97	97	96	49 796	0.000	7.31
5–9	105	97	104	111	99	110	100	94	99	101	89	90	5 838	0.005	6.62
10–39	103	104	110	107	113	98	95	97	95	95	92	93	13 076	0.000	6.72
40–74	111	112	118	113	112	100	78	78	92	91	96	100	5 586	0.000	13.10
75–	133	144	123	93	99	98	81	62	61	81	102	122	1 102	0.000	25.44
All	104	107	113	109	105	96	90	91	97	96	95	96	75 398	0.000	7.09

Note: for a definition of the meaning of the column headed 'Prob.', see p. 329. The monthly index figures are corrected for the varying length of the month.
Source: Cambridge Group reconstitutions.

326

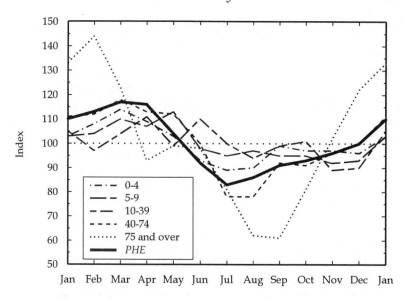

Figure 6.26 *The seasonality of deaths by age (monthly average = 100)*
Note: the monthly index numbers are corrected for the varying length of the month.
Sources: Cambridge Group reconstitutions. PHE line: Wrigley and Schofield, *Population history of England*, tab. 8.3, p. 294.

showed that there was very little difference in seasonality between narrower age bands within each group. Both for this section, dealing with general patterns of seasonality, and for the following section, relating principally to the first two years of life, experiment also showed that it was unnecessary to approach the question of seasonality by considering separately data from the four groups and producing a composite picture, as with most other aspects of mortality. Although the *level* of mortality differed between the four groups in the periods when the groups overlapped one another, and it was therefore necessary to draw data from the four groups separately and adjust the resulting rates to produce consistent time series,[170] the *seasonality pattern* did not differ significantly between the groups in overlap periods. The results reported in this section, therefore, are based on data drawn from all the parishes in observation at any given time.[171] This has the advantage of increasing the size of the body of data available, thus reducing the scale of random fluctuations and simplifying analysis.

The standard deviations shown in the final column of table 6.33

[170] See pp. 214–6 above.   [171] See tab. 2.1, pp. 22–3.

provide a convenient summary measure of the variability of monthly figures round the mean. They were calculated from monthly index figures where 100 represents the monthly average. Thus, if the total number of deaths in an age group were 840, the monthly average therefore 70, and the total in, say, March was 105, the index figure for March would be 150 (105/70 × 100 = 150). The arithmetic was a little less simple than indicated since the monthly index values in all the seasonality calculations were corrected for the varying length of the different months. The series of twelve monthly index values was then used to calculate the standard deviation for the age group in question. In the first three age groups, 0–4, 5–9, and 10–39, the standard deviations were 7.31, 6.62, and 6.72 respectively.

Table 6.33 shows that there were very many more deaths in the 0–4 age group than in any other, more indeed than in all the others combined. This is in part a reflection of the high risk of death in infancy, but is also due to the effect of migration, which meant that, the longer a man or woman lived, the more likely he or she was to die away from his or her parish of birth. As a result of the dominant influence of the 0–4 age group, the standard deviation of all deaths in table 6.33 was only modestly higher than that for the first five years of life. This accounts also for the lower variability of all deaths in the table than in the aggregative data which appear as a heavy line in figure 6.26. The standard deviation of the monthly index figures for the aggregative data for the whole period 1538–1837 was 11.20 compared with a figure of 7.09 for all deaths in table 6.33. If the seasonal patterns of the different reconstitution age groups were appropriately weighted, however, the resulting line would follow the aggregative line very closely.

The very large number of deaths in the age group 0–4 explains the relatively smooth regularity of the line representing the monthly behaviour of its index. There is a steady fall from a peak value of 114 in March to a low point of 89 in July, a peak to trough ratio of 1.28, and thereafter an almost equally smooth rise during the late summer, autumn, and winter, except that the figure for September is somewhat higher than would be expected if the progression were completely smooth.

Smaller numbers may account for the less regular pattern of the monthly values for the age groups 5–9 and 10–39. Their peak values occur in April and May respectively, and in both these age groups the lowest value occurs in November. Although the number of events on which the monthly index numbers in these two age groups were based was smaller than in the first age group, the patterns are highly significant in a statistical sense, and this is true even for the highest age group, where the numbers were far lower still, as may be seen from the 'probability' figures in the penultimate column of table 6.33. These figures represent the likelihood of the observed pattern not being significantly different from an even distribution of deaths month by month, and therefore occurring by chance. In most cases the probability is not expressed to a sufficiently large number of places of decimals for any figure other than nought to appear, and the highest probability shown represents only 5 in 1000.[172]

In general the pattern of seasonality of death by age group in early modern England was a very simple one. In the first 40 years of life seasonality was muted. Above the age of 40 seasonality became steadily more pronounced. The standard deviation doubled between the age group 10–39 and the age group 40–74, from 6.72 to 13.10, and almost doubled again, to 25.44, among those aged 75 and over. Amongst the most elderly age group it would seem that temperature may have played a major role in determining the seasonality of death, since deaths reached a peak in February and a low point six months later, the index figures for August and September being closely similar and well below those for any other month. The peak to trough ratio for the age group is 2.36, in marked contrast with that for the youngest age group. Among children in the first 5 years of life the number of deaths in the most fatal month was only 28 per cent higher than in the healthiest month, whereas among those aged 75 years or more, the comparable figure was 136 per cent. For those in the age group 40–74, the seasonality of mortality was less pronounced than in the oldest age group, but much

---

[172] The tests employed here were derived from Watson's and Maag's tests for 'circular' data: Watson, 'Goodness of fit tests'; Maag, 'A k-sample analogue of Watson's U^2 statistic'. They were used in the form developed by Brown and Gunn. Watson's statistic measures departure from an expected distribution; Maag's statistic measures the difference between two or more empirical distributions. A 'circular' test is needed because conventional tests of the differences between ordered distributions, such as the Kolmogorov–Smirnov test, are inappropriate. Aggregation of parish register data in the form of monthly totals produces a time series with a natural origin at the start of registration, as long as information about both year and month is used. But if the data are simply categorised by month, the natural origin is lost, even though the seasonal ordering is retained. A circular test, since it does not require an origin, avoids the problem that otherwise the results can be affected by the arbitrary point at which the circle is cut to create an origin. Brown and Gunn have developed Watson's and Maag's tests for use on frequency data. The test is sensitive to successive values and not simply to individual readings. Thus, a run of values extending over several months, all of which are above 100 or below 100 may be taken to be significant, even though a set of values which were on average equally far from 100, but where some were above and others below 100, might fail to be significant. The seasonal pattern in almost all the individual five-year age groups is significant at the 5 per cent level.

more marked than in the earlier decades of life. The peak to trough ratio was 1.51, with the peak occurring in March and the trough in July and August, a repetition of the pattern found among the youngest age group. Increasing age brought with it increasing vulnerability to the progression of the calendar.

Statistical tests showed that there was no significant difference in the seasonality of mortality by sex in early modern England in any of the major age groups used in figure 6.26.[173]

In all age groups death was most likely to occur towards the end of the winter season when ambient temperatures were low and the nights long, and was least likely when the population had enjoyed for some time the benefit of warmth and light, though this benefit stayed with those in youth and early adulthood through into the late autumn, but was lost earlier by infants and the elderly. Whether the link between temperature and mortality was direct to any significant extent, or whether the linkage was indirect cannot, of course, be inferred confidently from evidence such as this. If a larger body of data were available, more progress might be made, since it would then be possible to consider the patterns of death by age in years when the winters were exceptionally cold or the summers unusually hot. Using the very much larger body of seasonal aggregative data which formed the empirical basis of the *Population history of England*, Lee was able to specify the nature of the links between exceptionally cold winters or unusually hot summers and fluctuations in overall mortality, though not, of course, in age-specific death rates. It is of interest in this regard, that, as might be expected, very cold winter weather was associated with increased mortality, but that unusually hot summers also *increased* mortality, even though the warmer temperatures of summer were associated with the seasonal trough in deaths.[174]

The contrast between the winter and summer fortunes of the elderly may be brought home by a simple device. Assume for argument's sake that the seasonal index figures shown in table 6.33 referred to a population characterised by level 10 mortality in the Princeton North tables, representing an expectation of life at birth for the sexes combined of about 41 years. During the month of August when mortality was at its lowest (monthly index = 70), those aged 70–4 would be experiencing the same death rates as those found in the table for level 17 (that is, an expectation of life at birth 17.5 years greater than level 10), while in the

[173] The method used for this and the previous statistical test was Maag's U^2, and the criterion was the conventional one, that the probability of the observed difference arising by chance should be less than 5 per cent.

[174] Lee in Wrigley and Schofield, *Population history of England*, ch. 9, esp. pp. 384–98.

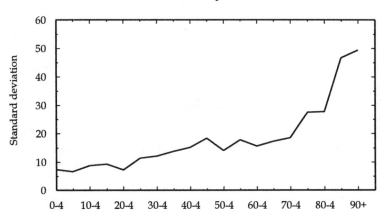

Figure 6.27   *The variability of the seasonal index of deaths by age*
Note: the standard deviation was calculated from the monthly index figures where the
mean monthly value = 100. Corrected for the varying length of the month.
Source: Cambridge Group reconstitutions.

month when mortality was at its height (monthly index = 134), the
comparable mortality level would be level 5 (with an e_0 12.5 years less
than level 10). Because seasonality of death was even more extreme in
the age group 75–9, the spread of mortality levels calculated in the same
way on either side of level 10 is even greater, with a high in the best
month of level 24 (equivalent to the annual mortality level in an
advanced country today, with an e_0 of almost 78 years) and a low in the
worst month of level 3 ($e_0 = 23.6$ years). In the course of the year,
therefore, there was a sense in which the elderly passed from months in
which the mortality regime was of extreme severity to months when it
might be almost as mild as the average experience of those in the same
age groups today.

The degree to which increasing age resulted in increasing variability
in the seasonal index of deaths is further clarified in figure 6.27 in which
the standard deviation in the monthly index figures from the average
figure of 100 is shown for five-year age groups throughout the whole
age span. It was very low and stable for the first 20 years of life, never
exceeding 10; rose slightly but remained at a modest level for the next 20
years, during which it normally lay between 10 and 15; and continued to
rise above the age of 40, though not exceeding 20 in any age group until
75–9. Thereafter it rose dramatically, reaching extraordinary heights in
extreme old age, even rising eventually as high as 50, though in the
highest age groups the number of deaths was very small, and the

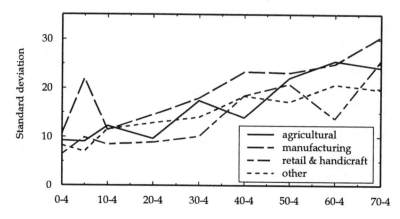

Figure 6.28   *The variability of the seasonal index of deaths by age and parish occupational type*
Note: the standard deviations were calculated from the monthly index figures where the mean monthly value = 100. Corrected for the varying length of the month.
Source: Cambridge Group reconstitutions.

recorded standard deviations should therefore be treated with circumspection.

The seasonality of death, therefore, was plainly much affected by age, although seasonality patterns do not appear to have been greatly influenced either by period or by sex. The nature of the local economy, however, may have played a part in determining seasonality patterns. If the 26 parishes are divided into four 'occupational' groups according to the occupational structure of the parish at the time of the 1831 census, a statistically significant difference in one aspect of the seasonality pattern is found between 'manufacturing' parishes and other types, as may be seen in figure 6.28.[175]

Two points distinguish manufacturing parishes from the other three groups: the standard deviation of deaths shows a marked peak in manufacturing parishes in the age group 5–9 which is not visible in the other groups; and seasonality of death was consistently more pronounced in manufacturing parishes throughout all the age groups. Since only three parishes, Birstall, Gedling, and Shepshed, fall into the manufacturing group, this is flimsy evidence. A much larger body of evidence would be needed to consolidate the point, and it should not be forgotten that the occupational structure of the manufacturing parishes

---

[175] For a definition of the criteria used in dividing the 26 parishes into these four groups, see p. 272.

sometimes only became distinctive in the course of the eighteenth century, so that for a part of their history these parishes were much more agricultural than was the case in 1831. Nevertheless, the contrast with the other three types is suggestive, especially as the other three categories, 'agricultural', 'retail trade and handicraft', and 'other', appear broadly similar to each other.[176]

If monthly seasonality of death by occupational type is plotted in the same fashion as was done for different age groups in figure 6.25 above, the manufacturing parishes again appear distinctive. The spring peak of deaths in manufacturing parishes came earlier than in the other groups, in February rather than in March or April, and there was a much more clear-cut trough in deaths in the late summer and early autumn in manufacturing parishes than elsewhere. For example, the September index figure for the manufacturing parishes was 84, whereas in the other three groups the comparable figures were 98, 100, and 100.

The first two years of life

A part of the analysis which follows makes use of the illuminating contrast in the seasonal patterns visible in the data when they are marshalled both in a cohort and in a period fashion. Since this mode of treatment may be unfamiliar in the context of infant mortality, it may prove useful to specify the nature of the distinction between them. The *period* measure of infant mortality is obtained by determining the mortality which would occur if a group of infants were subject to the mortality risks of a given month throughout the whole of the first year of life. The logic is exactly analogous to the construction of a period life table. The period life table for England in 1995, for example, is constructed as if a group of individuals were born in 1995 and lived the whole of their first year of life in that year, and then during the second year of life were again exposed to 1995 risks for the second year of life, and so on for each successive year of their lives. In Lexis diagram terms the data are all taken from a vertical column. Similarly, a period measure of infant mortality for March, for example, may be obtained by calculating the deaths and associated exposure of children exposed to March risks in their first month of life, and then exposed again to March risks in their second month of life, and so on for each month of life up to and including the twelfth. In contrast a *cohort* measure for March

---

[176] The retail trade and handicraft group of parishes are, however, also identified as significantly different from the overall pattern, though the difference is much less clear-cut than in the case of the manufacturing parishes.

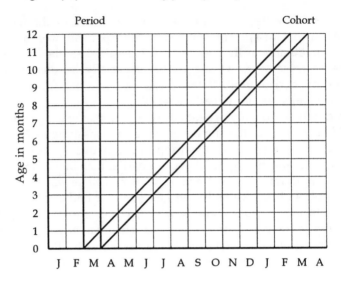

Figure 6.29   *Illustration of period and cohort infant mortality for the month of March (Lexis diagram)*

concatenates, say, the experience of children all of whom were born in March, and who therefore spent the whole of their first month of life in either March or April with the subsequent history of the cohort until the end of its first year. Thus data for their second month of life will relate to deaths and exposure occurring partly in April and partly in May, for their third month to deaths and exposure partly in May and partly in June, and so on. In Lexis diagram terms the cohort data are all taken from a diagonal. The nature of the contrast is illustrated in figure 6.29.

We have already seen that the convention whereby mortality within the first year of life is treated as an entity to be kept separate from mortality later in childhood may prove unfortunate when describing the pattern of rates by age. The same proves also to be true of the seasonality of deaths early in life. It is therefore convenient to consider the seasonality patterns both in the first and in the second year of life at the same time for some purposes, rather than confining attention solely to the first year.

Figure 6.30 shows how marked are the differences between the infant mortality patterns revealed by the period and cohort measures, although, of course, the body of data upon which one measure is based is exactly the same as that upon which the other is based, though marshalled in a different fashion. The values indexed are q_xs, so that the

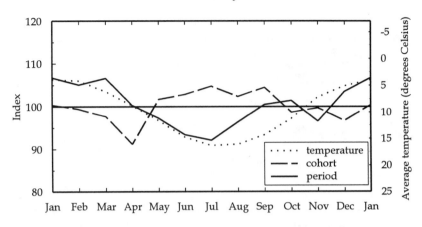

Figure 6.30   *The seasonality of period and cohort infant mortality by month*
(q_x values converted to indexed form where mean monthly rate = 100)
Source: Cambridge Group reconstitutions.

seasonality visible in the figure is uninfluenced by the fact that births displayed a marked seasonality.

The cohort data reveal that April was the least dangerous month in which to be born, with July and September the most dangerous.[177] The four month block from June to September was consistently unfavourable to infant life. This finding is remarkable in that July was the month in which fewest children were born and April was close to the point in the year when the greatest number of births took place. The data presented in the *Population history of England* show clearly that July was a low point in the annual birth cycle, with its flanking months of June and August also low, and that March was probably the peak month,[178] but with February and April also running at a high level. The timing of births was thus very 'efficient' in minimising the early loss of life. Whether this pattern is the product of chance, or reflects some form of selective pressure on the timing of conception, is unclear. If the latter, the nature of the linkage would be a matter of the highest interest.

The period infant mortality rates show that, although April was a

[177] There are few data with which to compare the pattern revealed by this analysis, but it is interesting to note that in Belgium in the 1840s, although there is a degree of similarity in the monthly cohort pattern, the peak in mortality came earlier, from March to July, rather than from July to September. Vilquin, 'La mortalité infantile', fig. A, p. 1140.

[178] Wrigley and Schofield, *Population history of England*, tab. 8.1 and fig. 8.1, pp. 287–8. Establishing the location of peaks and troughs in the eighteenth century or later is complicated by the increasing time lag between birth and baptism.

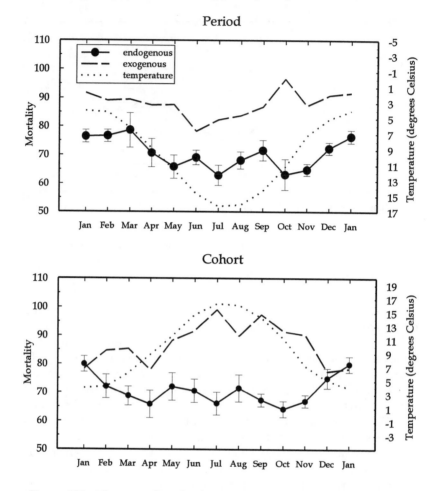

Figure 6.31   *The seasonality of endogenous and exogenous infant mortality by month: period (upper panel) and cohort (lower panel) (1000d_x)*
Source: Cambridge Group reconstitutions.

good month in which to be born, it was only an average month generally for children during the first year of life, and that, even though July was very unfavourable as a birth month, it was a very healthy month overall for children under 1. The temperature graph included in the figure suggests that period mortality in the first year of life was inversely related to the thermometer. When the temperature scale is inverted, as in the figure, the two lines trace out very similar paths. The colder months of the year were dangerous to infants: when warmer weather returned mortality was materially reduced. This apparent coincidence is, however, somewhat misleading, as more detailed analysis, with a fuller breakdown by age within the first year of life, will show.[179]

Figure 6.31 allows the seasonality of infant death to be further explored. In it the seasonality of exogenous and endogenous mortality is shown both by period and by cohort. The error bars step out two standard deviations from the large points representing the level of endogenous mortality, and therefore embrace the range within which there is a high probability that the true level lay. Their length varies substantially from one month to the next, since the precision of the estimate is affected by the straightness of the line of points representing cumulative mortality in the first year of life from which they were estimated.[180] Period and cohort endogenous mortality show broadly similar seasonal patterns, as might be expected since for any given month they share a triangle comprising half of the information used to calculate the monthly rate (figure 6.29). Mortality was higher in the winter months than in the summer, but the inverse link to temperature is not clearly visible in the warmer months, when mortality, though lower than in winter, was almost 'flat', suggesting the possibility of a threshold effect which broke the link with temperature in the warmer months of the year. The similarity between the period and cohort patterns was, however, not perfect. Indeed, it is a testimony to the variability of endogenous mortality from one month to the next that the differences in detail between the two graphs were quite marked.

Period and cohort exogenous mortality, in contrast, did not display similar patterns. Cohort exogenous infant mortality was at its height among children born in the later part of the summer from July to September. Consider the July cohort. Given the nature of exogenous mortality, most deaths within the first year of life would occur within the first three or four months from July onwards, principally in the period from August to November. A glance at the pattern of period exogenous mortality makes it clear why the July cohort suffered relatively severely. Much the same holds true for cohort exogenous mortality in all the late summer months. In the case of cohort mortality the endogenous and exogenous seasonal patterns offset one another to a considerable degree, resulting in a comparatively flat overall pattern of seasonality (figure 6.30). The very marked April dip in the overall index occurred because endogenous and exogenous mortality both dipped in that month. Period exogenous seasonality, in contrast, was not dissimilar from the period endogenous pattern, which meant, of course, that

179 See below pp. 343–7.   180 See above pp. 224–7.

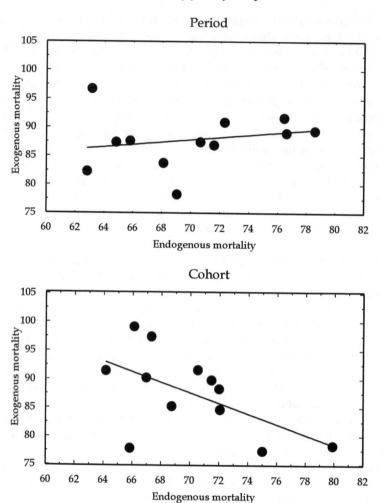

Figure 6.32   *The relative levels of endogenous and exogenous infant mortality by month: period (upper panel) and cohort (lower panel) (1000d$_x$)*
Source: Cambridge Group reconstitutions.

the overall index mirrored the behaviour of each of its two component elements (figure 6.30). In both cases, cold weather brought higher mortality, while in the summer months rates were significantly lower. In the case of the exogenous rate it would appear that the digestive tract ailments which tended to become more widespread in summer weather were less destructive than the upper respiratory tract infections which peaked in the winter. As already noted, however, further analysis, with a more complete age breakdown within the first year of life, shows that the apparent simplicity of the seasonal path of exogenous period infant mortality is deceptive.[181]

The contrast between the period and cohort seasonality patterns of endogenous and exogenous mortality is further explored in figure 6.32. In the upper panel the monthly period endogenous and exogenous rates are plotted against one another. There is little or no relationship between them (adj.$r^2 = 0.03$). It is not possible, from a knowledge of the level of one of the two rates, to predict the level of the other. But the same is not true of the pair of cohort rates, which are negatively correlated with each other (adj.$r^2 = 0.25$). High endogenous rates were followed by low exogenous rates, but babies born in the months when endogenous mortality was low, between June and October, suffered from an above average exogenous mortality later in their first year of life. The outlier, combining low endogenous and and exogenous mortality, whose presence accounts for the relatively low level of correlation between the endogenous and exogenous rates as a whole, was the month of April.

The second year seasonality of mortality can, of course, be measured by period and cohort, just like first year mortality, as may be seen in figure 6.33. Cohort seasonality displays a broadly similar pattern in both years. Apart from the marked dip in April in the first year index, which is not visible in the second year, the two lines trace out similar paths. It appears, for example, that the broadly favourable winter and unfavourable summer patterns are common to both years of life. A child born in September, for example, suffered above average mortality not only in the first year of life, but in the second also, while, for a child born in the winter months from November to March, the lower than average mortality experienced in the first year of life is paralleled by a relatively benign regime in the second year also. Any differences between first and second year seasonality were too small for the two patterns to differ in a statistically significant fashion. Moreover, as might be expected, the similarity between the seasonal pattern of cohort exogenous mortality in the first year of life (figure 6.31) and the second year pattern is still closer than when the comparison is made with the full first year pattern (figure 6.30).

Period mortality in the second year of life, in contrast, did differ in a statistically significant fashion from the first year pattern. Several points are notable about second year period seasonality. First, the inverse relationship to temperature, visible in the endogenous, exogenous, and overall period patterns in the first year, has disappeared in the second.

---

[181] See below pp. 343–7.

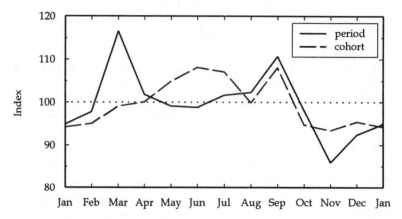

Figure 6.33   *The seasonality of second year period and cohort mortality by month*
(q$_x$ values converted to index form where mean monthly rate = 100)
Source: Cambridge Group reconstitutions.

In the summer the second year index is consistently close to 100, rather than falling to a nadir at that season, as in the first year of life. The healthiest part of the year occurred in the colder months of the late autumn and early winter. Secondly, some features become more pronounced in the second year. In particular, the March peak and the November trough stand out much more clearly. However, the most significant change in seasonality occurring over the first two years of life is not readily visible when comparing seasonality for the whole of the first and second years. A more appropriate grouping of the seasonality data by age reveals the existence of much more striking changes in seasonality, which may plausibly be explained, in large measure, by the timing of weaning in early modern England. This possibility is further examined in the next two sections.

The seasonal concentration of death

As a prelude to the further analysis of the seasonality of death in the first two years of life, but also because of its intrinsic interest, consider the data on the seasonal concentration of death, shown in figure 6.34. The measure used is so constructed that it can vary between 0.0 and 1.0. If all deaths occurred in one single month of the twelve it would register 1.0: if deaths were distributed in a perfectly uniform manner throughout the year it would register 0.0.[182] The horizontal scale is logarithmic, and the

[182] See Batschelet, *Circular statistics*.

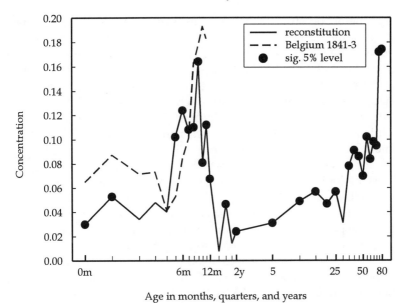

Figure 6.34 *The seasonal concentration of deaths by age*
Note: the horizontal scale is logarithmic. The individual points refer to months in the first year of life, to quarters in the second year of life, and thereafter to the age groups 2–4, 5–9, and so on by 5-year age groups until a final open age group comprising all deaths above the age of 80. For method of calculation and for notes on the significance of the solid circles and on the plotting of the points, see accompanying text.
Source: English data: Cambridge Group reconstitutions; Belgian data: Vilquin, 'La mortalité infantile', tab. 1, p. 1141.

individual points refer to each month in the first year of life, to each quarter in the second, and thereafter to the age groups 2–4, 5–9, and so on by five-year age groups until a final open-ended age group comprising all deaths above the age of 80. In the first two years of life the measure used is the mortality rate (q_x): thereafter totals of deaths rather than a mortality rate were used. The points marked by solid circles are those where the measure of concentration is significant at the 5 per cent level.[183] The points are placed at the beginning of the age interval to which they refer.

The pattern revealed is striking. In the main the degree of concentration is low, but between the fifth and eleventh months it increases

---

[183] In the sense that the degree of concentration differed significantly from 0.00 and the number of deaths was sufficient to result in a significant result.

sharply before reverting to the same low level as obtained in the first few months of life. From the 5–9 age group onwards, however, it shows a general tendency to rise and among the elderly, above the age of 75, it regains the peak level found in the second half of the first year of life. The increase appears to accelerate when plotted on a logarithmic horizontal scale, but would appear much less dramatic if the scale were natural. The data for Belgium in the early 1840s, published by Vilquin, to which reference was made earlier, can be reordered in the same fashion. They cover only the first year of life, but the shape of the Belgian curve for this age strongly suggests that the pattern found in England reflects biological, physiological, or epidemiological influences that were widely present.[184]

Before discussing further the seasonal concentration of mortality, it may be helpful also to note where 'centre of gravity' of mortality lay. The centre of gravity for any age group is the point in the year which minimises the sum of the squared distances of all deaths from that point. This point may for convenience be termed the mean month of death, which is plotted in figure 6.35. A fairly regular pattern is found. For those in the first few months of life the mean month of death lies between the late autumn and midwinter. In the first month of life the mean month is December, followed in the second and third months by November, in the fourth month by October, and in the fifth month by November again.[185] Thereafter the mean month moves steadily later in the calendar into the spring or even, in the second year of life, a little later, though in this age period the pattern is irregular. The move to a later month in the calendar occurs during the period when the seasonal concentration of death rises so sharply. In the years of life from the age of 2 onwards, in the great majority of age groups the mean month is either February, March, or April. Once again, the pattern found in Belgium in the early 1840s, relating to the first year of life, is almost uncannily similar to that found in England in the parish register era.

The standard deviation from the centre of gravity of deaths can be calculated as an interval in months. At all ages, with remarkable constancy, the standard deviation in England was about 2.6 months,

---

[184] Vilquin, 'La mortalité infantile', tab. 1, p. 1141. The q_xs in the table were converted to l_xs and then the separate mortality rates for males and females were converted into a combined sex figure by assuming a male/female sex ratio at birth of 105:100. The earlier reference to Vilquin is on p. 335, n. 177.

[185] Because of the nature of the calculation of the centre of gravity, the plotted points are located where the exact mean lies, and therefore often part way through the month in which they fall. As a result, for example, the points representing the second and third months, though both in November, are not joined by a horizontal line.

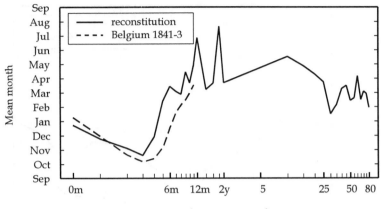

Age in months, quarters, and years

Figure 6.35   *The mean month of death by age*
Note: the horizontal scale is logarithmic. The individual points refer to months in the first year of life, to quarters in the second year of life, and thereafter to the age groups 2–4, 5–9, and so on by 5-year age groups until a final open age group comprising all deaths above the age of 80. The points are plotted on the lower bound of the interval to which they refer, except for month 0, which is plotted in the middle of that month. The mode of calculation is such that the exact location of a reading may be at any point within the band representing a given month. Thus, the points for two adjacent age groups may both be in the same month but the line joining them need not be horizontal.
Source: English data: Cambridge Group reconstitutions; Belgian data: Vilquin, 'La mortalité infantile', tab. 1, p. 1141.

which implies that over the great bulk of the life span just over two-thirds of all deaths will have occurred within a spread of about 5.2 months centring on the late spring. At the periods of the greatest seasonal concentration, in the second half of the first year of life and in old age, the standard deviation falls to about 2.5, indicating a slightly stronger concentration within a briefer span, but the most striking feature of this statistic is its stability.

Unconventional age divisions within the first two years of life

The graph of the seasonal concentration of death shown in figure 6.34 identifies months 5–11 as a distinctive period in the development of seasonality in relation to age, suggesting that it may be of interest to consider the seasonality profile of death during these months as well as its seasonal concentration. Figure 6.36 shows the result of such an exercise. The seasonal pattern of months 5–11 stands in striking contrast

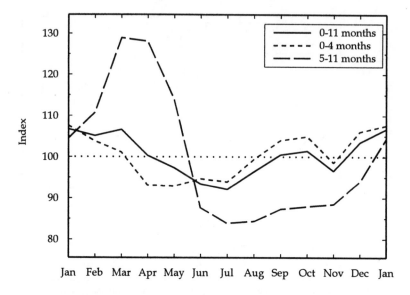

Figure 6.36   *The seasonality of period infant mortality by month (q_x values converted to indexed form where mean monthly mortality rate = 100)*
Source: Cambridge Group reconstitutions.

with that of the first five months of life (months 0–4). The earlier graphs of the seasonality of period infant mortality can now be seen to be somewhat misleading. Because most first year deaths occur in the early months of life, endogenous, exogenous, and overall infant mortality seasonality patterns are all dominated by such deaths (endogenous mortality, of course, exclusively so). The distinctive nature of mortality in the second half of the first year of life, therefore, remains hidden. Whereas the seasonal pattern of months 0–4 shows a general tendency for mortality to follow the inverse of the temperature graph, and therefore to be lower in the warmer months than in the colder part of the year, in months 5–11 there is a very marked late winter or early spring peak in March and April, and a far more clear-cut summer minimum which lasts right through the rest of the year, though with a slight rising trend in the last quarter of the year.

This pattern is very similar to that found during the bulk of adult life, though more pronounced, as may be seen by comparison with figure 6.26. Indeed, though the timing of the peak and trough is not identical, the overall seasonal pattern bears a strong resemblance to that found during the other period of life when the seasonal concentration of deaths is most marked, among the oldest groups in the population (those aged 75 and over in figure 6.26). The reason for the abrupt change

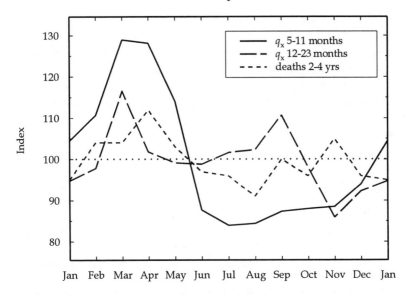

Figure 6.37   *The seasonality of period infant and child mortality by month*
Note: for 5–11 and 12–23 months q_x values were converted to indexed form where the mean monthly mortality rate = 100. For 2–4 years totals of deaths expressed as monthly indexed values corrected for the varying length of the month.
Source: Cambridge Group reconstitutions.

in the timing and acuteness of the seasonality of death part way through the first year of life is unclear. Evidently, however, the relative importance of the different causes of death must have changed markedly between the first and second half of the first year of life.[186]

The appearance of a pattern of seasonality dominated by a late spring peak and a summer minimum did not, however, herald the establishment of a pattern that would then vary only modestly during the rest of life. This is very clear from the information contained in figure 6.37, which reproduces again the seasonal pattern for months 5–11, but also shows the pattern for the second year of life and for the next three years of life, that is for children aged 2–4 years. During the second year of life the pronounced spring peak, so prominent in the 5–11 month data, was greatly reduced in size, but whereas the summer and autumn had been periods of very low mortality for months 5–11, in the second year of life they became a period of above average mortality, especially in Septem-

---

[186] Although the data are not directly comparable, it would appear that there was a remarkably similar sharp differentiation between the first and second halves of the first year of life in Belgium in the mid-nineteenth century: Vilquin, 'La mortalité infantile', pp. 1142–7.

ber. The proportional change from the preceding months is very marked. Thereafter, however, in the years 2–4, seasonality was much dampened and already foreshadowed the pattern to be found for most of the rest of childhood, youth, and early adulthood.[187]

A possible explanation of the sudden appearance of a radically different seasonality in the course of the second year of life relates to the effects of weaning on the vulnerability of the child to infection. Fertility data suggest that weaning occurred primarily in the second year of life of the child, peaking at the age of about 18 months.[188] Digestive tract ailments were particularly likely to cause infant death when the child first ceased to be wholly dependent on breastmilk. Exposure to infection was increased by this change and simultaneously any remaining benefit associated with the transfer of antibodies from mother to child through breastmilk was lost. At any season weaning would increase the danger of death but that risk was more acute towards the end of summer with the sharp rise in the contamination of food by insect-borne infective agents.

If the second year of life is divided at 18 months, the early autumn peak is more pronounced in the first of the two halves of the year, though clearly visible in both. Since the analysis of fertility data suggests that weaning was roughly equally spread on either side of the mean interval of 18 months, this might appear to represent a conflict of evidence between the implications of the fertility and mortality analyses. However, it is likely that weaning became progressively less dangerous as the age of the child increased, and therefore that weaning might result in more deaths if undertaken when the child was, say, 12 months old than when it was 20 months old. If this were the case, the mean age at weaning and the distribution of weaning implied by the fecundability data are not inconsistent with the seasonality of child deaths in the second year of life.

The particular form of this hypothesis associating the changed seasonality of deaths in the second year of life with the dangers of weaning should be recognised, however, to be open to question. In particular it assumes by implication that weaning was spread fairly evenly through the year, and that the concentration of mortality in the late summer reflects the additional hazards of weaning at that time of year. But the observed pattern might in principle have arisen not because weaning was more hazardous in the late summer, but because weaning occurred more commonly at that time, perhaps because of the increased demand for labour at harvest time. If this were so, the risk of dying as a result of being weaned might be no greater in late summer

---

[187] See fig. 6.26, p. 327.   [188] See fig. 7.10, p. 490, and associated text.

than at other times of the year. The peak would reflect the timing of weaning rather than the seasonal pattern of the degree of danger associated with it. That the seasonality of death in the second year of life was influenced by the hazards of weaning, however, appears probable. It is reasonable to speculate that, but for the influence of weaning on the seasonality of death, the late spring peak and late summer trough in mortality, which was first established in months 5–11, and reemerges in the third year of life in a less marked form, would also have been visible in the second year. Any alternative explanation would need to identify a cause of death, or group of such causes, peculiar to this age, and relatively unimportant both in slightly younger and in slightly older children.

Conclusion

The national mortality history of England in the early modern period was largely free from devastating brief mortality shocks of the kind that occurred in some countries until a much later date.[189] In the parish register period the worst such episode occurred in the late 1550s, in time to figure in aggregative studies but too early to be covered by reconstitution. Even that mortality surge was not especially dramatic by the general standards of the pre-industrial world.[190] Within the period

---

[189] After the end of the sixteenth century the year with the highest CDR in England was 1729 when it reached 44.7 per 1000. This compares with an average CDR in the 10 surrounding years (that is the preceding five years and the succeeding five years) of 31.4 per 1000. It was therefore a little over 40 per cent higher than the local average. In Norway in 1773 the CDR reached 47.5 per 1000: this was more than double the average rate in the 10 surrounding years (22.7 per 1000). In Sweden in the same year the rate was 52.5 per 1000, almost double the average of the preceding and succeeding quinquennia (26.9 per 1000). Both these mortality spasms were dwarfed by the catastrophe which struck in Finland in 1868 when the CDR reach 77.6 per 1000. This peak was more than three times as high as in the surrounding 10 years (25.3 per 1000). Wrigley and Schofield, *Population history of England*, tab. A3.3, pp. 531–4; Drake, *Population and society*, tab. 7, pp. 192–3; *Historisk statistik för Sverige*, part 1, Befolkning 1720–1967 (Stockholm, 1969), tab. 28, pp. 91, 93; *Bijdrag till Finlands officiela statistik*, VI, Befolkningsstatistik, 33, Hufvuddragen af Finlands befolkningsstatistik 1750–1890 (Helsinki, 1902), tab. 182, p. 297.

[190] The crude death rate in 1558, the worst year, reached 54 per 1000, a high figure by comparison with the English norm, but not by the standards of many traditional societies. In the Indian state of Berar, for example, which had a population approaching 3 million in the late nineteenth century, the crude death rate averaged 40.6 per 1000 in the 40 years 1881–1920, but the rate was as low as 23.4 per 1000 on two occasions (1888 and 1898), yet reached more than 50 per 1000 on five occasions, with forbidding peaks as high as 82.4 per 1000 in 1900 and 111.3 per 1000 in 1918. Wrigley and Schofield, *Population history of England*, tab. A3.3, p. 531. Dyson, 'The historical demography of Berar', app., pp. 193–4.

covered by the reconstitution data, the 1680s and the late 1720s were the most mortal years. Between 1678 and 1686 the population fell by almost 200 000 from 5.06 to 4.87 million, while between 1727 and 1730 the fall was slightly greater in absolute numbers, from 5.48 to 5.27 million, a fall of 210 000, though proportionately very similar.[191] By comparison with the losses suffered by many other countries in the early modern period, these were modest setbacks. Aggregative methods of analysis can usually establish the scale of dramatic episodes of this type, though reconstitution will add illuminating detail about, for example, the age structure of mortality in crisis periods. But the value of reconstitution data in complementing aggregative work is still clearer in relation to secular mortality change.

Back projection had earlier revealed that secular mortality change took a relatively simple form in England in the early modern period. Death rates were low in Elizabethan England, except in the brief periods of crisis, such as the late 1550s or 1597, but rose steadily during the first half of the seventeenth century. Expectation of life at birth estimated in this way fell by seven or eight years between the late sixteenth and the late seventeenth centuries. Thereafter for half a century there was no decisive improvement. Only after the early 1740s did death rates begin a steady if unspectacular fall, causing expectation of life in the early nineteenth century to revert to much the same level as in the late sixteenth century.

Reconstitution does not controvert this account but can both add much illuminating detail to the rather stark outline that is the most that back projection can provide, and bring into focus a variety of important topics for future research. Back projection, when used without independent evidence of the age structure of mortality and its changes over time, was capable of capturing only general, stylised shifts in mortality, expressed as expectation of life at birth. This it did by selecting within a family of life tables a level which, given a particular population size and age structure, 'absorbed' all the deaths occurring in a given interval of time. It then reported the age-specific rates to be found in the life table in question, but the reported rates were simply a function of the character of the life table and had no independent validity. Thus, if mortality improved it would appear to improve at all ages. And, similarly, the relative level of rates at different ages was fixed by the life table system employed.

[191] Wrigley and Schofield, *Population history of England*, tab. A3.3, pp. 532–3. These totals and population falls are somewhat changed by using the revised aggregative totals of events suggested by the findings of reconstitution, and by the use of generalised inverse projection in place of back projection: see app. 9.

One of the most striking discoveries to emerge from the analysis of the English reconstitution data is that it is dangerous to assume that life tables whose structure reflects the mortality experience of contemporary populations, or those of the recent past, are appropriate for the more distant past. Viewed in terms of the Princeton North or West model life tables adult mortality was far too high relative to rates in infancy and childhood in the seventeenth century. If the only information available were the adult rates, and one were to extrapolate from them to estimates of expectation of life as a whole, using the Princeton tables, the result would be a radical underestimate of expectation of life at birth. A similar but opposite overestimate of expectation of life at birth would have resulted from the use of infant and child mortality data in the same way. In the course of the first half of the eighteenth century there was a period of revolutionary change. Adult rates improved very sharply while rates in infancy and childhood remained high (figure 6.15). By the second half of the century, the relationship between childhood and adult rates had assumed the character made familiar by the Princeton tables.

This finding has great significance for the interpretation of the more scattered data about adult mortality that exist for still earlier times. Monastic records and the *Inquisitiones post mortem*, for example, both provide evidence about adult male mortality in medieval times for elite groups, and both, when viewed in terms of the assumptions that seem natural from familiarity with model life tables, suggest extremely high levels of mortality. For example, e_{20} in the fifteenth century among the Canterbury monks was about 27.6 years,[192] which in turn suggests a world in which e_0 was only about 18 years, if the extrapolation is made using model North tables, but if it is made with an eye to the age-specific pattern to be found in England 200 years later, it would be more appropriate to suppose that e_0 was much higher, probably above 30 years.

The radical change in the relationship betweeen mortality in infancy and childhood and mortality later in life is a particularly striking finding, but it is by no means unique. The age structure of mortality in the past was plastic and flexible in other respects. Equally instructive, for example, are the relative changes in mortality rates in the first few years of life which took place in the parish register era.

Infant and child mortality in general reached a peak in the late seventeenth and early eighteenth centuries but the extent both of the rise in individual rates before this saddleback ridge of high rates and of their

---

[192] This figure is obtained by averaging the cohorts of monks admitted during the century; Hatcher, 'Mortality in the fifteenth century', tab. 2, p. 28.

subsequent fall varied to a remarkable extent. Between the late sixteenth century and the early eighteenth century (1580–99 and 1700–24), the rate in the third quarter of the first year of life almost doubled and rates between the second and sixth month, and again from the ninth to the fifteenth month, also rose markedly, by about one third to one half, but the proportionate rise was much less marked at higher ages; $_{10}q_5$ rose by little more than one tenth (tables 6.10 and 6.11). The rise was also less marked at the other end of the age range. Mortality in the first month scarcely rose at all between the same periods (by about 4 per cent), while in the second month the rise was about one tenth (table 6.4). After the period of high rates in the early eighteenth century, the pattern of change also differed greatly by age group. Rates which had previously risen most subsequently declined least. Between the third and twenty-fourth months there was no retreat from the peak in rates reached in the early eighteenth century; the peak in short proved to be the edge of a plateau. But at younger and older ages, where the earlier rise had been modest, the later fall was substantial; $_{10}q_5$ fell by more than one third between 1700–24 and 1800–24 , while the falls in the first and second months (almost one half and one quarter) were equally striking. The changes are shown in summary form in figure 6.38. In this figure the age divisions were chosen with an eye to grouping the rates for still finer age divisions into sets with a large measure of internal homogeneity in change over time.

The extent of the contrast between mortality trends in the first month of life and those between the third month and the end of the second year of life is vividly clear. First month mortality was substantially the higher of the two in the early seventeenth century. By the early nineteenth century it was less than half as high. The changes in the other rates afford less strong contrasts, though they suggest diversity of experience (compare, for example, $_3q_2$ and $_5q_5$).

The complex pattern of relative mortality changes at all ages was necessarily invisible when using aggregative techniques of analysis. Such methods may reveal a mortality line but not a mortality surface, so to speak. They may result in a series representing expectation of life at birth or a crude death rate, but cannot reveal intricate changes, such as those shown in figure 6.38. Once revealed, the mortality surface prohibits simplistic explanations of mortality trends. Changes in real incomes, or in occupational structure, or in the urban/rural balance, or in contact patterns induced by a greater dependence on the exchange of goods, may each have played a part in producing the observed trends but they can only have been indirectly influential in engendering the relative shifts in rates brought to light by reconstitution. The changes

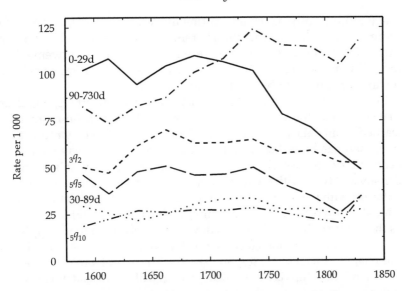

Figure 6.38   *Infant and child mortality with unconventional age divisions*
$(1000q_x)$
Source: Cambridge Group reconstitutions.

were at once complex and yet at the same time strongly patterned. The trends of mortality at different ages were clear and often sustained but far from uniform between one age range and another. They are a salutary reminder that biological, epidemiological, and social history will probably prove at least as important as economic history in enabling better sense to be made of the history of mortality in England.

Because reconstitution provides complex information about demographic behaviour, it can be tabulated and retabulated to probe particular issues as their characteristics gradually become clear. This virtue of the data was well illustrated in studying the seasonality of mortality. The overall patterns of the seasonality of death are familiar from many studies based on aggregative data, but the possibility of cross-classifying seasonality by age, and of using both period and cohort methods of marshalling the information, proved illuminating. The clues provided by the extent of the seasonal concentration of death by age (figure 6.34), for example, led to a reconsideration of the seasonality of deaths within the first and second years of life (figures 6.36 and 6.37); to the discovery that the seasonality of infant death in the second half of the first year of life was radically different from that of younger or older infants; and to the uncovering of evidence suggesting that weaning took place chiefly during the second year of life. It may be more than coincidental that the age range within the second half of the first year of life, over which there was little or no improvement in mortality in the eighteenth century, was also the age range with a distinctive and much higher level of seasonality.

In relation to this aspect of mortality, as with many others, it is clear that so far only the surface has been scratched. There is far more to be learned, from data as rich and intricate as those afforded by reconstitution, than has been discovered as yet. There were, or may well have been, differences associated with urban and rural life; with settlement density and type; with the frequency and distance of human movement patterns; with the nature of house construction; with contact with farm animals; with occupational structure; with environmental factors such as the nature of the local sources of water supply; with food supply, as well as the more obvious factors which have been used as variables in this chapter, such as age, sex, and season. The teasing out of the nature of such relationships is a dialectical process which will lead not only to a fuller understanding of the determinants of demographic characteristics but to a better knowledge of the factor in question.

It is premature as yet even to list and categorise many of the determinants of demographic behaviour, far less to try to effect a convincing synthesis of them in order to account for what can already be measured. It is unlikely that this task will be undertaken successfully until comparative data from other countries have been assembled, together with a greater volume of English material. For example, a suggestion was made about a link between mortality patterns in the second year of life and weaning. But if it transpired that similar breastfeeding and weaning practices were to be found in other parts of Europe with dissimilar mortality patterns, it would be hard to continue to maintain this hypothesis.

Even though a convincing explanation for many of the patterns revealed by reconstitution may still be lacking, the findings are valuable in several ways. Not only do they set an implicit research agenda for the future, they also have other significance. It may be difficult as yet to move 'upstream' to the causes of the changes, but some of the 'downstream' consequences deserve to be considered. *Ceteris paribus*, for example, the dramatic improvement in adult mortality in the first half of the eighteenth century will have increased the joint life expectancy of a newly married couple substantially, thereby raising age of widowhood and reducing the percentage of marriages in which one or both partners were widowed, as well as significantly changing the likelihood of becoming an orphan. Fertility, no less than nuptiality, will also be affected. In the absence of offsetting changes, the fall in adult mortality will raise fertility, both because fewer women will die before reaching the end of the childbearing period, and because fewer will lose their partners while still young. Remarriage, though possible, almost always involved an interval between births much longer than would otherwise have been the case.

A similar list of examples of the consequences of mortality falls (or rises) early in life could be made. If nuptiality and fertility are assumed to remain constant, for example, a fall in infant and child mortality will produce a rise in the number of surviving children with important implications for the proportion of families which lack heirs or have 'surplus' sons.[193] A rising intrinsic growth rate may also help to induce a changing propensity to migrate, and play a part in altering the balance between urban and rural populations, more especially if the improvement in mortality is differentially pronounced in towns.

This chapter, however, has been principally concerned with description of mortality change in England in the quarter-millenium from *c.* 1580 to *c.* 1840 and it would be inappropriate to stray too far into wider issues, however tempting. No system of recording births and deaths can ever be completely free from error and omission. Anglican parish registration can lay no claim to perfection in this regard. But it is also possible to carry scepticism to excess. Provided that registers are carefully selected and rigorously tested for accuracy and completeness (in relation, of course, only to members of the established church), it seems feasible to produce from them tolerably accurate measurements of mortality change in the period between their institution in 1538 and their supersession by a civil system in 1837. A variety of exercises were carried out in the course of this chapter to test the validity of particular findings.[194] In every case the upshot was reassuring. This proved so when information from the latest decades of reconstitution was compared with the early mortality returns of the Registrar-General; when comparison was made with other evidence about mortality levels and mortality change; and when specific issues were taken up, such as the proportion of all deaths in the first year of life that occurred on the first day, the history of maternal mortality in England and in other countries, or the relative level of singleton and twin infant mortality. Accordingly, it seems fair to claim that many aspects of mortality history which could previously only be examined back to 1837 using the Registrar-General's returns can now be reviewed with almost equal confidence over a much longer span of time.

---

[193] Wrigley, 'Fertility strategy for the individual and the group'.
[194] See above pp. 217, 231–6, 240–2, 258–9, 261–3, 272–8, 285–93, 313–7, 340–3.

7

Fertility

The technique of family reconstitution was devised by Louis Henry primarily as a means of investigating the phenomenon of human fertility; what determined the spacing between births, the phenomenon of teenage subfecundity, the gradual extinction of the capacity to bear children associated with increasing age, and a host of cognate questions. In the years immediately after the Second World War Henry was faced by the instructive and ironic paradox that countries in which birth control within marriage was still largely absent did not collect reliable and sophisticated demographic data, while countries which did collect such data were universally countries where the deliberate restriction of fertility within marriage was common. To study the biological parameters of fertility it was necessary to secure data from a society which did not deliberately restrict fertility within marriage. Henry therefore turned to the past to provide the data which was otherwise out of reach, first making use of the genealogies of the Genevan bourgeoisie and then creating his own genealogies, so to speak, by reconstituting the families of the parish of Crulai in Normandy.[1]

Family reconstitution has proved a most fruitful source of information about the characteristics of fertility, both for the study of the matters which first caused Henry to use historical data, and more generally in providing accurate and detailed pictures of the fertility histories of many communities during the period when parish registers represented the equivalent of a modern state-run vital registration system. Family reconstitution, however, is not without limitations when attempting to recover information about fertility in the past. Just as adult mortality estimates relate only to those who marry, because unmarried adults escape effective observation, so the fertility of those who married can be studied in great detail and with satisfactory precision, but the

---

[1] Henry, *Anciennes familles genevoises*; Gautier and Henry, *Crulai*.

Table 7.1 *Age-specific marital fertility rates (per 1000 woman-years lived)*

	15–9	20–4	25–9	30–4	35–9	40–4	45–9	TMFR 20–49
1600–24	329.6	400.8	377.3	325.6	259.8	142.3	19.4	7.63
1625–49	386.4	408.1	362.5	320.4	251.9	128.1	21.4	7.46
1650–74	376.7	383.9	335.8	285.5	225.5	125.3	23.7	6.90
1675–99	343.4	391.7	351.6	315.4	244.5	98.3	19.3	7.10
1700–24	280.3	414.5	385.3	318.7	235.8	120.9	22.5	7.49
1725–49	350.6	419.6	361.2	323.1	261.0	132.7	23.1	7.60
1750–74	486.7	415.7	366.9	312.7	248.0	128.7	20.3	7.46
1775–99	505.3	423.1	370.3	302.8	237.4	147.8	20.3	7.51
1800–24	547.6	424.8	381.4	310.5	254.9	142.3	19.2	7.67
1600–1824	406.6	410.5	366.1	313.2	246.3	130.1	21.1	7.44

Source: Cambridge Group reconstitutions.

fertility of those who did not marry lies beyond effective reach. The reason is the same in both cases. Reconstitution enables demographic rates to be calculated by measuring events against exposure and, because the presence or absence of unmarried persons in a parish is so difficult to establish, rates relating to them cannot be determined with any accuracy. The date of each birth taking place outside marriage may be known, but the corresponding period of risk of unmarried women cannot be measured.

The most familiar approach to the measurement of fertility is through the use of age-specific marital fertility rates (ASMFRs). This measure relates the total of legitimate births occurring to married women in a given age group to the total of woman-years lived by such women in that age group. This measure is readily calculated from family reconstitution data. For example, in table 7.1 ASMFRs for each quarter-century of the period covered by reconstitution data are set out, together with the associated total marital fertility rates (TMFRs). They show that marital fertility was not constant over time. There were substantial changes in the TMFRs and much more substantial changes in the rates for individual age groups. For example, the rates for 15–9 rose from 280.3 to 547.6 per 1000 between 1700–24 and 1800–24; or, at the other end of the age range, rates for 40–4 rose from 98.3 to 147.8 per 1000 between 1675–99 and 1775–99. Clearly there is much in the table to warrant further examination. But the history of fertility in England is better understood if table 7.1 is regarded as an end point rather than a beginning. The factors contributing to the determination of marital fertility rates were complex and it makes better sense to consider the component elements of fertility before commenting on the overall fertility changes which resulted from the changes in these elements or other aspects of fertility behaviour in the past.

Accordingly, we turn to a discussion of the problem of identifying and measuring the factors determining marital fertility levels in the population of early modern England. The first main section of the chapter, which is divided into several subsections, is based largely on data drawn from completed families. Such data are best suited to the analysis of the components of fertility and their changes. There then follow sections devoted to particular influences on fertility characteristics; to long-run overall fertility trends; to fecundability; and to the characteristics of individual parishes, before a short concluding section. The chapter deals only with legitimate fertility. There were many illegitimate births in early modern England. Procreation outside marriage was both important as an element in overall fertility and a topic of great interest in its own right,[2] but reconstitution depends upon data taken from FRFs, each of which begins either with a marriage or a legitimate birth. Within the context of an FRF events can be related to exposure with confidence. In the case of illegitimate births, however, while events may be recorded, there is no way of estimating a matching period of exposure, and therefore no possibility of deriving measures of illegitimate fertility to parallel those which can be calculated for legitimate fertility.

In the two preceding chapters, dealing with nuptiality and mortality, data from all 26 reconstitution parishes were used. In this chapter no data from Birstall have been used because in the reconstitution of Birstall no FRFs were created for childless marriages. Marital fertility rates calculated from Birstall FRFs, therefore, would be too high since, although all events would be counted, exposure would be understated. This problem does not arise, of course, in relation to the measurement of birth interval data, but it would introduce needless complication to include Birstall for one aspect of fertility measurement but to exclude it from others. It is appropriate also to recall that Birstall was one of the two parishes which were counted only at half-weight in all demographic calculations. This was done to ensure a better match between the occupational characteristics of the sample of reconstitution parishes and those of the country as a whole.[3] The other parish, Shepshed, remains in the sample of 25 parishes from which data were drawn for this chapter. As a result, as previously, some tables will contain apparent absurdities, such as 94.5 births as the numerator in the calculation of a fertility rate.

---

[2] See, for example, Laslett, 'Long-term trends in bastardy in England'; Adair, 'Regional variations in illegitimacy'; and, more generally, Laslett, Oosterveen, and Smith, eds., *Bastardy and its comparative history*.   [3] See above pp. 43–8.

In order to secure unbiased time series for nuptiality and mortality measures, it was necessary to correct for the effects of compositional change in the parishes in observation by the use of four parish groups. In order to decide whether a similar strategy was needed in studying fertility, two tests were required: first, a test to determine whether there was any significant difference between paired groups in the overlap periods; and second, if this test were negative, a test to establish whether a series constructed from the entire data set differed from one construc- ted by taking data from the four groups as was done with mortality and nuptiality. The first test was carried out exactly as for mortality and nuptiality. Using the TMFR 20–49 as a summary measure of fertility, the ratio of the TMFR for group 2 to that of group 1 in the 50-year overlap period was 0.996; that between the comparable ratio of the TMFRs for group 3 and group 2 was 1.005; and that between group 4 and group 3 0.999. These ratios are so close to unity that there is evidently no reason to suppose any systematic difference between the successive groups.[4]

There remained a possibility, however, that, although no adjustment was needed in moving between one group and the next, the rates derived from the use of the four groups might differ from those for the data set as a whole, because during the period covered by any one group the same parishes were in observation throughout, whereas within the whole data set the passage of parishes in and out of observation might cause changes not reflected in the behaviour of the four groups. When TMFRs for the whole data set were compared with those drawn from the four groups, however, the results showed that the fear that the two series might drift apart was unfounded. The rates from the groups were invariably almost indistinguishable from the rates for the whole data set. There seems no reason, therefore, to do other than use data drawn from the whole sample of parishes in the study of the characteristics of fertility change.

The evidence from completed marriages

The measurement of fecundity and fertility

Fecundity refers to the capacity of an individual or couple to reproduce; fertility to the scale of reproduction which actually takes place. The

---

[4] The TMFR 20–49 was used in preference to that for 15–49 because, even over a period as long as 50 years the number of woman-years in observation in the age group 15–9 was quite small, with the consequent danger that differences in the 15–9 fertility rates might be due to random effects. For example, in the period 1600–49 the total of woman-years lived by women in group 2 in the age group 15–9 was 209.2 years, compared with 1555.4 years for the age group 20–4.

standard basic measure of fertility among married women, age-specific marital fertility, may be regarded as the product of the interplay of three more fundamental variables which jointly determine the level and trend of the ASMFR, one of which is fecundity. In order that the subsequent discussion should be clear it may be useful at this point to define the three variables and give them distinctive names since two of them are defined in a way that differs somewhat from conventional usage. The discussion in both this section and the next may appear somewhat dry and technical but it constitutes a necessary preliminary to the subsequent analysis of the changing determinants of fertility among married women in early modern England.

In the following discussion B_{leg} = total of legitimate live-born children; Exp_f = exposure of fecund married women in woman-years lived; Exp_{nf} = exposure of non-fecund married women in woman-years. Conventional ASMFRs will be termed marital fertility rates and may be defined as $B_{leg}/(Exp_f + Exp_{nf})$. Fecund marital fertility rates are defined as B_{leg}/Exp_f. Fecund marital fertility rates will always be higher than marital fertility rates at the same age because of the presence among the population of married women of some who were never fecund (or, more strictly, of couples who were never fecund) or who had ceased to be fecund. The state of being fecund is the complement of the state of being sterile (so that if 15 per cent of women are sterile, 85 per cent are fecund). It is convenient to distinguish between two types of sterility; a first type referring to women who were never at any stage in their married lives capable of conceiving a child and carrying it to term, and a second type referring to the transition from a previously fecund state to an irreversibly infecund or sterile state. The latter might occur because of the trauma of childbirth, the effect of some types of disease on either partner, or because of the process of aging, which makes it certain that every couple is sterile when the woman has ceased to be fecund by the age of 50, or in exceptional cases soon thereafter. Of these three factors, that of aging was normally the dominant influence, at least from the mid-30s onwards.

In order to study the interplay of these three variables it is convenient initially to consider only marriages in which the wife survived in marriage to age 50. This makes good sense because it avoids the problem of competing risks when studying the duration of fecundity. The onset of sterility in historical populations has to be measured from data concerning the date of birth of the last child in a family. In the set of all marriages the timing of the last birth may be determined not only by the exhaustion of fecundity but also by the death either of the wife or of her husband. She is subject to the competing risks of sterility and death.

But if the set of marriages used is restricted to completed marriages the timing of the last birth is unaffected by the risk of death. By the age of 50 a woman may be presumed to have become sterile, and her age at the birth of her last child affords reliable evidence about the onset of sterility, which is not the case where either she or her husband dies before she reaches 50.[5]

Marriages in which the wife survived in marriage to age 50 may conveniently be referred to as completed marriages. Marriages in which the wife did not survive to age 50 in marriage, whether because of her own death or that of her husband, will be referred to as incomplete marriages. Having examined the components of fertility from data drawn from completed marriages, the characteristics of the population as a whole can then be identified with greater confidence.

In a population in which virtually every woman married and all who married did so at an early age, and in which there was no deliberate limitation of fertility, the proportion of women who were never fecund might be taken to be accurately measured as the percentage of first marriages which lasted, say, 10 years or more and which were childless.[6] This type of sterility is often termed *primary* sterility, and the adjective would be appropriate when applied to the percentage of marriages that proved childless if all populations were like late nineteenth-century India, where teenage marriage for women was universal. In populations in which many marriages were celebrated much later in life, however, to describe the proportion of women whose marriage proved childless as primarily sterile is potentially misleading since a woman who married at, say, 35 and remained childless might well not have been so, if she had married 15 years earlier.[7] The same process, conventionally referred to as the advent of *secondary* sterility, which will, by the age of 35, have rendered sterile some women who

[5] In a marriage in which the husband was much the older of the pair, of course, it may be his aging rather than his wife's that renders the couple sterile.

[6] The chance of bearing a first child after more than 10 years of married life in a population in which contraception is not practised is very small.

[7] Wilson, who edited the English-language edition of Pressat's demographic dictionary, proposes the following definition relating to sterility, 'A distinction is made between *primary* sterility where a woman has never been able to have a child and *secondary* sterility which occurs after the birth of at least one child': Pressat, *Dictionary of demography*, p. 214. The definition reflects normal usage, but the inconvenience often attaching to the use of the term primary sterility is clear from Wilson's own work. In his joint article with Knodel on the fecundity of German village populations, there is an accurate definition of the concept of primary sterility (p. 63) but the term is subsequently equated with the proportion of women who bore no children after marriage and the calculation of its change over time includes data for women married at all ages up to 50 years. Knodel and Wilson, 'The secular increase in fecundity'.

married at 20 and who were previously fecund, will be the reason why many women who married later in life failed to bear a child. The level of secondary sterility in one group of women and of primary sterility in the other would both be principally due to the same influence.

Accordingly it seems preferable to use terminology which is less likely to give rise to misunderstanding. In the attempt to clarify the factors which resulted in a given level of marital fertility it is convenient to attempt to measure, first, fecund marital fecundity (that is the rates which characterised those who were still fecund); second, entry sterility (the proportion of women in a given age at marriage group who were not fecund), whose complement is entry fecundity; and, third, subsequent sterility (the proportion of women in a given age at marriage group who had once been fecund but who had ceased to be so), whose complement is subsequent fecundity. The two latter may be defined as S_{entry} and S_{subs} whose complements are Fec_{entry} and Fec_{subs}. Fecund marital fecundity, entry sterility, and subsequent sterility are the three variables mentioned earlier which in combination determine marital fertility. The impact of the two types of sterility, which can also be readily combined as a measure of overall sterility (S_{over} and its complement Fec_{over}), will then represent the difference between fecund marital fertility rates and marital fertility rates.

The three variables possess the convenient property that they will, when multiplied together, yield a product equal to marital fertility rates (conventional ASMFRs), and any change in the latter can then be explained in terms of shifts in one or more of the three variables, whose relative importance in causing the change can be measured: that is, $B_{leg}/(Exp_f + Exp_{nf}) = (B_{leg}/Exp_f) \times Fec_{entry} \times Fec_{subs}$. This property is illustrated in table 7.2. In table 7.2 the data refer to all spinsters who married in the age group 20–4 taking bachelors as their spouses, the largest of all the female age at marriage groups. All these were women who passed the age of 50 while still in their first marriage. In the first column the fecund marital fertility rates are set out. The ratio in the second column represents the entry fecundity proportion (that is, 96.16 per cent of women were fecund on entry into marriage). This ratio does not change with age, of course, since all women enter in the first age group. Subsequent fecundity is specified in the third column, showing the proportion of women who had had at least one child but had not yet become sterile. Thus, in the age group 35–9, 72.02 per cent of such women remained fecund, while 27.98 per cent had ceased to be fecund. It might seem surprising that the figure in the entry age group is not 1.000 since all women must have at least one child to figure in this column, but the figure for each five-year age group measures the

Table 7.2 *Fecund marital fertility rates, entry fecundity, subsequent fecundity, and marital fertility rates of bachelor/spinster marriages in which the wife was aged 20–4 at marriage and where the marriage lasted until the wife was aged 50 or more*

Wife's age	(1) Fecund marital fertility rate[a]	(2) Entry fecundity	(3) Subsequent fecundity	(4) Overall fecundity (2) × (3)	(5) Implied marital fertility rate (1) × (4)[a]	(6) Observed marital fertility rate[a]	(7) Ratio (5)/(6)
20–4	474.6	0.9616	0.9948	0.9566	454.0	455.0	0.998
25–9	397.0	0.9616	0.9611	0.9242	366.9	366.6	1.001
30–4	361.7	0.9616	0.8679	0.8346	301.8	301.8	1.000
35–9	362.0	0.9616	0.7202	0.6925	250.7	251.0	0.999
40–4	338.0	0.9616	0.3940	0.3789	128.1	128.6	0.996
45–9	333.3	0.9616	0.0574	0.0552	18.4	18.3	1.005

[a] Rates per 1000 woman-years lived.
Note: for definitions of the measures used see text.
Source: Cambridge Group reconstitutions.

proportion of all years lived in that age group lived by women who were still fecund. A small number of women had ceased to be fecund before the end of the entry age group, even though they had borne a child within it. The fourth column shows the overall level of fecundity in each age group, and is the product of the entry and subsequent fecundity ratios. The fifth column gives the fertility rates obtained by multiplying the column 1 rates by the ratios in column 4, while the sixth column shows marital fertility, that is the conventional ASMFRs. Finally, in column 7 the ratio between the rates in columns 5 and 6 is given to enable the closeness of fit between the calculated and observed rates to be noted. The ratios are all close to unity. The fact that some are slightly above or below unity is partly attributable to rounding, and partly to minor inaccuracies inherent in the construction of indices for five-year periods from data relating to single years in relatively small data sets.

The duration of fecundity

Before discussing further the patterns to be seen in table 7.2, a brief digression on the subject of the duration of fecundity is needed, since this must be known in order to measure both fecund fertility and subsequent sterility. In both cases it is necessary to define a point in the life of each woman at which she ceased to be capable of bearing children. It is simplest to discuss the matter initially in relation to fecund fertility rates. The age of each woman at the birth of her last child is known (all these, it will be recalled were women who survived to the age of 50 in marriage). When should she be regarded as having become sterile? A lower bound is set by the date at which her last child was conceived, 9 months before the last birth. It is reasonable to suppose that, in any large group of women, some would have ceased to be fecund in the months immediately following their last conception, even though in fact they went on to bear a last child. On the other hand, in many cases fecundity did not cease with the birth of a last child. Postpartum amenorrhoea, anovulatory cycles, and the effects of breast-feeding would prevent a further conception for a while (though in the absence of these factors a new conception might well have taken place) and thereafter, a woman might remain for a time capable of conceiving, even though no conception took place, since the chance of conceiving in each monthly cycle was relatively low.[8]

It is impossible directly to measure the point in the lifetime of each woman at which fecundity ceased, but an approximate solution is feasible, and, with some margin of error, the validity of any proposed solution can be tested indirectly. The beginning of the period during which fecundity declined and eventually ceased may be taken to be 9 months before the birth of the last child, and there must be a point in time after the birth of the last child when fecundity has been lost by all women. If, by way of illustration, this happened 40 months after the birth of the last child, then on the assumption that mean fecundity declined linearly over this 49-month period, the average duration of fecundity would then be 24.5 months from its start, or 15.5 months after the birth of the last child.

A hypothesis of this sort can be tested by taking advantage of the fact that any given length of birth interval implies a particular rate of childbearing among fecund women. For example, a mean birth interval of 30 months implies a fecund fertility rate of 400 per 1000 (30 months = 2.5 years; $1/2.5 \times 1000 = 400$). Therefore the rates implied by birth interval data and the rates obtained by relating events to exposure among women who were still fecund should agree in any given population.

In table 7.3 the result of a comparative exercise of this sort is shown. The rates derived from relating events to exposure were obtained by

---

[8] See below pp. 464–72.

assuming that, over most of the childbearing age range, a woman remained fecund for 17.5 months on average following the birth of her last child. However, since there is an upper limit to the fecund age range, the interval of 17.5 months following the birth of the last child must shrink as the limit is approached. The arbitrary solution adopted for the purpose of this exercise was to add 16.5 months if the last birth occurred at age 46, 15 months at age 47, 12 months at age 48, and 6 months at age 49, except that if the last birth occurred at any age above 49.5 years sterility was assumed to supervene on reaching 50.

It can be seen in table 7.3 that, on these assumptions about the timing of the onset of subsequent sterility, there is a very close agreement between the two sets of rates except in the first five-year period. It is particularly significant that the agreement remains good in the later five-year duration periods. It is necessarily the case that in these periods a higher and higher proportion of all exposure will consist of the period following the birth of the last child, and therefore, if the assumptions made about the correct amount of time to add after the last birth were flawed, the two sets of rates would tend to drift further and further apart. The fact that this does not happen suggests that a broadly correct allowance for the period of fecundity following a last birth has been made. Because of the problems associated with small numbers, the ratios shown on the bottom line of each panel of table 7.3 for the later duration periods are not always close to unity, but there is no tendency for the ratios to be consistently above or below unity. In every age at marriage group the overall ratio, in the final main column of the table, is, reassuringly, very close to unity.[9]

In considering the rates in table 7.3 it should be noted that the birth intervals were allocated to five-year age groups by the timing of the midpoint of the interval. This is an unusual procedure, but necessary to avoid the distortions involved if birth intervals are allocated to age groups by their opening or closing dates. The former method causes the mean length of the birth interval to decline in the highest age groups because to be included in, say, the age group 45–9 the birth interval must begin within that age group. Short final birth intervals will therefore be included but long birth intervals, which are more likely to bridge across between the age groups 40–4 and 45–9, will be included in the earlier of

---

[9] It is easy to show that other assumptions about the length of the fecund period following a last birth, say 15 months or 20 months added after the birth of the last child, would produce a substantially poorer agreement. In some cases inherently improbable results would ensue, such as that fecundity ratios rise with the age of the woman, a result readily obtained by assuming an average period of fecundity following a last birth of, say, 10 months.

Table 7.3 *The fecund fertility rates implied by birth interval data and duration-specific fecund marital fertility rates: bachelor/spinster completed marriages*

(1) Birth intervals in months.
(2) Fecund fertility rate implied by birth interval (per 1000 woman-year lived)
(3) Duration-specific fecund marital fertility rates (per 1000 woman-years lived).

Wife's age at marriage		Duration of marriage (years)						Number of birth intervals or births on which rate based
		0–4	5–9	10–4	15–9	20–4	5 and over	
15–9	(1)	21.80	31.25	31.09	30.92	35.64	31.62	
	(2)	550.5	384.0	386.0	388.1	336.7	379.5	853
	(3)	444.4	387.4	380.3	381.9	360.2	367.0	931
	(2)/(3)	1.239	0.991	1.015	1.016	0.935	1.034	
20–4	(1)	22.02	32.38	32.95	34.29	36.76	33.12	
	(2)	545.0	370.6	364.2	350.0	326.4	362.3	2 845.5
	(3)	437.0	373.8	366.2	349.3	328.8	356.5	3 202.5
	(2)/(3)	1.247	0.991	0.995	1.002	0.993	1.016	
25–9	(1)	22.65	33.34	35.98	36.27	21.03	34.48	
	(2)	529.8	359.9	335.5	330.9	570.6	348.0	1 393.5
	(3)	425.1	356.8	338.8	332.6	336.6	352.1	1 650.5
	(2)/(3)	1.246	1.009	0.984	0.995	1.695	0.988	
30–4	(1)	22.83	33.84	38.54	33.50		34.92	
	(2)	525.6	354.6	311.4	358.2		343.6	345.5
	(3)	410.4	361.5	313.9	375.7		339.7	458.5
	(2)/(3)	1.281	0.981	0.992	0.953	1.012		

All ages at marriage							
(1)	22.32	32.79	33.77	33.77	35.99	33.39	
(2)	537.6	366.0	355.3	355.3	333.4	359.4	5 479.5
(3)	427.4	367.0	356.5	352.1	339.7	358.6	6 311
(2)/(3)	1.258	0.997	0.997	1.009	0.982	1.002	

Notes: the birth intervals were allocated to duration of marriage divisions by their midpoints. The rates for the duration of marriage period 20–4 years were based on small numbers. A very small total of births occurred in the 25–9 year duration period in the 15–9 and 20–4 age at marriage groups but, because the number of events was so small, the results are not listed, though they have been included in the 5 and over column. See pp. 362–3 for assumptions made about the interval between the last birth and the onset of sterility, which affects the measurement of exposure in calculating the fecund marital fertility rate.
Source: Cambridge Group reconstitutions.

Table 7.4 *Mean birth intervals tabulated by age of mother at the opening of the interval, at its midpoint, and at its end (months: bachelor/spinster completed marriages)*

	15–9	20–4	25–9	30–4	35–9	40–4	45–9	All
Age of mother								
Opening	19.66	23.18	27.98	30.63	32.15	33.47	29.47	28.68
Midpoint	12.66	20.02	25.92	30.48	33.23	36.01	43.02	28.68
Closing	10.70	17.04	23.69	29.03	32.97	38.17	47.06	28.68
Number								
Opening	263.5	1 800.5	2 780.0	2 675.0	1 913.5	491.0	22.0	9 945.5
Midpoint	146.5	1 432.5	2 576.0	2 702.0	2 179.0	849.0	60.5	9 945.5
Closing	99.0	1 113.5	2 334.5	2 621.5	2 324.0	1 257.0	196.0	9 945.5

Source: Cambridge Group reconstitutions.

366

the two age groups. If, conversely, the birth intervals are allocated according to the age of the mother at the close of the birth interval, there is an opposite bias.

The scale of the effect produced by alternative ways of allocating birth intervals is shown in table 7.4. In the top panel the mean birth intervals by age of mother are shown, tabulated in three ways; by age at the opening of the interval, by age at the midpoint of the interval, and by age at the close of the birth interval. In the lower panel the number of cases relating to each cell in the upper panel of the table is shown. The contrasts are striking. If intervals are tabulated by the closing event, there are about nine times as many cases in the final age group, 45–9, as if they are tabulated by the opening event, and the mean interval is 60 per cent longer in the former case than in the latter. The 'opening' and 'closing' methods of allocating birth intervals represent extreme alternatives, unsuitable for the present purpose. The third method whereby the intervals are tabulated by the midpoint of the interval is, however, akin to the method by which the duration-specific primary fertility rate is calculated.

Even using the midpoint method, however, the rates will fail to agree in the first five-year period because longer than usual birth intervals occurring at the end of the first five-year period will be excluded from that period since their midpoint falls in the second five-year period, though short birth intervals will be included. In later five-year periods, however, the problem is minimised because, even though this effect is again present, it tends to be balanced by an opposite effect at the beginning of each period. By definition, the balancing effect is absent in the first five-year period. Rates based on birth intervals are therefore higher than those conventionally calculated in this period. In later five-year periods, however, as is evident in table 7.3, the fecundity rates derived in these two different ways correspond closely.

The data in table 7.3, despite appearances, do *not* constitute proof that fecundity subsisted on average for 17.5 months after the birth of the last child. It is possible that fecundity experience prior to the birth of the last child, which is the only aspect of fecundity that can be directly observed, is not a reliable guide to what happens after the birth of the last child, but it is at least plausible to assume the close agreement between the two fertility series in table 7.3 is strong *prima facie* evidence that adding a period of 17.5 months, with the modifications described above at ages over 45 years, is reasonable in the early modern period in England.

It may be of interest to note in this connection that a different test of the assumption made about the duration of fecundity leads to the same conclusion. Exposure and events can be tabulated for each woman for

Table 7.5 *Age-specific fecund marital fertility rates calculated (1) from events and exposure until the age group next before that in which the last birth occurred, and (2) where sterility is assumed to have supervened 17.5 months after the birth of the last child[a] (per 1000 woman-years lived)*

(1) Age-specific fecund marital fertility rates calculated from events and exposure in five-year age groups up to and including the age group next before that in which the last birth takes place.
(2) Age-specific fecund marital fertility rates with exposure taken to extend to 17.5 months after the birth of the last child.
(3) = (1)/(2).

| | Wife's age at marriage | | | | | |
| | 15–9 | | | 20–4 | | |
Age	(1)	(2)	(3)	(1)	(2)	(3)
15–9	493.9	496.7	0.994			
20–4	415.1	416.2	0.997	474.0	474.6	0.999
25–9	393.3	392.5	1.002	397.8	397.0	1.002
30–4	392.4	387.1	1.014	361.1	361.7	0.998
35–9	361.2	369.2	0.978	348.9	362.0	0.964
40–4	263.3	331.1	0.795	261.4	338.0	0.773
	25–9			30–4		
	(1)	(2)	(3)	(1)	(2)	(3)
25–9	450.9	452.4	0.997			
30–4	374.7	375.9	0.997	441.9	449.0	0.984
35–9	336.5	345.9	0.973	337.9	350.6	0.964
40–4	255.5	332.7	0.768	311.9	361.0	0.864

[a] Note that there can be no comparison of rates for the age group 45–9, since no births occur above age 50, which prevents calculating a figure for this age group for col. 1. Therefore, since sterility above age 45 does not enter into the calculation of the col. 2 rates, the interval between the last birth and the onset of sterility is always 17.5 months.
Source: Cambridge Group reconstitutions.

each five-year age group up to, but not including, the age group in which she bore her last child. This was the method employed by Henry in his pioneering study of the demographic history of Crulai.[10] Rates calculated in this way must by definition relate to fecund women. Such rates for the reconstitution parishes are shown in table 7.5.

The ratios given in column 3 of the table show that the rates calculated on this basis are very similar to fecund fertility rates calculated by the

[10] Henry, *Crulai*, pp. 113–6.

method just described in all except the last two age groups in each age at marriage set. The divergence in the last two age groups is to be expected since unusually long last birth intervals are more likely to bridge into the next age group than short ones. As a result FRFs with these characteristics are disproportionately likely to be present in the later age groups when tabulations are made for the rates given in column 1, and the same characteristic which places the last birth in another, higher age group will cause rates in the last age group counted, and even to a minor degree in its predecessor, to be misleadingly low.[11] Where this influence is absent, however, the agreement between rates shown in columns 1 and 2 is very close. Since, in the case of the rates shown in column 2, a part of the exposure even in the younger age groups will consist of the 17.5 months added after the last birth, the fact that the ratios in column 3, other than the last, are close to unity, and not consistently above or below it, constitutes further confirmation that the added exposure is broadly correct.

Fecund marital fertility rates fell only modestly with age. If the first rate in column 2 is ignored in each of the four age at marriage sets, because the entry rate for any age at marriage group is inflated by prenuptial conceptions, the slightness of any subsequent fall is evident.

Subsequent fecundity also can be calculated from data about age of mother at birth of last child. If 17.5 months are added to her age at this event, or an appropriately smaller figure above age 45, an age at sterility is defined. The subsequent fecundity data in column 3 of table 7.2 were obtained in this way. For each year of age the proportion still fecund can readily be calculated, or the individual figures for each year of age in a five-year age group can be averaged, to provide a figure for the age group as a whole.[12] Thus among women who married in the age group 20–4 just over 13 per cent had become sterile 10 years later when they were aged 30–4 (in table 7.2 the relevant cell shows that 0.8679 were still fecund).

[11] Trussell and Wilson, for example, using English reconstitution data concluded that there was a fall of a third in fecund marital fertility between the age groups 25–9 and 40–4, and that the bulk of this fall occurred between 35–9 and 40–4. This finding was inevitable given the method employed. Trussell and Wilson, 'Sterility in a population with natural fertility', tab. 7, p. 281 and p. 282. It may be noted that the fall in col. 1 of tab. 7.5 closely parallels Trussell and Wilson's estimates, as might be expected. This point has a wider significance in that Henry assumed that the fertility of fecund women who ceased to be fecund in a particular age group was the same as the fertility of fecund women who remained fecund until a later age group. This assumption affects one method for the calculation of the proportion of sterile women in each age group. Leridon, *Human fertility*, pp. 100–1.   [12] For details, see app. 8.

Table 7.6 Fecund marital fertility rates, entry fecundity, subsequent fecundity, and marital fertility rates: bachelor/spinster completed marriages

Wife's age at marriage	Wife's age	(1) Fecund marital fertility rate[a]	(2) Entry fecundity	(3) Subsequent fecundity	(4) Overall fecundity (2) × (3)	(5) Implied marital fertility rate (1) × (4)[a]	(6) Observed marital fertility rate[a]	(7) Ratio (5)/(6)
15–9	15–9	496.7	0.9735	1.0000	0.9740	483.6	484.3	0.999
	20–4	416.2	0.9735	0.9849	0.9590	399.0	399.4	0.999
	25–9	392.5	0.9735	0.9054	0.8814	345.9	345.8	1.000
	30–4	387.1	0.9735	0.7894	0.7685	297.5	298.2	0.997
	35–9	369.2	0.9735	0.6628	0.6452	238.2	238.2	1.000
	40–4	331.1	0.9735	0.3517	0.3424	113.4	114.1	0.993
	45–9	323.3	0.9735	0.0396	0.0386	12.5	12.4	1.009
20–4	20–4	474.6	0.9616	0.9948	0.9566	454.0	455.0	0.998
	25–9	397.0	0.9616	0.9611	0.9242	366.9	366.6	1.001
	30–4	361.7	0.9616	0.8679	0.8346	301.8	301.8	1.000
	35–9	362.0	0.9616	0.7202	0.6925	250.7	251.0	0.998
	40–4	338.0	0.9616	0.3940	0.3789	128.0	128.6	0.996
	45–9	333.3	0.9616	0.0574	0.0552	18.4	18.3	1.005
25–9	25–9	452.4	0.9207	0.9913	0.9127	412.8	414.8	0.995
	30–4	375.9	0.9207	0.9189	0.8460	318.0	317.7	1.001
	35–9	345.9	0.9207	0.7463	0.6871	237.7	238.2	0.998
	40–4	332.7	0.9207	0.4066	0.3744	124.5	123.8	1.006
	45–9	310.7	0.9207	0.0621	0.0572	17.8	17.5	1.014

30–4	30–4	449.0	0.8564	0.9928	0.8502	381.7	388.0	0.984
	35–9	350.6	0.8564	0.8712	0.7461	261.6	261.5	1.000
	40–4	361.0	0.8564	0.4692	0.4018	145.0	145.3	0.999
	45–9	321.5	0.8564	0.0996	0.0853	27.4	27.4	1.002
35–9	35–9	405.0	0.7575	0.9540	0.7227	292.7	302.8	0.967
	40–4	352.1	0.7575	0.5483	0.4153	146.2	148.5	0.985
	45–9	326.8	0.7575	0.1227	0.0929	30.4	30.6	0.993

[a] Rates per 1000 woman-years lived.
Source: Cambridge Group reconstitutions.

371

The variables determining fertility

We are now in a position to consider the same data for all age at marriage groups as were given for the 20–4 age at marriage group in table 7.2, and these are set out in table 7.6. It will be recalled that these data refer only to bachelor/spinster marriages which lasted until the wife had passed the age of 50 and so had completed her childbearing.

The closeness of fit between the implied fertility rates (column 5) and the observed marital fertility rates (column 6) which was visible in table 7.2 for the 20–4 age at marriage group is also found in each of the other age at marriage groups covered in the table (the number of spinster/bachelor marriages taking place when the bride was over 40 was too small to justify extending the table further). In each age at marriage group fecund fertility rates declined with age, but only moderately, so that rates for women in their mid-40s were at about four-fifths of their level for women 20 years younger (the initial fecund fertility rate in each age at marriage group should be disregarded in this connection: the much higher level of the initial rates is due to the relatively high proportion of prenuptially conceived first births).

The difference between the fecundity rates in column 1 and the implied rates in column 5, or the observed fertility rates in column 6, occurs because of the growing impact of sterility with age. In the younger age groups, when most women were still fecund, the difference between the fecund marital fertility rates and the conventional marital fertility rates was modest, but with increasing age sterility becomes the dominant factor in determining the latter (that is, the ratios in column 4 change radically). Clearly, therefore, the characteristics of entry and subsequent sterility are of the first importance in understanding the patterns of marital fertility by age.

Rearranging the data in table 7.6 makes it possible to see the effect of age at marriage on a given variable by looking along a row. The top panel of table 7.7, for example, shows the proportions of those who had once been fecund who were still fecund. Thus in the second column 72 per cent of those marrying at age 20–4, and who had had at least one child, were still fecund in the age group 35–9. In this panel there is a steady and substantial rise in the proportion still fecund moving along each row, or, in other words, the later a woman married the higher the proportion still fecund. However, this pattern largely disappears in the second panel, showing overall fecundity. In this panel any tendency for the proportion still fecund to rise moving from left to right along each row is muted and not fully consistent, especially in the three central columns covering the age at marriage groups

Table 7.7 *Subsequent fecundity, overall fecundity, fecund marital fertility rates, and marital fertility rates by age and age at marriage: bachelor/spinster completed marriages*

	Age at marriage				
Age	15–9	20–4	25–9	30–4	35–9
Subsequent fecundity					
15–9	1.0000				
20–4	0.9849	0.9948			
25–9	0.9054	0.9611	0.9913		
30–4	0.7894	0.8679	0.9189	0.9928	
35–9	0.6628	0.7202	0.7463	0.8712	0.9540
40–4	0.3517	0.3940	0.4066	0.4692	0.5483
45–9	0.0396	0.0574	0.0621	0.0996	0.1227
Overall fecundity					
15–9	0.9740				
20–4	0.9590	0.9566			
25–9	0.8814	0.9242	0.9127		
30–4	0.7685	0.8346	0.8460	0.8502	
35–9	0.6452	0.6925	0.6871	0.7461	0.7227
40–4	0.3424	0.3789	0.3744	0.4018	0.4153
45–9	0.0386	0.0552	0.0572	0.0853	0.0929
Fecund marital fertility rates[a]					
15–9	496.7				
20–4	416.2	474.6			
25–9	392.5	397.0	452.4		
30–4	387.1	361.7	375.9	449.0	
35–9	369.2	362.0	345.9	350.6	405.0
40–4	331.1	338.0	332.7	361.0	352.1
45–9	323.3	333.3	310.7	321.5	326.8
Marital fertility rates[a]					
15–9	484.3				
20–4	399.4	455.0			
25–9	345.8	366.6	414.8		
30–4	298.2	301.8	317.7	388.0	
35–9	238.2	251.0	238.2	261.5	302.8
40–4	114.1	128.6	123.8	145.3	148.5
45–9	12.4	18.4	17.5	27.4	30.6

[a] Rates per 1000 woman-years lived.
Source: tab. 7.6.

20–4 to 30–4, which include the great bulk of all marriages. The change in pattern occurs, of course, because a much higher proportion of late marrying women were already sterile at marriage. When this influence is taken into account by conflating entry and subsequent sterility to produce an overall figure, differences by age at marriage are far less pronounced.

The second panel of table 7.7 suggests, in other words, that the principal determinant of sterility is age rather than parity. The fact that a woman had already had several children appears to have had only a limited effect in increasing her risk of sterility compared with a woman of the same age who had had many fewer children. Consider, for example, the lines for the age groups 25–9, 30–4, 35–9, and 40–4, excluding the ratios in the first column.[13] There are then two ratios on the first row, three on the second, and four on the third and fourth. On these four rows values are normally slightly higher moving to the right along the row, but, considering that in, say, the column referring to women marrying 20–4 mean parity will be about four children higher than in the column referring to those marrying 30–4, it is clear that any impairment of fecundity associated with childbearing must have been modest in this population.

Another way of illustrating the same point is to compare the overall sterility proportion with the entry sterility proportion. If the two were identical it would suggest that childbearing had no influence in causing an increase in sterility. The entry fecundity proportions for the age groups 20–4, 25–9, 30–4, and 35–9 are 0.9616, 0.9207, 0.8564, and 0.7575 (table 7.6). Comparable overall fecundity proportions can be obtained by weighting the figures for each age at marriage group contributing to a particular age group by the relative number of woman-years lived by women in each age at marriage group. This produces fecundity estimates of 0.9566, 0.9215, 0.8408, and 0.7012, figures which are respectively 99.5, 100.1, 98.2, and 92.6 per cent of the first set of proportions. Fecundity is almost identical in the two series initially, though a difference appears as the weight of marriages of long duration increases in the fecundity figures for the second set, but the percentages again suggest that increasing parity affected fecundity only modestly and that age effects were dominant.

The two lowest panels of table 7.7 contain comparable information about fecund marital fertility and ordinary marital fertility rates. If the rate given at the top of each column is ignored, because it is heavily influenced by prenuptial pregnancy, the other rates in the body of the panel devoted to fecund fertility suggest strongly that there was little if any effect from duration of marriage upon the rates. Looking along each row reveals that there was no consistent tendency in any given age

---

[13] There were few teenage brides and the data in the first column are therefore more subject to random influences than those in the other columns.

group for fecund fertility either to rise or to fall with age at marriage. Rates declined moderately with age, but appear unaffected by age at marriage. In the final panel, however, where the conventional marital fertility rates are shown, there is a tendency at any given age for rates to be higher the more recent the marriage, reflecting, of course, the pattern by age and age at marriage to be found in the second panel, devoted to overall fecundity. Since marital fertility rates are the product of fecund fertility rates and overall fecundity, and fecund fertility rates were broadly unaffected by duration of marriage, the pattern present in overall fecundity, which fell sharply with age, must be reflected in marital fertility rates.

Change in the components of fertility over time

It is natural to wonder whether the fecundity and fertility characteristics just discussed were stable over time. This issue is addressed in tables 7.10 and 7.11. In these tables the parish register period as a whole is divided into three roughly equal parts. Further subdivision, though attractive, would have involved the risks attaching to rates based on a relatively small total of events, especially in the higher age groups.

Table 7.8 is in the same general format as table 7.6 in that the first three columns consist of an implied fertility rate, an observed fertility rate, and the ratio between the two, but the implied fertility rate is produced by a method that differs slightly from that of table 7.6. In table 7.6 the individual fecundity rate, entry fecundity ratio, and subsequent fecundity ratio for each age group within each age at marriage group were multiplied together to produce an implied fertility rate (fecundity rate x entry fecundity ratio x subsequent fecundity ratio = implied fertility rate). Table 7.8, rather than showing data for each age at marriage group separately, consists of rates and ratios produced by collapsing together the experience of all age at marriage groups contributing to any given age group. Thus, the observed marital fertility rate in 1650–1749 for the age group 35–9, at 241.7 per 1000, is the rate for all women of that age, irrespective of their age at marriage.

To preserve consistency with the calculation of the observed marital fertility rate, the calculation of an implied rate from its component elements had to be treated in a parallel fashion. This was done by weighting the implied age-specific marital fertility rates for each separate age at marriage group (that is, implied rates such as those in table 7.6) by the proportionate share of the total of woman-years lived in a given age group by that age at marriage group. Thus, using the data in

Table 7.8 *The changing levels of the components of marital fertility: bachelor/spinster completed marriages*

Wife's age	(1) Implied marital fertility rate[a]	(2) Observed marital fertility rate[a]	(3) Ratio (1)/(2)	(4) Fecund marital fertility rate[ab]	(5) Entry fecundity ratio[b]	(6) Subsequent fecundity ratio[b]
1538–1649						
15–9	470.1	470.1	1.0000	470.1	1.0000	1.0000
20–4	440.7	439.3	1.0031	456.5	0.9719	0.9940
25–9	369.3	368.9	1.0011	401.2	0.9581	0.9609
30–4	313.8	314.5	0.9979	373.2	0.9437	0.8932
35–9	245.7	246.6	0.9963	349.5	0.9317	0.7602
40–4	122.9	123.0	0.9992	322.3	0.9176	0.4231
45–9	16.8	16.8	1.0029	286.9	0.9071	0.0631
1650–1749						
15–9	388.6	384.9	1.0097	411.8	0.9437	1.0000
20–4	419.4	420.8	0.9967	440.7	0.9611	0.9895
25–9	371.5	372.6	0.9971	409.7	0.9505	0.9546
30–4	309.4	309.9	0.9984	374.4	0.9356	0.8842
35–9	241.0	241.7	0.9971	359.1	0.9203	0.7337
40–4	117.4	118.0	0.9955	342.6	0.9071	0.3842
45–9	17.8	18.0	0.9920	314.9	0.8998	0.0660
1750–1837						
15–9	613.4	617.6	0.9932	618.6	0.9915	1.0000
20–4	450.2	451.3	0.9976	470.2	0.9662	0.9922
25–9	385.0	384.7	1.0009	418.4	0.9497	0.9697
30–4	324.0	324.6	0.9981	386.5	0.9366	0.8960
35–9	263.0	263.3	0.9988	361.4	0.9293	0.7855
40–4	150.1	151.4	0.9914	350.7	0.9176	0.4734
45–9	24.1	24.2	0.9956	333.8	0.9077	0.0829
All						
15–9	483.6	484.3	0.9985	496.7	0.9735	1.0000
20–4	435.5	436.3	0.9982	454.9	0.9656	0.9914
25–9	376.4	376.7	0.9991	411.3	0.9522	0.9615
30–4	314.9	315.5	0.9982	377.8	0.9380	0.8902
35–9	248.8	249.6	0.9971	357.5	0.9248	0.7566
40–4	128.9	129.5	0.9953	340.0	0.9117	0.4224
45–9	19.8	19.9	0.9965	321.8	0.9031	0.0716

[a] Rates per 1000 woman-years lived.
[b] The rates or ratios shown in these columns were calculated by weighting the rates or ratios for individual age at marriage groups by the number of woman-years lived by each age at marriage group in the age group in question in the data set as a whole.

table 7.6, and considering the implied 'All' rate for the age group 25–9, it will be obvious that three rates are involved, those for the age at marriage groups 15–9, 20–4, and 25–9 (345.9, 366.9, and 412.8). The proportionate share of each age at marriage group in the total of woman-years lived in the age group 25–9 was 0.1392, 0.5909, and 0.2699. The implied consolidated rate for the 25–9 age group for the 'All' category in table 7.8, therefore, is 376.4 per 1000 ((345.9 × 0.1392) + (366.9 × 0.5909) + (412.8 × 0.2699) = 376.4). Since it would be wearisome to list all the component elements in such calculations, only the implied rates are given in table 7.8.

The implied and observed rates for the three subperiods in the table were calculated using the overall weights for the whole data set so that the resulting rates are controlled for changes in the relative size of different age at marriage groups. Note, however, that this operation is not algebraically equivalent to treating fecund fertility, entry fecundity, and subsequent fecundity separately, weighting the three different age at marriage rates or ratios with the weights just given, and multiplying the resulting rate and ratios to produce an implied rate. Therefore, the task of identifying the relative importance of changes in these three variables in causing changes in marital fertility cannot be discharged simply by measuring proportionate changes in rates or ratios calculated in this fashion (or, to make the same point in a different way, the product of the rates and ratios in columns 4, 5, and 6 does not equal the implied marital fertility rate in column 1). However, fecund fertility rates and entry and subsequent fecundity ratios can readily be calculated in this way (that is, weighted by the overall total of woman-years lived in each age group by each age at marriage group), and they give a clear impression of the scale of proportionate change in each variable. Such rates and ratios are therefore shown in the last three columns of the table.

Before considering the trends over time visible in table 7.8, it is important to list factors to be discussed later which affect the interpretation of trends. At this stage only a preliminary review of the evidence, as it were, can be attempted. A more considered and shaded assessment will be possible only when some other influences on fertility trends have

Notes to table 7.8 (*cont.*)

Note: the ratios in column 3 were calculated from unrounded rates in the first two columns so that they may differ very slightly from the figure that would be produced by considering the printed rates in columns 1 and 2. *Source*: Cambridge Group reconstitutions.

been analysed. Two points in particular, which are examined at greater length later, need to be borne in mind since each affects the measurement of 'true' trends in fecundity and fertility over time.

The first is prenuptial pregnancy. Any woman who had a first child which was prenuptially conceived contributed less to the total of exposure than should be the case. The birth event takes place after marriage, but a part of the exposure which should be related to it takes place before marriage and so is not counted. The proportion of first births prenuptially conceived was sometimes large but varied greatly over time in early modern England. Trends both in fecund marital fertility and in marital fertility are subject to distortion from changing proportions of prenuptial first births. The distortions are most pronounced, of course, in the age group 15–9 since all women in this age group were recently married and a very high proportion of all births were first births. But rates for the next two age groups, 20–4 and 25–9, were also affected by the same phenomenon, and even later age groups, though to a much more limited extent.

Secondly, changes in the level of infant mortality will affect mean birth intervals and hence fertility rates. Since the interval between two successive births was more than 8 months shorter if the earlier of the two died in infancy than if he or she survived the first year, a fall in infant mortality must, other things being equal, cause the mean birth interval to increase and fertility rates to fall.[14]

The convenient property found in table 7.6, that the implied marital fertility rates are very close to the observed rates, has not been lost in table 7.8, even though the individual age at marriage groups have been collapsed into a single expression for each age group. The implied and observed rates are never more than 0.5 per cent apart in the 'All' section, where random effects are minimised by the larger data base, and very seldom more than 0.5 per cent elsewhere, except in the youngest and oldest age groups where the number of births was much smaller than in other age groups.

A glance at column 2 of table 7.8 shows that marital fertility rates, after making allowance for the fact that the proportion of first births that were prenuptially conceived was at a low level in the middle period, changed very little between the early and middle periods. Between the middle and late periods, in contrast, there was a rise in each age-specific rate. Once again, in the younger age groups this was principally to do with the prevalence of prenuptial first births, but there were also pronounced

---

[14] See tab. 7.35, pp. 438–9, for data on birth intervals according to whether the earlier child of a pair died in infancy or survived.

differences in the rates later in life when few prenuptial births occurred. The rates in the age groups 35–9, 40–4, and 45–9 in the period after 1750 were higher than the equivalent rates in the middle period by 9, 28, and 34 per cent respectively. These are unexpectedly large changes and the relative importance of the three underlying variables deserves investigation.

The first step is to recast the information in table 7.8 into a form which lends itself to clarifying the components of change. In table 7.9 the middle period, when marital fertility rates were lowest, is represented as 1000 in each panel and the comparable rates and ratios in the early and late periods are indexed to the middle period figures. The relative scale of the changes in marital fertility, fecund marital fertility, entry fecundity, and subsequent fecundity are clear from the table, and the relative importance of each of the three last variables in producing changes in marital fertility rates is suggested by the scale of the proportionate changes in each of them.

The long-term pattern of change in fecund fertility is relatively clear and simple, if the influence of prenuptial pregnancy is taken into account. Prenuptial pregnancy was commoner in the early and late periods than in the middle period, and affected young age groups disproportionately. Prenuptiality is examined in detail later, but a brief digression at this point may serve to substantiate the point that, when the effect of prenuptiality is eliminated, fecund marital fertility did not greatly change in early modern England and that the apparently dramatic changes in fecund marital fertility in the younger age groups are an illusion.

In table 7.10 standardised fecund marital fertility rates are given for women who had no prenuptially conceived children together with the associated TMFRs. Both the rates and the TMFRs are also shown in an indexed form in the lower half of the table.

Both in the first age group, 15–9, and in the last, 45–9, the number of events was small and the rates are therefore a more uncertain guide to behaviour than those for other age groups. The rates for the age groups between 20 and 40 deserve special attention since the great majority of all births were to women in this age range. Fecund marital fertility rates in these age groups were about 2 per cent lower in the first period than in the middle period, while in the last period rates were about 2.5 per cent higher than in the middle period. The differences were moderately consistent across all the individual age groups, so that it seems safe to assert that, when the effect of the changing levels of entry fecundity has been removed, fecund marital fertility rose slowly throughout the parish register period, by a little less than 5 per cent overall. Such a

Table 7.9 Indexed changes in marital fertility, fecund marital fertility, entry fecundity, and subsequent fecundity (1650–1749 = 1000)

	Fecund marital fertility rates			Entry fecundity ratios			Subsequent fecundity ratios			Marital fertility rates		
	1538–1649	1650–1749	1750–1837	1538–1649	1650–1749	1750–1837	1538–1650	1650–1749	1750–1837	1538–1649	1650–1749	1750–1837
15–9	1 142	1 000	1 502	1 060	1 000	1 051	1 000	1 000	1 000	1 221	1 000	1 605
20–4	1 036	1 000	1 067	1 011	1 000	1 005	1 005	1 000	1 003	1 044	1 000	1 072
25–9	979	1 000	1 021	1 008	1 000	999	1 006	1 000	1 016	990	1 000	1 032
30–4	997	1 000	1 032	1 009	1 000	1 001	1 010	1 000	1 013	1 015	1 000	1 047
35–9	973	1 000	1 006	1 012	1 000	1 010	1 036	1 000	1 071	1 020	1 000	1 089
40–4	941	1 000	1 024	1 012	1 000	1 012	1 105	1 000	1 232	1 042	1 000	1 283
45–9	911	1 000	1 060	1 008	1 000	1 009	956	1 000	1 256	933	1 000	1 344

Source: tab. 7.8.

380

Table 7.10 *Standardised fecund marital fertility rates of women who had no prenuptially conceived children (per 1000 woman-years lived)*

	Wife's age							TFMFR		
	15–9	20–4	25–9	30–4	35–9	40–4	45–9	20–44	20–49	15–49
1538–1649	423.0	395.9	396.9	368.7	343.6	314.7	272.4	9.10	10.46	12.58
1650–1749	337.0	405.4	400.5	367.1	358.6	344.9	319.2	9.38	10.98	12.66
1750–1837	387.3	417.5	406.8	379.1	366.7	346.2	345.9	9.58	11.31	13.25
1538–1649	1 255	977	991	1 004	958	912	853	970	953	994
1650–1749	1 000	1 000	1 000	1 000	1 000	1 000	1 000	1 000	1 000	1 000
1750–1837	1 149	1 030	1 016	1 033	1 023	1 004	1 084	1 021	1 030	1 047

Notes: for the method of standardisation see tab. 7.8, note *b*.
Source: Cambridge Group reconstitutions.

change is consonant, say, with a small decline in the mean length of breastfeeding during the parish register period. For example, a fall of a month or slightly more in the mean length would probably produce this effect. Because the length of the intergenesic interval is so heavily influenced by breastfeeding, and breastfeeding practices in turn can vary so strikingly, this explanation is, so to speak, a port of first resort when seeking an explanation. These issues are considered further when trends in birth intervals are discussed.[15]

The net effect of the trends in fecund marital fertility rates and the two fecundity ratios is reflected in the marital fertility rates. Broadly speaking, and after making an allowance for the effect of the relatively high proportion of prenuptially conceived first births in the first period compared with the second, there was no great difference in marital fertility between the first two periods (fourth panel, table 7.9). But in the final period marital fertility was substantially higher than it had previously been. This was a period in which prenuptially conceived first births were very common, so that the high ratio in the first two age groups may be largely discounted, but in the age groups between 25 and 34 marital fertility was about 4 per cent higher than in the middle period, and the difference increased in the next higher age group (35–9) to 9 per cent, before growing still larger in the two highest age groups when it was about 31 per cent. In every age group from 25–9 upwards marital fertility in the final period was also much higher than in the first period. Between 25 and 34 the higher marital fertility after 1750 owed more to higher fecund marital fertility rates than to higher fecundity. Above the age of 35, however, the roles were reversed, with change in subsequent fecundity the dominant influence in producing the high marital fertility rates.

All the changes in fecund marital fertility rates shown in table 7.9 were modest in scale, with changes in individual age groups in the range from 0 to 6 per cent between the middle period and the last, apart from the two youngest age groups where the rates were affected by the prevalence of prenuptially conceived first births. But the pronounced rise in marital fertility rates above the age of 35 in the later eighteenth century was far more dramatic, and, given the multiplicative nature of the relationship between fecund marital fertility, fecundity and marital fertility, it implies the existence of equally large changes in fecundity. Indeed, it is reasonable to claim that this is the most striking feature of the fertility history of early modern England. Changes in entry fecundity played little part in bringing this about. Apart from the age group

---

[15] See below pp. 445–6.

15–9, where the substantial differences from one period to the next were probably the result of the small numbers involved, differences were very minor, never much exceeding 1 per cent between adjacent periods, though the lowest rate in each age group was almost always in the middle period. The rise in marital fertility, therefore, was principally a question of sharply rising subsequent fecundity in the later age groups in the period after 1750. Possible reasons for this development are discussed below,[16] but, to provide a more informative background to the discussion of fecundity change, and also because the phenomenon is of great intrinsic interest, entry and subsequent fecundity trends are first considered in greater detail.

Entry sterility estimates (the complement of entry fecundity) are obtained by determining what proportion of women in each age at marriage group never bore a child. The total number of women in the data set of completed bachelor/spinster marriages is only just over 2000. When divided into three periods and further into five-year age at marriage groups, the cell sizes become small at the two ends of the age range, because such a high proportion of all marriages occurred when the bride was in her 20s or early 30s.

The problems associated with small numbers are immediately evident in table 7.11. The percentages are fairly stable in the age range 20 to 34, within which 82 per cent of all marriages took place, but fluctuate wildly in the other age groups. For this reason two weighted averages have been included in the table. The first, which relates to all marriages, is arrived at by the same standardisation procedure that was employed in table 7.8, though based on totals of marriages rather than woman-years lived (for example, 37 per cent of all the marriages involved women aged 20–4, and the primary sterility percentage for that age group was therefore multiplied by 0.3700 in arriving at the weighted average). The second uses the same principle to summarise the information relating to the three age groups in which more than four-fifths of all the marriages took place.

The two sets of weighted averages present a broadly similar picture. The overall weighted average suggests that primary sterility was marginally lowest in the latest of the three subperiods, with a peak in 1650–1749. The weighted averages based on marriages in the age range 20–34 suggest, if anything, a slight rise in sterility over time, but the differences are so slight in both cases that, in view of the numbers involved, the safest conclusion must be that entry sterility was essential-

---

[16] See below pp. 385–7.

Table 7.11 *Entry sterility: bachelor/spinster completed marriages*

Age at marriage	1538–1649	1650–1749	1750–1837	All
15–9	0.00	5.63	0.85	2.65
20–4	4.24	3.00	4.66	3.84
25–9	6.25	8.85	8.00	7.93
30–4	15.69	13.99	13.70	14.36
35–9	17.86	30.43	11.76	24.25
40–4	86.67	59.32	81.48	69.31
45–9	100.00	100.00	[100.00]	100.00
Weighted average[a]	9.59	10.30	9.52	9.97
Weighted average 20–34[b]	7.04	7.13	7.52	7.24

[a] This average was obtained by giving each percentage for the different age at marriage groups a weight proportional to the share of all marriages in that age group for all periods to the overall total of marriages for all periods.
[b] This average was obtained in the same fashion as that described in note *a* except that only marriages in the age groups 20–4 to 30–4 were considered.
Note: there were no first marriages in which the bride was aged 45–9 in the period after 1750. The figure in square brackets in the appropriate cell is therefore an attributed figure.
Source: Cambridge Group reconstitutions.

ly stable throughout the parish register period.[17] The data on entry fecundity in table 7.8, of course, suggest the same thing.[18] When overall fecundity rose or fell, it did so principally because of changes in subsequent fecundity.

Subsequent fecundity ratios are set out in table 7.12. The top four

[17] Entry sterility might in principle be strongly influenced by social convention. If, for example, only women who had demonstrated their fecundity and become pregnant were marriageable, then entry sterility would be an underestimate of its level in a random sample of women, because sterile women would be unable to find a marriage partner. In these circumstances a high level of prenuptial pregnancy would be associated with a low level of entry sterility, *ceteris paribus*, and vice versa. Conclusive evidence about this topic is lacking for early modern England, but the stability of entry sterility over a 250-year period during which the level of prenuptial pregnancy varied markedly suggests that there was no linkage between demonstrating fecundity and the possibility of marrying in this period.
[18] Trussell and Wilson, employing two different methods of measuring sterility, and using data referring to all marriages rather than to bachelor/spinster marriages, produced entry sterility estimates from a subset of the English reconstitution data used in tab. 7.11 which are generally similar to those in tab. 7.11, though their estimates were higher in the younger, but lower in the older age at marriage groups. Trussell and Wilson, 'Sterility in a population with natural fertility', tab. 8, p. 281, and tab. 9, p. 283. See also figs. 7.2 and 7.3, pp. 395 and 396.

panels of the table show subsequent fecundity ratios in each of the five main age at marriage groups for each of the three subperiods and for the period as a whole. The table immediately suggests why, although fecund fertility, after allowing for prenuptiality, rose only slightly over time, and there was also little change in entry sterility, overall marital fertility nevertheless fluctuated much more markedly. In the early age groups subsequent fecundity patterns were not greatly different in the three subperiods, though usually highest in the final period and lowest in the middle period. Above the age of 35, however, differences are far more pronounced. Subsequent fecundity was much higher after 1750 in these age groups than in the previous centuries, and especially than in the period 1650–1749. The figures for the earliest period usually lie between those for the two later periods. The scale of the differences between the final period and the two earlier ones for age groups above the age of 35 may be seen in the middle panel of table 7.12 where the ratios for the period before 1650 and for 1650–1749 have been indexed against the ratio for the period after 1750, which is taken as 1000.

The differences in fecundity between the subperiods were partly a matter of level but also a matter of shape. It is instructive to compare the first and last periods in this regard. Before 1650, the pattern of fecundity of women who married aged 25–9, from the age of 35 onwards, was broadly similar to that found in the period after 1750. But before 1650 the fecundity of women who married young, in the age groups 15–9 or 20–4, was far lower above the age of 35 than the fecundity of those marrying aged 25–9, whereas after 1750 the fecundity above the age of 35 of younger marrying women was little different from those marrying in the 25–9 age group. In the later period, in other words, there was little or no duration of marriage effect on subsequent fecundity. In both the two earlier periods this effect was strong, so that, for example, subsequent fecundity among women marrying 15–9 when they were in their early 40s was only 60–80 per cent as high as for women who married aged 25–9.

The last point is most easily grasped by referring to the last four panels of table 7.12, where the ratios at other ages have been indexed on the level in the 25–9 age at marriage group. This shows very clearly that for women marrying 15–9, 20–4, and 25–9 in the final period after 1750 there were only slight differences between the age at marriage groups, even towards the end of the childbearing period. In either of the two earlier periods, but perhaps most markedly in the middle period, the indexed figures show vividly that in their late 30s and early 40s women who had married in their teens had far lower subsequent fecundity than those marrying in their late 20s. In the period 1650–1749, for example,

Table 7.12 *Subsequent fecundity ratios*

Wife's age at marriage	Age						
	15–9	20–4	25–9	30–4	35–9	40–4	45–9
1538–1649							
15–9	1.0000	0.9925	0.9100	0.7950	0.6625	0.2950	0.0200
20–4		0.9948	0.9601	0.8731	0.7137	0.3664	0.0598
25–9			0.9887	0.9193	0.7523	0.4377	0.0593
30–4				0.9933	0.9178	0.5481	0.1333
35–9					0.8838	0.4891	0.0239
1650–1749							
15–9	1.0000	0.9851	0.8776	0.7485	0.5955	0.2955	0.0276
20–4		0.9917	0.9543	0.8669	0.7003	0.3596	0.0502
25–9			0.9949	0.9163	0.7416	0.3744	0.0588
30–4				0.9886	0.8155	0.4012	0.0770
35–9					0.9849	0.5482	0.1536
1750–1837							
15–9	1.0000	0.9795	0.9342	0.8325	0.7402	0.4547	0.0557
20–4		0.9986	0.9701	0.8663	0.7489	0.4523	0.0652
25–9			0.9873	0.9227	0.7485	0.4311	0.0706
30–4				1.0000	0.9349	0.5246	0.1103
35–9					0.9543	0.6089	0.1467
All							
15–9	1.0000	0.9849	0.9054	0.7894	0.6628	0.3517	0.0396
20–4		0.9948	0.9611	0.8679	0.7202	0.3940	0.0574
25–9			0.9913	0.9189	0.7463	0.4066	0.0621
30–4				0.9928	0.8712	0.4692	0.0996
35–9					0.9540	0.5483	0.1227

The top panel indexed: 1750–1837 = 1000

	15–9	20–4	25–9	30–4	35–9	40–4	45–9
1538–1649							
15–9					882	649	300
20–4					953	810	917
25–9					1 005	1 015	840
30–4					982	1 045	1 209
35–9					926	803	163
1650–1749							
15–9					805	650	414
20–4					935	795	770
25–9					991	868	833
30–4					872	765	698
35–9					1 032	900	1 047

The top panel indexed: wife's age at marriage 25–9 = 1000

	15–9	20–4	25–9	30–4	35–9	40–4	45–9
1538–1649							
15–9			1 920	865	881	674	337
20–4			971	950	949	837	1 008
25–9			1 000	1 000	1 000	1 000	1 000
30–4				1 080	1 220	1 252	2 248
35–9					1 175	1 117	403

Table 7.12 (*cont.*)

Wife's age at marriage	Age						
	15–9	20–4	25–9	30–4	35–9	40–4	45–9
1650–1749							
15–9			882	817	803	789	469
20–4			959	946	944	960	854
25–9			1 000	1 000	1 000	1 000	1 000
30–4				1 079	1 100	1 072	1 310
35–9					1 328	1 464	2 612
1750–1837							
15–9			946	902	988	1 055	945
20–4			983	939	1 001	1 049	923
25–9			1 000	1 000	1 000	1 000	1 000
30–4				1 084	1 249	1 217	1 562
35–9					1 275	1 412	2 078
All							
15–9			913	859	888	865	638
20–4			970	944	965	969	924
25–9			1 000	1 000	1 000	1 000	1 000
30–4				1 080	1 167	1 154	1 604
35–9					1 278	1 348	1 976

Source: Cambridge Group reconstitutions.

the ratios for the age groups 35–9 to 45–9 among women marrying 25–9 were on average 46 per cent higher than among those who married when in their late teens. After 1750 the comparable percentage was under 4 per cent. Before 1650 it was 60 per cent. The very marked gains in marital fertility towards the end of the parish register period were largely a function of this remarkable rise in subsequent fecundity among early marrying wives.

Changes in subsequent fecundity will be reflected, of course, in changes in the mean age at birth of last child. In table 7.13 this summary statistic is shown for each age at marriage group in each of the three subperiods and for the whole reconstitution period. The mean age is necessarily lower among women who marry young since women may bear a last child at any age subsequent to marriage. If, therefore, a woman marries young she will be at risk of becoming sterile when still in her 20s, whereas a woman marrying ten years later cannot become sterile until in her 30s or later. Late marrying women do not, of course, escape the physiological changes which result in sterility, but this will

Table 7.13 *Mean age at birth of last child (years): bachelor/spinster completed marriages*

Wife's age at marriage	1538–1649	1650–1749	1750–1837	All
15–9	36.98	36.19	38.62	37.24
20–4	38.41	38.19	39.06	38.55
25–9	39.31	39.00	39.35	39.18
30–4	41.55	40.04	41.47	40.77
35–9	40.64	42.11	42.27	41.81
40–4	42.94	44.22	44.70	44.21
Weighted mean age[a]	39.17	38.80	39.68	39.16
W'ted mean 15–24[b](a)	38.14	37.81	39.98	38.30
W'ted mean 30 and over(b)	41.35	40.79	41.82	41.20
Difference (b) – (a)	3.21	2.98	2.84	2.90

[a] The weighted mean age was obtained by giving each mean age at birth of last child for each age at marriage group a weight equal to the share of all marriages in that age group in all periods as a proportion of the overall total of marriages for all periods.
[b] The weighted mean was calculated as described in note *a* except that the overall totals were for marriage in the age range indicated rather than for all marriages.
Source: Cambridge Group reconstitutions.

appear in a higher proportion being sterile on entry into marriage compared with younger marrying women.

In almost all age at marriage groups the mean age at birth of last child was lowest in the period 1650–1749, and the duration of childbearing therefore least in this period. In all age at marriage groups except one it was highest in the period after 1750. *Ceteris paribus* a rise in the mean age at birth of last child will increase marital fertility because childbearing is continued to a later age. It will also increase age-specific fertility rates in the higher age groups more than in the lower age groups, a prominent feature of the standardised marital fertility rates in table 7.8. Age at last birth rose slightly more between the middle and later periods in the early marrying age groups than among women who were older at marriage, as may be seen in summary form in the weighted mean ages at last birth for women marrying aged 15–24 compared with those marrying when aged 30 or more, shown towards the foot of the table. This is not surprising since physiology limits the size of the possible rise if mean age at last birth is already high. The effect, however, will be to cause marital fertility rates in the higher age groups to rise more among those who married young than among older brides. This change also explains the fact that the difference between age at last birth among those marrying aged 15–24 and those marrying over 30 was less in the post-1750 period than earlier (bottom line of table 7.13), a phenomenon which helps to explain the subsequent fecundity patterns visible in table 7.12.

Reviewing entry and subsequent fecundity separately is, of course, a somewhat artificial exercise. In table 7.14 levels of overall fecundity by age and age at marriage are set out. The table takes the same form as table 7.12 but the subsequent fecundity ratios shown in the upper panel of table 7.12 have been multiplied by the entry fecundity ratios which are the complements of the entry sterility ratios shown in table 7.11. Thus, the entry fecundity ratio for women aged 20–4 at marriage in the first period was 0.9576 and therefore each subsequent fecundity ratio on the appropriate line of table 7.12 was multiplied by this ratio to yield an overall fecundity ratio to be entered on the comparable line of table 7.14. As an example, the first figure on the second row of the top panel of table 7.12 is 0.9948, which, multiplied by 0.9576, gives 0.9526, the figure in the parallel cell of table 7.14. The ratios in each cell should be interpreted as representing the proportion of woman-years lived in a given age group by a given age at marriage group by women who were still fecund. The middle panel of the table repeats the kind of exercise carried out in the lower panel of table 7.12, while the bottom panel indexes the ratios found in each cell of the first and last subperiods to the ratio found in the comparable cell in the middle period.

The merging of entry and subsequent fecundity into a single overall ratio does not greatly change the patterns visible in the table devoted to subsequent fecundity. Under the age of 35 there is no consistent difference in fecundity in the different periods in either level or 'shape' (that is, in the patterns in a given age group by age at marriage), apart from the ratios for the 15–9 age at marriage group in the middle period which are lower than in the other two periods. This reflects a low entry fecundity figure which is probably an aberration associated with the small number of women married in their teens. The total in this period was 71, of whom 4 were sterile, resulting in an unusually low entry fecundity ratio of 0.9437. Apart from this, the slight differences up to the age of 35 are probably essentially random.

Above the age of 35, however, the uniformity visible at earlier ages disappears. Fecundity was substantially lower in the middle period than either earlier or later. In general the highest fecundity ratios are to be found in the post-1750 period. In some instances the rise during the century after 1650–1749 was striking. For example, in the age group 40–4

Table 7.14 *Overall fecundity ratios*

Wife's age at marriage	15–9	20–4	25–9	30–4	35–9	40–4	45–9
1538–1649							
15–9	1.0000	0.9925	0.9100	0.7950	0.6625	0.2950	0.0200
20–4		0.9526	0.9194	0.8360	0.6834	0.3509	0.0572
25–9			0.9269	0.8619	0.7053	0.4103	0.0556
30–4				0.8374	0.7738	0.4621	0.1124
35–9					0.7260	0.4018	0.0196
1650–1749							
15–9	0.9437	0.9296	0.8282	0.7064	0.5620	0.2789	0.0261
20–4		0.9620	0.9257	0.8409	0.6793	0.3488	0.0487
25–9			0.9069	0.8352	0.6759	0.3412	0.0536
30–4				0.8503	0.7014	0.3451	0.0662
35–9					0.6852	0.3814	0.1068
1750–1837							
15–9	0.9915	0.9733	0.9226	0.8280	0.7432	0.4420	0.0590
20–4		0.9521	0.9258	0.8301	0.7181	0.4359	0.0605
25–9			0.9092	0.8494	0.6894	0.3974	0.0631
30–4				0.8630	0.7989	0.4452	0.0974
35–9					0.8421	0.5373	0.1294
All							
15–9	0.9735	0.9594	0.8812	0.7712	0.6518	0.3431	0.0370
20–4		0.9566	0.9246	0.8360	0.6944	0.3813	0.0546
25–9			0.9128	0.8462	0.6874	0.3751	0.0568
30–4				0.8503	0.7447	0.4005	0.0860
35–9					0.7226	0.4153	0.0929

The above indexed: wife's age at marriage (20–4 = 1 000)

	15–9	20–4	25–9	30–4	35–9	40–4	45–9
1538–1649							
15–9		1 042	990	951	955	841	350
20–4		1 000	1 000	1 000	1 000	1 000	1 000
25–9			1 008	1 031	1 032	1 169	972
30–4				1 002	1 132	1 317	1 965
35–9					1 062	1 145	343
1650–1749							
15–9		966	895	840	827	800	536
20–4		1 000	1 000	1 000	1 000	1 000	1 000
25–9			980	993	995	978	1 101
30–4				1 011	1 033	989	1 359
35–9					1 009	1 093	2 193
1750–1837							
15–9		1 022	997	997	1 035	1 014	975
20–4		1 000	1 000	1 000	1 000	1 000	1 000
25–9			982	1 023	960	912	1 043
30–4				1 040	1 113	1 021	1 610
35–9					1 173	1 233	2 139

Table 7.14 (*cont.*)

Wife's age at marriage	15–9	20–4	25–9	30–4	35–9	40–4	45–9
All							
15–9		1 003	953	922	939	900	678
20–4		1 000	1 000	1 000	1 000	1 000	1 000
25–9			987	1 012	990	984	1 040
30–4				1 018	1 072	1 050	1 575
35–9					1 041	1 089	1 701
Indexed ratios for 1538–1649 and 1750–1837 (1650–1749 = 1 000)							
1538–1649							
15–9	1060	1 068	1099	1 125	1 179	1 058	766
20–4		990	993	994	1 006	1 006	1 175
25–9			1 022	1 032	1 043	1 203	1 037
30–4				985	1 103	1 339	1 698
35–9					1 060	1 053	184
1750–1837							
15–9	1 051	1 047	1 114	1 172	1 322	1 585	2 261
20–4		990	1 000	987	1 057	1 250	1 242
25–9			1 003	1 017	1 020	1 165	1 177
30–4				1 015	1 139	1 290	1 471
35–9					1 229	1 409	1 212

Sources: entry fecundity from tab. 7.11 (the complement of entry sterility); subsequent fecundity from tab. 7.12.

in the five age at marriage groups from 15–9 to 45–9 the ratio in the latest period was 59, 25, 17, 29, and 41 per cent higher than in the middle period. Above the age of 35, ratios in the pre-1650 period were also consistently higher than in the middle period, except for two ratios in the age group 45–9. They were usually, though not invariably, higher after 1750 than in either of the two earlier periods.

The last two panels of table 7.14 summarise the levels of the fecundity ratios in the first and last periods relative to the middle period. Beneath the age of 35 all the values which relate to marriages contracted between 20 and 35 are close to 1000. There are higher values on the top row but this is a product of the aberrantly low level of entry fecundity in this age at marriage group in the middle period, which was discussed above when entry fecundity was described.[19] Above the age of 35 large differences appear: there can be no doubt that fecundity in the older age groups was considerably lower in the late seventeenth and early

[19] See above p. 389.

eighteenth centuries than at other times in the parish register period.

Differences between the three subperiods were not confined to level; they are also found in the 'shape' of the ratios, which may be observed by reading down the columns, or, in other words, by considering how much, in any given age group, the level of fecundity was affected by length of marriage. Here the middle and later periods have much in common and the earliest period stands out. The patterns are evident from the middle set of panels of table 7.14. Here ratios at other ages are indexed within each column on the ratio for those who married aged 20–4, the age group in which the largest number of marriages took place. If the bottom row and final column of the data relating to the period after 1750 are ignored (in the former case because the absolute fecundity ratios were low and in the latter case because the number of marriages was small), there is little evidence that duration of marriage influenced fecundity. Instead of values rising down each column (that is, fecundity being highest among those recently married), values close to 1000 are almost universal. Over the great bulk of the age range and age at marriage range, duration of marriage effects were slight.

In general, the 'shape' characteristics of the post-1750 period are also to be found in the middle period, but in the earliest period there was a more consistent, though still not pronounced, tendency for marriages of shorter duration to have higher fecundity at any given age.

Standardised figures for overall fecundity for each age group as a whole are helpful as summary measures and can readily be produced.[20] The resulting data for each subperiod are shown in figure 7.1 indexed against the overall fecundity ratios for the period as a whole. The overall fecundity ratios for the five-year age groups 15–9 to 45–9 are 0.9735, 0.9576, 0.9154, 0.8344, 0.6972, 0.3796, and 0.0612. The age groups are plotted by their midpoints, except in the case of the first age group 15–9 which is plotted at 18.5 years in view of the distribution of ages at marriage within the age group. Displaying the data in this form makes it easy to identify the extent of the change in overall fecundity over time. The lines are almost indistinguishable from one another down to the age group 30–4, except that the figure for the 15–9 age group for 1650–1749 is low. This may reasonably be regarded as an aberration resulting from the very small number of teenage brides and the consequent danger that ratios are unreliable. Below the age of 35 there is no indication of major differences over time. Above the age of 35, however, the line for the

---

[20] For any particular age group this can be achieved by weighting the individual overall fecundity ratios in tab. 7.14 for any given age at marriage group by the number of woman-years lived in that age group by the age at marriage group in question over the parish register period as a whole.

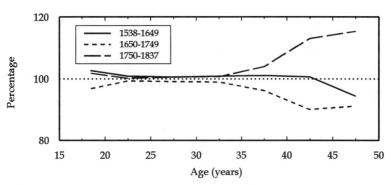

Figure 7.1   *Standardised overall fecundity ratios for three subperiods indexed to the overall average (100)*
Source: tab. 7.16.

period after 1750 lies well above the other two lines, and the middle period sags below the average. Given that age-specific fecund marital fertility rates were broadly constant over time, it is obvious that, towards the end of the parish register period, age-specific marital fertility rates must have risen substantially in the higher age groups because of rising overall fecundity.

The data themselves do not, of course, provide any direct evidence about the cause of the change. There was a significant decline in mean birth intervals during the eighteenth century.[21] Other things being equal, short birth intervals are likely to be associated with a later age at last birth, since, assuming an unchanging pattern of the advent of sterility, a last birth will occur at a higher age if birth intervals are short. But this would not account for any relative change in fecundity by age at marriage. A change in behaviour seems a more plausible possibility. If, for example, the frequency of coitus both by age and by duration of marriage fell off less steeply after 1750 than before, this would produce a change of the kind observed, as would a comparable change in complete abstinence from intercourse. But while such changes might provide proximate reasons for the change, they would only explain it in a somewhat trivial sense. Such changes in behaviour themselves require an explanation. For example, they might have arisen as a response to an appreciation of the rising value of children. Many couples who married young would have had a large surviving family by the time they reached their later 30s, and might have wished to avoid adding to their burdens in one era, but have viewed matters differently in altered

[21] See below fig. 7.4, p. 448.

economic circumstances; or the change might have come about because the economics of family formation appeared in one light to couples dependent solely upon wage income but differently to those who had a holding or a craft workshop. If this were so, a change in the relative proportion of these two groups in the population might have resulted in the kind of change which occurred.[22] At present, however, both the proximate and more distant determinants of fertility behaviour are a matter for speculation rather than demonstration.

Comparative data on *overall* fecundity to provide a setting for those shown in figure 7.1 do not exist, but it may be of interest to consider *entry* fecundity (expressed in the form of its complement entry sterility) for a number of populations to compare with the data given in table 7.11.[23] Figure 7.2 shows such material for the reconstitution parishes over the parish register period as a whole and for six other populations which were used by Pittenger in devising his model of female sterility.[24] The data points themselves are plotted, together with linear regression line for the six other populations which makes it easier to appreciate how closely the populations resemble each other. The vertical scale is logarithmic and the scattering of individual points round the regression line suggests that the growth of sterility with age was broadly exponential in character. Given the disparate nature of the sources from which the data were drawn, the strong resemblance between them is striking. There appears to have been nothing distinctive about early modern England in respect of entry sterility. The individual reconstitution data points fall slightly below the regression line related to the other populations, but any difference is very slight.

Since overall sterility ratios are the product of entry and subsequent sterility ratios, they might be expected to provide estimates of the level of sterility invariably lower than those based on entry sterility only. In figure 7.3 the two sets of estimates are compared. The figure shows point estimates of sterility at 18.5 years, 22.5 years, and then every five years until 42.5 years, and in the case of overall sterility at 47.5 years. They represent data for the age groups 15–9, 20–4, etc. The first reading is

---

[22] This argument resembles that used by Goldstone in a similar connection; Goldstone, 'The demographic revolution in England'.

[23] Evidence that fecundity levels in early modern England were similar to those in comparable populations elsewhere may be found, however, in Knodel, *Demographic behavior in the past*, esp. ch. 10, for 14 German village populations, and for the four 'quarters' of France in Henry, 'Fécondité des mariages dans le quart sud-ouest'; Henry, 'Fécondité des mariages dans le quart sud-est'; Henry and Houdaille, 'Fécondité des mariages dans le quart nord-ouest'; and Houdaille, 'La fecondité des mariages dans le quart nord-est'.

[24] Pittenger, 'An exponential model of female sterility', tab. 2, p. 116.

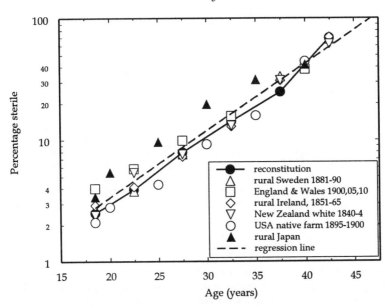

Figure 7.2   *Entry sterility: comparative data*
Sources: reconstitution data: tab. 7.13. Other data: Pittenger, 'An exponential model of
female sterility', tab. 2, p. 116.

plotted at 18.5 years since there were very few brides in the earlier part
of this age group. That there is no point at 47.5 years for entry sterility
reflects the fact that no woman in the reconstitution set contracted a first
marriage in the 45–9 age group.

Figure 7.3 reveals several points of interest. The overall sterility
estimates are slightly higher than those for entry sterility but the
differences are minor except at 37.5 and 42.5 years where the overall
sterility estimate is first significantly higher and then somewhat lower
than the entry sterility estimate. From the nature of their construction
(that is, because the figure for each age group represents the combined
experience of all the contributing age at marriage groups), the overall
sterility readings, except at the first two age points, are dominated by
the experience of women who had been married for many years and had
borne several children on average. And, whereas the entry sterility
estimates are based on progressively thinner evidence because fewer
and fewer women married for the first time with advancing age, the
overall sterility estimates are based on a steadily increasing number of
woman-years of exposure because all the data are drawn from marriages which continued until the wife was 50 or older. Given the nature
of their construction, the fact that the overall sterility estimates are so

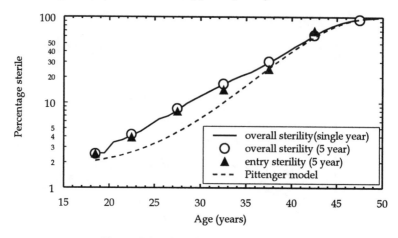

Figure 7.3   *Overall and entry sterility*

Note: the overall sterility estimates for each age group were obtained by weighting the proportions sterile in each age at marriage group by the number of woman-years lived by each age at marriage group in the age group in question in the data set as a whole.

Sources: see source note to fig. 7.2 for entry sterility and Pittenger. Overall sterility: Cambridge Group reconstitutions (overall sterility is the complement of overall fecundity).

similar to those for entry sterility again underlines the slightness of any sterility penalty attached to childbearing. Women who were long married and had already borne several children were only slightly more likely to be sterile than those recently married. And the far more extensive empirical base from which the overall sterility estimates are derived in the higher age groups makes it likely that they are a safer guide to the pattern of increasing sterility with age. The points representing overall sterility lie closer to a straight line than those of entry sterility.

The solid line in figure 7.3 represents single-year estimates of the level of overall sterility. The pattern traced out by the line is of interest in relation to the question of the relationship between advancing age and growing sterility. Pittenger considered the possibility that the process could be described by a simple exponential function but was impressed by both the evidence for a break in the sterility curves between the ages of 30 and 35 and the improbability that such a function could describe the last few years before the age of 50 since extrapolation of the exponential line would usually imply an end to all childbearing well before age 50. He opted instead for a sterility function which produces a shallow S-shaped curve flattened both at the beginning and at the end, which was intended to capture the lowest levels of sterility at each age which might be expected to occur in human populations.[25] The dotted line in figure 7.3 reproduces the outcome of his sterility model. It might be described as an attempt to model the minimum possible level of sterility implied by a mixture of empirical and theoretical considerations. The reconstitution data on overall fecundity, in contrast, suggest that the rise in sterility is well described by a simple exponential function from the youngest ages until the early 40s with a flattening of the curve only in the last few years of childbearing. Until the early 40s the straightness of the line encourages a belief that a more complex formulation is unnecessary. There is no break in the early 30s and little to suggest any flattening in its early stages, though it is proper to add that the fact that very few marriages were contracted by women in their teens means that for this part of the curve the empirical evidence is limited.

For reasons already noted, the sterility estimates for the later years of childbearing are based on a comparatively large body of data when derived from overall fecundity, whereas sterility estimates based on entry fecundity are least dependable in the later 30s and 40s since few first marriages took place in this age range. Pittenger's latest point estimates were for the age group 40–4, and centred therefore on 42.5 years.[26] The behaviour of the reconstitution line in figure 7.3 above the age of 40, therefore, may afford more reliable empirical evidence of the progress of sterility in this age range than has previously been available.[27] In view of this, it is noteworthy that from the age of 40

---

[25] Ibid., fig. 1, p. 117, and, more generally pp. 117–21.   [26] Ibid., tab. 1, p. 116.

[27] While it is unlikely that any alternative procedures would significantly change this conclusion, two points should be noted in connection with the construction of the overall sterility estimates shown in fig. 7.3. First, they reflect the method of defining the date of the onset of sterility in each woman described in pp. 361–71 above. Second, the weighting process which produced estimates for each year of age involved two short-cut procedures which fall short of the ideal. The weighting of the woman-years lived should in principle be done separately for each year of age, but the weights used were those for five-year age groups (that is the same weights were used for, say, ages 30, 31, 32, 33, and 34, with another set of weights for the next block of five years, and so on). Since the annual weights changed only slowly this simplification can have had only a marginal effect. Further, the entry sterility component in the calculation of overall sterility was also taken for five-year age groups rather than individual years. This procedure was unavoidable given the small number of marriages contracted in some of the age groups, which would have caused individual annual estimates of overall fecundity to fluctuate excessively. Fortunately, however, this procedure once again makes only a marginal difference to the outcome of the calculations. Indeed, in the later age groups, where the overall fecundity figures are dominated by experience of long-married women, any difference introduced by the use of five-year age groups is negligibly small.

upwards the Pittenger model and the reconstitution empirical data agree remarkably well.

Duration of marriage effects on fertility rates

The issues just described are closely linked to a question that has attracted attention in a number of studies of marital fertility based on parish register data. It has often been remarked that at a given age fertility was lower among women who had been long married than among those who had been married more recently. As a rough-and-ready rule it has sometimes appeared that for each additional five years of marriage fertility rates in a given age group were between 5 and 10 per cent lower. Thus ASMFRs for women who had married aged 15–9 in the age group 35–9 were to be expected to be perhaps 15 per cent lower than for those who had married aged 25–9. Neither the fecund fertility rates in table 7.7 nor the fecundity ratios in table 7.14 suggested that this pattern would be prominent in early modern England. It is no surprise, therefore, that the patterns of ASMFRs displayed in table 7.15 show only a limited duration of marriage effect, except in the period 1650–1749. The figures on the left-hand diagonal of each section of the table should be ignored since they are so heavily influenced by prenuptial conceptions. The figures in the final column of each section may also be ignored. They are based on only a few births which can result in violent but largely meaningless fluctuations in the rates. Elsewhere in the table the effect of duration of marriage, which might be expected to cause the rates to rise steadily down each column, though visible, is relatively muted and inconsistent. If rates based on fewer than 50 births are also ignored because the associated rates are likely to be unreliable (these rates are italicised in table 7.15), the average percentage rise in rates for each additional five years of marriage, holding age constant, is 4.2 per cent overall. In the three long subperiods the percentages are 2.1, 8.6, and 4.7 respectively, so that in two of the three subperiods the effect is comparatively slight.

Parity progression ratios

No discussion of fecundity would be complete without considering a different form in which the information about fecundity is often presented, the parity progression ratio. This ratio measures the proportion of cases in which at a given parity the interval following the birth of a child is closed by the birth of a further child. Thus a ratio of 0.950 at

Table 7.15 *Age-specific marital fertility rates: bachelor/spinster completed marriages (per 1 000 woman-years lived)*

Wife's age at marriage	15–9	20–4	25–9	30–4	35–9	40–4	45–9
1538–1649							
15–9	*470.1*	430.7	341.2	334.3	292.3	*116.3*	*18.9*
20–4		447.8	348.5	309.6	255.5	128.7	*20.7*
25–9			430.5	323.6	244.1	132.7	*12.5*
30–4				375.4	248.5	152.9	*33.9*
35–9					295.4	*148.5*	*4.5*
40–4						52.7	*0.0*
45–9							—
1650–1749							
15–9	*385.5*	388.3	344.4	241.1	205.3	*77.8*	*5.2*
20–4		437.3	361.6	299.7	238.7	104.2	*12.3*
25–9			409.8	306.0	229.1	120.8	*18.3*
30–4				390.5	253.9	134.5	*25.6*
35–9					299.8	128.8	*37.6*
40–4						*114.3*	*33.8*
45–9							—
1750–1837							
15–9	*616.3*	392.1	349.9	331.4	244.8	140.6	*15.4*
20–4		478.4	380.3	300.8	260.2	147.6	*22.1*
25–9			408.7	330.4	247.4	123.1	*18.6*
30–4				396.1	286.7	157.1	*29.0*
35–9					*317.9*	*206.2*	*31.1*
40–4						*175.0*	*0.0*
45–9							—
All							
15–9	484.3	399.4	345.9	298.2	238.2	114.1	*12.4*
20–4		455.0	366.6	301.8	251.0	128.6	18.3
25–9			414.8	317.7	238.2	123.8	17.5
30–4				388.1	261.5	145.3	*28.4*
35–9					302.8	148.5	*30.6*
40–4						*115.9*	*19.8*
45–9							—

Note: the italicised rates are based on fewer than 50 births.
Source: Cambridge Group reconstitutions.

parity 0 indicates that in 95 per cent of cases a marriage was followed by the birth of a child; a similar ratio at parity 1 would indicate that, following the birth of a first child, in 95 per cent of cases a second was born; and so on. At some stage in the life history of every woman, of course, an open interval must occur, when sterility supervenes. In any substantial population, the advent of sterility in individual cases ensures that each parity progression ratio (PPR) will be less than unity. Multiplying a succession of PPRs reveals what proportion of women reach a given parity. Thus, if the PPRs at parity 0, parity 1, and parity 2 were each 0.9, this would imply that approximately 73 per cent of those who married had three or more children (since $0.9 \times 0.9 \times 0.9 = 0.729$).

In their most general form PPRs are uninformative. Women of widely different ages may share the same parity but have very different chances of bearing a further child since fecundity is so closely linked to age. The point is evident if the information is set out in the form of table 7.16. This shows, for women marrying aged 20–4, how age and parity influence the ratios. The number of cases is also shown to make it clear that many of the ratios are based on very small numbers. The position is simplest in the first cell of the first row. This shows that 742.5 women were married in this age group and that of these 96.2 per cent proved fecund (this is, of course, the same figure as appears for this age at marriage group in table 7.11 for entry fecundity).[28] There being no other entry age group for this age at marriage group, this figure carries down to the bottom row as the overall ratio for parity 0. Other bottom row figures then define the progression ratios at other parities. The ratios fall slowly with parity because by, say, the fifth parity women are on average well into their 30s and the effects of the steady rise in subsequent sterility with age are increasingly felt. The PPR for this parity is 0.874. However, a glance up the column above this figure shows that it relates to women of widely differing age. A total of 529.0 women reached parity 5, of whom 74.5, or about 14 per cent, had reached this parity while still under 30, whereas at the other extreme 1 woman reached this parity when aged between 45 and 50. Differentiated by age in this way, there are striking differences in the progression ratio for parity 5. 96 per cent of those who were under 30 when reaching parity 5 went on to bear a sixth child, and almost as high a percentage of those whose fifth child was born when they were in their early 30s also progressed to a higher parity, but the comparable figure for those who had a fifth child in their early 40s fell to only 29 per cent, and the one woman who reached parity 5 in her later 40s had no further child.

Looking along the rows in the table reveals a feature that might be thought self-evident. In general the PPR rises from left to right. To reach a high parity at a relatively early age implies short birth intervals and therefore a good chance that a further birth will take place before the

---

[28] It should be noted that in tab. 7.11 the figure referred to relates to entry sterility, the complement of entry fecundity. The figure given in tab. 7.11 is 3.84 per cent: $100 - 3.84 = 96.16$.

Table 7.16 *Parity progression ratios for women marrying 20–4:*
bachelor/spinster completed marriages

				Parity				
Age	0	1	2	3	4	5	6 and over	All
20–4	0.962	0.979	0.982	1.000	1.000			0.971
25–9		0.933	0.935	0.976	0.956	0.960	1.000	0.953
30–4		0.615	0.710	0.875	0.925	0.953	0.952	0.922
35–9			0.667	0.630	0.532	0.766	0.820	0.782
40–4					0.200	0.286	0.388	0.381
45–9					0.000	0.000	0.078	0.075
All	0.962	0.963	0.932	0.940	0.878	0.874	0.694	0.863
Number of women from which the ratio was derived								
20–4	742.5	513.5	220.5	39.5	4.0			1 520.0
25–9		194.0	414.5	419.0	229.0	74.5	20.0	1 351.0
30–4		6.5	46.5	159.5	285.5	287.0	324.0	1 109.0
35–9			6.0	23.0	77.0	145.5	664.5	916.0
40–4					5.0	21.0	438.5	464.5
45–9					2.0	1.0	64.0	67.0
All	742.5	714.0	687.5	641.0	602.5	529.0	1 511.0	5 427.5

Source: Cambridge Group reconstitutions.

onset of sterility. The ratios in the final column show the progression
ratio for each age group irrespective of parity. They bear a general
resemblance to the measure of subsequent fecundity given in table 7.13.
An identity is not to be expected, however, since subsequent fecundity
is a measure of the proportion of all woman-years lived in a given age
group which is lived by fecund women, whereas the parity progression
ratio for a given age group measures the proportion of all births
occurring in the age group which is followed by a subsequent birth to
the same woman.

In exceptional circumstances the two different methods of measurement may lead to widely different figures for the same age group. For
example, if 10 per cent of women in a given age at marriage group had a
child in the 45–9 age group and in each case the child was born on the
46th birthday of the woman but none of them went on to bear a further
child at a still higher age, the parity progression ratio for the age group
45–9 would be 0.000. The subsequent fecundity measure for the same
women, however, would be 0.0475 since, allowing for the estimated 16.5
months of fecundity following the birth of the last child, each of the

women who bore a child would be fecund for 28.5 months out of the 60 months in the age group $(0.0475 = (28.5/60) \times 0.1)$. If, however, 20 per cent of the women in question had gone on to bear a further child, the parity progression ratio would be 0.200 rather than 0.000, whereas the subsequent fecundity ratio would rise only modestly on this revised assumption, the extent of the rise depending on the timing of the later births.

It would be possible to provide an analysis like that in table 7.16 for each age at marriage group and for each major subperiod, but this would occupy much space and might bring only limited additional insight into the history of fertility in pre-industrial England. In table 7.17, however, some additional PPR material is set out. In the upper panel of the table each row shows the PPR for all women of a given parity and age, whatever their age at marriage. The figures in the first column are, of course, identical to the entry fecundity figures implied by the entry sterility proportions given in table 7.11. In the lower panel of the table the ratios equivalent to those given on the bottom line of the top panel are given for each subperiod. Since the data in table 7.17 recapitulate fecundity data given in a different guise previously, additional comment is unnecessary.

Particular influences on fertility characteristics

Fertility and mortality

There are several sources of difficulty in making an assessment of fecundity and fertility change over time because of the influence of factors which distort apparently 'pure' measures. One of these is infant mortality. There was a large difference between the average birth interval that occurred if the previous child in the family had died as an infant and that occurring when the previous child survived. The chance of a new conception taking place was greatly reduced while a child was being suckled. If, therefore, the child at breast died, the next conception usually happened sooner than would otherwise have been the case. This phenomenon is discussed further below.[29] Here it is sufficient to note that the average length of the birth interval following an infant death was more than 8 months shorter than when the preceding child did not die.[30]

An apparent fall in age-specific fertility, therefore, in an era of falling infant mortality is consonant with an unchanging 'real' fertility once the fall in the latter has been taken into account. The point is important since

[29] See below pp. 438–46.   [30] See tab. 7.35, pp. 438–9.

Table 7.17 *Parity progression ratios: bachelor/spinster completed marriages*

	Parity							
Age	0	1	2	3	4	5	6 and over	All
15–9	0.974	0.988	1.000					0.980
20–4	0.962	0.980	0.977	0.970	0.885	1.000		0.970
25–9	0.921	0.944	0.945	0.972	0.955	0.941	0.951	0.946
30–4	0.856	0.916	0.880	0.915	0.925	0.948	0.952	0.917
35–9	0.757	0.772	0.727	0.734	0.689	0.810	0.819	0.778
40–4	0.307	0.357	0.346	0.333	0.369	0.411	0.382	0.376
45–9	0.000	0.250	0.000	0.167	0.219	0.051	0.106	0.107
All	0.900	0.926	0.888	0.876	0.818	0.814	0.668	0.832
Subperiods (all ages)								
1538–1649	0.911	0.926	0.910	0.869	0.821	0.802	0.659	0.846
1650–1749	0.885	0.914	0.873	0.854	0.804	0.785	0.640	0.823
1750–1837	0.917	0.944	0.894	0.908	0.832	0.848	0.691	0.835

Source: Cambridge Group reconstitutions.

infant mortality rose somewhat in England during the seventeenth century and then fell markedly in the course of the eighteenth century. To estimate trends in 'pure' fertility, therefore, entails taking cognisance of this effect.[31] Similarly, in comparing the marital fertility rates of a parish in which infant mortality was very low, such as Hartland, with a parish like Gainsborough where the infant mortality rate was more than twice as high, the relationship between high infant mortality and relatively short birth intervals should be borne in mind. The order of magnitude of the effect depends, of course, on the extent of any difference in infant mortality. For example, in a parish in which the infant mortality rate was 300 per 1000, and in which the birth interval following an infant death was 24 months, but was otherwise 32 months, the average birth interval would be 4 per cent shorter on average than in a parish where the same birth intervals were found, but in which the infant death rate was 150 per 1000. A fall in the infant death rate from 200 to 150 per 1000 (which is comparable to that which occurred in

---

[31] Furthermore, it is also important to consider this point when making any comparison between fertility in England and fertility in most parts of continental Europe in the early modern period. English fertility rates were usually lower than those found elsewhere, but any difference is partly a function of the fact that infant mortality rates were generally lower, and often much lower than on the continent.

England between the early eighteenth and early nineteenth centuries), on the same assumptions, would cause a rise in the average birth interval of 1.3 per cent.

The assumptions embodied in the calculation in the last paragraph are, however, over simple. For example, when an infant death occurred but the child was the last in the family, there was no subsequent birth interval to be affected. This suggests that the effect on fertility of changes in infant mortality rates will be overstated by the method described.[32] Other developments in infant mortality may also in principle affect any correction process. In the eighteenth century, for example, there was a major decline in mortality within the first month of life but not later in the first year. Such a change will slightly increase the average length of the subsequent birth interval compared with a preceding period in which the proportion of early deaths was higher, though the effect is minor.[33] The order of magnitude of the effect of changes in the level of infant mortality may be captured, however, by the method used to construct the data given in table 7.18.

Table 7.18 lists age-specific marital fertility rates for each of the three long subperiods used in this analysis of the fertility. The rates refer to all marriages in which the age of the mother and the date of the end of the marriage are known. One set of rates shows conventional 'uncorrected' ASMFRs. In the other, the 'corrected' rates are always lower because, whenever a child died under the age of 1 year and there was a subsequent birth in the family, 8 months has been added to the exposure for that family. In other words, the interval following the death of an infant has been increased to equal that which would have prevailed if the child had not died. This is an artificial procedure in that, in a small proportion of cases, there might have been no subsequent child if the earlier child had not died because the woman would have become sterile in the additional period of time. But, though artificial, the procedure does permit the effect of changing levels of infant mortality to be assessed.

To make the comparison simple, in the lower panel of the table the rates are shown in an indexed form with the rate in 1650–1749, the period of lowest fertility, used as a base. It can be seen that, if an allowance is made for the effect of changing levels of infant mortality,

---

[32] But the issue is further complicated by the fact that in a proportion of cases an infant death occurring towards the end of the fertile period may, by the forced ending of breastfeeding, cause a woman to conceive again and produce a further child, where she would have failed to conceive again if the child had not died, because she had become sterile before the end of the period of breastfeeding.   [33] See below, pp. 440–1.

Table 7.18 *Age-specific marital fertility rates with and without correction for the effects of infant mortality (per 1000 woman-years lived)*

	Uncorrected			Corrected		
Age	Up to 1649	1650–1749	1750 and after	Up to 1649	1650–1749	1750 and after
15–9	376.6	339.4	501.0	369.6	328.6	486.1
20–4	405.6	404.2	422.1	392.6	390.3	411.1
25–9	372.6	360.8	373.8	361.1	350.2	363.9
30–4	325.0	312.5	309.0	316.6	304.8	302.7
35–9	258.2	242.9	248.3	253.8	238.1	244.1
40–4	137.8	120.9	139.4	136.7	120.0	138.3
45–9	20.3	22.3	21.6	20.3	22.3	21.6
Indexed 1650–1749 = 100						
15–9	111.0	100	147.6	112.5	100	147.9
20–4	100.3	100	104.4	100.6	100	105.3
25–9	103.3	100	103.6	103.1	100	103.9
30–4	104.0	100	98.9	103.9	100	99.3
35–9	106.3	100	102.2	106.6	100	102.5
40–4	114.0	100	115.3	113.9	100	115.3
45–9	91.0	100	96.9	91.0	100	96.9

Note: for explanation of the difference between uncorrected and corrected see text.
Source: Cambridge Group reconstitutions.

the rise in fertility between the middle and later periods is emphasised, but only slightly. The effect is most marked in the younger age groups and eventually disappears with increasing age since the proportion of last births in the total rises steadily with age. The slightness of the changes shown in the indexed figures is, however, somewhat misleading. The very long subperiods used in the table tend to mask the extent of the fall in infant mortality. The legitimate infant mortality rate fell between the middle and the final period from 182.5 to 150.4 per 1000.[34] But the fall from the decades of peak infant mortality in the late seventeenth and early eighteenth centuries to its lowest point early in the nineteenth century was twice as great. When, therefore, the indexed numbers in table 7.18 show, for example, that, whereas the apparent rise in the ASMFR between the middle and later periods for women aged 20–4 was 4.4 per cent, and the rise taking infant mortality into account

[34] Tab. 6.1, p. 215.

was 5.3 per cent, it should be borne in mind that from peak to trough of infant mortality the 'true' rise was over 6 per cent and the distorting effect of infant mortality on the ASMFR is no longer trivial, though still small.

The examination of the effect of changing levels of infant mortality on fertility is an instance of the ways in which mortality influenced fertility in the past. But it is neither the only instance nor necessarily the most important. A large proportion of women, especially of women who married young, did not survive in marriage to the end of the childbearing period and yet bore many of the children who enter into the measures of marital fertility that are most widely employed. If the only difference between women who did and did not survive in marriage to 50 lay in the mere fact of their survival or failure to survive, the picture painted for women who completed their fertility histories in marriage might stand for the community as a whole. Clearly, however, it is entirely possible that marriages which ended early displayed characteristic differences from those which endured longer. For example, if ill health on the part of either spouse both contributed to an early end to the marriage and reduced the fertility of the couple in the years before the end of the marriage, the fertility characteristics of the community as a whole would be different from those of the fortunate couples whose marriages lasted a long time.

Table 7.19 suggests at first blush that this is an issue of importance. Age-specific fertility rates of women whose marriages lasted throughout the childbearing period were generally, though not invariably, higher than those whose marriages were brought to an earlier end by the death of one or other partner. It will be obvious that in the later age groups the proportion of all years lived in marriage that were lived by women who survived in marriage to age 50 or more will be much higher than in the younger age groups. To emphasise the extent of the change in the relative proportions of the two types of women in each age group, the table also shows the numbers of years lived in marriage by the 'survivors' and the others in each age group.

In most age at marriage groups ASMFRs were lower where the marriage was broken early than when it lasted throughout the wife's childbearing life. In the two age at marriage groups 25–9 and 35–9 this was not the case, but elsewhere, apart from several instances in the 45–9 column, the ratio of the rate in the top panel to the comparable rate in the lower panel was almost always below unity. Excluding the cells in the 45–9 column, and the diagonal rates, where the level of prenuptial pregnancy was so influential, the 'incomplete' rates in the other 15 cells were between 3 and 4 per cent lower on average than the equivalent 'completed' rates. The difference is not marked, but might be taken to be significant.

One obvious possible explanation of these differences, for example, is that the lower rates found in incomplete marriages were a result of a decline in fertility in the years immediately preceding the end of a marriage when the woman or her husband might have suffered from declining health, later leading to death. To test this possibility ASMFRs were calculated for incomplete marriages *excluding* the last five years of each such marriage. The resulting rates, however, are lower rather than higher than the 'full' rates. For the age groups 15–9 to 40–4 (there is, of course, no rate for 45–9 if the last five years of observation are excluded) the rates for marriages if the last five years in observation were ignored, expressed as a percentage of the 'full' rate, were 95.5, 98.1, 97.3, 97.1, 97.9, and 98.9 respectively. Clearly, therefore, the explanation cannot lie in a lowering of fertility in the years immediately prior to the end of the marriage.

The issue cannot be further explored in exactly the same way as for the discussion of fertility in completed marriages, because neither fecund fertility nor subsequent fecundity can be calculated for incomplete marriages. However, an exercise that is closely equivalent is possible, since birth interval data provide information similar to that obtained from fecund fertility rates. Table 7.20 shows the birth intervals found in the two classes of marriages.

Comparison of cells in the same location in the two matrices shows that there is no consistent tendency for either set of birth intervals to be the shorter of the two. Summary measures of the two data sets are bound to be somewhat arbitrary. The birth interval means on the diagonals are best ignored since they are heavily affected by the scale of prenuptial pregnancy, and the means in the higher age groups are volatile because they are based on small numbers of births. However, 87.9 per cent of all birth intervals in the completed marriages and 95.9 per cent of all intervals in the incomplete marriages are concentrated in the 10 cells of ages up to 40 discounting the cells on the diagonals. The means in the 10 cells can be weighted to produce a single mean figure either by the relative number of birth intervals in each of the 10 cells in the completed marriage set, or by the comparable relative totals among the incomplete marriages. The latter procedure, of course, gives a greater weight to the means in the younger age groups.[35]

If the weighting is based on completed marriage data, the mean

[35] In the nature of the case there must be a higher proportion of all birth intervals in the younger age group in incomplete than in completed marriages. See the lower panels of tab. 7.19.

Table 7.19 *Age-specific marital fertility rates of completed and incomplete marriages: bachelor/spinster marriages (per 1000 woman-years lived)*

Rates

Wife's age at marriage	Age						
	15–9	20–4	25–9	30–4	35–9	40–4	45–9
Wife aged less than 50 at end of marriage							
15–9	384.9	356.3	296.9	269.5	180.4	90.0	21.6
20–4		423.3	351.6	298.9	220.5	120.5	23.2
25–9			433.6	348.8	279.1	150.0	46.4
30–4				357.4	263.1	135.7	28.5
35–9					365.2	168.8	111.1
40–4						189.8	45.4
45–9							123.1
All	384.9	395.7	361.7	317.7	244.6	131.9	36.6
Wife aged more than 50 at end of marriage							
15–9	484.3	399.4	345.9	298.2	238.2	114.1	12.4
20–4		455.0	366.6	301.8	251.0	128.6	18.3
25–9			414.8	317.7	238.2	123.8	17.5
30–4				388.1	261.5	145.3	28.4
35–9					302.8	148.5	30.6
40–4						115.9	19.8
45–9							0.0
All	484.3	436.6	376.7	315.5	249.6	129.6	19.9
Combined rate	407.4	410.4	368.2	316.6	247.6	130.2	21.6

Woman-years lived

Wife's age at marriage	Age						
	15–9	20–4	25–9	30–4	35–9	40–4	45–9
Wife aged less than 50 at end of marriage							
15–9	698.9	1895.8	1485.5	1100.0	720.7	389.1	138.9
20–4		2709.5	4634.1	3412.4	2356.3	1323.2	432.0
25–9			1986.8	2771.1	1868.8	1066.5	301.5
30–4				777.7	910.5	489.9	175.5
35–9					180.7	207.3	63.0
40–4						42.2	33.0
45–9							16.2
All	698.9	4605.3	8106.4	8061.3	6036.9	3518.2	1160.1

Table 7.19 *(cont.)*

Woman-years lived

Wife's age at marriage	Age						
	15–9	20–4	25–9	30–4	35–9	40–4	45–9
Wife aged 50 or more at end of marriage							
15–9	204.4	850.0	850.0	850.0	850.0	850.0	850.0
20–4		1 717.7	3 712.5	3 712.5	3 712.5	3 712.5	3 712.5
25–9			1 676.7	3 025.0	3 025.0	3 025.0	3 025.0
30–4				809.1	1 480.0	1 480.0	1 480.0
35–9					401.3	670.0	670.0
40–4						138.1	252.5
45–0							19.9
All	204.4	2 567.7	6 239.2	8 396.6	9 468.8	9 875.6	10 009.9
Combined total	903.3	7 173.0	14 345.7	16 457.9	15 505.8	13 393.7	11 170.1

Source: Cambridge Group reconstitutions.

interval in completed marriages is 32.0 months and in incomplete marriages 31.4 months. If the weighting is based on data from incomplete marriages, the means are 31.3 and 30.8 months respectively. The ratio of the mean for incomplete to the mean for completed marriages is 0.981 in the former case, 0.984 in the latter case. It is clear that the birth intervals of the two types of marriage were very similar, but that if anything the mean was *shorter* rather than longer in incomplete marriages. This is equivalent, in terms of the earlier analysis of fertility, to showing that the fertility of fecund women was slightly higher in incomplete marriages than in completed marriages, and suggests that there must have been substantial differences either in entry or in subsequent fecundity to account for the observed differences in fertility rates.

In table 7.21 the entry sterility percentages for each age at marriage group are shown for completed and incomplete marriages. Calculating the former presents no problem since in every completed marriage it is clear whether the couple were fecund or not. Calculating the latter is less straightforward since many incomplete marriages ended childless, but before it was clear whether the couple were sterile. Accordingly, the percentages for incomplete marriages in table 7.21 refer only to marriages which lasted for 10 years or more, a period long enough to make it very improbable that a first child would be born at some later date. This explains why it is that there are no incomplete marriages after

Table 7.20 *Birth intervals in completed and incomplete marriages: bachelor/spinster marriages (months; birth intervals classified by midpoint of birth interval)*

Wife's age at marriage	Age							
	15–9	20–4	25–9	30–4	35–9	40–4	45–9	All
Wife aged less than 50 at end of marriage								
15–9	15.6	28.1	31.3	31.9	35.5	36.1	—	27.1
20–4		17.6	29.3	32.6	34.4	38.1	30.1	26.5
25–9			18.2	30.4	32.9	36.4	32.9	25.7
30–4				19.0	31.0	32.6	14.6	23.9
35–9					19.2	35.1	44.6	22.9
40–4						15.6	9.9	15.3
45–9							8.0	8.0
All	15.6	20.8	25.6	29.7	32.3	35.5	28.0	26.2
Wife aged 50 or more at end of marriage								
15–9	12.7	27.4	31.4	30.9	33.1	35.3	46.3	28.5
20–4		17.4	29.6	33.5	33.9	36.8	44.0	29.0
25–9			18.6	31.8	35.3	37.3	38.2	28.8
30–4				19.0	33.6	35.0	44.9	27.7
35–9					20.4	34.3	46.8	25.5
40–4						22.1	63.0	26.0
All	12.7	20.0	25.9	30.5	33.2	36.0	43.8	28.7

Source: Cambridge Group reconstitutions.

the 35–9 age group. It is immediately clear that a substantial part of the differences between the fertility of completed and incomplete marriages, visible in table 7.19, can be attributed to differences in entry sterility, even though its measurement presents some problems where incomplete marriages are concerned. In the age at marriage groups in which the fertility of completed marriages is higher than that of incomplete marriages, the entry sterility of the former is the lower of the two, while the reverse is the case in age at marriage groups in which the fertility of incomplete marriages is the higher of the two.

It is noteworthy that if the entry sterility percentages are cumulated and standardised, the differences between completed and incomplete marriages become trivial. For example, in the 35–9 age group, the last for which there are entry sterility percentages in both categories, the proportion of all the women in the age group, irrespective of their age at marriage, who were sterile at marriage, was 8.01 per cent in completed

Table 7.21 *Entry sterility in completed and incomplete marriages:*
bachelor/spinster marriages

(1) Wife aged less than 50 at end of marriage.
(2) Wife aged 50 or more at end of marriage.

Wife's age at marriage	(1)	(2)	(3) (1) – (2)
Percentages			
15–9	7.80	2.65	15.15
20–4	6.15	3.84	2.31
25–9	4.47	7.93	–3.46
30–4	19.91	14.36	5.55
35–9	0.00	24.25	–24.25
40–4		69.31	
45–9		100.00	
Totals			
15–9	282.0	170.0	
20–4	666.5	742.5	
25–9	380.0	605.0	
30–4	110.5	296.0	
35–9	16.5	134.0	
40–4			
45–9			

Note: in incomplete marriages (where the marriage ended before the wife reached her 50th birthday) only marriages which lasted at least 10 years were taken into account. If such a marriage were childless the couple were taken to be sterile.
Source: Cambridge Group reconstitutions.

marriages and 7.72 per cent in incomplete marriages . This calculation is made by weighting the entry sterility percentages for each age at marriage group by the percentage of woman-years lived by all women of that age at marriage group in the age group 35–9. In spite of the volatility of the estimated sterility percentages for the successive age at marriage groups in incomplete marriages, therefore, it seems likely that entry sterility was not significantly different in the two types of marriage.

A simple way in which to picture the influence of entry sterility on the overall ASMFRs is to calculate a TMFR for each age at marriage group and to express the difference between age at marriage TMFRs for completed and incomplete marriages as a ratio figure. For the successive age at marriage groups 15–9 to 35–9 in table 7.19, the ratio of the incomplete to complete TMFRs is 0.839, 0.940, 1.108, 0.952, and 1.181

respectively.[36] The effect of entry sterility can then be removed by recalculating the rates as if there were no entry sterility in either set of women. If this is done, the ratios change to 0.887, 0.964, 1.069, 1.017, and 0.896. The first set of ratios differ from unity on average by 0.112, the latter by 0.068, so that correcting for differences in entry sterility reduces by 40 per cent the difference in fertility between completed and incomplete marriages. In the three age at marriage groups which are numerically dominant (20–4, 25–9, and 30–4), the ratios are on average very close to unity. This is to be expected in view of the close similarity in the birth interval data for the two groups of women.

If it is acceptable to argue that the differences in entry sterility which caused the ASMFR differences conceal underlying similarities between complete and incomplete marriages, even in respect of entry sterility, then it would seem, upon deeper examination, that there is little firm evidence that the fertility of incomplete marriages was significantly different from that of completed marriages. And, if this is so, the fuller analysis of fertility and fecundity that is feasible in relation to the latter, may reasonably be thought to hold true also for the former.

The fertility of different marriage rank combinations

We have concentrated so far exclusively upon the history of bachelor/spinster marriages, always by far the commonest type of marriage, as the type of marriage into which the great majority of all children were born. But many marriages fell outside this category, of course. Were the fertility characteristics of these marriages different from those of bachelor/spinster marriages? The question is most conveniently tackled by considering completed marriages since any differences in ASMFRs can then be analysed in terms of fecund fertility, entry fecundity, and subsequent fecundity. This clarity is bought, however, at the cost of working with a relatively restricted empirical base. Indeed completed bachelor/widow and widower/widow marriages were too few in number to provide an adequate basis for other than a rather impressionistic treatment.

Table 7.22 shows the ASMFRs and TMFRs for the four main categories of marriage rank combinations. Rates are given only when in any given age at marriage group the number of woman-years lived

---

[36] These are based on the TMFRs 15–44 rather than 15–49 to avoid the volatility of the rates in the age group 45–9 which, in the case of incomplete marriages, are derived from very few marriages.

exceeds 50 in at least one cell. Substantial differences are visible in the rates. Marriages between widowers and spinsters (2+/1) in most age at marriage groups had lower fertility than those between bachelors and spinsters (1/1). In the 15–9 age at marriage group the difference is very marked. In the few cells providing rates for bachelor/widow marriages (1/2+) and widower/widow (2+/2+) marriages, the rates do not differ markedly or consistently from the 1/1 rates. However, the column which shows the number of FRFs on which the rates are based immediately suggests great caution in drawing any conclusions about systematic differences between the four marriage rank combination groups. A review of the fecund fertility, entry fecundity, and subsequent fecundity characteristics of the four groups tends to underline the danger of believing that the ASMFR differences are 'real'.

Consider first fecund fertility. In table 7.23 some summary data giving the total fecund marital fertility rates (TFMFRs) for age at marriage groups from 15–9 to 35–9 are set out. They are based on the same women as those whose ASMFRs were given in table 7.22. Each figure relates to the cumulative fertility of a particular age at marriage group, excluding the rate for the 45–9 age group. Even in a large population this rate is based on a very small number of woman-years in observation. In a small population the observational base is tiny and the rate therefore volatile.[37] Given the small empirical base for the TFMFRs apart from those for 1/1 marriages, the very close grouping of the rates strongly suggests that there were no substantial or consistent differences in fecund fertility between the different age at marriage groups.

Entry fecundity and subsequent fecundity are described in table 7.24. The entry fecundity ratios underline the dangers of basing an analysis on small numbers of cases. For example, the figure of 0.7000 for 2+/1 marriages in the age at marriage group 15–9 arises because 3 women out of the 10 in this group did not have any children. It is little wonder that the ASMFRs for this group of women were much lower than that of the 170 women in their 1/1 equivalents. Given the slim evidential base, however, it is probably reasonable to conclude that there was little difference in entry fecundity by marriage rank combination.

The subsequent fecundity ratios for each age group are weighted averages of the individual age at marriage ratios. Once again, it is well to be cautious in making inferences from the data because, at least for 1/2+ and 2+/2+ marriages, the numbers involved are very small. Yet there is a

---

[37] In some instances, indeed, there were no years in observation of women still fecund in the 45–9 age group.

Table 7.22 Age-specific marital fertility rates by marriage rank combinations (per 1000 woman-years lived: completed marriages only)

Bachelor/spinster: 1/1. Bachelor/widow: 1/2+. Widower/spinster: 2+/1. Widower/widow: 2+/2+.

Wife's age at marriage	Marriage rank combination	ASMFR							TMFR 15–49	Number of FRFs from which data taken
		15–9	20–4	25–9	30–4	35–9	40–4	45–9		
15–9	1/1	484.3	399.4	345.9	298.2	238.2	114.1	12.4	9.46	170.0
	2+/1	308.3	340.0	200.0	160.0	100.0	20.0	0.0	5.64	10.0
	1/2+									
	2+/2+									
20–4	1/1		455.0	366.6	301.8	251.0	128.6	18.3	7.61	742.5
	2+/1		359.6	371.9	301.8	231.6	115.8	28.1	7.04	28.5
	1/2+									
	2+/2+									
25–9	1/1			414.8	317.7	238.2	123.8	17.5	5.56	605.0
	2+/1			393.4	296.1	186.3	90.2	11.8	4.89	51.0
	1/2+			435.6	400.0	327.3	109.1	0.0	6.36	11.0
	2+/2+									
30–4	1/1				388.0	261.5	145.3	28.4	4.12	296.0
	2+/1				389.8	295.1	153.7	24.4	4.32	41.0
	1/2+				409.9	322.6	148.4	51.6	4.66	31.0
	2+/2+									

414

35–9	1/1					302.8	148.5	30.6	2.41	134.0
	2+/1					284.5	163.0	9.9	2.29	40.5
	1/2+					273.3	157.6	18.2	2.25	33.0
	2+/2+					320.9	120.0	0.0	2.20	10.0
40–4	1/1						115.9	19.8	0.68	50.5
	2+/1						183.5	78.9	1.31	35.5
	1/2+						257.2	48.7	1.53	18.5
	2+/2+						83.6	0.0	0.42	21.5
All	1/1	484.3	436.6	376.7	315.5	249.6	129.6	19.9		
	2+/1	308.3	351.0	353.9	301.6	231.7	129.4	26.0		
	1/2+		386.5	513.1	401.8	310.8	161.4	30.4		
	2+/2+			271.0	443.3	284.9	151.7	0.0		

Note: where, in a particular cell, the woman-years in observation were fewer than 50, no rate has been given for that cell, since such slim evidence is apt to result in misleading figures. This gives rise to apparent anomalies, such as two rates appearing in the 'All' panel on the 2+/2+ line for which there are no matching cells in the individual age at marriage panels, or a rate in the 'All' panel which is higher or lower than any of the component rates in the upper panels. If fuller details had been given, however, these anomalies would disappear.

Source: Cambridge Group reconstitutions.

415

Table 7.23 *Total fecund marital fertility rates (to age 44)*

Bachelor/spinster: 1/1. Bachelor/widow: 1/2+. Widower/spinster: 2+/1. Widower/widow: 2+/2+.

Marriage rank	Wife's age at marriage				
	15–9	20–4	25–9	30–4	35–9
1/1	11.96	9.67	7.53	5.80	3.79
2+/1	11.71	9.64	7.50	5.82	4.00
1/2+			7.71	6.06	4.12
2+/2+					4.24

Source: Cambridge Group reconstitutions.

Table 7.24 *Entry and subsequent fecundity by marriage rank combinations*

Bachelor/spinster: 1/1. Bachelor/widow: 1/2+. Widower/spinster: 2+/1. Widower/widow: 2+/2+.

Age	Entry fecundity Marriage rank combinations				Weighted subsequent fecundity Marriage rank combinations			
	1/1	2+/1	1/2+	2+/2+	1/1	2+/1	1/2+	2+/2+
15–9	0.9735	0.7000			1.0000	1.0000		
20–4	0.9616	0.9649	1.0000	1.0000	0.9914	0.9568	1.0000	1.0000
25–9	0.9207	0.8824	1.0000	0.0000	0.9615	0.9082	1.0000	1.0000
30–4	0.8564	0.8781	0.8710	1.0000	0.8902	0.8472	0.9007	0.9980
35–9	0.7575	0.7284	0.6667	0.6000	0.7566	0.6724	0.8178	0.9706
40–4	0.3069	0.4789	0.5135	0.1860	0.4224	0.3537	0.4653	0.8673
45–9	0.0000	0.0000	0.0500	0.0000	0.0716	0.0557	0.0496	0.0746

	N			
15–9	170.0	10.0		
20–4	742.5	28.5	4.5	1.0
25–9	605.0	51.0	11.0	1.0
30–4	296.0	41.0	31.0	9.0
35–9	134.0	40.5	33.0	10.0
40–4	50.5	35.5	18.5	21.5
45–9	9.0	16.5	20.0	22.5
All	2 007.0	223.0	118.0	65.0

Note: the subsequent fecundity ratios were obtained by weighting the ratio for each age at marriage group contributing to a particular age group by the number of woman-years lived in the age group by the age at marriage group in question.

Source: Cambridge Group reconstitutions.

hint of a pattern here that would repay further investigation when a larger body of information is available for analysis. Comparison of the 1/1 and 2+/1 columns suggests that in widower/spinster marriages, when the husband was substantially older than his wife, the marriage became sterile earlier than when they were of like age or when the husband was the younger of the two, as would be the case in the other marriage rank combinations.

To summarise, there is no ground for supposing that fecund fertility differed between the four marriage rank combinations. Nor is it clear that there were consistent differences in entry fecundity between them, though, because of effects attributable to the small number of cases involved, the ratios for the different age at marriage groups sometimes vary widely on the same line. When a single indicator of entry fecundity is calculated for each marriage rank combination as a weighted average using data from each age group, any differences are much reduced. The fluctuations from one marriage rank combination to another in entry fecundity by age at marriage were sufficient, however, to produce substantial differences in ASMFRs in some instances. With subsequent fecundity the case may have been different. Pending the accumulation of a larger body of data to settle the matter, the evidence of table 7.24 provides reason to think that in 2+/1 marriages where the husband was, on average, considerably older than his wife, subsequent fecundity declined more rapidly than in any of the other three marriage rank combinations where the spouses were close to one another in age or where the husband was the younger of the two.

Fertility and age difference between spouses

The question of the effect on fertility of the age gap between spouses can, of course, be examined directly. Since, once again, it is valuable to be able to separate out the constituent elements determining ASMFRs, the appropriate data set for this purpose is all completed 1/1 marriages, but their number in this instance is reduced compared with similar earlier exercises because the age of the husband as well as the wife must be known. This cuts the total of FRFs by about a half. All such marriages were divided into four groups: where the husband was younger than his wife; where he was the older by 0–4 years; where he was the older by 5–9 years; and where he was the older by a still wider margin.

In table 7.25 the TMFRs of the different age gap categories are given for the age at marriage groups from 15–9 to 30–4.[38] Two sets of TMFRs

---

[38] Above the age of 35 there were no marriages in the category in which the husband is more than 10 years older than his wife.

Table 7.25 *Age gap between spouses and total marital fertility rates*
(to age 49)

(1) Husband younger than wife.
(2) Husband older than wife by 0–4 years.
(3) Husband older than wife by 5–9 years.
(4) Husband older than wife by 10 years or more.

Wife's age at marriage	Based on all age groups				Based on all age groups except the entry age group			
	(1)	(2)	(3)	(4)	(1)	(2)	(3)	(4)
Bachelor/spinster completed marriages								
15–9	11.20	9.70	10.15	*8.43*	*5.20*	*7.19*	*7.80*	*5.83*
20–4	7.89	7.50	7.50	6.06	5.57	5.23	5.04	3.76
25–9	6.03	5.95	5.84	4.42	3.85	3.73	3.66	2.40
30–4	4.51	4.48	*3.00*	*3.52*	2.35	2.33	*1.27*	*2.00*
Completed and incomplete marriages combined, all marriage rank combinations								
15–9	11.71	9.53	9.39	7.28	7.05	7.24	7.29	5.56
20–4	7.91	7.23	7.58	5.63	5.67	5.06	5.17	3.73
25–9	6.20	5.91	5.78	4.42	3.98	3.68	3.77	2.39
30–4	4.44	3.88	4.01	2.87	2.38	2.04	2.12	1.30

Note: the italicised rates were based on data drawn from fewer than 10 FRFs.
Source: Cambridge Group reconstitutions.

are shown in the two panels: for all age groups, and for all except the entry age group. The latter measure has the advantage of eliminating any possible influence from differing levels of prenuptially conceived first births. Where the data were drawn from fewer than 10 FRFs the rates are shown in italics.[39] The upper panel consists of the rates for 1/1 completed marriages. The lower panel shows the rates for all marriages, whether completed or not and for all marriage rank combinations: it is based on a much bigger empirical base, many times larger in the younger age groups where completed families are swamped by incomplete, and about three times as large even in the highest age group 45–9. The reason for including both was to test how representative the restricted data set is. If the two are similar, it is reasonable to think that any differences in the three underlying fertility variables that determine the ASMFRs in the restricted set would also apply to age gap fertility differences generally.

[39] See tab. 7.26 for the totals of marriages in each age at marriage group.

The first point to note is that the TMFRs in the larger data set, though normally slightly lower than in the restricted set, display a very similar pattern, and it is probable that any analytical features that hold good in the restricted set will also be true of the larger one. Secondly, marital fertility was broadly similar in the categories shown in the first three columns of each segment of the table, though in general the rates declined slightly from left to right. But fertility was considerably lower in the fourth column, consisting of marriages in which the husband was much older than his wife. It seems clear, therefore, that a large positive age gap between husband and wife was associated with lower marital fertility. It remains to determine in what proportion this was due to differences in fecund marital fertility, entry fecundity, and subsequent fecundity.

Table 7.26 provides information about the components of marital fertility to enable this question to be answered. The entry fecundity ratios in the first panel are based on small numbers in the case of the third and fourth columns but both these data and also the weighted figures in the second panel suggest that there was little difference in entry fecundity between the different age gap classes. The same is broadly true of fecund marital fertility. All three of the TFMFRs shown in the lower part of the fourth panel tend to support the conclusion that fecund marital fertility was somewhat lower where husbands were much older than their wives than in the other age gap classes. But the difference was moderate, of the order of 5–10 per cent depending upon which summary measure is used and with which other class the comparison is made. There is also a hint that fecund fertility was highest where the husband was the younger of the two and that it then fell off slightly in the next two categories, where he was 0–4 and where he was 5–9 years the elder, but the differences are quite modest.

There was, however, a much more decided difference between the fourth category and the other three in subsequent fecundity. The first three categories show essentially the same pattern but in the fourth category the ratio falls off more sharply with age of wife. Above the age of 30 the difference was marked and appears to have been progressive. This mirrors the finding in the previous section, devoted to marriage rank combinations, and suggests that the reason for the lower marital fertility in widower/spinster marriages is to be sought in the age difference between them. It is, of course, a corollary of a large age gap between spouses that women in their 30s and 40s were married to men in late middle life or older. Age of husband may therefore have been the key factor. The evidential base is slim and the finding about the effect of a wide positive age gap between spouses will not be fully established

Table 7.26 Age gap between spouses and fecund marital fertility, entry fecundity, and subsequent fecundity

(1) Husband younger than wife.
(2) Husband older than wife by 0–4 years.
(3) Husband older than wife by 5–9 years.
(4) Husband older than wife by 10 years or more.

Wife's age	Entry fecundity (1)	(2)	(3)	(4)	Weighted entry fecundity (1)	(2)	(3)	(4)	Subsequent fecundity (1)	(2)	(3)	(4)	Fecund marital fertility rate[a] (1)	(2)	(3)	(4)
15–9	0.8000	0.9783	1.0000	1.0000	0.8000	0.9783	1.0000	1.0000	1.0000	1.0000	1.0000	1.0000	1283.8	515.5	471.5	519.9
20–4	0.9398	0.9614	0.9714	0.9630	0.8927	0.9671	0.9811	0.9754	1.0000	0.9891	0.9958	0.9951	485.1	459.0	471.1	428.0
25–9	0.9371	0.9415	0.8857	0.9000	0.9196	0.9584	0.9523	0.9511	0.9861	0.9577	0.9747	0.9120	434.2	399.4	381.1	395.6
30–4	0.9268	0.8462	0.7343	0.7500	0.9231	0.9449	0.9206	0.9236	0.9270	0.8825	0.9032	0.7861	407.3	373.7	367.7	340.2
35–9	0.8125	0.8333	1.0000		0.9188	0.9334	0.9109		0.7750	0.7490	0.7761	0.6536	366.2	356.5	354.5	357.8
40–4	0.4000				0.9087				0.4558	0.4065	0.4824	0.3081	354.5	343.3	320.1	289.5
45–9	0.0000				0.9013				0.0814	0.0672	0.0735	0.0384	324.2	304.3	372.6	305.1

Wife's age	N (1)	(2)	(3)	(4)
15–9	2.5	46.0	39.0	6.0
20–4	83.0	194.5	70.0	27.0
25–9	159.0	85.5	35.0	10.0
30–4	102.5	19.5	7.5	4.0
35–9	48.0	6.0	1.0	
40–4	20.0			
45–9	4.0			
All	419.0	351.5	152.5	47.0

TFMFR	(1)	(2)	(3)	(4)
15–49	18.28	13.76	13.69	13.18
20–49	11.86	11.18	11.34	10.58
20–44	10.24	9.66	9.47	9.06

[a] Rates per 1000 woman-years lived.

Note: the entry fecundity figures in the first panel refer to age at marriage groups rather than age groups. The weighted entry fecundity figures in the second panel were obtained by weighting the ratio for each age at marriage group contributing to a particular age group by the number of woman-years lived in the age group by the age at marriage group in question. The subsequent fecundity ratios are also weighted figures obtained in the same way.

Table 7.27 *The prevalence of prenuptially conceived first births*
(percentages)

	Months since marriage						
	0–2	3–6	7–8	0–8	9 and over	All	N
1538–99	6.7	11.9	10.0	28.6	71.4	100.0	2 634.0
1600–24	5.7	12.6	8.4	26.6	73.4	100.0	2 607.5
1625–49	3.8	7.7	9.9	21.4	78.6	100.0	2 400.0
1650–74	2.7	6.5	9.6	18.8	81.2	100.0	2 191.5
1675–99	3.1	5.5	7.9	16.4	83.6	100 0	2 392.5
1700–24	4.1	8.4	8.3	20.8	79.2	100.0	2 948.5
1725–49	6.0	9.9	7.4	23.3	76.7	100.0	2 697.5
1750–74	7.1	15.2	8.7	31.0	69.0	100.0	3 079.5
1775–99	7.5	18.7	9.0	35.1	64.9	100.0	2 700.5
1800–37	8.9	20.4	8.3	37.6	62.4	100.0	3 027.5
All	5.7	12.0	8.7	26.4	73.6	100.0	26 679.0

Source: Cambridge Group reconstitutions.

until a larger body of relevant information has been gathered, but a preliminary conclusion must be that age gap had little if any influence on entry fecundity and only a modest effect on fecund fertility, but a much more decided impact on subsequent fecundity.

Prenuptially conceived births

A relatively high proportion of prenuptially conceived first births was a prominent feature of English fertility history at times. Table 7.27 provides an overview of the phenomenon, showing both that the prenuptially conceived percentage was far from constant, and that within the overall total of prenuptially conceived births the relative importance of 'early' and 'late' births changed markedly. In the late seventeenth century prenuptiality was subdued. Only 16.4 per cent of all first births were prenuptially conceived in the quarter-century 1675–99, and, moreover, almost half of these were 'late' births, conceived within a couple of months of the marriage of the couple in question, and born in the eighth and ninth months after marriage. By the early nineteenth century, in contrast, not only were there proportionately far more prenuptially conceived births, but a much higher fraction of them were 'early' births, conceived many months before the marriage took place. In the early decades of the nineteenth century 37.6 per cent of all first births were prenuptially conceived, and of these almost four-fifths were baptised within the first seven months of marriage. If all births within the first seven months are regarded as 'early', then the proportion of early first births reached a low point of 8.6 per cent in 1675–99, but had risen to 29.3 per cent at the beginning of the nineteenth century. Late prenuptially conceived births, in contrast, varied only within a narrow band between 7.4 and 10.0 per cent and were without a decided trend over time. It is also worthy of note that prenuptiality in Elizabethan England was at levels not exceeded thereafter until the second half of the eighteenth century.

The history of prenuptiality lies as much or more with the history of marriage and of illegitimacy as with that of fertility. Births conceived well before marriage were probably more closely akin to illegitimate births than to those prenuptial conceptions which took place immediately before marriage. The latter class of prenuptially conceived births were arguably the product of behaviour licensed by formal betrothal and this may account for the relatively stable proportion of this type of prenuptially conceived birth over time. In contrast, the former class of prenuptially conceived births shared many of the characteristics of illegitimate births and their frequency changed over time in very close harmony with trends in illegitimacy.[40]

In one respect, however, prenuptiality is an important issue in the history of fertility. The issue is less to do with behaviour prior to marriage than with the subsequent fertility history of women who had had a prenuptially conceived birth. It might be expected that such women would display higher fertility during the balance of their childbearing life than women whose first child was born more than nine months after marriage, since it might be supposed that women of high fecundity, or perhaps with a greater appetite for sexual activity, would have higher fertility and would be more likely to become pregnant before marriage than others. Indeed, a moment's reflection will show that they are certain to experience higher fertility throughout marriage than women who were not pregnant at marriage, because by definition prenuptially pregnant women experience no entry sterility. All entry sterility will be found exclusively among those who were not prenuptially pregnant. This must reduce the fertility of this group as a whole by adding all non-fecund women to it alone.

The scale of the difference between the fertility of prenuptially pregnant women (pnp) and others (non-pnp) will be clear from table

[40] See Wrigley, 'Marriage, fertility and population growth', pp. 155–63.

Table 7.28 *Marital fertility rates of women who were prenuptially pregnant compared with those who were not (per 1000 woman-years lived)*

	Age						
Age at marriage	15–9	20–4	25–9	30–4	35–9	40–4	45–9
Prenuptially pregnant							
15–9	720.5	410.1	321.3	310.2	221.8	142.5	15.4
20–4		628.2	387.2	319.2	254.5	137.8	19.7
25–9			565.0	355.1	261.7	146.2	16.6
30–4				611.4	310.8	173.6	41.3
35–9					494.7	177.1	28.8
40–4						477.1	90.6
45–9							2 275.7
All	720.5	542.2	421.7	355.9	268.4	152.0	24.1
Not prenuptially pregnant							
15–9	299.7	351.2	308.8	266.2	202.5	89.0	11.8
20–4		364.4	345.7	288.8	228.8	118.5	18.4
25–9			369.4	319.0	247.1	122.0	20.2
30–4				315.1	255.5	134.6	25.3
35–9					267.1	148.3	26.4
40–4						97.5	31.1
45–9							5.0
All	299.7	359.5	346.4	300.4	239.6	122.7	21.0

Source: Cambridge Group reconstitutions.

7.28. There must, of course, be a marked difference between the two panels in the table in all the rates down the two diagonals since all the first born child of pnp women will contribute to the rates on the diagonal of the top panel whereas there is no comparable boost to fertility to rates down the diagonal of the bottom panel. However, the other rates in the top panel are consistently and substantially higher than those in the bottom panel. If the rates in the final column are ignored because they are based on a relatively small number of births and are apt to be volatile, there remain 15 cells in each table other than those on the diagonals. The difference between two rates in any pair of parallel cells taken from the upper and lower panels can be expressed as a ratio. Thus, for example, the rates for the age group 25–9 among women who married aged 20–4 were 387.2 and 345.7 respectively in the lower and upper panels, a ratio of 1.120. The average of all 15 such ratios is 1.176. Clearly, there was a large difference in fertility between the two groups of women, quite apart from that associated with the prenuptially

Table 7.29 *Marital fertility rates of women who were prenuptially pregnant compared with those who were not: bachelor/spinster completed marriages (per 1000 woman-years lived)*

	Age						
Age at marriage	15–9	20–4	25–9	30–4	35–9	40–4	45–9
Prenuptially pregnant							
15–9	761.5	405.4	329.7	327.9	236.0	149.5	18.0
20–4		618.7	380.9	312.0	260.0	145.3	21.3
25–9			545.0	350.8	257.7	136.1	14.7
30–4				601.6	317.8	158.1	40.3
35–9					425.0	153.8	15.4
40–4						411.9	0.0
45–9							—
All	761.5	546.2	412.3	348.7	267.0	145.8	21.1
Not prenuptially pregnant							
15–9	364.4	396.5	353.7	283.8	239.3	96.9	9.6
20–4		380.3	360.4	297.4	247.1	121.4	17.0
25–9			368.7	306.1	231.4	119.5	18.5
30–4				327.2	245.8	141.7	25.1
35–9					286.5	147.9	32.2
40–4						93.5	21.1
45–9							0.0
All	364.4	385.6	361.9	302.5	243.2	123.8	19.5

Source: Cambridge Group reconstitutions.

conceived birth itself. The point at issue is how far this was due simply to differences in entry sterility between them and how far to other fertility characteristics.

The data in table 7.28 referred to all marriages for which age-specific rates could be calculated, including many, of course, that were not of completed fertility and for which, therefore, it is not possible to estimate fecund marital fertility rates or subsequent fecundity ratios. But if attention is confined to completed marriages this can be done.

In table 7.29 the ASMFRs for completed marriages between bachelors and spinsters are set out, divided between pnp and non-pnp women as in table 7.28. It is clear that the same pattern is visible in both tables, though the differences are not quite so prominent among completed marriages as in the previous table. The average difference in the 15 cells of table 7.29, equivalent to the figure given above for all marriages, is

Table 7.30 *Fecund marital fertility, entry fecundity, subsequent fecundity, and marital fertility in pnp and non-pnp women: bachelor/spinster completed marriages*

Age	Entry fecundity		Subsequent fecundity		Fecund marital fertility[a]		Marital fertility[a]	
	pnp	non-pnp	pnp	non-pnp	pnp	non-pnp	pnp	non-pnp
15–9	1.0000	0.9607	1.0000	1.0000			761.5	364.4
20–4	1.0000	0.9449	0.9843	0.9950	416.2	416.2	546.2	385.6
25–9	1.0000	0.8930	0.9549	0.9645	393.0	397.7	412.3	361.9
30–4	1.0000	0.8164	0.8894	0.8903	375.4	368.0	348.7	302.5
35–9	1.0000	0.7314	0.7538	0.7557	354.0	356.5	267.0	243.2
40–4	1.0000	0.2632	0.4204	0.4187	348.8	336.5	145.8	123.8
45–9	—	0.0000	0.0691	0.0716	311.8	320.5	21.1	19.5

[a] Rates per 1000 woman-years lived.

Notes: the entry fecundity ratios indicate for each age at marriage group (not each age group) the proportion of women who were fecund on marriage. The other rates and ratios refer to all women in each age group and were obtained by weighting the rates or ratios for each age at marriage group represented in the age group by the proportionate share of woman-years lived by each age at marriage group in the age group. The fecund marital fertility rates were obtained after excluding the rate for the first age group from the set of rates for each age at marriage group.

Source: Cambridge Group reconstitutions.

1.133, to be compared with 1.176. Nevertheless, it seems reasonable to pursue the question of the source of the differences between pnp and non-pnp rates using data from completed marriage in the expectation that what proves true of completed marriages would also be true of the population as a whole.

Within the category of completed marriages pnp/non-pnp differences can be analysed by studying the component elements of age-specific marital fertility rates: fecund marital fertility, entry fecundity, and subsequent fecundity. In table 7.30 these three elements are set out in summary form, together with the ASMFRs. Except in the case of entry fecundity, the summary figures have been arrived at by weighting the contributions of each age at marriage group to any given age group figure by the proportion of the total of woman-years lived in that age group by each age at marriage group. It should be noted that, since fecund marital fertility rates, no less than ASMFRs, are affected by the prevalence or otherwise of prenuptial pregnancy, the fecund marital fertility rates given in the table were obtained by excluding from observation the first five-year age group in each age at marriage group. Thus, for example, among women marrying aged 20–4, the first rate used is that for this group of women in the age group 25–9.[41]

The resulting picture is clear-cut. Fecund fertility rates for pnp and non-pnp women are almost identical. The TFMFRs are virtually identical, at 10.97 for pnp women and 10.98 for non-pnp women (TFMFRs calculated over the age range 20–49). There is no evidence here that the fecundity of women who were pregnant at marriage was any different from those who were not.

The subsequent fecundity of the two groups may also be regarded as identical. The individual age group figures are always close to one another, with the non-pnp slightly the higher of the two. It is plain, therefore, that the key difference between pnp and non-pnp women must be entry fecundity, and this is borne out by a calculation based on the entry fecundity figures in table 7.30. Using them it is possible to recalculate the ASMFRs given in table 7.29 for non-pnp women by taking into account the effect of entry fecundity on the rates. For example, entry fecundity in the 20–4 age at marriage group was 0.9449. If, therefore, there had been no entry sterility in the age group, the age-specific marital fertility rate for women aged 25–9 from this age at marriage group would have been 360.4/0.9449 = 381.4 per 1000, rather than 360.4. The revised rates for non-pnp women can then be compared with the original rates for pnp women, ignoring once more any rates on the diagonal since these, but only these, are affected by prenuptiality in the case of pnp women. The TMFRs for pnp women for the age at marriage groups 15–9 to 30–4, excluding the entry age group in each case, are 7.33, 5.60, 3.80, and 2.58. The comparable rates for non-pnp women after correction for entry sterility are 7.18, 5.52, 3.78, and 2.53. The ratio of the latter set of rates to the former set is 0.980, 0.986, 0.995, and 0.981 respectively.

It is therefore evident that the great bulk of the difference between the ASMFRs of pnp and non-pnp women is attributable to the fact that there is no entry sterility in the former group. If allowance is made for this, the remaining differences are very small, less than 2 per cent.[42]

Since the pattern of differences between the ASMFRs of pnp and

---

[41] An alternative method of comparing the fecund fertility of pnp and non-pnp women which also eliminates the effect of prenuptiality is to begin observation from immediately after the birth of the first child in each family. This method also suggests that fecund fertility was slightly higher in pnp marriages, though the differences are again small, of the order of 2 or 3 per cent. This finding closely parallels the experience of German village populations in the eighteenth and nineteenth centuries; Knodel, *Demographic behavior in the past*, tab. 9.11, p. 237.   [42] See n. 41.

non-pnp women in completed marriages (table 7.29) and in all marriages (table 7.28) is so similar, it is probably safe to assume that entry fecundity disparities were the dominant reason for the wide difference in age-specific fertility in the two groups of women. The level of prenuptiality changed strikingly over time in early modern England, but there is little ground for supposing that pnp and non-pnp women formed groups with significantly different fertility characteristics except in that all entry sterility was concentrated among the latter group.

Inasmuch as fertility *was* higher among pnp women, it should not be assumed, of course, that this was the result of a selection process in which women who were more likely to conceive for physiological reasons were thereby more likely to have a prenuptially conceived first birth. Other explanations are also possible. For example, it might be that pnp women were disproportionately drawn from a particular sector of society which was relatively indifferent to intercourse outside marriage, and that women from this background were accustomed to breastfeed their children for a marginally shorter period on average than women from the rest of society.

Fertility and 'occupation'

There were wide variations in mortality both between individual parishes and between the four parish groupings devised to reflect differences in occupational structure.[43] In fertility, however, interparochial differences were much less pronounced. Summary statistics relating to individual parishes are reported below,[44] but it is of interest also to consider separately the 'agricultural', 'manufacturing', 'retail trade and handicraft', and 'other' groupings which were used in the discussion of mortality differences.

Table 7.31 shows the standardised ASMFRs for these four groupings in the three long time periods which have been used frequently in this chapter, and for the parish register period as a whole. They were standardised by weighting the rates for individual age at marriage groups by the numbers of woman-years lived by the population overall by each age at marriage group in each age group. The associated TMFRs are calculated for the 20–49 age range to minimise any distorting effects associated with prenuptiality or with the small number of events on which rates for the age group 15–9 were based. The differences between the groups were never very marked. Indeed, over the period as a whole the differences were trivial among three of the four, with 'other' about

---

[43] See tabs. 6.16 and 6.17, pp. 270–1 and 274.   [44] See pp. 501–7.

Table 7.31 *Standardised marital fertility rates by parish occupational groupings (per 1000 woman-years lived): bachelor/spinster marriages[a]*

Age	Agricultural	Manufacturing	Retail trade & handicraft	Other
1538–1649				
15–9	423.3	348.6	406.5	345.3
20–4	392.1	394.4	427.9	407.7
25–9	348.1	361.0	397.1	362.0
30–4	299.6	328.5	332.5	315.7
35–9	229.5	300.8	257.1	243.2
40–4	111.4	136.5	152.7	122.5
45–9	9.3	18.3	28.4	19.6
TMFR 20–49	6.95	7.70	7.98	7.35
1650–1749				
15–9	294.1	392.9	361.2	354.1
20–4	426.9	398.9	400.3	399.4
25–9	356.7	373.8	374.9	361.4
30–4	312.4	300.6	332.0	310.4
35–9	248.4	226.9	249.1	243.0
40–4	131.0	120.1	121.7	109.9
45–9	20.9	22.8	21.0	16.8
TMFR 20–49	7.48	7.22	7.50	7.20
1750–1837				
15–9	536.9	565.3	460.8	560.4
20–4	429.2	470.1	407.4	397.9
25–9	374.6	383.0	376.8	362.9
30–4	331.6	325.2	288.1	307.8
35–9	275.9	269.4	232.6	229.1
40–4	162.4	161.6	127.2	129.5
45–9	33.5	19.7	16.3	23.7
TMFR 20–49	8.04	8.15	7.24	7.25
All				
15–9	425.6	485.0	397.7	382.1
20–4	421.1	431.2	414.2	401.5
25–9	361.4	376.8	383.2	361.5
30–4	316.1	315.5	323.8	310.2
35–9	253.5	255.5	248.8	239.7
40–4	138.0	141.5	129.7	118.7
45–9	23.2	20.0	22.6	19.5
TMFR 20–49	7.57	7.70	7.61	7.26

[a] See text for details of the method used in standardising fertility rates.
Source: Cambridge Group reconstitutions.

5 per cent lower than the other three. But there were some changes in the relative standing of the four groups. Initially, the agricultural group had the lowest TMFR but ended with the second highest, whereas the reverse happened in the retail trade and handicraft group, which began highest and ended lowest. In one case the TMFR fell steadily, in the other it fell from one time period to the next, a development all the more remarkable in that fertility tended to rise overall during the parish register period. It should be remembered, however, that there was a more marked fall in infant mortality in this group than in any other. Other things being equal, a fall in infant mortality, by reducing the proportion of short birth intervals, must tend to increase the average length of birth intervals as a whole and thus to reduce fertility rates. Manufacturing parishes experienced the highest rate overall, but, in view of the fact that they were heavily agricultural in nature in the earliest period, it would be unwise to suppose that this fact signifies something distinctive about dependence upon manufacturing employment. The 'other' group changed very little over time, and was only lowest in one of the three subperiods, and then only marginally, but experienced somewhat lower fertility overall.

Fecund marital fertility rates, entry fecundity ratios, and subsequent fecundity ratios were also calculated for the four parish groupings. They are not reproduced here. None showed large differences between the groupings, though the fecund marital fertility data suggested that the rise in ASMFR in agricultural parishes was partly due to a rise in fecund marital fertility. It is also clear that subsequent fecundity rose more markedly in agricultural parishes than in the retail trade and handicraft group, though not more decisively than in the other two groupings.

This lengthy section on particular influences on fertility characteristics has covered a number of factors which affected fertility levels. It suggests that the interpretation of the level and trend of fertility in the past needs to take account of many potentially distorting influences. The discussion has, however, been less sophisticated than the ideal because it has considered a series of factors in isolation, even though there may be important interactions between them in some instances. For example, as we have noted, 'occupational' differences might in principle be partly a by-product of differences in infant mortality levels. Because of the constraints of space, we have, in general, stopped short of undertaking such analysis while recognising both that it would be desirable and that it might well prove repaying.

Long-run trends

Birth intervals and long-run fertility trends

The analysis of data relating to bachelor/spinster completed marriages has shown that there were significant changes in marital fertility in England in the course of the parish register period, and in particular that there was a marked contrast in subsequent fecundity between the late seventeenth and early nineteenth centuries. But although data from marriages of this type lend themselves well to the breakdown of age-specific marital fertility rates into the component elements which determined marital fertility, they represent a relatively slim empirical base. The total number of births to marriages of this type which were used in constructing the data given in table 7.8, for example, was only 10 061.5. This is no more than 5.5 per cent of the total of 181 612 births on all the FRFs from the 26 parishes from which all the reconstitution data were derived.[45] In order to produce age-specific fertility rates, it is necessary, of course, to know both the date of birth of the wife and the dates at which the marriage took place and at which it ended. Because of the frequency of migration in early modern England these dates are known only for a minority of marriages. Reducing the data set further by focusing principally on completed marriages between bachelors and spinsters means another sharp fall in the percentage of all births which enter into the analysis.

Fortunately, one fundamental aspect of fertility, the fertility of fecund women, can be studied effectively by using birth interval data, which is closely equivalent to the use of fecund marital fertility rates.[46] Birth intervals can be measured from FRFs of all types, including those where there is no date of end of marriage, and even from dummy marriages, though they lack a date of marriage. It is therefore possible to base the measurement of changes in birth intervals over time upon a far larger body of data than any other aspect of fertility. In order to be confident that such data can be used as an indicator, however, it is, of course, first necessary to discover whether birth interval data from, say, dummy marriages are a reliable source of information. It is important both to know more about the characteristics of birth intervals as a category of

---

[45] This is the total that results from applying the same criteria as were applied for most of the tabulations used in this chapter. The crude total of births on all the FRFs of the 26 parishes is much higher, approximately 250 000. This total includes births in years outside the period of good quality data in each parish and the births in the very large parish of Birstall which was excluded from the fertility tabulations for the reason given on p. 356 above.   [46] See tab. 7.3, pp. 364–5, and accompanying text.

Table 7.32 *Birth intervals of parity 2 or higher classified by the opening of the interval, by its midpoint, and by the closing of the interval: bachelor/spinster completed marriages (months)*

	Age of mother				Number			
	34 and under	35–9	40 and over	All	34 and under	35–9	40 and over	All
Birth intervals of parity 2 or above (not last)								
Opening	29.7	28.5	26.4	29.4	4 159.5	1 066.0	120.0	5 345.5
Midpoint	29.0	30.2	29.5	29.4	3 697.5	1 400.5	240.5	5 338.5
Closing	27.9	31.1	33.2	29.4	3 195.0	1 660.5	479.0	5 334.5
Birth intervals of parity 2 or above (last)								
Opening	46.5	40.2	35.7	41.0	460.5	717.0	377.0	1 554.5
Midpoint	42.0	41.9	39.6	41.0	297.0	613.5	640.0	1 550.5
Closing	33.7	40.4	42.8	41.0	181.5	456.0	911.0	1 548.5

Source: Cambridge Group reconstitutions.

information, and to discover whether different types of FRFs can provide equally reliable data.

In relation to the first point, it is convenient once more to begin by considering completed marriages, partly because their other characteristics are now familiar, and partly because completed marriages provide fuller information than other types of marriage not only about such variables as parity and age of mother but also about last birth intervals, which are often impossible to identify unambiguously in other categories of FRFs.

It is well to begin by emphasising again a point which surfaced earlier in this chapter. Table 7.4 showed how greatly the apparent relationship between age of mother and length of birth interval is affected by whether the birth intervals are tabulated by the age of the mother at their opening, midpoint, or closing. In table 7.32 some similar data relating to birth intervals of parity 2 or higher are set out (to be referred to subsequently as 2+ intervals).[47] The birth intervals are divided between last birth intervals and others to make clear the scale of the difference between them. The age grouping was made in the knowledge that last births take place chiefly when women are in their later 30s and 40s.

The lower panel of the table shows how strongly the method of

---

[47] A parity 0 birth interval is that between marriage and a first birth, a parity 1 birth interval that between a first and a second birth, and so on.

classifying the intervals affects the apparent pattern. If classified by the age of the mother at the opening of the interval, last birth intervals decline in length with increasing age; if classified by the closing of the interval, they increase in length; and, if classified by the midpoint, the length varies only slightly with age. The same effect is also visible in the upper panel, which refers to parity 2+ birth intervals other than last birth intervals. Classifying by the opening of the interval tends to ensure that only short intervals can appear in the highest age group. In the lowest age group, on the other hand, long birth intervals are disproportionately favoured. If a woman were in her early 30s at the opening of her last birth interval, for example, she would be included in the under 35 group only if the interval in question were a short one. Classifying by the closing of the interval has an opposite effect. The least misleading procedure is, perhaps, to use the midpoint, and this method is adopted in the following birth interval tables.

Table 7.32 also shows that when a parity 2+ birth interval was also a last birth interval, it was on average 11.6 months longer than other intervals of the same parity which were not last intervals. Since mean intervals did not vary much with age in either category, it is clear that the difference in length between last and other intervals was not the result of last intervals occurring disproportionately among older women. It is also clear that the average of all parity 2+ birth intervals must rise with age because the proportion of last birth intervals rises with age.

Table 7.33 cross-tabulates the parity of birth intervals by the wife's age at marriage in bachelor/spinster completed marriages. The tabulation is shown for all birth intervals other than the last, for last birth intervals, and for the two categories combined. The number of birth intervals is given at the foot of each column.

Parity 0 birth intervals were, of course, much shorter than all higher parities because at parity 0 there was no period of postpartum amenorrhoea associated with the breastfeeding of an earlier child. Moreover, their length was further compressed by the prevalence of prenuptial conceptions. Very few were both first and last intervals and, therefore, the overall average length of parity 0 intervals was only slightly greater than the average where the first birth was not also the last. The characteristics of parity 0 birth intervals are described more extensively below when considering fecundability.[48]

Parity 1 birth intervals were little influenced by wife's age at marriage but they were always considerably shorter than parity 2+ birth intervals, by almost 2 months. Since all births intervals of parity 1 or higher

[48] See below pp. 464–72.

Table 7.33 *Birth intervals by parity: bachelor/spinster completed marriages (months)*

Wife's age at marriage	0	1	2	3	4	5	6 and over	All	N
All birth intervals other than last									
15–9	14.7	26.6	30.0	31.1	32.0	28.9	26.5	26.7	1 223.0
20–4	14.2	28.4	30.4	30.9	30.0	30.3	27.2	26.7	4 278.0
25–9	15.8	27.6	30.4	31.2	29.2	27.8	25.7	25.9	2 373.5
30–4	14.7	26.5	28.1	27.7	26.6	25.1	24.2	23.1	720.5
35–	16.6	26.1	28.9	30.7	38.9			21.4	142.5
All	15.0	27.7	30.1	30.7	29.9	29.3	26.8	26.1	8737.5
N	1799	1600	1397.5	1141.5	925	690	1184.5	8737.5	
Last birth intervals									
15–9	29.2	48.1	33.2	33.0	40.9	53.8	38.5	40.3	173.5
20–4	29.3	46.4	49.8	47.7	46.2	45.0	38.7	41.9	751.0
25–9	28.4	42.5	47.2	42.1	45.1	42.2	35.0	40.4	583.5
30–4	39.3	44.4	41.0	39.2	41.5	35.2	31.5	39.8	260.5
35–	23.5	32.7	35.6	33.2	30.5	43.4		30.6	117.0
All	29.9	42.1	44.1	42.5	44.3	43.6	37.6	40.3	1 885.5
N	141	194	192.5	247	209.5	232.5	669	1885.5	
All birth intervals									
15–9	14.9	27.5	30.2	31.2	32.9	32.9	29.6	28.4	1 396.5
20–4	14.8	29.6	31.6	32.9	32.0	33.1	31.2	29.0	5 029.0
25–9	16.6	29.1	32.6	33.7	33.2	32.9	30.4	28.7	2 957.0
30–4	17.9	29.8	31.6	32.2	33.1	30.9	28.2	27.5	981.0
35–	18.8	29.4	33.1	32.4	33.9	43.4		25.5	259.5
All	16.0	29.2	31.8	32.8	32.6	32.9	30.7	28.6	10 623.0
N	1940	1794	1590	1388.5	1134.5	922.5	1853.5	10623	

Source: Cambridge Group reconstitutions.

share the same 9-month period of pregnancy, the difference must be attributed to other components of the interval and is proportionately greater than appears at first sight. For example, the mean length of parity 1 birth intervals, excluding last birth intervals, was 27.7 months. The comparable figure for parity 2+ birth intervals was 29.4 months (table 7.34), but, subtracting 9 months in each case, the figures to be compared are 18.7 and 20.4 months. This difference must spring from differences in pregnancy wastage through miscarriage, in the length of the period of postpartum amenorrhoea, in coital frequency, or in the interval following the resumption of ovulatory cycles before a new conception occurs. Differences in the length or intensity of breastfeeding, which has a marked effect on the average length of postpartum amenorrhoea, are perhaps the most plausible possible explanation, at least in the sense that, in most European populations in the past, postpartum amenorrhoea took up many more months than either the wait time to conception or time lost through pregnancy wastage.[49] A relatively small proportional difference in this variable could therefore account for the difference in the birth interval means, whereas only very striking proportional differences in the other variables would have the same effect. On the other hand, it does not seem inherently likely that first children would be breastfed for a shorter period on average than their younger siblings, so that the causation remains obscure.[50] It should be noted that the infant mortality of first born children was higher than that of children of higher parity, and this accounts for a part of the difference because birth intervals following an infant death were much shorter than the average. That this is only a partial explanation, however, is clear from the data in table 7.35, which show that there was a substantial difference between parity 1 and parity 2+ birth intervals even when all intervals following an infant death have been removed from the data set.

---

[49] As an example of the orders of magnitude involved, Leridon suggests that mean time to conception (that is, the mean interval to conception after a woman has resumed fecundable ovulatory cycles) may vary from 4 to 10 months; that time lost to pregnancy wastage may vary between 1 and 2 months; and that time lost because of the length of the non-susceptible period may vary between 2 and 17 months. Leridon, *Human fertility*, tab. 3.2, p. 34; pp. 75–81; and tab. 10.1, p. 146. The second of these two estimates represents a calculation based on Leridon's observations, rather than the reporting of a figure advanced by Leridon himself. Estimates of the length of the non-susceptible period are not, of course, exactly the same as the period attributable to breastfeeding. Leridon estimated the non-susceptible period as 2 months even when the child is weaned at birth because of the effects of parturition itself. However, the upper end of his estimate of the length of the non-susceptible period is entirely attributable to the effect of prolonged breastfeeding.   [50] But see p. 496 below.

Birth interval lengths changed very little between parities 2 and 5. This is true both of last intervals and of other intervals. Nor, allowing for the vagaries affecting means based on small numbers, did they vary much by wife's age at marriage. At parity 6 and above, on the other hand, both last and other birth intervals were considerably shorter, and shorter also in the 'All' category forming the bottom panel of the table, even though there was a rising proportion of last birth intervals in the higher parities, a feature which ensures that the 'All' category has a flatter distribution of means than either of the other two. The explanation, of course, is that to reach a high parity a quick tempo of reproduction was necessary and mean birth intervals in such families were therefore shorter than in other families. Nevertheless the change in mean at higher parities was not strongly marked.

The issue of birth interval characteristics may be pursued further by making use of a tabulation in which all parity 2+ birth intervals are tabulated by age of mother and by wife's age at marriage. This is done in table 7.34. The upper panel of the table is directly comparable with the previous table in that all parity 2+ birth intervals given in table 7.33 are shown in table 7.34 tabulated by age of mother. This section of the table, however, like its predecessor, refers only to births taking place in completed marriages. The bottom half of the table shows comparable data for incomplete marriages, though only for the 'All' category, since in an incomplete marriage it is not possible to identify last births separately.

Table 7.34 displays some features that are predictable, given its nature. For example, parity 2+ birth intervals under the age of 25 were shorter than those at higher ages because only women with closely spaced births could reach such parities early in life. On the other hand, whereas the mean of parity 2+ birth intervals fell sharply at high parities for birth intervals other than the last (table 7.33), such intervals did not change greatly with increasing age, falling only modestly above the age of 40, evidence that a considerable proportion of birth intervals above that age were not of high parity. Much the same is true of last birth intervals, shown in the second panel of the table, but when the two types of birth intervals are combined, in the third panel of the table, the tendency of the mean length of the birth interval to rise with increasing age becomes quite marked, brought about by the steadily increasing proportion of last births in the total of births. In this panel, however, there is clear evidence that the mean length of all 2+ birth intervals was almost the same for all age at marriage groups.

The fourth panel of table 7.34, which contains data for incomplete marriages comparable to those in the third panel for completed

Table 7.34 *Birth intervals of parity 2 or higher: bachelor/spinster marriages, completed and incomplete (months)*

Wife's age at marriage	Wife's age							
	15–9	20–4	25–9	30–4	35–9	40 and over	All	N
Completed marriages								
All birth intervals other than last								
15–9	19.2	27.4	30.7	29.6	27.8	30.0	29.1	871.0
20–4		22.2	28.1	31.4	30.5	29.8	29.6	2 831.5
25–9			23.1	29.3	31.5	28.9	29.5	1 314.0
30–				22.9	28.1	29.4	27.6	322.0
All	19.2	25.4	28.2	30.3	30.2	29.5	29.4	5 338.5
N	5.5	320.5	1 381.5	1 990	1 400.5	240.5	5 338.5	
Last birth intervals								
15–9		25.1	33.5	47.5	44.5	37.4	40.2	164.0
20–4		22.0	36.1	49.4	42.6	39.5	42.1	673.0
25–9			32.5	39.1	42.6	40.5	41.1	489.5
30–				25.7	36.3	39.5	38.2	224.0
All		24.8	35.1	45.3	41.9	39.6	41.0	1 550.5
N		11	72	214	613.5	640	1 550.5	
All birth intervals								
15–9	19.2	27.3	30.9	31.1	33.0	35.8	30.9	1 035.0
20–4		22.2	28.4	33.2	34.1	37.1	32.0	3 504.5
25–9			23.6	30.3	35.0	37.4	32.6	1 803.5
30–				23.1	30.5	36.1	31.9	546.0
All	19.2	25.4	28.5	31.7	33.8	36.8	32.0	6 889.0
N	5.5	331.5	1 453.5	2 204	2 014	880.5	6 889	
Incomplete marriages								
All birth intervals								
15–9	27.2	27.1	30.7	31.7	34.9	36.3	30.1	1 260
20–4		21.7	27.7	32.0	34.3	38.3	30.1	2 774
25–9			21.5	29.2	32.9	35.7	30.1	1 329
30–				22.3	27.9	31.5	28.0	240
All	27.2	25.4	28.0	30.8	32.9	35.9	30.0	5 603
N	12	597.5	1 728.5	1 914	1 107.5	243.5	5 603	

Source: Cambridge Group reconstitutions.

marriages, shows that parity 2+ birth intervals were very similar in completed and incomplete marriages, though in most cells of the table the mean was slightly lower in the latter than in the former. The similarity between the third and fourth panels ensures that the data for both kinds of marriages combined is little different from either of the two taken separately, and it is encouraging since it suggests that taking data on birth intervals from other types of marriage, which may combine in varying proportions parity 2+ birth intervals which were last intervals and those which were not, may be merged with those for the more fully observed marriages without running the risk of introducing serious distortions.

Tables 7.35 and 7.36 provide grounds for thinking that trends in fecund marital fertility can be established by using birth interval data from all FRFs rather than simply from those which include a date of marriage or on which the wife's date of birth is recorded. The first of the two tables showed that there were no major differences in mean birth intervals by parity from the second birth onwards, except at high parities, while the second showed that when all parity 2+ birth intervals were tabulated by age of mother the mean increased steadily with age, though when last birth intervals and other birth intervals were tabulated separately, this effect was not visible. In these two tabulations the mean interval tended to grow with age initially, but then declined in most instances. Both characteristics are at least partly attributable to the selection effect which exists in both the early and late age groups. Age at marriage had little effect on mean birth intervals. The increase in mean interval with age visible when all birth intervals are pooled is due to the steady increase in the proportion of last birth intervals with age. Incomplete and completed marriages share much the same mean birth interval patterns.

It remains to discover whether, moving to the general mass of FRFs from the restricted data set that enables tabulations to be made by parity, age of mother, age at marriage, and so on, reveals similar or different mean birth intervals in different categories of FRFs. In table 7.35 mean birth intervals are shown for four subgroups of FRFs and for the four combined. It will be evident that there can be no birth intervals on FRFs either with no births at all or with only one birth,[51] nor can FRFs which lack a date of marriage be used unless they contain at least three births. This restriction applies because if there are only two births on the FRF and no date of marriage it is impossible to determine whether the

---

[51] The interval from marriage to first birth is often treated as a birth interval, and can, of course, be measured on any FRF which contains both a date of marriage and at least one birth, but such cases are of no value in this context.

Table 7.35 Long-term trends in birth intervals (months)

1. Bachelor/spinster completed marriages.
2. Date of marriage and wife's date of birth known.
3. Date of marriage known, wife's date of birth not known.
4. Dummy marriages (date of marriage not known).
5. All.

	First child of birth interval died under 1					First child of birth interval survived				
	(1)	(2)	(3)	(4)	(5)	(1)	(2)	(3)	(4)	(5)
Parity 1										
1550–99	21.86	18.19	22.67		22.09	32.22	29.89	30.53		30.50
1600–24	18.41	20.90	23.25		22.29	30.11	29.27	31.05		30.46
1625–49	20.90	22.52	21.89		22.04	28.68	29.69	31.15		30.44
1650–74	18.50	23.09	24.55		23.64	29.61	31.72	31.51		31.39
1675–99	26.53	21.83	22.72		22.65	30.67	28.82	30.28		29.92
1700–24	20.25	21.19	21.13		21.08	31.01	29.21	29.93		29.84
1725–49	23.49	23.36	24.14		23.83	31.96	28.94	30.25		30.09
1750–74	25.38	23.04	22.94		23.25	29.57	28.07	28.72		28.64
1775–99	25.73	22.30	23.49		23.31	29.50	28.46	28.85		28.79
1800–37	14.95	22.52	24.39		23.18	29.46	28.42	28.81		28.67
All	22.47	22.11	22.94		22.65	30.21	29.06	30.05		29.77
N	239.5	990	2012.5		3242	1553.5	5115.5	10442		17111

438

Parity 2+

1550–99	17.48	21.96	23.39	22.54	22.86	34.20	31.61	32.99	32.51	32.71
1600–24	23.92	22.65	22.71	23.67	23.15	34.54	33.33	32.71	32.31	32.78
1625–49	21.40	22.84	23.31	23.79	23.29	34.66	32.98	33.20	33.22	33.27
1650–74	23.20	24.18	21.52	24.29	23.51	33.62	33.01	34.00	33.23	33.42
1675–99	25.66	21.37	23.98	22.91	23.17	34.09	31.48	33.17	32.15	32.46
1700–24	27.46	21.30	24.50	23.58	23.69	33.09	31.32	32.38	31.32	31.78
1725–49	23.72	23.29	24.33	23.52	23.77	33.04	32.05	32.36	31.97	32.24
1750–74	24.21	23.90	22.19	23.87	23.27	31.94	31.57	31.51	31.42	31.55
1775–99	28.73	22.87	23.49	24.21	23.98	32.73	31.15	30.90	30.59	31.10
1800–37	25.36	24.29	24.10	25.01	24.50	31.27	31.15	31.17	30.52	30.99
All	24.82	22.96	23.41	23.64	23.52	33.01	31.85	32.32	32.03	32.18
N	862	2 232.5	4 524.5	5 450	13 069	6 023	12 902	26 508.5	31 101	76 534.5

Source: Cambridge Group reconstitutions.

interval in question is of parity 1 or of parity 2+, but with three births it must be the case that the second interval is of parity 2+. All other FRFs must yield at least one usable birth interval and will therefore figure in one of the categories of table 7.35.

The four subgroups in the table are those from bachelor/spinster completed marriages; from marriages in which there is a date of marriage and a wife's date of birth; from marriages in which there is a date of marriage but no wife's date of birth; and from dummy marriages. The four groups are mutually exclusive and between them comprise all usable birth intervals. An indication of their relative size may be had from the numbers of birth intervals given at the foot of each column. The information is given separately for parity 1 intervals and for parity 2+ intervals because the former interval was always substantially shorter than the latter. Each tabulation is also divided according to whether or not the first child of the pair involved in any one interval died when less than 1 year old, since birth intervals following the early death of an older sibling were much shorter than when the older child of the pair survived. There are, of course, no parity 1 birth intervals for dummy marriages since only parity 2+ birth intervals can be identified in such marriages.

Before considering the trends revealed by table 7.35, it is first important to consider two possible criticisms of the form in which the data are presented. Both relate to their compressed format. The first concerns the left-hand panels of the table in which birth intervals following an infant death are presented. It might be expected that birth intervals would be significantly longer where the first child of the pair died towards the end of the first year of life than when it died soon after birth. In the eighteenth century there was a very marked fall in the proportion of infant deaths taking place in the first month of life,[52] which might have been expected to increase the mean interval following an infant death, other things being equal, which in turn would affect the interpretation of any time trend or the absence thereof.

There was such an effect, but it was much more modest than might have been expected. The mean birth interval following the death of the first child of the pair at less than 1 month was 22.67 months in parity 1 cases; where the first child died aged between 1 and 12 months the mean was 22.63 months: in parity 2+ cases the comparable figures were 23.09 and 23.96 months. The first difference is negligible; the second, though not negligible, is too slight to justify separate tabulation. It is slight because, when the first child died very young, the effects of parturition

---

[52] Tab. 6.4 , p. 226.

delayed a new conception even though breastfeeding had ceased, while in cases where the first child died at between 1 and 12 months, a high proportion died towards the lower end of the age range rather than late in the first year. Hence the birth intervals in the two cases differed surprisingly little. Deaths under 1 month as a proportion of all deaths under 1 fell from 55.7 per cent in 1700–24 to 33.8 per cent in 1800–37,[53] a compositional change which would have increased the mean birth interval following an infant death by only 0.20 months. This increase might call in doubt the apparent slight increase in the mean birth interval in the final period in the bottom left-hand panel of table 7.35, but does not qualify the general picture of a broad stability over time.

The second possible criticism of the form in which the data are presented in table 7.35 is potentially more serious. The right-hand panels of the table conflate two different types of birth interval. These panels are headed 'First child of birth interval survived'. But this category embraces both cases where the first child is *known* to have survived its first year, because the register records his or her burial or marriage, and those where the date of death is *unknown*. The second category deserves careful attention. Failure to register a death was most likely to occur when the child was very young, and in these circumstances the mean birth interval of children whose date of death was unknown would be shorter than the mean birth interval of children known to have survived their first year, since birth intervals following an infant death were much shorter than other birth intervals. Comparison of these two types of birth interval, therefore, constitutes a searching test of the quality of registration. The test was employed in chapter 4 for this purpose. On that occasion the percentage frequency distribution of the two types of birth interval was compared using the Kolmogorov–Smirnov test with reassuring results.[54] Since the present context is different, it is useful to pursue the matter further.

At first sight the difference in the means of the two types of birth interval which were used in table 7.35 appears substantial and the propriety of amalgamating the two data sets therefore doubtful. There are 109 956 birth intervals in all in table 7.35, of which 93 645.5 are cases in which either the child is known to have survived its first year (33 821.5), or its fate is unknown (59 824). The mean length of the birth interval in the former case is 32.00 months, in the latter 31.59 months, a difference of 0.41 months. The latter is, therefore, more than 1.3 per cent shorter than the former, a potentially significant difference. A more appropriate exercise, however, produces a different outcome.

[53] Ibid.   [54] See p. 103 above.

Two adjustments to the data sets are needed before a truer comparison can be made. The first is suggested by the fact that the 'unknown' mean is actually the higher of the two in the data set which has been heavily used in this chapter, that consisting of bachelor/spinster completed marriages.[55] In these marriages the last birth interval recorded on the FRF is always a last birth interval in the more technical sense that the woman in question had no further children though exposed to the risk of childbearing until the end of her fecund life. In many other marriages, however, the last birth interval is only the last in the sequence recorded on the FRF. Either death or migration may have prevented it being the last in the technical sense. Since last birth intervals were on average substantially longer than earlier birth intervals, it is prudent to ensure that observed differences in means are not the product of differing proportions of last birth intervals in the data sets. This can be done by discounting the last birth interval on every FRF. This will remove many intervals that were not last birth intervals in the technical sense, but does at least make it certain that all true last birth intervals are excluded.

Secondly, it is important to take into account the possible influence of parity on the length of birth intervals. In principle a difference in overall means might be the result simply of parity composition.[56] To be able to carry out parity-specific comparisons, however, means excluding data taken from dummy marriages since, although all birth intervals in this data set are known to be of parity 2 or greater,[57] exact parity cannot be specified for any birth in a dummy marriage.

When the data sets have been reduced by removing last birth intervals and data from dummy marriages, the difference between the overall means falls to 0.20, a figure only 49 per cent as large as the original crude difference derived from the unadjusted data sets.[58] Moreover, if a comparison is made on a parity basis rather than overall, the issue of whether any difference at all exists appears even more problematic. For the six successive parities beginning at parity 1 and ending with all birth intervals of parity 6 or greater, the signed differences ('known' minus 'unknown') are +0.44, +0.28, −0.06, +0.03, 0.00, and −0.12, an average difference of only +0.11 months, or about 3 days whereas the average birth interval was about 30 months. From

---

[55] The means are 32.29 months for the 'known' intervals, and 32.55 months for the 'unknown' intervals.

[56] Or, equally, the absence of a difference in overall means might conceal a 'true' difference which would be revealed in parity-specific comparisons.

[57] See above pp. 437 and 440.

[58] The means were 29.48 and 29.28 months respectively for 'known' and 'unknown' intervals.

parity 3 upwards 'unknown' birth intervals were slightly longer than 'known' intervals on average.

Given the uncertainty that surrounds any comparison of this type, and especially the difficulty of ensuring that like is being compared with like, it would be unsafe to draw a categorical conclusion from this evidence about the existence of a difference of means between the two types of birth interval or about its size, if it exists, especially in view of the absence of any positive difference of means between the two categories in bachelor/spinster completed marriages. So far as the measurement of fertility trends by the use of birth interval data is concerned, however, it seems clear that the 'known' and 'unknown' birth intervals in cases where the earlier child survived the first year of life may be amalgamated into a single data set without the risk of introducing any but the slightest distortion.

Having considered some characteristics of the birth interval data presented in table 7.35, we may now focus on the light thrown by the table on long-term fertility trends in early modern England. It is notable that there was a greater volatility of means in the smaller data sets, a feature particularly marked in the smallest data set in column 1. This column also tended to have higher means than the other columns, a feature especially well marked in parity 2+ birth intervals where the earlier child did not die young. This characteristic is readily intelligible since every completed family included a last birth interval, whereas in the other three groups there were many families without a last birth interval.

The right-hand section of the bottom panel of the table is based on far larger numbers of birth intervals than any other section and shows a coherent pattern of change. The final column of this section is based on more than 76 000 birth intervals, and, as might be expected, displays the greatest stability, though the other columns in the same section all conform to the same pattern. In the final column there is a slow, though uninterrupted rise in the mean from 32.7 months in the late sixteenth century to 33.4 months in the third quarter of the seventeenth century, but thereafter a decline to 31.0 months in the early nineteenth century.

The decline was perfectly regular apart from a slight rise between the first and second quarters of the eighteenth century. The fall was sharpest down to the mid-eighteenth century. It continued thereafter but at a much slower rate. The fall from peak to trough was about 7.3 per cent. This agrees very closely with the rise in fecund fertility shown in table 7.10. In table 7.10 the TFMFR 20–49 rose between 1650–1749 and 1750–1837 by 3 per cent (the exact percentage varies according to the age range over which the TFMFR is calculated). If the birth interval data in the right-hand section of the bottom panel of table 7.35 is grouped into the same time periods a similar, if slightly higher, result is obtained. Regrouping birth interval data into shorter rather than longer time periods, on the other hand, naturally suggests a bigger peak to trough fall in the length of the interval of about 10 per cent, as appears below from the decadal data in table 7.36.

The comparable data for first birth intervals (top panel, right-hand section) is based on only a quarter as many birth intervals as for parity 2+ intervals but it shows a very similar course of events. The mean was broadly stable from the late sixteenth century until the third quarter of the seventeenth century (the figure for 1650–74 was sharply higher than either its predecessor or successor, but the height and abruptness of the peak may be deceptive: if a mean is calculated for the whole of the second half of the seventeenth century it is very close to earlier means). Thereafter the decline was pronounced, though it was complete by the middle of the eighteenth century. The fall was larger in absolute terms than in the previous case and therefore greater proportionately since the means for parity 1 birth intervals were smaller than for parity 2+ birth intervals.

The pattern of change for birth intervals where the earlier child survived forms a striking contrast with that for birth intervals where the earlier child died in infancy. In the latter case, the interval increased rather than declined: for parity 1 birth intervals from 1725 onwards; for parity 2+ birth intervals, which had been exceptionally stable from the beginning until 1775, it grew only towards the very end of the parish register period. The relatively small totals of cases for parity 1 result in greater volatility, making it difficult to distinguish trend from random fluctuation. The 'true' trend in both series, however, can be seen to be flat or even slightly declining if account is taken of the change in the mean age of infant deaths. During the late sixteenth and seventeenth centuries this statistic was almost invariant, averaging 2.02 months. During the eighteenth century it rose to 2.65 months in 1700–49 and 3.07 months in 1750–99, before rising still further to 3.61 months in the period after 1800.[59] The interval between the death of the earlier child and the birth of the later child, therefore, did not rise, even though the interval between the two *births* rose by about 1 month. Since the death of the earlier child of the pair was in most cases the reason why birth intervals of this type were much shorter than other birth intervals, the overall

[59] See pp. 217–42 above for the changing age patterns of infant mortality in the parish register period. In the eighteenth century, there was a large fall in mortality in the first month of life, not matched in the later months of the first year.

length of the birth interval should be adjusted to take account of any changes in the mean age at death of the earlier child. When this is done, the uniformity of experience throughout the whole parish register period is apparent.

The contrasting trends in birth intervals of the two types is instructive (that is, between cases where the earlier child died in infancy, on the one hand, and where he or she survived, on the other). It is most unlikely that coital frequency changed in one case but not in the other,[60] and even less likely that there were changes in the frequency of spontaneous miscarriage affecting one class of women but not the other. It is much more likely that the length of the period of postpartum amenorrhoea associated with breastfeeding changed for women whose earlier child survived but remained the same for those whose earlier child died.[61]

Since birth intervals were shortening in the former case but were broadly stable in the latter, the difference between the two shrank over time. Parity 2+ birth intervals of the former type averaged 32.9 months before 1700 but only 31.5 months after 1700, while intervals of the latter type averaged 23.2 and 23.8 months in the two periods. The difference therefore decreased from 9.7 to 7.7 months, a fall of 2.0 months. The comparable figures for parity 1 intervals were 30.5 and 29.2, 22.5 and 22.9, 8.0 and 6.3, and 1.7 months. If the length of the period of postpartum amenorrhoea is the key both to the difference between the two types of birth interval and to the fall in the 2+ interval, then the scale of the fall, approaching 2 months in the two long subperiods before and after 1700, but considerably more from peak to trough, suggests a substantial reduction in the average period during which children were breastfed. Wilson hazards the estimate that 12 to 18 months of breastfeeding is associated with a postpartum non-susceptible period of 10 to 12 months, which suggests that a reduction in mean birth interval of 2 months, if solely due to a change in breastfeeding practice, would imply an abbreviation of the average duration of breastfeeding of 2 to 3

[60] It is theoretically possible that the resumption of coitus remained unchanged over the centuries in the case of an early infant death, but occurred progressively earlier where the previous child survived, but there is no evidence to support this possibility.

[61] It seems unlikely that there was any general tendency to refrain from intercourse during breastfeeding in early modern England, comparable to the taboo observed in some African populations. The evidence presented below in the sections dealing with fecundability suggests that the mean length of breastfeeding was about 19 months in early modern England where the child did not die in infancy. If there were no intercourse until after an average interval as long as this, it would be hard to reconcile this evidence with an average birth interval of 30–2 months when the earlier child of the pair survived (tab. 7.35, pp. 438–9).

months.[62] If, therefore, the fall in mean birth intervals were solely attributable to a reduction in the normal duration of breastfeeding, this would imply a substantial change in breastfeeding practices during the eighteenth century, conceivably related to other demands upon the time of married women.[63]

An argument related to breastfeeding is consistent with the facts as they are currently known, but, of course, other explanations are possible. If, for example, there were a relationship between the nutritional levels and the speed with which amenorrhoea came to an end when a women was breastfeeding, and if there were a sustained improvement in nutritional standards, or, what might be an equivalent development, a significant decrease in the prevalence and severity of infectious ailments among the adult population, breastfeeding habits might have remained unchanged but the average birth interval would nevertheless have fallen. Or again, changes in fecundability, by affecting the speed with which conception took place following the resumption of ovulatory cycles, might explain a part of the observed fall in the mean birth interval.[64]

The markedly shorter interval following first births compared to that following later births irrespective of the fate of the earlier child is very difficult to account for, even speculatively. The difference did not change significantly over time. The difference was proportionately less pronounced where the earlier child died young than where the earlier child survived (the ratio was 0.963 in the former case but 0.925 in the latter), but it was still substantial. This appears to rule out breastfeeding as a sufficient explanation since parity 1 and parity 2+ children who died as infants must have represented an almost identical breastfeeding burden to their mothers. It is not easy to light upon either a physiological or a behavioural explanation, nor any combination of the two, which 'saves the phenomenon' effectively.[65]

The chief attraction of turning to birth interval data drawn from all FRFs as a source of information about fertility trends is their very large number. There are almost 110 000 birth intervals represented in the four sections of table 7.35. This allows a finer subdivision by time than would

---

[62] Wilson, 'Marital fertility in pre-industrial England', p. 153. Wilson's conclusion is broadly consonant with the data summarised in Huffman and Lamphere, 'Breastfeeding performance and child survival', tab. 1, p. 107.

[63] There is some limited direct evidence of a fall in age at weaning in the eighteenth century, presented in Fildes, *Breasts, bottles and babies*, ch. 15.

[64] See below pp. 473–7.

[65] Some further light on the phenomenon, however, is thrown by the data relating to fecundability. See below pp. 495–6.

Table 7.36 *Long-term trends in birth intervals: all parities except parity 0: earlier child of pair survives infancy (months)*

Decadal		3-point moving average		5-point moving average	
(1)	(2)	(3)	(4)	(5)	(6)
1550–79	31.11				
1580–9	32.21	1550–99	32.33		
1590–9	33.68	1580–1609	32.58	1550–1619	32.34
1600–9	31.86	1590–1619	32.79	1580–1629	32.60
1610–9	32.83	1600–29	32.36	1590–1639	32.66
1620–9	32.41	1610–39	32.58	1600–49	32.57
1630–9	32.52	1620–49	32.72	1610–59	32.79
1640–9	33.23	1630–59	32.90	1620–69	32.95
1650–9	32.96	1640–69	33.27	1630–79	32.91
1660–9	33.64	1650–79	32.92	1640–89	32.74
1670–9	32.18	1660–89	32.51	1650–99	32.59
1680–9	31.71	1670–99	32.11	1660–1709	32.27
1690–9	32.45	1680–1709	31.84	1670–1719	31.75
1700–9	31.37	1690–1719	31.61	1680–1729	31.85
1710–9	31.02	1700–29	31.69	1690–1739	31.75
1720–9	32.69	1710–39	31.65	1700–49	31.64
1730–9	31.24	1720–49	31.93	1710–59	31.61
1740–9	31.87	1730–59	31.44	1720–69	31.59
1750–9	31.21	1740–69	31.33	1730–79	31.14
1760–9	30.92	1750–79	30.85	1740–89	31.05
1770–9	30.44	1760–89	30.72	1750–99	30.80
1780–9	30.82	1770–99	30.62	1760–1809	30.78
1790–9	30.62	1780–1809	30.85	1770–1819	30.58
1800–9	31.12	1790–1819	30.54	1780–1837	30.63
1810–9	29.90	1800–37	30.57		
1820–37	30.69				

Note: The 3- and 5-point moving average figures in the second and third vertical panels are means of the individual decadal figures in the first panel (though it should be noted that the first 'decadal' figure covers a 30-year period because the number of birth intervals was small at the beginning of the data).
Source: Cambridge Group reconstitutions.

otherwise be feasible without running the risk that small numbers would prohibit confident interpretation. In table 7.36 parity 1 and parity 2+ birth intervals for all cases where the child survived infancy have been combined and a mean for each decade has been calculated. Three- and five-point moving averages are also given, covering 30- and 50-year periods, respectively. In almost all decades the total of birth intervals

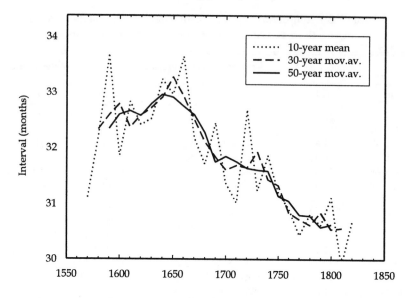

Figure 7.4   *Long-term trends in birth intervals (all parities except parity 0: earlier child of pair survives infancy)*
Note: the individual readings on each line represent data for 10-year, 30-year, and 50-year periods. The 30-year period is the average of 3 decennial periods; the 50-year period the average of 5 decennial periods. The following plotting convention was followed: a point plotted at, say, 1650 refers to 1650–9, 1640–69, or 1630–79 depending on the series plotted. *Source*: tab. 7.38.

lies between 3000 and 4500: the three- and five-point moving averages of the means are therefore based on very large totals of events. The same information is shown graphically in figure 7.4.

The smoothest series is, of course, that in column 6 of the table, where each figure refers to a 50-year period. This series suggests a slight rise in the length of the birth interval down to the mid-seventeenth century, followed by an almost uninterrupted fall, which, from a high point in the period 1620–69 (32.95 months) declined by 7.2 per cent to a low point in 1770–1819 (30.58 months). The other series display the same general pattern, though, as might be expected, the figures tend to be more erratic and the scale of the fall from a seventeenth-century maximum to an early nineteenth-century minimum is more pronounced in these series. The 30-year, or three-point, moving average reaches a maximum in 1640–69 (33.27 months) and a minimum in 1790–1819 (30.54 months), a fall of 8.2 per cent, while the comparable figures in the decadal series are 1660–9 (33.64 months), 1810–9 (29.90 months), and 11.1 per cent. The fall was largely complete by about 1770, about a century after it was first clearly evident. The earlier rise, from the start of the series until the mid-seventeenth century, though less spectacular than the subsequent fall, was not trivial. The mean birth interval in the 30-year moving average, for example, rose by almost 1 month between the beginning of the series and its peak in 1640–69, or by just over 2.9 per cent.

The foregoing birth interval data justify the conclusion that fecund marital fertility, as measured by birth intervals unaffected by infant mortality, rose by roughly 10 per cent between the middle of the seventeenth century and the beginning of the nineteenth century. This is in some ways a better measure of fecund marital fertility than the fecund marital fertility rate since the latter would be affected by changes in the level of infant mortality even if the 'true' fecund marital fertility rate remained unchanged. A rise on this scale is far from trivial. It is a change that might produce, for example, an increase in a crude birth rate from 30 to 33 per 1000. To cause as great an increase in fertility by a change in marriage age would require a drop of more than a year in mean age at marriage.[66] At the time that the *Population history of England* was written it had seemed a reasonable working hypothesis to assume that fecund marital fertility was broadly constant in early modern England. It is now plain that both fecund marital fertility and, particularly, subsequent fecundity rose during the eighteenth century, thereby magnifying considerably the changes in marriage age, and in fertility outside marriage, all of which were causing overall fertility to rise towards a high peak early in the nineteenth century.

Conventional age-specific marital fertility rates

It will be clear from earlier sections of this chapter that, although conventional age-specific marital rates are a useful summary measure, they are the product of so many separate influences that they are seldom unproblematic if presented in isolation. Having begun this chapter with a table rehearsing ASMFRs for 25-year periods, however, it is convenient to return to them at this stage with the analytic information presented earlier in mind, even though such a review of conventional

---

[66] For example, if mean age at marriage fell from 24 to 23 years, and using the marital fertility rates set out in tab. 7.1, the resultant rise in fertility would be 9.3 per cent. A fall of one year in mean age at marriage represents a very substantial change. The difference between the maximum and minimum mean ages at marriage found in England in the parish register period was only about three years.

Table 7.37 *Age-specific marital fertility rates: 50-year averages (per 1000 woman-years lived)[a]*

	15–9	20–4	25–9	30–4	35–9	40–4	45–9	TMFR 20–49	TMFR 15–49
1590–1639	377	402	381	327	268	142	22	7.71	9.59
1600–49	357	408	370	323	257	135	21	7.58	9.36
1610–59	374	403	362	309	248	131	20	7.36	9.24
1620–69	367	405	350	305	243	125	19	7.24	9.07
1630–79	391	384	348	306	237	123	22	7.10	9.05
1640–89	354	398	345	301	235	119	20	7.09	8.86
1650–99	362	389	343	299	235	112	22	6.99	8.80
1660–1709	323	398	352	309	234	112	23	7.14	8.75
1670–1719	322	409	362	314	238	113	23	7.29	8.90
1680–1729	315	410	366	315	240	111	22	7.32	8.90
1690–1739	333	413	369	323	244	119	21	7.44	9.11
1700–49	323	419	374	320	249	127	23	7.56	9.17
1710–59	392	429	373	318	251	130	22	7.61	9.57
1720–69	414	419	371	318	249	128	22	7.53	9.60
1730–79	430	418	364	314	254	134	22	7.53	9.68
1740–89	455	414	368	303	247	137	21	7.45	9.73
1750–99	507	421	367	309	243	138	21	7.49	10.03
1760–1809	503	410	366	304	242	140	21	7.41	9.93
1770–1819	517	418	371	306	251	144	19	7.54	10.13
1780–1829	532	429	390	312	255	148	23	7.79	10.45

Note: The 50-year averages are the averages of 5 decadal figures rather than of 50 annual figures.
Source: Cambridge Group reconstitutions.

ASMFRs will contain few, if any, surprises. Such rates are frequently of use for comparative purposes. Moreover, their existence makes possible a valuable test of the general reliability of parish register derived fertility data.

Table 7.37 gives five-year age-specific marital fertility rates for overlapping 50-year periods beginning in 1590–1639 and ending with 1780–1829, while figure 7.5 both plots these rates and, in a second panel, shows the degree to which the decadal rates varied from 50-year periods centred on the decade in question. The data are drawn from all marriages for which the date of marriage, the date of end of marriage, and the date of birth of the wife are known. They therefore represent an amalgam of information taken from marriages that were previously often treated separately. They are drawn from both completed and incomplete marriages; they include both prenuptially and postnuptially

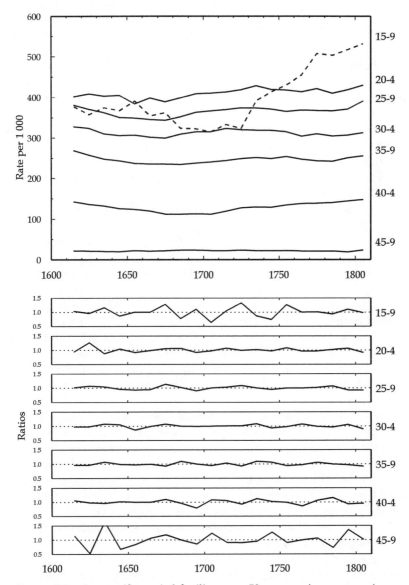

Figure 7.5   *Age-specific marital fertility rates: 50-year moving averages (upper panel); ratios of 10-year to 50-year rates (lower panel)*
Note: the individual readings on each line, representing a moving average, were plotted at the midpoint of the period covered.
Source: tab. 7.39.

conceived births; and they are taken from all varieties of marriage rank combination, provided that they meet the three stated criteria.

The effect of the several influences upon individual age-specific rates, which were described earlier in the chapter, did not in general result in significant changes in the 50-year rates over time. Over the age span within which most births took place, from 20 to 34, they were remarkably stable. The maximum rate for the 20–4 age group was 429 per 1000, the minimum 384 per 1000, so that the highest rate was 12 per cent higher than the lowest. For the age group 25–9 the comparable figure was 14 per cent (the maximum and minimum rates were 390 and 343 per 1000); while for the age group 30–4 the comparable figures were 9 per cent, and 327 and 299 per 1000. These are modest percentage differences. Nor was the situation different in the age group 35–9 (maximum rate 268, minimum rate 234, the former exceeding the latter by 15 per cent). But both in the 15–9 age group, where the maximum and minimum rates were 532 and 315 per 1000, and in the 40–4 age group, where maximum and minimum rates were 148 and 112 per 1000, the variations over time were far greater. The reasons for greater variability were quite different in the two cases. Fluctuating levels of prenuptial conceptions were the main reason for the first; changes in subsequent fecundity the main reason for the second. Between them they account for the bulk of the changes in the TMFR. For example, the TMFR 15–49 in 1780–1829 was 10.45, 19 per cent higher than the comparable figure for 1660–1709, at 8.75. But if the 15–9 and 40–4 rates in the earlier period had been as high as in the later period, the difference would have been less than 5 per cent.

The first panel of figure 7.5 shows how substantially teenage fertility rates fell short of those of women in their 20s after allowing for the distorting effects of prenuptial pregnancy. In the later decades of the seventeenth century, when prenuptial pregnancy was much lower than either earlier or later, the rates in the age group 15–9 were approximately on the same level as those for women aged 30–4, though by the end of the eighteenth century, with prenuptial pregnancy rife, the 15–9 rate was the highest of all. The phenomenon sometimes labelled teenage subfecundity is clearly evident.[67]

The second panel of figure 7.5 shows that the wider fluctuations in the 50-year rates found in the youngest and oldest age groups was matched by far more marked short-term variability in these rates. The number of

---

[67] The same pattern is visible in tab. 7.28, p. 423 above. The section of the table devoted to the marital fertility rates of women who were not prenuptially pregnant reveals rates of 300, 360, 346, and 300 per 1000 for the age groups from 15–9 to 30–4 respectively.

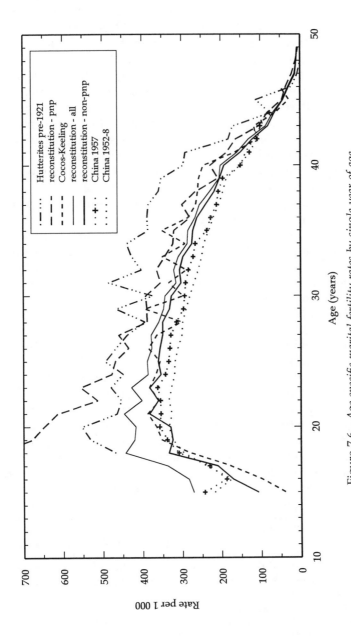

Figure 7.6 *Age-specific marital fertility rates by single year of age*

Sources: Cambridge Group reconstitutions. Cocos-Keeling: Smith, 'The Cocos-Keeling islands', tab. 8, p. 109. Hutterites: Eaton and Mayer, 'The social biology of very high fertility', tab. 13, p. 230. China: Lavely, 'Age patterns of Chinese marital fertility', app. tab., p. 432.

453

woman-years of observation was much lower in the 15–9 age group than in later age groups and the totals of births upon which the rates for the 45–9 age group were based were modest.[68] It is probable, therefore, that the 'true' variability of fertility rates in these age groups was no higher than in the other age groups but that random movements resulting from small numbers were much more pronounced.[69] It may be significant, for example, that the 15–9 rate became less volatile in the later eighteenth century at a time when teenage marriage was growing far more common and the observational base was therefore expanding. It is possible that some of the decadal changes were significant and represented a response to the particular circumstances of the time, but more likely that they are largely meaningless and would disappear or be greatly subdued if a larger body of data were to hand.

The examination of age pattern of fertility may be taken a step further by considering the age-specific rates by single year of age. Such information is rare, especially for populations not practising the deliberate control of fertility within marriage. Most individual reconstitution studies, of course, produce too few data to enable meaningful single-year rates to be calculated. The English reconstitution rates are shown in figure 7.6, together with some comparative data from studies of the Hutterite population, of the inhabitants of the Cocos-Keeling islands, and of China, the first relating to marriages contracted before 1921, the second to information recorded between 1888 and 1947, and the third to the 1950s.

As with the rates shown in figure 7.5, the English rates are based on all FRFs where the date of marriage, date of end of marriage, and date of birth of the wife are known. The solid, but light line in figure 7.6, therefore, recapitulates the information in table 7.37 by single year of age and consolidated for all periods. Since the rate for all women, however, is strongly influenced in younger women by the proportion of prenuptially conceived births, figure 7.6 also shows separately the rates for women who had a prenuptially conceived first child and for those whose first child was conceived in wedlock. The scale and nature of the

---

[68] The average number of woman-years upon which each decadal rate for women aged 15–9 was based was less than 50. The comparable figure for the age group 30–4, the age group in which the largest number of woman-years was lived, was 18 times as great. The average number of births per decade on which the 45–9 rate was based was only 12, whereas in the four principal childbearing age groups from 20–39, the decadal totals varied between 147 and 259.

[69] This impression is confirmed by a more formal test. The Z scores for the 10-year ASMFRs shown in fig. 7.5 reveal no differences between the seven age at marriage groups. The number of scores in each group that exceed the 5 per cent level is no greater than would be expected by chance.

differences in fertility between these two groups of women has already been discussed.[70] For present purposes the best guide to the age pattern of fertility is, of course, to be found in the line representing women who did not have a prenuptially conceived first child, which is shown as the solid, heavy line, since the other two lines are both affected by the lack of a true equivalence in the measurement of events and exposure, though the non-pnp line will be a little lower than a hypothetical 'true' line by about 2 per cent.[71]

The non-pnp line shows an initial rate at age 15 of just over 100 per 1000 woman-years, rising above 200 at age 17, and above 300 in the following year of age, to reach a peak value of just over 380 in both years 21 and 23. Thereafter there is a slow decline with the rates falling below 300 at age 33, below 200 at age 40, and below 100 at age 45, before dwindling to less than 10 in the final two years among women aged 48 and 49. Over the bulk of the whole span of the fertile years the rates are based on a substantial number of woman-years in observation. For each year from 25 onwards the total exceeds 2000 woman-years, except for age 49 where the total drops just below 2000. Between age 31 and 35, when the observational base is broadest the total of woman-years is always above 3000. Over the age range 25–49, therefore, it is likely that the rates are trustworthy, and the smooth pattern of change over these years suggests this. Below the age of 25, however, the observational base becomes progressively narrower with declining age because early marriage, and especially early marriage without a prenuptial pregnancy, was relatively rare in early modern England. The number of woman-years in observation was less than 1000 at age 21, and less than 100 below the age of 17. The rate for age 15 is derived from only 1 birth and just over 9 years in observation, while the comparable figures for age 16 are only 8 and 47. No reliance should be placed, therefore, on rates under the age of 18, though the phenomenon of teenage sub-fecundity is clear enough. The variability of rates in the late teens and early 20s is probably also a function of the narrow observational base. With larger numbers of woman-years lived, a smoother pattern would no doubt be visible.

There is an impressively close similarity between the non-pnp line and the Cocos-Keeling line, and it is therefore important to be aware of the differences between the two data sets. A first point to note is that the Cocos-Keeling data refer to confinements rather than births and there-fore understate the fertility rate by 1–2 per cent if appropriate allowance

---

[70] See above tabs. 7.28, 7.29, and 7.30, pp. 423, 424, and 425, and accompanying text.
[71] See above p. 426.

is made for twin births. Other differences are more significant. The English non-pnp rates refer only to married women and are the result of relating the number of events to the total of woman-years lived in the year of age in question. The Cocos-Keeling rates were obtained by relating confinements resulting in a live birth or births to years in observation of all women, whatever their marital status. As a result, the total of years of exposure is greatest for the very young and grows progressively smaller with age. The resulting rates are, however, more nearly comparable to the reconstitution-derived rates than might be supposed, because marriage took place very early by west European standards and few women remained unmarried. Moreover, it would appear that sexual relations were almost universal from an early age and a large proportion of women were pregnant on marriage.[72] The circumstances of all teenage women in the Cocos-Keeling islands, therefore, were not greatly dissimilar to those of teenage married women in early modern England. The observational base was wide for young women in the Cocos-Keelings and therefore the close match between their rates and the non-pnp English women suggests that the English rates, though based on such a tiny total of years in observation, may be moderately accurate.

The Chinese data are drawn from a 1 in 1000 fertility survey conducted in 1982. The number of women involved was very large and the resulting lines are therefore little affected by random influences. The information is subject, however, to the uncertainties associated with retrospective surveys of fertility and the construction of the rates involved making a number of assumptions about the proportions of women married at each age which are not directly verifiable.[73] It is fairly clear, too, that the rates for very young ages are unreliable, since it is inherently implausible to suppose that 'true' rates at the age of 15 were higher than at the age of 16, as suggested by the data for 1952–8 used in figure 7.6. The rates are available for each year from 1950 to 1981 and for single years of age from 15 to 44 but not from 45 to 49. At most ages the single-year rates were surprisingly variable from year to year. The years 1952–8 were chosen as being largely free from natural disasters or from major political crises and because they relate to a period before there was any significant evidence of parity-related control of fertility. The age-specific pattern in China is closely similar to that in England or in

---

[72] Smith, 'The Cocos-Keeling islands', pp. 104–7.
[73] The assumptions made in estimating the proportion of ever-married women currently married at each age were arbitrary, though not unreasonable. Lavely, 'Age patterns of Chinese marital fertility', p. 420.

the Cocos-Keeling islands, though the level was somewhat lower in China than in the other two populations. The year 1957 is also shown separately since in this year Chinese fertility was higher than in any other year of the period and the rates are close to those which typified early modern England.

Hutterite fertility was much higher than in any of the other three populations. Indeed, it is often taken as the population with the highest reliably recorded marital fertility rates. The shape of Hutterite fertility was similar to that of the other populations, except that the Hutterites preserved a high plateau of fertility to a later age than the other populations. The ratio of Hutterite fertility at the age of 40 to the peak reached about age 20 was distinctly higher than the comparable ratio in England or elsewhere. Small numbers mean fluctuating single-year rates among the Hutterites, however, and confident generalisation must be tempered by this fact. Marriage began late among the Hutterites, so that Hutterite data throw no light on fertility in the middle teens. All the data sets are in close agreement in regard to rates in the middle and later 40s.

The 'natural fertility' question

It has become customary, when considering a body of ASMFRs from a period prior to the onset of the widespread practice of birth control within marriage, to attempt to discover whether the population in question was a 'natural fertility' population. One of Henry's most valuable and influential contributions to the study of human fertility was his definition of the concept of natural fertility. Central to his concept was the criterion that natural fertility could be said to exist if the fertility behaviour of couples was not affected by parity. Equally, control was to be regarded as present if the number of children already born to married couples could be shown to influence their subsequent behaviour. Using this definition led to the conclusion that the *level* of age-specific marital fertility rates might vary considerably in natural fertility populations, but that their *shape* would be similar in all such cases.[74]

Subsequently Coale and Trussell, building on Henry's original

---

[74] Henry, 'Some data on natural fertility'. It should be noted that the shape of fertility by age might be 'natural' even though couples practised control of fertility within marriage, provided that they did so uniformly throughout marriage by some form of 'spacing' behaviour. That the shape of fertility by age was natural is not conclusive evidence, therefore, of the absence of fertility control within marriage.

insight, devised a means of summarising both the level and the shape of the marital fertility curves, expressed in two parameters, M and m, which may be calculated from any set of five-year age-specific marital fertility rates.[75] M is a scale factor intended to measure the level of fertility in a population relative to a standard schedule of natural fertility. It is so constructed as to equal 1.00 when the underlying fertility in the population in question matches the standard schedule. m is a shape parameter, devised as a means of testing departure from the age patterns of natural fertility, especially in populations moving towards the deliberate control of fertility within marriage.

Neither Henry's attempt to calculate a model schedule of age-specific natural fertility rates nor the assumptions underlying Coale and Trussell's work have escaped later criticism, but, equally, there has been widespread use of the Coale/Trussell measures M and m in historical demographic work. It is clear that, used uncritically, both M and m can produce misleading results. This is particularly liable to happen in small populations with characteristics such as those to be found in English parishes in the early modern period.[76] Nevertheless, since M and m have been routinely calculated in studies similar to this, it is of interest to note the results obtained by applying the Coale/Trussell technique to the rates shown in table 7.37. Because both the prevalence of prenuptial conceptions and the age pattern of marriage varied considerably over time, neither the exact values of M and m nor any apparent changes in their level over time should be thought unambiguous, unless the changes are pronounced, but low values of m may be taken as reinforcing the other evidence presented in this chapter that there was no significant practice of contraception in early modern England.[77]

M and m were calculated for the following half-century rates in table 7.37: 1590–1639, 1650–99, 1720–69, and 1780–1829. The rates were based on all the five-year ASMFRs from 15 to 49. The four periods include the lowest and highest TFRs found for any half-century in the parish register period (1650–99 and 1780–1829). A similar calculation was made for the entire reconstitution data set. The estimates of M and m

---

[75] Coale and Trussell, 'Model fertility schedules' and 'Erratum'.

[76] Some telling criticisms both of Henry and of Coale and Trussell are to be found in Wilson, Oeppen, and Pardoe, 'What is natural fertility?'.

[77] Wilson, Oeppen, and Pardoe discuss with illustrations the effect of prenuptial conceptions and marriage age distributions on the measurement of M and m; Wilson, Oeppen, and Pardoe, 'What is natural fertility?'. The data on subsequent fecundity and on mean age at birth of last child, given in tabs. 7.12 and 7.13 provide additional evidence that contraception was largely absent in this period.

were obtained using the maximum likelihood estimation method described by Broström.[78] The level of M in the four periods was 0.877, 0.832, 0.894, and 0.899 respectively: the level of m in the same periods was 0.058, 0.126, 0.128, and 0.102. For the whole parish register period combined M and m were 0.873 and 0.102 respectively. Such findings are valuable as a rough indication, though other readings might be obtained which would carry equal or greater plausibility. For example, the distorting effect of prenuptial pregnancy in raising ASMFRs in the earlier age groups can be eliminated by using data from families in which there was no prenuptially conceived birth (table 7.28, bottom line of lower panel). This results in a value of M of 0.795 and of m of 0.049. But one might also concentrate upon a particular age at marriage group, thus eliminating whatever distortions may attend a particular mix of age at marriage groups in producing a given age-specific rate. For example, the value of M and m among women who were not prenuptially pregnant, based solely on those married aged 15–9 and 20–4, were respectively 0.761 and 0.806, and 0.200 and 0.104 (table 7.28, lower panel, lines 1 and 2).

The values of M and m quoted above for the parish register period as a whole and for the four half-century periods are in general similar to those obtained by Wilson in his earlier review of English reconstitution data, though M is somewhat higher in the current exercise.[79] All suffer, however, from the fact that the shape of the model curve, which is assumed to capture the typical shape of natural fertility, is a fallible guide and that as a result both M and m values are at best rough approximations rather than precise readings.[80]

Figure 7.7 plots the levels of M and m for the parish register period as a whole and for the four half-century periods for which details have just been given, and also the 95 per cent confidence regions round the plotted points.[81] The confidence region for the whole period is much smaller than the other four because of the much larger number of woman-years of observation on which it is based. There is a large area of overlap between the confidence regions for 1590–1639, 1720–69, and

[78] Broström, *Estimation in a model for natural fertility*, and 'Practical aspects'. The advantages of using maximum likelihood estimation are discussed in Wilson, Oeppen, and Pardoe, 'What is natural fertility?'.

[79] Wilson, 'Natural fertility in pre-industrial England', tab. 4.1, p. 55. For all periods combined Wilson found $M = 0.816$ and $m = 0.041$ if estimated from the observed ASMFRs, and $M = 0.784$ and $m = 0.005$ if estimated from rates adjusted to eliminate the effects of prenuptially conceived first births.

[80] Wilson, Oeppen, and Pardoe, 'What is natural fertility?'.

[81] For details of the method used to derive the confidence regions, ibid., pp. 6–8. The effect of sample size on the size of the confidence region is also discussed in these pages.

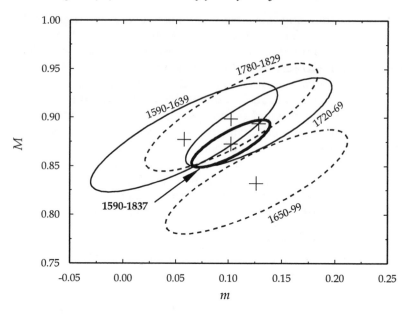

Figure 7.7   *The changing levels of* M *and* m *in England (with 95 per cent confidence regions)*
Source: Cambridge Group reconstitutions.

1780–1829, and indeed their similarity is emphasised further if similar plots are made using data which exclude the age-specific rates for the age group 15–9. The period 1780–1829 extends further 'north-east' than the other only because the age-specific fertility rate for 15–9 is much higher in this period than earlier because of the prevalence of prenuptially conceived first births at the time. The plot for 1650–99 stands clear of the other three periods, suggesting that the intervals between births were distinctly longer in this period than either earlier or later (it is M rather than m that appears significantly different). However, it was in this period that prenuptially conceived births were least common, and for this reason the period is less distinct from the others than appears at first sight.

In general the levels of M do not call for extensive comment. They are lower than those often found in reconstitution exercises in some other European countries, and lower than many of those used by Henry in constructing his model schedule of natural fertility,[82] but the reasons for

[82] The rates from which estimates of M and m can be derived are to be found in Henry, 'Some data on natural fertility'. The problems associated with their use, and especially the sample sizes on which they were based, are discussed by Wilson, Oeppen, and

this will be familiar in view of the evidence about the determinants of the length of birth intervals presented elsewhere in this chapter, especially in the section devoted to fecundability. The relatively low level of *m* reinforces the impression that early modern English parishes were communities in which 'natural fertility' was the norm. As a rough-and-ready rule, it has been suggested that a value of *m* greater than 0.20 may be taken as an indication that parity-related control of fertility within marriage may be occurring, and a value exceeding 0.30 may be taken as conclusive evidence of the same.[83] The levels quoted above for the four half-centuries were never as high as 0.13, and would have been lower still but for the distorting effect of prenuptially conceived births. The fact that *m* was low does not preclude the possibility that small groups may have been practising family limitation,[84] but the reconstitution evidence suggests that such behaviour was restricted to a small minority of the population, if present at all.[85]

The credibility of fertility estimates derived from parish registers

No registration system can hope to be perfectly accurate and comprehensive. The shortcomings of different systems, however, have varied enormously. Minor defects are of little consequence, but many vital registration systems have suffered from deficiencies so gross as to undermine the credibility of any analyses based upon them. The defects of Anglican registration are well known and have caused doubts to be expressed about the value of their exploitation as a source for the study of population behaviour in the past. The general issue of Anglican coverage has already been treated extensively, but the particular question of the accuracy of fertility measurement, especially in the last

Pardoe, 'What is natural fertility?'. By going back to the sources from which Henry derived his data, Wilson, Oeppen, and Pardoe also plot the confidence regions round the point estimates of each of the 10 fertility schedules used by Henry. These are plotted in fig. 4, p. 10, of their article. If the overall figures of *M* and *m* for early modern England had been plotted in this figure, there would have been 8 readings of *M* higher than the English figure and 3 lower, and 2 readings of *m* higher than the English figure with 9 lower.   [83] Knodel, *Demographic behavior in the past*, p. 297.

[84] A case in point is the fertility data for Colyton in the later seventeenth century, where the evidence for fertility control within marriage by a part of the community is persuasive, though the absence of comparable data for other parishes must raise doubts about its authoritativeness: Wrigley, 'Family limitation', and 'Marital fertility in seventeenth-century Colyton'; Morrow, 'Family limitation . . . a reappraisal'; Crafts and Ireland, 'Family limitation and the English demographic revolution'.

[85] As already noted (p. 457 n. 74), this evidence for the absence of family limitation relates only to parity-dependent behaviour. It throws no light on any possible parity-independent behaviour which may have taken place.

years of the period during which Anglican registers are by far the most important source of information, though touched on briefly in chapter 4, remains.[86] Fortunately, the data set out in table 7.37 permit a test of the reliability of Anglican coverage to be made.

The Registrar-General evinced far less interest in fertility than in mortality in the early decades of civil registration. No age-specific rates, for example, can be calculated from his data. But a test of the credibility of age-specific fertility rates derived from reconstitution data is nonetheless possible. The 1851 census provides a breakdown of the population by sex, marital status, and five-year age groups. The totals of married women by five-year age group are therefore known, and it is possible, by applying age-specific marital fertility rates taken from reconstitution data to age group totals of married women in 1851, to determine how many legitimate children would have been born if married women had experienced the same fertility rates as those found in the reconstitution parishes, and to compare the resulting totals of births with the totals recorded by the Registrar-General in his *Annual reports*.

The result of this exercise may be seen in table 7.38. Since all the reconstitution parishes are English, all the national data refer to England alone rather than to England and Wales.

The exercise is revealing. The reconstitution parishes appear to have been broadly representative of the English population as a whole, as appeared from the several tests made in chapter 3. If the rates which obtained in the reconstitution parishes in 1780–1829 are applied to married women in 1851, the total of births resulting is 10 per cent higher than the total recorded by the Registrar-General in a five-year period centring on 1851. Anglican registration was severely disrupted by the advent of civil registration in 1837. It is, therefore, not possible to calculate parish register fertility rates overlapping into the early years of civil registration. It is conceivable that if this had been possible, and, as a result, parish register-based ASMFRs were known for the 1840s and 1850s, they would reveal a sharp drop in marital fertility from the level prevailing in 1780–1829. This is unlikely, however, given the general stability of fertility rates throughout the parish register period. It is noteworthy in this connection that even if the fertility rates for the period 1700–49 are used, the resulting total is still more than 6 per cent higher than the civil registration total. It is therefore clear that the high level of prenuptial pregnancy in the late eighteenth and early nineteenth

[86] See above pp. 97–8.

Table 7.38 *English national birth totals derived from applying reconstitution marital fertility rates to census totals of married women compared with birth totals recorded by the Registrar-General*

	Legitimate births		1851 census: married women		Reconstitution ASMFRs (per 1000 woman-years lived)	
					1780–1829	1700–49
1849	505 167	15–9	21 301	15–9	532	323
1850	518 718	20–4	253 996	20–4	429	419
1851	538 971	25–9	424 004	25–9	390	374
1852	546 227	30–4	439 820	30–4	312	320
1853	537 275	35–9	394 793	35–9	255	249
Total	2 646 358	40–4	350 088	40–4	148	127
1849–53 average	529 272	45–9	280 632	45–9	23	23

Average annual total of legitimate births 1849–53	529 272 (a)
Total of births if 1780–1829 reconstitution ASMFRs had prevailed among married women in 1851	581 822 (b)
Total of births if 1700–49 reconstitution ASMFRs had prevailed among married women in 1851	561 843 (c)

Ratio (b)/(a) = 1.099   Ratio (c)/(a) = 1.062

Note: the totals of births recorded by the Registrar-General and the census totals refer to England only, rather than to England and Wales.
Sources: reconstitution ASMFRs: tab. 7.37. National totals of legitimate births: Registrar-General, *Annual reports*. 1851 census totals: *1851 census. Population tables II. Ages, civil condition, occupations and birth places of the people.*

centuries, which boosted age-specific rates in the younger age groups, is not a sufficient explanation of the difference between the reconstitution and civil registration totals, since prenuptial pregnancy was at a much lower level in the early eighteenth century.

It comes as no surprise that the registered totals of births should fall short of the true totals during the early years of civil registration. Before the 1874 Act there was no legal obligation laid upon parents to register the birth of a child.[87] Contemporaries such as William Farr, and many later scholars, have emphasised the substantial scale of underregistration during the early decades of the new system. For example, Farr, Glass, and Teitelbaum estimated the ratio of the true total to the recorded total in the decade 1841–51 as 1.065, 1.078, and 1.061 respectively, and for the following decade 1851–61 as 1.029, 1.042, and 1.028, while the comparable ratios for these two decades adopted in the *Population history of England* were 1.0780 and 1.0488.[88] The calculations in table 7.38 tend to confirm that the birth totals recorded in the early decades of civil registration were well short of the truth. The fact that the ratio of reconstitution to civil registration totals is higher than the ratios to be found in the work of Farr, Glass, and Teitelbaum may suggest either that a higher correction ratio for the Registrar-General's early returns is needed, or that the reconstitution parishes experienced a higher level of marital fertility than the country as a whole. Or again, there may have been some change in fertility levels between the early nineteenth century and its middle decades. At all events, the exercise does not suggest that the marital fertility rates calculated from reconstitution data quoted in table 7.37 need to be increased to allow for any significant degree of underregistration. No registration system is free from defects, and parish registers were certainly not complete records even of events occurring in the Anglican population, but suitably monitored and selected, they appear able to yield tolerably reliable fertility estimates.

Fecundability

The concept of fecundability

That the study of fecundity and the examination of the determinants of birth intervals are two sides of the same coin will be obvious from the earlier sections of this chapter. Important to the understanding of both is the concept of fecundability. The concept of fecundability refers to the probability of conceiving in the course of a single monthly cycle on the part of a woman who is capable of conceiving. The concept itself is simple, but it has proved difficult to match it with equally explicit and unambiguous empirical data. Insofar as measurements of fecundability exist, moreover, they refer almost exclusively to the early months of marriage. Reconstitution data, however, afford an opportunity to consider fecundability both early in marriage and in its later stages. This

---

[87] 37 & 38 Vict. c. 88.

[88] Wrigley and Schofield, *Population history of England*, tab. A8.4 and A8.5, pp. 635–6.

section, therefore, attempts both conventional and less conventional estimates of fecundability in early modern England.

In the case of married women there were often long periods after the beginning of fecundity and before the onset of sterility when a woman was not capable of conceiving, for example because she was pregnant or because she was amenorrhoeic as a result of breastfeeding a child. The fact that such periods were common makes the measurement of fecundability problematic. Its measurement usually presents fewest problems in relation to the first birth following a marriage. If there were no sexual intercourse before marriage, women would first become exposed to the risk of conception only after their marriage: none would be pregnant or engaged in breastfeeding. Moreover, it has been thought reasonable to suppose that intercourse will be frequent in the early months of marriage, thus enhancing the chance of conception, and leading to a maximum fecundability estimate.

In early modern England, of course, prenuptial pregnancies were frequent. If, however, births taking place less than 9 months after marriage are ignored, it is still possible to make estimates of fecundability, as Wilson has demonstrated.[89] What can be measured directly is *effective* fecundability, that is a conception which goes to term and results in a live birth (baptism). Since many conceptions failed to go to term a measure of effective fecundability will inevitably understate the frequency with which a conception takes place. Other features of social practice and Anglican registration in early modern England may have further compromised the possibility of measuring fecundability with accuracy and completeness. Two to which reference is often made are the delay between birth and baptism, which will cause the time elapsing between marriage and first birth to be overstated; and the alleged existence of the custom of baptising a first child in the parish of origin of the mother. This custom, where she was a 'foreigner', might mean that the first birth registered in the local parish register was the second rather than the first birth in the family.[90] The degree to which the measurement of fecundability is affected by such influences will become clearer when the data themselves have been examined.

Fecundability measured by the interval from marriage to first birth

In table 7.39 the basic data available for the estimation of fecundability from the interval between marriage and first birth are set out. They refer

[89] Wilson, 'Marital fertility in pre-industrial England', ch. 7.
[90] Though it should be noted, of course, that as a 'foreigner' it is also likely that she would have been married in another parish, and so cause no difficulty in this connection.

to the entire parish register period. The table is divided between cases where a date of marriage is known but the age of the wife at marriage is not known (column 1) and cases where both are known so that the data can be broken down by age at marriage (columns 2 to 9). The upper part of the table contains the 'raw' data; in the lower part, towards the foot of each column, there are some summary statistics conventionally used to measure fecundability and its concomitants.

It is vividly clear how frequently marriage did not represent the beginning of intercourse in early modern England. Although more children were born in the tenth month after marriage (that is, month 9) than in any other month, as might be expected, there were as many births in the months immediately preceding the peak, which may be taken as occurring in months 9–11, as there were in the months immediately succeeding the peak. Instead of a distribution of first birth intervals produced by intercourse following marriage, there were a variety of distributions superimposed on one another. The most important was that produced by the 'classic' inception of intercourse following marriage, but in addition groups of women, whose entry into the risk of conceiving dated back many months before their marriage, were also contributing to the observed totals of events, not merely during the first 9 months after marriage, but also after that point. The presence of births to women whose reproductive careers began well before marriage must inevitably complicate the measurement of fecundability from birth interval data. It is possible, therefore, that using conventional methods of estimating fecundability will tend to cause the true level of fecundability to be underestimated.

There is much of interest in table 7.39 apart from the information relating to fecundability. For example, a comparison of the lines which give the totals of births 0–8 months after marriage with those which give the totals for 9+ months brings out very clearly the far greater prevalence of prenuptiality among young brides than among older ones. Births in months 0–8 among teenage brides were 66 per cent as large as the total for 9+, but only 23 per cent as large among brides aged 35–9, with a regular progression by age in between. And among teenage brides 'late' prenuptial conceptions, which gave rise to births in the 8th and 9th months after marriage, were only 26 per cent of the 0–8 month total, but 45 per cent of the total among brides aged 35–9. Much of the far lower level of prenuptiality among older brides arose from intercourse which probably took place only after formal betrothal, whereas young brides were far more apt to have been pregnant long before their marriage took place, and often, probably, long before it was clear whether a marriage would take place.[91]

Bongaarts suggested a summary method that can yield acceptable estimates of fecundability using information about first birth intervals, derived from the ratio of births in months 9–11 after marriage to all births from 9 months onwards.[92] Bongaarts's method was in turn extended by Wilson who provided tables to enable either the ratio 9–11/9+ months or the ratio 9–11/9–23 months to be employed to estimate fecundability.[93] The two measures do not offer an unambiguous single estimate of fecundability since, when the raw data are translated into the fecundability estimates, using the two alternative methods, shown on the lines labelled Fec.(a) and Fec.(b), they prove to differ from one another. The latter (that is, 9–11/9–23) is consistently higher than the former. The differences between the two estimates are very small among the youngest marrying age groups but grow larger with age. The 9–11/9+ estimates suggest that fecundability is at its height among young women, with no evidence of lower fecundability among teenage brides, and a steady decline thereafter. The 9–11/9–23 estimates suggest a plateau of high fecundability in the 20s and early 30s but a slightly lower level of teenage fecundability and a decline above the age of 35.

This difference between fecundability estimates was noted by Wilson. In his discussion of the problem he favoured the ratio 9–11/9–23, which produces the higher fecundability estimates. He was moved to do so partly from a consideration of the proportion of all 9+ births which were 60+, remarking that this proportion, which is about 5 per cent when measured overall, was considerably higher than would be expected from fecundability models, which, at the levels of fecundability which appeared to have prevailed in early modern England, suggest a 60+/9+ ratio of about 2 per cent.[94] Wilson pointed out that there is evidence that women who were not born in the parish in which they had

---

[91] See, however, the discussion of older brides below, pp. 470–2, which illustrates the complexity of this issue. This issue is treated at greater length in Wrigley, 'Marriage, fertility and population growth', pp. 155–63. The issue of courtship practices and premarital pregnancy has attracted much attention and produced an extensive literature. See, for example, Laslett, *The world we have lost*; Quaife, *Wanton wenches*; Levine and Wrightson, 'The social context of illegitimacy'; and, more generally, Laslett, Oosterveen, and Smith, *Bastardy and its comparative history*.

[92] Bongaarts, 'A method for the estimation of fecundability'.

[93] Wilson, 'Marital fertility in pre-industrial England', app. 4, and esp. tab. A4.1. See also Wilson, 'The proximate determinants of marital fertility', pp. 212–9.

[94] Wilson, 'Marital fertility in pre-industrial England', pp. 111–3.

Table 7.39 Intervals from marriage to first birth and the estimation of fecundability (frequency counts)

Birth interval	Wife's age not known (1)	Wife's age at marriage						All (8)
		(2) 15–9	(3) 20–4	(4) 25–9	(5) 30–4	(6) 35–9	(7) 40 and over	
0	204.0	22.5	54.0	27.5	10.5	2.5	2.0	119.0
1	264.0	31.5	83.0	46.0	15.0	5.5	3.0	184.0
2	427.5	45.5	140.5	92.5	28.5	7.0	4.0	318.0
3	437.0	58.5	152.5	106.5	33.0	6.0	2.0	358.5
4	447.5	63.0	157.5	77.0	44.0	10.0	4.0	355.5
5	427.0	50.0	148.5	89.5	27.0	10.0	3.0	328.0
6	491.5	40.0	152.5	109.5	35.0	11.0	4.0	352.0
7	498.0	56.0	153.0	85.0	44.5	17.0	2.0	357.5
8	893.0	52.5	228.5	172.0	81.5	25.0	7.5	567.0
9	1706.5	92.5	447.5	317.0	131.5	40.5	10.5	1039.5
10	1429.5	86.5	379.5	257.5	142.5	35.0	8.0	909.0
11	1128.5	72.5	278.5	226.5	79.5	33.5	8.5	699.0
12	818.5	57.5	208.5	158.5	55.5	23.5	3.0	506.5
13	660.0	36.5	164.0	111.5	55.0	20.0	3.0	390.0
14	564.0	34.5	150.0	87.5	28.5	17.0	4.5	322.0
15	473.0	22.0	97.0	86.0	32.0	19.5	4.0	260.5
16	397.0	29.0	84.0	69.5	29.5	11.5	7.0	230.5
17	342.0	24.5	69.0	53.5	28.5	5.0	2.5	183.0
18	302.5	17.0	68.0	51.5	16.0	10.5	2.0	165.0
19	257.5	17.0	71.0	42.0	14.5	11.5	7.0	163.0
20	241.5	13.0	55.0	33.5	16.0	9.5	1.0	128.0
21	249.0	8.5	56.0	42.5	22.5	10.0	2.0	141.5
22	229.0	8.0	44.0	26.5	17.5	5.5	0.0	101.5
23	192.5	6.0	31.0	22.5	17.0	11.5	1.0	89.0

24–9	156.8	6.9	30.1	25.7	12.3	8.2	2.1	85.3
30–5	116.3	4.2	22.4	17.6	9.0	3.0	1.0	57.2
36–41	77.6	2.0	11.3	13.8	5.0	2.8	1.0	35.9
42–7	47.1	1.4	8.3	11.2	6.0	1.6	0.3	28.8
48–53	37.3	1.5	7.3	6.2	3.7	1.2	0.4	20.2
54–9	27.8	0.2	3.7	5.4	1.1	0.8	0.2	11.3
60+	11.5	0.2	1.3	2.0	1.2	0.7	0.1	5.5
All	16 546.0	1 050.5	4 051.5	2 990.5	1 299.0	503.5	133.0	10 028.0
0–8	4 089.5	419.5	1 270.0	805.5	319.0	94.0	31.5	2 939.5
9–11	4 264.5	251.5	1 105.5	801.0	353.5	109.0	27.0	2 647.5
9–23	8 991.0	525.0	2 203.0	1 586.0	686.0	264.0	64.0	5 328.0
9+	12 457.0	631.0	2 781.5	2 185.0	980.0	409.5	101.5	7 088.5
(a) 9–11/9+	0.342	0.399	0.397	0.367	0.361	0.266	0.266	0.373
(b) 9–11/9–23	0.474	0.479	0.502	0.505	0.515	0.413	0.422	0.497
Fec.(a)	0.18	0.22	0.22	0.20	0.19	0.13	0.13	0.20
Fec.(b)	0.22	0.23	0.25	0.26	0.27	0.17	0.18	0.25
60+/9+	0.055	0.014	0.029	0.055	0.073	0.098	0.074	0.046

Note: the frequency counts for rows 24–9 to 54–9 are the monthly averages for the 6 months comprising each period. In the row 60+ the overall frequency count was divided by 60 since the longest birth interval is 120 months.

Source: Cambridge Group reconstitutions.

settled with their husbands occasionally returned to their parish of origin to baptise their first children, and that, if this were the case, it would cause a proportion of second births to appear as first births in the local register, thus increasing the proportion of very long first birth intervals.[95] The alternative ratio, 9–11/9–23, he argued, is not subject to this potentially distorting influence and so produces a more reliable estimate.

The fuller data now available permit a new look at this issue. A first point to note is that the proportion of long intervals of more than 60 months is almost as high among brides whose age is known as it is amongst those whose age is not known (4.6 and 5.5 per cent respectively of all 9+ birth intervals: columns 1 and 8, table 7.39). The former group were all local-born, since to be able to calculate age at marriage the date of birth must be known, that is the baptism must appear in the register of the parish in question. The slightly higher ratio among those whose age is not known may have been due to the phenomenon which Wilson invoked, but may also be due to the inclusion of a higher proportion of older brides in this group. For example, the age of widows at marriage is known in a much smaller proportion of cases than the age of spinsters at marriage, so that the women figuring in column 1 would include proportionately more widows than those in the other columns. It seems clear, in any case, that the high proportion of 60+ birth intervals cannot be attributed to the presence of 'foreign' brides in the parish.

A striking feature of the ratios shown on the bottom line of the table is the steady and marked increase with age in the 60+/9+ ratio, from less than 2 per cent among teenage brides to almost 10 per cent among those marrying in their later 30s.[96] If age at marriage in England had been universally low with very few brides over 25 years of age at marriage, the proportion of long first birth intervals would not appear high. It is possible that the age of the wife may influence the 60+/9+ ratio. There are a number of possible mechanisms which might conceivably bring this about. For example, the proportion of miscarriages among older women might be higher in a first pregnancy. A lower frequency of intercourse with age would also point in the same direction. However, it is probable that the phenomenon is chiefly a function of another influence on the distribution of first birth intervals. This factor also helps to explain the divergence between the two sets of estimates of fecundability. Deficiencies in registration are not a plausible reason for the high level of the 60+/9+ ratio in marriage to first birth intervals. This is plain

---

[95] Ibid., pp. 118–9.

[96] The final, somewhat lower, figure for brides in their 40s is based on very small numbers and should probably not be regarded as significant.

from table 7.41 below which shows that the ratio is very low in the case of birth intervals later in marriage measured from the death of a child who died in infancy to the next birth in the family. The death of a child in infancy, by interrupting breastfeeding, creates a situation analogous to the interval from marriage to first birth. In these circumstances intervals greater than 60 months were well under 2 per cent of the total.

Table 7.39 shows a large number of very short marriage to first birth intervals. More than a quarter of all first births were prenuptially conceived: 26.5 per cent of all first births in the table occurred within the first 9 months after marriage. Almost 6 per cent occurred within the first 3 months of marriage. These early postnuptial births were matched by a large number of prenuptially conceived births. When illegitimacy was at its peak early in the nineteenth century about a quarter of all first births were illegitimate.[97] Many women who had had a first birth extra-nuptially later married, so that their second children would appear on an FRF as a first birth. Thus, a proportion of all the birth intervals that appear to be first birth intervals arose from a birth distribution for second or subsequent birth intervals rather than from a first birth interval distribution. For example, if a woman had a first birth, say, 1 month before marrying, the timing of her second birth, which would appear on her FRF as a first birth, would be determined by the factors influencing second rather than first birth intervals. For many months after marriage such a woman would be suckling and would experience a reduced likelihood of conception. Long apparent first birth intervals would then result.

The effect of the presence of a significant number of second birth intervals masquerading as first birth intervals cannot be determined without knowing the characteristic distribution of births prior to marriage in relation to the date of the marriage, and indeed of other factors, such as the frequency of intercourse in such circumstances in the interval between an earlier illegitimate birth and the subsequent marriage. But it is probable that the effect of the presence of such births would be to lower both the 9–11/9–23 and the 9–11/9+ ratios, and likely also that the effect would be greater in depressing the latter than the former. It seems rational, therefore, to follow Wilson in preferring the first of these two ratios as a measure of fecundability, though for somewhat different reasons than those which he discussed.

At the same time, this factor may also account, in part at least, for the

---

[97] The illegitimacy ratio in the late eighteenth and early nineteenth centuries was a little over 6 per cent (tab. 6.3, p. 224). A very high proportion of all illegitimate births were first births, and the proportion of all births which were first births was about a quarter. Thus roughly a quarter of all first births in this period were illegitimate.

changing proportion of 60+ birth intervals by wife's age at marriage. A very high proportion of teenage brides were prenuptially pregnant, but it is likely that relatively few of them had previously had a prenuptial birth. The briefness of the time available for such events following the inception of fecundity in the case of such women is sufficient reason to suppose that this is likely. There is also evidence to suggest that the mean age at first birth of women bearing a child outside marriage was much the same as for first births within marriage.[98] This, too, argues against any significant number of teenage brides having borne a child before marriage. With increasing age at marriage, the likelihood of having already borne a child outside marriage increased, and with it the chance that the first child appearing on an FRF was not the first child of the woman in question. A woman who was breastfeeding a younger child for, say, a year after marriage, other things being equal, would be more likely to have a long first birth interval after her marriage than a woman without previous children at marriage.

Levels of fecundability of about 0.25, such as are suggested by the 9–11/9–23 ratio in the final column of table 7.39, are in the middle or towards the upper end of the range of estimates available for other European populations in the past. In the German villages studied by Knodel, for example, the level in a combined sample, when standardised for age at marriage, was about 0.22 in the eighteenth century, rising substantially in the nineteenth century to the range 0.26 to 0.28.[99] It should be noted that, although the fecundability estimates are based on measures of *effective* fecundability (the conceptions which give rise to a live birth), the estimates themselves are of *recognisable* fecundability (defined by Bongaarts as 'the probability of a conception which is recognised at the end of the conception cycle by the nonoccurrence of the menstruation'[100]). The nature of the difference between recognisable and effective fecundability will become clearer in the section dealing with fecundability later in marriage.[101]

Change over time

Only the data for the whole parish register period have so far been considered. Studying data for subperiods is of value not only in showing whether fecundability changed over time, but also in order to

---

[98] Oosterveen, Smith, and Stewart, 'Family reconstitution and the study of bastardy', pp. 107–10, 130–2.

[99] Knodel and Wilson, 'The secular increase in fecundity', tab. 7, p. 68.

[100] Bongaarts, 'A method for the estimation of fecundability', p. 646.

[101] See especially p. 488 below.

discover how far some of the idiosyncrasies of English registration affected the data. For example, in table 7.39 the first birth interval distribution peaks less sharply at the tenth month (birth interval 9) than would be expected from models of fecundability. In both column 1 and column 8 this month is the highest figure in the series, but, especially in column 8, it is not as much larger than the eleventh month as might be expected. This is due, at least in part, to the lengthening of the conventional interval between birth and baptism during the eighteenth century, which would, of course, increase the measured interval from marriage to first birth (baptism), even though the true interval had remained the same.[102] By looking at tabulations for different time periods it is possible to see how much of the bluntness of the tenth month peak in the overall data set is due to the presence of material drawn from the period when late baptism was common.

In order to avoid taking up excessive space, only summary information about first birth intervals and fecundability estimates is given in table 7.40. The data are given for three subperiods. The age at marriage divisions have been reduced to three, 15–9, 20–34, and 35 and over. The first division was retained from the earlier table, since the possibility that teenage brides were of lower fecundability deserves examination. The amalgamation of the next three five-year age at marriage groups reflects the fact that fecundability, measured from the interval from marriage to first birth, appears to have varied very little between these age at marriage groups, and it is an advantage that merging the three groups means that the numbers of women involved are large and the estimates consequently more dependable. Finally, since the number of women who married above the age of 35 was always small, they are best treated as a single group when considering the three subperiods.

In the first two subperiods, shown in the two top panels of table 7.40, when there was normally only a brief interval between birth and baptism, the relative size of the totals of births in the tenth, eleventh, and twelfth months (months 9–11) conforms to expectation. The first of the three was much the highest total, and the twelfth month saw only 60–5 per cent as many births as the tenth month.[103] With the lengthening

---

[102] Schofield and Berry, 'Age at baptism'.

[103] There is a discussion of the relative size of 9-, 10-, and 11-month birth totals and their determinants in Bongaarts, 'A method for the estimation of fecundability', pp. 652–4. As an example, he estimated the relative proportions involved by fitting a model to empirical data drawn from a study of Tourouvre-au-Perche, a French parish with a level of fecundability similar to that in English parishes. In the case of Tourouvre-au-Perche the twelfth month total of births was 63.5 per cent of the tenth month total (tab. 3, p. 654).

Table 7.40 Fecundability estimates by time period

	Wife's age not known (1)	Wife's age at marriage					Wife's age not known (1)	Wife's age at marriage			
		(2) 15–9	(3) 20–34	(4) 35 and over	(5) All			(2) 15–9	(3) 20–34	(4) 35 and over	(5) All
			1550–1649						1650–1749		
9	515.0	20.0	221.0	13.5	254.5		746.5	44.0	403.0	25.5	472.5
10	395.5	16.0	168.5	12.0	196.5		605.5	24.0	342.0	19.0	385.0
11	330.0	18.5	125.0	9.0	152.5		467.5	25.0	260.5	20.5	306.0
9–11	1 240.5	54.5	514.5	34.5	603.5		1 819.5	93.0	1 005.5	65.0	1 163.5
9–23	2 768.0	138.0	1 052.5	84.0	1 274.5		3 785.0	182.0	1 952.0	157.0	2 291.0
9+	3 878.5	177.0	1 380.5	117.0	1 674.5		5 117.5	210.0	2 556.5	247.5	3 014.0
60+	196.0	1.0	56.0	9.0	66.0		273.5	3.0	112.0	24.0	139.0
All	5 229.0	234.0	1 885.5	147.5	2 267.0		6 346.5	289.5	3 244.5	288.5	3 822.5
(a) 9–11/9+	0.320	0.308	0.373	0.295	0.360		0.356	0.443	0.393	0.263	0.386
(b) 9–11/9–23	0.448	0.395	0.489	0.411	0.474		0.481	0.511	0.515	0.414	0.508
Fec.(a)	0.17	0.16	0.20	0.15	0.19		0.19	0.26	0.22	0.13	0.21
Fec.(b)	0.20	0.15	0.24	0.17	0.22		0.23	0.26	0.27	0.17	0.26
60+/9+	0.051	0.006	0.041	0.077	0.039		0.053	0.014	0.044	0.097	0.046
9+/all	0.742	0.756	0.732	0.793	0.739		0.806	0.725	0.788	0.858	0.788

1750–1837

						All				
9	445.0	28.5	272.0	12.0	312.5	1 706.5	92.5	896.0	51.0	1 039.5
10	428.5	46.5	269.0	12.0	327.5	1 429.5	86.5	779.5	43.0	909.0
11	331.0	29.0	199.0	12.5	240.5	1 128.5	72.5	584.5	42.0	699.0
9–11	1204.5	104.0	740.0	36.5	880.5	4 264.5	251.5	2 260.0	136.0	2 647.5
9–23	2438.0	205.0	1 470.5	87.0	1 762.5	8 991.0	525.0	4 475.0	328.0	5 328.0
9+	3 460.5	244.0	2 009.5	146.5	2 400.0	12 457.0	631.0	5 946.5	511.0	7 088.5
60+	218.5	5.0	104.5	14.5	124.0	688.0	9.0	272.5	47.5	329.0
All	4 970.5	527.0	3 211.0	200.5	3 938.5	16 546.0	1 050.5	8 341.0	636.5	10 028.0
(a) 9–11/9+	0.348	0.426	0.368	0.249	0.367	0.342	0.399	0.380	0.266	0.373
(b) 9–11/9–23	0.494	0.507	0.503	0.420	0.500	0.474	0.479	0.505	0.415	0.497
Fec.(a)	0.18	0.24	0.20	0.12	0.20	0.18	0.22	0.21	0.13	0.20
Fec.(b)	0.24	0.26	0.25	0.17	0.25	0.22	0.23	0.26	0.17	0.25
60+/9+	0.063	0.020	0.052	0.099	0.052	0.055	0.014	0.046	0.093	0.046
9+/all	0.696	0.463	0.626	0.731	0.609	0.753	0.601	0.713	0.803	0.707

Source: Cambridge Group reconstitutions.

delay between birth and baptism which occurred as the eighteenth century progressed, the sharp peak previously visible in the tenth month became flattened and there were as many births (baptisms) in the eleventh month as in the tenth in the period after 1750.

The fecundability estimates derived from the ratio 9–11/9–23 are very similar in the periods 1650–1749 and 1750–1837. Given the displacement of dates of 'birth' by the delay in baptism, one might speculate that fecundability was not the same in the two periods but had increased between them, since some births that should have been included in the 9–11 month period had been displaced into later months. But this effect, if present at all, seems to have been relatively slight in its impact, no doubt because the frequency of births in the ninth month after marriage (month 8), some of which would also be displaced to the right, largely offsets the later displacement.

It is possible to test whether the blunting of the peak has led to too low a 9–11 total, and a consequent underestimation of fecundability in the final period. If the true level of fecundability were higher after 1750 than before but this were concealed by the displacement of births to the right because of baptism delay, it is to be expected that if the ratio were calculated over a larger number of months after the tenth month peak, the ratio in the later period would be higher than in its predecessor. For example, one might expect that if a 9–13/9–23 ratio were calculated it would be higher after 1750 than before because the displacement effect would be more strongly present in one period than in the other. Experiment shows that this is not the case, and it is therefore reasonable to make the assumption that fecundability can continue to be estimated from the 9–11/9–23 ratio for the last period without serious risk of error. The possibility of a rise should not be excluded, however, since fecundability measured from cases where the wife's age was not known (column 1) rose slightly between the middle and last periods, and these estimates were based on a larger number of women than those for women whose age was known.

Table 7.40 suggests that fecundability was lower before 1650 than over the next two centuries, though after 1650 there was little change. In the main 20–34 age at marriage group the rise from the early to the middle period was similar in scale to that in the large group consisting of marriages in which the wife's age at marriage is unknown, a group in which a substantial majority of brides would have been in the 20–34 age group. After 1750 there was a small fall in the measure based on the 20–34 age at marriage group but a further modest rise in the group where age is unknown, suggesting a broadly stable situation. Among teenage brides there was a sharp rise between the early and middle periods, but thereafter little or no change. Fecundability in brides marrying above the age of 35 was the same in all three periods.

In each subperiod, as overall, estimates based on the two ratios 9–11/9–23 and 9–11/9+ are very similar for teenage brides but draw apart with increasing bridal age.

The proportion of 60+ births was always very small indeed in teenage brides and rose steadily with age in the three subperiods, just as in the parish register period as a whole. It may be significant that the 60+/9+ ratio is higher in the last period than in the middle period. Since illegitimacy was much higher after 1750 than in the preceding century, it is to be expected that there would be a rise in proportion of second births incorrectly identified as first births (because the first birth was illegitimate and preceded the marriage). This in turn might lead to an increase in very long intervals. However, there was also a rise in the 60+/9+ ratio between the first and second periods, though the level of illegitimacy was falling from a relatively high level in the late sixteenth century to a much lower level in the later seventeenth century, which suggests caution in drawing a firm conclusion.

In summary, therefore, the available data from first birth intervals suggest that fecundability in the age range 20–34 was about 0.26 after 1650, though somewhat lower in the preceding period. Fecundability was at a lower level among teenage brides than among those aged 20–34, and markedly lower in older brides above the age of 35. Given the prevalence of prenuptial births and of prenuptial conceptions, whose effect on the overall distribution of first birth intervals (that is, of the intervals from marriage to the first birth occurring after marriage) is difficult to quantify, these estimates lack the precision which might be achieved in a population where marriage and the beginning of the reproductive career coincided more closely, but they suggest moderately high fecundability levels in early modern England.

Fecundability later in marriage

Most studies of fecundability depend upon information about the distribution of first birth intervals. It is usually held to be difficult to measure fecundability at any other stage of a marriage, for reasons already discussed. If feasible, it would clearly be attractive to be able to measure fecundability later in marriage, for example to test the assumption that fecundability tended to fall with duration of marriage because the frequency of intercourse declined. The opportunity exists to explore issues of this kind by taking advantage of data relating to women who lost a child in infancy when still breastfeeding. Breastfeeding tended to induce amenorrhoea. Although women sometimes became pregnant while still breastfeeding, especially when the child at breast reached the age of 1 year or more, most women did not become pregnant again until after having ceased breastfeeding. The death of a child who was still being breastfed, therefore, normally signalled a return to exposure to the likelihood of a new pregnancy. Just as marriage represented a transition from a state with a relatively low risk of pregnancy to a state where the risk was much enhanced, so the same was true for the death of a suckling infant. If the infant died very young, say within the first month of life, the mother characteristically required some time to become fully fecund once more. When the infant had reached a greater age, the interval before the return of full fecundity was much shorter.[104] Accordingly, the subsequent peak in new births was sharper and more pronounced following a relatively late infant death than after an early death. In either case, the proportion of births which were conceived in the months immediately following the death of the previous child will yield a clue to levels of fecundability when a couple were well into married life rather than at its beginning.

Figure 7.8 provides a striking visual image of the pattern of fecundability following the death of the previous child in infancy. Each line in the four panels of the graph represents the subsequent fertility history of all women who had it in common that they lost their previous child in a particular month of its life. Each panel contains the details of six such groups, the first panel representing women who lost a previous child in months 0 to 5, the second in months 6 to 11, the third in months 12 to 17, and the fourth in months 18 to 23. Thus the first line (furthest to the left) in the top panel refers to all those who lost a previous child in the first month of life, the second line to those who lost a previous child in the second month of life, and so on. The first line in each panel is solid, the second broken, and so on, in a regular sequence. The heavy black line in each panel records the fecundability of women who did *not* lose the earlier child of a pair. The data were drawn from the whole period 1538 to 1837, and, to ensure maximum accuracy and consistency, all birth intervals beginning and ending with a baptism weighted *70 or *71 were excluded from the tabulations, since such weights indicate a degree of

---

[104] In women who do not breastfeed, modern studies suggest that normal ovulation is resumed between 45 and 120 days postpartum. If a breastfeeding woman loses a child within a few days or weeks of birth, therefore, there will be a longer period before the resumption of normal ovulation than where the child died at a greater age, because of the proximity of the birth. McNeilley, 'Breastfeeding and fertility', p. 391.

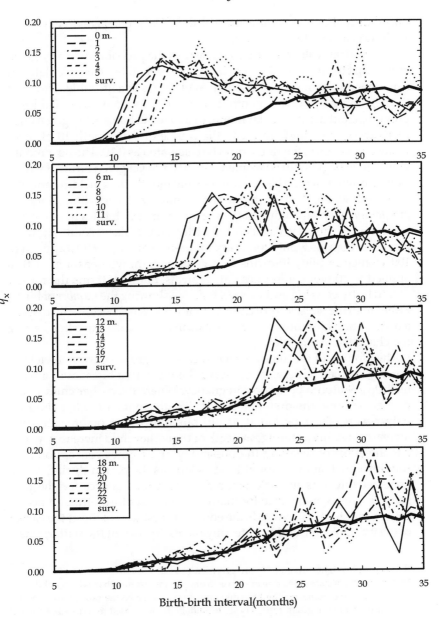

Figure 7.8 *Fecundability: probability of closing a closed birth interval following an infant death by age at death of earlier child of the birth interval*
Source: Cambridge Group reconstitutions.

uncertainty about the timing of the birth.[105] Only marriages in which the bride was a spinster were used.

The vertical scale in figure 7.8 measures the probability in any given month that the next child will be born. The probability was calculated in a manner analogous to the calculation of the q_xs in a life table. Thus if at the beginning of a given month there were 100 women who had lost a previous child in a particular month of its age but had not yet given birth to a subsequent child, and if in the course of that month 10 of these women gave birth, the rate would be calculated as 0.10. The next month would then begin with 90 women who had not yet given birth, of whom a given number would be delivered in that month, thus yielding another rate; and so on.[106] It is important to note that each line plots the *probability* of a birth taking place in a given month. It does not give any indication of the relative *number* of births taking place. A line showing d_xs rather than q_xs would look very different. Thus a q_x of 0.10 applied to 100 women implies 10 births in a given month, whereas a q_x of 0.50 applied to 10 women implies only 5 births, but in d_x terms the former would be twice as big as the latter. A d_x line showing the *number* of births rather than the *probability* of a birth would, of course, necessarily display a distribution far more concentrated in an early peak than a line having the character of a q_x plot.

The plotting of the lines for each successive group of women yields a notably regular pattern. The interval between two births will always include a 9-month period of pregnancy. Where the earlier child of the pair died within the first month of its life, the mother fed her child for only a very short period if at all, but the period of breastfeeding increases steadily as the age at death of the earlier child increases, which has the effect of delaying the possibility of a further conception by a roughly equal amount, for at least as long as the period during which breastfeeding was the sole or predominant food source for the new baby.[107] This remains true for many months after birth, though not, of course, indefinitely. Towards the end of the first year of life of the earlier of the two children, and to a steadily increasing extent thereafter, a new

---

[105] Details of weights *70 and *71 are given on p. 112.

[106] Eventually, of course, the rate must rise to unity in the last month in which a child was born since the numerator and the denominator will then be the same. However, the upward tilt to the graph representing fecundability by elapsed months since the last birth, imposed by this necessity, only affects the trend of the line towards its end. It may be ignored in studying the figures included in this chapter.

[107] The intensity of suckling is the chief determinant of the length of the postpartum absence of menses. Intense suckling can delay the resumption of menses by between one and two years. McNeilley, 'Breastfeeding and fertility', p. 393.

conception might occur even though the mother was still breastfeeding, as is clear, indeed, from the lines in figure 7.8.[108]

The pattern of the lines represents convincing evidence both of the small probability of conceiving while breastfeeding was taking place during the early months of the life of a new baby, and of the rapidity with which a new conception occurred following the death of an earlier child. Thus, the line representing births to women who lost their previous child in the first month of its life starts to climb abruptly after the eleventh month (month 10) after the birth of the child which died. Allowing for the fact that, on average, 9 months must elapse from conception to birth, this implies that a substantial proportion of women in this category became pregnant in the second month after losing their earlier child.[109] The line then rises steadily and quickly to reach a peak in the fifteenth month (month 14) after the preceding birth, corresponding to a peak in conception rates in the sixth month after the death of the earlier child. After the fifteenth month fecundability declines steadily, to form a rough plateau after about the twenty-fifth month. The subsequent lines display a markedly regular, similar pattern, succeeding one another like a series of overlapping waves.

The shape of the first few lines changes somewhat, showing a tendency to climb more steeply towards a sharper and higher peak, though the change is not uniform or regular. This pattern is probably due to the effects of parturition being superimposed on those associated with an abrupt end to breastfeeding. Close to the previous birth it will take longer for the normal monthly cycle of fecundable ovulation to establish itself following an infant death than is the case with a death occurring some months later.[110] The peak values for the lines representing cases where the earlier child died in the second, third, and fourth month after birth all occur in the fifteenth month (month 14), just as was

[108] The likelihood of conceiving is, however, reduced by breastfeeding even after menstruation has resumed. Breastfeeding women in these circumstances are only about one third as likely to conceive as those who have stopped breastfeeding. Ibid., p. 397.

[109] The presence of a very small number of births less than 9 months after the previous birth, evidently a physical impossibility, is attributable to defects in the data. For most of the parish register period it was the baptism rather than the birth date that was recorded in the register, and, since delay in baptism became increasingly common, especially during the eighteenth century, a number of 'impossible' intervals will arise when a delayed baptism is followed in the same family by the prompt baptism of the next child. For each birth interval that is too 'short', however, there will also be a birth interval that is too 'long', so that although the variance of true birth intervals will be exaggerated slightly by this defect in the data, the mean is not affected.

[110] See p. 478 n. 104 above.

the case where the earlier child died in the first month after birth. This suggests that the resumption of normal ovulation was more strongly affected by the after effects of the birth process than by the cessation of breastfeeding up to this point. Thereafter, however, the successive peaks are usually a month apart, though the feature is not entirely regular, no doubt due to the variability associated with small numbers of cases.

The pattern of the peak values is of interest. The tendency of peak values to increase in the first and second panels (that is until the peaks related to women who lost the earlier child when it was about a year old) suggests that the highest level of fecundability was not reached until well after the birth of the previous child, though whether this is to be attributed to the physiological effects of the previous birth, or to behavioural changes, for example a rising frequency of intercourse, to some combination of the two, or to other factors, is unclear.

All the women whose histories are represented in the heavy solid line escaped the loss of the earlier child of the pair and therefore their breastfeeding was not brought to an abrupt, premature halt.[111] Naturally, this line rises much less rapidly than the lines relating to cases where the earlier child died young and the period of breastfeeding was truncated as a result. However, in the course of time, as breastfeeding ceased to affect fecundability among those who did not lose the earlier child, and as the fecundability surge following the death of a child ceased to affect the level of the lines representing women whose earlier child had died, all the lines tend to converge and jointly form a fecundability plateau from about the thirtieth month after the birth of the earlier child. Moreover, the individual lines representing women who lost a child in infancy also lie close to the heavy line *before* the death of the earlier child, or, in other words, women who lost a child and those who did not were equally likely to become pregnant up to the point at which, in the case of the former, the child died. The child's death resulted in a discontinuity between the two lines for a time before the lines again converged.

The pattern of lines in the lower panels of the figure becomes increasingly hectic and the lines sometimes also move irregularly at a much earlier point. This is chiefly due to the small number of events on

---

[111] The cases which make up the heavy solid line fall into two categories: those where the child is known to have survived early infancy and those where the fate of the child is unknown, but it is reasonable to suppose that infancy was survived since the family remained in observation and no death was recorded. There is good reason to suppose that the assumption of survival to beyond the first birthday is justified in the latter case. See pp. 439–43 above.

which the probabilities were based in many cases. With larger numbers a smoother and more regular pattern should be visible. This suggests reordering the data shown in figure 7.8. If individual months whose character is fundamentally similar are merged into a single data set much of the random variability may be expected to disappear. If, however, this were all that was done, the result would be misleading. For example, if, say, months 6–11 displayed very similar patterns and data for these 6 months were consolidated into a single set, the resulting curve would have a lowered peak and a flat top because of the averaging out effect inherent in conflating what appear as a series of staggered peaks when the analysis is done month by month. The larger the number of months amalgamated in this way, the greater the degree to which the true height of the fecundability peak would be obscured.

There is, however, a simple solution to this problem. The phenomenon which caused fecundability to peak in the case of women who lost a child early in life was the death of the young child. This put an abrupt stop to breastfeeding. It is equivalent to knowing when a child was weaned in the case of a woman who did not lose the earlier child of a pair. As we shall see, if the date of weaning were known for such women, it is probable that a very similar pattern of fecundability would be found in all women, when measured from the date when breastfeeding ceased. To capture the peak level of fecundability, therefore, it is sensible, where a woman lost a child in infancy, to begin the measurement period from the death of the infant rather than from its birth. Doing so removes the stagger between the peaks which is such a striking feature of figure 7.8, and enables the data for groups of months with similar characteristics to be merged without causing the peak level of fecundability to be depressed.

The result can be seen in the top panel of figure 7.9. Experiment showed which groups of the months representing the age at death of the child, which were shown separately in the last figure, preserved their individual character without multiplying the entities involved any more than necessary. Within each grouping the component months displayed very similar characteristics. The groups are: 0, 1–2, 3–11, and 12–26 months. The death of an earlier child at any age greater than 26 months appeared, again by experiment, to have little or no effect on the subsequent pattern of fecundity of the women concerned. Up to 26 months, however, there is evidence that conceptions surged soon after the death of a child, which in turn demonstrates that a proportion of women were still breastfeeding not merely throughout the second year of a child's life, but into its third year. The number of cases of child deaths declined steadily with age, however, and was quite small at relatively high ages, such as 26 months, and the subsequent fecundability patterns are greatly affected by randomness, so that the decision about the last cut-off point was necessarily arbitrary.

In figure 7.9 the figure 0 on the horizontal axis represents the point in time when the earlier child died, so that a peak value at, say, 11 months (that is in the twelfth month) means that fecundability reached a high point in the third month after the death of the earlier child. A line representing fecundability patterns following marriage, and based on the interval between marriage and first birth, is included. It is the lighter of the two solid lines. In this case 0 on the horizontal axis represents marriage rather than the death of the earlier child. The heavy solid line once again represents the fecundability pattern of women whose earlier child did not die. In this case 0 represents not the birth of the earlier child of the pair, but a point in time 19 months after the birth of the earlier child. For reasons presented later, it is reasonable to suppose that the average length of breastfeeding of these women was 19 months, so that, both for such women and for those whose earlier child died, 0 represents the point at which breastfeeding ceased, though for the former it is less precisely located.[112]

The upper panel of figure 7.9 brings to light a number of points related to fecundability which are of great interest. For simplicity's sake the various lines in the figure will be referred to hereafter as line 0, line 1–2, and so on. Line 0 traces out, of course, a very similar shape to that in the last figure, differing only in that the date of death of the child is slightly later than the date of its birth. It never attains a peak as high as any of the other lines representing the experience of women who had lost a child in infancy. Line 1–2 is also relatively flat topped but records a peak earlier than line 0, in month 11 rather than month 13.[113] The after-effects of giving birth, however, superimposed upon those of the loss of a child, are still affecting the height and shape of the peak of the fecundability curve. Thereafter all the subsequent data concerning fecundability following the death of an earlier child are grouped into two sets, shown in line 3–11 and line 12–26. Both these groups sweep up to a higher and sharper peak than the other lines. The peak occurs in month 11 as with line 1–2 but is more pronounced and clear-cut. Since a twelfth month birth implies a third month conception, it is clear that normal ovulation took a few weeks to become reestablished following the death of the earlier child, or that intercourse was restrained for a period. Compari-

[112] See below pp. 489–92.

[113] It is more accurate to say that line 1–2 experiences a plateau of fecundability between months 11 and 13 than that it peaks in month 12. It is clear, however, that the peak comes earlier than with line 0.

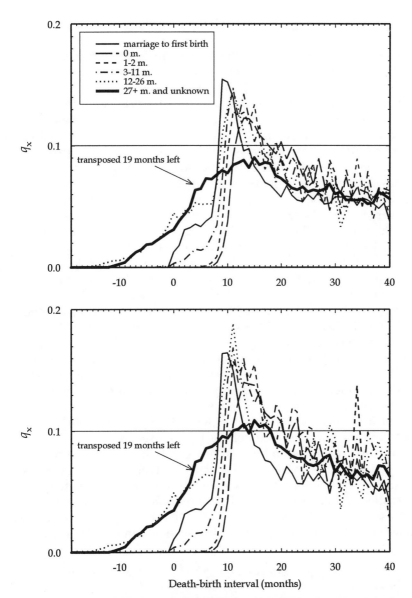

Figure 7.9 *Fecundability: probability of closing a closed birth interval following an infant death (upper panel, death–birth intervals: lower panel, death–birth intervals, excluding last births)*

Note: all the broken lines represent death to birth intervals. The key indicates how old the earlier child of a birth interval pair was at the time of its death. The thin continuous line shows the marriage to first birth interval. The thick continuous line relates to cases where either the earlier child is known to have survived to more than 27 months, or its fate is unknown, and represents birth to birth intervals.

Source: Cambridge Group reconstitutions.

son of lines 3–11 and 12–26 with the line representing marriage to first birth shows that fecundability could be virtually as high later in marriage as at its start, though the peak in the latter case occurs two months earlier than in the former, a pattern that occasions little surprise given the physiological changes and the emotional trauma associated with the death of a young child and the cessation of breastfeeding.

Some further light on breastfeeding and fecundability patterns is provided by the behaviour of the lines to the left of the point marked 0. Lines 3–11 and 12–26 show clearly that many women who lost the earlier child of the pair were already pregnant when the child's death occurred, since the later child was born less than 9 months after the death of its older sibling.[114] Furthermore line 12–26, which extends well to the left of 0, shows that the later child of the pair was sometimes not merely conceived but already born before the earlier child died. The path traced out by this line is notably similar to the line representing women who did not lose the earlier child of a pair until the effect of the death of the earlier child causes line 12–26 to move sharply up to its peak in month 11. In effect both lines have a common origin. The solid heavy line was transposed 19 months to the left. Virtually the same happens to line 12–26 since the average age at death of the children whose deaths gave rise to its construction will have been a little less than 19 months, and 0 will therefore be placed roughly 19 months after the birth of the earlier child on average.

The agreement between the two lines (12–26 and 27+) suggests that both groups of women were coming back into childbearing at a similar tempo. Many women in both groups would have resumed menstruation in the course of the second year of life of the earlier child, but their chance of conception would remain depressed as long as they were breastfeeding, at about one third of the 'normal' level.[115] In a proportion of cases in both groups of women, of course, breastfeeding would also have been discontinued, but sufficient women continued to breastfeed

---

[114] Strictly speaking, since the lines refer only to the probabilities of conception month by month, it is not possible to make any inference about the numbers of women in these categories who were already pregnant again when the earlier child died. However, a glance at the totals on the rows in tab. 7.41 on p. 498, referring to all births, and to births occurring more than 9 months after the death of the earlier child, shows the scale of the phenomenon. In the case of an infant death between 3 and 11 months 17.5 per cent of women were again pregnant when the death occurred, while for the 12 to 26 month category the comparable figure was 56.8 per cent (combining in each case the totals in the panels where the wife's age was known with the totals from the panel in which the wife's age was not known).   [115] See p. 481 n. 108 above.

until late in the second year and even beyond for the overall rate to remain relatively low.

All the lines tend to converge after about month 25 as the birth interval grows to the point where any breastfeeding effect has disappeared. The pronounced random variability of the individual lines in figure 7.8 obscured the convergence process, but in figure 7.9 it is clearly visible.

The upper panel of figure 7.9 provides strong evidence in support of the view that fecundability remained relatively constant over the childbearing years, or, in other words, that levels of fecundability calculated from marriage to first birth intervals were maintained for many years thereafter. However, a further refinement shows that the level of fecundability was higher over most of the fertile span than suggested by the upper panel, and that it may even have been less high at the start of a marriage than later. The lines in the upper panel are based on all birth intervals including the last. But last birth intervals were considerably longer than earlier birth intervals and it is therefore instructive to reconsider the fecundability evidence after having removed last birth intervals from the data set. The lower panel of figure 7.9 shows the results of doing this. It provides a more accurate estimate of the level of fecundability prevailing over the bulk of a woman's childbearing life.

Removal of the last birth interval presents no difficulties in the case of completed families, but in a proportion of the FRFs used in measuring fecundability, it is not clear whether the last birth recorded is a 'true' last birth in the sense that the woman had ceased to be fecund. Both out-migration and early death might mean that the last birth on the FRF was not the last birth in the more restricted, technical sense. To err on the safe side last birth intervals on all FRFs were barred from the tabulation of fecundability excluding last birth intervals, thereby ensuring that all 'true' last birth intervals were excluded, though at the cost of eliminating also some birth intervals that would have been retained if information were more complete.

The lower panel of figure 7.9 shows a somewhat changed picture compared with that given in the upper panel. The most obvious effect is to raise all the lines on the graph, but not all are raised in the same proportion. This is to be expected since the proportion of last births differed in the several data sets. The fecundability estimates based on the interval from marriage to first birth are raised only slightly. The peak value increases from 0.155 to 0.165, or by only 6–7 per cent. In the case of line 12–26, on the other hand, the peak value rises from 0.145 to 0.188 or by almost 30 per cent. In consequence, whereas these two peak values were at roughly the same height in the upper panel, the latter is substantially the higher of the two in the lower panel, conveying the general impression that, at least in the case of women who lost an earlier child when it was aged 3–11 months or 12–26 months, fecundability was higher in the middle years of marriage than at its beginning. Lines 0 and 1–2 in the lower panel, though also substantially raised by excluding last birth intervals, retain the same flattened top as was visible in the upper panel, no doubt for the reason already given, while the heavy solid line, representing cases where the earlier child survived, rises to a peak value in excess of 0.1 when last births are excluded, whereas otherwise the peak value is only about 0.09. As in the upper panel, the several lines converge after about the 30th month, except for the marriage to first birth line, which tends to remain slightly below all the others.

Figure 7.9 affords a convenient opportunity to consider further the distinction between recognisable and effective fecundability. It will be recalled that the distribution of marriage to first birth intervals suggested a level of recognisable fertility of about 0.25. It might therefore seem odd that the line in figure 7.9 representing these data reaches a peak of only 0.155, or 0.165 after the elimination of last birth intervals. The peak in the tenth month after marriage seems less high than might have been expected. The explanation lies principally in three considerations. The first is obvious from the definition of recognisable fecundability. Any loss of a foetus through spontaneous abortion will cause a proportion of women who become pregnant in the first month after marriage to fail to produce a live birth 9 months later. Secondly, a proportion of women who did conceive in the first month, and who went to term successfully, gave birth in month 8 or month 10 rather than in month 9 after marriage, thus causing a flattening of the month 9 peak. Thirdly, some women are more fecund than others. A figure for the fecundability of a population of women represents an averaging out of the experience of some women who were quick to conceive and others who were slow to do so. In other words, women are heterogeneous rather than homogeneous in respect of fecundability. This, too, may have the effect of causing the initial peak to be less pronounced than might have been expected. All three of these factors are discussed by Bongaarts.[116] Jointly, they reconcile the patterns visible in figure 7.9 with the estimate of recognisable fecundability of 0.25 to be found in table 7.39.

Heterogeneity is also the reason for the slow fall in the lines in figure

[116] Bongaarts, 'A method for the estimation of fecundability'.

7.9 after the initial peaks. The more fecund women are progressively removed from those at risk to conceive because they become pregnant, leaving the less fecund still in the pool from which later q_xs are calculated. For any one woman the chance of becoming pregnant may be constant in each monthly cycle, but for a group of women this is not so since their average fecundability declines as the composition of the group changes by the conceptions taking place among them.

Comparatively little has been said so far about the line representing women whose earlier child did not die. This line rises to a peak of only about 0.11, far below the maximum reached by line 12–26. Yet one might expect the fecundability of these women to be little different from the less fortunate mothers whose earlier child died. The cause of the upsurge to a high peak in the more dramatic lines in the figure was the enforced ending of breastfeeding brought about by the death of the earlier child. But women who did not lose their child all stopped breastfeeding too, though by choice, or from custom, or because of some physiological deficiency, rather than because of the death of a young child. It is therefore to be presumed that if it were possible to identify the date at which breastfeeding was discontinued by such women, and fecundability were measured from that date, just as fecundability was measured from the date of the death of the earlier child in figure 7.9, the resulting lines on a graph would show equally dramatic rises to similar peaks. No doubt the pattern might be a little less clear-cut if this could be done, because most women would not have stopped breastfeeding abruptly but would have tapered it off over a period whose length might vary. Nevertheless a broadly similar pattern might be expected.

Although it is impossible to discover when any individual woman ceased breastfeeding if she did not lose the earlier child of a pair, it is nonetheless possible to test whether such women in general experienced fecundability similar to those who were less fortunate and lost the earlier child. If the fertility experience of the two classes of women is assumed to be similar, and if a distribution of cessation of breastfeeding over time is assumed for women who did not lose the earlier child, then an expected fecundability curve can be generated which can be compared with the observed curve.

Suppose, for example, that the following assumptions, arrived at after much experimentation, hold true; 12.5 per cent of such women stopped breastfeeding between 12 and 14 months following the birth of the earlier child, 25 per cent between 15 and 17 months, 25 per cent between 18 and 20 months, 25 per cent between 21 and 23 months, and 12.5 per cent between 24 and 26 months; that is, a symmetrical distribution

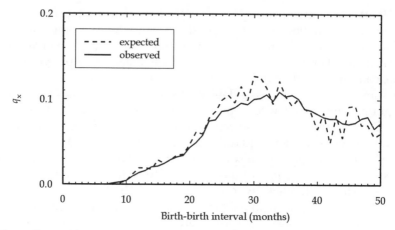

Figure 7.10   *Observed and expected fecundability where the earlier child of a birth interval survives (excluding last birth intervals)*
Note: see text for explanation of 'expected'.
Source: Cambridge Group reconstitutions.

round a mean of 19 months.[117] And suppose, further, that women who stopped breastfeeding, say, within the period 15–7 months after the birth of the earlier child were similar in fecundability to women who lost an earlier child after the same interval from the earlier birth, then, by weighting the fecundability data relating to women whose earlier child died at the appropriate age to reflect the assumptions made about the

---

[117] This may seem a high mean age of weaning to those accustomed to breastfeeding practices in industrialised countries, though not to those with knowledge of some Third World communities. It is interesting to note in this connection, therefore, that the normal period of paid breastfeeding of wetnurses in the service of the Spedale degli Innocenti in Florence was 18 months until the end of the eighteenth century. Nor was this simply an administrative prescription. Where wetnursing was not interrupted by the premature death of the child, the mean period of wetnursing was 16.3 months. Corsini, 'Breastfeeding, fertility and infant mortality', p. 66 and tab. 1, p. 67. Fildes has grappled with the limited evidence about practice in early modern England. The empirical evidence is very slight, is taken from literary sources, comes disproportionately from the upper social strata, and includes a number of instances of several cases being drawn from the same family. She concludes that the length of breastfeeding fell between the sixteenth and eighteenth centuries, though the evidence presented suggests rather that the median was probably between 12 and 18 months, and that any time trend is very uncertain. If the limited evidence is to be trusted, however, it would seem that weaning at less than 12 months was rare before 1700 but more common thereafter. Fildes, *Breasts, bottles and babies*, p. 315, and more generally pp. 352–76. She quotes data marshalled by Mondot-Bernard, showing that the average length of breastfeeding in a wide range of communities in rural Africa in recent decades was 24.1 months. Ibid., tab. 15.11, p. 436.

spread of the cessation of breastfeeding, an estimated rate for women whose earlier child did not die can be derived. Thus, if the five classes of women listed above, whose weights are 1, 2, 2, 2, and 1, experienced fecundability levels in a given month of 0.05, 0.09, 0.14, 0.15, and 0.08 respectively, the overall rate for the month would be $((1 \times 0.05) + (2 \times 0.09) + (2 \times 0.14) + (2 \times 0.15) + (1 \times 0.08))/8 = 0.111$.[118]

The outcome of this exercise may be seen in figure 7.10. The agreement between the expected and observed curves is close enough to encourage the conclusion that the fecundability history of women who did not lose the earlier of two children was substantially the same as those who were less fortunate. If they could be directly observed, the fecundability characteristics of all women following the end of breast-feeding, regardless of the reason for its ending, would probably be similar. Throughout the early months following the birth of the earlier child the expected and observed rates are almost identical. For about 10 months after about month 24 the expected line is the higher of the two, and thereafter the two are again much alike, the greater variability of the expected line being attributable to the small number of events on which its component elements were based. The peak value of the expected line is a little to the left of that in the observed line. Such slight differences between the observed and expected lines, however, are what might be expected if the weaning process were normally spread over a period of time rather than occurring abruptly, as happened when the earlier child died. This would tend to reduce the acuteness of any subsequent peak and in general 'blur' subsequent fecundability patterns.

In the observed curve there is nothing to suggest that any consider-able proportion of women either voluntarily weaned their children at birth, as happened in parts of Bavaria,[119] or were unable to breastfeed their children for other reasons. If this had been the case there would have been an upward 'blip' in the curve relating to women whose earlier child survived, at, say, 12–4 months, such as is visible in the curve representing women who lost an earlier child soon after birth. The observed curve appears to provide strong, perhaps conclusive, evi-dence that breastfeeding was well nigh universal and normally pro-longed for many months after childbirth.

It also appears fair to conclude, moreover, that where the earlier child survived and the end of breastfeeding was a matter of choice, at least in

---

[118] To simplify exposition, this illustration is given in what, in life table terms, would be called q_xs. The calculations were carried out, however, using the equivalent of l_xs and then converting to q_xs.

[119] Knodel described this phenomenon in 'Infant mortality and fertility'; see also Knodel, *Demographic behavior in the past*, app. F, 'Prevailing infant-feeding patterns'.

some measure, or of physiological differences between women, individual characteristics varied considerably. If, say, a very high proportion of all women had stopped breastfeeding when their baby was approximately 18 months old and very few at other ages, there would have been a much higher peak on the observed line in figure 7.10 than is the case. A relatively low, wide-spreading peak indicates a correspondingly wide dispersal in the timing of the ending of breastfeeding. In this exercise a spread of 14 months was assumed. A still wider spread would lead to a further flattening of the peak in the 'expected' curve without altering its other characteristics significantly.

How far it is possible to infer the empirical pattern of the timing of the ending of breastfeeding from the assumptions lying behind the construction of the expected line in figure 7.10 is a matter of opinion rather than conclusive demonstration. Experiment suggests that some assumptions would be hard to sustain. For example, if the start of the cessation of breastfeeding is put as early as 6 months and no women are assumed to continue beyond 18 months, with an intervening distribution peaking at about 12 months, the resulting expected line would peak well to the left of the observed peak and would lie well above the observed line for many months from the beginning. It seems clear, in other words, that many women continued breastfeeding well into the second year after the birth of a child, and that a proportion continued until the child was past its second birthday. It was probably the case that few stopped before the end of the first year. There is nothing sacrosanct in the choice of the distribution of cessation of breastfeeding embodied in the expected line. In the present state of knowledge, it is possible to make an informed choice between major differences in the assumed distribution, but not between minor ones.

The picture presented by figure 7.9 supports the view that the levels of fecundability that characterised women in the early months of their marriage did not thereafter change significantly. The graphical representations of fecundability suggest that, if anything, it may have been higher in the months after the end of breastfeeding than it was in the months following marriage. Nor does there appear to have been any significant difference in fecundability between cases where the earlier of two children died and cases where it survived.

Other aspects of fecundability

The apparent near constancy of fecundability levels throughout the years of childbearing is important in another context. Recent work has produced strong evidence that in the later decades of the nineteenth century, when fertility control within marriage began to be widespread, much of the fall is to be attributed to 'spacing' rather than 'stopping' behaviour on the part of married couples.[120] It is possible that this was a distinctively English trait not widely found in continental countries in which fertility was falling rapidly at much the same time. Abstinence, or other practices which led to widely spaced births, was common in England. If it were possible to gain access to the Registrar-General's records of births, marriages, and deaths and so to parallel the kind of fecundability measurements which have been made from parish register data, levels of fecundability would appear modest since the probability of conception in each monthly cycle would be low, especially in the later stages of marriage, though probably also even in its earlier stages. It is therefore of interest that the absence of any duration effect in fecundability measurements based on parish register data, combined with the relatively high levels of fecundability, suggest that spacing behaviour was a novel phenomenon in late nineteenth-century England.

In this connection, it is important to note that Santow's recent argument concerning the probable prevalence of spacing behaviour in the past, and of the practice of *coitus interruptus* in particular, appears to rest upon a misapprehension. Making use of Bracher's modelling of the effects of lactational amenorrhoea on birth spacing, she argued that spacing behaviour of this type could account for the fact that birth intervals were typically much longer than would be expected from Bracher's microsimulation of a breastfeeding population. Such behaviour, she noted, might be parity-independent and so would not result in a raised level of Coale and Trussell's m.[121] Moreover, it need not be inconsistent with a high level of fecundability in the course of married life, such as that found in early modern England, if fecundability is measured from the interval to next birth following an infant death, since in such circumstances parents might have been especially anxious to replace the lost child as soon as possible and so to have abstained from any practice which might delay a new conception.

There is, however, reason to question the assumptions made by Bracher in his modelling of birth intervals in a breastfeeding population. His data were drawn from a study of 101 Australian women who breastfed their children for a relatively long period, commonly exceed-

[120] Szreter, *Fertility, class and gender in Britain.*

[121] Santow, '*Coitus interruptus* and the control of natural fertility'. The reference to Bracher is on p. 24, while the discussion of the issue generally is to be found on pp. 20–9. Bracher, 'Breastfeeding, lactational infecundity'.

ing one year, and he concluded that, even in these circumstances, the median birth interval, in the absence of contraception, would be only 22.2 months.[122] These women he described as 'breastfeeding only'.[123] But the study from which the data were drawn made it clear that although the women in question continued to breastfeed for many months, supplementary feeding became increasingly common. 'Most infants were not given any supplement before 5 months. Almost all children, however, were receiving > 100 Kcal/24h by 9 months of age', and 'once the child was taking > 100 Kcal/d weaning had effectively commenced.'[124] Bracher's modelling of the effects of breastfeeding on the interval between births, therefore, was based on a population of women who were weaning their children at a relatively early age by the standards of early modern England.

The resulting birth intervals are no shorter than would be expected in these circumstances. This can be demonstrated by an exercise which parallels that underlying figure 7.10. If the point at which supplementary feeding exceeds 100 Kcal a day is regarded as equivalent to the cessation of breastfeeding brought about by the loss of a child, a distribution of subsequent birth intervals can be generated as the weighted sum of the birth intervals occurring when the earlier child of a pair died in infancy in the parish register period. The timing of the introduction of supplementary feeding at a rate exceeding 100 Kcal a day is known for each of the women in the Australian study.[125] The great majority of them began supplementary feeding on this scale between 5 and 9 months after the birth of the child, with extreme values as low as 2 months and as high as 16 months. The monthly totals in question provide the relative weights for generating a birth interval distribution from the empirical values found in early modern England following an infant death at the various ages in question. The resulting median birth interval is 21.5 months, a value very close to that arising in Bracher's model which he assumed to hold true for women 'breastfeeding only' for much longer periods. It is unnecessary to invoke abstinence or the practice of *coitus interruptus* to explain the length of birth intervals found in the past. Bracher's model does not produce birth intervals which are difficult to reconcile with empirical data. On the contrary, the two agree remarkably well.

---

[122] Bracher, 'Breastfeeding, lactational infecundity', p. 26.   [123] Ibid., fig. 2, p. 27.
[124] Lewis, Brown, Renfree, and Short, 'The resumption of ovulation', p. 533.
[125] Ibid., fig. 5, p. 534.

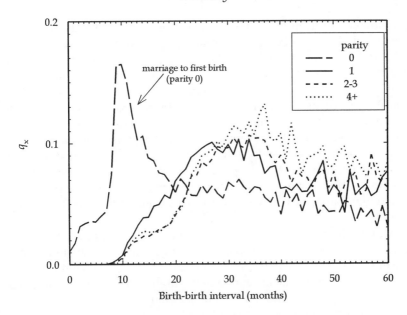

Figure 7.11 *Fecundability by parity*
Source: Cambridge Group reconstitutions.

Fecundability by parity

The fact that fecundability did not fall in the course of marriage, and may even have risen, in turn suggests that fecundability should also be studied by parity. It must be the case that to have a large number of children a woman must have closely spaced births, and it is probable that the close spacing may occur in part because such women have higher fecundability than others.

Figure 7.11 reorders the data used in earlier figures and demonstrates that fecundability varies according to parity. For reasons that will be familiar, the timing of the peak value of the 0 line differs markedly from that of the lines representing higher parities, which follow an earlier birth rather than a marriage. For present purposes it is the level of the lines to the right of their peaks which is of interest. The fecundability of women having a first birth is substantially and consistently below that of women of higher parity, and would be so even if the 0 line were shifted bodily to the right to offset the effect of its much earlier peak. Moreover, though not with perfect regularity, it is in general true of the other lines that the higher the parity, the higher the level of fecundability. All those who reach parity 4 and above must, of course, have previously contributed to the measurement of the fecundability of lower parities, but the reverse is not true. Those who were of low fecundability were more likely not to progress to a higher parity and their elimination leads to an increase in average fecundability. Since high parity is also associated with increased age, the parity effect after controlling for age is likely to be even more pronounced. This is a refinement of analysis which is not attempted here, but, armed with a larger data set, it might well prove illuminating. The positive relationship between parity and fecundability is, of course, an illustration of heterogeneity in the female population in respect of fecundability. Women of high fecundability are disproportionately well represented in the high parity births, women of low fecundability in the low parity births.

Another feature of figure 7.11 worth noting is the path of the 1 line between months 10 and 25. Although at longer intervals the 1 line shows lower fecundability than the lines for higher parities, from months 10 to 25 it is consistently and substantially the highest line. It will be recalled that parity 1 birth intervals were substantially shorter than later birth intervals both when the first child died and when it survived.[126] The behaviour of line 1 in figure 7.11 suggests that the shortness of the birth interval may be partly explained by unusually high fecundability in the early months following the birth of the first child, or possibly by higher coital frequency.

To complete this description of the graphical evidence relating to fecundability, it is of interest to note that when the data set was split by period to test whether fecundability in mid-marriage, measured from the intervals following an infant death, showed any change over time, the resulting graphs showed no clear evidence of significant change. As with fecundability relating to the interval between marriage and first birth, it is also possible to use mid-marriage data to test whether fecundability varied with age. Too little data exist to establish fecundability levels for teenage mothers, since there were relatively few cases of an infant death among mothers of this age. Sufficient data do exist, however, to compare the fecundability of women aged 20–34, when fecundability was at its peak, with that of women aged 35 and over. The resulting graphs, which are not reproduced here, showed slightly higher fecundability among the younger age group, but the differences were not marked. In these two respects, therefore, there was little to distinguish fecundability in mid-marriage from fecundability at the beginning of marriage, which was described earlier.

---

[126] See tab. 7.35, pp. 438–9 above.

An alternative method of measuring fecundability later in marriage

It remains to discover whether more conventional methods of measuring fecundability suggest the same conclusions as those which are supported by the preceding figures.

The shape of the fecundability curves shown in the preceding figures leaves no doubt that estimating the fecundability of women after the loss of a child in infancy by a measure such as the number of births 9–11 months after the death of the earlier child divided by the number 9–23 months after his or her death would produce a meaningless result, since the peak was reached later in post-infant death curves than in post-marriage curves, which must tend to cause fecundability in the former case to be underestimated. The extent to which this factor causes distortion when using the conventional methods of fecundability estimation may be seen in table 7.41. In this table the conventional ratios are given for both post-infant death and post-marriage data, but with them are also given ratios based not only on births within 9–11 months but also on births within 9–14 months as a numerator. Including a wider span of time from the earliest month in which a birth could occur accommodates the later peak characteristic of post-infant death fecundability. Since earlier analysis suggested that it is preferable to exclude last birth intervals when estimating fecundability, the estimates in table 7.41 are based only on birth intervals other than the last.

Table 7.41 is divided into three vertical panels: the first refers to cases where the age of the wife, whether at marriage or at the death of a child, is unknown; the second to cases where the wife was aged between 20 and 34 at marriage or at the death of a child; and the third to all cases in which the wife's age was known. The first and third categories may be regarded as broadly comparable in the sense that between them they include all available cases divided into two categories: where the age of the mother was known, and where it was not known. The second category was included because the years between 20 and 34 are normally the years of highest fecundability. The top half of the table consists of totals; the lower half of ratios derived from the totals.

Within each vertical panel there are three columns containing respectively data relating to the interval from marriage to first birth; to cases where the earlier child of a pair died aged between 3 and 11 months; and to cases where the earlier child died aged between 12 and 26 months. In the latter two cases the totals given in the top half of the table refer to births taking place in the indicated number of months since the death of the earlier child rather than since its birth, except in the case of the row entitled 'All' where the numbers refer to all births, including

Table 7.41 *Fecundability: comparison of estimates derived from marriage to first birth intervals with estimates derived from birth intervals following an infant death*

	Wife's age not known			Wife aged 20–34			All cases where wife's age known		
	Marriage to first birth	Infant death at 3–11 months	Infant death at 12–26 months	Marriage to first birth	Infant death at 3–11 months	Infant death at 12–26 months	Marriage to first birth	Infant death at 3–11 months	Infant death at 12–26 months
9–11	427.5	810.5	493.5	1 882.5	241.0	116.0	2 199.0	287.0	157.0
9–14	5 015.5	1 379.5	745.0	2 742.0	408.5	179.0	3 202.5	512.0	246.0
9–23	7 021.0	2 063.5	1 036.5	3 692.0	577.5	261.5	4 336.5	744.5	365.5
9–	9 337.5	2 494.0	1 273.0	4 760.0	685.5	319.0	5 563.5	885.0	455.0
60–	370.5	24.5	24.0	165.5	9.0	3.5	184.5	13.0	5.5
All	12 527.0	3 033.0	2 986.0	6 741.0	825.5	739.0	7 994.0	1 052.5	1 016.0
9–11/9–	0.367	0.325	0.388	0.395	0.352	0.364	0.395	0.324	0.345
9–14/9–	0.537	0.553	0.585	0.576	0.596	0.561	0.576	0.579	0.541
9–11/9–23	0.488	0.393	0.476	0.510	0.417	0.444	0.507	0.385	0.430
9–14/9–23	0.714	0.669	0.719	0.743	0.707	0.685	0.738	0.688	0.673
60–/9–	0.040	0.010	0.019	0.035	0.013	0.011	0.033	0.015	0.012
9–/all	0.745	0.822	0.426	0.706	0.830	0.432	0.696	0.841	0.448

Note: the upper panel contains totals; the lower panel contains ratios derived from the totals.
Source: Cambridge Group reconstitutions.

498

those where a further birth occurred *before* the death of the earlier child. Such cases were very rare in the 3–11 months column, but quite common in the 12–26 months column.

A first point to note is that the exclusion of last birth intervals causes a modest increase in the ratios derived from marriage to first birth data. In table 7.41 the 9–11/9–23 ratios in the three vertical panels are 0.488, 0.510, and 0.507. The comparable ratios in table 7.40, in which last birth intervals were not excluded, were 0.474, 0.505, and 0.497. If the ratios in table 7.41 are preferred as a measure, they imply, of course, slightly higher fecundability than the estimates given in table 7.40, raising the estimates of fecundability given in that table by about 0.01 on average (e.g. from 0.26 to 0.27, and so on).

Table 7.41 confirms the impression given by the graphical representation of fecundability patterns derived from deaths in infancy and early childhood. Because full fecundity appears to have taken some weeks to establish itself following the death of a child, the peak values of fecundability were reached more slowly in such cases than following marriage. As a result ratios calculated from births in the period 9–11 months after an infant death were normally considerably lower than the similar ratios calculated from marriage to first birth. But if the ratios are calculated from a 9–14 month period rather than from a 9–11 month period, the difference is much reduced. Indeed if the comparison is based on the 9–14/9+ ratio, there is a striking similarity between all three main categories (marriage to first birth; following the death of an earlier child aged 3–11 months; and following the death of an earlier child aged 12–26 months). Consideration of the row containing this ratio reveals that there is no consistent tendency for any of the three categories to be the highest or the lowest. The impression given by the data in table 7.41 is that, although the more widely used measures of fecundability cannot be applied to information about intervals from a child's death to the next birth, modified but similar measures support the view that fecundability varied surprisingly little over the course of married life in early modern England. Patterns following the early death of a child while its mother was breastfeeding are essentially similar to those following marriage. Furthermore, figure 7.10 suggested that these patterns also held true of women when the earlier child in a birth interval did not die.

The data in table 7.40 suggested that fecundability did not vary greatly over time in early modern England. That analysis was based on intervals between marriage and first birth. The same issue can be approached by analysing trends in the interval to the next birth following the death of a child in infancy. This evidence (not reproduced in tabular form here) also suggests no clear pattern of change over time. The differences between the three time periods (before 1650, 1650–1749, and after 1750) were small and the apparent changes measured on a 9–14/9–23 basis were not always consistent with those measured on a 9–14/9+ basis. Division of the whole data set into subperiods increases the likelihood that random influences may obscure underlying trends, if any, but the available evidence suggests that fecundability during the course of married life was broadly constant over time.

The very low ratios of birth intervals of more than 60 months expressed as a proportion of all intervals of greater than 9 months following an infant death, shown in table 7.41, is noteworthy. These ratios were much lower than the comparable ratios based on birth intervals after marriage. In all three categories the ratio is lower than it would otherwise be because of the exclusion of last birth intervals. For reasons already discussed, there were many births less than 9 months after marriage, and the same was true of the birth intervals after the death of the earlier child. Some of these, indeed, were negative when the earlier child died towards the end of the second year of life, because the birth of the later child preceded the death of the earlier child. This complicates any comparison of the observed ratios. The low level of the ratios following an infant death, however, is reassuring in relation to the question of the fullness of recording and level of undetected migration from the parish. If there had been many cases where one birth in a sequence of births was missed through negligence or because the couple had been absent from the parish for a time but had later returned, a higher proportion of birth intervals apparently exceeding 60 months would be likely to have occurred.

One final reflection on a cognate issue is appropriate before closing this long section on fecundability. Levels of marital fertility in early modern England were not as high as in many other parts of Europe at this time. Since the viability of Anglican parish registers as a source of information about population characteristics in the past has sometimes been called in question, the modest level of observed fertility has been held doubtful.[127] There are, however, good grounds for considering that, provided that only the best registers are used, Anglican registers can prove a reliable source.[128] The fecundability data throw additional

---

[127] The most persistent pessimist about the quality of the Anglican registration system in relation both to births and to deaths has been Razzell. If his doubts were justified, 60+/9+ ratios as low as those in tab. 7.41 could not have occurred. Nor could the exercise comparing reconstitution estimates of fertility with those derived from the censuses and the early civil registration system have produced the results described on pp. 461–4. Razzell's views are set out in his *Essays in English population history*.

[128] See ch. 4 generally and tab. 7.38, p. 463.

light on this issue. Levels of fecundability, measured from the analysis of the interval from marriage to first birth, were fairly high in early modern England, as high as or higher than those found in eighteenth-century Germany, for example, where the completeness of the information recorded in the *Ortsippenbücher* is normally regarded as excellent.[129] And there is strong evidence that the levels of fecundability which result from the analysis of marriage to first birth intervals were maintained or increased throughout the childbearing period. Relatively high fecundability may be accompanied by relatively modest levels of marital fertility, however, if prolonged breastfeeding causes women to be 'out of action', so to speak, for a substantial proportion of their fecund years. The fact that observed and 'expected' fecundability can be closely matched, as shown in figure 7.10, on the assumption that breastfeeding was common until well into the second year of life of the baby and sometimes extended into the third year, suggests that this situation obtained in early modern England. The bits of the jigsaw fit together surprisingly well.

The individual parishes

The fertility characteristics of individual parishes can be examined in exactly the same way as those for all parishes combined with the ASMFRs broken down into their component elements of fecund fertility, entry fecundity, and subsequent fecundity. To provide information in this form, however, would take up much space and would only be justified if there were notable differences between parishes. But uniformity rather than diversity of characteristics was the order of the day, and parochial statistics are therefore presented only in summary form in table 7.42.

The first group of columns of the table are taken up with the conventional ASMFRs for each parish derived from bachelor/spinster completed marriages, and with the total of woman-years lived by married women aged 30–4. There then follow in successive columns the TFMFRs (that is fecund TMFRs), entry sterility data, and two columns devoted to subsequent fecundity, before, finally, two further columns, the first showing TMFRs derived, like all the earlier columns, from bachelor/spinster completed marriages, and the second showing TMFRs from all marriages of every type. The entry sterility and subsequent fecundity data refer to women towards the end of the childbearing period. The entry sterility ratios show what proportion of

---

[129] Knodel, 'Ortssippenbücher als Daten', and 'Natural fertility in pre-industrial Germany'; Knodel and Shorter, 'The reliability of family reconstitution data'.

women were infertile in their early forties because of entry sterility. If, for example, the figure were 0.100, this would indicate that 10 per cent of women in this age group had never borne a child. This figure is an average of the separate figures for each age at marriage group weighted according to the proportionate share of each age at marriage group in the years lived in the age group 40–4 in the population as a whole. Similarly, the two columns for subsequent fecundity represent the average of the ratios for individual age at marriage groups weighted in the same way.

The reason for choosing to show the 40–4 entry sterility figure is that almost all first marriages had taken place by the age of 45 and this statistic therefore represents a good summary measure of the accumulated experience of women marrying at all ages. Similar figures for, say, an age group such as 25–9 are more liable to be distorted by a single aberrant figure for a particular age at marriage group. Comparable considerations governed the choice of the two subsequent fecundity ratios. In general this ratio was very high in the younger age groups where few women who were fecund at marriage had become sterile. Equally, by the 45–9 age group few women were still fecund, whatever their age at marriage group. The major changes occurred between 35 and 44 and any marked differences between different populations will show up best in these age groups.

In considering the data in table 7.42 two points should be borne in mind. First, some parishes were very small. The totals of woman-years upon which the age-specific rates for the age group 30–4 were based are shown in column 8 of the table. This is the appropriate age group to consider because in most parishes there was a greater total of woman-years in observation for this age group than for any other. In small parishes the age-specific rates were apt to be volatile; their level might reflect random influences rather than underlying reality. Accordingly, wherever the total of woman-years for this age group was less than 250 the data for the parish are shown italicised to emphasise the danger of placing reliance upon their accuracy. Secondly, the reconstitutions did not begin and end at the same time in all parishes.[130] Since fertility rose during the eighteenth century, a parish which began late tended, other things being equal, to have higher fertility rates than one which began early, especially if it also ended early. Ash began late; Reigate ended early. The high rates in the former and the lower rates in the latter are attributable in part to this.

Notwithstanding the last point, the predominant impression left by

---

[130] See tab. 2.1, pp. 22–3.

table 7.42 is of the absence of major contrasts. Both in France and in Germany contrasts were far more pronounced. In his study of data from the *Ortsippenbücher*, Knodel did not publish ASMFRs for the German parishes to which they referred, but he did provide age-standardised I_gs for seven individual parishes and for two groups of three and four parishes respectively. In these nine cases, in the period 1750–99, the maximum and minimum I_gs were 0.99 and 0.70; in 1800–24 the comparable figures were 0.90 and 0.60.[131] In the parish with the highest fertility, therefore, fertility was 40 to 50 per cent higher than in the parish at the opposite end of the spectrum, whereas in 12 English parishes the highest parish TMFR was only 16 per cent higher than the lowest (table 7.42, column 14, ignoring the relatively small parishes shown in italics). In France, for which a large number of reconstitution studies exists, an even wider range could be identified by taking extreme cases. More telling, perhaps, is a feature of the analysis carried out by Henry and Houdaille using data from reconstitutions of a random sample of parishes throughout France. The published tabulations are not for individual parishes but for the four 'quarters' of France, north-east, north-west, south-east, and south-west. The spread of fertility between *quarters* was greater than that between *parishes* in England (fertility in the north-east was 23 per cent higher than in the south-west).[132]

Consider, first, fecund fertility. In the 12 parishes, which are shown in roman rather than in italic type in the table, the TFMFR varied only between 9.2 and 10.5; 7 of the 12 were in the range 9.4 to 9.9. The highest rate was less than 5 per cent above, the lowest less than 5 per cent below the midpoint of the range. The rate was calculated for the age range 20–44 rather than 15–49 to minimise the impact of prenuptial pregnancy, which affected the age group 15–9 especially powerfully, and to

---

[131] Knodel, *Demographic behavior in the past*, tab. 10.1, p. 250.
[132] Henry and Houdaille published ASMFRs for each age at marriage group but not the overall ASMFRs. Since the age at marriage group that normally contains the highest percentage of women is the age at marriage group 20–4, TMFRs were calculated for this age at marriage group for each of the four quarters. This rate was highest in north-east France, 9.84, and lowest in the south-west, 7.97. The corrected rates were used in both cases, since Henry and Houdaille considered them to be more accurate. Because of the evidence in some parts of France of an early decline in ASMFRs, the rates were calculated only for the period down to 1739. In three of the four quarters the rates can be calculated for the period 1670–1739, but for the south-west data problems prevented as early a start as in the other three quarters, and therefore the TMFR for this quarter is for the period 1720–39. Henry, 'Fécondité des mariages dans le quart sud-ouest', tab. 1, p. 979; Houdaille, 'La fécondité des mariages dans le quart nord-est', tab. 9, p. 353.

Table 7.42 Fertility characteristics of the 26 parishes

| | ASMFR (1:1 completed marriages)[a] | | | | | | | Woman-years lived 30-4[b] | TFMFR 20-44[c] | Entry sterility 40-4[d] | Subsequent fecundity[e] | | TMFR 20-49[f] | TMFR (all women 20-49)[g] |
	(1) 15-9	(2) 20-4	(3) 25-9	(4) 30-4	(5) 35-9	(6) 40-4	(7) 45-9	(8)	(9)	(10)	(11) 35-9	(12) 40-4	(13)	(14)
Alcester	364.9	401.4	388.1	383.4	269.5	101.3	14.7	180	9.9	0.111	0.773	0.334	7.8	7.5
Aldenham	602.7	368.4	317.7	272.1	228.8	112.2	17.2	246	9.1	0.108	0.724	0.384	6.6	7.2
Ash	499.3	442.6	408.5	357.9	287.5	164.6	34.9	458	10.3	0.073	0.801	0.476	8.5	8.0
Austrey	0.0	402.9	410.1	360.5	254.6	102.6	20.0	36	9.3	0.081	0.816	0.589	7.8	8.0
Banbury	530.3	470.7	401.2	319.0	243.1	150.3	23.0	759	10.4	0.133	0.759	0.454	8.0	7.6
Bottesford	661.7	449.5	400.7	339.8	243.5	141.6	17.8	439	9.7	0.068	0.728	0.395	8.0	7.6
Bridford	0.0	458.2	441.9	244.3	174.0	94.1	11.8	66	9.1	0.045	0.615	0.287	7.1	6.3
Colyton	775.1	552.0	371.3	303.2	237.2	122.4	11.6	369	9.9	0.083	0.787	0.408	8.0	7.3
Dawlish	446.5	461.1	393.2	349.7	262.7	147.9	15.4	272	9.5	0.027	0.841	0.466	8.2	7.7
Earsdon	440.3	418.5	359.3	342.2	272.5	137.5	18.8	134	9.8	0.048	0.844	0.453	7.7	8.1
Gainsborough	425.0	457.0	405.8	324.1	246.3	125.1	25.4	923	10.5	0.113	0.735	0.427	7.9	7.5
Gedling	472.3	425.7	380.7	329.0	261.7	153.5	15.5	544	9.6	0.056	0.790	0.467	7.8	7.6
Gt Oakley	—	528.5	121.1	100.1	300.0	50.0	50.0	20	7.9	0.000	0.531	0.198	5.7	7.8
Hartland	0.0	430.9	369.0	271.1	231.6	126.5	15.1	594	9.4	0.087	0.723	0.424	7.2	6.9
Ipplepen	—	439.7	279.3	240.9	350.2	117.3	42.1	79	8.4	0.045	0.781	0.510	6.4	7.3
Lowestoft	619.1	366.2	326.6	266.1	208.8	98.9	9.8	282	9.2	0.101	0.650	0.353	6.4	7.6

March	*—*	*359.1*	*384.7*	*267.2*	*235.4*	*166.7*	*0.0*	*23*	*9.3*	*0.000*	*0.870*	*0.508*	*7.1*	*9.5*
Methley	*320.1*	*516.4*	*368.5*	*284.3*	*240.8*	*100.7*	*8.0*	*229*	*9.8*	*0.046*	*0.672*	*0.320*	*7.6*	*6.8*
Morchard Bishop	587.6	466.0	359.5	326.2	259.5	147.7	22.6	1049	9.6	0.056	0.800	0.450	7.9	7.8
Odiham	435.8	416.3	391.7	327.5	260.4	107.4	23.2	950	9.7	0.100	0.761	0.401	7.6	7.2
Reigate	286.0	419.0	396.6	262.3	206.3	97.1	5.7	153	9.8	0.111	0.630	0.331	6.9	6.8
Shepshed	676.3	383.5	365.7	307.7	260.4	123.4	23.7	326	9.2	0.080	0.761	0.417	7.3	7.6
Southill	270.3	359.2	344.1	367.2	289.1	108.3	29.2	204	9.4	0.012	0.710	0.358	7.5	7.5
Terling	166.7	458.7	354.4	267.4	225.7	115.2	0.0	153	9.2	0.109	0.720	0.314	7.1	6.5
Willingham	*618.0*	*417.3*	*327.9*	*338.5*	*173.7*	*71.4*	*28.6*	*65*	*9.6*	*0.062*	*0.577*	*0.208*	*6.8*	*7.1*

[a] Age-specific marital fertility rates of bachelor/spinster completed marriages (per 1000 woman-years lived).

[b] The number of woman-years lived in marriage by women aged 30–4 in bachelor/spinster completed marriages.

[c] Total fecund marital fertility rate 20–44 of bachelor/spinster completed marriages.

[d] Entry sterility proportions of all women 40–4 in bachelor/spinster completed marriages.

[e] Subsequent fecundity proportions of all women 35–9 and 40–4 in bachelor/spinster completed marriages.

[f] Total marital fertility rate 20–49 of bachelor/spinster completed marriages.

[g] Total marital fertility rate 20–49 of all marriages.

Note: where the number of woman-years lived 30–4 (col. 8) is less than 250 the data for the parish are shown italicised to emphasise the fragility of the estimates.

Source: Cambridge Group reconstitutions.

505

avoid including the rate for the age group 45–9, an age group where the TFMFR was still high but based on very few woman-years in observation, since few women were still fecund at this age. There is no evidence of regional differences. Devon, for example, is sometimes taken to be an area of low fertility, but fecund fertility in the larger Devon parishes was not below the general average. Perhaps the only point worthy of note is that the two largest parishes, Banbury and Gainsbo2rough, had the two highest TFMFRs, but infant mortality was very high in both of them. A crude correction for this suggests that for comparative purposes their rates might be reduced by about 3 per cent, which would substantially reduce the differential.[133]

The relative level of fecund fertility in a particular parish is not necessarily reflected in the ASMFRs since the intervening variables, entry sterility and subsequent fecundity, can substantially modify any rank order based on fecund fertility. Thus, both Banbury and Gainsborough experienced unusually high levels of entry sterility (13.3 and 11.3 per cent respectively: column 10) so that the ASMFRs in the two parishes were not unusually high. Entry sterility in the age group 40–4 was also relatively high, reaching or exceeding 10 per cent, in Alcester, Aldenham, Lowestoft, Odiham, Reigate, and Terling among the larger parishes, but was not as high as 12 per cent in any of them. Moreover, of these parishes, only Lowestoft and Odiham were 'large', and therefore shown in roman type. In a few parishes (Dawlish, Methley, and Southill) it was less than 5 per cent but all these parishes were small and such low entry sterility rates may simply be the result of small numbers.

Levels of subsequent fecundity were once again remarkably similar in the 12 parishes of sufficient size to yield tolerably reliable data. Among the larger parishes subsequent fecundity was unusually low in Lowestoft, but even here the empirical base is slim, and too much should not be made of such evidence.

It is no surprise, given the foregoing review of fecund fertility, entry sterility, and subsequent fecundity, that the TMFRs, whether measured overall in the conventional manner, or based solely on bachelor/spinster completed marriages, should be closely grouped with maximum and minimum values in each case less than 10 per cent above and below the midpoint of the range. Some of the variation was probably due to the

---

[133] In carrying out this calculation, which is merely illustrative, it was assumed that infant mortality in Banbury and Gainsborough was at 275 per 1000, that in the other parishes it averaged 175 per 1000, and that the mean birth interval following an infant death was 22 months but that where the earlier child survived infancy the mean birth interval was 30 months.

effects of small numbers and would be reduced if the parish data sets were larger; some is the result of the differing start and finish dates in the different parishes; and some is misleading in that it is due to the effects of differential *mortality* rather than differential fertility.[134] In view of these considerations, it is fair to assert that interparochial differences in fertility in England were subdued, a finding which underlines the conclusion already reached about the influence of 'occupation' on fertility. England appears to have been a singularly homogeneous society in those aspects of social and personal behaviour which influenced fertility characteristics in early modern times.

Conclusion

Where suitable data exist, the fertility of past populations makes a fascinating subject for study. The number of living children born to women was influenced by an astonishingly wide range of factors, physiological, behavioural, cultural, social, and personal. As a result fertility patterns in different societies varied greatly, even in the absence of deliberate measures to avoid conception or to procure an abortion.[135] Teasing out the way in which the factors affecting fertility interacted opens up the possibility of understanding what might be termed the ethology and ecology of the fertility behaviour of past populations.

Some distinctive features of the English scene have long been apparent. The period of fecundity varies considerably from woman to woman, but was probably on average about 25 years in length in early modern England. The average age at last birth was about 40 years. Fecundity will have lasted a little longer than this, having begun in the middle or later teens. The average age at first marriage varied between about 23 and 26 years, reducing the length of the period of full exposure to the risk of conception to between 15 and 18 years. Reproductive careers often began before marriage in England, of course, but even if allowance is made for this, for most women the span of time available for childbearing was restricted, since few married in their teens and many were in their later 20s or early 30s at marriage. Furthermore the pace of childbearing was deliberate except in the case of women who were unfortunate enough to lose a series of children in infancy. The

[134] That is, high infant mortality, by giving rise to a high proportion of short birth intervals, caused fertility levels to be higher than would otherwise have been the case.
[135] See, for example, Feng, Lee, and Campbell, 'Marital fertility control among the Qing nobility'.

analysis of fecundability shows that almost all women must have breastfed their children for quite a long time. It is likely that few stopped breastfeeding in less than a year from the birth of a child, and a significant number probably continued to breastfeed until after the beginning of the third year of life of the child. With birth intervals of about 30 months on average, except following an infant death, even if the marriage survived until the wife was too old to bear further children, only 6 or 7 children were likely to be born. Large families of 10 or more children ever born were rare, unless the bride married young or the couple lost several children in infancy.

In these circumstances, apparently small changes in the mean age of marriage could result in substantial swings in fertility, especially bearing in mind the fact that many marriages were cut short by the death of one or other of the parents before the completion of childbearing. If the wife was the survivor, she might remarry but this would cause a longer than usual gap between births, and in any case many widows did not remarry. The frequency with which marriages were cut short in this way exaggerated, of course, the proportional impact of any change in mean age at marriage, since the end of childbearing often came several years earlier than the onset of sterility.

The salient features of English nuptiality and fertility were all reflections of social conventions and personal choice. Late marriage for women, though common in much of western Europe for many centuries, was very rare until recently outside Europe. A large proportion of women who never married was even rarer outside a west European context. If it is to survive, every society must be so organised that a new generation arises to succeed the old . The conventions that secured this end elsewhere in the world, however, were such as to leave marriage for women largely a matter of physiological maturation, in the sense that a sexually adult woman was expected to be married. Other conventions prevailed in western Europe, where access to a viable economic niche in which to establish a new family was commonly a prerequisite for marriage. Both general economic conditions and personal economic circumstances, acting within a framework for decision-making about marriage set by convention, exercised a strong influence on the timing and extent of marriage in each rising English generation, both for men and for women.

Once couples were married, other social conventions came into play in helping to determine fertility levels. Fecundability was at a relatively high level in early modern England. This was true at the start of a marriage and remained the case throughout the period when the wife was fecund. This suggests both the rarity of physiological conditions, whether brought about by disease or by poor nutrition, which impaired either female or male fecundity, and that intercourse must habitually have been maintained at a moderately high frequency throughout the childbearing years. Furthermore, since what can be observed is effective fecundability, as evidenced by a live birth, it suggests that the rate of loss through miscarriage and spontaneous abortion was not at a high level. Because breastfeeding was apparently both nearly universal and normally lengthy, however, a high level of fecundability did not lead to a high level of fecund fertility.

Fecund fertility rates, which measure the fertility of women who have not yet become sterile, are always higher than conventional marital fertility rates because a proportion of women are sterile at marriage, and with increasing age all women eventually become sterile. Entry sterility varies with age. In early modern England the level of entry sterility in each successive age at marriage group was similar to the levels observed in other European populations in the past, and there is no clear evidence that these levels changed over time. Subsequent sterility, on the other hand, which measures the progressive loss of fecundity with increasing age on the part of women who were earlier fecund and produced children, was not constant over time. It decreased in the later eighteenth century, and was the principal reason for the increase in marital fertility that took place at that time.[136]

The change in subsequent sterility took an interesting form. In the first century of the parish register period overall sterility at any given age was lower in recently married women than in women who had been married longer. This feature is usually attributed to one of two factors, or to them both in combination. The first is that at any given age women who have been married for a long time will be of a higher average birth parity than those more recently married, and so will have suffered more exposure to the risk of becoming sterile as a result of birth complications. The second is that with increasing length of marriage the frequency of intercourse is assumed to have declined. After 1650, but especially after 1750, there was a narrowing in the difference in overall sterility at any given age between women who had been long married and those who had recently become brides. This did not occur because of changes in entry sterility but because of changes in the pattern of subsequent sterility by age and length of marriage.[137] As a result, among women in their later 30s or early 40s,

---

[136] This claim holds true only if, as seems proper, the effect of the sharp rise in the percentage of prenuptially conceived first births is discounted. ASMFRs in the younger age groups rose significantly in the later eighteenth century, but only because the proportion of pregnant brides increased so much.   [137] Tab. 7.12, pp. 386–7.

the fertility rates of women who had married in their teens or early 20s were little lower than those who had married in the later 20s or 30s in the period after 1750, whereas originally there had been a significant fertility gradient between them. For this reason marital fertility rates among older women rose more markedly than among younger women in the later decades of the parish register period. The assumption of broadly constant marital fertility throughout the parish register period, made in the *Population history of England* in order to obtain estimates of the proportion of the population which never married, on the basis of simpler fertility measures relating to a smaller group of reconstitutions, was mistaken.[138]

By taking advantage of the way in which fecund marital fertility rates can be translated into conventional marital fertility rates if the intervening variables of entry and subsequent sterility can be measured, the relative importance of changes in fecund fertility, entry sterility, and subsequent sterility in causing changes in marital fertility can be established. The third of these three variables, subsequent fecundity, played the largest role in producing the changes in marital fertility which they jointly determine.

No discussion of English fertility in the past would be complete without stressing one final point, the remarkable homogeneity of the patterns to be observed in the data for individual parishes. None of the three main variables affecting marital fertility, namely fecund fertility, entry sterility, and subsequent sterility, showed significant variation from parish to parish. There were neither significant regional differences so far as can be judged from these data, nor significant differences according to the economic type of the parish. Indeed, such differences as there were may have been due largely to random variation, given the relatively small size of the data sets in most cases. As a result, marital fertility rates also displayed only a limited range between 'high' and 'low' parishes. Much the same is true, as we have seen, of nuptiality, though there were very substantial differences in mortality by settlement size, and because of the influence of environmental factors. Because fertility was so heavily influenced by social conventions, this suggests that local cultural differences were more muted in England than on the continent, where local and regional fertility

---

[138] Wrigley and Schofield, *Population history of England*, tab. 7.28, p. 260. It follows, of course, that estimates of proportions never marrying, made using this method, stand in need of revision. The issue was, however, subsequently taken further by Weir, 'Rather never than late'; Henry and Blanchet, 'La population de l'Angleterre'; and Schofield, 'English marriage patterns revisited'.

differences were commonly much more pronounced. Women in Lorraine and women in Guyenne had very different fertility patterns. The same was clearly true of women in Bavaria when compared with those in East Friesland. But the same was not true of parishes in Yorkshire and Devon.

PART III

8

Reconstitution and inverse projection

This volume is the second of a pair which, from the beginning, were viewed as part of a single enterprise. It is important, therefore, to consider whether the evidence taken from parish reconstitutions agrees with that derived from aggregative data. The conversion of aggregative data into demographic estimates was originally carried out by using a method called back projection (BP), which has now been superseded by a more flexible and refined method known as generalised inverse projection (GIP), which belongs to a family of statistical techniques whose properties are better understood.

The estimates of fertility, mortality, and nuptiality which were published in the *Population history of England* were in principle open to correction and improvement in each of three different ways. First, the change from BP to GIP might produce different demographic estimates, even with unchanged input data and input parameters (that is, such matters as the assumptions made about the age structure of cohort migration). Second, the new knowledge gained from reconstitution might make it appear that different input data were to be preferred to those used earlier. And, third, reconstitution data might suggest that the input parameters should be altered to reflect, say, a revised view about changes in the age structure of mortality in the past. It is convenient to consider each of these points in turn.

Generalised inverse projection and back projection

In 1974 Lee achieved a breakthrough by developing a technique which he christened inverse projection (IP) to generate estimates of the demographic characteristics of a population from long-run aggregative data. IP converts a knowledge of totals of births and deaths over a period of time into estimates of fertility and mortality. It is well named since it inverts the conventional form of a population projection. Given a knowledge of population size and age structure at a point in time, and assumptions about the future course of expectation of life at birth and of the gross reproduction rate, it is straightforward to estimate annual totals of births and deaths over as long a period as is covered by the assumptions made. IP is inverse in the sense that *input* data consist of totals of births and deaths and the *output* consists of estimates of underlying fertility and mortality expressed as expectation of life at birth and the gross reproduction rate.

Lee demonstrated the practical utility of IP in relation to both national and local data sets.[1] In its original form, however, IP suffered from two limitations which restricted its value for use in conjunction with birth and death totals for early modern England. It assumed that there was no net migration, and it required as input estimates of population size and age structure at the date at which the continuous series of birth and death totals started, the point in time about which least was likely to be known.

Back projection was devised in an attempt to overcome these two limitations. It required information about population size and age structure at the end of the birth and death series rather than at their beginning (hence *back* projection), and it made no assumption of population closure, generating estimates of net migration as well as of such demographic variables as expectation of life at birth, the gross reproduction rate, and the intrinsic growth rate. BP was an *ad hoc* solution to the problem of making the most effective use of monthly estimated totals of births and deaths over a period of three centuries. It produced results for England that were consistent with knowledge gained by other methods and using other data about the population in the past.[2] And it was possible to show that, when similar data from other populations were converted into estimates of population size, net migration, fertility, and mortality, the results were reassuringly accurate. For example, detailed information exists for the population of Stockholm from 1815 onwards, and it is therefore possible to compare the output from BP, estimated solely from input data consisting of birth and death totals, and a knowledge of the size and age structure of the population in 1940, with independent information about net migration, age structure at earlier census dates, and other demographic variables.[3] BP proved able to reconstruct past reality effectively, though smoothing

[1] Lee, 'Estimating series of vital rates'.

[2] Wrigley and Schofield, *Population history of England*, app. 5.

[3] The technique of back projection is described by Oeppen in ibid., app. 15. The experiment with Stockholm data is described in ibid., pp. 733–6.

through short-term fluctuations, rather than tracking them accurately, even when migration rates were relatively high.

The technique of back projection and its application to English data, however, attracted criticism. In particular, Lee argued that it suffered from underidentification and from the problems associated with the existence of weak ergodicity in long-run population projections.[4] Ergodicity in a demographic context refers to the tendency of a population to 'forget' its own earlier history. The strong ergodic theorem is the basis of stable population theory. It was first proved by Lotka and Sharpe in 1911 and shows that if the age-specific fertility and mortality rates of a population remain unchanged for a sufficient time, its age structure will assume a particular form, regardless of its initial shape. The weak ergodic theorem proves that if two populations, whose initial age structure was different, experience the same sequence of changing age-specific vital rates, their age structures will become increasingly similar, though also continuing to change over time. Recent rates, in other words, exert great influence: the effect of the initial age composition is progressively reduced.[5]

Partially in response to Lee's criticism, Oeppen developed the concept of generalised inverse projection to characterise a wider class of models of which both inverse projection and back projection were members, and to examine their properties. He did so in a way that was intended to clarify the logical status of these techniques, making use of recent advances in the understanding of the non-stable dynamics of open population systems to characterise their nature, and taking up the two issues raised by Lee.[6] Subsequently both Lee and Oeppen have returned to this range of issues.[7] The problems involved are complex. It is, however, common ground that the application of GIP models to English historical data does not capture past demographic reality unambiguously and would not do so even if the totals of births and deaths were known with perfect precision. This is because a number of different paths are compatible with any given body of input data. The result will be influenced by the selection of input parameters, though if a sufficient number of independent 'targets' exist, such as, for example, a reliable early census total, the margin of uncertainty may become very small. It is reasonable to claim, however, that GIP 'selects the population surface that is, in a precisely defined way, as consistent as

[4] Lee, 'Inverse projection and back projection'.
[5] Arthur, 'The ergodic theorems of demography'.
[6] Oeppen, 'Back projection and inverse projection'.
[7] See, for example, Lee, 'Inverse projection and demographic fluctuations'; Oeppen, 'Generalized inverse projection'.

possible with the input data and with explicit assumptions built into the model'.[8]

In later sections of this chapter the nature of the input data and the explicit assumptions used to generate 'best guess' estimates of English population characteristics in the early modern period are described. In particular, the improvements in the model specification made possible by the new reconstitution findings are described and their impact on demographic series estimates are discussed. In this section, however, we consider only the extent of the change brought about by switching from BP to GIP. To do this involves two steps: first making a comparison between BP and GIP run with a life table set based on the third English life table (3rd ELT) linked to the Princeton model North system, and then comparing BP with GIP using a life table system of the Brass type.

A life table system must be selected for any exercise of the type represented by BP or GIP because the program must be able to distribute a given total of deaths between the age groups constituting the population at a particular point in time. BP used as a base a modified version of the 3rd ELT extended by model North.[9] The initial comparison should therefore be between BP and GIP using the same system, but it is convenient also to demonstrate that the same results are obtained by switching to a Brass system in which the β coefficient is set to mirror the modified 3rd ELT as closely as possible and the α coefficient then varies to match the total of deaths to be distributed.

Table 8.1 shows the population totals at half-century intervals which are produced by the three alternative methods. The birth and death totals used in all three series are those given in the *Population history of England*.[10] The input parameters were also the same or as closely similar as can be achieved given the characteristics of BP and GIP.

The population totals are much alike in all three series, showing that the change from BP to GIP and between two different ways of distributing deaths between the age groups has only a limited effect on the demographic estimates. The GIP Princeton series is higher than the BP series throughout, except in 1851, but the differences are small, except in 1551 when the GIP Princeton figure is almost 4 per cent higher than the BP figure. Otherwise the largest difference is 1.2 per cent in 1701. The GIP Brass series, in contrast, was always slightly lower than the BP series. Again, the differences are small. They increase very slowly moving backwards in time, exceeding 1 per cent in 1651, and reaching 2.2 per cent in 1551.

[8] Oeppen, 'Generalized inverse projection', p. 39.
[9] Wrigley and Schofield, *Population history of England*, app. 14.
[10] Ibid., tab. A2.3, pp. 496–502.

Table 8.1 *Estimates of population totals from back projection and generalised inverse projection (000s)*

	BP	GIP Princeton	GIP Brass
1551	3 011	3 126	2 946
1601	4 110	4 150	4 029
1651	5 228	5 251	5 159
1701	5 058	5 118	5 040
1751	5 772	5 789	5 741
1801	8 664	8 667	8 655
1851	16 736	16 706	16 725
Top panel GIP totals indexed against the BP total for the line (BP = 1000)			
1551	1 000	1 038	978
1601	1 000	1 010	980
1651	1 000	1 004	987
1701	1 000	1 012	996
1751	1 000	1 003	995
1801	1 000	1 000	999
1851	1 000	998	999

Note: the population totals refer to the midpoint of the years shown. For explanation of 'Princeton' and 'Brass' see text.
Sources: back projection: Wrigley and Schofield, *Population history of England*, tab. A3.1, pp. 528–9. Generalised inverse projection: Cambridge Group data.

The gross reproduction rate (GRR) and expectation of life can, of course, be calculated in an exercise of this type. The quinquennial figures from the BP series are not, however, directly comparable with those from the GIP series. The GRRs and e_0s from BP are for five-year periods centring on each 'census' date, 1541, 1546, and so on. Those for the two GIP series are for five-year periods beginning at each 'census' date.[11] Such differences are, however, minimised by taking 50-year blocks, comparing, for example, the period 1549–1603 in the BP series with the period mid-1551 to mid-1601 in the two GIP series, and so on. The results are shown in table 8.2.

As was to be expected in view of the population totals in table 8.1, the GRR and e_0 series in the BP and GIP columns are generally similar. Since the population totals in the GIP Princeton run were higher than in the BP series, the GRR is lower and the e_0 higher than in the original exercise, while, since the reverse was true of the population totals in the GIP Brass run, the GRR is higher in this case, though the e_0 is almost indistinguish-

[11] The GRRs and e_0s in these series were calculated in relation to age-group population totals which were obtained by interpolation between, for example, the 1541 and 1546 'censuses'.

Table 8.2 *Gross reproduction rates and expectation of life at birth from back projection and generalised inverse projection*

	Back projection			GIP Princeton		GIP Brass	
	GRR	e_0		GRR	e_0	GRR	e_0
1549–98	2.35	36.6	1551–1601	2.28	38.0	2.42	36.8
1599–1648	2.18	37.4	1601–51	2.16	37.8	2.20	37.0
1649–98	1.99	33.8	1651–1701	1.98	34.5	2.03	33.9
1699–1748	2.24	34.2	1701–51	2.22	34.9	2.27	34.6
1749–98	2.51	36.2	1751–1801	2.50	36.8	2.53	36.9
1799–1833	2.85	38.6	1801–36	2.83	39.3	2.83	39.4

Note: the gross reproduction rates and expectations of life in the GIP columns run from mid-year to mid-year, 1551–1601, 1601–51, etc.
Source: back projection: Wrigley and Schofield, *Population history of England*, tab. A3.1, pp. 528–9. Generalised inverse projection: Cambridge Group data.

able from the BP series. This suggests that the Brass-derived allocation of deaths between the different age groups differs sufficiently to raise estimates of expectation of life at birth to a slightly higher level under the Brass system than under that in which the Princeton North family of life tables was used to extend the third English life table.

Revised input data

The process by which national monthly totals of births, deaths, and marriages were estimated in the *Population history of England* involved a long series of operations designed to correct the raw totals of events, taken from the registers of 404 parishes, for periods of deficient registration; to cause the data collected to mirror the national pattern by reweighting parish totals to offset the untypical population size distribution of the aggregative sample; to compensate for the fact that, before 1662 and after 1811, the number of parishes in observation slowly shrank (between 1662 and 1811 data could be drawn from all the 404 parishes); to inflate the resulting totals by a factor intended to convert the resulting totals into national estimates; and, lastly, to estimate a final inflation ratio to offset the combined effects of the spread of nonconformity and residual non-registration.[12] The totals reached at the

[12] The effect of taking these successive steps is summarised in Wrigley and Schofield, *Population history of England*, app. 4.

penultimate stage, before applying the final inflation ratio, may conveniently be termed the totals of corrected baptisms and corrected burials.

The last of this series of actions was the most problematic. The scale of the gap between the totals of corrected baptisms and the true totals of births was gauged by taking advantage of the information about age structure given in the nineteenth-century censuses, and especially in the censuses of 1821 and 1841, the only two of the first five censuses to provide information about age structure. After making allowance for inaccuracies in the reporting of age in the censuses, and, in the case of the 1821 census, for the failure to report any age for 13.2 per cent of the population, it appeared that between 1821 and 1841 the mortality regime reflected in the third English life table, which was based on the deaths taking place in the seventeen-year period 1838–54, also held true in this earlier 20-year period. There was an excellent 'fit' between the age group totals recorded in 1821 and those obtained by inflating the appropriate age groups in 1841 according to the L_xs in the 3rd ELT.[13] This in turn meant that the total of births for the 1820s and 1830s could be estimated from the population totals in the age groups 0–9 and 10–9 in the 1841 census, once allowance had been made for the underregistration of the very young and the misreporting of age in the census.

If the 'true' total of births is known for a given decade, the total of deaths can also be estimated straightforwardly by deducting the intercensal increase,[14] and this opens the way to the calculation of final inflation ratios for converting the monthly and annual totals of corrected baptisms and burials to national totals of births and deaths.

Similar operations to that just described for the period 1821–41 were then carried out, using the age data in the 1821 census to yield estimates of decennial birth and death totals for the 30-year period stretching back from the 1821 census to 1791. The best 'fit' between the overall population totals in the censuses of 1801 and 1811 and the totals produced by inflating the age group totals in the 1821 census appeared to be secured by assuming a more severe mortality regime for the first 20 years of the century than for the period 1821–41. In order to facilitate a judgement of this kind, a family of life tables had been created, to which reference has already been made in the last section. The life tables were based on a modified 3rd ELT, and linked to the Princeton model North system, with 'levels' representing e_0s approximately 2.5 years apart, as

[13] Ibid., pp. 103–18.

[14] An assumption must, of course, be made about net migration in order to make an estimate of the total of deaths in this way. This issue is discussed in ibid., pp. 118–20.

in the Princeton system. The 3rd ELT represented level 10.[15] Level 9 was chosen as the most plausible mortality level for the 30-year period stretching back from the 1821 census, and totals of births and deaths were calculated accordingly. This in turn determined the final inflation ratios used to increase the totals of corrected baptisms and burials to match the number of births and deaths which were calculated to have occurred. The decision to use level 9 mortality in making these calculations appeared the more plausible in that, if mortality changed at all in the early decades of the nineteenth century, it seemed more credible to suppose that it might have improved than that it deteriorated.

The reconstitution findings suggested that the decisions about the prevailing levels of mortality made when working on the *Population history of England* were in need of review. In particular, the conclusion that mortality was more severe at the beginning of the century than later seemed difficult to sustain. Childhood mortality worsened over the first half of the nineteenth century. It will be recalled that there was a close agreement between the estimates of infant and child mortality obtained from reconstitution and those found in the 3rd ELT apart from $_4q_1$.[16] Infant and child mortality in these age groups in the reconstitution parishes was closely similar to the rates observed in the registration districts of which they formed part,[17] but it so happened that, even though infant mortality and mortality later in childhood were on average very similar to the national level, mortality in the age group 1–4 in these areas was distinctly lower than in the country as a whole, probably because none of the reconstitution parishes were situated in cities or large industrial agglomerations. The absolute level of $_{10}q_0$ in the reconstitution parishes in the early nineteenth century, therefore, was lower than in the country as a whole, but any *change* in $_{10}q_0$ in the reconstitution parishes probably reflected national trends.

In the 1820s and 1830s the reconstitution data suggest that $_{10}q_0$ was no different from its level during the years on which the 3rd ELT was based, 1838–54, confirming the conclusion reached in the *Population history of England*. They also suggest, however, that mortality was *less* severe in the first 20 years of the century than in the next two decades. In 1820–37 $_{10}q_0$ was 258.2 per 1000, but in 1800–19 only 246.6 per 1000.[18] The

---

[15] The 3rd ELT was modified in that above the age of 50 q_xs were derived from the Princeton North tables. These were used in preference to those in the 3rd ELT because at advanced ages the rates in the latter were clearly too low. Ibid., p. 110 and especially app. 14, where the evidence for distrusting the 3rd ELT in the higher age groups is reviewed.   [16] Tab. 6.13, p. 258.   [17] See tab. 4.3, p. 93.
[18] Tabs. 6.3 and 6.10, pp. 224 and 250–1.

difference between the two rates is the equivalent of about one half of a level in the Princeton North system, and therefore also in the system based on the 3rd ELT. Rather than assuming level 9 as the appropriate level to be used in calculating totals of births and deaths for the first 20 years of the century, it appeared that level 10.5 was the better choice for the years of childhood, especially as other research also suggests that mortality in infancy and childhood was worsening rather than improving during the early decades of the century.[19]

In summary, therefore, substantial changes needed to be made to the input data for GIP for the period 1791–1821. The reconstitution data do not suggest changing the assumption that level 10 mortality prevailed from 1821 to 1841, but they do suggest that infant and child mortality in the preceding 20 years should be treated as at level 10.5 rather than at level 9, and that late eighteenth-century mortality was also less severe than earlier assumed.

Before reviewing the implementation of this altered view of mortality in the late eighteenth and early nineteenth centuries, one other question must be considered. In making a new estimate of births and deaths in the period 1811–21, the only calculation to be made is $_{10}L_0/10l_0$, and the new evidence suggests that this should be done using level 10.5. But in making a comparable estimate for 1801–11 account must also be taken of $_{10}L_0/_{10}L_{10}$, since the age group 10–9 in the 1821 census must be converted into an estimate of those aged 0–9 in 1811 before being converted in turn into an estimate of the birth cohort in the period 1801–11 using level 10.5. In other words, a decision must be made about the level of mortality in the age group 10–9 as well as in the age group 0–9.

Unfortunately, the reconstitution rates for the age group 10–4 are based on relatively small totals of deaths, so that a change in this rate between one decade and the next may be influenced by random factors, and reconstitution can provide no direct evidence about the age group 15–9 since this was the time of life when many young people had left home, but almost none of them had married. Moreover, 1800–9 was the last decade for which an estimate of adult mortality was possible.[20] In these circumstances any decision about the level of $_{10}q_{10}$ in the next decade must be tentative and arbitrary. On balance it seemed best to assume level 10 rather than level 10.5 for this age group in 1811–21. Adult mortality at the beginning of the nineteenth century appears to have been at much the same level as in the mid-century at the time of the 3rd ELT,[21] and the same may also have been true of teenagers.

Table 8.3 shows the totals of births and deaths which resulted from

---

[19] See above pp. 256–7.   [20] See pp. 281–2 and app. 6.   [21] Fig. 6.14, p. 281.

Table 8.3 *Decennial totals of female births and deaths in England: old and new estimates*

	Old estimates			New estimates		
	Births	Deaths	Intercensal increase	Births	Deaths	Intercensal increase
1801–11	1 799 500	1 180 770	618 730	1 706 149	1 087 419	618 730
1811–21	2 131 683	1 311 263	820 420	2 044 837	1 225 272	819 565
1821–31	2 340 196	1 405 639	934 557	2 338 877	1 403 465	935 412
1831–41	2 470 590	1 563 598	906 992	2 455 674	1 558 285	897 389

Sources: old estimates: Wrigley and Schofield, *Population history of England*, tab. 5.16, p. 127. New estimates: see text.

the calculations made for the *Population history of England* and those produced by the new exercise. The totals are for females only. The female population was made the basis for this exercise, both because it is probable that levels of net migration were substantially lower for women than for men, and because male census totals in 1801 and 1811 were significantly distorted by the number of men in the army and navy.[22] It is, however, a straightforward matter subsequently to convert estimates of female births and deaths into combined sex totals by multiplying the female totals by 2.045 and 2.03 respectively.[23] Expressing the relationship of new totals to the old totals as ratios, the four successive figures from 1801–11 to 1831–41 are 0.9481, 0.9593, 0.9994, and 0.9940, while the comparable death ratios are 0.9209, 0.9344, 0.9985, and 0.9966. The changes are substantial in the first two decades, but trivial to the point of being barely visible in the two later decades.

It is convenient to consider first the very small changes in the period 1821–41 before turning to the more substantial changes in 1801–21.

The 1831–41 birth total, unlike the totals for earlier decades, was originally obtained by inflating the 0–4 and 5–9 age group totals of female children separately rather than by working from the 0–9 age group total as a whole. The same policy was pursued in the new exercise, and the new total differs from the old only in that the enumerated total for the age group 5–9 was preferred (884 314), rather than a total inferred from the enumerated total, on what now seems a somewhat flimsy argument. This has a knock-on effect on the female census total for 1841, reducing it by 9603, which in turn affects the total

[22] Wrigley and Schofield, *Population history of England*, pp. 104–5, 118–20.
[23] For the reasons for using these multipliers, ibid., pp. 126–9.

of female deaths for the decade, because it reduces the intercensal increase by the same amount.

The 1821–31 birth total is almost the same as its predecessor, differing by less than 0.06 per cent, a change due to a reestimation of the female population aged 10–9 in 1841, from which this decadal birth total was estimated. Since the reporting of the age of young women in their 20s was inaccurate and affected the age groups on either side, the total female population aged 10–39 was redistributed between the three age groups, 10–9, 20–9, and 30–9, on the assumption that their relative size would be captured accurately by using the data for the age groups 30–9 to 50–9 in the 1861 census in conjunction with the 3rd ELT, and estimating the total in each age group when it was 20 years younger. This was a very similar exercise to that carried out in the *Population history of England*, and described in greater detail there,[24] but it yielded marginally different results. The successive steps and population totals are rehearsed in table 8.4.

The intercensal increase in 1821–31 was slightly increased because the estimated total of children under 10 in 1821, which affects the estimated census total in that year, was slightly reduced, by 855. With the birth total and the intercensal increase both defined, the death total is obtained by subtraction.

The birth totals for 1801–11 and 1811–21 were derived from the estimated population totals for the age groups 0–9 and 10–9 in 1821, using the mortality assumptions already described. The 10–9 total (1 204 502) was obtained by correcting the distortions in the recorded totals of women in the decennial age groups between 10 and 39 (2 859 828) by using the census totals of women in the decennial age groups from 30 to 59 in 1841, employing exactly the same method as was used in carrying out the parallel correction for the same age groups in 1841, using 1861 census data. The 0–9 total (1 608 792) was inferred from the revised female total for the age group 20–9 in 1841. In both cases level 10 mortality was assumed for the 1821 to 1841 period. The series of operations, which closely parallel those employed in the earlier back projection exercise,[25] are summarised in table 8.4.

In column 1 of table 8.4 are shown the census totals to be used to monitor the recorded numbers in the same decennial cohorts 20 years earlier. The extent of any misreporting of age in the age groups from 30 to 59 was probably much less than when the same women were 20 years younger. The assumed mortality level between the two dates is shown in column 2, and the result of reverse surviving the three age groups is

---

[24] Ibid., pp. 113–5, and tab. 5.8, p. 115.   [25] Ibid., pp. 113–30.

Table 8.4 *The steps by which decennial totals of female births were estimated for the decades 1801–11 to 1821–31*

(1)	(2)	(3)		(4)	(5)	(6)	(7)	(8)	(9)
1861	Level 10	1841 estimate		1841 census total	1841 census revised	Level 10		Level 10.5	Birth cohort
30–9	$1\,279\,110 \times {}_{10}L_{10}/{}_{10}L_{30} = 1\,534\,282$		10–9	$1\,547\,350$	$1\,629\,638 \times {}_{10}L_0/{}_{10}L_{10} =$				$2\,338\,877$ (1821–31)
40–9	$997\,247 \times {}_{10}L_{20}/{}_{10}L_{40} = 1\,258\,231$		20–9	$1\,408\,389$	$1\,336\,430 \times {}_{10}L_0/{}_{10}L_{20} = 1\,608\,792 \times {}_{10}L_0/{}_{10}L_0 = 2\,044\,837$				$2\,044\,837$ (1811–21)
50–9	$683\,813 \times {}_{10}L_{30}/{}_{10}L_{50} = 920\,468$		30–9	$988\,004$	$977\,675$				
		$3\,712\,981$		$3\,943\,743$	$3\,943\,743$				

(1)	(2)	(3)		(4)	(5)	(6)	(7)	(8)	(9)
1841	Level 10	1821 estimate		1821 census total	1821 census revised	Level 10		Level 10.5	Birth cohort
30–9	$977\,675 \times {}_{10}L_{10}/{}_{10}L_{30} = 1\,172\,714$		10–9	$1\,172\,561$	$1\,204\,502 \times {}_{10}L_0/{}_{10}L_{10} = 1\,342\,326 = {}_{10}L_0/{}_{10}L_{10} = 1\,706\,149$ (1801–11)				
40–9	$729\,821 \times {}_{10}L_{20}/{}_{10}L_{40} = 920\,726$		20–9	$981\,918$	$945\,684$				
50–9	$513\,278 \times {}_{10}L_{30}/{}_{10}L_{50} = 690\,914$		30–9	$705\,349$	$709\,642$				
		$2\,784\,354$		$2\,859\,828$	$2\,859\,828$				

Notes: see text for explanation of the sequence of operations giving rise to birth cohort estimates. The derivation of the mortality levels based on the third English life table is described in Wrigley and Schofield, *Population history of England*, app. 14.

Sources: census totals for 1821 and 1841: ibid., tab. 5.3, p. 108 and tab. 5.11, p. 117. Census totals for 1861: *1861 Census*, Population tables II. Ages, civil condition, occupations and birth places of the people.

given in column 3. Column 4 shows the recorded census totals and column 5 the revised census totals produced by redistributing the same total of women to conform to the pattern suggested by the column 3 totals.[26] Thus, for example, in the top line of the table the revised census total 10–9 is 1 629 638, which is 3 943 743 × 1 534 282/3 712 981. The subsequent columns then show the conversion of an age group total into a total of births.

The birth cohort totals for 1801–11 and for 1811–21, shown in column 9 of table 8.4, taken in conjunction with the intercensal increases in the two decades, yield the totals of deaths given in table 8.3.

There remains the question of estimating the decennial totals of births before 1801. In moving earlier in time than the first census, any process of estimating birth totals becomes in one sense less securely based, but in another sense the margin of error is reduced, since the ratio between the corrected totals of baptisms and the 'true' total of births can be shown to have grown much less by the 1790s than in later decades, so that the band of uncertainty narrows.

Consider, first, the estimation of the birth total for 1791–1801. Reconstitution gives no warrant for supposing that the milder infant and child mortality levels of the first 20 years of the nineteenth century extended to an earlier period. Any estimate for the 1790s has to be related to the total of women aged 20–9 in 1821, who formed the birth cohort in the decade 1791–1801. Table 8.4 shows that they numbered 945 684 in 1821. They lived for most of their youth in the period of low death rates early in the century, but their childhood was not so favoured. A best guess is that the birth total from which they sprang may be approximated by assuming level 10 mortality over their lifespan to 1821, implying a birth total of 1 466 106.

In table 8.5 the birth totals (sexes combined) for the period 1791 to 1836 are set out together with the corresponding corrected baptism totals. The ratio between the birth totals and the corresponding baptism totals is shown in column 3. The corrected baptism totals, it will be recalled, included all the corrections and adjustments listed earlier apart from the inflation needed to offset the increasing importance of nonconformity and any residual escapes from registration. This gap is bridged by the final inflation ratio. The inflation ratio appropriate for the

[26] The total for women aged 30–9 shown in the first column of the second panel might be regarded as an illogical choice. The total is the revised rather than the recorded total for the age group (cols. 5 and 4 of the top panel). A decision between the two is arbitrary, but it has only a very small impact on the estimated birth total for 1801–11. Using the recorded rather than the revised figure would raise the birth total by about a thousand a year in each year of the decade, a trivially small difference.

Table 8.5 *Decennial English birth and corrected baptism totals,
nonconformist inflation ratios, and final inflation ratios*

	(1) Corrected baptisms	(2) Births	(3) Final inflation ratio (2)/(1)	(4) Nonconformist inflation ratio	(5) (3)/(4)[a]
1791–1801	2 709 950	2 998 188	1.1064	1.0396	2.69
1801–11	3 023 437	3 489 075	1.1540	1.0486	3.17
1811–21	3 387 237	4 181 692	1.2345	1.0563	4.17
1821–31	3 903 270	4 783 004	1.2254	1.0623	3.62
1831–6	2 105 062	2 462 403	1.1698	1.0682	2.49

[a] This ratio expresses the relationship between the percentage inflations in
the two columns. Thus 1064/396 = 2.69.
Sources: the birth totals are derived from the female birth totals in tab. 8.1
by multiplying the latter by 2.045. The totals in each case refer to 10-year
periods beginning in July and ending in June, rather than January and
December. The corrected baptism totals are taken from Wrigley and
Schofield, *Population history of England*, tab. 5.27, p. 140. Note, however, that
the totals for 1831–6 refer to a 5-year period ending in June 1836 (a slightly
different period from that in tab. 5.27, which ended in December 1836).

correction of nonconformity alone is shown in column 4, while in
column 5 the ratio between the percentage inflation linked to nonconformity and the percentage which includes both nonconformity and
other residual non-registration is shown.[27]

The total of baptisms recorded in nonconformist registers can be
estimated, and therefore the nonconformist ratio can be calculated, from
the origins of an independent nonconformity in the mid-seventeenth
century onwards. In the *Population history of England* the argument was
made that the final inflation ratio for periods before 1791 could be
inferred from the nonconformist ratio for each decade on the assumption that there was a stable relationship between the two ratios.[28] The
solution then adopted was to take the final inflation ratio as 2.5 times the
nonconformist inflation ratio. There seems no good reason to change
this decision. Indeed, if anything the ratios in column 5 of table 8.5
strengthen the case for it. The birth totals in the first two decades of the
nineteenth century are lower than in the previous exercise, suggesting
that the faltering in Anglican and nonconformist coverage of births was

[27] The comparable data and ratios which influenced the choice of final inflation ratios in
the earlier, back projection exercise are to be found in Wrigley and Schofield, *Population
history of England*, tabs. 5.23 and 5.24, pp. 135 and 137.   [28] Ibid., pp. 136–42.

significantly less pronounced than had earlier appeared, but having the same general pattern. The pattern conforms to the picture drawn by Krause when studying this issue.[29] At the beginning and the end of the period when Anglican coverage was at its weakest, in the 1790s and the 1830s, the evidence of table 8.5 suggests that the ratio between the two inflation factors is *c.* 2.5. Accordingly, this relationship was used in calculating all the final inflation ratios stretching back from the 1780s. They are, therefore, unchanged in the present exercise from those used in its predecessor, except that in the earlier exercise the 1780s were treated as a special case, but not in the present one.[30] As a result, the old and new totals are identical from the beginning until 1774. Similarly, the principles determining the final inflation ratios for burials, and therefore the totals of deaths, are unchanged from the *Population history of England*, and the totals of deaths are also unchanged from the beginning of the annual totals in 1538 until 1774. After that date the different final inflation ratio of the 1780s begins to take effect.[31]

Table 8.6 shows the old and new decennial totals of births and deaths. Before the decade 1771–81, and also after 1841, the totals are unchanged from the previous exercise. Neither the old nor the new totals of events are notable in the sense that they are surprising. They are well within the envelope of earlier estimates made by those who have studied the question, from Finlaison to Razzell.[32] When the old totals were published they were queried by Lindert.[33] He had no quarrel with the high totals of events when birth and death rates were at their peak early in the nineteenth century, but argued for much higher totals stretching back throughout the eighteenth century. The new estimates have something of the shape which he advocated but are well below the level which he thought probable.

The new estimates, however, help to resolve a problem highlighted by the work of Wilson and Woods. In a survey of long-term trends in fertility in England, they took up an issue which had previously received attention by Weir and Schofield.[34] Weir showed that if gross reproduction rates are known, and rates of marital fertility, marital

[29] Ibid., p. 130. Krause, 'Changes in English fertility and mortality'; and 'The changing adequacy of English registration'.
[30] Wrigley and Schofield, *Population history of England*, tab. 5.25, p. 138.
[31] The method by which the final inflation ratios chosen for each decade were implemented is described in ibid., pp. 139–42.
[32] Details of the estimates made by Finlaison, Farr, Brownlee, Griffith, Krause, Hollingsworth, and Razzell may be found in ibid., pp. 142–52.
[33] Lindert, 'English living standards'.
[34] Wilson and Woods, 'Fertility in England'; Weir, 'Rather never than late'; Schofield, 'English marriage patterns revisited'.

Table 8.6 *Old and new decennial totals of births and deaths*

	Births			Deaths		
	(1) New	(2) Old	(3) (1)–(2)	(1) New	(2) Old	(3) (1)–(2)
1771–81	2 442 912	2 438 551	+4 361	1 799 539	1 796 887	+2 652
1781–91	2 684 344	2 725 911	−41 567	1 981 416	1 995 527	−14 111
1791–1801	2 997 870	3 149 428	−151 558	2 099 175	2 183 981	−84 806
1801–11	3 490 498	3 680 048	−189 550	2 207 140	2 396 995	−189 855
1811–21	4 184 032	4 359 378	−175 346	2 488 799	2 662 116	−173 317
1821–31	4 783 116	4 786 007	−2 891	2 847 077	2 853 495	−6 418
1831–41	2 462 403	2 449 868	+12 545	1 532 915	1 537 501	−4 586

Note: the totals all refer to decades, or in the case of 1831–6 a quinquennium, beginning in July and ending in June (thus, July 1801 – June 1811). The totals are those resulting from applying the final inflation ratios to the totals of corrected baptisms and burials. They may therefore differ very slightly from the estimated decennial totals in tab. 8.5 because the monthly totals of baptisms and burials to which the ratios are applied do not change smoothly over time as the inflation ratios do in moving from one inflection point to another.
Sources: new: see text. Old: Wrigley and Schofield, *Population history of England*, tab. A2.3, pp. 500–1.

dissolution, and remarriage are either known or can be estimated, levels of nuptiality can be inferred. Further, if, say, age at marriage is known, the proportions ever marrying can also be calculated, on certain assumptions. Wilson and Woods, using the best information then available, and pursuing the same line of thought, came to the conclusion that 'During periods of very high fertility (for example, the early nineteenth century when the crude birth rate exceeded 40 per thousand) marital fertility almost certainly increased. Assuming that it did not, leads to implausibly high estimates of proportions married and thus levels of I_m.'[35] Their estimates of I_m, based on near-constant levels of marital fertility, show it reaching a particularly high level in the period 1801–25, quite out of keeping with any level previously attained.[36] Their surmise that marital fertility had risen, and that I_m was exaggerated, is sustained by the new evidence of falling birth intervals in the eighteenth century.[37] But the significant reduction in the total of births in this period is also helpful in resolving the problem. Age at marriage was low in this period, but it is not necessary to posit an exceptionally high

[35] Wilson and Woods, 'Fertility in England', pp. 405–6.   [36] Ibid., fig. 2, p. 405.
[37] Tab. 7.36, p. 447.

proportion of women marrying in order to reconcile fertility with nuptiality.

The effect of the new data on demographic estimates

Having described the considerations which have led to a revision of the estimates of birth and death totals in the later eighteenth and early nineteenth centuries, we may now turn to their implications for estimates of population size, fertility, and mortality. Since the quinquennial totals of births and particularly of deaths in the period 1791–1821 were significantly reduced, it will be obvious that levels of fertility and mortality in this period must be lower in the new than in the old sets of estimates, but, since the absolute differences between the totals of births and deaths were altered only modestly by these changes, the long-run implications of the changes need not be marked. In table 8.7 some benchmark data are set out to establish the extent of the changes that are due to the altered input totals of births and deaths. All other input parameters for the GIP program were the same as in the exercise designed to test the effect of moving from BP to GIP based on a Brass system. The population totals in the column headed '*PHE* totals' are, therefore, the same as those shown in the third column of table 8.1, headed 'GIP Brass' in that table.

Table 8.7 shows the population totals at decennial intervals from 1851 back to 1751, which was the period most affected by the changes which were made to birth and death totals, and at 50-year intervals before 1751. The gross reproduction rate and expectation of life at birth are given for each five-year period beginning at the date for which a population total is given.

The changed input totals make little difference to population totals after 1801. The nineteenth-century totals are very similar in the two series, never differing from one another by a total larger than 16 000, or 0.18 per cent (in 1801). Moving backward in time, however, the difference becomes more pronounced. It reaches 160 000 in 1781, a difference of 2.3 per cent. By 1751 the two population totals differ by 176 000, and the new total is 3.1 per cent the higher of the two. Thereafter the absolute difference decreases fairly rapidly, but the relative difference declines only very slowly, and eventually stabilises at *c*. 2.5 per cent over the first century from 1551 to 1651. The alteration to the birth and death totals in the period 1791 to 1821, therefore, not only changes population totals close to this period, but also influences estimates of earlier populations over the whole sweep of the exercise.

Table 8.7 *Estimates of population totals, and of gross reproduction rates and expectation of life at birth using old and new estimates of birth and death totals*

	Population 000s		GRR		e_0	
	(1) *PHE* totals	(2) New totals	(3) *PHE* totals	(4) New totals	(5) *PHE* totals	(6) New totals
1551	2946	3024	2.72	2.64	38.9	39.7
1601	4029	4126	2.30	2.24	37.7	38.5
1651	5159	5284	1.98	1.93	38.4	39.1
1701	5040	5198	2.43	2.35	37.9	38.9
1751	5741	5917	2.43	2.35	38.8	39.7
1761	6130	6306	2.42	2.35	34.4	35.3
1771	6448	6620	2.48	2.41	38.2	39.1
1781	7044	7204	2.50	2.44	35.1	35.8
1791	7734	7844	2.79	2.65	37.0	38.0
1801	8655	8671	2.86	2.68	38.2	40.1
1811	9875	9864	2.96	2.83	38.7	41.3
1821	11472	11457	2.95	2.93	39.8	40.5
1831	13252	13255	2.57	2.59	40.6	40.9
1841	14941	14939	2.44	2.45	41.7	41.7
1851	16725	16733	2.42	2.42	40.4	40.5

Notes: the population totals refer to the midpoint of the years shown. The GRRs and e_0s refer to quinquennia beginning in the year indicated at its midpoint: 1551–6, 1556–61, etc. For description of *PHE* and new totals, see text.
Source: Cambridge Group data.

Given that population totals are affected by changing the totals of births and deaths, it is inevitable that there should also be changes in the fertility and mortality estimates. Moving backwards in time, there are only slight differences between the two series of GRRs and e_0s between 1851 and 1821, but, as was to be expected, substantial differences appear directly related to the changed birth and death totals. In the three decades 1791–1801, 1801–11, and 1811–21, the new GRR is 5.0, 6.3, and 4.4 per cent lower than in the old one, while the comparable percentage rise in e_0 is 2.7, 5.0, and 6.7, respectively. The differences in both the fertility and the mortality series then decline sharply but remain affected by the differing population totals. The GRR in the new series is usually between 2.5 and 3.5 per cent lower with the new input data, while the e_0 is about 2 per cent higher.

Changing the input parameters

Both lack of knowledge and the limitations of back projection as a technique restricted the choice of input parameters used in generating the results published in the *Population history of England*. Reconstitution has improved matters in relation to the first point and generalised inverse projection in relation to the second. In this section the opportunity to modify and refine earlier assumptions is taken up. The point of departure is the situation summarised in table 8.7, where the effects of changing the input totals of births and deaths were examined, but where the assumptions were otherwise those of the *Population history of England*. The following issues are considered in turn: the changing mean age at maternity; the changes in the age structure of mortality which occurred in the first half of the eighteenth century; and the alternative ways of securing a best fit for the model.

Mean age at maternity

In order to generate estimates of the gross reproduction rate, it is necessary to make a decision about the mean age at maternity to be used in the model. Since mortality progressively reduces the number of women in each cohort as the cohort ages, a high mean age at maternity will result in a relatively high estimate of GRR, while if women are assumed to marry young, and therefore to have a low mean age at maternity, the GRR will be lower than in the alternative case. Some of the implications of a change in the mean age at maternity were examined in the *Population history of England*,[38] but an unchanging mean age at maternity of 32 years was assumed in the back projection exercise.

It is clear *a priori* that the effect of introducing a changing mean age at maternity must be slightly to reduce the extent of the difference between the trough of the GRR in the mid-seventeenth century and its peak early in the nineteenth century, since age at marriage was high in the earlier period and had fallen substantially by the later period. Table 5.7 shows that female mean age at first marriage in bachelor/spinster marriages was about 25.8 years on average, with little evidence of trend, between 1610 and 1724, and that after 1775 it was about 23.7 years. There was a slight further fall after 1775, but the main change was confined to the half-century between 1725 and 1775. The mean age of all first marriages was slightly higher than these figures, but for the purposes of an exercise of this sort, this is a refinement which may be ignored. Table 7.1 provides age-specific marital fertility rates for the parish register period

[38] Wrigley and Schofield, *Population history of England*, pp. 265–9.

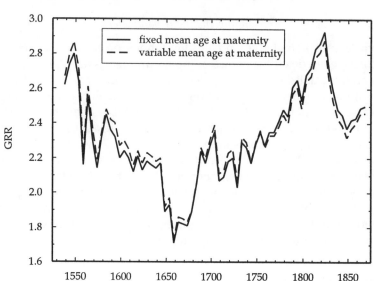

Figure 8.1   *Quinquennial gross reproduction rates: fixed and variable mean
age at maternity*
Source: Cambridge Group data.

as a whole. In a more exhaustive exercise, the changes in these rates
which occurred over time might be taken into account, but in the present
context simplicity is attractive, and it is adequate to assume that the
same rates prevailed throughout. Finally, account must be taken of
illegitimacy. Again, simplification seemed in order. In the period before
1725, 1.5 per cent of all births were taken as illegitimate; in the period
after 1775, 6.0 per cent. It was further assumed that the average age of
the mothers of illegitimate children was the same as the average age of
mothers of first-born legitimate children.[39] These various assumptions,
when combined, suggest that the mean age at maternity in the period
before 1725 was about 33.0 years, and in the period after 1775 31.3 years.
Between 1725 and 1775 the mean age was assumed to fall linearly
between the two figures. The assumptions used are crude and they
ignore the minor effect that lower levels of mortality will have had in
increasing the mean age. They also ignore the complications involved in
establishing the effects of remarriage in modifying the impact of

[39] Tab. 6.2, p. 219. Evidence exists to support the view that the age of the mothers of
illegitimate children when they had their first birth was very similar to that of mothers
of legitimate children at the same point in their reproductive career. Oosterveen, Smith,
and Stewart, 'Family reconstitution and the study of bastardy', pp. 107–8.

mortality. But they serve to show the order of magnitude of the impact of a changing mean age at maternity.

Figure 8.1 plots the quinquennial GRRs with a fixed and variable mean age at maternity. The peak GRR reached in 1806–31 is reduced slightly from 2.81 to 2.76 with a changing mean age at maternity, and in the period 1646–81, when the GRR was at its lowest, its level is raised from 1.84 to 1.87. The trough-to-peak rise is therefore less dramatic than with a fixed mean age at maternity. With a fixed age at maternity, the GRR rises by 53 per cent. With a variable age at maternity, it rises by 48 per cent. The rise is, therefore, somewhat less dramatic, but the exercise shows that the switch to a less rigid view of the mean age at maternity makes no large differences to the picture of fertility change over time.

Since the calculation of the GRR is independent of the working of other assumptions incorporated into the model, none of the other demographic measures produced by GIP is affected by the changes just described. Changes in several of the other input parameters, however, may have much more widespread effects. This is true, for example, of a change in the assumptions made about the structure of mortality in the early modern period.

The age structure of mortality

When expectation of life at birth was calculated by back projection, use was made of a family of life tables developed from the third English life table. The combined sex age-specific mortality rates (q_x) from the 3rd ELT were extended above the age of 50 from model North of the Princeton life tables to form level 10 of a family of tables, which was then built up from this base, again using model North as a guide.[40] Given a life table family of this type and a knowledge of the age structure of a population, a mortality level can always be identified which will absorb a particular total of deaths, and thus an e_0 for the period during which the deaths occurred can be established.

Model North was selected because the age structure of mortality in early modern England appeared to have conformed fairly closely to the North pattern, but once it became apparent that the age structure of mortality changed significantly in the parish register period, it was evident that adopting a life table system of this kind was likely to distort our vision of past reality by forcing the relative level of mortality at different ages to remain constant when it was actually in the course of change. One of the most intriguing discoveries made possible by the

[40] Wrigley and Schofield, *Population history of England*, apps. 14 and 15.

new reconstitution evidence is that in the course of the first half of the eighteenth century adult mortality improved radically while infant and child mortality did not. After 1750 the age structure of mortality was broadly consonant with the pattern captured in model North. Before 1700, in model North terms, adult mortality was relatively far higher than mortality in infancy and childhood.[41] A change of this type is potentially of signficance in a GIP exercise since a change from an era when adult mortality was relatively high to an era when this was no longer the case must alter the age structure of the population, and with it estimates of many variables which are influenced by age structure, such as the age-specific mortality rates or the gross reproduction rate.

A main reason for moving to a Brass system of defining the level and shape of mortality was the comparative ease with which altering the β coefficient captures the general nature of the changing age structure of mortality in England. The β coefficient defines the shape of the age pattern of mortality rates, where the α coefficient defines the level of mortality over the whole age range. Changing β, therefore, can capture a change in the level of adult mortality relative to mortality in childhood. The change in the β coefficient over time is shown in figure 8.2, in which the data for its calculation are those provided by reconstitution. The figure shows that from 1750 onwards the coefficient was very close to 1.0, and that before 1700 it was at a distinctly higher level. Between 1700 and 1750 it declined fairly regularly, reflecting the pronounced fall in adult death rates relative to those in infancy and childhood.[42] The small changes in β which took place before and after the major decline are probably attributable to random influences on particular sets of age-specific rates. Accordingly, to incorporate the major change into the GIP exercise, the change was modelled by assuming that the average level of β over the period 1640–89 represented the 'before' state, while the average level over the period 1750–1809 represented the 'after' state. This follows the line of thinking embodied in table 6.20.[43] Between 1690 and 1750 it was assumed that β declined linearly as the mortality age structure changed. Before 1640 β was assumed to remain at the level of the 1640–89 period: from 1810 onwards it was assumed to be 1.00 (that is, at the level of the modified third English life table). The mean value of β for the period 1640–89 was 1.1062, and for 1750–1809 1.0076. Within GIP, having specified the *shape* of mortality as an input parameter (the β coefficient), the model is free to select the most appropriate *level* of mortality (the α coefficient). Figure 8.2 also plots the α coefficient. It reveals nothing surprising. Mortality worsened during the seventeenth

---

[41] See above pp. 282–4.   [42] See above Fig. 6.15, p. 283.   [43] P. 291.

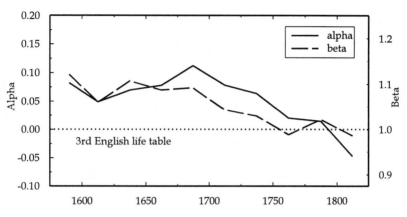

Figure 8.2 *Brass parameters: change over time*
Source: Cambridge Group reconstitutions.

century, but improved steadily thereafter, though if the plot were extended further into the nineteenth century, it would, of course, rise again, since it was calibrated as 0.0 in the third English life table.

Table 8.8 indicates the effect of moving from a fixed β coefficient to one in which β changes is shown. The changes to population totals and other demographic variables are too slight to be distinguishable if plotted on a graph and some representative data are therefore given in the form of a table. It parallels earlier tables in showing the population totals at half-century intervals under the two sets of assumptions, with GRR and e_0 estimates for five-year periods beginning at the dates shown. These will suffice to give a general impression of the slightness of the changes brought about by the adoption of a variable β. The population totals are uniformly slightly higher with a variable β but the differences are small. The maximum difference, in 1551, was less than 1.5 per cent. Moreover, the associated changes in age structure were such that GRR and e_0 changed even less than might have been expected from the changes in the population totals.

Other input parameters

Generalised inverse projection requires decisions to be made about other input parameters, besides those explicitly considered so far. It may be helpful to review them briefly at this point.

GIP generates estimates of net migration, and to do this requires a schedule of the age structure of migration. The assumptions made in

Table 8.8 *Estimates of population totals, gross reproduction rates, and expectation of life at birth with a fixed β and a variable β*

	Population 000s		GRR		e_0	
	Fixed β	Variable β	Fixed β	Variable β	Fixed β	Variable β
1551	3 024	3 065	2.64	2.64	39.7	39.6
1601	4 126	4 162	2.24	2.27	38.5	38.5
1651	5 284	5 308	1.93	1.94	39.1	39.1
1701	5 198	5 211	2.35	2.34	38.9	38.5
1751	5 917	5 922	2.35	2.37	39.7	39.8
1801	8 671	8 671	2.68	2.64	40.1	40.0
1851	16 733	16 732	2.42	2.38	40.5	40.5

Note: the population totals refer to the midpoint of the years shown. The GRRs are those obtained using a variable mean age at maternity. The GRRs and e_0s refer to quinquennia beginning in the year indicated at its midpoint: 1551–6, 1556–61, etc. For comments on the fixed and variable β assumptions, see text.
Source: Cambridge Group data.

this regard in the back projection exercise in the *Population history of England* have been retained throughout in the GIP runs described in this chapter.[44] Net migration estimates are made on a cohort basis. GIP is able to move to a period calculation of net migration, and in a more extended reconsideration of the derivation of demographic estimates from GIP it would be appropriate both to consider the effects of moving from a cohort to a period basis of calculating migration, and to examine the degree to which results are affected by changing the assumptions about the age structure of net migration. In this context, however, this would represent an unnecessary addition to an already complex operation.

GIP also requires a decision to be made about the relative importance to be attached to minimising departures from a set of objective functions. One of these relates to the degree to which migration is allowed to vary from one cohort to the next. The value given to the regularisation parameter λ determines this. A relatively high value of λ will make the system very reluctant to arrive at a solution in which there are major differences in the level of net migration between successive cohorts. It results in 'smooth' net migration estimates. In the series of GIP runs reported in this chapter λ was given the value of 0.1, an arbitrary decision, which, however, has the advantage of helping to

---

[44] Wrigley and Schofield, *Population history of England*, tab. 7.3, p. 201 and app. 15.

produce the relatively close agreement between BP and GIP reported in tables 8.1 and 8.2.[45]

Finally, it is necessary to provide as an input parameter an initial rate of population growth or its equivalent, since this will enable the 'blank triangle' in the Lexis surface to be filled, which is created by the absence of information about the size of the birth cohorts before the start date of the exercise. Such information is needed because, for example, the cohort of children born in 1531–6 will be present in the population until well into the seventeenth century. This cohort, and many others from the last century *before* the beginning of input data in 1541, spend part of their lifetimes in the century *after* 1541, and if deaths are to be distributed between members of all the cohorts with living members in the period from 1541 to 1641, the size of the pre-1541 cohorts at the point at which the exercise starts must be estimated. Thus, for example, it is possible to estimate the population growth rate from the rate of growth of birth totals *after* the beginning of the input data, and assume that this rate obtained *before* the beginning also, estimating the size of pre-1541 birth cohorts accordingly. However, in the several GIP exercises described in this chapter, in order to preserve parity with the original BP exercise, this input parameter was defined by using the same estimates of pre-1541 births which were used in the *Population history of England* back projection exercise.[46] The relative size of the pre-1541 cohorts is readily determined once a decision to use these data has been made.[47]

The new GIP estimates and reconstitution

The findings summarised in table 8.8 reflect the combined effects of adopting GIP, using new series of birth and death totals, adopting a variable schedule for the mean age at maternity, and allowing the age structure of mortality to vary over time. They represent a plausible set of estimates made from the revised aggregative data using GIP. It remains to compare these estimates with the findings of reconstitution. The tabulation of the results of a GIP exercise of this sort has a place in a book devoted to the presentation of reconstitution results only because it is instructive to compare the results obtained by

---

[45] For a fuller discussion of the part played by the setting of an objective function in the GIP system, and of the effects of altering the value of λ, see Oeppen, 'Back projection and inverse projection', pp. 248–52.

[46] Wrigley and Schofield, *Population history of England*, tab. A15.5, p. 736.

[47] On the questions raised by this procedure, see Lee, 'Inverse projection and demographic fluctuations', and Oeppen, 'Generalized inverse projection'.

reconstitution and GIP.[48] A good agreement between the two is a substantial endorsement of the accuracy of both since they stand quite independently of each other, except to the extent that results derived from reconstitution are built into GIP as input parameters.

A comparison of the reconstitution data with the results obtained by back projection and published in the *Population history of England* would be pointless, because the very different assumptions about mortality levels in the early nineteenth century used in the BP exercise would necessarily have produced a significant divergence between the two sets of estimates, especially during the period when there was a substantial revision of the birth and death totals, between *c.* 1780 and *c.* 1820, in the light of the reconstitution findings. The pointlessness of such a comparison is visible in figures 6.14 and 6.17.

The successive experiments reported in this chapter enabled both the effect of using GIP rather than BP and, similarly, the effect of adopting revised birth and death totals and the introduction of a variable mean age at maternity and a variable β in the Brass system to be assessed. They showed that, while the introduction of new birth and death totals had a substantial effect over the whole sweep of the exercise apart from the post-1821 period, the other changes made only small differences. We are now, therefore, in a position to make the reconstitution/GIP comparison. In doing so, it is reasonable to use the GIP results which incorporate two input parameter changes derived from reconstitution, that concerning a variable mean age at maternity and that designed to take into account the changing age structure of mortality. These two reconstitution-derived changes are helpful to include as approximating reality more closely, but, since they did not make a great difference to the results obtained by GIP before introducing these two refinements,[49] a close agreement is not guaranteed, or perhaps even made more likely, by the inclusion of information drawn from reconstitution as input parameters in GIP.

The most appropriate summary way of testing the agreement between reconstitution and GIP is to compare the estimates of expectation of life at birth produced by the two methods. Expectation of life at birth is a surer method of comparing the results of reconstitution and GIP than the main fertility measure generated by GIP, the gross reproduction rate. The GRRs produced by GIP suffer from the disadvantage that

---

[48] Although the results summarised in tab. 8.8 are not necessarily the best obtainable by GIP, since their form is constrained by the nature of this book, it may be of interest to present them in a fuller form. The most comprehensive summary table in the *Population history of England* was that given in tab. A3.1, and in app. 9 a similar table has been constructed to provide a comparison between the 'new' and 'old' reconstructions using aggregative data.   [49] See above pp. 533–7.

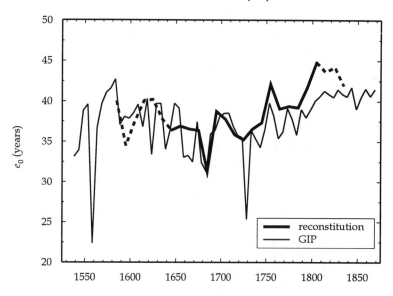

Figure 8.3   *Estimates of expectation of life at birth from reconstitution and by generalised inverse projection*
Source: Cambridge Group reconstitutions and Cambridge Group data.

the data make no distinction between males and females. This does not prohibit the construction of a GRR, but it forces assumptions to be made about a similarity in age structure between males and females and about their relative numbers in the childbearing age groups, even though there may be no direct evidence on either point. Equally, although reconstitution produces an abundance of fertility information, all fertility data relate to married women only and a GRR can only be calculated from reconstitution data by making assumptions about the proportion of unmarried women in each age group. Expectation of life at birth for the sexes combined, in contrast, can be calculated directly using reconstitution data and is immediately comparable with the estimates of e_0 produced by GIP.

Figure 8.3 shows that estimates of e_0 from the two sources agree remarkably well from the earliest dates for which they are available. Before 1640–9 and after 1800–9 the reconstitution line is shown as broken to indicate that the e_0s are partly based on modelled life tables in these periods. After 1810 the e_0s are estimated from data about infant and child mortality, while before 1640 some adult rates could not be measured directly for lack of information and are therefore estimated from the age groups for which there are empirical data.

Given that the two series of e_0s track one another so closely it is probable that both are close to the truth. For example, while it is possible to argue that, say, deaths were deficient equally in both cases, with the implication that mortality was higher than appears, it would require a very improbable conjunction of other circumstances to sustain this possibility. If this were a problem which affected deaths but births were more fully registered, the level of natural increase implied would cause population totals or net migration totals to assume implausible levels. Alternatively, if both births and deaths were equally underregistered, this, too, because of the internally consistent nature of demographic accounting within GIP, would produce a cumulative effect that was increasingly implausible. The obvious conclusion, that the agreement between the two series suggests that they are recovering past experience with tolerable accuracy, is also the one that is easiest to accept, especially as other checks upon the accuracy of the reconstitution mortality estimates all suggested that registration was reliable.[50]

Figure 8.4 reinforces the view that the two sets of results are mutually consistent by comparing partial life expectancies from the two sources for the age groups 0–14, 25–44, 45–64, and 65–84. The first of these comparisons is especially interesting in that the reconstitution data cover a longer period, from 1580 onwards, rather than from 1640 onwards, and therefore allow the comparison to cover a substantially longer period. The close agreement in $_{15}e_0$ between the two sources in the late sixteenth century is therefore additionally telling. The tendency for the reconstitution line to drift apart from the GIP line during the second half of the eighteenth century, which is the chief reason for a similar pattern in the two lines on figure 8.3, is principally due to the lower level of $_4q_1$ in the reconstitution data. It will be recalled that the agreement between the reconstitution data and the third English life table is good, apart from this age group.[51] In the 3rd ELT, however, $_4q_1$ was at a significantly higher level. A plausible explanation of the difference is that the reconstitution parishes do not include any from big cities or the major new industrial areas. GIP imposes an age structure of mortality that reflects the 3rd ELT, and which therefore allocates a relatively high proportion of deaths to the age group 1–4.

In the adult age groups, shown in the lower panel of figure 8.4, the agreement is good for $_{20}e_{25}$ and $_{20}e_{65}$, but less so for $_{20}e_{45}$. This suggests that the use of the Brass two-parameter system may be insufficiently flexible to mirror historical reality in this respect, though it enables the model to parallel empirical change much more effectively than would

---

[50] See, for example, pp. 93–7.   [51] See tab. 6.13, p. 258, and accompanying text.

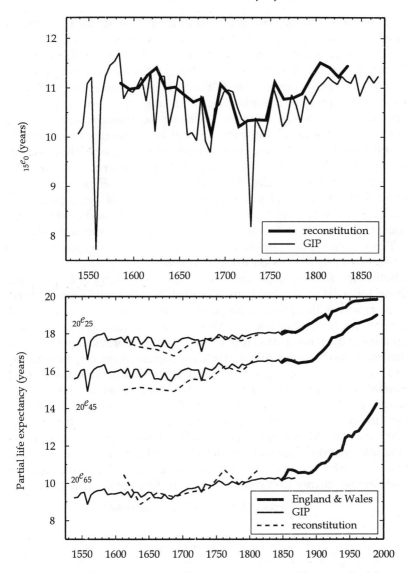

Figure 8.4 *Partial life expectancies from reconstitution and by generalised inverse projection: upper panel $_{15}e_0$, lower panel $_{20}e_{25}$, $_{20}e_{45}$, and $_{20}e_{65}$*
Sources: national data for England and Wales: *The Chester Beatty life tables*. Other data: Cambridge Group reconstitutions and Cambridge Group data.

be possible within, say, one of the Princeton model life table systems. It may prove rewarding in future work to consider the use of other systems, such as one of the Ledermann model life tables,[52] to try to model the empirical data more effectively. It is also encouraging that both the reconstitution and the GIP partial life expectancies match the national trends from the mid-nineteenth century onwards so closely. The latter are shown as heavy lines in the figure. Though there are minor departures from trend, the improvement in mortality which began in the later seventeenth century appears to have continued without serious interruption thereafter. The levelling off in the national trend lines for the elderly in the later decades of the nineteenth century may be no more than the effect of the improving accuracy of age reporting in causing mortality rates to appear to rise, and hence partial life expectancies to fall, after an initial period when the rates were understated.

These patterns are intriguing and suggestive. In the context of this book, however, the reason for a digression into GIP was to discover whether the findings reported in the *Population history of England* and those reported in this book are compatible with each other. A direct comparison with earlier findings made no sense because there are compelling reasons to take a different view of mortality in the early decades of the nineteenth century from that taken previously. Once this correction has been incorporated into the picture, however, the simplest and most testing comparison that can be made, that concerning estimates of expectation of life at birth, yields a result that strongly suggests that no incompatibility exists. Further, reconstitution helps to identify the most plausible path for GIP to follow. The nature of GIP, when considered in conjunction with the limited amount of independent information about early modern England that can be incorporated into a GIP exercise as a constraint, means that reconstitution guide posts will narrow further uncertainties about results obtained with GIP.

[52] Ledermann, *Nouvelles tables-types de mortalité.*

9

Conclusion

Two long hot summers enclose the bulk of the work which resulted in the *Population history of England* and this volume. In 1976 work on the analysis of the aggregative data used in the *Population history of England* was in its very early stages. Primary collection of the raw material for the book was already complete, and, of the 530 aggregative tabulations which had been returned to the Cambridge Group by the volunteers who carried out the work, a total of 404 had been selected to form the empirical basis of the enterprise. In the summer of 1995 the last chapters of this present volume were being written under a brilliant sun and in unusual heat.

Between them the two volumes have substantially enhanced what is known about English population history. They have also altered its standing in two respects.

First, there is no other country for which detailed and internally consistent demographic information is available over such a long period. In the early decades of the twentieth century the longest coherent and accessible national data series was that for Sweden, due in large measure to the efforts of Sundbärg.[1] The data were continuous from the middle of the eighteenth century. In Sweden there could be no doubt that the acceleration in population growth rates in the nineteenth century was due to falling mortality, with fertility for many decades remaining at the level of the late eighteenth century.[2] For a time it was widely assumed that the pattern of change in other countries conformed

---

[1] Sundbärg, *Bevölkerungsstatistik Schwedens*.

[2] Marital fertility in Sweden showed no sign of falling below its eighteenth-century level until the last quarter of the nineteenth century. For example, the marital TMFR 20–49 was 8.26 in 1871–5, compared with 7.29 a century earlier in 1771–5, though mortality had already fallen substantially during the same hundred years. Hofsten and Lundström, *Swedish population history*, tab. 2.3, p. 30.

to the Swedish model. That this was not the case only became clear much later.[3] In the mid-1970s Henry and Blayo provided a sketch of French national population changes from 1740 onwards.[4] It showed that fertility and mortality both began to fall from much the same date in France. In contrast to most other countries, therefore, France never experienced a major surge in the population growth rate in the eighteenth and nineteenth centuries. Neither in Sweden nor in France, however, was it possible to provide estimates of national trends in fertility and mortality before the mid-eighteenth century. Much the same has proved to be true of Norway.[5] But for England from mid-Tudor times onwards, as a result both of the findings of generalised inverse projection and of those from reconstitution, there are now detailed estimates of a wide variety of demographic indicators, ranging from simple variables such as population size, to measures which are intrinsically complex, such as fecundability. Furthermore, English history proved to differ from both the Swedish and French examples, since the acceleration in the rate of population growth in the 'long eighteenth century' from *c.* 1680 to *c.* 1820 was the joint product of rising fertility and declining mortality, a pattern reminiscent of many Third World countries in the recent past, though due to very different demographic circumstances, and occurring over a very different time scale.[6]

Second, no other branch of British social or economic history is blessed by such a fully quantified picture of change over time. Thirty-five years ago, demographic data were subject to as great a degree of uncertainty as estimates of wheat yields per acre or of the scale of iron production. Deane and Cole had then just completed their admirable attempt to frame a coherent account of British economic growth from 1688 onwards.[7] They made a sustained effort to ensure that the inferences they drew about population size and trends were well supported and mutually consistent but found that 'Although there are enough data available to provide reasonable estimates of the broad trends involved, the specific turning points cannot be located and causes of the initial changes are still a matter of controversy.'[8] They noted that work was still heavily dependent on the parish register

[3] Wrigley and Schofield, *Population history of England*, pp. 246–8.
[4] In four connected articles in a special issue of *Population*, 30 (1975), devoted to historical demography: Blayo, 'Mouvement naturel', 'La proportion des naissances illégitimes', and 'La mortalité en France', and Henry and Blayo, 'La population de la France'.
[5] Drake, *Population and society*.
[6] Dyson and Murphy, 'The onset of fertility transition'.
[7] Deane and Cole, *British economic growth*.   [8] Ibid., p. 5.

abstracts which had been returned at Rickman's behest. The views of Habakkuk and Krause were then newly available,[9] and, influenced especially by Krause, they concluded a chapter devoted to population change by accepting the view that the role of mortality decline had probably been exaggerated and that, at least in the areas most affected by industrial growth, fertility had risen substantially.[10]

It is an interesting commentary on Deane and Cole's work that new 'stories' have been constructed about the path of British growth in the industrial revolution period and later which differ considerably from theirs, notably by Crafts. Such revisions, however, have diverged from Deane and Cole not, in the main, because new and better data have been assembled, but because the data used by them to construct indices of growth have been made to sustain different interpretations, principally by reweighting the component elements of national output.[11] The reweighting of elements such as cotton output can have a substantial impact on measures of aggregate growth because cotton output grew so rapidly.[12] In contrast with most other series concerning the main economic and social variables, however, information about population in early modern England is markedly fuller and richer now than 30 or 40 years ago.[13]

It is fortunate that progress has taken place in enriching and refining knowledge of English population in the early modern period, since it is true both that the course of English population history in the early modern period was most unusual, and that it is centrally important to achieving a better understanding of the economic and social history of the period. It was unusual in that English population growth was much more rapid than elsewhere. Germany, Italy, Spain, and France were the four main western European national groups in this era. Their rate of growth provides a convenient measure of English progress.[14] Between 1550 and 1820 the populations of Germany, Italy, Spain, and France rose by broadly similar percentages; 51, 67, 56, and 79 per cent respectively. In the same period the population of England rose by more than 280 per

[9] Habakkuk, 'English population in the eighteenth century'; Krause, 'Changes in English fertility and mortality', and 'The changing adequacy of English registration'.

[10] Deane and Cole, *British economic growth*, pp. 133–5.

[11] Crafts, 'British economic growth', and *British economic growth*, pp. 22–34.

[12] This issue, and others related to it, are discussed in Wrigley, *Continuity, chance and change*, pp. 105–12.

[13] A notable exception to the general lack of new research on major economic series is Feinstein's work on capital formation. Feinstein, 'Capital formation in Great Britain', and 'National statistics, 1750–1920'.

[14] The scale of the progress as reflected in increasing effectiveness in international power struggles is well captured in the collection of essays in Stone, ed., *An imperial state at war*.

cent.[15] The available data are of variable quality, and the apparent precision of the percentages is spurious, but the broad similarity of growth in the four large countries, and the striking contrast between them and England, are not in doubt.

In 1550 the average population of the four large countries was 12.25 million (ranging from 9 million in Spain to 17 million in France), and the English population (3 million) was only 24 per cent of this figure. In 1820 the average population of the four had risen to 20.25 million, but growth in England had been so rapid that the country by then supported a population of 11.5 million, 57 per cent as large as the big four average.

Furthermore, while attempts to measure output per head or real incomes per head are fraught with many problems in the early modern period, there can be no doubt that they were higher in England than elsewhere in 1820, and little doubt that this was not the case 270 years earlier.[16] Plainly, the implications of such simple statistics for the relative rates of growth of gross national product in England and in Germany, Italy, Spain, and France are striking and intriguing. If, for example, one were to assume that output per head rose, say, by one third in these four countries between 1550 and 1820, but in England by three-quarters, this implies that the average increase in GNP in the four was c. 120 per cent over the period $((100 \times (20.25/12.25) \times 1.33) - 100)$, whereas in England the comparable change was 570 per cent $((100 \times (11.5/3) \times 1.75 - 100)$. Much of this disproportionate growth occurred well before the conventional date for the beginning of the industrial revolution.

The bare outlines of this extraordinary contrast have long been known. The early nineteenth-century population totals are census-based and therefore relatively precise. In the case of England, there has been no major change in estimated population sizes, even for distant periods. The most recent estimates of population size in the mid-sixteenth century produced by generalised inverse projection are little different from those of Russell or Cornwall, made several decades ago.[17] Indeed, they are broadly comparable with Rickman's calculations, derived from the parish register abstracts, and published in the 1841 census. But until recently the demographic changes underlying the

---

[15] Wrigley, 'The growth of population', p. 122.

[16] Maddison, 'A comparison of levels of GDP per capita'; Bairoch, 'Niveaux de développement économique'; de Vries, 'Population and economy of the preindustrial Netherlands'.

[17] Russell, *British medieval population*, pp. 22, 270–2; Cornwall, 'English population in the early sixteenth century'; Wrigley and Schofield, *Population history of England*, pp. 565–9.

surging population growth in early modern England were obscure and provoked much discussion. The *Population history of England* showed, if a drastic simplification is permissible, that for most of the parish register period, fertility change was more important than mortality change in altering growth rates, and that fertility change in turn chiefly reflected fluctuations in nuptiality. By drawing attention to the apparently close relationship between secular change in nuptiality and secular change in real incomes per head, and the absence of such a link between real incomes per head and mortality changes, the book gave a new currency to a debate about the interlinkage beween demographic and economic variables which had taken its origin in the description of two limiting possibilities by Malthus.

Had he but known it, Malthus might well have dubbed a preventive-check society, in which marriage acted as the demographic regulator, as 'English' to balance his designation of a positive-check society, where the regulator was mortality, as 'Chinese'.[18] The English case shows in an especially clear-cut fashion that a country with a 'low-pressure' demographic/economic system is just as readily capable of rapid population growth as a country with a 'high-pressure' system.[19] Indeed, it suggests the instructive possibility that population growth may occur more readily in the former than in the latter, if low pressure connotes a relatively high level of real incomes per head and a structure of aggregate demand favourable to the growth of industry. England was probably closer to the 'low-pressure' end of the spectrum of possible systems than any other country in western Europe yet experienced much faster population growth.[20]

The present volume largely confirms the sketch of English demographic history given in the *Population history of England* and therefore consolidates the evidence pointing to the central importance of the institution of marriage as the principal determinant of secular demographic change in England. The reconstitution evidence concerning age at marriage is clear and consistent. Age at marriage fell substantially from the end of the first quarter of the eighteenth century. By the early

---

[18] Malthus, *Essay on population* (1798), p. 49.

[19] 'Low-pressure' refers to a situation in which a balance between fertility and mortality is maintained when both are at a low level; 'high-pressure' to a situation in which a balance is maintained when both are at a high level. The range of possibilities is discussed in Wrigley and Schofield, *Population history of England*, pp. 457–66, while on p. 473 England is identified as having 'low-pressure' characteristics.

[20] For a discussion of value systems regulating interpersonal relationships in England in the past, contrasted with other possible scenarios, see Schofield, 'Family structure'; and for comparative data on the susceptibility of European populations to poor harvests and high prices, see Galloway, 'Basic patterns'.

nineteenth century women were marrying about two-and-a-half years younger than their great-grandmothers, a large enough fall in marriage age to have produced a marked rise in fertility, other things being equal. Moreover, the trend to earlier marriage was remarkably uniform among the 26 parishes, though they differed greatly in size, location, occupational structure, and in other respects.[21] With nuptiality, as with mortality and fertility, the picture in outline remains unchanged, though the richness of detail afforded by reconstitution floods the canvas with additional colour.

Any valedictory remarks about the work of the Cambridge Group over the past quarter-century on the population history of early modern England, however, should not simply rehearse what is known and what has been achieved, but should also stress what is still obscure and what remains to be done. Much may have been accomplished but much more remains to be tackled. This is especially true of wider issues of interpretation. The sheer richness of detailed information which reconstitution yields has led to this book focusing more on the trees than on the wood. In addition, there were the complexities of establishing what could safely be inferred from the information available for analysis; of testing the accuracy of the data employed; of devising methods of dealing with sources that were sometimes refractory; and of testing the plausibility of the results. All these have tended to stand in the way of a synoptic vision. This is true not only of the wider issues of the relationship between the economy and society of early modern England and its demography, but also of demographic interrelationships. There have been separate chapters on nuptiality, mortality, and fertility, but only limited attempts to explore the interplay between them. This is regrettable in that some of the most interesting issues are to be found here, though their neglect ensures a full agenda for future research. A few examples of such issues are touched on below.

Equally regrettable is the abandonment of what had originally been envisaged as the prime reason for a reconstitution volume. The nature of reconstitution, in which information is built up from individual FRFs, is intrinsically well adapted to investigating the ways in which the economic and social circumstances of individual families influenced their demographic behaviour, and vice versa. And what can be done for individual families can also, of course, be done for larger local groupings by amalgamating information from FRFs: for those who lived in a

---

[21] Tabs. 5.3 and 5.18, pp. 134 and 184–5.

particular district, if, for example, environmental factors are thought to have a dominant influence on mortality; for those who formed a particular occupational grouping; for those who died without male heirs; for those in receipt of poor relief; for those who were not natives of the parish; for the parish as a whole. In some cases, of course, paucity of other information about family members to be merged with that taken from the parish register may frustrate a particular investigation, but analyses of this type are often feasible, and are likely to prove illuminating. It was originally intended to create a series of such textured local studies in order to complement the national picture obtained from aggregative data with evidence of the extent and nature of local variation. But the wish to provide a fuller account of national trends and characteristics frustrated this intention, though it is to be hoped that the frustration will prove only temporary.

Even within the restricted range of topics treated in this book, much remains to be done. For example, although there is a brief description of the age structure of infant and child mortality when death rates were exceptionally high,[22] much more could be done to elucidate the question of whether, when death rates rose to unusual heights, the age structure of mortality changed significantly, and, if so, whether such changes were consistent or varied from one crisis to another. Earlier work suggested that there is reason to expect variety,[23] but the volume of available reconstitution data offers opportunities in this regard which did not previously exist. Or again, the major improvement in adult mortality in the first half of the eighteenth century, caused in part by a large reduction in maternal mortality, must have made a substantial difference to the mean duration of marriages, which has implications for fertility, for the frequency and timing of remarriage, and for issues such as the proportion of children who were orphaned in childhood. This is a topic which could be tackled both by modelling and by the assembly of empirical data, but which was foregone in order to concentrate upon the core demographic variables. Lists of this kind, especially those involving the interplay of several different variables, could be greatly extended.

Wider issues linking demographic with economic and social change have been almost entirely neglected, though they are ultimately of greater significance than the attempt to establish the facts of population

---

[22] See above pp. 267–8.

[23] For example, a study of Ludlow in the late sixteenth and early seventeenth centuries, with a rough division of deaths between infants, children, and adults, suggested that years of high mortality in one age category were seldom years of high mortality in all three categories: Schofield and Wrigley, 'Infant and child mortality', pp. 84–8.

history.[24] One example may suffice to illustrate the kind of issue which would repay further research. It seems clear that age at marriage and proportions marrying changed substantially in early modern England. The changes were large enough to alter the intrinsic growth rate considerably, *ceteris paribus*. Marriage decisions were strongly influenced by economic factors, thus ensuring a feedback between economic and demographic change of a kind which may serve to explain some important features of English society during the centuries immediately preceding the industrial revolution.

In contrast, it also seems clear that mortality changes were not closely linked to economic factors such as changes in real incomes per head.[25] But overall mortality changed substantially between the sixteenth century and the nineteenth century, first worsening from a relatively mild regime in late Elizabethan times to the rigours of the 1680s before improving markedly by the later eighteenth century. So much was known from earlier work. Reconstitution has shown that age-specific mortality rates did not all follow the pattern suggested by overall measures, such as expectation of life at birth. This must complicate any satisfactory explanation. Moreover, preliminary work on other data sets shows that privileged groups, such as the peerage, Members of Parliament, Scottish advocates, or members of tontines, appear to have experienced changes in adult mortality very similar to those in the general population between the mid-seventeenth and the mid-eighteenth century.[26]

Since differences in status and income were associated with very different levels of nutrition, types of diet, and general living standards, the absence of major differences in level or trend in adult mortality across much of the social scale may appear surprising and should prove instructive. Either other factors were offsetting the apparent advantages of wealth and status, or mortality in this period and among these age groups was largely determined by non-economic influences. The improvement in adult mortality was striking. Reconstitution data show that in the period between 1640–89 and 1750–1809 mortality rates between the ages of 25 and 60 fell by an average of 31 per cent.[27] If a

---

[24] The types of demographic data which can provide revealing clues to the changing conventions of society extend well beyond those which have been reported in this book. Analysis of the distribution of baptisms, burials, and marriages between the days of the week, for example, can yield fascinating insights into social practice and its changing sensitivity to social, economic, and other pressures; Schofield, 'Monday's child is fair of face'.   [25] Wrigley and Schofield, *Population history of England*, chs. 10 and 11.

[26] Razzell, 'The growth of population'; Houston, 'Mortality in early modern Scotland'.

[27] Tab. 6.20, p. 291.

change as large as this is properly attributable to factors which were not primarily economic or social, it underlines the potential importance of biological or epidemiological history and the limitations of the treatment of such topics using conventional historical categories. It may not prove easy to resolve the issue of the causes of the observed fall in adult mortality, but the opportunity exists to pursue the matter much further than has so far been attempted, especially through the assembly of comparative data from different environmental settings and different countries.

In this connection, the contrast between the mortality history of the first half of the eighteenth century and that of the second half of the nineteenth century is instructive. These were both periods in which mortality fell substantially. In the latter period, setting aside the special case of infant mortality, which maintained its earlier level, mortality fell earliest and proportionally most in the younger age groups. Broadly speaking, the higher the age group, the later the onset of the decline and the shallower its course.[28] In the first half of the eighteenth century, in contrast, childhood rates showed no tendency to fall even though adult rates declined sharply.[29] In the later period, one point at least is clear. Mortality rates fell and expectation of life improved because infectious diseases were killing fewer people, and the age groups in which exogenous causes of death were relatively the most important benefited the most. The proximate cause, therefore, is evident in this instance, though the social, economic, or epidemiological circumstances which underlay it are still the subject of debate.[30] In the case of the early eighteenth-century change, not even the proximate cause is clear, though some of the consequences are obvious.

Reconstitution has brought to light several previously unknown features of the mortality history of early modern England. A principal reason for this was that acceptable estimates of adult mortality were secured. Most earlier reconstitution studies concentrated exclusively or primarily on infant and child rates. Because both adult and child rates are now available for seventeenth- and eighteenth-century England, some puzzling and intriguing features of English mortality history have become visible, and a new research agenda has thereby been brought into being.

Reconstitution was originally developed with a prime focus on the

---

[28] The age pattern is very clear, for example, in McKeown and Record, 'Decline of mortality', fig. 2, p. 100. [29] See pp. 282–4 above.

[30] Szreter has been a prominent participant in this debate. See especially Szreter, 'The importance of social intervention', and his survey of the debate in 'Mortality and public health'.

characteristics of fertility, and questions related to fertility have received more attention than mortality questions in most previous reconstitution-based studies. The fertility data provided by reconstitution for early modern England yield no dramatic surprises, but add a considerable amount to preexisting knowledge. It was already known that fertility was not as high as in some other European populations in the period before there was any considerable degree of fertility limitation within marriage. It was well below the level found in French Canada or early nineteenth-century Bavaria, for example, but similar to the levels found in the south-west of France, or in German East Friesland.[31] The principal reasons for the comparatively modest level of marital fertility were probably the customary length of breastfeeding and the low level of infant mortality. The two variables were, of course, related. Both tended to increase the mean interval between births, the first by delaying the return of ovulation, the second because the death of an infant, by bringing breastfeeding to an end, increased the chance of an early conception.

Again, it came as no surprise that marital fertility showed remarkably little variation between the 26 parishes.[32] It is, however, new knowledge that fertility rose steadily, though only slowly, in the course of the eighteenth century. The mean birth interval was 33.27 months in 1640–69, but had fallen to 30.54 months by 1790–1819.[33] A fall of 8.2 per cent in the mean birth interval is not spectacular but, in conjunction with falling marriage age, was sufficient to cause a substantial rise in general measures of fertility, such as the gross reproduction rate, especially as the proportion of all births which were illegitimate rose markedly. In a stylised calculation, designed only to establish an order of magnitude, a rise in marital fertility of just over 8 per cent, allied to a fall in mean age at marriage of two years, from 26 to 24 years, reinforced by a rise in the proportion of all births that were illegitimate from *c*. 1.5 to *c*. 6.0 per cent would, *ceteris paribus*, cause the gross reproduction rate to rise by over 40 per cent.[34]

The fertility data provided by reconstitution allow analysis to go well

---

[31] For French Canada, Henripin, *La population canadienne*, tab. 14, p. 60, and Charbonneau et al., *Naissance d'une population*, tab. 55, p. 88; for Bavaria and East Friesland, Knodel, *Demographic behavior in the past*, tab. 10.1, p. 250; for south-west France, Henry, 'Fécondité des mariages dans le quart sud-ouest', tab. 1, pp. 978–9.

[32] Tab. 7.42, pp. 504–5.

[33] Tab. 7.36, p. 447. The means include all birth parities, except parity 0, but exclude cases where the earlier child of the pair died, in order to exclude the influence of changing levels of infant mortality on the birth interval.

[34] The calculation was based on the average age-specific marital fertility rates given in tab. 7.1, p. 355.

beyond the construction of a few standard measures, and some innovations were made in this regard, encouraged by the scale of the data available which made refined analysis much easier than where a single parish is the object of study. A feature of the analysis described in chapter 7 was the introduction of a method of measuring age-specific fecund marital fertility, entry fecundity, and subsequent fecundity.[35] By definition, the product of these three variables is an age-specific marital fertility rate, and any change in marital fertility can therefore be broken down into these three constituent elements. It can be shown that the fit between the age-specific marital fertility rates estimated from these variables and the empirically observed rates is very good.[36]

As a result it was possible to show that fecund marital fertility rose throughout the parish register period, though only modestly, by about 5 per cent. Other things being equal, this must, of course, raise marital fertility commensurately, but after 1750 marital fertility, especially above the age of 35, rose by a much greater margin, and this change was due primarily to a major increase in the level of subsequent fecundity in these age groups. The onset of sterility was delayed in this period compared with earlier centuries. The change occurred immediately after the striking improvement in adult mortality in the first half of the eighteenth century, but whether this was more than a coincidence is as yet unclear. Entry fecundity changed little, but because of the much more marked change in subsequent fecundity, and because overall fecundity is the product of entry and subsequent fecundity, overall fecundity in the higher age groups rose in parallel with the change in subsequent fecundity.[37] Entry fecundity in each five-year age group was almost indistinguishable in early modern England from the average of a variety of other populations prior to the adoption of fertility limitation within marriage.[38]

The extent of the rise in subsequent fecundity among older women was due to a marked change in the fecundity characteristics of women who married young, rather than to a general change among all women. The fecundity of women marrying in their teens or early 20s declined far less rapidly after 1750 than had been the case in earlier times. Above the age of 35 there was little to distinguish their subsequent fecundity from that of women who had married much older, in their 30s, where previously there had been a clear duration of marriage effect.[39] This, too, constitutes a conundrum whose elucidation will proved instructive.

Fecundability can also be studied from parish register data, and here,

[35] For a definition of these terms, which may be unfamiliar, see pp. 358–61.
[36] See above pp. 360–1.   [37] These changes are described on pp. 389–93 above.
[38] Fig. 7.2, p. 395.   [39] Tab. 7.12, pp. 386–7.

as in other aspects of the study of fertility, some innovation was feasible. By comparison with other populations, fecundability was at a relatively high level among English women at the time of their marriage during the early modern period.[40] The analysis of the interval from marriage to a first birth is the conventional way to estimate fecundability. Fecundability is therefore normally only known in the early months of marriage, and is widely assumed to have declined in the later years of marriage because of a decline in the frequency of coitus and perhaps also for other reasons linked to the birth of previous children. However, it is also possible to study fecundability directly throughout the course of marriage, and not just at its beginning, by using data relating to birth intervals following the death of a previous child in infancy. The outcome suggested that fecundability was at a broadly constant level throughout marriage, and did not decline because of a fall in the frequency of coitus, or for other reasons.[41] Moreover, an extension of the analysis suggested that fecundability was as high when a woman did not lose the previous child as after an early infant death.[42] In other words, the maintenance of a high level of fecundability later in marriage does not appear to be restricted to women who had recently lost a child, and who might therefore have wished to replace it quickly. It will be interesting to see if comparable analyses reveal a similar pattern in other pre-industrial populations.

'To travel hopefully is a better thing than to arrive, and the true success is to labour', Robert Louis Stevenson wrote. Slightly adapted, this might stand as a motto for all research. Success in research might as justly be measured by the range of new problems revealed as by the solution of the problems known to exist when the research was first undertaken. And research which is not in some sense its own reward soon becomes a burden rather than a delight. The enduring attraction of work in historical population studies lies in the fact that the process by which one generation is replaced by another, the process of reproduction broadly defined, is fundamental to all other human activities. Just as *production* is necessary to enable life to continue, so also is *reproduction*. That the understanding of economic success or failure is impossible unless account is taken of almost all aspects of the life of a community is widely appreciated. The same is true of demographic success or failure. It is intimately related to a host of social, economic, technological, political, and biological factors, and, because demographic behaviour is mensurable, the relative importance of the different influences can

[40] Tab. 7.39, pp. 468–9, and pp. 465–72.   [41] See pp. 477–89.   [42] See pp. 489–92.

sometimes be quantified. Furthermore, it is an advantage in such research that the structure of many demographic characteristics is tightly constrained by the biology of life. Death rates among 60-year olds cannot plausibly be lower than those among 30-year-olds in the same population, save in the most exceptional circumstances. Nor is it credible that birth intervals should be less than, say, 20 months on average. This feature of many demographic variables serves to enable scraps of reliable information to be used to great advantage, since it may be possible to infer the unknown from the known with comparatively small margins of possible error.

The combination of characteristics such as these with the riches provided by Anglican parish registers makes it feasible to reconstruct English population history from the mid-sixteenth century onwards in greater detail and with a smaller margin of error than any other aspect of the economic or social life of the country in the early modern period. The parish registers have often been criticised for their shortcomings. Certainly they should be used with discretion, but compared, say, with the difficulties of inferring grain yields from inventories, the comparative precision with which population characteristics can be defined from the information contained in Anglican parish registers is striking. For once, amid the baffling complexities of reconstructing the history of any aspect of human behaviour in the past, a topic of fundamental importance is matched by the opportunity to do it justice. This is a branch of history where it is not necessary to adopt a purely relativist stance, assuming that each generation writes its own history. We shall never arrive, in the sense of establishing a body of knowledge which cannot be refuted or further refined, but we may travel hopefully, because successive generations of scholars will benefit from and build upon their predecessors' work. Even the most striking advances in cumulative empirical knowledge will not, of course, necessarily resolve issues of interpretation. But such advances can 'réduire le champ de l'arbitraire' by identifying hypotheses that are incompatible with established knowledge.

Work on aggregative data and on reconstitution has been in progress at the Cambridge Group since its foundation. Given the scale of the labour involved, it might sometimes have seemed tempting to hope that at some point it would be possible to draw a line under the project and declare that it had achieved its purpose. But to adopt such a position would have been to connive at failure. The most successful research is that which remains incomplete. Just as reproduction is necessary for the survival of a population, so good research must breed new problems. Accordingly, it is neither desirable nor probable that all that is contained in this volume should be accepted, but it would be a disappointment if it did not help to maintain the momentum of research which it has been a pleasure to foster over the past two decades.

APPENDICES

1

A list of the reconstituted parishes from which data were drawn and of the names of those who carried out the reconstitutions

Even a small reconstitution carried out by hand takes many hundreds of hours of work. Where a large reconstitution is undertaken the work load may be measured in thousands of hours. The work is tedious but, for long periods, requires unremitting concentration. The extent of our debt to those who carried out the reconstitutions listed below is very great. Their generosity in undertaking to collaborate in the task was both touching and inspiring. All at some stage must have wondered whether they had been foolhardy in making such a commitment. Any favourable attention which this book may attract should redound as much to the credit of those whose labours produced the empirical foundation of the work as of those whose names appear on the title page.

Parish	County	Person carrying out the reconstitution
Alcester	Warwicks	Mrs P. Ford
Aldenham	Herts	Mr W. Newman-Brown
Ash	Kent	Mrs A. Newman
Austrey	Warwicks	Dr V. Brodsky
Banbury	Oxon	Mrs S. Stewart
Birstall	Yorks, WR	Mr H. Thwaite
Bottesford	Leics	Prof. D.C. Levine
Bridford	Devon	Dr R.R. Sellman
Colyton	Devon	Prof. E.A. Wrigley
Dawlish	Devon	Dr R.R. Sellman

Earsdon	Northumbs	Mrs J.B. Hodgkiss
Gainsborough	Lincs	Mrs L. Clarke
Gedling	Notts	Mrs J.D. Young
Great Oakley	Essex	Mrs R. Barker
Hartland	Devon	Mrs S. Stewart
Ipplepen	Devon	Dr R.R. Sellman
Lowestoft	Suffolk	Mr D. Butcher
March	Cambs	Miss G. Reynolds
Methley	Yorks, WR	Prof. M. Yasumoto
Morchard Bishop	Devon	Miss M.C. Phillips
Odiham	Hants	Dr B. Stapleton
Reigate	Surrey	Mr J. Greenwood
Shepshed	Leics	Prof. D.C. Levine
Southill	Beds	Mr J.D. Asteraki
Terling	Essex	Prof. D.C. Levine
Willingham	Cambs	Miss G. Reynolds

2

Examples of the slips and forms used in reconstitution and a description of the system of weights and flags employed

The method used for the reconstitution of families from parish register data by hand has been described in detail elsewhere.[1] It may be useful, nonetheless, to provide examples of the slips used in the process of reconstitution and of the larger FRF. The four types of slips are reproduced in figure A2.1 together with an FRF. The slips are designed so as to be able to transfer to each of them from a parish register the information contained in a single entry of baptism, marriage, or burial. Once transferred to slips the information relating to a single family can be articulated and transferred in turn to an FRF. Two slips are made out for each marriage, because the bride and groom will have different surnames before marriage and it is convenient to be able to manoeuvre the information relating to the marriage separately for the two individuals concerned.

Nothing needs to be said about most of the information which is to be found on an FRF, but, in order to illustrate the way in which distinctions can be made between information of differing degrees of precision, it may be of interest to describe briefly the nature of a system of date weights which was extensively employed in the course of each reconstitution. The weights were designed to indicate increasing imprecision, so that, for example, a weight of 104 (shown by adding *104 to a particular date) indicates less possible inaccuracy than a weight of *112. Imprecision can arise in several different ways. For example, although the exact date of an event may be unknown, it may be clear that it occurred between two dates that are known, as when a date in a register

---

[1] Wrigley, ed., *English historical demography*, ch. 4.

Baptism slip

| Baptised 18-10-1792 | christian name ROBERT | surname DRURIE |

born

(male) / female / unknown
bastard / twin
stillborn / abortion

Father
name Xpher
residence .... t.p.
occupation

Mother
name Sarah   maiden name
mother's father's name
residence .... t.p.
occupation

Remarks

E.S.1   viii 61

Parish

No. ....

Burial slip

| Buried 6-11-1816 | christian name CHRISTOPHER | surname DRURY |

died .... t.p.
residence HARTBORN
age 84   occupation
bachelor / spinster / widow(er) / bastard

son
daughter   of ....
residence .... t.p.
occupation
and .... maiden name

husband
wife   of ....
widow(er)   residence .... t.p.
occupation .... maiden name

Remarks

E.S. II   viii 64

Parish

No. ....

Marriage slips

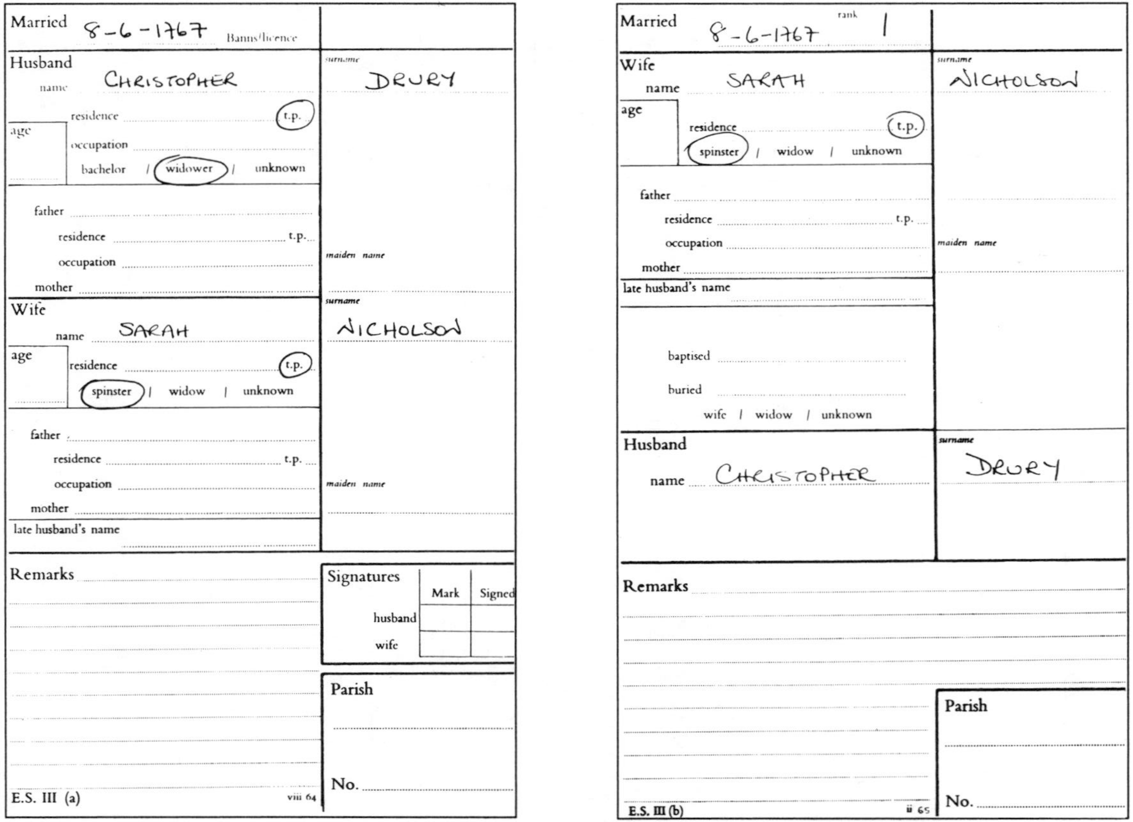

Figure A2.1   *Examples of extraction slips and a family reconstitution form*

Figure A2.1 (cont.)   A family reconstitution form (FRF)

MARRIAGE

	no.	place	date	date of end	date of next
M	/ 345	EARSDON	18-6-1767 /		

LITERACY

	husband	wife
L /		/

HUSBAND

	surname	name(s)	date of baptism(birth)	date of burial (death)	order of marr.	earlier FRF no.	later FRF no.	residence at baptism
H /	DRURY	/Christopher	/-(6-5-1732* 19)	/ 6-11-1816	/ ≥ 2	/10166	/	/

residence (occupation) at marriage	residence (occupation) at burial	date	residence (occupation)	date	residence (occupation)
tp	H	1775 / H (pitman)		1800 / H (poor)	

Husband's father					Husband's mother		
surname	name(s)	residence (occupation)	FRF no.		surname	name(s)	
HF /	/	/	/	HM /	/	

WIFE

	surname	name(s)	date of baptism(birth)	date of burial (death)	order of marr.	earlier FRF no.	later FRF no.	residence at baptism
W /	NICHOLSON	/ Sarah	/	/	/ 1	/	/	/

residence (occupation) at marriage	residence (occupation) at burial	date	residence (occupation)	date	residence (occupation)
tp					

Wife's father					Wife's mother		
surname	name(s)	residence (occupation)	FRF no.		surname	name(s)	
WF /	/	/	/	WM /	/	

CHILDREN

		sex	date of baptism(birth)	date of burial (death)	status	name(s)	date of marriage	FRF no. of first marr.	surname of spouse	age at bur.	age at marr.	birth inter-val	age of mother
1	C	/ F/	20-3-1768	/	/	/ Mary	/14-8-1790 /	54					
2	C	/M/	22-7-1770	/ 2-9-1777	/	/ John	/						
3	C	/M/	22-7-1770	/ 22-7-1770	/	/ James	/						
4	C	/M/	18-10-1772	/ 29-12-1831	/	/ Robert	/ 23-2-1802 /	346					
5	C	/ F/	1-10-1775	/	/	/ Margaret	/						
6	C	/M/	9-11-1777	/ 6-10-1778	/	/ Aaron	/						
7	C	/ M/	13-2-1780	/	/	/ John	/						
8	C	/M/	19-5-1782	/ 3-5-1783	/	/ James	/						
9	C	/ F/	18-9-1785	/	/	/ Ann	/23-8-1809 /	994					
10	C	/	/	/	/	/							
11	C	/	/	/	/	/							
12	C	/	/	/	/	/							
13	C	/	/	/	/	/							
14	C	/	/	/	/	/							
15	C	/	/	/	/	/							
16	C	/	/	/	/	/							

COMMENTS		Husband	Wife	Age group	Years marr.	No. of births
F/C2/2/C3/Z2				15 - 19		
	Age at marriage			15 - 19		
	Age at end of marriage			20 - 24		
	Age at burial			25 - 29		
	Length of widowhood(mths)			30 - 34		
	Length of marriage (years)			35 - 39		
		total	sons	daughters	40 - 44	
FRF iv 6	Number of births				45 - 49	

566

is illegible, or torn away, or defaced but the event is recorded between two others whose dates are known. If the two enclosing dates are only a week apart, the maximum imprecision will be less than if the two enclosing dates are two months apart, and the weights allocated in these two circumstances will reflect this fact. Similarly, the date of a birth may be known approximately, even though the individual in question was not born in the parish, because an age was recorded when he or she died. If the age is given in days or weeks the uncertainty surrounding the date of birth is very much less than if the age is given as, say, 55 years. Here, too, differing weights would be used as appropriate. In the specimen FRF Christopher Drury is given a date of birth calculated from the fact that he was recorded as 84 years old when he died on 6 November 1816. The weight *119 attached to his birth date indicates that he was over 40 years old at death (the date of birth allocated to him allows for the fact that, on average, a person giving his or her age accurately will have lived a half year longer than the stated age, and is therefore 6 May 1732 rather than 6 November 1732). Or again, there are weights to indicate that a date is known to have occurred before (*126), or after (*127) a known date.

The existence of a system of weights makes it possible to specify which items of information should be included or excluded from a particular tabulation. Thus, it is more important to know age with precision when studying patterns of mortality within the first year of life than when studying age at marriage, where it may be tolerable to know age with, say, a band of uncertainty of two months centring on the apparent age, even though this would not be acceptable for the former purpose. Rather than burdening each table in the book with notes about the degree of precision required for each tabulation, and for the sake of brevity, information under this head has been concentrated in a single location. Appendix 10 is devoted exclusively to such information.

In addition to a system of weights, a system of flags was also employed. Flags serve a different purpose. They add to the information available, rather than qualifying its accuracy. Flag information is recorded in the area of the FRF reserved for comments. In the FRF above, the flags indicate that the second and third children on the FRF were twins and that the third child was stillborn (C3/Z2, where 'Z' indicates stillborn, and '2' a twin). Or again, if a woman died and at her death she was recorded as 'Anne, wife of William', it is apparent that John survived his wife and that her date of death was also the date at which the marriage ended, even though the date of William's death is unknown. The fact that he was still alive when his wife died is also useful information in connection with the study of adult mortality. In the circumstances described, the fact that William survived would be indicated by adding a W-flag (widower) to the information relating to him. This would appear as F/H/W in the comments section. Other flags indicate that a child was posthumous, or that a man at his death was a pauper, and so on.

It would be wearisome to describe either the system of weighting or the system of flags in detail. However, a set of instructions describing their use was devised at the Cambridge Group for the benefit of those carrying out reconstitutions, and a copy of these instructions can be obtained on request from the Cambridge Group.

𝕭

Truncation bias and similar problems

Conventional demographic measurements are either period or cohort in type. The latter is perhaps the simpler in conception. Cohort measures relate to the experience of a group of individuals over a whole or a part of their lifetimes. Thus, a *cohort* measure of expectation of life at birth is obtained by accumulating data relating to a group of individuals all of whom were born in the same year, quinquennium, or other time period. For example, 100 000 children might be born in a given country in the year 1700. All will have died by the year 1800 or shortly thereafter. The period of time from which data are taken for a cohort calculation of this sort, therefore, will span a century. If the age at death of each individual is known, mean expectation of life at birth can readily be calculated.[1]

Alternatively, a *period* measure of expectation of life for the year 1700 may be obtained by securing data from the many cohorts which were all in existence in that year and using them to construct an 'artificial' cohort. This exercise will show what expectation of life would have been if the mortality levels prevailing in each age group in 1700 had continued to hold true long enough for a cohort born in that year to have been completely exhausted by mortality. Some of the cohorts involved in the construction of the period rate will, of course, have been born 80 years or more before the children whose success or failure in surviving their first year of life will provide the data needed to calculate an infant mortality rate for the year 1700 itself. The nature of the difference between the two methods of marshalling demographic data is illustrated in figure A3.1 in the form of a Lexis diagram.

It will be obvious that, if figure A3.1 had been extended further to the

---

[1] A cohort can, of course, be identified by other characteristics than a common year of birth. Marriage cohorts, for example, may share a common year, or other time period, of marriage.

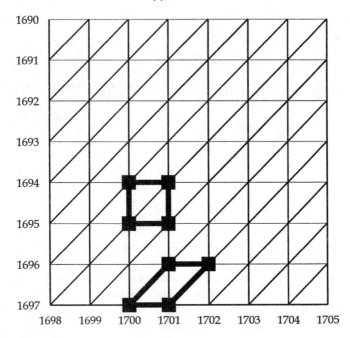

Figure A3.1 *Cohort and period rates illustrated by a Lexis diagram*

left, each of the birth cohorts, whose year of birth is identified by the labelling on the left-hand vertical axis, would have taken their origin on the horizontal axis of the figure, just as the years from 1698 to 1704 may be seen to do. The Lexis diagram makes it easy to appreciate that, before reaching their first birthdays, all the children born in 1700 will have spent part of their first year of life in 1701. Indeed, one half of the period between the births and first birthdays of the cohort in question will have been spent in 1701 rather than 1700, as is clear from the two triangles comprising the parallelogram in the figure. These two triangles represent the first year in the life history of the cohort born in 1700. By adding comparable pairs of triangles, representing each subsequent year in their life history, the experience of the cohort can be established completely.

The nature of period measures is also visible in figure A3.1. Whereas in a cohort measure, data drawn from two calendar years are required in order to describe the experience of one year of life of a cohort born in a given calendar year, in a period measure data drawn from two annual cohorts are needed in order to calculate the period rate for a single year of age. Thus, both those born in 1697 and those born in 1698 will

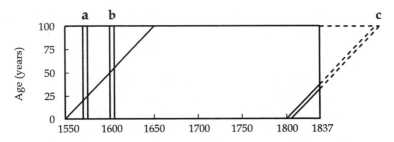

Figure A3.2   *Illustrations of truncation bias*

contribute to the calculation of a mortality rate for 2-year olds in 1700. Again, the relevant triangles have been indicated in the figure.

Reflection upon the characteristics of cohort and period measures will show that their nature must be taken into account if unbiased estimates of demographic behaviour are to be obtained from reconstitution data.

Consider figure A3.2, covering more than three centuries. It shows parish registration beginning in 1550 and ending in 1837. It will be obvious that all those who were present in the parish in 1550 and who married or died at a later date will be of unknown age. If, for example, the register records a marriage between William Greensmith and Elizabeth Hodge in that year, there can be no possibility of determining the age of either the bride or the groom by subtracting the date of his or her baptism from the date of their marriage, since both were born before the inception of parochial registration. By 1575 the age of anyone who was born in the parish and married below the age of 25 can be known by making use of the relevant baptism and marriage entries, but the ages of brides or grooms who were older than 25 in that year cannot be determined since their births will have occurred before the register was begun. The triangle in the north-west corner of the figure, though within the period of parochial registration, represents an area in which the individual ages of men and women whose marriages and deaths are recorded must remain unknown. Not until a full century has elapsed after the beginning of registration is it possible to establish the age of all those who were baptised in the parish, whatever their current age. Only then would a man or woman aged 100 have moved into an area of the diagram which ensures that his or her baptism is available.

The potential for obtaining an inaccurate estimate of the level and trend of marriage age in these circumstances is illustrated by columns **a** and **b** in figure A3.2. Column a represents a period estimate of female mean age at first marriage for the years 1575–9, column **b** for the years 1600–4. Assuming that the true mean age at first marriage was unchanging in the two periods, it is inevitable that the true level will be underestimated for the earlier period because the age of women who were over 25 on marriage cannot be established in the year 1575, nor those aged 30 and over at the end of the period represented by column **a**. If, for the sake of simplicity, we assume that no first marriage takes place above the age of 50, on the other hand, the column **b** estimate of mean age at first marriage will not be affected by truncation bias. There will therefore appear to be a rising trend in marriage age where none in reality existed. All period measures are subject to truncation bias in the early years of registration, though the period which must elapse before this danger is over will vary according to the nature of the phenomenon under study. Failure to take the possibility of bias into account will leave uncertain the status of any results which are reported.

Cohort measures are free from truncation bias at the beginning of registration provided that the earliest cohort used was born after the beginning of registration, but the boot is on the other foot as the end of registration is approached. Thus the cohort represented by the diagonal labelled **c**, which was born in 1800–4, will live out much of its life history in the dashed triangle in the north-east corner of the figure. Only those cohorts born up to the beginning of the year 1738 will have exhausted their entire life histories before the end of the period when parish registers were the prime source of information in 1837, whereas period measures in principle remain unaffected by truncation problems until registration ends. Which should be the latest cohort from which data are drawn will again depend upon the nature of the phenomenon under study.

The approach of the end of registration may, however, bring with it subtler problems than those mentioned so far, and these may affect period measures as well as cohort measures. For example, a date of end of observation must be established for each FRF for each type of demographic calculation. It was one of Henry's most important achievements to suggest how to do this without introducing bias into subsequent tabulations.[2] Often the date of end of observation is set by the end of the marriage itself with the death of the first spouse to die. As the end of registration approaches a marriage in which one of the partners dies young will be more likely to have a date of end of observation than one in which the couple survive together into old age, other things being equal. If, therefore, there is reason to think that these are families in which children as well as adults are more likely to die than in the rest of the population, there is evidently a danger that high

[2] See p. 13.

mortality families will be overrepresented. Or again, from 1813 onwards, under the provisions of Rose's Act, age at death was routinely recorded in Anglican registers, and the year of birth of any individual who is buried in the parish can therefore be established by subtraction, even if he or she was not baptised in the parish, though dates of birth calculated in this fashion attract a high weighting to indicate the uncertainty attaching to them.[3] This circumstance also produces a problem. Consider, for example, two cohorts of women, one born in the period 1790–4, the other in the period 1800–4, and a period calculation of age at marriage for the period 1830–4. If age at marriage is calculated solely by subtracting a date of baptism from a date of marriage, no bias arises, but if age of marriage is known because of an age given at a subsequent death, then during the balance of the period of parochial registration, 1835–7, there will be a greater chance of women from earlier cohorts dying before the end of registration because death rates rise with age, and this in turn may distort the calculation of a mean age at marriage, if ages derived in both ways are used.

In carrying out the tabulations which gave rise to the tables included in this volume, care was taken not only to obey what might be termed the 'mechanical' rules for avoiding bias which are suggested by the points which can be illustrated from figure A3.2, but also to try to avoid the kind of distortion which may arise indirectly because of the selection effects that may cause certain kinds of FRFs to contribute disproportionately to data drawn from the opening or closing years of parochial registration. Details of the action taken for each table may be found in appendix 10.

[3] The weight *111 was attached to the birth of anyone whose birth year was known from an age at death of less than 40, while the weight *119 was attached to the birth date of someone dying above the age of 40, since the degree of uncertainty regarding the accuracy of age statements increased with increasing age at death. The system of weights and their uses are discussed in app. 2.

4

Tests for logical errors in reconstitution data

Physiology and social conventions may both set limits to the range of demographic phenomena, and therefore permit tests to be made on FRFs after their input into a machine-readable form. The tests are made in order to detect errors that may have been made either in the original process of reconstitution or subsequently, in the course of data input. As a result the quality and consistency of the data used in demographic tabulations is enhanced. The following tests were carried out on all the FRFs from the 26 parishes that form the empirical basis of this book.

On all individuals

1 That the date of birth was less than or equal to the date of baptism. Note that if the date of birth was not known directly from the register it was set equal to the date of baptism but given a weight, so that knowledge of the provenance of the information could be used as appropriate in subsequent tabulations.
2 That, similarly, the date of death was less than or equal to the date of burial. Here, too, if the date of death was not recorded in the register, it was set equal to the date of burial with the addition of a weight.
3 That the date of birth was less than or equal to the date of death.
4 That the date of death was less than the date of birth plus 105 years.

On all husbands

1 That the date of marriage was greater than or equal to the date of birth plus 15 years.

2 That the date of marriage was less than the date of birth plus 60 years if the marriage was known to be the first marriage of the husband; otherwise that the date of marriage was less than the date of birth plus 105 years.
3 That the date of marriage was less than or equal to the date of death.
4 That if the rank of marriage was not known from the register (that is, if the groom was not stated to be either a bachelor or a widower), the rank was set as greater than or equal to one.

On all wives

The same tests as for husbands, *mutatis mutandis*.

On all children

1 That there is a date of birth.
2 That the date of birth is greater than or equal to the date of the marriage of the child's parents.
3 That the date of birth is less than the date of marriage plus 35 years.
4 That the date of birth is greater than or equal to the wife's date of birth plus 15 years, and less than or equal to the wife's date of birth plus 50 years.
5 That the date of birth is less than or equal to the wife's date of death.
6 That the date of birth is less than or equal to the husband's date of death, except that if the child is flagged as posthumous, the date of the child's birth must be less than the husband's date of death plus 300 days.[1]
7 If the child line contains a date of marriage, the marriage date must be greater than or equal to the date of birth plus 15 years and less than or equal to the date of birth plus 60 years.
8 If the child line contains both a date of marriage and a date of death, the latter must be greater than or equal to the former.

Intergenesic interval (the interval between two successive birth events in the same family)

1 If the intergenesic interval is between two successive baptisms it must be either less than 30 days or more than 184 days, or, if between

---

[1] See app. 2 for a description of the nature and functions of flags.

successive births, it must be greater than 270 days (if, however, the second event is a stillbirth the interval must be greater than 180 days).

2 That the intergenesic interval is less than 12 years.

The date of the end of the marriage

This date was set by program according to the following rules.

1 If the dates of death of both spouses to the marriage were known, then the earlier of these two dates.

2 If the date of death of only one spouse is known, it is taken as the date of the end of the marriage if it is known that the other spouse remarries or is flagged as having been widowed. This might happen, for example, if the surviving spouse is described as a widow or a widower at the death of a child of the marriage.

3 If a child to the marriage is flagged as posthumous, but the death of the husband is not recorded, the date of the end of the marriage is set at the child's date of birth less 122 days and a weight is added to the date. This action reflects the assumption that the death of the husband occurred half way through the pregnancy of the wife, which is here taken as about 8 months in length.[2]

Most of these rules call for no further comment; for example, it is unnecessary to insist that birth must precede death. The additional assumptions underlying particular tests include the following:

1 The maximum span of life was 105 years.

2 No-one contracted a marriage when under 15 years of age, nor a first marriage when older than 60, but there is no upper age limit for the contraction of a second or subsequent marriage other than the overall limit to the span of life.

3 Women were not fertile when under 15 or over 50.

4 Intergenesic intervals. A distinction was made between cases where the 'true' interval can be measured because the register provides dates of birth, and those where the register only provides dates of baptism. In the former case the normal length of pregnancy, 270 days, was taken as the minimum interval. In the latter case a more complex rule was needed. Accepting a very short interval (less than 30 days) is to treat the two baptisms in question as a case of twins. The reason for allowing this interpretation is that in some instances a dying twin was baptised early while the survivor was only taken to the font at a later date, but the fact that the two were twins may or may not be made

---

[2] See app. 2 for a discussion of the logic used in constructing the system of weights.

explicit. The variability of the interval between birth and baptism is the reason for accepting an interval as brief as 184 days. No two successive birth events occurring to the same woman can be separated by so short an interval, but if the earlier of the two was baptised late and his or her younger sibling was baptised early, relatively short intervals may occur. The rough and ready rule of at least 184 days is at best informed guesswork. Since the average interval between birth and baptism varied considerably both over time and from parish to parish, it may be broadly appropriate in one period or place but too liberal or too restrictive in another. The number of cases of intervals between 185 and 269 days was, however, very modest.[3] Finally, it was assumed that the maximum interval between two successive births to the same couple was 12 years.

All these assumptions involve an element of judgement. Occasionally, perhaps, an individual did live to an age greater than 105 years, but it seems probable that most apparent instances represent an error in transcription or linkage. Similarly, a very small number of children will have been born to women under 15 or over 50, but the accuracy of the reconstitution as a whole is probably enhanced by treating such cases as spurious.

The limits to age at first marriage reflect assumptions about social practice rather than biological characteristics. The pattern of the distribution of observed ages at first marriage, however, is such as to encourage the belief that apparent ages at first marriage under 15 or over 60 were highly likely to be the result of inaccurate linkage.

One further point should be noted in reference to the tests described above. For simplicity each rule is set out as if it were universally applicable. In very many cases, however, it will be inapplicable for lack of information. To discover whether a wife was over 50 at the birth of a child, for example, depends on knowing her date of baptism, but frequently she will have been born and baptised elsewhere.

---

[3] It was consistently about 0.3 per cent of the total of baptisms throughout the parish register period.

5

Correcting for a 'missing' parish in making tabulations of marriage age

This appendix describes the method used to maximise the period of time over which age at marriage was calculated in chapter 5. The problem arises because the parishes making up a particular group may not all begin to produce reliable data from the same date. To wait until all were yielding reliable data would mean a late starting date, but to make no correction for 'missing' parishes in the early decades of a tabulation would carry the risk that apparent changes were due simply to the entry of a new parish into the group at a particular point in time. It is necessary to produce a series in which a 'missing' parish contributes in a rational, if arbitrary, fashion to the mean for the group as a whole even before it has come 'on stream'.

Consider the case of Birstall and group 2 using the data contained in table 5.2.[1] The table suggests that a correction for Birstall is only necessary for 1630–9 and earlier decades, since the parish made a contribution to the group total in 1640–9 at much the same level as in the next decade. Appearances are deceptive, however. Reconstitution began in Birstall in 1595, so that, if truncation bias is to be avoided, marriage age information can only be used from 1645 onwards, and the proportional contribution of Birstall in the 1640s shown in table 5.2,

---

[1] It is worth noting that a problem that affects the measurement of fertility in the case of Birstall does not complicate the measurement of age at first marriage. The reconstitution of Birstall originally lacked FRFs in the case of childless families. This obviously makes for problems in the measurement of marital fertility and could do the same for age at marriage, since women who remained childless were older on average at marriage than those whose marriages proved fertile. However, it was possible to recover age at marriage data for all such marriages as would have been included in a conventional reconstitution and no allowance need therefore be made for childless marriages in age at marriage calculations.

therefore, is based on a total of marriages for 1645–9 rather than for the whole decade. Clearly, a replacement value for the whole period before 1645 needs to be calculated for Birstall.

The first issue is the calculation of the parish's proportional contribution during a representative base period. It is important both that this should be long enough to include a significant number of marriage ages so that the difference between the parish and the rest of the group can be estimated with confidence, but also that it should be short enough to avoid the danger of blurring the effects of unusually fast or slow growth.[2] Birstall, for example, was a rapidly growing parish. If its proportional share were calculated over the whole period from 1650 to 1729 this would exaggerate its importance in the early decades of the seventeenth century when it was a much less dominant element in the set of parishes in group 2 than was later to be the case. Our arbitrary solution was to relate the calculation to the first two decades after the parish was fully in observation: in the case of Birstall this meant taking the period 1645–64.

In this period there were 72.5 bachelor/spinster marriages for which the age of the bride was known with an average age of 24.56 years.[3] The average age of the 797.5 brides in the other parishes in group 2 in 1645–64 was 25.68 years, a difference of 1.12 years. Birstall brides tended to marry a little earlier in life than those in the rest of group 2. The marriages on which the calculation of marriage age in Birstall was based formed 8.3 per cent of the total of 870 marriages taking place in group 2 in 1645–64. To derive an estimated revised marriage age figure for group 2 for 1640–4, therefore, it was assumed that if Birstall had been fully represented during that quinquennium there would have been not 235.5 marriages (the total recorded in the other 19 parishes) but $235.5 \times (100/(100 - 8.3)) = 256.9$ marriages. If the 21.4 additional 'Birstall' marriages are then given an appropriate marriage age, a revised figure for the group can be calculated. The average age at marriage in the other 19 parishes in this period was 25.96: since the expected age in Birstall was 1.12 years lower than in the other parishes in the period when the parish was first fully in observation, the expected overall figure is $((256.9 \times 25.96) - (21.4 \times 1.12))/256.9 = 25.86$ years.

The procedure just described becomes more complicated when more

[2] This procedure has many points in common with that adopted to solve a comparable difficulty when dealing with monthly totals of events drawn from parish registers in an earlier exercise: Wrigley and Schofield, *Population history of England*, pp. 60–2.

[3] The apparently odd total of 72.5 marriages occurs because Birstall and Shepshed were both given half-weight in the reconstitution tabulations to obtain a better balanced parish sample. See pp. 43–8.

than one parish is lost to a group. It will be clear from table 5.2, for example, that in the 1630s as in the 1640s correction needs to be made only for Birstall, but that in the 1620s, when Bottesford was also missing, the calculation must make allowance for both the missing parishes. The same basic algorithm, however, can be used as easily for two parishes as for one. In the 1610s the situation is further complicated by the need to include Banbury, Gainsborough, and Gedling among the 'missing' parishes. Reconstitution began in Banbury in 1564, and in Gainsborough and Gedling in 1565. Allowing for the necessary 50-year 'run-in' period to avoid the danger of underestimating average age at marriage, data could be used in Banbury only after 1614 and in the other 2 parishes only after 1615. The 3 parishes were treated in the 1610s as Birstall and Bottesford had been previously. Before the 1610–9 decade, however, the number of 'missing' parishes becomes so large that it would be artificial to repeat the procedure.

6

The estimation of adult mortality

The use of reconstitution data for the estimation of adult mortality has always posed greater problems than its use for the estimation of infant and child mortality. The first problem in this connection does not appear capable of resolution. The parish registers do not yield any information which can be used to establish the presence of unmarried adults in the parish. The deaths of bachelors and spinsters may be registered as punctiliously as those of husbands and wives, but, if there is no way of establishing their presence in the parish except at the time of their death, no dependable mortality rate can be calculated. Flow can be measured but stock cannot. Any adult mortality rate, therefore, refers only to the married population. Since most men and women did marry, a rate which refers to the married population is likely to be broadly representative of the population as a whole, but, in considering the adult mortality rates produced from reconstitution data, this limitation should always be borne in mind.

The measurement of the mortality of married adults, however, also involves difficulties. Anglican registers very rarely provide information about age at marriage before Hardwicke's Act, and even after that act came into force the ages of the bride and groom were seldom given. If any information was given it might often take the form of stating that the bride or groom was over 21, or 'a minor', or 'of full age'. Even when an age is given with apparent precision, it is not necessarily trustworthy. Consequently, it is not possible to include all those who marry in a parish in the study of adult mortality. The study of adult mortality must be based exclusively on the lives of men and women who were born in a given parish and were subsequently married there. For such grooms and brides either a date of death (burial) is known from an entry in the register, or there is no such entry, implying that the man or woman had died elsewhere. In the former case, the available information can readily be used in the calculation of standard mortality rates (m_x). For example, if a man were married on his 28th birthday and died on his 81st birthday, he would contribute 2 years at risk to the denominator of the mortality rate for the age group 25–9, 5 years to each subsequent age group up to 75–9, and 1 year to the age group 80–4. In the final age group he would also contribute 1 death to the numerator of the mortality rate for the age group. In the earlier age groups there would, of course, be no addition to the numerator of the mortality rate.

Matters are less straightforward in the latter case, where the death occurs outside the parish and where therefore the date of death is unknown. At some point the individual in question must have migrated from the parish, but this may have taken place many years after the marriage occurred. To fail to take such periods of residence in the parish into account must, of course, cause the mortality rate to be overestimated since the numerator would be known accurately (all adult deaths of those who were both baptised and buried in the parish), but the denominator would consist solely of the period at risk of those who died in the parish. It is essential to include also the period at risk of those who lived for part of their lives after marriage in the parish but who ultimately died elsewhere, and therefore it is essential to be able to estimate the length of their residence in the parish before their departure. What is required may be expressed more formally as follows. The death rate (m_x) of those aged, say, 30–4, is $1000 \times (d_{30-4}/\exp._{30-4 \text{(stay.)}} + \exp._{30-4 \text{(leav.)}})$, where d = the total of deaths; exp. = the totals of years at risk; stay. = stayers; and leav. = leavers. The problem lies, of course, in estimating the final term, $\exp._{30-4 \text{ leav.}}$. If a satisfactory way of solving this problem can be found, however, the result is exactly what one might want in that it will define with precision the mortality prevailing *in the parish*, as opposed, for example, to that characterising a particular birth cohort.

Fortunately, although there are no parochial sources which provide systematic evidence about the timing of migratory moves, FRFs contain a comparative wealth of information which helps to define the period of continued residence in the parish. For example, a couple whose marriage caused an FRF to be created may have a string of children baptised. The succession of baptisms and of occasional child burials is evidence of the continued presence of the parents in the parish. And the abrupt end of such a sequence affords persuasive evidence about the timing of the family's migration from the parish.

Blum brought this issue into clearer focus by defining minimum and maximum periods of exposure for leavers. His minimum required no great leap of the imagination. It was specified by assuming that the date of the last event relating to an individual in the parish register was the date at which he or she left the parish. Thus, if the date of her marriage is the last reference to a bride on the FRF, she is assumed to have left the parish on that date. Or again, if she had a third child at the age of 34, and thereafter no entry stating or implying her presence, its baptism is evidence of her continued presence in the parish until that time.

Blum's maximum, which represented an ingenious innovation, was obtained by matching an individual who left the parish as closely as possible to a group of individuals who remained in the parish and whose subsequent life history is therefore known. For example, suppose that a 30-year-old woman had had two children baptised in the parish but that there were no subsequent events recorded on her FRF. She may be presumed to have left the parish at some point after the date of the baptism of her second child. Other women of similar age and with a similar family pattern, but who were stayers rather than leavers, are then identified, and a choice is made at random among these matched stayers. If the woman selected had a third child three years after the birth of her second, the migrant woman is assumed to have had an exactly similar life history and therefore to have spent a further three years in the parish before migrating. In other words, she is assumed to have left the parish on the day before her next child would have been born, an event which would have caused a further entry on her FRF.[1] This represents the maximum possible additional exposure. If the method is dependable, the true mortality rate must lie somewhere between the maximum and minimum rates arrived at in this way by identifying minimum and maximum periods of exposure. The determination of the interval to next event which in turn decides the scale of maximum exposure to risk on the part of migrants is therefore the key issue in this regard.

Ruggles has subsequently pointed to logical difficulties with Blum's method of estimating maximum exposure and has attempted to demonstrate their magnitude by a simulation exercise. The basic problem arises because of the existence of competing risks. The matched individuals between whom Blum chooses at random consist only of stayers. But amongst all those whose prior history resembled that of the migrant there will also be some leavers, and ideally the determination of the characteristics of the intervals to next event should include information about the leavers as well as about the stayers. Failure to take leavers into account would not matter if stayers and leavers could be counted on to display a similar range of intervals to next event, but even if the

---

[1] Blum, 'Estimation de la mortalité locale', pp. 44–9.

prior history of leavers and stayers were similar, the distribution of intervals to *next* event will differ in the two groups. On average the intervals will be longer among leavers than among stayers because the longer the interval to the next event, the more likely it is that the individual in question will have left the parish. Where the next event is the death of the migrant, the problem may be especially acute.[2] The longer someone lives, the greater the chance that he will migrate, and therefore to select only among intervals to death among stayers must cause too high a proportion of intervals to be short.[3]

Ruggles conducted a simulation exercise to explore this issue further. It appeared to show that in certain circumstances Blum's maximum estimate of exposure would cause the minimum estimate of mortality to be slightly *higher* than the true rate. In arriving at this conclusion Ruggles was, in effect, juggling with two variables with opposite implications so far as the average interval to next event was concerned. On the one hand, his recognition of the competing risk issue caused the average interval to next event to rise relative to Blum's estimates. On the other hand, his use of a migration schedule in which the propensity to migrate declined sharply with age tended to limit the length of the interval to next event.

Even though it is clear that Blum's approach, while providing a most important breakthrough, is open to criticism, it is no easy matter to devise an alternative that is unequivocally better. In the first place, there is little or no accurate historical information available about migration schedules for married people. Most migration schedules, especially in the younger age groups, primarily reflect the migration propensities of the unmarried. It is probable, however, that if a migration schedule for married people existed, it would be very different from that for the unmarried. Marriage is punctuated with events which are strongly related to migration. For example, if a marriage takes place in which the age of the bride but not that of the groom is known, and the marriage is the last event relating to the couple to be recorded in the register, it is highly likely that the couple left the parish immediately after marrying to return to the parish of the groom. It would be artificial to estimate the length of continued residence in the parish for such a bride from a list of 'similar' cases where the next event was the baptism or burial of a child to the marriage.

A similar point applies to cases where the last known event is the death of a spouse, and he or she is still alive at the time. Here the next

---

[2] This point was appreciated by Blum. Ibid., p. 49.
[3] Ruggles, 'Migration, marriage, and mortality', pp. 514–7.

event will always be the death of the surviving spouse estimated from data concerning stayers. This will often produce a long interval to next event. But in a substantial proportion of such cases the death of the spouse will have triggered a decision to leave the parish. Once again, it is somewhat artificial to make use of matching data as if the circumstances of the migrant and those of the stayers were similar. In real life, in other words, although the competing risk consideration will mean that, other things being equal, estimating interval to next event from stayers will cause the interval to be underestimated, other things were sufficiently unequal to leave the situation unclear. It may also be true of married couples that, as they acquired goods and an increasing stake in the community, they became progressively less willing to move in a more decided fashion than other groups in the population. Another incentive to stay which may have weighed increasingly strongly with married couples was their settlement in the parish and the entitlements which went with it. For these reasons it seems plausible to suppose, though as yet impossible to demonstrate, that, under Blum's procedure, where the interval to next event is chosen randomly from the experience of a set of matched individuals, long intervals will be given too great a weight. If, say, the procedure suggests an interval to next event of 30 years on the part of a man of 50 when his last event occurs, it is much more probable that his move took place in the early part of the interval than towards its end. Accordingly, Blum's inclination to treat migration as occurring half-way through the interval between his minimum and maximum exposure dates when making a 'best guess' estimate of exposure probably sets the point of migration too far from the minimum date.[4]

The sensitivity of estimated mortality rates to particular solutions to the problem of imputing additional exposure for leavers will depend, of course, upon the proportion of total exposure represented by the imputation. In calculating a mortality rate (m_x) the total of deaths in a given age group is readily obtained directly from the FRFs, as also the exposure in that age group of all those who died in the parish. Moreover, much of the total exposure in that age group will consist of years lived in the parish *before* the date of their last known event by people who later migrated from the parish. This exposure, too, is readily calculated. There will, however, also always be some imputed exposure to be added for leavers whose last event took place in the age group in question in respect of the additional time they spent in the parish. Expressed more formally, and as an elaboration of the definition offered

---

[4] Blum, 'Estimation de la mortalité locale', p. 50.

Table A6.1 *Adult mortality: the totals of years at risk contributed by stayers (those dying in the parish) and leavers (those dying elsewhere), the latter divided between residence to last recorded event and imputed subsequent exposure before migration*

Age	Totals				Totals indexed			
	(1) Stayers exp·stay	(2) Leavers (known) exp·leav.pre	(3) Leavers (imputed) exp·leav.post	(4) Total	(5) Stayers exp·stay	(6) Leavers (known) exp·leav.pre	(7) Leavers (imputed) exp·leav.post	(8) Total
25–9	32 746	12 074	1 921	46 741	701	258	41	1 000
30–4	42 524	11 467	2 081	56 072	758	205	37	1 000
35–9	44 195	8 223	2 233	54 651	809	150	41	1 000
40–4	42 114	4 597	2 432	49 143	857	94	49	1 000
45–9	38 085	2 120	1 987	42 192	903	50	47	1 000
50–4	33 111	1 138	1 077	35 326	937	32	30	1 000
55–9	27 327	700	515	28 542	957	25	18	1 000
60–4	21 716	396	328	22 440	968	18	15	1 000
65–9	15 830	222	156	16 208	977	14	10	1 000
70–4	10 241	129	63	10 433	982	12	6	1 000
75–9	5 638	60	42	5 740	982	10	7	1 000
80 and over	3 501	89	14	3 604	971	25	4	1 000

Source: Cambridge Group reconstitutions.

earlier, total exposure = exp.$_{(stay.)}$ + exp.$_{(leav.pre)}$ + exp.$_{(leav.post)}$, where leav.pre. refers to the exposure of migrants before their last event, and leav.post refers to the imputed exposure of migrants after their last event. The first two components are known directly and with precision. Only the third is uncertain. If, therefore the size of the third component relative to the other two is very small, whatever the assumptions made in deriving an imputed figure for this element, it is clear that it can make only a slight difference to the resulting rate.

Table A6.1 shows the relative size of the three components of exposure in each age group from the age of 25 upwards. The data refer to group 2 (1600–1729) rather than to the whole body of reconstitution data, but would differ very little from one period to another. The rules followed in calculating imputed exposure are detailed below. They are broadly similar to those proposed by Blum, though differing significantly in some particulars. It is convenient, however, first to consider the patterns revealed by the table.

The proportion of total exposure contributed by those dying in the parish rises steadily and rapidly from 70 per cent in the age group 25–9 to about 95 per cent by about age 55, before reaching a high plateau of about 98 per cent above the age of 65, though there is a small dip in the final age group, consisting of those over 80 (column 5). In the early age groups, therefore, migrants make a very substantial contribution to total exposure, of approximately 30 per cent. However, the bulk of this exposure relates to their residence in the parish before the last registered event which testifies to their presence, which, as a source of information about exposure, is as reliable as that relating to stayers (column 6). Imputed exposure, that is exposure attributed to leavers after their last registered event, was about 4 per cent in the youngest age groups, rising to a peak of almost 5 per cent in the age group 40–4, but then declining quickly to less than 1 per cent from age 65 onwards (column 7). The most significant uncertainty about adult mortality rates, therefore, concerns the age groups from about 25 to 50. In these age groups, on very extreme assumptions about minimum exposure, a rate perhaps 2 per cent higher than that resulting from the assumptions embodied in the table is conceivable, while equally extreme assumptions about maximum exposure would result in a rate about 2 per cent lower. In other age groups the band of uncertainty would, of course, be narrower. In the highest age groups, there is little room for any uncertainty related to imputed exposure. If separate tables are constructed for males and females, there is a general similarity between them, though both exp.$_{(leav.pre)}$ and exp.$_{(leav.post)}$ are higher for women than for men, especially in the younger age groups.

The imputed exposure in table A6.1 is the mean of the minimum and the maximum, the solution which appealed to Blum.[5] The minimum of imputed exposure follows Blum's suggestions exactly. For each leaver the minimum was zero, since migration was assumed to take place on the day on which the last observed event establishing the presence of the individual in the parish was recorded. The maximum differs somewhat from Blum's definition. The maximum, it will be recalled, is the interval between an event similar to that experienced by the leaver (last event) and the next event which would have established his or her presence in the parish (next event). The last and next events were both defined somewhat differently from Blum's suggestions, and some other rules also differed. Moreover, rather than using Blum's technique of 'hot-decking', that is choosing at random between a group of matched individuals to attribute an imputed interval of further residence, a different method was used, which will result in the same mean interval, *ceteris paribus*, but without reproducing the variance of the intervals from which the mean is derived.

Before considering these issues further, it is convenient to describe in turn the kinds of events used to define the earliest date at which an individual could have migrated (last event), and then those which were used to identify the date of the closure of the subsequent interval (next event), that is the event that would next have occurred in the life of a leaver if he or she had remained in the parish. Events of these types define the opening and closing of the intervals relevant to the calculation of imputed exposure. All closed intervals bounded by the events listed were used for this purpose. They were drawn from the FRFs of both stayers and leavers.

The dates which might represent the 'last event' were the following. The latest of such dates in a particular life on an FRF was identified as the last event before migration.

1 The marriage of x.
2 The baptism of a child to the marriage where x is mentioned or where his or her presence may be presumed, unless x is male and the reference to x is posthumous in which case the date is 9 months earlier.
3 The burial of a child under the age of 15 under the same conditions as in (2) (this implies that below the age of 15 a child is presumed to have been normally resident in the parental household, and that the recording of the child's death is evidence of the continued presence of the family).

[5] Ibid.

4 The burial of a spouse of x where x is mentioned, and not posthumously, and is therefore presumptively still living (that is where the date of burial of the husband or wife is the date of the end of the marriage).

In each of these cases only dates whose weights show that the date of the event is known to within a month are used.

The comparable dates for identifying the 'next event' were the following.

1 As (2) above.
2 As (3) above.
3 As (4) above.
4 The burial of x.

Once again, only dates known to within less than a month were used.

The next event most likely to occur will clearly differ according to the age of the individual in question. For a young married woman in her 20s, by far the most probable next event in her life was the birth of a new child or the death of one of those already born. For a woman beyond the age of childbearing the probabilities would evidently be very different.

Table A6.2 and A6.3 provide some information about the relative frequencies of the different types of closed intervals and about their average length for husbands and for wives. They show the data from two contrasting perspectives. In table A6.2 all the data are classified by the event which opened the interval. Thus, for example, in the case of husbands aged 20–4 the average length of interval to next event which followed the birth of a child was 2.75 years, and intervals begun by a birth in this way constituted 45.6 per cent of all the intervals recorded on the FRFs of husbands in this age group (column 2 in the two top panels). The next event which followed the birth might be another birth, the death of a child, the death of the wife, or his own death. One such event happened on average 2.75 years after a birth. The 4184 intervals for husbands in this age group represent data drawn either from the families of men who were stayers or from families of leavers, but at a period when the family in question was still resident in the parish and so the interval was closed by a later event recorded in the register. The overall mean interval for each age group is shown in bold in column 5.

The differences in the means in the first four columns are, in general, readily intelligible. The shortest intervals during the childbearing age groups are to be found in columns 2 and 3, since the wives in question were all fecund and events related to the birth or death of children in the family succeeded one another in quick succession. In the prime

Table A6.2 Imputing exposure: the relative importance of different categories of events opening the interval and the mean periods of exposure associated with each

(1) Marriage.
(2) Birth of child.
(3) Death of child.
(4) Death of spouse.
(5) Overall mean.

Age	Mean length of interval (years)					Percentage distribution				N
	(1)	(2)	(3)	(4)	(5)	(1)	(2)	(3)	(4)	
Male										
15–9	3.34	2.41	5.85	20.47	3.34	61.2	31.1	6.9	0.7	289
20–4	2.79	2.75	2.77	23.91	3.07	44.0	45.6	9.0	1.4	4184
25–9	2.94	3.12	3.08	21.55	3.42	22.6	62.9	12.6	1.9	8497
30–4	3.73	3.49	3.60	18.46	3.96	10.9	68.9	17.4	2.8	8732
35–9	5.02	4.48	4.49	17.37	5.02	7.9	68.4	19.8	3.8	6956
40–4	5.33	5.11	5.84	15.16	5.84	6.1	65.8	22.6	5.5	4753
45–9	8.72	5.83	7.21	13.46	7.03	7.1	60.0	24.2	8.6	2504
50–4	9.48	5.71	7.32	14.03	8.06	8.2	48.1	23.7	19.9	1230
55–9	8.11	4.97	7.29	11.00	8.09	11.7	33.6	14.7	40.0	1598
60–4	6.42	5.55	8.33	9.75	8.29	11.4	22.0	11.1	55.4	1377
65–9	7.26	3.72	5.92	9.04	7.83	7.9	15.9	7.1	69.0	1239
70–4	5.89	3.43	5.34	6.34	5.99	7.1	9.6	4.1	79.2	1197
75–9	3.96	2.72	3.17	4.50	4.36	1.0	5.2	3.1	90.6	96
80 and over	3.98	—	5.09	3.96	3.98	7.0	0.0	2.3	90.7	43

Female

15–9	3.06	2.32	2.17	16.85	**2.83**	58.6	34.8	6.0	0.6	1 150
20–4	2.28	2.74	2.14	13.21	**2.61**	35.0	54.6	9.6	0.9	5 908
25–9	2.84	2.96	2.59	15.17	**3.02**	18.1	66.2	14.6	1.1	8 797
30–4	3.66	3.31	2.63	15.60	**3.45**	9.8	69.8	18.5	1.9	8 289
35–9	6.02	4.55	3.99	16.09	**4.88**	6.0	68.1	22.6	3.2	6 220
40–4	10.52	7.93	7.58	15.14	**8.46**	4.9	60.4	27.8	6.9	2 993
45–9	14.12	10.71	12.03	16.19	**13.01**	8.5	31.6	30.5	29.4	838
50–4	11.30	—	12.71	15.49	**14.54**	9.2	0.0	20.1	70.7	304
55–9	10.15	—	9.91	13.48	**13.09**	5.8	0.0	5.4	88.8	224
60–4	15.73	—	15.16	11.76	**11.79**	0.5	0.0	0.5	99.1	211
65–9	8.36	—	—	8.43	**8.43**	2.4	0.0	0.0	97.6	168
70–4	—	—	—	7.47	**7.47**	0.0	0.0	0.0	100.0	109
75–9	—	—	—	5.42	**5.42**	0.0	0.0	0.0	100.0	57
80 and over	—	—	—	4.60	**4.60**	0.0	0.0	0.0	100.0	29

Source: Cambridge Group reconstitutions.

Table A6.3 Imputing exposure: the relative importance of different categories of events closing the interval and the mean periods of exposure associated with each

(1) Own death.
(2) Birth of child.
(3) Death of child.
(4) Death of spouse.
(5) Overall mean.

	Mean length of interval (years)					Percentage distribution				N
	(1)	(2)	(3)	(4)	(5)	(1)	(2)	(3)	(4)	
Male										
15–9	21.99	1.82	0.34	11.75	3.34	6.2	82.4	7.6	3.8	289
20–4	19.70	1.80	0.74	10.61	3.07	5.5	80.5	9.6	4.4	4 184
25–9	18.54	2.12	0.99	11.38	3.42	6.1	76.6	12.5	4.8	8 497
30–4	18.13	2.29	1.15	11.43	3.96	8.5	68.5	17.3	5.7	8 732
35–9	17.76	2.36	1.41	13.99	5.02	12.6	61.0	18.7	7.7	6 956
40–4	15.73	2.38	1.48	13.66	5.84	19.1	51.5	19.7	9.7	4 753
45–9	14.73	2.38	1.64	13.14	7.03	28.1	40.2	19.4	12.2	2 504
50–4	13.42	2.35	1.70	11.38	8.06	43.3	30.9	14.6	11.2	1 230
55–9	11.38	2.36	1.22	9.31	8.09	58.9	23.1	10.4	7.7	598
60–4	9.99	2.42	1.20	8.98	8.29	73.7	14.3	6.4	5.6	377
65–9	9.01	2.07	1.58	11.28	7.83	79.5	12.1	5.4	2.9	239
70–4	6.22	2.21	2.54	12.81	5.99	89.8	6.1	2.5	1.5	197
75–9	4.49	1.11	0.85	6.37	4.36	94.8	2.1	2.1	1.0	96
80 and over	4.01	—	—	2.70	3.98	97.7	0.0	0.0	2.3	43

Female

15–9	19.50	1.75	0.62	12.47	**2.83**	5.1	84.8	7.7	2.4	1 150
20–4	14.23	1.92	0.86	11.34	**2.61**	4.7	82.2	10.7	2.4	5 988
25–9	15.04	2.19	1.01	12.88	**3.02**	5.3	76.8	14.8	3.0	8 797
30–4	14.18	2.35	1.14	11.87	**3.45**	7.7	69.3	18.6	4.4	8 289
35–9	15.56	2.35	1.37	14.25	**4.88**	13.1	56.9	21.5	8.6	6 220
40–4	16.77	2.22	1.97	15.06	**8.46**	27.0	30.0	24.5	18.4	2 993
45–9	17.58	1.65	1.95	13.62	**13.01**	55.8	8.5	15.5	20.2	838
50–4	15.34	—	2.25	11.08	**14.54**	86.8	0.0	2.6	10.5	304
55–9	13.32	—	1.17	10.31	**13.09**	93.8	0.0	0.4	5.8	224
60–4	11.77	—	—	15.73	**11.79**	99.5	0.0	0.0	0.5	211
65–9	8.49	—	—	4.98	**8.43**	98.2	0.0	0.0	1.8	168
70–4	7.47	—	—	—	**7.47**	100.0	0.0	0.0	0.0	109
75–9	5.42	—	—	—	**5.42**	100.0	0.0	0.0	0.0	57
80 and over	4.60	—	—	—	**4.60**	100.0	0.0	0.0	0.0	29

Source: Cambridge Group reconstitutions.

childbearing years the average closed interval was between three and four years in length.[6] With increasing age the level of sterility also increased and the intervals grow steadily longer. The phenomenon is much more clear-cut among wives than among husbands, since a proportion of relatively elderly husbands might still have wives of an age to bear children, whereas for wives there is no entry for any age group higher than 45–9 in the column for intervals begun by a birth, and in that age group the mean interval in column 2 rises to almost 11 years. The overall mean for the age group is over 13 years. Intervals that began with a marriage are somewhat longer than those begun by a child's birth or death, partly because a proportion of marriages were infertile and partly because the interval could never be closed by the death of a child. In contrast to the other three types of interval, intervals that began with death of a spouse tend to become shorter with increasing age, since such intervals were closed predominantly by the death of the surviving spouse, which was naturally a more distant event when the surviving partner was young than when he or she was older. Occasionally, however, in the younger age groups the death of a child might be the reason for the closing of an interval of this type.

The right-hand panel of table A6.2 gives the relative frequency with which each type of event was the opening event of the interval. Once again the patterns are those which might be expected from first principles, with child-related events providing the bulk of the cases throughout the main years of childbearing, though in the earliest age groups the marriage itself claimed a major share of the total. With advancing years, and especially beyond the age of 50, the death of a spouse dominated the distribution, though the absolute number of cases declined rapidly. Once again, the male and female patterns were broadly similar, save that the female patterns were the more clear-cut, since husbands might father children to a relatively advanced age, but end of childbearing for women was concentrated into a short span of years.

In table A6.3 the same intervals are categorised by the closing event rather than the opening event. The categories change somewhat. No

---

[6] In view of the fact that the mean birth interval was shorter than this (tabs. 7.33 and 7.35, pp. 433 and 438–9), it may seem illogical that the mean closed interval was as long as this, but it should be borne in mind that a proportion of births, even in the younger age groups, were last births, and where this was the case, the interval to the next recorded event might be much longer than the mean birth interval. This influence outweighed the fact that the interval to the next event in families in which the wife was still fecund was somewhat shorter than the interval to the next birth, since the death of an earlier child sometimes took place between two births (baptisms).

interval could end with a marriage, nor could any interval begin with the death of the individual whose life history is being used to build up a picture of mean intervals relevant to the life histories of leavers. As in the previous table the male and female patterns are generally similar. Intervals closed by the death of a child were often very short indeed, since in many cases the death was that of the child whose birth had opened the interval. At the other extreme, intervals closed by an own death or the death of a spouse were long, though in the former case declining with great regularity with increasing age in the case of men, though more irregularly in the case of women. Because the birth of a child was the dominant closing event in the younger age groups, overall average intervals were short, in spite of the great length of the own death intervals in these age groups. The steady rise in the proportion of all closing events which were own deaths caused the overall mean to rise steadily even though the average length of such intervals declined with age. The peak value in the overall means occurred in intervals beginning when the men and women concerned were in their 50s, that is when childbearing was over for women and largely complete also for men, but before old age caused the own death and death of spouse means to fall.

The object of this exercise, of course, was to make it possible to calculate the imputed additional exposure to be added for each leaver (migrant from the parish) to represent time spent in the parish and therefore at risk after the last known event and before migration actually took place. The amount to be added on was calculated separately for each five-year age group, as suggested by the format of tables A6.2 and A6.3. As already noted, it was taken to be half of the mean of the intervals. The relevant means are those shown in column 5 of tables A6.2 and A6.3.

The data employed in the calculation of imputed exposure were drawn from the whole time span of reconstitution and the results were applied to populations throughout the parish register period. Small changes in the average intervals between successive events will have occurred with changing patterns of fertility and mortality in early modern England, but any such changes were quite modest in scale, and it was attractive to make use of as a large a body of data as possible in estimating mean intervals. Clearly, the larger the body of data employed, the less the averages are affected by random factors.

In considering the use of the data set out in table A6.2 and A6.3, the following points should be noted.

(1) Where the date of birth of the wife is known but that of her husband is not known, and the last recorded event on the FRF is the

marriage itself, it was assumed, for reasons given above, that the couple left the parish immediately after the wedding, and, therefore, no addition was made to the total of imputed exposure.[7]

(2) Where a husband or wife died and the surviving spouse remarried, either once or, because of further deaths, more than once, the resulting 'chain' of marriages was treated as a series of separate periods of exposure, rather than as a single continuous sequence. In other words, the period between marriages was not counted, since it is less certain that the individual in question was continuously resident in the parish in the interval between marriages than in the course of a marriage.

(3) Appropriate periods of imputed exposure were calculated separately for men and women, and attributions made accordingly. However, there was one exception to this rule. In the case of marriages in which the dates of birth of both partners to the marriages were known, but the dates of death of the two were both unknown, it must be assumed that the pair left the parish together and it therefore appears illogical to attribute to each spouse a different period of imputed exposure after the last event and before migration. The circumstance can, of course, only arise following a marriage or the birth or death of a child. When it did arise the same imputed exposure was given to both spouses, and the amount of imputed exposure was taken from the female table. Experiment shows that the totals of exposure were scarcely altered whether the male or female imputed exposure tables were used, or the average of the two.

(4) This fourth and last point was by far the most important in changing the amount of imputed exposure. It represents an attempt to offset an asymmetry between the two sexes in the information routinely recorded in parish registers on the death of a spouse. When a wife died but her husband was still living the form of the entry in a good parish register makes this clear by recording her death as that of '*x*, wife of *y*'. This means that even if the husband's date of death is unknown (that is, he was a leaver), it is plain that he was still living when his wife died. But when a husband died leaving a surviving wife, the corresponding entry in the register simply records the name of the deceased man without affording any clue as to whether the marriage was ended by his death, or had already ended. If the wife's date of death is unknown, therefore, her presence in the parish until her husband's death cannot be established and her 'last event' will often be many years earlier than her husband's death. To repeat, where a wife died it is clear from the form of

---

[7] See p. 584.

entry whether or not her husband survived her, but it is relatively rare for this to be clear for a wife from an entry relating to a husband. Where the date of death of only one spouse is known this asymmetry will make it much more difficult in the case of women than in the case of men to demonstrate that the individual was still in the parish at the time of the spouse's death.

The loss of information which occurs because the information given when a husband died was less complete than when a wife died is important. There was often a long gap within the history of a family between the last date relating to the birth or death of a child and the date of the end of the marriage, which occurred with the death of the first of the two spouses to die. Up to the date of the end of the marriage, it is reasonable to assume that both spouses were still resident in the parish. If, when the marriage ended, the form of entry relating to the death of the husband or wife was explicit that the marriage had ended, by implying the continued existence of the other spouse ('x, the wife of y'), it was clear that observed exposure (exp.$_{(leav.pre)}$) extended to that date, and that imputed exposure (exp.$_{(leav.post)}$) should be added thereafter. But if this was not the case, exp.$_{(leav.post)}$ would have to be calculated from the last event occurring in the marriage *before* the date of death of the spouse. Because of the asymmetry of information, therefore, a far higher proportion of women suffered from a premature truncation of exp.$_{(leav.pre)}$ and were therefore credited with less exposure than should have been the case. For example, if a woman had a last child at a date 20 years before the death of her husband, and the form of entry relating to her husband's death was such that the fact that she survived her husband could not be established, her exp.$_{(leav.pre)}$ must be taken to end with the birth of her last child, and her exp.$_{(leav.post)}$ would be calculated as from the birth of a child in the appropriate age group. Only the poverty of information in the entry relating to her husband's death would, in these circumstances, prevent her from being credited with a much greater exposure.

The effect of the asymmetry, if left uncorrected, is to underestimate the exposure of married women and therefore to cause female mortality rates to be overestimated. As a result, without correction for this problem, female mortality will be overestimated relative to male rates. Accordingly, a rough and ready solution was adopted, which is arbitrary but unlikely to be far from the truth.

First, it is necessary to identify all cases in which the date of death of the wife but not that of the husband is known, and then to establish, for each age group of the husband, in what proportion of such cases the wife's death represented the end of the marriage. Clearly, the proportion will be high in the younger age groups, since, if the wife died while her husband was still young, he is very likely to have survived her. With increasing age, the proportion must fall: the husband will often have predeceased his wife and she will therefore be termed a widow at her death. While it is arbitrary, and cannot be entirely accurate, to suppose that a pattern observed for husbands can be expected to be mirrored by wives, there must be a broad similarity between the two patterns. Therefore, it was assumed that the date of death of the husband in each age group represented the end of the marriage in the same proportion of cases as happened with the date of death of the wife. This makes it possible in a much increased proportion of cases to treat the death of the husband as the last event for the wife, and so to increase the exp.(leav.pre) for wives to a more realistic level. For example, suppose that in the husbands' age group 30–4 in 75 per cent of all cases when a wife died she was described as 'wife of' when she was buried, and it was therefore clear that the marriage ended with her death and not before, even though the husband's date of death was unknown. In all these cases his last event would be the death of his wife. But suppose further that in the wives' age group 30–4 it was clear in only 10 per cent of the cases that she survived her husband. In the other 90 per cent of the cases the last event for the wife would probably be the birth or death of a child some years previously, unless some correction were made. To prevent this information asymmetry from biasing the calculation of mortality rates, it was assumed that in reality in 75 per cent of the deaths of husbands in the age group, the wife survived her husband, just as was the case in the parallel situation with the deaths of wives. Therefore, a balance of 65 per cent of cases of husbands' deaths should be treated as last events for wives and exp.(leav.pre) increased accordingly. Further exp.(leav.post) would then be calculated from the death of a spouse rather than from the birth or death of a child. To secure this result, for each relevant death of a husband a decision by random number was made about whether or not to treat the event as the end of the marriage (and therefore to determine whether or not the wife survived her husband), with the probabilities so ordered that an appropriate proportion of all such deaths were given this character. In the particular illustration used, the procedure would, of course, raise the percentage of cases in which the husband's death was the end of the marriage to 75 per cent.

One further issue requires a brief consideration. The calculation of adult mortality involves identifying individuals who left the parish and died elsewhere, and attributing to them an appropriate amount of exposure to the risk of dying after their last known events and before their departure from the parish. Towards the end of any reconstitution a

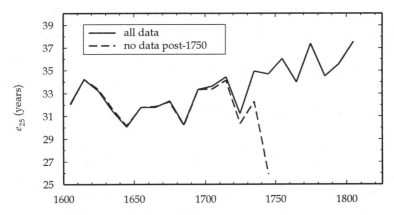

Figure A6.1 *An illustration of the increasing inaccuracy of the measurement of exposure in adult mortality towards the end of a reconstitution exercise: expectation of life at age 25*
Source: Cambridge Group reconstitutions.

problem arises in that the proportion of husbands and wives with an unknown date of death will rise, not because an increasing proportion were migrants, but because their death occurred after the end of registration in the parish. If they are treated as leavers, the amount of exposure attributed to them will be much too low since many were in the parish and at risk to die until the end of the reconstitution period. In these circumstance, it is inevitable that mortality rates will be exaggerated because exposure will become increasingly underestimated, unless migrants can be distinguished from those who remained in the parish until the end of the reconstitution in some other fashion. English registers do not afford any information which can enable this to be done.[8] Accordingly it is important to be able to identify the point at which adult mortality rates are liable to be inaccurate, given the nature of this problem.

Figure A6.1 illustrates the characteristic divergence of the calculated rate from the true rate which occurs toward the end of a reconstitution. The group of parishes from which the data were drawn for this exercise were those which were members of all four groups. There is therefore no danger that the level or trend of the observed rates will be affected by a change in the composition of the group. The solid line on the figure traces e_{25} throughout the whole parish register period, while the broken

[8] Combining information from parish registers with information drawn from the census enumerators' books might overcome this problem, of course, but this solution was too laborious to have been undertaken for this study.

line shows what happens if all information after 1750 is ignored. It is apparent that in the last decade, 1740–9, e_{25} in the latter data set is radically deflected below its true path. In earlier decades the divergence is far less pronounced, though far from negligible in the 1730s and even in the 1720s. If the table of q_xs underlying the lines on the graph are consulted, it appears that the rates from the full data set and that truncated in 1750 showed no divergence before the decade 1700–9.[9] In 1700–9 the rates in half the age groups are again identical or differ by less than 1 per cent. In no age group is the difference as great as 3 per cent. Overall e_{25} is depressed by only 0.23 years (from 33.61 to 33.38 years). These discrepancies are too slight to warrant concern. Much the same is true for the decade 1710–9. The overall measure of mortality, e_{25}, is still only 0.28 years below its true level (34.43 and 34.15 years respectively), though the divergence in some individual age groups is more pronounced than in 1700–9. Since the two e_{25}s differ by less than 1 per cent, it seems acceptable to make use of data from this decade. In the following decade, 1720–9, however, the e_{25} taken from the data set truncated in 1750 is 0.87 years, or 2.8 per cent below its value in the full data set and it seems unwise to use it as a source of information.

In view of these findings, no data drawn from a period less than 30 years from the end of an individual reconstitution were included in the tables and figures relating to adult mortality presented in chapter 6. It will be evident from the foregoing that, since the individual q_xs may be slightly above their true level, and summary measures, such as e_{25}, may therefore be very slightly understated, a slight question mark attaches to rates from the last quoted decadal rate in a reconstitution series. The possible extent of any distortion is, however, very modest, and it is attractive to include as long a run of estimates as is reasonably possible.

[9] The slight divergence between the solid and dotted lines in fig. A6.1 before 1700 arises because the process by which the asymmetry of information between husbands and wives is corrected (see pp. 596–8) involves an element of random choice so that no two runs will produce exactly the same results.

7

Adjusting mortality rates taken from the four groups to form a single series

The research design which led to the division of the 26 reconstitution parishes into four groups has been described elsewhere, as has the reason for treating group 2 as the reference group to which data drawn from the other groups should be aligned.[1] The issue covered in this appendix is the implementation of this strategy when dealing first with infant and child mortality, and then with adult mortality.

Infant and child mortality

The four groups were chosen so that there were long overlaps between them. It will be recalled that group 1 covers the period 1580–1729 (15 parishes); group 2, 1600–1729 (20 parishes); group 3, 1680–1789 (18 parishes); group 4, 1680–1837 (8 parishes).[2] The separate tabulations for each group showed that in overlap periods infant and child mortality rates in the groups differed, sometimes considerably, and that therefore adjustment between the rates for each pair of adjacent groups was necessary to produce a single series. The adjustment process might appear to involve reconciling two conflicting desiderata. On the one hand, it is the ratio of rates drawn from two adjacent groups over a period close to the changeover between them which is at issue. Therefore, adjustment ratios based on a brief overlap period are attractive since there is no certainty that the appropriate adjustment ratio would be constant over the whole period of a long overlap. On the other hand, the shorter the overlap period, the more slender the empirical base upon which the calculation of the adjustment ratio must

---

[1] See pp. 24–8, 133.
[2] For a full list of the parishes in each group, see tab. 2.2, p. 26.

be based and the greater the danger of random influences causing a misestimation.

In the event, adjustment ratios proved by experiment to be relatively invariant with respect to the length of the overlap period used. It therefore seemed sensible to use a long overlap period as the basis for the calculation of the adjustment ratios. Adjustment ratios were calculated separately from period rates for $_1q_0$, $_4q_1$, $_5q_5$, and $_5q_{10}$. The overlap periods were as follows: group1/group2 1600–49, group 2/group 3 1680–1729, group 3/group 4 1740–89. Group 1 data formed the basis for the adjusted rates for the period 1580–99. Group 2 data could be used without adjustment from 1600 to 1729, since group 2 is the reference group. Group 3 data were used with adjustment for 1730–89, and group 4 data, also after adjustment, for 1790–1837.

As an illustration of the nature and scale of the adjustment process, consider the adjustment ratios for infant mortality, $_1q_0$. Over the period 1600–49 infant mortality in group 1 was 159.32 and in group 2 159.18, an inconsiderable difference. Since group 2 was the reference group, all the rates for the series as a whole could be taken direct from group 2 for the whole of the period 1600–1729, but for the period 1580–99 the group 1 rates were multiplied by 0.9991 (159.18/159.32). Thus, the group 1 rate for 1580–9 was 168.57 but the adjusted rate became 168.42 (168.57×0.9991).

The adjustment ratio of infant mortality in group 2 to that in group 3 in the second overlap period, 1680–1729, was 1.1226 (the rates in question were 189.52 in group 2 and 168.83 in group 3). Therefore, the group 3 rates in the period 1730–89 were multiplied by 1.1226.

Finally, in the period 1740–89 the adjustment ratio between rates in group 3 and group 4 was 1.0629 (the rates in question were 148.56 in group 3 and 139.78 in group 4). The group 4 rates, however, were to be adjusted to group 2 rather than to group 3 since group 2 was the reference group and therefore infant mortality rates from 1790 onwards taken from group 4 were multiplied by 1.1931 (1.1226×1.0629). Thus the group 4 rate for 1790–9 was 126.81, but after adjustment the rate became 151.30.

The same procedures were employed to produce adjustment ratios for the three childhood rates, $_4q_1$, $_5q_5$, and $_5q_{10}$.

Adult mortality

It was desirable that the overlap period should be at least as long as for infant and child mortality so that the volume of data upon which the calculation of any adjustment ratio was based would be sufficient to provide a reliable estimate of the difference between two groups. But to secure a 50-year overlap in data between two groups is a much more demanding condition with adult than with infant and child mortality. The nature of the problem can be put quite simply. Individuals can live for up to 100 years. If period rates are used for the comparison, therefore, the comparison period can begin only 100 years after the beginning of the data since only after a century can mortality rates for all age groups be calculated. This in turn implies that, if the comparison period is 50 years broad, 150 years of data must be common to any two groups between which an adjustment ratio is to be calculated. If the comparison is between cohort rates, the same constraints apply, as may be seen in figure A7.1, which shows both a 50-year birth cohort parallelogram of 1600–49 and a 50-year period block of 1740–89. The choice of period or cohort rates for the comparison is therefore a matter of taste. In essence the two operations are very similar. Cohort rates were used to calculate adjustment ratios in this exercise.

The periods of overlap between the groups clearly preclude the possibility of meeting the ideal requirements for the calculation of adjustment ratios. In order to make it possible to estimate adjustment ratios, therefore, the following modifications to the ideal scheme were made. First, instead of making the comparison over the maximum span of life, 100 years, it was made over the first 80 years of life. The great majority of deaths occurred below the age of 80, so that this modification involved little sacrifice of information. The change implied that the overlap period should be 130 years rather than 150 years. Adjustment ratios based on mortality experience below the age of 80 were applied to mortality rates above that age. Adopting this procedure solved the problem as far as the group1/group 2 comparison is concerned since a Lexis parallelogram with a base in 1600–49, and therefore with a top in 1680–1729, can be constructed entirely within the overlap between the two groups.

The group 3/group 4 comparison can also be accommodated without major problems within this framework. Both groups begin in 1680.[3] The fact that the groups begin in 1680 appears at first sight to prohibit a comparison exercise which requires 130 years of overlapping data since group 3 ends in 1789. However, sound data begin before 1660 in all the constituent parishes of the two groups except for 3 parishes in group 3: Earsdon, 1679; Great Oakley, 1673; and Ipplepen, 1671. 2 of the 3 are very small indeed, and the third of only moderate size. A comparison

[3] See tabs. 2.1 and 2.2, pp. 22–3 and 26.

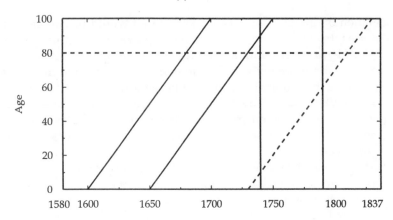

Figure A7.1 *Estimating adjustment ratios between groups to produce a single adult mortality series*

parallelogram with a base in 1660–1709 and a top in 1740–89 can therefore be used with only a trivial risk that compositional change might affect the comparison.

The third comparison pair, group 2/group 3, present more considerable problems. Their solution involved a further relaxation of the ideal procedure. Group 2 ends in 1729, while group 3 begins in 1680, which appears to prohibit the identification of a suitable comparison parallelogram of the same dimensions as those used for the group 1/group 2 and group 3/group 4 comparisons. However, it will be recalled that in chapter 2, in discussing the data available for each parish, a distinction was drawn between the outer limits of registration and the final limits, the former representing the period within which baptisms, burials, and marriages were all recorded, while the latter represented the boundaries within which the data seemed to be of high quality. In many cases the outer limits were considerably wider than the final limits.[4] If, therefore, a somewhat poorer average quality of registration is acceptable for a particular purpose, the period during which data are available can often be extended substantially. The group 2/group 3 comparison was made using the outer limits for the parishes in each group.

If outer limit data are used, the same comparison parallelogram can be used as for the group 3/group 4 comparison, with a base in 1660–1709 and a top in 1740–89. There are no difficulties with the earliest date, 1660, in group 2 and only one parish begins later than 1660 on the 'outer limits' criterion in group 3 (Ipplepen, 1671). The end date presents no

[4] Tab. 2.1, pp. 22–3.

problems so far as group 3 is concerned. In all the constituent parishes in this group the reconstitution continues to a date beyond 1789. In the case of group 2, reconstitution ends before 1789 in 3 cases: Lowestoft, 1730; March, 1751; and Reigate, 1769. There will therefore be some compositional change in group 2 during the comparison period, but the 3 parishes in question contribute fully to the data for group 2 during most of the period of comparison, and represent only a small proportion of the 20 parishes in group 2. It is improbable that the calculation of the adjustment ratio will be significantly distorted by this problem.

The risk of misestimating the adjustment ratio as a result of adopting this more relaxed strategy would probably have been slight in any such comparison, but any risk is further reduced because of the nature of the calculation used to measure adult mortality rates. Since the date of death of many of those who enter into adult mortality calculations is unknown, a technique of imputation is used, which increases the period of exposure appropriately to allow for the fact that migrants were exposed to the risk of dying in their parish of origin not merely up to the date of the last recorded event that proves their continued residence in the parish but for a further period after that date. If such an adjustment is not made, exposure is understated relative to the number of recorded deaths.[5] Because adult mortality rates are calculated in this way, minor changes in the quality of the data will have a lesser impact than if conventional measures of deaths and periods of risk were used.

Table A7.1 shows the mortality rates in each age group in the three pairs of groups, while figure A7.2 depicts the relative levels of the mortality rates in groups 1, 3, and 4, indexed to group 2, which is represented by the 100 line. As with infant and child mortality rates, group 2 was taken as the reference group to which the rates in other groups were to be aligned. In general, the relative rates are remarkably stable across all age groups in the group 1/group 2 comparison. The rates in group 1 were almost always the higher of the two, but the differences were slight, never exceeding 10 per cent. All group 1 rates were therefore adjusted by the average of the percentage differences in the 11 age groups from 25 to 79. Since the group 1 rates were on average 1.0460 times higher than those in group 2, this meant multiplying the group 1 rates by 0.9560 (1/1.0460 = 0.9560).

The pattern of differences between group 2 and group 3 suggests that group 3 rates were substantially lower than those in group 2 in the younger age groups, but that the differences tended to decline with age. It was assumed that the underlying change was linear but that random

---

[5] See app. 6 for details of the system of imputed exposure used in this connection.

Table A7.1 A comparison of the mortality rates ($1000q_x$) in the overlap periods between the groups

Age	Group1	Group2	Ratio gp1/gp2	Group 3	Group 2	Ratio gp3/gp2	Group 4	Group 3	Ratio gp4/gp3
25–9	66.9	67.2	0.9955	54.4	65.0	0.8369	52.1	54.4	0.9577
30–4	80.9	76.2	1.0617	64.7	70.2	0.9217	62.3	64.7	0.9629
35–9	102.3	98.2	1.0418	80.2	85.2	0.9413	75.6	80.2	0.9426
40–4	95.4	90.3	1.0565	73.7	82.9	0.8890	57.7	73.7	0.7829
45–9	123.2	112.6	1.0941	90.0	96.9	0.9288	87.6	90.0	0.9733
50–4	146.4	138.1	1.0579	103.2	113.8	0.9069	105.5	103.4	1.0203
55–9	201.3	190.8	1.0550	153.4	160.9	0.9534	158.2	153.3	1.0320
60–4	233.8	228.9	1.0214	187.3	194.3	0.9640	200.8	187.5	1.0709
65–9	284.3	278.9	1.0194	238.9	248.3	0.9621	238.4	238.5	0.9996
70–4	393.4	378.3	1.0399	340.5	350.7	0.9709	346.7	339.9	1.0200
75–9	531.2	499.7	1.0630	449.4	446.6	1.0063	468.1	444.3	1.0536

Source: Cambridge Group reconstitutions.

606

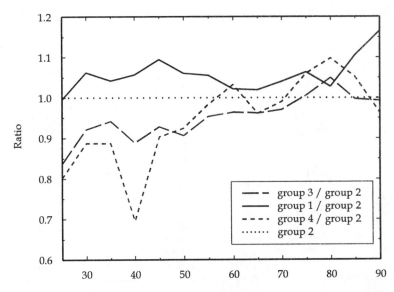

Figure A7.2   *The relative levels of adult mortality rates (q_x) in groups 1, 2, 3, and 4*
Source: Cambridge Group reconstitutions.

factors caused minor departures from a straight path. Accordingly, the mean of the ratios in the first three age groups was taken to be the initial adjustment ratio for the youngest age group, and, similarly, the mean of the last three age groups was taken as the final ratio (1.1111 and 1.0204, respectively: table A7.2). The relationship between the rates in group 3 and group 4, shown in table A7.1, also displayed a general, if erratic, tendency to rise with age. The group 4 rates were the lower of the two initially, but had become modestly the higher of the two in the higher age groups. The exceptional ratio for the age group 40–4 is plainly the product of random influences.

The group 4/group 3 ratios could be used to align group 4 rates with those drawn from group 3 to form a single sequence. Since the object of the exercise, however, is to bring rates in the other groups into alignment with those in group 2, the adjustment to be made to group 4 rates is the product of the ratios for group 3/group 2 and group 4/group 3. For example, the group 3/group 2 ratio for the age group 50–4 is 1.0658, and the group 4/group 3 ratio for the same age group is 1.0120, with the result that the group 4/group 2 ratio is 1.0786 (1.0658 × 1.0120). The results of all these manipulations may be seen in table A7.2.

The adjustment ratios shown in table A7.2 were applied to the rates in

Table A7.2 *Adjustment ratios to enable rates from other groups to be aligned with those for group 2*

	Adjustment ratios				
	(1) Gp1/gp2	(2) Gp2	(3) Gp3/gp2	(4) Gp4/gp3	(5) Gp4/gp2
25–9	**0.9560**	1.0000	**1.1111**	1.0478	**1.1642**
30–4	**0.9560**	1.0000	**1.1020**	1.0406	**1.1467**
35–9	**0.9560**	1.0000	**1.0930**	1.0335	**1.1296**
40–4	**0.9560**	1.0000	**1.0839**	1.0263	**1.1124**
45–9	**0.9560**	1.0000	**1.0748**	1.0192	**1.0954**
50–4	**0.9560**	1.0000	**1.0658**	1.0120	**1.0786**
55–9	**0.9560**	1.0000	**1.0567**	1.0048	**1.0618**
60–4	**0.9560**	1.0000	**1.0476**	0.9977	**1.0452**
65–9	**0.9560**	1.0000	**1.0385**	0.9905	**1.0286**
70–4	**0.9560**	1.0000	**1.0295**	0.9834	**1.0124**
75–9	**0.9560**	1.0000	**1.0204**	0.9762	**0.9961**
80+	**0.9560**	1.0000	**1.0204**	0.9762	**0.9961**

Note: The ratios shown are those by which age-specific mortality rates in group 1 (col. 1), group 3 (col. 3), and group 4 (col. 5) are to be multiplied in order to bring them into alignment with those of group 2. The rates in question are shown in bold. The rates in col. 4 are not shown in bold because they represent an intermediate step (see accompanying text).

successive cohorts as follows: to the cohort born in 1580–99 the ratios shown in column 1; to the cohort born in 1600–1729 the ratios shown in column 2; to the cohort born in 1730–89 the ratios shown in column 3; and to the cohort born in 1790–1837 the ratios shown in column 5. The revised rates produced in this fashion extending down a given diagonal were then combined to produce period rather than cohort mortality estimates by taking the appropriate rates from a Lexis diagram column. This might mean, of course, taking data from successive diagonals which had been adjusted by differing ratios. As an example, in figure A7.1 the period rates for 1740–89 are shown as being derived by combining data drawn from two different group cohorts, which will have been adjusted by differing factors. The broken diagonal line represents the boundary between the group 2 and group 3 cohorts.

The birth cohorts whose mortality rates are to be modified by using the adjustment ratios shown in table A7.2 should logically be those of the parishes comprising the four groups, changing from one group to the next at 1600, 1730, and 1790, the dates marking the transition between the groups. To proceed in this way, however, involves sacrifice of data without compensating advantages. Experiment showed clearly that estimated mortality rates towards the end of a reconstitution become distorted, rising well above their true level. The divergence begins about 30 years before the end of the data.[6] This means that no information should be drawn from the last three decades of a reconstitution. If, for example, the final limit of observation in a given parish, that is the end of reliable data, were 1760, no adult mortality data should be used after 1730. Since the final limit dates vary from parish to parish, some coinciding with the final year of a given group, others occurring many years later, it is not possible to preserve an invariant parish composition for a given group throughout the period associated with the group, as, for example, the period 1600–1730 in the case of group 2, except by sacrificing a relatively large amount of data from some reconstitutions. In these circumstances, the best and simplest policy appeared to be to use the adjustment ratios set out in table A7.2 and apply them to the birth cohorts of 1580–99 (group 1), 1600–1729 (group 2), 1730–89 (group 3), and 1790–1837 (group 4), drawing data from all parishes whose final limits meant that data could properly be drawn from them for a birth cohort of a given period. The parishes from which data were drawn for a birth cohort, say, of the decade 1720–9 might not be solely those of the group 2 set, therefore, but any slight blurring of the normal group membership which occurs by proceeding in this fashion is of little effect. In other words, the adjustment ratios are applied to birth cohorts arising within the periods associated with a group rather than strictly to the parishes comprising that group. This maximises the quantity of data available while paying only a negligible price in that there is a slight discrepancy between the data sets from which the ratios were calculated and those to which they were subsequently applied.

[6] See app. 6, pp. 598–600.

8

The calculation of the proportion of women still fecund at any given age

The method of calculation used to derive a proportion of women still fecund for individual years of age or for five-year age groups is illustrated in figure A8.1, which refers to this calculation for women in the age group 35–9. In the figure a part of the life history of eight women is shown by lines within the figure representing events in their lives between the ages of 34 and 41. A cross represents a birth, a bold cross a last birth, while the point at which fecundity ceases is indicated by a small vertical line 17.5 months later than a bold cross. The subsequent history of the woman is then shown as a broken line.[1] To simplify matters a year is taken as 365 days and 17.5 months is taken as 533 days.[2] The age of the individual at the birth of the last child, and again at the point at which fecundity ceases, is shown in years and days. In two cases the birth of the last child takes place after the age of 41 years, and in another case the last birth occurs during the 41st year. There is also one case in which, although the date of birth of the last child is less than 40 (38 years and 300 days), the age of the woman when her fecundity ceases is greater than 40 years. Four women in all, therefore, are fecund throughout the age group. One woman had already become infecund before her 35th birthday, at 34 years and 248 days, while in the other three cases infecundity occurred within the age group at 35:198, 36:233, and 39:268 years and days respectively.

The proportion still fecund was taken as the proportion of all days lived in the single year of age or in the age group as a whole by women

---

[1] It will be recalled that all the women survived to age 50 in marriage since only completed marriages were used in the estimation of fecundity.

[2] In the calculations which gave rise to the tables in ch. 7 greater precision was used, with the year, for example, taken as 365.25 days in length.

610

Table A8.1 *Proportions of women still fecund*

	Age					
	35	36	37	38	39	35–9
	Woman-days lived					
1	365	365	365	365	365	1 825
2	365	365	365	365	365	1 825
3	365	365	365	365	365	1 825
4	365	365	365	365	365	1 825
5	365	365	365	365	268	1 728
6	365	233	0	0	0	598
7	168	0	0	0	0	168
8	0	0	0	0	0	0
Days lived fecund	2 358	2 058	1 825	1 825	1 728	9 794
Total days lived	2 920	2 920	2 920	2 920	2 920	14 600
Proportion fecund	0.808	0.705	0.625	0.625	0.592	0.671

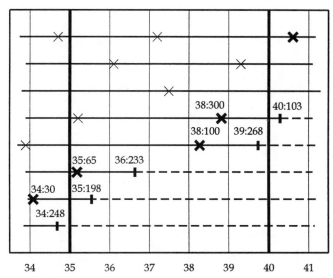

Figure A8.1   *The identification of the onset of infecundity*
Note: the ages noted on the figure are given in years and days. Thus, 38:300 indicates 38 years and 300 days.

who had not yet become infecund. The calculation is shown in table A8.1.

The total of days lived in each year is 2920 (8 × 365). The total of days lived by women still fecund is 2358, 2058, 1825, 1825, and 1728 days respectively for the five years 35–9 and the proportion still fecund in each year is therefore 0.808, 0.705, 0.625, 0.625, and 0.592, while for the 35–9 age group as a whole the proportion is 0.671.

9

Summary of quinquennial demographic data using revised aggregative data and produced by generalised inverse projection

This appendix is included to provide a comparison between the findings published in the *Population history of England*, which were obtained using the technique of back projection, and those resulting from the use of generalised inverse projection applied to national totals of births and deaths which have been revised in the light of the evidence afforded by reconstitution. The results also reflect a mean age at maternity which changes over time and, similarly, provision for a changing relationship over time between the level of infant and child mortality on the one hand and adult mortality on the other hand. Fuller details may be found in chapter 8. The form of the table which is appended is designed to parallel table A3.1 in the earlier work.[1] Note, however, that the fertility and mortality measures in table A9.1 relate in every case to the five-year periods between successive 'censuses' for which population totals are given, whereas in the parallel table in the earlier work, the comparable data always refer to five-year periods centring on the 'census' dates. In table A9.1, therefore, the rates on the line for 1541 refer to the period 1541–6. For the purpose of calculating the rates given here, it was assumed that populations and their component elements changed exponentially between any two successive 'censuses'. The censuses relate to the midpoint of the year, and the rates therefore run, for example, from July 1541 to June 1546, and so on. All data refer to England only (excluding Wales).

---

[1] Wrigley and Schofield, *Population history of England*, tab. A3.1, pp. 528–9.

Table A9.1 *Quinquennial demographic data produced by generalised inverse projection*

Year	Pop.	CGR	GRR	NRR	e_0	ITR	Mig.	CBR	CDR	CRNI	CMR
1541	2 830 459	0.54	2.72	1.34	33.94	0.92	3 990	37.17	30.34	6.83	12.54
1546	2 908 465	1.05	2.80	1.58	38.82	1.42	4 197	37.88	25.98	11.90	12.53
1551	3 065 168	0.94	2.64	1.52	39.59	1.31	4 410	35.62	24.82	10.80	10.20
1556	3 212 504	−1.13	2.17	0.68	22.38	−1.17	4 394	30.24	40.16	−9.92	10.32
1561	3 035 687	0.89	2.56	1.37	36.66	0.97	4 582	37.06	26.70	10.36	10.37
1566	3 173 512	0.84	2.32	1.34	39.67	0.91	4 883	34.16	24.21	9.94	9.65
1571	3 310 219	0.82	2.15	1.28	41.06	0.77	5 016	32.37	22.73	9.64	9.87
1576	3 447 944	1.04	2.30	1.39	41.56	1.02	4 946	34.20	22.43	11.77	9.88
1581	3 631 442	1.12	2.42	1.51	42.70	1.27	5 064	34.12	21.56	12.56	9.47
1586	3 840 645	0.50	2.36	1.28	37.05	0.75	5 387	32.09	25.70	6.38	9.48
1591	3 937 846	0.59	2.35	1.30	38.05	0.81	5 676	32.12	24.75	7.36	9.37
1596	4 056 575	0.51	2.23	1.23	37.82	0.63	5 884	31.50	24.95	6.55	8.61
1601	4 161 784	0.70	2.27	1.27	38.53	0.75	6 138	33.24	24.77	8.47	9.12
1606	4 310 420	0.76	2.22	1.28	39.59	0.76	6 252	33.05	24.07	8.98	8.76
1611	4 476 311	0.41	2.13	1.14	36.79	0.41	6 231	31.60	26.14	5.45	8.61
1616	4 568 410	0.76	2.21	1.30	40.31	0.81	6 284	32.30	23.37	8.93	8.53
1621	4 744 972	0.07	2.14	1.04	33.39	0.11	6 361	30.91	28.85	2.05	7.19
1626	4 761 955	0.68	2.20	1.27	39.69	0.74	6 515	31.81	23.68	8.13	8.12
1631	4 926 322	0.65	2.18	1.26	39.72	0.71	6 652	31.66	23.80	7.86	8.19
1636	5 089 826	0.16	2.14	1.06	34.03	0.18	6 647	31.47	28.59	2.88	8.46
1641	5 130 124	0.39	2.17	1.15	36.32	0.43	6 595	31.97	26.79	5.18	7.78
1646	5 231 238	0.29	1.90	1.10	39.74	0.29	6 560	27.79	23.63	4.16	6.71
1651	5 307 979	0.31	1.94	1.11	39.14	0.31	6 631	28.55	24.22	4.33	8.82
1656	5 390 763	−0.42	1.71	0.82	33.04	−0.60	6 523	25.74	28.68	−2.94	7.86
1661	5 279 735	−0.19	1.83	0.89	33.27	−0.38	6 405	28.22	28.92	−0.70	7.49
1666	5 229 233	−0.27	1.82	0.86	32.48	−0.47	6 231	28.53	30.03	−1.51	6.94
1671	5 158 920	0.10	1.81	0.99	37.41	−0.04	5 994	28.40	26.25	2.15	6.71
1676	5 184 564	−0.29	1.87	0.88	32.40	−0.39	5 647	28.91	30.75	−1.84	7.21
1681	5 109 031	−0.29	2.03	0.92	31.27	−0.26	5 335	30.32	32.14	−1.82	7.91
1686	5 036 098	0.23	2.23	1.17	35.93	0.47	5 229	31.87	28.56	3.31	7.17
1691	5 093 749	0.10	2.16	1.14	36.35	0.42	5 217	30.05	28.06	1.99	6.61
1696	5 118 433	0.36	2.27	1.26	38.06	0.71	5 210	31.25	26.67	4.58	7.70
1701	5 210 623	0.47	2.34	1.31	38.47	0.83	5 251	32.06	26.39	5.66	7.72
1706	5 333 593	0.18	2.07	1.16	38.50	0.45	5 317	28.48	25.67	2.81	7.05
1711	5 382 324	0.17	2.09	1.12	36.89	0.34	5 432	29.47	26.77	2.71	8.03
1716	5 428 308	0.27	2.19	1.13	35.75	0.38	5 533	31.65	27.91	3.74	8.21
1721	5 502 742	0.36	2.22	1.13	35.49	0.39	5 621	32.80	28.21	4.60	9.01
1726	5 602 228	−0.68	2.05	0.74	25.34	−0.95	5 461	31.16	36.99	−5.83	9.00
1731	5 414 320	0.67	2.30	1.20	36.34	0.58	5 318	35.13	27.46	7.67	9.16
1736	5 598 933	0.44	2.28	1.16	35.26	0.46	5 262	33.79	28.47	5.32	7.99
1741	5 723 209	0.20	2.18	1.08	34.27	0.24	5 169	31.71	28.78	2.94	8.15
1746	5 781 806	0.48	2.30	1.21	36.47	0.62	5 060	32.68	27.02	5.65	8.11
1751	5 921 905	0.75	2.37	1.37	39.77	0.99	5 145	32.97	24.61	8.36	8.05
1756	6 148 553	0.52	2.27	1.26	38.12	0.75	5 331	31.87	25.82	6.05	8.50
1761	6 310 338	0.43	2.34	1.21	35.37	0.61	5 426	33.48	28.29	5.19	8.88
1766	6 448 730	0.53	2.33	1.23	36.19	0.68	5 486	33.88	27.69	6.18	8.79
1771	6 623 358	0.86	2.38	1.36	39.09	1.01	5 754	34.90	25.47	9.43	8.48
1776	6 913 474	0.83	2.44	1.35	37.74	0.99	6 363	35.76	26.57	9.19	8.67
1781	7 206 139	0.62	2.40	1.26	35.81	0.76	6 027	34.86	27.81	7.04	8.57
1786	7 433 690	1.08	2.56	1.46	38.97	1.25	6 650	36.89	25.23	11.66	8.56
1791	7 845 678	1.02	2.60	1.45	37.92	1.22	7 197	37.17	26.07	11.10	8.38
1796	8 256 323	0.98	2.49	1.42	38.93	1.15	7 389	35.51	24.82	10.69	8.19
1801	8 671 439	1.25	2.64	1.54	40.02	1.43	8 746	37.60	24.08	13.52	8.90
1806	9 232 494	1.32	2.67	1.59	40.58	1.52	9 422	37.90	23.68	14.22	8.08
1811	9 863 955	1.49	2.77	1.67	41.25	1.69	10 203	39.18	23.25	15.93	8.42
1816	10 628 380	1.50	2.81	1.68	40.84	1.70	10 272	39.48	23.54	15.95	7.91
1821	11 456 808	1.54	2.88	1.70	40.47	1.75	12 933	40.22	23.73	16.49	8.35
1826	12 373 740	1.37	2.66	1.61	41.43	1.56	14 824	37.30	22.40	14.91	7.70
1831	13 254 058	1.24	2.53	1.51	40.89	1.36	16 806	36.03	22.43	13.60	8.12
1836	14 099 516	1.15	2.43	1.44	40.56	1.19	18 371	35.27	22.47	12.80	7.96
1841	14 936 706	1.26	2.39	1.46	41.71	1.23	21 035	35.61	21.61	13.99	8.23
1846	15 910 019	1.01	2.32	1.33	38.99	0.92	20 771	35.06	23.71	11.35	8.46
1851	16 732 114	1.22	2.38	1.40	40.46	1.11	20 185	35.98	22.65	13.33	8.87
1856	17 780 540	1.30	2.40	1.45	41.53	1.22	17 618	35.89	21.92	13.97	8.61
1861	18 975 496	1.27	2.46	1.46	40.62	1.24	16 796	36.30	22.71	13.59	8.69
1866	20 222 174	1.31	2.46	1.49	41.47	1.31	16 433	35.95	22.06	13.89	8.39
1871	21 500 720										

				Age structure (percentages)						
0–4	5–14	0–14	15–24	25–44	45–64	65–84	25–59	60+	DR	Year
13.30	21.23	34.53	17.46	25.61	17.06	5.23	39.43	8.58	758	1541
13.95	21.19	35.14	17.90	25.26	16.50	5.10	38.54	8.43	772	1546
14.86	21.72	36.58	17.78	24.94	15.62	4.99	37.48	8.16	810	1551
14.13	23.27	37.40	17.56	25.10	14.93	4.87	37.13	7.92	829	1556
9.81	23.39	33.20	19.51	26.69	15.54	4.95	39.27	8.02	701	1561
14.25	18.29	32.55	20.81	26.64	15.20	4.71	39.04	7.60	671	1566
13.59	19.64	33.24	19.55	27.36	15.23	4.52	39.83	7.38	684	1571
13.07	22.87	35.94	15.44	28.58	15.52	4.43	41.24	7.38	764	1576
13.60	21.80	35.59	16.51	27.91	15.48	4.42	40.61	7.29	751	1581
13.88	21.92	35.80	18.94	25.29	15.49	4.38	37.98	7.28	757	1586
12.52	22.78	35.30	18.43	25.72	16.05	4.41	38.87	7.41	745	1591
12.64	21.65	34.29	18.90	25.35	16.87	4.50	39.34	7.47	717	1596
12.39	20.76	33.16	19.65	25.86	16.70	4.55	39.63	7.56	687	1601
13.12	20.54	34.66	18.58	27.93	15.17	4.58	39.93	7.83	709	1606
13.17	20.95	34.12	17.66	27.97	15.39	4.77	39.95	8.27	736	1611
12.32	21.72	34.05	17.69	27.67	15.40	5.11	40.20	8.06	727	1616
12.97	20.97	33.94	18.06	27.36	15.67	4.88	40.89	7.11	696	1621
11.66	20.97	32.62	18.95	27.05	17.08	4.20	40.90	7.53	671	1626
12.72	20.19	32.91	18.33	26.89	17.24	4.54	40.99	7.77	686	1631
12.67	20.22	32.90	18.00	27.30	16.94	4.75	41.19	7.92	690	1636
11.95	21.03	32.98	17.63	27.49	16.94	4.87	41.11	8.28	703	1641
12.41	20.22	32.63	17.81	27.80	16.59	5.10	41.05	8.52	699	1646
11.23	20.49	31.72	18.56	27.40	16.91	5.31	41.22	8.50	673	1651
11.46	20.04	31.50	18.00	27.71	17.47	5.22	42.00	8.50	667	1656
9.79	19.38	29.17	18.71	28.74	17.99	5.28	43.52	8.60	607	1661
10.70	17.88	28.58	18.57	28.91	18.54	5.27	43.93	8.92	600	1666
10.73	17.20	27.93	17.83	30.15	18.45	5.52	44.98	9.27	592	1671
11.25	18.05	29.30	16.31	29.64	18.87	5.76	45.01	9.38	631	1676
10.87	18.60	29.47	15.73	29.45	19.42	5.82	45.17	9.63	642	1681
11.22	18.42	29.64	16.65	28.13	19.52	5.94	44.18	9.54	644	1686
12.37	18.28	30.66	16.81	26.62	20.00	5.78	42.77	9.76	678	1691
11.76	19.83	31.60	16.48	26.16	19.63	6.01	41.96	9.96	711	1696
12.35	20.22	32.58	16.32	25.66	19.18	6.15	41.16	9.95	740	1701
12.66	20.14	32.79	17.45	25.60	17.91	6.12	39.57	10.18	754	1706
11.29	21.14	32.43	17.97	25.86	17.20	6.41	39.46	10.14	741	1711
11.44	20.22	31.66	18.13	26.78	16.97	6.31	40.15	10.05	716	1716
12.05	18.92	30.97	18.88	27.01	16.78	6.20	40.79	9.36	676	1721
12.38	19.32	31.70	17.86	27.84	16.75	5.68	41.37	9.07	689	1726
10.33	19.75	30.09	17.27	29.57	17.24	5.66	43.45	9.20	647	1731
13.25	17.79	31.05	17.36	28.31	17.53	5.59	42.48	9.11	671	1736
12.65	19.22	31.87	17.07	27.70	17.58	5.62	42.14	8.92	689	1741
11.79	21.17	32.97	15.69	27.43	18.22	5.55	42.36	8.98	723	1746
12.41	19.94	32.35	16.95	26.32	18.67	5.56	41.37	9.32	714	1751
12.91	19.83	32.74	18.31	25.05	17.94	5.81	39.58	9.37	727	1756
12.33	20.92	33.25	17.26	25.94	17.54	5.86	39.91	9.58	749	1761
12.56	20.67	33.23	17.34	26.12	17.20	5.97	39.67	9.76	754	1766
12.80	20.23	33.03	18.23	26.04	16.48	6.07	39.36	9.38	736	1771
13.52	20.55	34.07	17.73	26.76	15.56	5.72	39.21	8.99	756	1776
13.65	21.29	34.93	17.14	26.43	15.91	5.44	39.16	8.77	776	1781
13.08	21.90	34.98	17.53	26.07	15.92	5.33	39.05	8.44	767	1786
14.20	21.30	35.50	17.95	25.79	15.54	5.06	38.79	7.77	762	1791
14.17	21.77	35.94	18.14	25.43	15.74	4.63	37.97	7.96	782	1796
13.71	22.69	36.40	17.71	25.37	15.52	4.87	37.91	7.98	798	1801
14.56	22.18	36.74	17.99	25.31	14.98	4.85	37.58	7.69	800	1806
14.73	22.43	37.16	18.46	24.93	14.67	4.65	36.79	7.58	810	1811
15.26	23.04	38.29	17.91	24.90	14.22	4.57	36.31	7.49	844	1816
15.28	23.49	38.77	17.95	24.73	13.92	4.51	36.11	7.17	850	1821
15.47	23.78	39.25	18.28	24.38	13.69	4.29	35.58	6.89	857	1826
14.58	24.18	38.76	18.75	24.72	13.49	4.17	35.72	6.76	836	1831
14.08	23.85	37.92	19.26	24.95	13.64	4.11	36.05	6.77	808	1836
13.78	22.90	36.68	19.76	25.49	13.81	4.15	36.80	6.76	768	1841
14.04	22.30	36.33	19.46	26.10	13.86	4.14	37.53	6.68	755	1846
13.52	22.37	35.89	18.88	26.86	14.17	4.09	38.43	6.80	745	1851
14.01	22.00	36.01	18.47	26.95	14.30	4.17	38.62	6.89	751	1856
14.09	22.00	36.08	18.36	26.68	14.53	4.24	38.66	6.89	754	1861
14.11	22.38	36.49	18.03	26.32	14.84	4.22	38.53	6.95	768	1866
14.08	22.43	36.51	18.01	26.03	15.08	4.27	38.45	7.03	771	1871

Appendix 9

The abbreviated column headings in the table should be read as follows; Pop.: population total; CGR: compound annual growth rate per 1000; GRR: gross reproduction rate; NRR: net reproduction rate; e_0: expectation of life at birth; ITR: intrinsic growth rate; Mig.: average annual net migration total; CBR: crude birth rate per 1000; CDR: crude death rate per 1000; CRNI: crude rate of natural increase per 1000; CMR: crude marriage rate per 1000; DR: dependency ratio ($1000 \times$ ((0–$14 + 60$plus)/15–59)). The age structure percentages are taken from the 'censuses' for the years shown.

10

Selection criteria used in compiling the tables in chapters 5 to 7

The purpose of this appendix is to provide fuller specification of the tabular reconstitution material than can conveniently be presented in the main body of the book. Chapters 5, 6, and 7 contain the chief empirical findings of this book. The data were derived from information contained on family reconstitution forms, and the chapters deal respectively with nuptiality, mortality, and fertility. The tables which appear in the other chapters were simple counts of totals of events, or are fully described in the accompanying text, or were obtained from tabulations which parallel those used for the tables in chapters 5 to 7. Accordingly, the table specifications given below refer exclusively to tables in these three chapters.

The three main types of criteria which are reflected in the listed specifications relate to the degree of precision required in the data; to the wish to avoid truncation and censoring bias; and to conventions which reflect biological realities. An example of the first type is the requirement in the fertility chapter that the date of birth of the wife must be accurate to within a month. This rule ensures that, in the study of marital fertility, age is known with adequate precision. The requirement in tables 5.1 to 5.11 that the date of marriage should be at least 50 years after the start of the reconstitution is an example of the second type. It avoids the danger that the calculated mean age at marriage would be biased downwards in the early decades of a reconstitution without such a rule.[1] Reproductive physiology suggests that a marriage must last until the wife has reached her 50th birthday if it is to be used in the study of completed fertility. This is an example of the third type of criterion.

[1] See above app. 3.

It may be helpful to recall at this point that, except where otherwise indicated, data taken from the reconstitutions of Birstall and Shepshed were given half-weight only in all the tabulations in this book.[2]

Throughout this appendix the phrases 'in quality' or 'quality data' are used as a shorthand to refer to periods during which in a given parish the data are reliable. The time periods in question are shown separately for each of the 26 parishes in column 8 of table 2.1, which is headed 'Final limits'.[3]

Chapter 5

In contrast with chapters 6 and 7, the most distinctive feature of the tabulations for chapter 5 is the absence of a requirement that all data must be in quality. The reasons for relaxing this requirement were discussed at length in chapter 5.[4] In brief, they derive from a consideration of the nature of the basic operation underlying all marriage age calculations. Age at marriage is obtained by subtracting a date of birth (baptism) from a date of marriage. In a period when registration in a given parish appears not to have been fully reliable and which, in consequence, is treated as outside quality, it would be foolish to use the data for the measurement of fertility and mortality, but the same is not true of nuptiality. An infant mortality rate might be underestimated using data from such a period, but a link between a birth (baptism) and a marriage may still yield an accurate estimate of age at marriage. If some births went unrecorded, some ages at marriage which might have been used would be lost, but those which are calculable should be no less accurate. Unless, therefore, there is reason to think that the ages at marriage which can be obtained are unrepresentative, or other, more subtle sources of bias are present, the requirement that all data used must be in quality can be relaxed without significant penalty.

Tables 5.1 to 5.11	Date of marriage must be known to the day and be at least 50 years after the start of the reconstitution: *and* date of birth (baptism) in all cases must be known to the day.
Table 5.12	Parents' date of marriage must be known to the day: *and* all marriages of parents must be bachelor/spinster marriages:

[2] The reasons for giving these two parishes half-weight are set out on pp. 43–8.
[3] Tab. 2.1, pp. 22–3.   [4] See pp. 126–8.

	and child's marriage must occur at least 50 years after the start of the reconstitution.
Table 5.13	As table 5.12:
	and father's date of death (burial) must be known to within a year and must occur at least 75 years before the end of the reconstitution.
Tables 5.14 to 5.17	Both dates of marriage must be known to the day:
	and first spouse's date of death (burial) must be known to within a month and must occur at least 10 years before the end of the reconstitution.
Tables 5.18 to 5.21	As table 5.1

Chapter 6

Since the calculation of adult mortality involves complex rules and remains a matter which attracts controversy, the rationale of the procedure used for the adult mortality tables in this chapter has been set out at length in appendix 6. Accordingly, the specifications set out here for the tables dealing either exclusively or in part with adult mortality (tables 6.19, 6.20, 6.21, 6.26, and 6.27) should be read in conjunction with appendix 6.

The nature of the information available about age at death changed with the coming into force of the provisions of Rose's Act in 1813. From 1813 onwards age at death was almost invariably recorded when a burial was recorded. Before 1813 age at death was seldom recorded, and therefore age can only be known for those born in the parish (by subtracting a date of birth (baptism) from a date of death (burial)). For the calculation of infant and child mortality rates the change in registration practice is irrelevant since only children whose date of birth (baptism) is known enter into the study. The change in convention creates a danger of bias in the case of adult mortality, however, because it might favour the long-lived. For example, consider two marriages taking place in 1780 between individuals, all of whom were of much the same age and for none of whom a date of birth (baptism) was known. Suppose further that in one case the partners had both died before 1813, whereas in the other case both had survived. In this event, the ages at death of the partners to the latter marriage would enter into the calculation of adult mortality if the change which occurred in registration practice in 1813 were ignored, whereas the deaths at a younger age of the partners to the former marriage would not.

To avoid this danger all marriage partners whose births were weighted *111 or *119, who were married before 1813, and whose implied date of birth lay between 1713 and 1812, were excluded from adult mortality calculations (weights *111 and *119 were attached to birth dates obtained by subtracting a stated age at death from a date of death).

All data used in the tables in chapter 6, both for infant and child mortality and for adult mortality calculations, were drawn from periods of quality data.

Tables 6.1 to 6.4	Date of birth (baptism) and death (burial) of child must be known to within a month: *and* date of end of marriage must be known to within a month.
Table 6.5	As table 6.1 for infant mortality: *and* date of death (burial) known to within a month for maternal deaths.
Tables 6.6 to 6.18	As table 6.1.
Tables 6.19 to 6.20	Date and birth (baptism) and death (burial) of adult must be known to within a month: *and* note that, whereas exposure is normally measured from the date of marriage, in the case of Birstall women it begins from the birth (baptism) of the first child, because all women on Birstall FRFs had at least one child which implies no mortality for women between marriage and first birth.[5] For Birstall men exposure begins at marriage or 9 months before the first birth, whichever is the later, since husbands are at risk to die before the birth but not before the conception.
Table 6.21	As table 6.1 for infant and child mortality: *and* as table 6.19 for adult mortality.
Tables 6.22 to 6.23	As table 6.1.
Table 6.25	As table 6.1.
Table 6.26	As table 6.19.
Table 6.27	As table 6.1 for infant and child mortality: *and* as table 6.19 for adult mortality.

[5] See above p. 356. It should be noted that, strictly speaking, exposure is measured not from the date of birth of the first child but from the date of birth of the first child whose date of birth (baptism) is known to within a month.

Tables 6.29 to 6.31	Date of death (burial) known to within a month.
Table 6.32	Date of death (burial) known to within a month *and* date of birth (baptism) known to within a year.
Table 6.33	Date of death (burial) known to within a month.

Chapter 7

For reasons explained in the text the parish of Birstall was excluded from many of the tabulations in this chapter.[6]

Only marriages with at least one child were used in the tables in chapter 7 except when measuring ASMFRs and sterility.

Where the tabulation relates to an interval closed by a birth, no interval beginning less than 10 years from the end of quality data was used, to ensure that long intervals were not differentially excluded.

No restrictions relating to the precision of the dating of a birth (baptism) were imposed for the tabulations in this chapter. Thus 'dummy' births were included, and also the very small percentage of births whose date was not known to the day. This policy was adopted to guard against the danger that a more exclusive rule would have selected against marriages which produced a large number of children. It should be noted that, as far as mean birth intervals are concerned, any inaccuracy of dating is, *ceteris paribus*, self-cancelling, since an interval x which, through some imprecision, is overestimated, will be balanced by an interval $x+1$ which will be underestimated, and vice versa.

A substantial number of tabulations were based on a selection of marriages that represent the completed marital fertility of bachelor/spinster marriages (marriages that meet the sets of conditions listed under A and B below). Since both A and B in combination and A alone were frequent requirements, and it would have been wearisome to repeat them, A and B are used as summary expressions to represent them.

All data used in the tables in chapter 7 were drawn from periods of quality data.

A   date of marriage known to within a month
    date of end of marriage known to within a month

[6] See above p. 356.

wife's date of birth (baptism) known to within a month
wife's age at marriage in the range 15–49 years

B   first marriage for wife
     first marriage for husband
     marriage must survive until wife is aged 50
     period from date of marriage to wife aged 50 must lie within
     quality

Table 7.1	A.
Tables 7.2 to 7.17	A + B.
Table 7.18	A.
Tables 7.19 to 7.20	A:
	and first marriage for both spouses.
Table 7.21	A:
	and first marriage for both spouses:
	and from date of marriage to wife's 50th birthday must be in quality:
	and marriage survives 10 years or until wife aged 50.
Tables 7.22 to 7.24	A:
	and from date of marriage to wife's 50th birthday must be in quality:
	and marriage survives until wife aged 50.
Tables 7.25 to 7.26	A:
	and marriage survives until wife aged 50:
	and from date of marriage to wife's 50th birthday must be in quality:
	and husband's date of birth (baptism) known to within a month.
Tables 7.27 to 7.28	Date of marriage known to within a month:
	and wife aged 15–49 at marriage.
Tables 7.29 to 7.30	A + B.
Table 7.31	A:
	and first marriage for both spouses:
	and from date of marriage to wife's 50th birthday must be in quality.
Tables 7.32 to 7.33	A + B.
Table 7.34	As table 7.31.
Tables 7.35 to 7.36	Marriage produces at least two children.
Table 7.37	A.
Tables 7.39 to 7.41	Date of marriage known to within a month.
Table 7.42	A + B (last column just A).

Bibliography

SECONDARY LITERATURE

Adair, R.L., 'Regional variations in illegitimacy and courtship patterns in England 1538–1754' (unpub. PhD thesis, University of Cambridge, 1991).

Adams, J., *Index villaris* (London, 1700).

Armstrong, W.A., 'The trend of mortality in Carlisle between the 1780s and the 1840s: a demographic contribution to the standard of living debate', *Economic History Review*, 2nd ser., 34 (1981), pp. 94–114.

Arthur, W.B., 'The ergodic theorems of demography: a simple proof', *Demography*, 19 (1982), pp. 439–45.

Bairoch, P. , 'Niveaux de développement économique de 1810 à 1910', *Annales, ESC*, 20 (1965), pp. 1091–117.

Bardet, J.-P., *et al.*, 'La mortalité maternelle autrefois: une étude comparée (de la France de l'Ouest à l'Utah)', *Annales de démographie historique* (1981), pp. 31–48.

Batschelet, E., *Circular statistics in biology* (London, 1981).

Berry, B.M., and Schofield, R.S., 'Age at baptism in pre-industrial England', *Population Studies*, 25 (1971), pp. 453–63.

Bideau, A., 'A demographic and social analysis of widowhood and remarriage: the example of the Castellany of Thoissey-en-Dombes, 1670–1840', *Journal of Family History*, 5 (1980), pp. 28–43.

'Accouchement naturel et accouchement à haut risque. Châtellerie de Thoissey-en-Dombes, 1660–1814', *Annales de démographie historique* (1981), pp. 49–66.

Bland, R., 'Some calculations on the number of accidents or deaths which happen in consequence of parturition', *Philosophical Transactions of the Royal Society*, 71, pt. II (1781), pp. 355–71.

Blayo, Y., 'Mouvement naturel de la population française de 1740 à 1829', *Population*, num. spéc., 30 (1975), pp. 15–64.

'La proportion des naissances illégitimes en France de 1740 à 1829', *Population*, num. spéc., 30 (1975), pp. 65–70.

'La mortalité en France de 1740 à 1829', *Population*, num. spéc., 30 (1975), pp. 123–42.

Blum, A., 'Estimation de la mortalité locale des adultes à partir des fiches de familles', *Population*, 42 (1987), pp. 39–56. (English language version 'An estimate of local adult mortality based on family cards', *Population*, 44, English selection no. 1 (1989), pp. 39–56).

Bongaarts, J., 'A method for the estimation of fecundability', *Demography*, 12 (1975), pp. 645–60.

Botham, F.W., and Hunt, E.H., 'Wages in Britain during the industrial revolution', *Economic History Review*, 2nd ser., 40 (1987), pp. 380–9.

Boulton, J.R., 'Itching after private marryings? Marriage customs in seventeenth-century London', *London Journal*, 16 (1991), pp. 15–34.

Bourgeois-Pichat, J., 'La mesure de la mortalité infantile', *Population*, 6 (1951), pp. 233–48, 459–80.

Bracher, M., 'Breastfeeding, lactational infecundity, contraception and the spacing of births: implications of the Bellagio consensus statement', *Health Transition Review*, 2 (1992), pp. 19–47.

Brändström, A., and Sundin, J., 'Infant mortality in a changing society: the effects of child care in a Swedish parish 1820–94', in A. Brändström and J. Sundin, eds., *Tradition and transition. Studies in microdemography and social change*, Report 2, The Demographic Data Base, Umeå (Umeå, 1981), pp. 67–104.

Brass, W., 'On the scale of mortality', in W. Brass, ed., *Biological aspects of demography*, Symposia of the Society for the Study of Human Biology, 10 (London, 1971), pp. 69–110.

Broström, G., *Estimation in a model for marital fertility*, Statistical Research Report (University of Umeå, 1983).

'Practical aspects on the estimation of the parameters in Coale's model for marital fertility', *Demography*, 22 (1985), pp. 625–31.

Brown, B.M., and Gunn, P.A., 'The significance of seasonal effects: goodness-of-fit test for circular data', unpub. MS.

Brown, R.L., 'The rise and fall of Fleet marriages', in R.B. Outhwaite, ed., *Marriage and society: studies in the social history of marriage* (London, 1981), pp. 117–35.

Burn, J.S., *The history of parish registers in England*, 2nd edn (London, 1862).

Cabourdin, G., 'Le remariage', *Annales de demographie historique*, 1978, pp. 305–32.

'Qu'est-ce qu'une crise?', in J. Dupâquier *et al.*, *Histoire de la population française. II. De la Renaissance à 1789*, 4 vols. (Paris, 1988), pp. 175–92.

Cavalli-Sforza, L.L., and Bodmer, W.F., *The genetics of human populations* (San Francisco, 1971).

Chalklin, C.W., *The provincial towns of Georgian England: a study of the building process, 1740–1820* (London, 1974).

Charbonneau, H., *et al.*, *Naissance d'une population. Les français établis au Canada au XVIIe siècle* (Montréal, 1987).

The Chester Beatty Research Institute serial abridged life tables (London, 1962) and the *Supplement* thereto (London, 1970). Compiled by R.A.M. Case, C. Coghill, J.L. Harley, and J.T. Pearson (*Supplement* compiled by Case and Coghill).

Coale, A.J., and Demeny, P., *Regional model life tables and stable populations* (Princeton, 1966).

Coale, A.J., and Trussell, J.T., 'Model fertility schedules: variations in the age structure of childbearing in human populations', *Population Index*, 40 (1974), pp. 185–258.

'Erratum', *Population Index*, 41 (1975), p. 572.

Cornwall, J., 'English population in the early sixteenth century', *Economic History Review*, 2nd ser., 23 (1970), pp. 32–44.

Corsini, C.A., 'Breastfeeding, fertility and infant mortality: lessons from the archives of the Florence Spedale degli Innocenti', in S.F. Matthews Grieco and C.A. Corsini, *Historical perspectives on breastfeeding* (UNICEF, Florence, 1991), pp. 63–87.

Cox, J.C., *The parish registers of England* (London, 1910).

Crafts, N.F.R., 'British economic growth, 1700–1831: a review of the evidence', *Economic History Review*, 2nd ser., 36 (1983), pp. 177–99.

British economic growth during the industrial revolution (Oxford, 1985).

Crafts, N.F.R., and Ireland, N.J., 'Family limitation and the English demographic revolution: a simulation approach', *Journal of Economic History*, 36 (1976), pp. 598–623.

Creighton, C., *A history of epidemics in Britain*, 2 vols., 2nd edn with additional material by D.E.C. Eversley, E.A. Underwood and L. Ovenall (London, 1965).

Deane, P., and Cole, W.A., *British economic growth 1688–1959* (Cambridge, 1962).

Desjardins, B., 'Bias in age at marriage in family reconstitutions: evidence from French-Canadian data', *Population Studies*, 49 (1995), pp. 165–9.

de Vries, J., *The Dutch rural economy in the golden age* (New Haven, Conn., 1974).

'The population and economy of the preindustrial Netherlands', in R.I. Rotberg and T.K. Rabb, *Population and economy. Population and history from the traditional to the modern world* (Cambridge, 1986) pp. 101–22.

Dobson, M.J., 'Population, disease and mortality in southeast England 1600–1800 (unpub. DPhil. thesis, University of Oxford, 1982).

'The last hiccup of the old demographic regime: population stagnation and decline in late seventeenth and early eighteenth-century England', *Continuity and Change*, 4 (1989), pp. 395–428.

'Mortality gradients and disease exchanges: comparisons from old England and colonial America', *Society for the Social History of Medicine* (1989), pp. 259–97.

Drake, M., *Population and society in Norway 1735–1865* (Cambridge, 1969).

Dupâquier, J., Hélin, E., Laslett, P., Livi-Bacci, M., and Sogner, S., eds., *Marriage and remarriage in populations of the past* (London, 1981).

Dyson, T., 'The historical demography of Berar, 1881–1980', in T. Dyson, ed., *India's historical demography: studies in famine, disease and society* (London, 1989), pp. 150–96.

Dyson, T., and Murphy, M., 'The onset of fertility transition', *Population and Development Review*, 11 (1985), pp. 399–440.

Eaton, J.W., and Mayer, A.J., 'The social biology of very high fertility among the Hutterites: the demography of a unique population', *Human Biology*, 25 (1953), pp. 206–64.

Eccles, A., 'Obstetrics in the seventeenth and eighteenth centuries and its implications for maternal and infant mortality', *Society for the History of Medicine Bulletin*, 20 (1977), pp. 8–11.

Edin, K.A., 'Studier i Svensk fruktsamhetsstatistik', *Ekonomisk Tidskrift*, 9 (1915), pp. 251–304.

Falkus, M.E., and Jones, E.L., 'Urban improvement and the English economy in the seventeenth and eighteenth centuries', *Research in Economic History*, 4 (1979), pp. 193–233.

Farr, W., *Vital statistics* (London, 1885).

Feinstein, C.H., 'Capital formation in Great Britain', in P. Mathias and M.M. Postan, eds., *The Cambridge economic history of Europe*, VII, pt. 1 (Cambridge, 1978), pp. 28–96.

'Part II. National statistics, 1750–1920', in C.H. Feinstein and S. Pollard, eds., *Studies in capital formation in the United Kingdom, 1750–1920* (Oxford, 1988), pp. 259–471.

Feng, W., Lee, Y., and Campbell, C., 'Marital fertility control among the Qing nobility: implications for two types of preventive check', paper for IUSSP, Committee on Historical Demography, Workshop on *Abortion, infanticide and neglect in the Asian past: Japan in an Asian comparative perspective*, Kyoto, Japan (1994).

Fildes, V., *Breasts, bottles and babies* (Edinburgh, 1986).

Fildes, V., ed., *Women as mothers in pre-industrial England: essays in memory of Dorothy McLaren* (London, 1990).

Finlay, R., *Population and metropolis. The demography of London 1580–1650* (Cambridge, 1981).

Flandrin, J.-L., *Families in former times: kinship, household and sexuality* (Cambridge, 1979).

Fleury, M., and Henry, L., *Nouveau manuel de dépouillement et d'exploitation de l'état civil ancien*, 3rd edn (Paris, 1985).

Flinn, M.W., 'The stabilisation of mortality in pre-industrial western Europe', *Journal of European Economic History*, 3 (1974), pp. 285–318.

Flinn, M.W., *et al.*, *Scottish population history* (Cambridge, 1977).

Floud, R., Wachter, K., and Gregory, A., *Height, health and history. Nutritional status in the United Kingdom, 1750–1980* (Cambridge, 1990).

Galloway, P.R., 'Basic patterns in annual variations in fertility, nuptiality, mortality, and prices in pre-industrial Europe', *Population Studies*, 42 (1988), pp. 275–303.

Gardner, D.E., and Smith, F., *Genealogical research in England and Wales*, 2 vols. (Salt Lake City, 1956 and 1959).

Gautier, E., and Henry, L., *La population de Crulai: paroisse normande* (Paris, 1958).

Gillis, J.R., 'Conjugal settlements: resort to clandestine and common law marriage in England and Wales, 1650–1850', in J. Bossy, ed., *Disputes and settlements: law and human relations in the west* (Cambridge, 1983), pp. 261–86.

For better, for worse: British marriages, 1600 to the present (Oxford, 1985).

Glass, D.V., 'A note on the under-registration of births in Britain in the nineteenth century', *Population Studies*, 5 (1951), pp. 70–88.

Numbering the people: the eighteenth-century population controversy and the development of census and vital statistics in Britain (Farnborough, 1973).

Goldstone, J., 'The demographic revolution in England: a re-examination', *Population Studies*, 40 (1986), pp. 5–33.

Goubert, P. , *Beauvais et le Beauvaisis de 1600 à 1730*, 2 vols. (Paris, 1960).

Gutierrez, H., and Houdaille, J., 'La mortalité maternelle en France au XVIIIe siècle', *Population*, 38 (1983), pp. 974–94.

Habakkuk, H.J., 'English population in the eighteenth century', *Economic History Review*, 2nd ser., 6 (1953), pp. 117–53.

Hajnal, J., 'European marriage patterns in perspective', in D.V. Glass and D.E.C. Eversley, eds., *Population in history: essays in historical demography* (London, 1965), pp. 101–43.

'Two kinds of pre-industrial household formation', in R. Wall, ed., *Family forms in historic Europe* (Cambridge, 1983), pp. 65–104.

Harvey, B., *Living and dying in England 1100–1540: the monastic experience* (Oxford, 1993).

Hatcher, J., 'Mortality in the fifteenth century: some new evidence', *Economic History Review*, 2nd ser., 39 (1986), pp. 19–38.

Henripin, J., *La population canadienne au début du XVIIIe siècle* (Paris, 1954).

Henry, L., *Anciennes familles genevoises. Etude démographique: XVIe–XXe siècles* (Paris, 1956).

'La fécondité naturelle: observation, théorie, résultats', *Population*, 16 (1961), pp. 625–36.

'Some data on natural fertility', *Eugenics Quarterly*, 18 (1961), pp. 81–91.

Manuel de démographie historique (Paris, 1967).

'Fécondité des mariages dans le quart sud-ouest de la France de 1720 à 1869', *Annales, ESC*, 27 (1972), pp. 612–40, 977–1023.

'Fécondité des mariages dans le quart sud-est de la France de 1670 à 1829', *Population*, 33 (1978), pp. 855–83.

Techniques d'analyse en démographie historique (Paris, 1980).

Henry, L., and Blanchet, D., 'La population de l'Angleterre de 1541 à 1871', *Population*, 38 (1983), pp. 781–826.

Henry, L., and Blayo, Y., 'La population de la France de 1740 à 1860', *Population*, num. spéc., 30 (1975), pp. 71–122.

Henry, L., and Houdaille, J., 'Fécondité des mariages dans le quart nord-ouest de la France de 1670 à 1829', *Population*, 33 (1973), pp. 873–924.

Hofsten, E., and Lundström, H., *Swedish population history: main trends from 1750–1970*, Urval no. 8, Skriftserie utgiven av statistiska centralbyrån (Stockholm, 1976).

Hollingsworth, T.H., *The demography of the British peerage*, supp. to *Population Studies*, no. 2, 18 (London, 1964).

Houdaille, J., 'La fécondité des mariages de 1670 à 1829 dans le quart nord-est de la France', *Annales de démographie historique* (1976), pp. 341–91.

Houston, R.A., 'Mortality in early modern Scotland: the life expectancy of advocates', *Continuity and Change*, 7 (1992), pp. 47–69.

Huck, P., 'Infant mortality in nine industrial parishes in northern England, 1813–1836', *Population Studies*, 48 (1994), pp. 513–26.

Huffman, S.L., and Lamphere, B.B., 'Breastfeeding performance and child survival', *Population and Development Review*, in W.H. Mosley and L.C. Chen, eds., *Child survival strategies for research*, supp. to vol. 10 (1984), pp. 93–116.

Hyrenius, H., *Estlandssvenskarna. Demograkiska studier* (Lund, 1942).

'Fertility and reproduction in a Swedish population group without family limitation', *Population Studies*, 12 (1958), pp. 121–30.

Imhof, A.E., 'La surmortalité des femmes mariées en age de procréation: un indice de la condition féminine au XIXe siècle', *Annales de démographie historique* (1981), pp. 81–7.

Ingram, M., *Church courts, sex and marriage in England, 1570–1640* (Cambridge, 1987).

Jackson, R.V., 'Inequality of incomes and lifespans in England since 1688', *Economic History Review*, 47 (1994), pp. 508–24.

Keyfitz, N., and Flieger, W., *World population: an analysis of vital data* (Chicago, 1968).

Knodel, J., 'Infant mortality and fertility in three Bavarian villages: an analysis of family histories from the 19th century', *Population Studies*, 22 (1968), pp. 297–318.

'Two and a half centuries of demographic history in a Bavarian village', *Population Studies*, 24 (1970), pp. 353–76.

'Ortssippenbücher als Daten für die historische Demographie', *Gesellschaft und Geschichte*, 1 (1975), pp. 288–324.

'Natural fertility in pre-industrial Germany', *Population Studies*, 32 (1978), pp. 481–510.

Demographic behavior in the past: a study of fourteen German village populations in the eighteenth and nineteenth centuries (Cambridge, 1988).

Knodel, J., and Lynch, K.A., 'The decline of remarriage: evidence from German village populations in the eighteenth and nineteenth centuries', *Journal of Family History*, 10 (1985), pp. 34–59.

Knodel, J., and Shorter, E., 'The reliability of family reconstitution data in German village genealogies (Ortssippenücher)', *Annales de Démographie Historique* (1976), pp. 115–54.

Knodel, J., and Wilson, C., 'The secular increase in fecundity in German village populations: an analysis of reproductive histories of couples married 1750–1899', *Population Studies*, 35 (1981), pp. 53–84.

Krause, J.T., 'Changes in English fertility and mortality, 1781–1850', *Economic History Review*, 2nd ser., 11 (1958), pp. 52–70.

'The changing adequacy of English registration, 1690–1837', in D.V. Glass and D.E.C. Eversley, eds., *Population in history* (London, 1965), pp. 379–93.

Kussmaul, A., *Servants in husbandry in early modern England* (Cambridge, 1981).

Landers, J., *Death and the metropolis: studies in the demographic history of London 1670–1880* (Cambridge, 1993).

Laslett, P., *The world we have lost* (London, 1965).

'Introduction: the history of the family', in P. Laslett and R. Wall, eds., *Household and family in past time* (Cambridge, 1972), pp. 1–89.

'Long-term trends in bastardy in England', in P. Laslett, *Family life and illicit love in earlier generations* (Cambridge, 1977), pp. 102–55.

'Characteristics of the western family considered over time', *Journal of Family History*, 2 (1977), pp. 89–115.

'Introduction: comparing illegitimacy over time and between cultures', in P. Laslett, K. Oosterveen, and R.M. Smith, eds., *Bastardy and its comparative history* (London, 1980), pp. 1–65.

Laslett, P., Oosterveen, K., and Smith, R.M., eds., *Bastardy and its comparative history* (London, 1980).

Lavely, W.R., 'Age patterns of Chinese marital fertility, 1950–81', *Demography*, 23 (1986), pp. 419–34.

Laxton, P., and Williams, N., 'Urbanization and infant mortality in England: a long term perspective and review', in M.C. Nelson and J. Rogers, eds., *Urbanisation and the epidemiological transition*, Reports from the Family History Group, Department of History, Uppsala University, no. 9 (Uppsala, 1989).

Ledermann, S., *Nouvelles tables-types de mortalité* (Paris, 1969).

Lee, R.D., 'Estimating series of vital rates and age structures from baptisms and burials: a new technique with applications to pre-industrial England', *Population Studies*, 28 (1974), pp. 495–512.

'Population homeostasis and English demographic history', *Journal of Interdisciplinary History*, 15 (1985), pp. 635–60.

'Inverse projection and back projection: a critical appraisal, and comparative results for England, 1539 to 1871', *Population Studies*, 39 (1985), pp. 233–48.

'Inverse projection and demographic fluctuations: a critical assessment of new methods', in D.S. Reher and R. Schofield, eds., *Old and new methods in historical demography* (Oxford, 1993), pp. 7–28.

Leridon, H., *Human fertility. The basic components* (Chicago, 1977).

Levine, D., 'The reliability of parochial registration and the representativeness of family reconstitution', *Population Studies*, 30 (1976), pp. 107–22.

Family formation in an age of nascent capitalism (New York, 1977).

Levine, D., and Wrightson, K., 'The social context of illegitimacy in early modern England', in P. Laslett, K. Oosterveen, and R.M. Smith, eds., *Bastardy and its comparative history* (London, 1980), pp. 158–75.

Lewis, P.R., Brown, J.B., Renfree, M.B., and Short, R.V., 'The resumption of ovulation and menstruation in a well-nourished population of women breastfeeding for an extended period of time', *Fertility and Sterility*, 55 (1991), pp. 529–36.

Lindert, P.H., 'English living standards, population growth, and Wrigley–Schofield', *Explorations in Economic History*, 20 (1983), pp. 131–55.

Livi-Bacci, M., *Population and nutrition: an essay on European demographic history* (Cambridge, 1990).

London inhabitants within the Walls 1695, introd. by D.V. Glass (London Record Society, 1966).

Loudon, I., *Death in childbirth. An international study of maternal care and maternal mortality 1800–1950* (Oxford, 1992).

Maag, U.R., 'A k-sample analogue of Watson's U^2 statistic', *Biometrika*, 53 (1966), pp. 579–83.

McDowall, M., 'Long term trends in seasonal mortality', *Population Trends*, 26 (1981), pp. 16–9.

Macfarlane, A., 'Illegitimacy and illegitimates in English history', in P. Laslett, K. Oosterveen, and R.M. Smith, eds., *Bastardy and its comparative history* (London, 1980), pp. 71–85.

Marriage and love in England: modes of reproduction 1300–1840 (Oxford, 1986).

McKeown, T., *The modern rise of population* (London, 1976).

McKeown, T., and Record, R.G., 'Reasons for the decline of mortality in England and Wales during the nineteenth century', *Population Studies*, 16 (1962), pp. 94–122.

McNeill, W.H., *Plagues and peoples* (New York, 1976).

McNeilley, A.S., 'Breastfeeding and fertility', in R. Gray, ed., with H. Leridon and A. Spira, *Biomedical and demographic determinants of fertility* (Oxford, 1993), pp. 391–412.

Maddison, A., 'A comparison of levels of GDP per capita in developed and developing countries, 1700–1980', *Journal of Economic History*, 43 (1983), pp. 27–41.

Malthus, T.R., *An essay on the principle of population* (1798), in E.A Wrigley and D. Souden, eds., *The works of Thomas Robert Malthus*, 8 vols. (London, 1986), I. *An essay on the principle of population*, 6th edn (1826), in E.A. Wrigley and D. Souden, eds., *The works of Thomas Robert Malthus*, 8 vols. (London, 1986), II and III.

Marshall, J., *Mortality in the metropolis* (London, 1832).

Meuvret, J., 'Les crises de subsistance et la démographie de la France de l'Ancien Régime', *Population*, 1 (1946), pp. 643–50.

Mills, D.R., 'The christening custom at Melbourn, Cambs.', *Local Population Studies*, 11 (1973), pp. 11–22.

Mitchell, B.R., *British historical statistics* (Cambridge, 1988).

Morrow, R.B., 'Family limitation in pre-industrial England: a reappraisal', *Economic History Review*, 2nd ser., 31 (1978), pp. 419–28.

Mortara, G., *Methods of using census statistics for the calculation of life tables and other demographic measures*, United Nations, Department of Social Affairs, Population Studies no. 7 (New York, 1949).

Notestein, F.W., 'Population: the long view', in T.W. Schulz, ed., *Food for the world* (Chicago, 1945), pp. 36–57.

Oeppen, J., 'Back projection and inverse projection: members of a wider class of constrained projection models', *Population Studies*, 47 (1993), pp. 245–67. 'Generalized inverse projection', in D.S. Reher and R. Schofield, eds., *Old and new methods in historical demography* (Oxford, 1993), pp. 29–39.

Oosterveen, K., Smith, R.M., and Stewart, S., 'Family reconstitution and the study of bastardy: evidence from certain English parishes', in P. Laslett, K. Oosterveen, and R.M. Smith, eds., *Bastardy and its comparative history* (London, 1980), pp. 86–140.

Pearl, R., *Studies in human biology* (Baltimore, 1924).

Peller, S., 'Studies on mortality since the Renaissance', *Bulletin of the History of Medicine*, 13 (1943), pp. 422–61.

Perrenoud, A., 'Surmortalité féminine et condition de la femme (XVIIe–XIXe siècles). Une vérification empirique', *Annales de démographie historique* (1981), pp. 89–104.

Phelps Brown, H., and Hopkins, S.V., *A perspective of wages and prices* (London, 1981).

Pittenger, D.B., 'An exponential model of female sterility', *Demography*, 10 (1973), pp. 113–21.

Porter, R., 'Cleaning up the Great Wen: public health in eighteenth-century London', in W.F. Bynum and R. Porter, eds., *Living and dying in London, Medical History*, supp. no. 11 (London, 1991), pp. 61–75.

Power, M.J., 'East London housing in the seventeenth century', in P. Clark and P. Slack, eds., *Crisis and order in English towns 1500–1700* (London, 1972), pp. 237–62.

Pressat, R., *The dictionary of demography*, ed. C. Wilson (Oxford, 1985).

Preston, S.H., Keyfitz, N., and Schoen, R., *Causes of death. Life tables for national populations* (New York and London, 1972).

Quaife, G.R., *Wanton wenches and wayward wives: peasants and illicit sex in early seventeenth century England* (New Brunswick, 1979).

Razzell, P., *The conquest of smallpox. The impact of inoculation on smallpox mortality in eighteenth century England* (Firle, 1977). 'The growth of population in eighteenth-century England: a critical reappraisal', *Journal of Economic History*, 53 (1993), pp. 743–71.

Essays in English population history (London, 1994).

Rotberg, R.I., and Rabb, T.K., eds., *Hunger and history: the impact of changing food production and consumption patterns on society* (Cambridge, 1983).

Ruggles, S., 'Migration, marriage, and mortality: correcting sources of bias in English family reconstitution', *Population Studies*, 46 (1992), pp. 507–22.

Russell, J.C., *British medieval population* (Albuquerque, 1948).

Santow, G., '*Coitus interruptus* and the control of natural fertility', *Population Studies*, 49 (1995), pp. 19–43.

Schofield, R., 'Anatomy of an epidemic. Colyton, November 1645 to November 1646', in *The plague reconsidered, Local Population Studies*, supp. (1977).

'English marriage patterns revisited', *Journal of Family History*, 10 (1985), pp. 2–20.

'Did the mothers really die? Three centuries of maternal mortality in "The world we have lost"', in L. Bonfield, R.M. Smith, and K. Wrightson, eds., *The world we have gained. Histories of population and social structure* (Oxford, 1986), pp. 231–60.

'Family structure, demographic behaviour, and economic growth', in J. Walter and R. Schofield, eds., *Famine, disease and the social order in early modern society* (Cambridge, 1989), pp. 279–304.

'Automated family reconstitution: the Cambridge experience', *Historical Methods*, 25 (1992), pp. 75–9.

'British population change, 1700–1871', in R. Floud and D. McCloskey, eds., *The economic history of Britain since 1700*, 2nd edn, 3 vols. (Cambridge, 1994), I, pp. 60–95.

'Monday's child is fair of face', in T.K. Hareven, R. Wall, and J. Ehmer, eds., *Family history and new historiography* (forthcoming)

Schofield, R.S., and Berry, B.M., 'Age at baptism in pre-industrial England', *Population Studies*, 25 (1971), pp. 453–63.

Schofield, R.S., and Wrigley, E.A., 'Infant and child mortality in England in the late Tudor and early Stuart period', in C. Webster, ed., *Health, medicine and mortality in the sixteenth century* (Cambridge, 1979), pp. 61–95.

Sharlin, A., 'Natural decrease in early modern cities', *Past and Present*, 79 (1978), pp. 126–38.

Sharpe, P., 'Literally spinsters: a new interpretation of local economy and demography in Colyton in the seventeenth and eighteenth centuries', *Economic History Review*, 44 (1991), pp. 46–65.

'Locating the "missing marryers" in Colyton, 1660–1750', *Local Population Studies*, 48 (1992), pp. 49–59.

Slack, P., *The impact of plague in Tudor and Stuart England* (London, 1985).

Smith, A., *An inquiry into the nature and causes of the wealth of nations*, ed. E. Cannan, 2 vols., orig. pub. 1904 (Chicago, 1976).

Smith, R.M., 'Some reflections on the evidence for the origins of the "European marriage pattern" in England', in C. Harris, ed., *The sociology of the family: new directions for Britain* (Keele, 1979), pp. 74–112.

'Fertility, economy and household formation in England over three centuries', *Population and Development Review*, 7 (1981), pp. 595–622.

'Demographic developments in rural England, 1300–48: a survey', in B.M.S. Campbell, ed., *Before the Black Death: studies in the 'crisis' of the early fourteenth century* (Manchester, 1991), pp. 25–77.

'Influences exogènes et endogènes sur le "frein préventif" en Angleterre, 1600–1750; quelques problèmes de spécification', in A. Blum, N. Bonneuil, and D. Blanchet, eds., *Modèles de la démographie historique* (Paris, 1992), pp. 175–91.

Smith, T.E., 'The Cocos-Keeling islands: a demographic laboratory', *Population Studies*, 14 (1960), pp. 94–130.

Steel, D.J., *National index of parish registers. I. Sources of births, marriages and deaths before 1837 (1)* (London, 1968).

Stone, L., *The family, sex and marriage in England 1500–1800*, abridged edn (Harmondsworth, 1979).

Stone, L., ed., *An imperial state at war: Britain from 1689–1815* (London, 1994).

Sundbärg, G., *Bevölkerungsstatisik Schwedens 1750–1900* (Stockholm, 1907), reprinted in *Skriftserieutgiven av statistiska centralbyrån*, Urval no. 3 (Stockholm, 1970).

Sundt, E., *On marriage in Norway*, trans. with an introd. by M. Drake (Cambridge, 1980).

Szreter, S.R.S., 'The importance of social intervention in Britain's mortality decline c.1850–1914: a reinterpretation of the role of public health', *Social History of Medicine*, 1 (1988), pp. 1–37.

'Mortality and public health, 1815–1914', *ReFresh*, 14 (1992), pp. 1–4.

Fertility, class and gender in Britain, 1860–1940 (Cambridge, 1995).

Teitelbaum, M.S., *The British fertility decline: demographic transition in the crucible of the industrial revolution* (Princeton, 1984).

Thomas, D.S., *Social and economic aspects of Swedish population movements, 1750–1933* (New York, 1941).

Trussell, J., and Wilson, C., 'Sterility in a population with natural fertility', *Population Studies*, 39 (1985), pp. 169–86.

Urdank, A.M., *Religion and society in a Cotswold vale: Nailsworth, Gloucestershire 1780–1865* (Berkeley and Los Angeles, 1990).

Utterström, G., 'Some population problems in pre-industrial Sweden', *Scandinavian Economic History Review*, 2 (1954), pp. 103–65.

Vallin, J., and Meslé, F., *Les causes de décès en France de 1925 à 1978* (Paris, 1988).

Vandenbroeke, C., van Poppel, F., and van der Woude, A.M., 'De zuigelingen-en kindersterfte in België en Nederlanden in seculair perspectief', *Tijdschrift voor Geschiedenis*, 94 (1981), pp. 461–91.

van der Woude, A., 'Population developments in the northern Netherlands (1500–1800) and the validity of the urban graveyard effect', *Annales de démographie historique* (1982), pp. 55–75.

Vann, R.T., and Eversley, D.E.C., *Friends in life and death: the British and Irish Quakers in the demographic transition* (Cambridge, 1992).

Vilquin, E., 'La mortalité infantile selon le mois de naissance', *Population*, 33 (1978), pp. 1137–53.

Wall, R., 'The age at leaving home', *Journal of Family History*, 3 (1978), pp. 181–202.

Walter, J., and Schofield, R., 'Famine, disease and crisis mortality in early modern society', in J. Walter and R. Schofield, eds., *Famine, disease and social order in early modern society* (Cambridge, 1989), pp. 1–73.

Watson, G.S., 'Goodness of fit tests on a circle', *Biometrika*, 48 (1961), pp. 109–14.

Weinberg, E., 'Pregnancy and resistance to infectious disease', *Review of Infectious Diseases*, 6 (1984), pp. 814–31.

Weir, D., 'Rather never than late: celibacy and age at marriage in English cohort fertility, 1541–1871', *Journal of Family History*, 9 (1984), pp. 341–55.

Wilson, A., 'Childbirth in seventeenth- and eighteenth-century England' (unpub. DPhil thesis, University of Sussex, 1982).

'William Hunter and the varieties of man-midwifery', in W.F. Bynum and R. Porter, eds., *William Hunter and the eighteenth-century medical world* (Cambridge, 1985), pp. 344–69.

'Participant or patient? Seventeenth-century childbirth from the mother's point of view', in R. Porter, ed., *Patients and practitioners: lay perceptions of medicine in pre-industrial society* (Cambridge, 1985), pp. 129–44.

'The perils of early modern procreation: childbirth with or without fear?', *British Journal of Eighteenth-Century Studies*, 16 (1993), pp. 1–19.

The making of man-midwifery: childbirth in England, 1660–1770 (London, 1995).

Wilson, C., 'Marital fertility in pre-industrial England, 1550–1849' (unpub. PhD thesis, University of Cambridge, 1982).

'Natural fertility in pre-industrial England', *Population Studies*, 38 (1984), pp. 225–40.

'The proximate determinants of marital fertility in England 1600–1799', in L. Bonfield, R.M. Smith, and K. Wrightson, eds., *The world we have gained* (Oxford, 1986), pp. 203–30.

Wilson, C., Oeppen, J., and Pardoe, M., 'What is natural fertility?: the modelling of a concept', *Population Index*, 54 (1988), pp. 4–20.

Wilson, C., and Woods, R., 'Fertility in England: a long-term perspective', *Population Studies*, 45 (1991), pp. 399–415.

Woods, R., *Theoretical population geography* (Harlow, 1982).

'On the historical relationship between infant and adult mortality', *Population Studies*, 47 (1993), pp. 195–217.

Wrigley, E.A., 'Family limitation in pre-industrial England', *Economic History Review*, 2nd ser., 19 (1966), pp. 82–109.

'A simple model of London's importance in changing English society and economy 1650–1750', *Past and Present*, 37 (1967), pp. 44–70.

'Mortality in pre-industrial England: the example of Colyton, Devon, over three centuries', *Daedalus*, 97 (1968), pp. 546–80.

Population and history (London, 1969).

'The process of modernization and the industrial revolution in England', *Journal of Interdisciplinary History*, 3 (1972), pp. 225–59.

'Some problems of family reconstitution using English parish register material: the example of Colyton', *Proceedings of the Third International Conference of Economic History*, Munich 1965, Section VII, Demography and Economics (Paris, 1972), pp. 199–221.

'Clandestine marriage in Tetbury in the late seventeenth century', *Local Population Studies*, 10 (1973), pp. 15–21.

'Baptism coverage in early nineteenth century England: the Colyton area', *Population Studies*, 29 (1975), pp. 299–316.

'Births and baptisms: the use of Anglican baptism registers as a source of information about the numbers of births in England before the beginning of civil registration', *Population Studies*, 31 (1977), pp. 281–312.

'Fertility strategy for the individual and the group', in C. Tilly, ed., *Historical studies of changing fertility* (Princeton, 1978), pp. 135–54.

'Marital fertility in seventeenth-century Colyton: a note', *Economic History*

Review, 2nd ser., 31 (1978), pp. 429–36.

'Marriage, fertility and population growth in eighteenth-century England', in R.B. Outhwaite, ed., *Marriage and society. Studies in the social history of marriage* (London, 1981), pp. 137–85.

'The growth of population in eighteenth-century England: a conundrum resolved', *Past and Present*, 98 (1983), pp. 121–50.

'Urban growth and agricultural change: England and the continent in the early modern period', *Journal of Interdisciplinary History*, 15 (1985), pp. 683–728.

Continuity, chance and change. The character of the industrial revolution in England (Cambridge, 1988).

'The effect of migration on the estimation of marriage age in family reconstitution studies', *Population Studies*, 48 (1994), pp. 81–97.

Wrigley, E.A., ed., *An introduction to English historical demography from the sixteenth to the nineteenth century* (London, 1966).

Wrigley, E.A., and Schofield, R.S., 'Nominal record linkage by computer and the logic of family reconstitution', in E.A. Wrigley, ed., *Identifying people in the past* (London, 1973), pp. 64–101.

'English population history from family reconstitution: summary results 1600–1799', *Population Studies*, 37 (1983), pp. 157–84.

The population history of England 1541–1871: a reconstruction, 1st pbk edn with new introduction (Cambridge, 1989).

Yasumoto, M., *Industrialisation, urbanisation and demographic change in England* (Nagoya, 1994).

OFFICIAL SOURCES

Annual report of the Registrar-General for England and Wales, 1838– (London, 1839–).

1801 Census. Enumeration, *PP* 1802, VII.

1811 Census. Preliminary observations, *PP* 1812, XI.

1831 Census. Enumeration abstract, vols. I and II, *PP* 1833, XXXVI and XXXVII.

1851 Census. Population tables I. Numbers of the inhabitants in the years 1801, 1811, 1821, 1831, 1841 and 1851, *PP* 1852–3, LXXXV.

Population tables II. Ages, civil condition, occupations, and birth place of the people, vols. I and II, *PP* 1852–3, LXXXVIII, pts I and II.

1861 Census. Population tables II. Ages, civil condition, occupations, and birth place of the people, *PP*, 1863, LIII, pts I and II.

Lists of non-parochial registers and records in the custody of the Registrar-General of births, deaths, and marriages (HMSO, London, 1859).

Manual of the international statistical classification of disease, injuries, and causes of death, vol. I (World Health Organisation, Geneva, 1977).

The Registrar-General's statistical review of England and Wales, 1921– (London, 1923–).

Name index

635

Place index

209, 282, 285, 289, 292–3, 309, 315,
319–20, 322, 394, 473, 503, 546–8,
554

Gainsborough, 29, 43, 48, 84–6, 133, 183,
186, 217, 269, 272, 279, 403, 506, 562,
580
Gedling, 25, 29, 43–4, 84–6, 90, 94, 186,
214, 272, 278, 332, 562, 580
Geneva, 13, 309, 354
Germany, 9, 108, 157, 165–6, 176, 182,
208, 315–6, 319–20, 322, 359, 394, 426,
472, 501, 503, 547, 554
Glasgow, 257
Grantham, 96
Great Ayton, 29
Great Oakley, 25, 35, 43, 50, 84, 86, 183,
191, 218, 272–3, 275, 562, 603
Guyenne, 511

Hampshire, 562
Hartland, 25, 35–6, 43, 84–6, 183, 190,
204, 233, 269, 273, 403, 562
Hartley, 34
Hartley Wintney, 94, 96
Hawkshead, 29
Helsinki, 347
Hertfordshire, 561
Holsworthy, 36, 233

India, 122, 347, 359
Ipplepen, 25, 36, 50, 84, 86, 186, 273, 279,
562, 603–4
Ireland, 92, 136, 242
Irthlingborough, 42
Italy, 547

Kent, 283, 561
Kenton, 29

Lancashire, 42
Ledbury, 221
Leicestershire, 561–2
Lincolnshire, 562
Linton, 33
Little Clacton, 218
Liverpool, 233–4
London, 100, 202, 204, 209, 218, 233, 256,
269, 273, 275, 308, 315–7
Lorraine, 511
Loughborough, 96
Lowestoft, 29, 43, 63, 65, 84–6, 183, 190–1,
217, 268, 272, 506, 562, 605
Ludlow, 551
Lyon, 177

March, 29, 84, 86, 183, 190–1, 217–8, 233,
260, 269, 272–3, 279, 562, 605
Mediterranean, 122
Methley, 29, 84, 86, 110, 133, 183, 186,
273, 278, 506, 562
Morchard Bishop, 29, 50, 84, 86, 183, 273,
562
Moretonhampstead, 29

Netherlands, 204, 548
Newton Abbot, 96
Northampton, 42
Northamptonshire, 42
Northumberland, 562
Norway, 124, 347, 546
Nottinghamshire, 562

Odiham, 25, 29, 84–6, 94, 186, 214, 230,
273, 506, 562
Oxford, 316
Oxfordshire, 561

Prussia, 221, 240

Reeth, 221
Reigate, 25, 36–7, 65, 84–6, 183, 190, 268,
273, 502, 506, 562, 605

St George in the East, 233
St Georges, Lyon, 177
Sandwich, 218
Scotland, 242, 257, 283, 552
Seaton, 34
Serbia, 122
Shefford, with Campton, *see* Southill
Sheppey, 218
Shepshed, 37, 42–5, 48, 50, 57, 71, 84–5,
110, 127–8, 186, 272, 278, 332, 356, 562,
579, 618
South Benfleet, 218
Southchurch, 218
Southill, 37, 51, 84, 86, 186, 194, 506, 562
Spain, 547–8
Stockholm, 347, 516
Suffolk, 562
Surrey, 562
Sweden, 3, 125, 203–4, 208, 240, 259–60,
310, 312–3, 315–6, 320, 322, 347, 545–6

Tavistock, 29
Terling, 37, 43, 72, 84, 86, 191, 273, 506,
562
Thurleston, 29
Tollesbury, 218
Tourouvre–au–Perche, 473

Wales, 158, 232, 243, 256, 299, 303, 307,
   316, 462
Warwickshire, 561
Wellingborough, 42
Wetherby, 221
Whickham, 29

Willingham, 25, 38, 84–6, 111, 183, 191,
   218, 272–3
Wisbech, 233
Witchford, 233, 260

Yorkshire, 42, 110, 511, 561–2

Subject index

abortion, 319, 488, 507, 509
  see also maternal mortality;
    miscarriage; stillbirths
abstinence, sexual, 393, 493–4
adult mortality, 11, 211, 238, 280–95, 298,
    301–2, 309, 317, 352, 523, 536,
    541–2, 551–3, 555, 619, app. 6
  see also childhood mortality; infant
    mortality; maternal mortality;
    mortality; seasonal mortality
  by age, 289–92
  cf. childhood mortality, 283–4
  English life table, third, 291
  estimation, 211–3, app. 6
    bias, 16, 211, app. 6
    Blum method, 582–5
    inmigrants, 581
    interaction with migration, 584–5
    outmigrants, 582
    Ruggles's criticisms, 583–4
    unmarried, 581
  exposure imputation, 605, app. 6
    celibacy, 581, 584
    closing events, 588, 594–5
    competing risk, 583–5
    composition effect, 599
    frequency by event type, 589–95
    hot–decking, 588
    interval distributions, 584, 594
    interval to next event, 582–5, 587–9,
      594–8
    maximum, 582–5
    method, 588–99
    migration, 582–5, 587–9, 595–6, 599
    migration schedule, 584
    minimum, 582–3, 585
    opening events, 588–9, 594–5
    posthumous birth, 588–9

  random imputation, 583, 588, 595,
    598, 600
  remarriage, 596
  residence, 582, 584, 587–9, 596–7
  scale, 585–7
  simulation, 583–4
  special cases, 595–8
  sterility, 594
  truncation, 597–600
  weights, 589
  widowhood, 598
  cf. France 291–2
  groups of parishes, app. 7
    splicing, 280, 602–9, app. 7
  model life tables, 282, 284–5
  partial life expectancy, 287–9
  cf. *PHE* and France, 281–2, 285, 287–9
  cf. Registrar-General, 281–2
  trends, 150, 281–2
  by age, 289–92
advocates' mortality, 283, 552
age at marriage, 17, 28, 122, 549–50, 552,
    554, app. 2
  see also marriage rank; nuptiality;
    remarriage; widowhood
  adult mortality, 149
  age gap between spouses, 122, 151–3,
    191
    distribution, 152
    by period and rank combinations,
      151–3
  bachelor/spinster marriages, 128–49,
    182–94, 533
    distribution, 139–49, 151, 159, 164–6
    by groups of parishes and sex,
      140–8, 182–94
    trends, 149
  bias in age estimation, 160–4

641

Cambridge Studies in Population, Economy and Society in Past Time

Titles available in paperback are marked with an asterisk